AFTER SAN JACINTO

The Texas-Mexican Frontier, 1836–1841

THIS BOOK IS PUBLISHED WITH THE ASSISTANCE OF THE

Dan Danciger Publication Fund

AFTER SAN JACINTO

The Texas-Mexican Frontier, 1836-1841

By JOSEPH MILTON NANCE

UNIVERSITY OF TEXAS PRESS · AUSTIN

Library of Congress Catalog Card No. 62–9789

Copyright © 1963 Joseph Milton Nance

Printed in the United States of America

International Standard Book Number 0-292-73156-6

Second Printing, 1970

TO

MRS. LOUISE HUTCHISON NANCE

WHOSE DEVOTION

INSTILLED IN HER CHILDREN

A DESIRE FOR KNOWLEDGE

AND THE TRUTH

PREFACE

One of the most interesting, but also one of the most neglected, phases of the history of Texas is that dealing with the southern and southwestern frontiers of the Republic. It is the story of Texas-Mexican relations along a thinly populated borderland between two contrasting civilizations—one virile, aggressive, restless and frequently lawless; the other proud, traditional, militaristic, and often corrupt. Both civilizations were projected upon a third and older culture—the Indian— which played an important role in the contest between the two stronger parties. Here, on the southern and southwestern frontier of Texas, Mexican, Anglo-American, and Indian met, mingled, and fought either singly or in some form of alliance of one with another against the third. Plots and expeditions, as much as the peaceful extension of settlement and trade, are important phases of the history of this frontier. Here men of many nations, adventurers and soldiers of fortune, spies, vigilantes, rangers, "cow-boys," government agents, merchants, lawyers, restless politicians, farmers, ranchers, cutthroats, and freebooters rubbed elbows, fought, and died.

Because of the clandestine operations of many of the characters involved, secrecy was often their motto; yet, enough of the written record on both sides has come down to us to permit the story of this frontier to be told. This is as much the story of Mexican history as it is Texan. No serious effort has been made by scholars in the past to write the history of this phase of Texas-Mexican relations, although it was a phase which engendered deep and long-lasting bitterness on both sides. The full story is much too long and complicated to be told in a single volume; so, the current work is confined to the period between the battle of San Jacinto and the Mexican seizure of San Antonio in March 1842.

Preface

The materials for this study are found for the most part in manuscript and newspaper collections in the Latin American and Eugene C. Barker Texas History libraries of the University of Texas, the Texas State Archives, the General Land Office in Austin, the Rosenberg Library at Galveston, the San Jacinto Museum of History, the National Archives in Washington, and in transcripts from the National Archives of Mexico, the State Archives of Coahuila at Saltillo, and the archives of Béxar, Laredo, and Matamoros.

Grateful acknowledgment is due to the custodians of the collections enumerated for courteous and considerate assistance, and especially to the late Miss Harriet Smither, long-time State Archivist; Miss Winnie Allen, retired Archivist, The University of Texas Library; the late Mr. E. W. Winkler, former Librarian and later Bibliographer of the University of Texas Library; the late Mr. E. R. Dabney, former Custodian of the Newspaper Collection, The University of Texas Library; Mrs. B. Brandt, former Assistant State Archivist; Miss Llerena Friend, Librarian, Eugene C. Barker Texas History Center, The University of Texas Library; and Mrs. Lavelle Castle of the Cushing Memorial Library of The Agricultural and Mechanical College of Texas. I am also much indebted to my wife (Mrs. Eleanor Hanover Nance) for the preparation of the maps.

JOSEPH MILTON NANCE

College Station, Texas

CONTENTS

ILLUSTRATIONS

Following page 306

MAPS

AFTER SAN JACINTO

The Texas-Mexican Frontier, 1836–1841

The Trans-Nueces Country

THE OFFICIAL BOUNDARY of the little Republic of Texas was set by the first session of the First Congress of Texas on December 19, 1836, through a resolution presented by Thomas Jefferson Green, representative from Béxar.[1] The boundary was defined as "beginning at the mouth of the Sabine River and running west along the Gulf of Mexico three leagues from land, to the mouth of the Río Grande, thence up the principal stream of said river to its source, thence due north to the forty-second degree of north latitude, thence along the boundary line as defined in the treaty between the United States and Spain to the beginning." Thus, Texas had two frontiers to defend. One frontier—the Indian—extended from the Red River on the north along the edge of the great prairie to the Río Grande, a distance of some 500 miles; the other—the Mexican—stretched from the vicinity of Presidio del Río Grande to the mouth of that stream, an approximate distance of 325 miles. It is the latter frontier that is the principal concern of this study.

In spite of the Texan claim, however, the area between the Nueces and the Río Grande, long regarded under Spanish law as a part of the province of Nuevo Santander and under Mexican law as a part of the states of Tamaulipas and Coahuila and often referred to by both Spaniards and Mexicans as *El Desierto Muerto*,[2] was after 1835 virtu-

---

[1] Francis R. Lubbock, *Six Decades in Texas: or Memoirs of Francis Richard Lubbock*, p. 91; *Laws of the Republic of Texas*, I, 133–134.

[2] I. J. Cox, "The Southwest Boundary of Texas," *Quarterly of the Texas State Historical Association*, VI (1902–1903), 95–96; William C. Binkley, *The Expansionist Movement in Texas, 1836–1850*, pp. 7–10. "Los limites de Téjas son ciertos y recondidos: jámas han passado del Río de las Nueces; y sin embargo, el ejército Americano ha salvado la linea que separa a Tamaulipas de aquel departamento." (Translated: "The limits of Texas are certain and recognized; never have they extended beyond the river Nueces; notwithstanding which, the American army has crossed the line separating Tamaulipas from that department.") Francisco

ally a no man's land over which for nearly a decade a predatory and guerrillalike warfare was waged between Mexicans and Texans, with first one and then the other, or both sides, aided by Indians. Although by early June 1836, all Mexican military forces in Texas had withdrawn beyond the historic boundaries of Texas and across the Río Grande, except for small units retained at Laredo and Brazos Santiago, Mexico never willingly relinquished her claims to the lost province; and maintained at the latter place (a rather insignificant establishment near the Pontón de Santa Isabel) a customhouse within the claimed boundary of Texas, whose revenues furnished the main support for her military forces in the north. With the reopening of the Texas-Mexican frontier trade after 1838 those revenues dropped more than three-fourths with a corresponding effect upon Mexican military strength in the north.[3]

Under the Spanish regime the territory lying between Matamoros and the east line of the Reinosa *porciónes,* and northward from the Río Grande to Los Olmos Creek had been allotted to wealthy cattle owners and Spaniards of reliability, and was not open to town settlement. After Mexico gained her independence in 1821, the state of Tamaulipas was formed from the old Spanish Provincio del Nuevo Santander, whose northern boundary had come to be regarded as the Nueces River. By successive land laws enacted between 1828 and 1836 the state of Tamaulipas distributed to prominent Mexican citizens and soldiers "all vacant lands then found as such between the Río Grande and the Nueces."[4] The only civilized settlements were at Béxar, Goliad, and Refugio,[5] all well east of the Nueces and lying along the southwestern frontier. Besides these, there were a number of small towns on or only a short distance from the Río Grande, including Santa Fé, El Paso, Presidio del Norte, Presidio del Río Grande, Laredo, Dolores,[6]

Mejía, "El general en gefe de las fuerzas avanzadas sobre el enemigo, á los habitantes de este departamento y á las tropas de su mando," Matamoros, Marzo 18 de 1846, in United States Congress, *House Executive Documents,* 30th Cong., 1st sess., no. 60, pp. 125–127.

[3] Message of President M. B. Lamar to Congress, Austin, Nov. 3, 1841, in Harriet Smither (ed.), *Journals of the Sixth Congress of the Republic of Texas,* I, 7–25.

[4] Frank C. Pierce, *A Brief History of the Lower Río Grande Valley,* p. 21.

[5] The town of Refugio was incorporated by an act of the Texas Congress, approved February 1, 1842. H. P. N. Gammel (ed.), *Laws of Texas,* II, 758–759.

[6] In May 1837, Dolores was entirely depopulated. Joseph Baker, [Chief Justice of the County Court], to Secretary of State, Béxar, May 1, 1837, in State Depart-

Carolitas, San Ygnacio, Guerrero, Mier, Reinosa Viejo, Reinosa Nuevo, Camargo, and Matamoros. The area between the two lines of settlement just mentioned was occupied by herds of wild horses and cattle and almost every conceivable species of native animal, and was infested by thieves, robbers, and murderers. The rivers and creeks abounded in fish.

The Comanches claimed the area as their hunting ground and were ever ready to wage a war of extermination upon all who trespassed within its borders. Even Mexican traders feared to go through these vast plains, given up, as they were, to various wandering tribes of Indians, freebooters, ladrones, and bands of Mexicans holding "roving commissions" from the Mexican military commander in the north, "to plunder all traders from Texas passing through that region." [7] Long after the claim of Texas to this region was established, the Nueces was called the "dead line for sheriffs." Sometimes the Republic of Texas was at peace with one enemy and sometimes with another, but she was practically never at peace with both the Mexicans and the Indians at the same time. She often fought them both simultaneously. "War was the rule, the commonplace of daily life, and death was the price of defeat, for the savage enemies of Texas knew no mercy." [8]

The terrain itself was commonly regarded as of very little value. For the first fifteen or twenty miles inland from the coast, the land was generally a flat prairie, composed of alluvial soil and sedimentary ocean deposits in alternate layers; here and there were valuable salt lakes. The rivers in the area were heavily impregnated with lime, making the soil rich, black, and too "surcharged" for some types of vegetation. Throughout the whole region were spots "devoid of vegetation and encrusted with a white saline deposite." Generally, however, the vegetation was a luxuriant coarse grass which grew waist-high, with an occasional clump of live oak bordering the wet places. Farther in-

ment (Texas), Department of State Letterbook, no. 2 (Nov. 1836–Mar. 1841), ms, pp. 37–39; hereafter cited as State Department Letterbook, no. 2.

[7] J. D. Affleck, "History of John C. Hays," pt. I, p. 140, ms. See also *Daily Texian* (Austin), Jan. 13, 1842; John C. Hays, Captain, Company of Spies, to T. B. [Branch T.] Archer, Secretary of War, San Antonio, April 14, 1841, *Telegraph and Texas Register* (Houston), April 28, 1841; C. A. Gulick and Others (eds.), *The Papers of Mirabeau Buonaparte Lamar*, IV, 232–233 (hereafter cited as *Lamar Papers*); *Jack Hays: The Intrepid Texas Ranger*, p. 6.

[8] Walter Prescott Webb, "The Texas Rangers," in E. C. Barker (ed.), *Texas History for High Schools and Colleges*, p. 595.

land beyond the belt of prairie was a low ridge of sand hills, which seemed to have marked the ancient limits of the coast, and here for the first time going toward the interior, one encountered clumps of post oaks, called "motts." The trees were crooked, wind-beaten, and generally unfit for lumber.[9] The vegetation began to assume a spinose stunted character; and as one approached within a few miles of the Río Grande, it was almost entirely chaparral. The river bottoms were well wooded with oak, pecan, walnut, and hackberry. West of the Nueces, and between it and the Río Grande, the country suffered from excessive and long-continued droughts, and the aridity of the area became more marked as the Río Grande was approached. This region was traversed by deep gullies, called arroyos. Immense and starkly beautiful, the barren lands of the trans-Nueces country could scarcely be expected, in the early days of the Republic, to support a handful of towns and ranches. Yet, it was in and across these lands that an intense border warfare was to be fought for years.

Passing through Laredo in 1822 on his way to Mexico City, Stephen F. Austin described the country between the Medina River and the Río Grande as "the poorest I ever saw in my life. It is generally nothing but Sand, entirely void of Timber, covered with scrubby thorn bushes and Prickly Pears." [10] Laredo, he wrote, "is as poor as sand banks, and drought, and indolence can make it." The country between the Nueces and the Río Grande, wrote the editor of the *Galveston Civilian* in 1843, is represented by travelers "as unfit for any purpose but grazing," and even for this it is lacking in water and grass, except immediately upon the rivers by which it is bounded.[11] Ten years later (1853), the picture had not materially changed, although there were a few more inhabitants in the area. It was still the range of wild cattle and horses, and was inhabited only along the rivers and there sparsely. "It is infested by thieves, robbers, and murderers from Mexico and Texas, and a few outrages committed there under these circumstances

[9] William H. Emory, *Report on the United States and Mexican Boundary Survey, Made under the Direction of the Secretary of the Interior*, I, 55–56.

[10] Stephen F. Austin to James E. B. Austin, Loredo, March 23, 1822, in Eugene C. Barker (ed.), *The Austin Papers*, in *Annual Report of the American Historical Association for the year 1919*, vol. II, pt. I, 487–488. See also, *Telegraph and Texas Register*, Dec. 8, 1841; Branch T. Archer to Messrs. Roman, Price, McDonald, Cunningham, O'Riley and Newcombe, War Department, Austin, July 14, 1841, in *ibid.*, Aug. 11, 1841.

[11] Quoted in *Telegraph and Texas Register*, July 12, 1843.

test the value of the defense," reported Colonel Freeman.[12] "The country from San Antonio," wrote a Texan volunteer in the Mexican War,
"is not fit for a hog to live in—nothing but a sandy desert . . . no house
from San Patricia to Goliad—none on the other side of Goliad for a
long distance"; [13] and General Vicente Filisola, who had ample reason
for disliking Texas in 1836, pronounced it a country of "mud and sand,"
and left it, never to return.[14] While in command of the military forces
at Mexico City on December 25, 1839, Filisola, when asked by a friend,
"What of Texas?" is alleged to have shaken his head, screwed up his
shoulders and replied, "My Friend, Texas is lost to Mexico. We will
never be able to retake it." [15] Many of the rank and file among the
Mexican troops of 1836 "swore they would never enter Texas again." [16]
And to ex-President Lamar, embittered in 1847 by years of political
strife, Texas was "very little more than Big Drunk's big Ranch." [17]

The face of the country from San Antonio to the Río del Norte [Río
Grande] is very uniform, [wrote Thomas W. Bell, a member of the Mier
Expedition] it consists of prairies covered with the finest grass, and generally the shrubby musquit growing over it. Sometimes these shrubs in
common with Prickly pear, or as the Mexicans term it the nopal, cover the
whole face of the country. . . . The soil is generally fertile and particularly
the vallies, which are extremely productive. On these wild and luxuriant
pastures nurtured alone by nature's care, roam undisturbed, thousands of
wild Cattle, Buffalo and Mustangs. Not far to the northward sets in a

[12] W. G. Freeman, "Report of an Inspection of Eighth Military District, April
23, 1853," Appendix V, pp. 5–6, Old Records Section, A. G. O., War Department,
Washington, D. C., ms.
[13] Eugene C. Barker (ed.), "James K. Holland's Diary of a Texas Volunteer
in the Mexican War," *Southwestern Historical Quarterly*, XXX (1926–1927), 8.
[14] H. Yoakum, *History of Texas from Its First Settlement in 1685 to Its Annexation to the United States in 1846*, II, 167.
[15] A. S. Wright to William Bryan, Mexico City, Dec. 25, 1839, in George P.
Garrison (ed.), *Diplomatic Correspondence of Texas* in *Annual Report of the
American Historical Association*, 1908, II, 518–520. Hereafter cited as Garrison,
Diplomatic Correspondence of Texas.
[16] Edward Hall to D. G. Burnet, New Orleans, June 20, 1836, in William C.
Binkley (ed.) *Official Correspondence of the Texan Revolution, 1835–1836*, II,
807–808.
[17] [M. B.] Lamar to David G. Burnet, Laredo, March 1847, in *Lamar Papers*,
IV, 165. "Big Drunk" was Lamar's appellation for Sam Houston, the name being
that of a Choctaw chief, so named for his habit of getting drunk when in the
settlements.

7

mountainous district, but there still is the finest pasturage and game in the greatest abundance.[18]

The whole region between the Nueces and the Río Bravo [Grande] was a fine grazing country, and "the number of horses and cattle that ranged it, belonging to the settlers on the Río Bravo under . . . Spanish rule prior to 1825, . . . [was] incredible. To this day," wrote Major Emory, who visited the area in 1852, "the remnants of this immense stock are running wild on the prairies between the two rivers." [19] Large ranches of sheep, goats, cattle, and horses along the Río Grande, on both the north and south banks, date from the founding of San Juan Bautista, Reinosa, Camargo, Reveilla (Guerrero), Mier, Dolores, and Laredo in the mid-eighteenth century. In subsequent years, "ranching north of the Río Grande gradually increased and extended northward, reaching the Nueces River" within a few years.[20] It was not entirely a northward movement, for ranching on a limited, and sometimes on an extensive scale, developed in the vicinity of all the mission establishments and fanned out in every direction. Ranching was begun in the neighborhood of La Bahía del Espíritu Santo, located first on the Garcitas and later on the San Antonio at Goliad, and extended southward. By 1776 Blas María de la Garza Falcón, founder and captain of Camargo, had established his Rancho de Santa Petronilla "within five leagues of the mouth of the Nueces, 'with a goodly number of the people, a stock of cattle, sheep and goats, and cornfields'." [21] Some of the ranches and herds were of enormous size. Fifty thousand head of cattle belonging to one cattle baron was reported destroyed by a flood inundating Padre Island in 1791.[22] El Rancho San Juan de Carricitos contained 600,000 acres. Around 1770 the Mission of Espíritu Santo claimed 40,000 head of cattle, branded and unbranded, "that ranged between the Guadalupe and San Antonio rivers, while the neighboring Mission of Rosario claimed 10,000 branded cattle and 20,00 unbranded cattle, ranging westward." [23] It has been estimated that three million

[18] Thomas W. Bell, *A Narrative of the Capture and Subsequent Sufferings of the Mier Prisoners in Mexico, Captured in the Cause of Texas, Dec. 26th, 1842 and Liberated Sept. 16th, 1844*, p. 15.

[19] Emory, *Report of the United States and Mexican Boundary Survey*, I, 56.

[20] Herbert E. Bolton, *Texas in the Middle Eighteenth Century*, pp. 300–301.

[21] *Ibid.*, p. 301. Don Blas' ranch was located on what is now Petronita Creek.

[22] Curtis Bishop and Bascom Giles, *Lots of Land*, pp. 11, 13.

[23] J. Frank Dobie, "The First Cattle in Texas and the Southwest Progenitors of the Longhorns," *Southwestern Historical Quarterly*, XLII (1938–1939), 177.

head of stock, including goats, sheep, and horses, as well as cattle, occupied the area between the Río de las Nueces and the Río Grande in 1835.[24]

The defense of the trans-Nueces region was not intentionally neglected by the Republic of Texas, but due largely to an impoverished financial condition, the great distances involved, the scarcity of population, and often the nature and character of the persons upon whom it depended for military service, the government's policy lacked continuity in both planning and leadership. This is not to say that the average Texan did not make a good fighter or that the Republic did not have a number of competent military officers, but that various and sundry conditions served as handicaps. These will be noted as we progress with our story. In the meantime, a brief résumé of the military establishment of Texas during the days immediately following the battle of San Jacinto may be in order at this point.[25]

[24] United States Congress, "Difficulties on the Southwestern Frontier," *House Executive Documents,* 36th Cong., 1st Sess., no. 52, p. 25.

[25] For an able discussion of the military organization of Texas from its establishment by the Consultation of 1835 and the Convention of 1836 through the battle of San Jacinto, see Eugene C. Barker, "The Texan Revolutionary Army," *Quarterly of the Texas State Historical Association,* IX (1905–1906), 227–261.

CHAPTER TWO

Mexican Threats and the Texan Military Establishment: May 1836-December 1838

A FEW DAYS AFTER the battle of San Jacinto General Sam Houston left the army to go to New Orleans for treatment of the wound he had received in the battle. At that time the command of the army was turned over to Thomas J. Rusk, who resigned his position as Secretary of War to accept the rank of brigadier general with the understanding that Houston would remain nominally in command. Rusk assumed command of the army on May 4 and led it westward in the wake of the retreating Mexicans to be sure that they abandoned the country as they had promised. Lieutenant Colonel Juan N. Seguin commanded the detachments stationed at Béxar (San Antonio).

The main army remained for a while at Victoria, and while it was there word was received in Texas that the Mexicans were preparing to renew their campaign. News of the proposed invasion had reached Texas in a rather unusual manner. Following the victory at San Jacinto, Colonel Henry W. Karnes and Captain Henry Teal were sent as commissioners to Matamoros to negotiate with General José Urrea about the exchange of prisoners provided for in the treaty of Velasco. There they were held prisoners at Matamoros by Filisola in retaliation for General Rusk's detention of General Adrián Woll, who had entered the Texan camp at San Jacinto under a flag of truce. While in prison Karnes and Teal learned of Urrea's preparation for another invasion of Texas to start in the summer, and with the help of William P. Miller and others managed to send out letters concealed in a whip handle telling of the Mexican preparations. This is known as the "Whip-handle Dispatch."[1] An unidentified Mexican was sent as courier to

[1] R. M. Potter, "Escape of Karnes and Teal from Matamoros," *Quarterly of the Texas State Historical Association*, IV (1900–1901), 71–85, 232–233; W. P. Miller to T. J. Rusk, Matamoros, June 9, 1836, in William C. Binkley (ed.), *Official Correspondence of the Texan Revolution, 1835–1836*, II, 766–767, 888–

deliver the whip handle to General Rusk, but he was captured by a Texan patrol near the Nueces River and the dispatch was sent to Secretary of War Alexander Somervell at Velasco. Before it was sent, however, a copy of the letters had been made and forwarded to New Orleans, where one of them appeared in the *New Orleans Picayune*. This letter, when the paper had been received at Matamoros, resulted in close confinement for Teal and Karnes. Teal had written that 4,000 men would leave Matamoros in a few days for La Bahía (Goliad) and that there were plans for an equal number to proceed by water from Vera Cruz to Copano or some other point along the Texas coast.[2] This information elicited a proclamation on June 20 from Acting President Burnet "to the people of Texas" urging every able-bodied man between the ages of sixteen and fifty to enroll for military duty. It also led to repeated requests from Burnet to the Texan agent in New Orleans to hurry on volunteers to defend the country[3] against General Urrea, "The cold blooded, heartless murderer of the gallant Fannin and his noble band," now leading a "vandal host" for the subjugation of Texas.

This alarm seemed justified. Before the remnants of Santa Anna's army had recrossed to the left bank of the Río Bravo, the Mexican Congress on May 20 decided to continue the war against Texas. General Urrea was given command, on June 5, of the troops destined for a new campaign in Texas and he immediately informed those at Matamoros that he would lead them into Texas as soon as the government so ordered him.[4] This was alarming news to every Texan, for Rusk's

---

890; William Bryan to David G. Burnet, Agency of Texas, New Orleans, June 20, 1836, in *ibid.*, II, 808–809; *Telegraph and Texas Register* (Houston), Aug. 30, 1836.

[2] Henry Teal to T. J. Rusk, June 9, 1836, in *Niles' Weekly Register* (Baltimore), L (July 23, 1836), 350.

[3] David G. Burnet, President, and A. Somerville [*sic*], Secretary of War, [Proclamation, to the People of Texas]. . . . Done at Velasco, the 20th day of June, 1836, broadside; also in Binkley (ed.), *Official Correspondence of the Texan Revolution*, II, 802–804; Executive Records (Texas), book 35, ms., pp. 68–71; David G. Burnet to Thomas Toby, Executive Department, Velasco, June 20, 1836, and also letters of Same to Same, June 23, 28, July 2, 22, 1836, in Binkley (ed.), *Official Correspondence of the Texan Revolution*, II, 802–804, 804–805, 813–815, 819–820, 836–837, 880–881.

[4] Thomas Maitland Marshall, *A History of the Western Boundary of the Louisiana Purchase, 1819–1841*, p. 176; José Urrea, *Proclama. José Urrea, general de brigada y comandante de la division de reserva en el ejército de operaciones sobre*

force at Victoria numbered only 350 men [5] on June 17 when Rusk wrote Thomas Jefferson Green urging the immediate concentration of the Texan troops to meet the Mexican advance. When Green reached Rusk's army, however, he refused to be commanded by General Rusk and held aloof, claiming that his commission was older than Rusk's.[6] "God help the work when the army of Texas is commanded by such a man [as Green]," commented David Macomb.[7]

On the following day Rusk wrote General Edmund P. Gaines, commander of the United States troops on the southwestern frontier at Fort Jesup, telling of the Mexican advance, and imploring his help against the butchers whose motto was, "Extermination to the Sabine, or death." [8] In the face of this report and of others concerning recent Indian depredations and hostilities along the frontier, General Gaines again called upon the governors of Kentucky, Mississippi, and Louisiana for troops as he had done on April 8 under similar circumstances. In a letter to General Alexander B. Bradford of the Tennessee volunteers, Gaines declared, "I am resolved, in case the Mexicans or Texians employ the Indians against the people of either side of the imaginery line to inflict on the offenders serious and severe punishment." [9]

General Rusk followed up the President's proclamation with a call upon his fellow-citizens to shoulder their rifles and repair to the field to sustain their rights.[10] Rusk let it be known that, "He that claims a home and a habitation in Texas—must now *fight for it, or abandon it,* to some one who will."

"It is my opinion," wrote David Ayres from Brazoria, "That the hardest battle is yet to be fought and unless the whole of Texas turn out and meet the enemy, on the Guadeloupe or the West side of the Colorado, we shall all have to remove again with our families. . . . I am

Téjas, á las tropas de su mando. Matamoros, Junio 5 de 1836, broadside; José Urrea, *Proclama. José Urrea, general en gefe del egército de operaciones sobre Téjas, á los valientes que lo forman.* Matamoros, Junio 8 de 1836, broadside.

[5] *Niles' Weekly Register* (Aug. 6, 1836), L, 383–384.

[6] Thomas J. Rusk to Thomas J. Green, Victoria, June 17, 1836, in *ibid.,* L, 383–384.

[7] D. B. Macomb to James Morgan, Steam Saw Mill, San Jacinto, July 28, 1836, in Binkley (ed.), *Official Correspondence of the Texan Revolution,* II, 897–899.

[8] James W. Silver, *Edmund Pendleton Gaines: Frontier General,* p. 204.

[9] E. P. Gaines to Gen. A. B. Bradford, Camp Sabine, June 28, 1836, in *Niles' Weekly Register* (Aug. 6, 1836), L, 384.

[10] Thomas J. Rusk, [Proclamation to the People of Texas], Guadaloupe-Victoria, June 27, 1836, broadside.

afraid that unless we all act united promptly, and forthwith all will be lost." [11] From New Orleans on June 20, the Texan agent reported a large Mexican force (supposedly some 15,000 men) preparing to advance into Texas at an early date, and stated that he had ordered a number of extra men aboard the Texan public vessels in that port and would despatch them immediately to Texas for orders.[12] Meanwhile, quite a number of vessels, including a few under Mexican registry, loaded at New Orleans in June and July with provisions and merchandise, and weighed anchor for Matamoros,[13] which port was opened by a decree of July 16 to the importation of provisions during the war with Texas.[14] This same decree exempted from seizure mules and wagons carrying supplies within Mexico to the army being fitted out for the Texas campaign. Furthermore, no vessels from Mexican ports had reached New Orleans in some time, a fact which led both New Orleans and Texas observers to conclude that they were being retained at home to transport the large numbers of troops and supplies said to be accumulating on the Mexican seaboard. In consequence, President Burnet proclaimed on July 21 a blockade of the port of Matamoros.[15]

Lieutenant Colonel Seguin was ordered to evacuate San Antonio and to fall back to army headquarters near Victoria. In preparing to leave Béxar, he appealed to the local inhabitants to drive off the cattle to places where the enemy could not make use of them. Here was an opportunity for the Mexicans of San Antonio to prove their loyalty to the newly established government of Texas. "Fellow citizens: your conduct on this day," warned Seguin, "is going to decide your fate

[11] David Ayres to D. G. Burnet, Brazoria, June 18, 1836, in Domestic Correspondence (Texas), 1836–1846, ms.

[12] William Bryan to D. G. Burnet, Agency of Texas, New Orleans, June 20, 1836, in Consular Correspondence (Texas), ms.; copy in Executive Department Journals (Texas), Mar. 1836–Sept. 1836, pp. 317–318.

[13] Thomas Toby and Brother to David G. Burnet, New Orleans, July 11, 1838 [1836?], in Consular Correspondence (Texas), ms.; copy in Executive Department Journals (Texas), Mar. 1836–Sept. 1836, pp. 340–343 (dated 1838).

[14] José Justo Corro, [Decree of the *Congreso general*, approved by José Justo Corro, President *ad interim*, July 16, 1836, opening the port of Matamoros to the importation of provisions during the war with Texas, assigning those provisions to the expeditionary force, and exempting from seizure mules and wagons carrying supplies to that army from within the country]. Mexico, Julio 16 de 1836.

[15] David G. Burnet, "A Proclamation of Blockade of the Port of Matamoros, Velasco, July 21, 1836," in *Telegraph and Texas Register*, Aug. 16, 1836.

before the general government of Texas. If you maintain your post as mere lookers-on; if you do not abandon the city and retire into the interior of Texas, that its army may protect you, you will, without fail, be treated as real enemies, and will suffer accordingly." [16]

On July 11 it was rumored at New Orleans that 4,000 Mexican troops were embarked at Vera Cruz and another 4,000 at Matamoros for Texas, and that these were to be supported by 4,000 troops to enter Texas by land; but, declared Thomas Toby, "as it is like many others got up by the opposition, there is no ground for it." [17] Toby's appraisal of the summer invasion prospects were confirmed by reports from Tampico in mid-July that the troops at Matamoros under General Urrea were in such a state of wretchedness that they could not advance in a new campaign against Texas before the elapse of two or three months.[18] Near the middle of August, Peter Suzeman reached Columbia from Matamoros, which place he left on July 12, to report numerous desertions from Urrea's force and to say that many of the Mexican troops were openly avowing that they would never again enter Texas.[19]

In the meantime, the Mexican authorities at Matamoros were reported endeavoring to engage 8,000 Indians to join them against Texas. Late in June fourteen or fifteen chiefs including six or seven representing themselves and other tribes from Texas held conferences at Matamoros with General Urrea and Colonel Ugartechea relative to joining the Mexicans against the Texans. A correspondent of the *New Orleans Commercial Bulletin* reported from Matamoros on July 1, that "every movement appears to confirm the belief that the negociation is concluded, with a promise to the Indians of land and cattle, should they assist and succeed in exterminating the population of Texas." [20]

Back in Tennessee at the end of May, Richard G. Dunlap had called the attention of the Texan Secretary of State Samuel P. Carson, then in Nashville, to plans to muster out of service between June 10 and June 22 the Tennessee volunteers that had been enrolled under Gen-

[16] John N. Seguin, Lieut.-Colonel of the Army of Texas, to the Inhabitants of Béxar, Béxar, June 21, 1836, in *ibid.*, Sept. 21, 1836. Very few of the Mexican inhabitants of San Antonio heeded Seguin's admonition. *Ibid.*, Nov. 9, 1836.

[17] Thomas Toby and Brother to D. G. Burnet, New Orleans, July 12, 1836, in Consular Correspondence (Texas), ms.; copy in Executive Department Journals (Texas), Mar. 1836–Sept. 1836, pp. 347–349.

[18] *Telegraph and Texas Register*, Aug. 9, 1836.

[19] *Ibid.*, Aug. 16, 1836.

[20] *Ibid.*

eral Gaines' call of April 8. At that time Gaines had asked for a brigade of volunteers each from Alabama, Mississippi, and Tennessee, and for a battalion of mounted men from Louisiana for the defense of the United States frontier, where the Indians were restless on account of the war in Texas. On May 31 Dunlap wrote Carson that the defeat of Santa Anna at San Jacinto had induced a belief that the war with Texas was over, but "if you do require further aid, I wish to be allowed today to state this to the three companies that will be mustered and discharged, as I am confident an appeal to the sons of Tennessee will be answered as becomes gallant spirits." [21] Dunlap declared he had joined the volunteers, believing that they would not be detained long in the service of the United States and that, in that event, he would be able to take the whole volunteer corps to Texas.[22] Carson immediately informed Dunlap that the war in Texas was not over and that he hoped Dunlap would form the men into a volunteer unit and go as soon as practicable to the seat of war.[23]

Early in July 1836, Dunlap received a letter from his close and long-time friend, General Houston (Dunlap, like Houston, was a favorite of Andrew Jackson), expressing regrets at his delay in bringing volunteers to Texas, for "we will need your aid, and that speedily," declared Houston.

[T]he enemy in large numbers are reported to be in Texas; their forces are estimated at from 8 to 12,000. It is impossible to ascertain, but I think it somewhat exaggerated. We can meet and beat them with one-third the number. The army with which they first entered Texas is broken up, and dispersed by desertion and other causes. If they get another army of the extent proposed, it must be composed of new recruits, and men pressed into service, will not possess the mechanical efficiency or discipline which gives the Mexican troops the only advantage they have[.] [T]hey will be easily routed by a very inferior force[.] [F]or a portion of that force we shall be obliged to look to the U. States. It cannot reach us too soon. . . .

March as speedily as possible with all the aid you can bring, and I doubt not you will be gratified with your reception, and situation. Come the most exped[it]ious route, and do not encumber yourself with baggage.[24]

[21] R. G. Dunlap to Samuel P. Carson, Nashville, May 31, 1836, in Garrison (ed.), *Diplomatic Correspondence of Texas*, 1907, I, 94–95.

[22] Same to Same, Nashville, June 1, 1836, in *ibid.*, 1907, I, 97.

[23] Sam P. Carson to Gen. R. G. Dunlap, Nashville, May 31, 1836, in *ibid.*, 1907, I, 95–96.

[24] Sam Houston to Gen. R. G. Dunlap, Nashville, Tenn. [dated:] Near Sabine,

Dunlap was delayed in getting volunteers off to Texas. Yet, it was not long before a considerable number of them began to reach Texas, anxious and determined to fight. The Texan force, consisting mostly of volunteers from the United States soon numbered over 2,000 men.[25] Among those bringing volunteers to Texas were Captain G. L. Postlethwaite, who sailed from New Orleans on July 2 with about 100 men and landed at Galveston on the 6th, and Colonel Edward J. Wilson, who arrived at the latter place on July 19 from North Carolina with a number of volunteers.[26]

With continued reports from Texas on Indian movements of a hostile nature, presumably based on rumors of the return of the Mexican army to Texas,[27] Gaines, acting under the broad discretionary authority conferred upon him by the United States Secretary of War Lewis Cass and with permission granted by the government of Texas,[28] ordered Lieutenant Colonel William Whistler's Fourth Infantry to Nacogdoches on July 11 to investigate the Indian situation, and especially the attack upon Robertson's settlement, feeling confident that some of the Indians who had participated in the raid were from the United States.[29] Whistler was instructed to occupy and fortify the town with a small breastwork and blockhouses. Additional troops, consisting of six companies of infantry and three companies of dragoons were ordered to Nacogdoches from Fort Towson. The first of the troops from Gaines' command reached Nacogdoches toward the end of July and they remained until December.

While encamped at Nacogdoches, the American troops were in close touch with the Texan army. General Houston and his staff visited

---

July 2, 1836, in Amelia Williams and Eugene C. Barker (eds.), *The Writings of Sam Houston*, I, 431 (hereafter cited, *Writings of Sam Houston*).

[25] Hubert Howe Bancroft, *History of Texas and the North Mexican States*, II 282.

[26] Edward J. Wilson and G. L. Postlethwaite to the Public, from the *Lexington* (Kentucky) *Intelligencer*, reproduced in *Telegraph and Texas Register*, Nov. 12, 1836.

[27] S. F. Austin to Gen. Edmund P. Gaines, Columbia, July 4, 1836, in Eugene C. Barker (ed.), *The Austin Papers*, III, 384–385; Barker, *Life of Stephen F. Austin*, pp. 435–436.

[28] Silver, *Edmund Pendleton Gaines*, p. 205; David G. Burnet to James Collinsworth and Peter W. Grayson, Executive Department, Velasco, July 8, 1836, in Garrison (ed.), *Diplomatic Correspondence*, I, 104–105.

[29] Marshall, *Western Boundary of the Louisiana Purchase*, pp. 176–180; Silver, *Edmund Pendleton Gaines*, pp. 204–209.

Nacogdoches late in July. The *Pensacola Gazette* reported that many of the United States soldiers deserted to the Texan army which was increasing rapidly owing to the threatened invasion from Mexico.[30] An American officer, sent to reclaim them, found two hundred men wearing the uniform of the United States army, who refused to return. The occupation of Nacogdoches by Gaines' troops caused General Urrea on August 10 to issue a proclamation to his troops saying that this action on the part of the United States amounted to a declaration of war by that government.[31]

Meanwhile, in Texas, before the rumor of an invasion, Rusk had asked to be relieved of his command, and, on June 25, President Burnet had appointed Mirabeau B. Lamar as major general and commander of the army. Lamar had served as Secretary of War from May 4 to May 30, when he resigned in protest against the plans to return Santa Anna to Mexico. During his brief tenure in the War Office, he had not particularly ingratiated himself with Rusk; in regard to the withdrawal of Mexican forces from Texas, he had specifically instructed him to "keep your troops in motion, moving in the rear of the enemy, but not approaching near enough to create any collision between the armies." Rusk had no sympathy with such a temporizing policy.[32] The first intimation of Lamar's appointment reached Rusk in a curt note from the President which read as follows: "The honorable Mirabeau B. Lamar has been appointed Major General and invested with the command of the Texian army. You will be pleased to receive and recognize him as such." [33] So, when Lamar arrived at army headquarters at Guadalupe-Victoria (Victoria), the army refused to accept him as its commander. Instead, with Felix Huston, Thomas Jefferson Green, and Rusk (now laboring under the excitement of an invasion) intriguing against Lamar, the army chose as its commander Felix Huston. Huston, known as "Old Longshanks" and sometimes as "Old Leather-Breeches," [34] was a turbulent and overbearing soldier of fortune from

[30] Marshall, *Western Boundary of the Louisiana Purchase*, pp. 179–180.

[31] José Urrea, *Proclama. El general en gefe del egército de operaciones sobre Téjas á sus subordinados*, Matamoros, Agosto 10 de 1836, broadside.

[32] *Lamar Papers*, I, 404; Frank W. Johnson, *A History of Texas and Texans*, I, 457; Mirabeau B. Lamar to Thomas J. Rusk, May 7, 1836, in Thomas J. Rusk Papers, ms.

[33] David G. Burnet to Thomas J. Rusk, June 27, 1836, in Thomas J. Rusk Papers, ms.

[34] William Preston Johnston, *The Life of Gen. Albert Sidney Johnston: Em-*

Kentucky who had emigrated to Mississippi. From there he had started to Texas in May 1836, having allegedly incurred a personal debt of some $40,000 in raising and equipping about five hundred volunteers.[35] Huston possessed neither military education nor experience, but had more than once witnessed civilians employ a brief military career as a steppingstone to political preferment and was determined to let no golden opportunity pass to achieve distinction on the fair field of Texas.

Lamar now left the army, and Rusk, reconsidering his request to be relieved of his post, actually continued to command the army, with Sam Houston addressing communications to it as commander in chief. Rusk advanced his headquarters on August 1 from Victoria to the Coleto, about fifteen miles east of Goliad, but when the Mexican troops did not advance from the Río Grande, discipline in the Texan army began to decline very rapidly. Soon most of the resident Texans in the army left for home, where there were many important things to do, and the army came to be made up largely of newcomers from the United States, who were alternately encouraged to come on or advised to hold up as rumors flowed in of a Mexican army assembling or not assembling below the Río Grande. Thus, during the summer of 1836 the army changed from a force composed largely of men who had defended their homes and their rights to one, almost three times as large, consisting of men who as yet had neither homes nor rights in Texas to defend.

Such muster rolls as can be found for the months of July and August 1836, show fifty-three companies with a total of 2,503 officers and men, not counting regimental and staff officers or members of the ranger force. Fourteen of the companies, containing a total of 672 men, were largely Texan, and the remaining thirty-nine, with a total of 1,813 men, were composed chiefly of individuals who had arrived in Texas since the battle of San Jacinto. Of the captains of the Texan companies one had been a staff officer at San Jacinto, three had been lieutenants, three had been privates, and the remaining seven had not participated in the

---

bracing His Services in the Armies of the United States, the Republic of Texas, and the Confederate States, p. 75.

[35] Walter Prescott Webb and H. Bailey Carroll (eds.), *The Handbook of Texas,* I, 869 (hereafter cited as *Handbook of Texas*); A. K. Christian, "Mirabeau Buonaparte Lamar," *Southwestern Historical Quarterly,* XXIII (1919–1920), 164–165. Charles DeMorse in a letter to W. P. Johnston, dated January 25, 1875, reports that Huston did not bring more than 100 to 125 men to Texas. DeMorse was serving as Adjutant General of the Army at the time. Johnston, *Life of Gen. Albert Sidney Johnston,* p. 74.

battle. Of the thirty-nine captains of the immigrant companies, two had been privates at San Jacinto, five had participated in earlier military operations of the Revolution, and the remaining thirty-two had arrived in Texas since April 21.[36]

The volunteers did not yield patiently to discipline, subordination, or effective organization. They had sworn vengeance against the Mexicans, and on reaching Texas were disappointed to find that the fighting was over.

Here were gathered those indomitable men of battle whom Santa Anna pointedly characterized as the *tumultuario* of the Mississippi Valley; the ardent youth of the South, burning for glory and military enterprise. Here enthusiasts of constitutional freedom were mingled with adventurous soldiers from Europe; and souls as knightly, generous, and unstained as Bayard's with outlaws and men of broken and desperate fortunes. Some of the best and some of the worst people in the world were thrown into contact [with one another]; but in one quality all were alike, a hardihood that no danger could check.[37]

Thus commented William P. Johnston, son of the renowned Confederate general Albert Sidney Johnston.

The Anglo-Americans in camp became impatient, and Green suggested to Rusk that, in view of the war talk, he should keep the ball rolling, since the expectation of immediate action against the enemy was the only adhesive force within the army.[38] Four alternatives for the army seemed possible to Green: (1) retire eastward toward the settled area of Texas and go into summer quarters, but this he believed would be unsatisfactory because of the increased danger to the health of the army and because it would project the army into the politics of the country; (2) station the army at some point of advantage on Copano Bay and fortify there, but this would require the effective

36 William C. Binkley, "The Activities of the Texan Revolutionary Army after San Jacinto," *Journal of Southern History*, VI (1904), 340; David G. Burnet to Col. R. Triplett, Velasco, June 3, 1836, in Executive Department Journal (Texas), Mar. 1836–Sept. 1836, p. 114; Same to Thomas Toby, Texas Agent, New Orleans, [dated:] Executive Department, Velasco, June 20, 1836, *ibid.*, pp. 123–125; also letters of Same to Same, June 28, July 2 and 22, 1836, *ibid.*, pp. 126, 127–128, 136–138.

37 Johnston, *Life of Gen. Albert Sidney Johnston*, p. 70.

38 T. J. Green to T. J. Rusk, Aug. 1, 1836, in Thomas J. Rusk Papers, ms.; also quoted in Mrs. Ina Kate (Hamon) Reinhardt, "The Public Career of Thomas Jefferson Green in Texas," p. 42, Masters' thesis.

cooperation of the government in supplying the army by sea; (3) march directly to San Antonio and there fortify, collect provisions, and await recruits from the United States, but it would be necessary to treat with the Comanches and gain their confidence; and (4) march immediately against Matamoros. The latter possibility seemed to Green to be the most desirable, but if a descent could not be made now upon northern Mexico, then he believed that the next best policy would be to move the army to San Antonio and prepare to advance against the line of the Río Grande in the fall.

No Mexican campaign in Texas, however, was immediately forthcoming, owing to internal strife in the interior of Mexico and to a deplorable condition within the Mexican frontier army. Felix Huston appraised the Mexican situation in a letter to Houston. The Mexican advance, he wrote, had been delayed on account of the lack of money for supplies and for the payment of the troops and on account of the unwillingness of the Mexican troops to re-enter the country they had so disgracefully left. Because of the dispersed and disorganized condition of the Mexican army, he believed a favorable opportunity now existed for Texas to subject the whole Río Grande country to conquest, and thus retaliate on Mexico for her devastation of Texas—"make her feel the desolation of war, destroy her resources and means of again invading us—repay our citizens for their great loss of property; and . . . aid our negotiation and make Mexico ask a peace on the terms of defraying the expenses of the war." In the negotiation, he thought, Mexico should be compelled to recognize the independence of Texas. A successful campaign against the northern frontier of Mexico, he believed, could be carried out easily by a force of 2,000 men, and the objectives of such an expedition, including the capture of Matamoros, could be accomplished in the space of one month. Such a campaign would establish the national character of the infant republic, giving it respectability both at home and abroad.[39]

On the other hand, A. C. Allen and John J. Linn believed that any campaign against Mexico ought to await cooler weather and the outcome of the negotiations being carried on through the United States. In the event the negotiations failed or seemed to bog down, Allen informed his "fellow citizens in arms and the Volunteers from the United States" on July 23, that perhaps the best course would be to pursue

[39] Extract of a letter from Gen. Felix Huston to Gen. Sam Houston, n. p., n. d., in *Telegraph and Texas Register*, Aug. 30, 1836.

the war with vigor, by gaining the cooperation of the Comanches through a friendly trade in horses, mules, sheep, and cattle plundered from the inhabitants of Tamaulipas, Coahuila, and Chihuahua, and by laying waste the northern Mexican states.[40]

Others suggested driving off the numerous herds of cattle on the Nueces, San Antonio, and other streams, and removing "the provisions in the country about San Antonio; and . . . [compelling] the Mexican citizens there to manifest their intentions with respect to the war," by moving either to the east or to the west.[41] On August 8 Burnet authorized R. R. Royall to raise a company of "Independent Rangers," numbering one hundred or more men as the commanding general of the army might determine, to be employed in collecting and driving in the large herds of cattle between the Nueces and the Río Grande that "have no ostensible owner and many of which are supposed to belong to Mexican citizens resident beyond the Río Grande."

If the war was renewed, it would be extremely difficult for the Mexican army to cross an extended wilderness, from which the stock had been driven off; whereas, the supply of cattle and horses for the Texan army would have been increased. Should the Mexicans be able to march an army to the Guadalupe without finding any supplies along its route, the men would probably be unfit for duty from fatigue for having packed provisions so far.[42] General Huston sought to support Royall in securing what cattle the Mexicans had not driven from the Nueces and San Antonio rivers in their evacuation of Texas. He offered to volunteers who would get up an expedition to drive cattle from that part of the country an interest in the stock thus obtained. An officer of the army was to accompany the expedition, and an adequate supply of ammunition was promised the unit for use against attacks by parties of Indians or Mexicans. Soon an expedition was in the process of being formed in the vicinity of the Navidad and the Lavaca, in the neighborhood of the Texan army at Camp Johnston on the Lavaca,

---

[40] A. C. Allen to My Fellow Citizens in Arms and the Volunteers from the United States, Head Quarters, Texian Army, Victoria, July 23, 1836, in *ibid.*; John J. Linn to William H. Jack, Secretary of State, New Orleans, August 11, 1836, in Executive Department Journals (Texas), Mar. 1836–Sept. 1836, pp. 72–79.

[41] *Telegraph and Texas Register*, Oct. 25, 1836.

[42] *Ibid.*; David G. Burnet to [R. R. Royall], Executive Department, Velasco, Aug. 8, 1836, in Executive Department Journals (Texas), Mar. 1836–Sept. 1836, pp. 139–140.

to move west for the triple purpose of keeping a watch to the west, preventing the numerous herds of cattle from falling into the hands of the enemy, and providing the army with a winter's supply of beef.[43]

James S. Mayfield, who was soon to become a strong supporter of the Lamar faction in Texas, did not think that merely laying waste the country west of the Guadalupe would help to end the war, unless measures were adopted to defend the country and property east of it.[44] Mayfield believed it would be wise for the government to establish two garrisons on the Guadalupe, which in time of need could be re-enforced quickly by the militia. Such an arrangement would accord some security to the people then living west of the Colorado.

About the time Allen made his address to the troops, President Burnet was expressing thanks to the citizens of Cincinnati for their gift of the two six-pound cannon, better known as the "twin sisters," used in the battle of San Jacinto. He declared that Texas had no desire "to extend her conquests beyond her own natural and appropriate limits, but if the war must be prosecuted against us, other land than our own must sustain a portion of its ravages," and "the voices of the *twin sisters* . . . will yet send their reverberations beyond the Río Grande." [45] With a new army composed largely of "emigrant" soldiers eager for action, Rusk soon joined Green, Huston, Branch T. Archer, Stephen F. Austin, and others in advocating an attack upon Matamoros, and it was not long before President Burnet accepted the idea. His purpose, however, may have been to turn the restless volunteers' attention toward Matamoros with the hope of avoiding further conflicts at home between the civil authorities and the army. Whatever the reason, by August 13 the idea of a movement toward Matamoros seems to have become a policy of the government, for on that date Burnet wrote confidentially to the Texan agent at New Orleans that "at the earnest instance of the officers of the Army we have resolved to make a movement toward Matamoros" and enclosed a list of supplies and munitions needed, "subject to being ordered to Brazos Santiago." [46] "Our army is moving westward, and is

---

[43] *Telegraph and Texas Register*, Dec. 17, 1836.

[44] J[ames] S. M[ayfield] to the Editors [of the *Telegraph*], n. p., n. d., in *ibid.*, Nov. 12, 1836.

[45] David G. Burnet to Daniel Drake and Others, Executive Department, Republic of Texas, Velasco, July 22, 1836, in *ibid.*, Aug. 30, 1836.

[46] David G. Burnet to Messrs. T. Toby and Brother, Executive Department, Velasco, Aug. 13, 1836 (Confidential); Same to Same, Velasco, Aug. 18, 1836;

impatient under the lassitude of an idle camp," he informed Memucan Hunt, an agent in the United States. "They want employment, and we have concluded to give it to them. An expedition against Matamoros is resolved on, and we are now busily engaged in arranging matters for it. The troops will probably commence their march in about two weeks." [47] Major Thomas W. Ward was sent to New Orleans to recruit volunteers in an unofficial and indirect way, for the laws of the United States would not have permitted a foreign government to establish an official recruiting station within its boundaries.

Hearing rumors at Nacogdoches that the Texan army was itself about to march upon Matamoros "to reciprocate the friendly feelings manifest for us," [48] and that Huston had advanced with some five hundred men to San Patricio where he had taken up a position near the Nueces,[49] General Houston wrote Rusk that he saw "no reason in support of the project. I cannot see what can be gained by it." Should the Texan army succeed in taking Matamoros, it would be difficult to hold the place against an aroused Mexican citizenry who could be expected to put forth every effort to expel an invader from a port upon which so large a portion of the Mexican people were dependent for commerce. Cooperation by sea would be necessary. Furthermore, Mexico might avail herself of the absence of any sizable military force in Texas to launch a counterinvasion by way of Laredo and San Antonio, or, using transports and supported by warships, she might seize the country's principal seaports. The most sanguine expectations of spoils from the enemy could not possibly be an adequate compensation for such a wild adventure. "The great object of our Military operations," declared Houston, "ought to be to guard our frontier against invasion, and to resist it if attempted. . . . I am, therefore, most positively opposed to any movement of this kind. . . . Our policy is to hazard nothing—let us act on the defensive." [50]

Two weeks later Houston again wrote Rusk a long letter opposing any movement of the Texan army toward the Río Grande. He pointed

Same to Same, Velasco, Sept. 3, 1836; all in Executive Department Journals (Texas), Mar. 1836–Sept. 1838, pp. 143–144, 149, 152.

[47] David G. Burnet to Memucan Hunt, Aug. 18, 1836, in Binkley (ed.), *Official Correspondence of the Texan Revolution*, II, 946.

[48] *Telegraph and Texas Register*, Aug. 23, 1836.

[49] Bancroft, *History of Texas and the North Mexican States*, II, 290.

[50] Sam Houston to Gen. [Thomas J.] Rusk, Nacogdoches, Aug. 8, 1836, in *Writings of Sam Houston*, I, 436–439.

out the difficulty of supplying the army owing to the lack of funds and the absence of effective naval support. Furthermore, he believed that the United States would look with displeasure upon any offensive operation against Mexico since both Mexico and Texas had requested the United States to mediate their differences. As commander in chief of the army, Houston wrote, "I have always abhorred the thought of attacking Matamoras, for the reason that no benefit could result from it." He continued;

It cannot be that the Army has nothing to do at home. The Colorado is swept of its inhabitants from the Frontier settlements to Moseleys Cotton Gin. The inhabitants have fled to the Brazos. Had the Army taken post on the Navidad, it could easily by throwing out its Cavalry have given protection to the inhabitants and chastised the Indians. It would have also been in a better situation to have given protection to the Coast. What protection could it now render if a force were to be landed at any point East of Matagorda? Then I take it, it can render no aid in its present condition to our Western borders, or to our Coast. . . . If a few Indians can break up our settlements is it not an argument against carrying the war into the enemy's Country, while we leave our own without protection? Let us husband our resources, and act defensively, and our independence will be established.[51]

In early September the reports from Matamoros were that the Mexican army was being daily diminished by desertion. By mid-September, in Texas, the idea of a campaign against Matamoros had floundered, partly because of the opposition of Houston and other men of influence and more particularly for the want of supplies for a campaign. Houston's popularity with the electorate was a warning to those who agitated in favor of an offensive operation against Mexico. "The Ma——s expedition will I apprehend," wrote *ad interim* President Burnet, "be postponed. The army have been a good deal divided on the subject. We are moving on in an easy trot, without much variety of incident to diversify the events of the day." Everyone seemed to be awaiting the forthcoming change in administration in Texas. Meanwhile, the Mexicans continued to drive off cattle from the Nueces country and to send their scouts into Texas as far as the Guadalupe River. The three months volunteers, Burnet wrote the Texan agent in New Orleans,

[51] Same to Same, Nacogdoches, Texas, Aug. 25, 1836, in *ibid.*, I, 443–445.

have multiplied too rapidly upon our hands. They never have and never will do Texas any good; but much evil, independent of the cost, results from them. I therefore request you will furnish no more facilities or aid of any kind to persons of this description. They are mere Leeches. We have no use for and do not want any men for a less period than one year or during the war. Such we will be happy to receive.

The supplies at Galveston were nearly played out, and both troops and prisoners were beginning to feel the pinch of want.[52]

By September 4 whatever danger there may have been from Indians or Mexicans, operating independently or jointly, had passed. On that date Whistler wrote from Nacogdoches that there had never been any disposition on the part of the Indians along the border to attack the United States frontier and that if they had had any intentions of warring on the Texans, the presence of his troops had discouraged them. On October 13 he complained that his men had suffered the hardship of a long march in coming to Nacogdoches to accord protection to a foreign state.[53] The Indians, he reported, had made no disturbances, but were quietly pursuing their various occupations. He found the stories that had been circulated to the prejudice of the Indians to be entirely false. Yet, at the end of November 1836, there were still 428 regulars of the United States army at Nacogdoches. Shortly thereafter, on December 19, in view of the state of affairs on the Mexican frontier and because of the desire of the Jackson administration not to irritate Mexico unnecessarily but to maintain strict neutrality, these troops were withdrawn from Nacogdoches and returned to the United States.[54]

In the meantime, on August 5, Jackson suspended the movement of the Tennessee volunteers to the Sabine, and on August 12 informed Amos Kendall, Postmaster General and presidential confidant, "I have no doubt [it] was intended by Gaines to get troops there who would at once went over to the Texan army; but I have stopped it in the bud." [55] Mexico felt outraged at Gaines' conduct, and her special

[52] David G. Burnet to T. Toby and Brother, Executive Department, Velasco, Sept. 12, 1836, in Executive Department Journals (Texas), Mar. 1836–Sept. 1836, pp. 155–156. See also Same to Same, Sept. 12 (second letter), 13, 20, 21, 24, 1836, in *ibid.*, 156–157, 160–165, 170; *Telegraph and Texas Register*, Nov. 30, 1836.

[53] Silver, *Edmund Pendleton Gaines*, p. 212.

[54] Marshall, *Western Boundary of the Louisiana Purchase*, 184–185.

[55] Andrew Jackson to Amos Kendall, Hermitage, Aug. 12, 1836, in John S. Bassett (ed.), *Correspondence of Andrew Jackson*, V, 420–421.

minister to Washington, M. E. de Gorostiza, demanded his passports and left. It is a "very singular coincidence," he said, "that only when the Mexican troops are advancing in Texas, these accounts of the excess of the Indians are invented or exaggerated, in order that they may, without doubt, reach the ears of General Gaines." [56] On October 15, as he prepared to leave, Gorostiza wrote that the premeditated attacks on the American frontier had existed only in the minds of the Texans and their supporters in the United States. The early rumors of an Indian uprising were invented "solely for the purpose of inducing General Gaines to approach the Sabine, as he in fact did." After the Texan victory at San Jacinto the fear of an Indian uprising quickly disappeared and the volunteers were disbanded. When it became known that Mexico was preparing a new advance, "Immediately, as if by enchantment, the hostile Indians again appeared," declared the Mexican diplomat.[57]

Idleness in the Texan army on the lower frontier of Texas gave an opportunity for venturesome spirits to create many problems, not the least of which were the interference with the government's plan to return Santa Anna to Vera Cruz, the demand that the erstwhile "Napoleon of the West" be sent to camp for trial by court-martial, the plot to kidnap President Burnet and members of his cabinet, and the talk of advancing on Matamoros.[58] A secret traffic in ardent spirits made discipline difficult, and when several of the smugglers of liquor were arrested, a mutiny developed. About fifty men rushed upon the guard at midnight and freed the prisoners, thus making the camp a scene of riot and confusion. The next day, seven of the principal leaders were arrested and quiet was temporarily restored in camp.[59] Towards the end of September the army began to disband, and when Houston became President in October, Rusk was named Secretary of War, Green became a member of Congress from Béxar County, and Huston succeeded to the command of the army. Shortly after inauguration, Houston learned with deep astonishment and regret that many officers

[56] M. E. de Gorostiza to Asbury Dickins, Aug. 4, 1836, in U. S. Congress, *Senate Executive Documents*, 24th Cong., 2nd Sess., Vol. I, doc. 1, pp. 48–49.

[57] Same to Same, Oct. 15, 1836, in *ibid.*, pp. 100–105.

[58] J. J. Linn to William H. Jack, Secretary of State, New Orleans, Aug. 11, 1836, in Executive Department Journals (Texas), April 1836–Oct. 1836, pp. 72–73; Binkley, "The Activities of the Texan Revolutionary Army after San Jacinto," *Journal of Southern History*, VI (1902–1903), 344–345.

[59] Johnston, *Life of Gen. Albert Sidney Johnston*, p. 82.

were at the seat of government, absent from duty, and that others had the habit of leaving at will the army or the special commands to which they had been assigned. "Such practices and conduct being at variance with all military rule and subordination," declared the President, "is forbidden. When in [the] future such cases occur it will be considered that either the officer has vacated his office, or that he is a *deserter* from his command."[60] Congress provided by a law of November 21 a set of rules and articles for the government of the armies of Texas.[61]

Soon after the permanent government under the Constitution of 1836 was installed, the administration, trying not to offend the United States, revoked the blockade of the port of Matamoros on November 1, and as further evidence of its desire for international goodwill issued on December 16, at Columbia, a proclamation recalling within forty days all privateers' commissions and letters of marque and reprisal then in force.[62]

Again, however, there was strong talk in Mexico of a renewal of the Texas campaign. General Huston reported to the War Department that the Mexicans were making formidable preparations for an immediate invasion of Texas under the leadership of General Nicolás Bravo, who had replaced[63] Urrea as commander in chief of the Army of the North.[64] On October 15 President *ad interim* José Justo Corro

[60] "General Orders, Executive Office, Columbia, Texas, October 24th, 1836," in *Telegraph and Texas Register*, Nov. 2, 1836.

[61] "An Act, For Establishing Rules and Articles for the Government of the Armies of the Republic of Texas," approved November 21, 1836, by Sam Houston, in *ibid.*, Dec. 9, 1836.

[62] *Telegraph and Texas Register*, Dec. 27, 1836; *Writings of Sam Houston*, I, 508–509.

[63] Nicolás Brabo [Bravo], *El general en gefe del Ejército del Norte, á las tropas de su mando*, Cuartel general en San Luis Potosí, Noviembre 9 de 1836, broadside; José Tornel y Mendivil, [Circular giving the organizational set up of the staff of the army which is to undertake the campaign against Texas. Dated and signed at the end:] Mexico 5 de Octubre de 1836; José J. de Herrera, [Letter of the Secretary of War, dated October 5, 1836, to Nicolás Bravo, General in Chief of the Army of the North, relating to the decree of the same date on the organization of the staff for the war in Texas. Dated and signed at end:] Mexico Octubre 11 de 1836. See also Thomas W. Streeter, *Bibliography of Texas*, III, 165–166.

[64] Proclamation of Nicolás Bravo, General-in-Chief of the Army of the North, to the Forces under His Command, Camp in San Luis Potosí, Nov. 9, 1836, in *Telegraph and Texas Register*, Feb. 10, 1837. The proclamation begins: "Soldiers! You are destined to form an important part of the army that returns to Texas."

27

by decree extended the order of July 16 (opening the port of Matamoros to provisions for the army) to all ports of the north where
forces were being assembled for another Texas campaign.[65] At the
same time a commissary department was ordered to be set up for the
expeditionary force to Texas.[66] A *manifiesto* issued at Matamoros on
October 16 by the officers of the Mexican army, including the commander in chief, Juan V. Amador, and Major General Woll, affirmed
their loyalty to the government and stated their unanimous desire to
renew the Texas campaign, once Santa Anna had been ransomed or
released.[67]

Upon the receipt of Huston's communication, President Houston,
through his Acting Secretary of War, William G. Cooke, issued a general order on November 30 for the immediate organization of the
militia and for each militiaman to provide himself at once with a sound
horse, a good rifle or gun, and one hundred rounds of ammunition.
The plan of organization required each company to consist of fifty-six
men, rank and file, with one captain, one first, and one second lieutenant.[68] On December 6 a new militia law was approved by the
President.[69]

Again there was great excitement in the country. From New Orleans
it was reported that one hundred men had enrolled for two years (or
for the duration of the war) as a part of General Memucan Hunt's
brigade and were about to leave for Texas.[70] Because there were, at
that time, so many unauthorized persons in Texas and in the United
States wearing the uniform and insignia of the army and navy of Texas
and having "by their licentious and unprincipled conduct, and many

[65] José Justo Corro, [Decree of José Justo Corro, Presidente *ad interim,* dated
July 16, 1836, is extended to all the ports at the north occupied by the expeditionary forces against Texas], Mexico, Octubre 15 de 1836.

[66] José Justo Corro, [Decree of José Justo Corro, President *ad interim,* promulgated October 15, 1836, by Alas, Secretary of the Treasury, establishing a commissary department for the army now proceeding to Texas], México a 15 de
Octubre de 1836, broadside.

[67] Juan V. Amador and Others, *Manifiesto del ejército que ha operado contra
los téjanos á la nación méjicana.* [Dated and signed at end:] Cuartel General en
Matamoros, Octubre 16 de 1836. El General en Gefe, Juan V. Amador. El Mayor
General, Adrián Woll [and twenty-three others], broadside.

[68] General Orders, Columbia, November 30, 1836, signed by William G. Cooke,
Acting Secretary of War, and by E. Morehouse, Adjutant General, in *Telegraph
and Texas Register,* Nov. 30 and Dec. 27, 1836.

[69] See this work, p. 38.   [70] *Telegraph and Texas Register,* Dec. 9, 1836.

impositions practiced upon the friends of Texas abroad, reflected disgrace on the country and service, which they pretend to represent," declared Acting Secretary of War Fisher, it became his duty to declare as "imposters" all such persons without proper authorization.[71]

Colonel Seguin was once more at San Antonio in command of eighty regular troops, largely Anglo-American, and some two hundred "Mexican citizen volunteers" under good subordination.[72] "Deaf" Smith, one of the best Texan scouts, left the capital at Columbia on December 8 hurriedly for Béxar, to investigate the report of a sizable Mexican army advancing towards the Texas frontier.[73] "Let every man . . . perform his duty," declared the editor of the *Telegraph*, and "we shall avoid the necessity of again running away from a poor miscreant band of hirelings. . . . Are there not," he asked, "freemen enough in Texas, to rise and at once crush the abject race, whom, like the musquetoe, it is easier to kill, than endure its annoying buzz?" [74]

By a joint resolution of Congress, approved December 22, 1836, the President was authorized to receive into the army any number of volunteers up to 40,000, to meet the new invasion threat from Mexico.[75] The authorization was more braggadocio than realism for a young country whose total white population probably did not exceed that figure. Obviously, the principal source of supply was expected to be volunteers from the United States. Already a letter from General Huston intended to encourage volunteers to enter Texas from the United States had found its way into the New Orleans newspapers and into the Mobile *Commercial Register*. Huston expressed the opinion that the war with Mexico was not yet over. "The war," he wrote, "must be terminated beyond the Río Grande." [76] To lend encouragement to those who might wish to volunteer, the editor of the *Telegraph* [77] gave a glowing report of the Texan army which he described as well clothed and provisioned, and in high spirits, ready to meet the enemy should he dare to enter the country. Albert Sidney Johnston departed Texas around the middle of November for New Orleans to make arrangements for the forwarding of volunteers to the Republic. The disap-

[71] General Orders, War Department, Columbia, Dec. 19th, 1836 [signed by:] William S. Fisher, Acting Secretary of War, in *ibid.*, Dec. 27, 1836.

[72] *Telegraph and Texas Register*, Dec. 17, 1836.

[73] *Ibid.*, Dec. 9, 1836.   [74] *Ibid.*, Dec. 27, 1836.

[75] H. P. N. Gammel (ed.), *Laws of Texas*, I, 1285.

[76] *Telegraph and Texas Register*, Nov. 12, 1836.

[77] *Ibid.*, Dec. 9, 1836.

pointment of men like Wilson and Postlethwaite, who had returned
to the United States after the threat of an invasion in the summer had
died down, because they had not been permitted to pillage, plunder,
and rob,[78] did not help the recruiting efforts of the Texan agents in
that country. Wilson and Postlethwaite published statements in the
Kentucky press declaring that "Texas was unworthy of public aid or
sympathy," and accused the mass of people in Texas, "from the highest
functionary of their pretended government, to the humblest citizen
(with but few exceptions) . . . [of being] animated alone by a desire
of plunder," and of appearing "totally indifferent whom they plunder,
friends or foes." [79]

While the government of Texas prepared to fend off the new threat
from Mexico, Congress took a look at the military defenses of the
country. It provided for a reorganization of the army of Texas, then
consisting of some 2,000 or 2,500 men, predominantly adventurers and
soldiers of fortune restlessly clamoring to attack Matamoros.[80] Aside
from volunteers, mounted riflemen, and militiamen, the permanent
military establishment was to consist of one regiment of cavalry, one
regiment of artillery, and four regiments of infantry, with a certain
number of engineers and ordnance officers. The entire force was to be
commanded by a major general appointed by the President. Also, there
were to be two brigadier generals, one adjutant general, one inspector
general, one quartermaster general, one commissary general of subsistence, one paymaster general, one surgeon general, and other lesser
officers.[81]

President Houston submitted to the Senate on December 20, 1836,
the names of Thomas Jefferson Green for senior brigadier general and
Felix Huston for junior brigadier general of the army. The Senate at
first refused to confirm either, but upon reconsideration the next day

[78] *Ibid.*, Dec. 22, 1836.

[79] Edward J. Wilson and G. L. Postlethwaite to the Public, from the *Lexington*
(Kentucky) *Intelligencer*, reproduced in the *Telegraph and Texas Register*, Nov.
12, 1836.

[80] Gammel (ed.), *Laws of Texas*, I, 1112, 1223–1226; Sam Houston, *Rules and
Regulations Promulgated by the President, for the Direction of the Army and
Navy of Texas;* see also *Writings of Sam Houston*, IV, 39–44.

[81] An Act to Organize and Fix the Military Establishment of the Republic of
Texas, Approved December 20, 1836, by Sam Houston, in *Telegraph and Texas
Register*, Jan. 3, 1837.

consented to the appointment of Huston but not Green.[82] The following day (December 22) Albert Sidney Johnston, whose brothers had
participated in the Gutiérrez-Magee filibustering expedition to Texas
in 1812–1813, was nominated by the President for the rank of senior
brigadier general and the Senate readily approved.[83] Johnston's previous experience in Texan military affairs had been short-lived.[84] General Rusk had appointed him on August 5 adjutant general with the
rank of colonel; and four days later he had been named by Houston
as an aide-de-camp with the rank of major.[85] Johnston served in the
latter position for a few weeks, but in September he left the army for
Columbia, the capital, to discharge the duties of adjutant general. On
November 16 he started for New Orleans "on a nominal furlough of
three months, but actually in the interests of the Texan Government," [86]
to make arrangements for volunteers to come to Texas. News reached
him in New Orleans on January 11, 1837, of his appointment to the
command of the army, but it was not until January 31, after his return
to Texas, that he was ordered to assume the command which had been
exercised by Huston after Rusk left the army to become Secretary of
War in the new administration.

General Huston and his friends resented the appointment of Johnston, and, on February 4, 1837, when the latter reached Camp Independence, on the east side of the Lavaca River about four or five miles
from Texana, to take command, Huston challenged him to a duel.[87]
In the duel that followed the next day Johnston was severely wounded
on the sixth shot and could not take charge of the army for some time.
Huston continued in command of it, later turning the command over
to Johnston, under whom he served for a time. The two became friends.

Further information brought into Texas late in December 1836, by
three Anglo-Texan prisoners who effected their escape from Matamoros, caused Secretary of War Fisher to repeat on the last day of

[82] E. W. Winkler (ed.), *Secret Journals of the Senate: Republic of Texas,
1836–1845*, pp. 35, 40.

[83] *Ibid.*, pp. 40–41.

[84] Johnston, *Life of Gen. Albert Sidney Johnston*, pp. 67–69.

[85] *Ibid.*, p. 73.

[86] *Ibid.*, p. 74.

[87] Felix Huston to General A. S. Johnston, Headquarters Camp Independence,
Feb. 4, 1837; and A. Sidney Johnston to Brigadier-General Felix Huston, Headquarters Camp Independence, Feb. 4, 1837, *ibid.*, pp. 75–79.

December Cooke's order of November 30 for an immediate organization of the militia to meet the expected Mexican invasion. Fisher added to the list of necessary equipment for each militiaman the requirement of ten days' provisions.[88] The day before, Brigadier General Green, then preparing to go on a recruiting expedition to the United States, issued from the capital a rather curious address, urging upon the men in the army "those principles of subordination and duty of which I have at all times taught you lessons, and to your present brave and gallant leader, General Huston," he concluded, "I most fervently recommend you." [89] This was, indeed, a strange piece of advice coming from one who so often flouted authority.

Thirty Mexican prisoners, allegedly spies, taken at various places and times along the frontier were moved from army headquarters to Columbia on January 5, 1837. Denying that they were spies, the Mexicans declared that they had only been engaged in the trading of horses and in the smuggling of tobacco into Mexico. Late in January five Mexicans direct from Laredo were captured near San Antonio by Colonel Seguin and sent to army headquarters.[90] Seguin also reported the concentration of Mexican troops along the Río Grande confirming to a substantial degree the confidential information President Houston received from Matamoros. The latter reports placed the Mexican forces at Matamoros on January 26 at 2,855 and at Saltillo at 2,500 with a combined total of twenty-eight cannons and two mortars. By March 1837, it was said that the Mexican forces in the north had been augmented to 8,000 men.[91]

Discipline was poor in the Mexican army at Matamoros, and it was said that the soldiers there, having gone unpaid for two months, were "stating they would not march for Texas until their arrears were paid up, and measures taken to have a regular commissariat behind the army, after having marched." [92] On the other hand, discipline in the

[88] General Orders, War Department, Columbia, December 31, 1836, signed by William S. Fisher, Secretary of War, in *Telegraph and Texas Register*, Jan. 3, 1837.

[89] Thomas J. Green to Fellow Soldiers and Late Companions in Arms, Columbia, December 30, 1836, in *Telegraph and Texas Register*, Jan. 11, 1837.

[90] *Telegraph and Texas Register*, Feb. 14, 1837.

[91] Johnston, *Life of Gen. Albert Sidney Johnston*, p. 81.

[92] Report from Matamoros dated January 2, 1837, in *Telegraph and Texas Register*, Feb. 3, 1837. See *Impugnación*, Matamoros, Febrero 23 de 1837 [by] Varios Gefes del Egército, amigos de la verdad, broadside. This is an attack by several army officers on the editors of the government organ, the *Diario del*

Texan army seems to have been somewhat better at this time. In January 1837, President Houston visited the army and, it was announced publicly, had found it in extraordinary health and in fine spirits, and considered it to be very efficient and daily improving in discipline and in military science.[93] Two months later, Secretary of War Fisher, returning to the nation's capital after a visit to the army, declared that "he never reviewed a finer body of troops, or one whose general appearance more fully indicated the beneficial effects of a strict military discipline and a well regulated camp police." [94] In an idle, ill-provisioned army, it was no easy matter to maintain discipline. Judging from the comments of a member of the army, beef seems to have been the main bill of fare. Wrote Joshua H. Davis in late May 1837,

> The Army has been quiet, feeding on Bull beef for so Long a time the Animal will occasionally rise and Bellow out[.] The officers have then to do their duty and Bring the soldiers back to their duty and all is over. . . . And I may add . . . Oh what fun we do have eating Beef Boiled-Stewed-Baked and Roasted. Notwithstanding the fare we are fat[,] raged and saucy—and feel as if we could whip our weight in Wild Cats And five times our weight in Mexicans.[95]

The Mexican army was expected to enter Texas in February, and early in that month news from the western frontier gave the distribution of the Mexican forces destined for Texas as 1,000 at Monterey, 2,000 at Saltillo, 2,000 at Matamoros, and 100 at Laredo. The troops were pictured as being "in a state of insubordination, badly clothed, and worse fed"; many of them were in irons and those who were not were quoted as saying that they would stay in Mexico and would fight if their country was invaded but that they would not and could not be forced into Texas.[96] By late February General Bravo left the command of the army and returned to Mexico City, but the Texans could find little consolation in this change on the Mexican frontier, for it was

Gobierno (Mexico City) for withholding information that the troops destined for a Texas campaign had received only a fraction of their pay and that they and their families were as a result undergoing great privation.

93 *Telegraph and Texas Register,* Jan. 21, 1837.

94 *Ibid.,* March 28, 1837.

95 Joshua H. Davis to Mrs. Pamela Davis, Morganfield, Ky. [dated:] Camp Bowie [Texas], May 31, 1837, in *Quarterly of the Texas State Historical Association,* X (1906–1907), 348–349; XI (1907–1908), 72 n.

96 *Telegraph and Texas Register,* Feb. 10, 1837. See also *ibid.,* May 2, 1837.

reported that small detachments from the Army of the North would soon be sent to capture San Antonio and Goliad, then unoccupied, after which the Mexican government would make an effort to conclude a definitive peace treaty with Texas, acknowledging her independence.[97]

The one effort made during Houston's first administration to extend the flag of Texas over the area claimed under the law of December 1836 met with a rebuff from the President himself. Ranging west of San Antonio with a force of twenty-one men, Erastus ("Deaf") Smith and John C. Hays set out from their camp on the Medina on March 6, 1837, without authorization from the government, to plant the Texan flag of independence on the spire of the church at Laredo and to learn something about the Mexican military buildings in the north. They arrived on the evening of March 16 at the old San Ygnacio Ranch on the Arroyo Chacón, about five miles northeast of Laredo, where they discovered five Mexicans, who fled instantly toward Laredo to give the alarm of the approach of the Texan force. Smith was unable to overtake the fleeing Mexicans. Early the next morning "Deaf" Smith, accompanied by one of his men, went out to view the road leading to Laredo, hoping to take a prisoner who could give him information about the town's defenses. While reconnoitering, he discovered the trail of a party of cavalry sent out from the town to intercept him. He forthwith returned to camp to prepare to defend himself. After waiting unsuccessfully until 1 o'clock for the enemy to put in his appearance, Smith determined to fall back a few miles to where his horses could get a little grass, as they had not had any during the night. Having proceeded about two miles, he again discovered the enemy, not more than one mile distant, "advancing in fine order." Smith quickly ordered a retreat to the camp he had just left, which had been located in a deep wash in the bed of a river, then dry. Before reaching the dry river bed, however, Smith discovered that a portion of his men were about to be cut off by the pursuing force of forty cavalrymen from the Laredo garrison. Consequently, he and his men found it necessary to take cover in a nearby mesquite thicket, to secure their horses, and to prepare for immediate action. The Texans had scarcely prepared themselves for battle when the enemy commenced firing on their right and left at a distance of about 150 yards, while a portion of the Mexican force advanced rapidly to the rear of the Texans. From their positions the Mexicans moved toward the thicket,

[97] *Ibid.*, Feb. 21, 1837.

keeping up a brisk fire all the time. When the attacking force arrived within some 50 yards of the Texans, Smith ordered his men to commence firing.

After an engagement, lasting about forty-five minutes, the Mexicans withdrew, leaving ten of their number dead on the field and carrying off several wounded. Two Texans were wounded. Smith reported later to the Secretary of War that he decided not to attempt to enter Laredo after learning from a wounded Mexican left on the battlefield that a considerable enemy force was in the town. The Texans returned to San Antonio on the evening of March 26 with the twenty horses they had captured from the Mexicans and after a fatiguing march of ten days. "No shout of exultation welcomed our return to Béxar," reported Smith, "the inhabitants plainly evidencing that their sympathies were with the enemy."

Concerning the escapade, President Houston wrote to Colonel Henry W. Karnes, commander of the Texas cavalry on the frontier, as follows: "I am afraid our friend Deaf Smith and his men have acted badly, if reports are true. . . . You will let him know if you should meet him that he is to draw no more goods on the merchants of San Antonio, for either his men or himself without your order." [98] Houston's policy was not to antagonize the Mexicans, although if Mexico wished to

[98] Sam Houston to Henry K. [W?] Karnes, Columbia, Texas, March 31, 1837 (Private), in *Writings of Sam Houston*, II, 76–78. See also Report of "Deaf" Smith to W. S. Fisher, Secretary of War, San Antonio de Béxar, March 27, 1837, in Army Papers (Texas), ms.; also in *Telegraph and Texas Register*, April 11, 1837; Defunciones, vol. II, p. 24, entries nos. 108–110, Archives of San Augustine Church, Laredo, ms.; Seb. S. Wilcox, "Laredo during the Texas Republic," *Southwestern Historical Quarterly*, XLII (1938–1939), 98; J. D. Affleck, "History of John C. Hays," pt. I, p. 40, typed ms.; Ed. Kilman and Lou W. Kemp, *Texas Musketeers: Stories of Early Texas Battles and Their Heroes*, pp. 119–120; *Jack Hays: The Intrepid Texas Ranger*, pp. 3–6; *Telegraph and Texas Register*, March 17, 1838.

Smith reported that Captain Nicholas Dawson, late of the army, "by his cool and intrepid conduct afforded great encouragement to the younger soldiers," during the fight with the Mexicans before Laredo. On March 27 the men elected Dawson captain of the company. The following men comprised Smith's unit: Nicholas Dawson, Captain; D. W. Babcock, orderly sergeant; J. C. Boyd; Owen B. Hardiman; Daniel Winchell; Abm. Goshay; John L. Bray; J. F. Johnson; J. C. Morgan; W. Williams; Perry James; M. B. Lewis; C. W. Egery; Peter Conrad, slightly wounded; Antonio Lockmar; James M. Jett; Stephen Jett; George Dolson, slightly wounded; F. W. White; L. B. Henderson; James S. Lee, necessarily detained at San Antonio, privates.

renew the campaign he would willingly and forcefully meet the challenge.

W. P. Benson, one of the prisoners captured at San Patricio in February 1836 by General Urrea's forces, arrived in Texas early in April by way of New Orleans after a long confinement at Matamoros. He gave the number of Mexican troops there as mustering between 3,600 and 3,800 men with only about 400 horses, "very old and very poor, and no grain to feed them." General Woll was "almost constantly engaged in superintending a Monte-bank." "A regiment of volunteers *rushed* to join the troops at Matamoros lately," commented the editor of the *Telegraph,* "all well handcuffed and urged onward by the well applied whips of two regiments of regulars." [99] The express mail between Mexico City and Matamoros was captured near Monterey in April by a Texan named J. Powell and brought to Houston on May 10, giving further information concerning the deplorable condition of the Mexican army.

As real danger of an invasion by Mexico waned, even though talk of renewing the Texas campaign continued in that country, Houston planned to curtail heavy expenditures and a mushrooming debt by reducing the huge military outlay of the Republic. Furthermore, Huston's failure to maintain discipline in the army no doubt caused some dissatisfaction on the part of the President, and the vociferous agitation carried on by many persons within and without the army for an attack upon Matamoros found little sympathy with a President who sought to promote peace and prosperity for the young nation. Having been promised letters of marque and reprisal by the President, Samuel A. Plummer and Huston were reported secretly planning "to cause a lawless invasion of Mexico, commencing at Matamoros and extending to Tampico" with General Huston at the head of the band.[100] An excellent steamship had already been procured for the expedition. The fiery factions in the army, easily stirred to turbulence and mutiny by the demagogues in the camp, threatened to become more terrible to the Republic than to its enemies. In March Huston started for New Orleans to raise men and money for the army. He stopped at the seat of government to confer with the administration, and from there on March 28 wrote General Johnston:

[99] *Telegraph and Texas Register,* April 4, 1837.
[100] J. Pinckney Henderson to Sam Houston, New Orleans, July 30, 1837, State Department Letterbook, no. 2, ms., pp. 57–58.

I hope little from the war policy of the Administration. The facility of arriving at the same conclusions from the most opposite state[ment]s of fact renders it entirely useless to argue or reason with the President on the subject. . . . As to our waging active war, he will not hear of it. I am in very low spirits as to our prospects, and deem Texas in a very critical situation.[101]

On May 19, 1837, General Huston was back in Houston from New Orleans [102] in time for the election of major general of the Texas Militia.

Suffering from poor health on account of his wound and being unable to ride on horseback, General Johnston, on May 7 turned over command of the army to Colonel Rogers.[103] On May 17 Johnston received a furlough to visit New Orleans to seek the assistance of certain eminent surgeons; and about midnight, while Huston was visiting the capital to secure the support of Congress in a campaign against Mexico, Houston dispatched his Secretary of War Fisher with sealed orders dated May 18 to the army to furlough three of the four regiments.[104] This was accomplished, leaving only about six hundred men under arms. Gradually these were disbanded by additional furloughs, desertions, or expiration of terms of enlistment.[105] Thereafter for defense against the Indian and Mexican, and for the maintenance of order on

[101] Quoted in Johnston, *Life of Gen. Albert Sidney Johnston,* p. 81.

[102] *Telegraph and Texas Register,* May 26, 1837.

[103] Johnston, *Life of Gen. Albert Sidney Johnston,* p. 83.

[104] William Carey Crane, *Life and Select Literary Remains of Sam Houston of Texas,* p. 128; Herbert Pickens Gambrell, *Mirabeau Buonaparte Lamar: Troubadour and Crusader,* pp. 192–193.

[105] On May 6, 1837, the Secretary of War began furloughing soldiers of the army in accordance to an order of the President. *Telegraph and Texas Register,* March 17, 1838. From San Antonio late in July 1837, Joseph Baker, Chief Justice of Béxar County and member of the First and Second Congresses, wrote:

As regards the Military I regret to say that some discontent prevails, not to a greater extent however. . . . than might reasonably be expected, in any Garrison neither paid, clothed, nor half fed. Although every exertion appears to be made by the officers in command to maintain a strict discipline, it must be acknowledged that under present circumstances it hardly can be expected. I would respectfully take the liberty of suggesting to the Government that propriety of withdrawing the Troops to a situation where they will be prevented from committing those little acts of plunder and pillage which are unavoidable in a well regulated Army.

Joseph Baker to Secretary of State, Béxar, July 24, 1837, State Department Letterbook, no. 2, ms., p. 50.

the frontier, the government depended upon the militia, upon ranger companies, and occasionally upon regular troops enlisted for reasonably long periods of time.

Although a decree of the General Council of the provisional government of Texas, approved by Governor Henry Smith on November 27, 1835, provided for the early organization of the militia, the law "To provide for the National Defence by Organizing the Militia," approved by President Houston on December 6, 1836, came to be the basic law establishing the militia of the Republic.[106] A few months after the furloughing of the army, a supplement to the Militia Act of 1836 was passed over the President's veto on December 18, 1837.[107]

The militia of the Republic consisted of one division commanded by a major general elected, before 1837, by the field officers of his division. After 1837, and until the supplementary Militia Act of January 24, 1839, the major general was elected by a joint vote of both houses of Congress. After 1839 all officers of the militia were to be chosen by the people in an election held under the supervision of a person appointed by the President.[108]

The militia was divided into four brigades, each commanded by a brigadier general elected, before December 1837, by the commissioned officers of the brigade. After that date the initial election was to be by Congress and thereafter, whenever a vacancy occurred, it was to be filled by the officers of the brigade. Each regiment was to have as its commander a colonel elected by the members of the regiment. Each company was to have one captain, two lieutenants, four sergeants, four corporals, one drummer, and one fifer or bugler. The captain and lieutenants were to be elected by the members of their company and the noncommissioned officers and musicians were to be appointed by the captain. At no time was a company to consist of less than thirty-two privates, and if at any time a company should be reduced to less than that number, it was to be incorporated with the adjoining companies while such disabilities existed.

The Republic was divided into four military districts. All counties west of the Brazos were to constitute one brigade; all between the Brazos and Trinity rivers, another; all between the Trinity and Sabine rivers, a third; and all north of the Sabine and Red rivers, a fourth district.

[106] Gammel (ed.), *Laws of Texas,* I, 932–934, 1114–1128.
[107] *Ibid.,* I, 1427–1428.
[108] *Ibid.,* I, 1427-1428; II, 88–89.

By the amended act of 1837 the counties were to be divided into militia precincts, varying in number according to the number of men subject to militia duty. One militia company of not less than fifty-six men, rank and file, was to be raised in each precinct. After the militia had been organized it was the duty of the colonel of each regiment, through his adjutant,

. . . to visit the respective company beats, and cause, by lots, the privates of said beats to be enrolled in class number one, two, and three, which class shall be liable, in the order in which they stand, to be called into actual service by the president, to serve for any period of time not less than three months, nor longer than six . . . and no class shall serve twice until all the others have been called out.[109]

The same division of newly enrolled members into three categories was thereafter to be made by the captain and his officers by lot.

The President had authority, when he thought necessary, to call into the service of the Republic any part of the militia that he deemed expedient, subject to the limitation that a "tour of duty" was to be estimated at three months and that no militia might be required to serve more than two "tours" without discharge. When in service the militia was to be governed by the articles of war and the rules and regulations adopted for the army,[110] and was to receive the same pay and rations as the army. The penalty established in the law of 1836 for failure "to perform a tour of duty when called on" was a fine of $100, but by an amendment of June 7, 1837,[111] this penalty was repealed and thereafter personal responsibility for rendering service became more lax. A further weakening of the militia laws occurred in May 1838, when another enactment was passed over President Houston's veto, divesting the executive of all power over the militia and conferring his "constitutional rights" upon the major general.[112] The

---

[109] *Ibid.*, I, 1427–1428.

[110] Houston, *Rules and Regulations for the Direction of the Army and Navy of Texas;* also found in the *Telegraph and Texas Register*, May 12, 16, and 19, 1838, under the following caption: "Rules and Regulations of the Different Departments of Government and of the Army and Navy"; and in *Writings of Sam Houston*, IV, 39–43.

[111] Gammel (ed.), *Laws of Texas*, I, 1300.

[112] Sam Houston to the House of Representatives, Washington, January 14, 1843, in *Writings of Sam Houston*, III, 292–297. The writer has been unable to locate the law of May 1838.

law "providing for the defence of the frontier" required the President to order out a sufficient number of mounted gunmen from each brigade to commence active operations against the hostile Indians on the frontier and to place at the disposal of a quartermaster, appointed by the major general, $20,000 to take care of the expenses. The President considered the law an infringement upon his constitutional prerogative to call out the militia when he should deem it necessary to do so, and believed that the appointment of a quartermaster by the major general would encroach upon the constitutional grant of power to the President and Senate.[113]

The day the December 1837 militia law was passed over the President's veto Congress proceeded to elect the officers contemplated under it. For major general, it elected Thomas J. Rusk; for brigadier general of the First Brigade (district west of the Brazos), Edward Burleson; for the Second Brigade (district lying between the Brazos and the Trinity), Moseley Baker; for the Third Brigade (district east of the Trinity and to the Sabine), Kelsey H. Douglass; for the Fourth Brigade (district north of the Sabine and up to the Red River), John H. Dyer; and as adjutant general, Hugh McLeod.[114] A year later Congress, with the approval of the President, declared that in the absence of regularly commissioned officers the militiamen were to choose their own officers and Congress pledged itself "to ratify and legalize all such elections." [115]

Every free able-bodied male citizen of the Republic over seventeen and under fifty years of age, unless exempt according to law, was subject to militia duty and was required to enroll in a militia company within a specified period of time of coming of age, of becoming a citizen, or of entering the district. Within ten days after enrolling, he was to "provide himself with a good musket, a sufficient bayonet and belt, six flints, knapsack and cartridge box, with twenty-four suitable ball cartridges; or with a good rifle, yauger, or shot gun, knapsack, shot pouch, powder horn, fifty balls suitable to the calibre of his gun, and half a pound of powder." [116]

The organization of the militia proceeded slowly under the law of

[113] Same to Same, Executive Department, City of Houston, Texas, May 25, 1838, in *ibid.*, II, 238–240.

[114] Texas Congress, *Journal of the House of Representatives of the Republic of Texas; Called Session of September 25, 1837, and Regular Session, commencing November 6, 1837,* p. 291.

[115] Gammel (ed.), *Laws of Texas,* II, 5.

[116] *Ibid.*, I, 1427–1428.

December 1836, and after two years it was still quite incomplete in many sections of the country. Finally, by a supplementary act, approved January 24, 1839, the President was instructed to appoint such persons as might be necessary to organize the militia in conformity with the previous laws; provided, however, that all the officers were to be "elected by the people, under the direction of the person [or persons] so appointed by the President." A penalty for noncompliance in fulfilling one's militia obligation was now revived and made more severe. "Any person," said the law, "refusing to obey such draft or order, shall forfeit a sum of not less than five hundred dollars, to be assessed by court martial." [117] On February 15, 1839, President Lamar issued a proclamation ordering the completion of the organization of the militia under the direction of the chief justices of the counties, assisted by the sheriff, if necessary.[118] In the absence of a chief justice, the duty of organizing the militia devolved upon the sheriff of the county.[119]

Another arm of defense in the Republic was the various companies of mounted riflemen and rangers. A battalion of mounted riflemen, consisting of 280 men was authorized by congressional act of December 5, 1836, for the protection of the frontier. The term of service for the corps was set at twelve months or upwards. Each man was "to furnish himself with a suitable, serviceable horse, a good rifle, and one brace of pistols," if they could be procured. Although pay and discipline were the same as in the army, an additional $15 per month was allowed the rifleman for furnishing his own horse and arms.[120] The mounted riflemen were intended for service in the counties of Gonzales, Mina [Bastrop], and Shelby.[121]

[117] *Ibid.*, II, 88–89.

[118] Proclamation [by Mirabeau B. Lamar] Ordering the Chief Justices to Aid in the Organization of the Militia, February 15, 1839, Record of Executive Documents from the 10th Dec. 1838 to the 14th Dec. 1841, ms., pp. 54–55.

[119] Under this law Frank Hardin was elected Colonel of the 2nd Regiment, 2nd Brigade, Texas Militia, and Edwin Morehouse was chosen brigadier general with headquarters at Houston. John Henry Brown, *Indian Wars and Pioneers of Texas*, p. 414.

[120] Gammel (ed.), *Laws of Texas*, I, 113–114; *Telegraph and Texas Register*, Dec. 13, 1836.

[121] President Houston on December 14, 1836, submitted the names of the officers for the battalion of mounted riflemen to the Senate, which gave its immediate approval. Winkler (ed.), *Secret Journals of the Senate*, pp. 30–31; R. Scurry, Secretary of the Senate, to Sam Houston, Senate Chamber, Dec. 15, 1836,

By an act approved June 12, 1837, after the furloughing of the greater portion of the army and near the expiration of the term of enlistment of the battalion of mounted riflemen, a corps of six hundred mounted men, rank and file, was ordered raised by voluntary enlistment for a term of six months for the protection of the northern frontier. The corps was to be made up of ten companies divided into three divisions, to each of which was to be attached a company of spies. Each officer and private was required to provide himself with "a substantial horse, well shod all round, and extra shoeing nails, a good gun, two hundred rounds of ammunition," and all other necessary equipment and provisions, except beef, which was to be supplied by the government.[122] The officers were to receive the same pay as those of like rank in the ranging service, and the privates were to be paid $25 per month. A bounty of 640 acres each of land was to be given to both officers and privates.

With the outbreak of Federalist revolutionary activities in northern Mexico, the establishment of the French blockade of Mexican ports in April 1838, the increased lawlessness of the southwestern frontier (where an unofficial trade was springing up with northern Mexico), and the constant threat of hostile, pilfering Indians, Congress determined in May 1838 to create a "Corps of Regular Cavalry" of not more than 280 men enlisted for a term of not less than one, nor more than three years, as the President might deem suitable, for the protection of the southwestern frontier.[123]

Recruiting officers were appointed and recruiting stations were opened at Houston, Galveston, and Matagorda.[124] Enlistments in this

---

in State Department Letterbook, no. 2, ms., p. 81. For the County of Gonzales— First Company: William H. Eastland, Captain; Joel Robinson, First Lieutenant; Nathan Mitchell, Second Lieutenant; for the County of Mina—Second Company: Micah Andrews, Captain; J. H. Wade, First Lieutenant; Nicholas Wren, Second Lieutenant; for the County of Shelby—Third Company: Robert O. Lusk, Captain; John P. Applegate, First Lieutenant; David Strickland, Second Lieutenant; Fourth Company: Thomas H. Barron, Captain; Charles Curtis, First Lieutenant; David W. Campbell, Second Lieutenant; Fifth Company: David Monroe, Captain; William H. Moore, First Lieutenant; ——— McLaughlin, Second Lieutenant. For Major of Battalion, William H. Smith; Surgeon of Battalion, A. Ramsay; Assistant Surgeon of Battalion, R. Montgomery.

[122] Gammel (ed.), *Laws of Texas*, I, 1334–1335.

[123] *Ibid.*, I, 1480–1481.

[124] Report of the Secretary of War to Sam Houston, Department of War, City of Houston, Oct. 31, 1838, in Sam Houston, *Documents from the Heads of De-*

regular military establishment went forward slowly. The several companies recruited in Brazoria and Galveston were mustered at Houston in mid-October 1838, before being assigned to duty on the frontier. Western citizens were calling loudly for aid in checking the border warfare, in maintaining peace and security, and in affording protection and encouragement to the Mexican traders, who were exceedingly desirous of continuing a friendly intercourse with the Texans. Every messenger from the west, reported the *Telegraph*, brings "intelligence of new depredations committed either by lawless bands of our own citizens, or by parties of Mexican marauders." [125]

For several months after their formation, the mounted companies were stationed near Béxar and Gonzales for the protection of the western counties, but they were withdrawn in May 1839, for a contemplated Indian campaign to the upper Brazos and Trinity; and the company of rangers that remained at Seguin as a part of Captain Mathew Caldwell's command was disbanded on May 15 at the expiration of the term of service for which the men had enlisted.[126]

A combination arsenal and armory was constructed at Houston under the supervision of Colonel George W. Hockley. By the end of October 1838 it was under the command of Samuel W. Jordan, acting captain of ordnance, and was described as being in excellent shape and possessing eighteen well-trained workmen. Many of the old muskets taken from the Mexicans in the battle of San Jacinto had been completely repaired at a cost of less than three dollars each.[127] According to the report of the Secretary of War in October 1838, the Republic's military stores consisted of the following items, located at Houston, Galveston, and Post West Bernard: [128]

Cannon		*Howitzers*	
Fit for service	11	In good order	2
Unfit for service	14	*Mortars*	1

---

partments, Submitted to Congress by the President. By order of Congress, p. 13.

[125] *Telegraph and Texas Register,* Oct. 20, 1838.

[126] *Ibid.,* May 21, 1839; Report of the Secretary of War to Sam Houston, Department of War, City of Houston, Oct. 31, 1838, in Houston, *Documents from the Heads of Departments,* p. 13.

[127] S. W. Jordan, Acting Captain Ordnance, to G. W. Hockley, Secretary of War, Houston, Oct. 6, 1838, in Houston, *Documents from the Heads of Departments,* pp. 13–14.

[128] Report of the Secretary of War to Sam Houston, Department of War, City of Houston, Oct. 31, 1838, in *ibid.,* p. 13.

Cannon balls		In good order	204
Various sizes	992	Damaged	30
Shells	110	Belts	240
Muskets		Bayonet scabbards	71
Complete	988	Bayonets	609
Needing repairs	440	Musket cartridges	16,770
Damaged & unfit		Musket balls	1 keg
for service	129	Powder	
Rifles	7	Good	189 kegs
Swords & Sabres	84	Damaged	127 kegs
Cartouch boxes			

Wagons, harness, armories, blacksmith's
and carpenter's tools

Of the muskets, 300 were at Houston, 35 at Galveston, and 653 at Post West Bernard. The latter were described as out of order, although they were included in the number listed as "complete." Two pieces of artillery were at Houston, one at Bastrop, and one near Live Oak Point, and several at Galveston. It had been hoped that considerable arms and munitions could have been acquired from the United States government at New Orleans upon the arrival there of the volunteers who had fought the Seminoles in Florida, but the arms had been sent to Baton Rouge and to Natchez where they could not be procured for cash.[129] At this time the Republic had only one hospital for the care of its sick and wounded soldiers, and this was the General Military Hospital at Houston.[130] Such a military establishment was certainly not an imposing one.

[129] Ibid.; The "two pieces of hollow ware" styled the "twin sisters of San Jacinto" were brought to the armory at Houston on August 13, 1838, and were reported to be in "excellent condition." Telegraph and Texas Register, Aug. 18, 1838.

[130] Ashbel Smith to George W. Hockley, Surgeon General's Office, Oct. 27, 1838, in Houston, Documents from the Heads of Departments, pp. 22–24.

CHAPTER THREE

Cattle Raids and Frontier Marauders

THE LARGE MEXICAN RANCHES on the southwestern frontier were broken up by the inroads of hostile Indians in 1834–1836; and, except for those in the vicinity of the Río Grande, their owners universally abandoned them after the defeat of Santa Anna at San Jacinto, fleeing hastily across the Río Grande, leaving thousands of head of cattle to run wild in the region, where the ranges had never been fenced and cattle [1] and horses roamed as freely as the deer or buffalo. Although some of the ranchers returned after the "scare" subsided, many of the restored ranches, as well as those which had survived the earlier disasters, were broken up during the succeeding decade. The repeated incursions of hostile Indians in the area immediately to the north of the Río Grande, occurring at almost every full moon, compelled most of the frontier inhabitants "to abandon their stock farms and remove to the south side of the Río Grande" [2] and even farther inland from the frontier line. In the latter part of July 1837, a party of Comanche Indians, numbering about a thousand warriors, approached to within a few miles of Matamoros; attacked an army outpost, killing a Colonel Cortina and eight or ten Cherokees; burned several ranchos; and escaped with a large quantity of mules, horses, and other plunder. About the middle of April 1840, the Comanches again raided to within two leagues of Matamoros, killed a number of the inhabitants on the Texas side of the river, and escaped with several captives, a number of horses and mules, and other loot.[3]

[1] The wild cattle were trimly made, with legs and feet built for speed, and horns "set forward to kill like the buffalo's." They were different from the domestic cattle in that they ran primarily to one color, that being black with brown backs and bellies. J. Frank Dobie, *The Longhorns*, p. 23.

[2] D. W. Smith to John Forsyth, Matamoros, Aug. 4, 1837, Consular Dispatches (U.S.), 1837–1839, (Matamoros), no. 127, ms., microfilm; see also *Telegraph and Texas Register* (Houston), Aug. 22 and Sept. 16, 1837.

[3] D. W. Smith to John Forsyth, Matamoros, May 26, 1840, Consular Dispatches (U.S.), 1840–1848 (Matamoros), no. 166, ms., microfilm.

With the abandonment of the herds, the number of wild cattle increased. Later, many of these wild and semiwild cattle were taken from this trans-Nueces wilderness by the Texas quartermaster corps for food. Learning in the summer of 1836 that between the Nueces and the Río Grande roamed large herds of cattle which had no ostensible owner, and many of which supposedly belonged to Mexican citizens resident beyond the Río Grande, and "it being important for the subsistence of the Army, to secure supplies of beef as convenient as possible," President Burnet authorized R. R. Royall to raise and organize a company of "Independent Rangers" of one hundred men to collect and drive in such cattle for the use of the government. Under the direction of Brigadier General Thomas J. Rusk, the army "erected their first cattle pens at Goliad, out of cedar posts and rawhide, and their first sweep resulted in the capture of 327 head, which were driven to headquarters." [4] After the disbandonment of the army,

[4] David G. Burnet to R. R. Royall, Velasco, Aug. 8, 1836, in William C. Binkley (ed.), *Official Correspondence of the Texan Revolution, 1835–1836*, II, 912–913; Commission dated Velasco, August 8, 1836, and signed by David G. Burnet and F. A. Sawyer, Acting Secretary of War, authorizing R. R. Royall to raise a company of Independent Rangers, in Executive Department Journal (Texas), Mar. 1836–Sept. 1836, pp. 139–140. Curtis Bishop and Bascom Giles, *Lots of Land*, p. 209 n. Jackson M. Parker was killed near the Nueces in the late summer of 1837 by a party of Tonkawa Indians while engaged with others in collecting cattle for the army. *Telegraph and Texas Register*, Aug. 22, 1837.

In reference to the driving of beeves from the frontier of Texas, Colonel Henry W. Karnes, with considerable acrimony wrote President Houston in the summer of 1837:

The neglect and indifference that I have recently received from you has aroused my feeling to the highest pitch of indignation, and under what I believe to be correct impulse I deem it my duty to inform you with all the frankness of a soldier that all feelings save those of eternal enmity are entirely rooted from my heart . . . When we last parted did you not promise me that I should have command of the whole country west of the Lee Baccay [Lavaca?] You did; but faithless to this solemn pledge you have, as I understand, fitted out two companies to range west of me and authorized them to rob and steal everything that they may meet with in their progress. O, consistency thou art a jewel. . . . Now that we have a Constitution and laws . . . is it a time to license bands of plunderers? Yet I have been credibly informed that Congress and your excellency have sent forward two companies of this description, offering them 7 cents per pound for the beeves they may drive in. Had the base and perjured Congress, instead of licensing marauders, provided means to raise 500 cavalry, I could not only have paid for five times that number of horses but fed our army and paid off the troops under my command with the public spoils which, by this time, I should have taken. Unless you fulfill your solemn pledges and pay more attention to my communications than you have hitherto done I

many of the cattle beyond the Nueces were rounded up by discharged soldiers, adventurers, and other enterprising Texans for private ownership, to replace losses sustained during the revolution, or to drive to markets as far east as New Orleans and Natchez.[5]

The Texas "cowboys" raiding into the area west of the Nueces, drove out cattle from the Mexican ranches at Viejo,[6] Anaquitas, Las Animas, San Juan de Carricitos, Norias, San Antonio, Los Fresnos, Colorado, El Mulato, Jaboncillos, Santa Rosa, Mota, Santa Margarita, Santa Gertrudis, San Diego, Los Angeles, El Pato, La Parida, San Patricio, Salmoneño and others, some of which had been abandoned.[7] Occasionally the raiders were excused on the grounds that the Consultation at San Felipe in November 1835, had decreed that all persons leaving the country without permission from the proper authorities, to avoid participation in the "struggle" with Mexico, would "forfeit all or any lands they may hold or may have a claim to, for the benefit of this government; *provided, nevertheless,* that widows and minors are not included in this provision." [8] This same provision was essentially repeated in the Constitution of 1836. General Provisions, Section 8, of that document declared: "All persons who shall leave the country for

---

will resign and retire to the walks of private life, for I will not be treated with neglect and indignity by any man, however exalted his official status may be. In the next breath, so to say, Karnes thought better of his threat and decided to quit forthwith. "Having solemnly pledged yourself," he wrote, "to accept my resignation, those pledges I now call upon you to redeem, and as I wish you to consider this communication as a tender of the same I now sir withdraw to private life." H. W. Karnes to [Sam Houston], Béxar, July 4, 1837 (Private), in Henry W. Karnes Papers, ms.; *San Antonio Daily Express,* March 10, 1910, p. 35, cols. 2 and 3.

[5] Joseph Eve to James F. Ballinger, Galveston, April 26, 1842, in Joseph Milton Nance (ed.), "A Letter Book of Joseph Eve, United States Chargé d'Affaires to Texas," *Southwestern Historical Quarterly,* XLIII (1939–1940), 486–491.

[6] Located three leagues north of Matamoros.

[7] Many of these ranches are listed in Antonio García y Cubas, *Atlas geográfico estadístico é histórico de la republica mexicana,* no. 6; T. J. Rusk to A. Somervill, Head Quarters, Victoria, June 22, 1836, in Binkley, (ed.), *Official Correspondence of the Texan Revolution,* II, 810–811; Vicnte Filisola, "Representación dirigida al supremo gobierno por el General Vicente Filisola, en defensa de su honor y declaración de sus operaciones como general en gefe del ejército sobre Tejas," reprinted and translated in Carlos E. Castañeda, *The Mexican Side of the Texan Revolution,* p. 187; José Urrea, "Diario de las operaciones militares de la division que al mando del General José Urrea hizo la campaña de Tejas," reprinted and translated in *ibid.,* pp. 212–214.

[8] H. P. N. Gammel (ed.), *Laws of Texas,* I, 542.

the purpose of evading a participation in the present struggle, or shall refuse to participate in it, or shall give aid or assistance to the present enemy, shall forfeit all rights of citizenship, and such lands as they may hold in the Republic." [9] The forfeitures included all property, such as horses, mules, cattle, and other items whose owners, being without citizenship, received no protection under the law for their property.[10] Often those whose loyalty had not been in question suffered at the hands of unscrupulous persons.

Many of the ranches abandoned near the Río Grande were later reoccupied, although Texan raids often extended to Matamoros, Guerrero, and Laredo. Reports were afloat in Texas that immense herds of cattle driven from the western counties of the Republic were pasturing on the prairies beyond the Río Grande.[11] Occasionally the bold, daring, and ruthless Texas raiders crossed the Río Grande and got more cattle and horses, many of which were not really wild, justifying their action under the "law of retaliation" for property either destroyed or carried off without compensation by the Mexican army in its retreat from Texas.[12] The debatable land between the Río Grande and the Nueces often became the scene of hostile meetings between the Mexicans and Texans, and the raids into the area were frequently conducted at the risk of spending a couple of months in a Matamoros jail "jess because I stole some horses from 'em to pay for them they stole from Texas." [13]

The word "cowboy" was not meant as a term of reproach, and as war existed between Texas and Mexico, the operations of the "cowboys" were considered legitimate, so long as they did not involve robbery or murder of citizens of Texas. Wild horse driving was an important phase of the cowboy's business. The area between the Sal Colorado (also known as Arroyo Colorado) and Agua Dulce was the favorite hunting ground for the small, wiry Spanish pony, commonly

[9] *Ibid.*, I, 1079.

[10] John Henry Brown, *Indian Wars and Pioneers of Texas*, p. 686.

[11] *Telegraph and Texas Register*, April 28, 1838.

[12] It was reported in New Orleans that the Mexican army drove off five thousand head of cattle, and that the Mexican soldiers half-starved and half-clothed "sneaked" into Matamoros "like thieves and murderers." Edward Hall to D. G. Burnet, New Orleans, June 20, 1836, in Binkley (ed.), *Official Correspondence of the Texan Revolution*, II, 807–808.

[13] John C. Duval, *The Young Explorers*, p. 133; see also Sam Houston to Col. H. W. Karnes, Commanding Texian Cavalry [dated:] Columbia, Texas, March 31, 1837, in Henry W. Karnes Papers, ms.

called "mustang." The maps of the day often showed the area as the "Wild Horse Desert." "There were hundreds of mustang pens between the Nueces and the Río Grande," recorded John S. Ford.[14]

A party of Mexicans from Camargo between October 20 and 25 was engaged in collecting cattle near the Carricitos when it was surprised by fifteen Texan cowboys and two of its members were captured and taken as far as the Mugeres before being released. Upon the return of the two rancheros to Camargo, they reported that the Texans had carried off upwards of a thousand head of cattle. Thus, not only have "the Indians plundered . . . the horses and mules," commented the editor of the *Mercurio de Matamoros,* but "the rascally *colonists,* aware that our troops are prevented from pursuing them, by the rise of the waters, band together in perfect security" to carry off the little stock that remains which might serve for a future campaign against Texas.[15]

The Mexicans who engaged in catching wild horses were a rough lot. Many of them paid little heed to the laws governing the rights of property and a wayfaring man was about as secure in meeting a band of Comanches as in encountering a party of "mustangers." The Mexicans were also good at raiding, often crossing the Nueces at the Santa Margarita Crossing and at other points. Late in December 1837, or early January 1838, Major W. Thompson with a few comrades penetrated to the Río Grande near Reinosa and returned to report that the party of Mexicans which recently visited San Patricio consisted of five hundred soldiers from Matamoros, supported by two field pieces and one hundred rancheros. From a couple of Mexicans he captured at a point about seventy miles west of the Nueces, Major Thompson learned that the troops recently at San Patricio had driven a thousand head of cattle from the vicinity of the Nueces to Matamoros. Near San Patricio the Mexicans had taken eight or ten prisoners, including

14 John S. Ford, "Memoirs," III, 531, ms. Patrick Burke related that the mustangers around San Patricio in the early days who wanted to capture wild horses would take one wild one and tie "an imitation man upon him and let him loose. Of course he would make for the herd, which would try to outrun him. This would start every mustang for miles around to running and the noise from these running horses, which sometimes numbered thousands, often sounded like the terrific roar of a passing cyclone. After they had run themselves down we could guide them into the pens with long wings which we had built for capturing them." Quoted in Mrs. I. C. Madray, *A History of Bee County with Some Brief Sketches about Men and Events in Adjoining Counties,* p. 5.

15 *Mercurio de Matamoros* quoted in *Telegraph and Texas Register,* Dec. 2, 1837.

a man named W. J. Cairns, whom "they treated in a very cruel manner." "When last seen they were dragging him along upon a cannon to which he had been tied." [16] Another captive was a spy belonging to Colonel Lysander Wells' company who was taken about twenty-five miles from San Patricio by a party of a hundred Mexicans. They sent him to San Patricio to another unit of their force, and there he was severely flogged. At night he made his escape.

During the week of March 3, 1838, a band of eight Mexican marauders believed to have been led by a renegade Mexican from San Antonio, named Antonio Viña, being apprised of the defenseless state of Copano House and of a considerable quantity of tobacco stored there decided to rob the place. On the road toward Goliad, six miles from Copano Landing, they met Reuben H. Roberts on his way to attend to business concerning land surveys. They arrested Roberts and forced him to proceed to Copano to help pack their horses with the contents of the warehouse. The robbers carried off most of the tobacco, and ripped open those bales that they could not take away, strewing tobacco all over the house with the object of wasting and spoiling it.[17] Roberts was carried as far as the Nueces and released.

Disasters of this nature, however, did not discourage the hardy pioneer and enterprising trader who sought to do business with the Mexicans below the Nueces. By midsummer, Willis Roberts, brother to Reuben H. Roberts, had nearly completed his house at Aransas; and Colonel James Power, a former *empresario*, was engaged in an active mercantile business at Live Oak Point. Three schooners had recently been to Aransas. The *Alexander* from New Orleans had returned some of the families who had formerly resided at the Mission of Refugio, and the *Empress* from Mobile was on July 12 preparing to cross the bar into the bay.[18] Although commercial activities showed considerable optimism, the business continued to be hazardous.

A party of Mexican marauders entered Goliad in June, and drove off a number of horses and mules. The party then proceeded in the direction of Copano. En route it captured near Refugio two American traders with loaded pack animals. Continuing northward from Refugio, the Mexicans ambushed on the rising ground near the San Nicolás

[16] *Telegraph and Texas Register,* Jan. 13, 1838.

[17] [Willis] Roberts to Genl. Mirabeau B. Lamar, Live Oak Point, March 3, 1838, in *Lamar Papers,* II, 41–43.

[18] W. Roberts to Mirabeau B. Lamar, Aransas, July 12, 1838, in *ibid.,* II, 183–184.

Lakes,[19] in Refugio County about nine miles north of Refugio, two Anglo-Americans and three Mexicans, including Rafael Herrera of Béxar, with four carts and one wagon loaded with clothing and provisions valued at several thousand dollars. The attacking party killed one of the Americans, who sought to use his arms, and wounded the other, who died several days later. The three Mexicans, who had made no resistance, were bound and taken with the carts and wagon to the Mexican camp, which was some distance from the point where the attack had occurred. The Mexican force, when united, consisted of approximately a hundred regulars and rancheros and twelve Indians under Captain Manuel Savariego. Savariego reproached the soldiers who brought the wounded American into camp. The other two Americans convinced the Captain that they were citizens of the United States, and he released them, but their goods were not restored. They demanded to be taken to Matamoros where they could protest this insult to the citizens of a friendly power, and so frightened the commander that he ordered their property restored to them at once. The day following the arrival of the prisoners in camp, the contents of the carts and wagon that could be carried were distributed among the troops and the remainder was destroyed. Savariego then released the empty vehicles and freed the wounded Anglo-American, Herrera, and several others whom units from his command had captured during the last few days. Three of the prisoners, however, were not released, because, he claimed, they were wanted by the authorities, and another, because, it was said, he owed more than $100 to a person named Falcón to whom he was a servant. The Mexican force then proceeded in the direction of Matamoros, having been unable to locate the party of Tahuacano Indians, who, they said, had stolen a *caballada* [20] and committed other damage.[21] This was the second outrage committed in 1838 by the Mexicans upon the western settlements, and with their plunder the marauders had gone off unmolested and, no doubt, elated with their success. Between Indians and Mexicans, wrote William McCraven from San Antonio in July 1838,

[19] The rising ground near the San Nicolás Lakes was a favorite camping ground for the Karankawa Indians. *Handbook of Texas,* II, 559.

[20] A *caballada* was a herd of horses.

[21] Erasmo Seguin, J[ustice of the] P[eace], al Señor Secret[ari]a de Estado, Béxar, 30 de Junio de 1838, in Domestic Correspondence (Texas), 1836–1846, ms.; *Telegraph and Texas Register,* July 7, 1838; *Matagorda Bulletin,* July 5, 1838, reported that seven carts of goods and stores were seized.

it is almost impossible to keep a horse. The latter I believe are almost as great a pest as the Indians. They come in from the Río Grande trading, bring in a drove of horses and mules.[22] They sell out and buy what merchandise they want and steal all the good horses they can lay their hands on to carry back with them. In most instances, the Indians bear the blame. There is at present a constant communication between the Mexicans on the Río Grande and this place. It is encouraged on account of the trade, but the policy appears to be exceedingly doubtful—for they steal almost as many horses as they bring in.[23]

"Something ought to be done for the protection of the West," declared the editor of the *Matagorda Bulletin*.[24] Shortly after retiring as Secretary of War, Colonel William S. Fisher, impatient with Houston's policy of leaving Mexico alone, wrote on February 6, 1838: "The people have lost faith in the Administration. They consider that the tendency of the whole of its measures is to prolong the war to an indefinite period, and then cry aloud for action and decided measures that will put an end to the harassing state of incertitude in which they now stand." [25]

There was increased talk in the west that nothing short of the taking of Matamoros and the establishment of Texan military posts there and at the various crossings of the Río Grande would remedy the situation. Meetings were held at Velasco, Brazoria, and other points in the west, demanding offensive action against Mexico. Texas, it was said, should

[22] A visitor to the Republic has left the following description of the Mexican *arrieros*, or muleteers, who braved the frontier dangers.

Mounted on Spanish horses, or well trained mules, with heavy Spanish saddles and bridles, enormous spurs, and large sombreros—hats covered with green oil cloth, with silver bands, and tassels, and buckles, and rich ponchos over their shoulders, their legs protected by mountain goat-skins from the brushwood and the rain, with long whips and *waccos*, or drinking shells made of gourd, a "wild and wonderful" appearance. The constant crack of the whip, and the oft repeated *vamos* to the mules and horses, produces a spell-bound and startling effect. [Frederic Benjamin Page], *Prairiedom: Rambles and Scrambles in Texas or New Estremadura, by a Suthron*, p. 98.

[23] William McCraven to Gen. M. B. Lamar, San Antonio, July 29, 1838, in *Lamar Papers*, II, 192–193.

[24] July 25, 1838.

[25] Quoted in William Preston Johnston, *The Life of Gen. Albert Sidney Johnston: Embracing His Service in the Armies of the United States, the Republic of Texas, and the Confederate States*, p. 85. William S. Fisher served as Secretary of War from December 21, 1836, to November 13, 1837. *Handbook of Texas*, I, 603.

have exclusive navigation of the Río Grande. This of course, could not be obtained except by conquest, which, in view of the French blockade and the numerous *pronunciamientos* in the north against Centralism, was believed to be no great difficulty at this time.[26] On the other hand, Thomas J. Green, who found Houston, Heaven, and Hell working against Lamar's candidacy for the presidency, believed that the frontier situation could be made to redound to Lamar's benefit in the forthcoming election. "I think it would be a national blessing at present," he wrote, "to have 20,000 Mexican soldiers east of the Río Grande, they could be easily whipped, and their presence would teach us the danger of placing at our head a respectable *old maid*, fit alone for the decencies of 'amiable Mediocrity'." [27]

In the meantime, on Tuesday, July 17, 1838, a trader by the name of Buckhanan discovered a schooner, presumed at the time to be the *Commanche* but later determined to be the *Lodi*, lying at anchor in the harbor at Corpus Christi. Suspecting that the Mexicans had taken possession of the bay of Corpus Christi, he landed seven men and drove off thirty Mexican cavalry, took possession of the schooner, and destroyed fifty barrels of flour.[28] Buckhanan then returned to Texana and reported the Mexican aggression within the claimed boundary of Texas. Shortly before his arrival at Texana, Colonel Pinckney Caldwell reached there to report that on Saturday, July 21, he met a party of Mexican cavalry proceeding towards Corpus Christi and that he had captured at some forty-five miles southwest of San Patricio the captain of the Mexican schooner which had been lying in the bay for two months. The Mexican ship captain, who was attempting to reach Matamoros by land, informed Caldwell

. . . that on account of the French blockade, Corpus Christi had been declared by the Mexican authorities a port of entry, that a customs house officer (from Matamoros) was then on board of his vessel, guarded by a considerable force and that re-inforcements were hourly expected, sufficient to enable them to hold the place against any force which might be sent against them.[29]

[26] *Matagorda Bulletin,* July 5, 1838.
[27] Thomas J. Green to Genl. M. B. Lamar, Velasco, July 11, 1838, in *Lamar Papers,* II, 181–182.
[28] *Telegraph and Texas Register,* July 28, 1838; William S. Fisher, Edwin Morehouse, and P. Caldwell to the People of Matagorda County, Texana, July 22, 1838, in *Matagorda Bulletin,* July 26, 1838.
[29] *Ibid.*

The report was that Filisola had dispatched General Adrián Woll with 400 men to protect the port of Corpus Christi, and that a part of his troops had already arrived. Since Caldwell had only 25 men with him, and 150 soldiers from Matamoros were expected to appear on the scene at any moment, he decided to release the captain of the *Commanche* and return to the settled area of Texas for re-enforcements. On his return toward San Patricio, Caldwell discovered, when about twenty-five miles from the place, a large Mexican cavalry unit of some 150 men in pursuit of him. The Mexicans, however, stayed at a respectful distance and permitted the Texans to cross the Nueces unmolested.

From his spies, Caldwell learned that Savariego with about seventy men had encamped on a small stream thirty miles west of the Frio, to which point he had recently escorted a party of thirty Cherokees, who had been to Matamoros to confer with the Mexican authorities and were proceeding eastward with mules loaded with ammunition and clothing. A treaty, it was said, had not been concluded between the Indians and the Mexicans, but the Indians were to return in two months to learn the determination of the Mexican government. It was also learned that a Mexican colonel had been among the Shawnees during the past spring, endeavoring to incite them against the Texans, but that he had apparently met with no success. Finally, Caldwell's spies had learned that the Mexican forces did not intend to cross the Nueces, but had received "express orders to continue in the vicinity of the bay of Corpus Christi and to act on the defensive."

Upon the arrival of this news at Texana, Colonel William S. Fisher, Brigadier General Edwin Morehouse, and Colonel Pinckney Caldwell issued a call to the people of Matagorda County to cooperate with them in expelling the invader, and set August 7, as the date for volunteers to rendezvous at Texana. The volunteers were duly fitted out, and left Texana on the 7th for Corpus Christi. En route they were joined by similar units from Matagorda and other places. A party of Tonkawa Indians [30] accompanied Caldwell. Ere the volunteers reached their destination, the truth of the Mexican intentions in respect to Corpus Christi was reported at Matagorda. It seems that the Mexican government had not contemplated establishing a customhouse at that place, but that the Mexican consul at New Orleans had sent out a

[30] The *Telegraph and Texas Register* of August 25, 1838, reports that forty Lipan warriors accompanied the Texans.

54

cargo or two of provisions, and since it would have been almost impossible, in the face of the French blockade, to have landed the supplies at some Mexican port, they were shipped to Corpus Christi, where they were met by a sufficient company of Mexicans from Matamoros and thereabouts with pack horses and mules to take them into northern Mexico by land.[31] By the time the Texans reached Corpus Christi, the Mexicans had gone, part of them returning to Matamoros in a light craft loaded with flour and other supplies.[32] A few days later the captain of the American schooner *Lodi* was at Aransas, awaiting the arrival of his vessel from Corpus Christi. From Aransas he intended to proceed to New Orleans for additional supplies of various kinds for the Mexican trade. Flour and all imported articles were described as selling at exorbitant prices in Matamoros.[33]

It was believed that the readiness with which the Texans had acted to defend the integrity of the national territory would be of good effect in showing the enemy that they would not lie supinely and suffer the country to be plundered or its territory used as a means of evading the French blockade. It would, at the same time, give the French no cause for complaint, and might incline that government to accord its recognition of Texan independence.

In the meantime, news of the Mexican incursion reached President Houston at Nacogdoches, and it was his determination that the enemy operating in the vicinity of Corpus Christi needed to be chastised and expelled. Accordingly, he authorized Colonel George W. Hockley, Secretary of War, to take the necessary steps to expel the enemy from within the boundary of Texas.[34] He suggested Lieutenant Colonel Lysander Wells or Colonel Henry W. Karnes, successor to Colonel Juan N. Seguin as commandant at San Antonio when the latter took leave to go to New Orleans late in 1837,[35] as the best qualified to lead the force to be dispatched to the lower Nueces. The exact size of that

[31] *Matagorda Bulletin*, Aug. 9, 1838.

[32] *Telegraph and Texas Register*, Aug. 25, 1838.

[33] *Ibid.*, Aug. 25 and Sept. 22, 1838.

[34] Sam Houston to Col. G. W. Hockley, Nacogdoches, Aug. 4–5, 1838, in Domestic Correspondence (Texas), 1836–1846, ms.; *Writings of Sam Houston*, II, 266–268.

[35] In his memoirs, written many years later, Seguin says he went to New Orleans in 1838 but it must have been some time earlier for he wrote Lamar on January 2, 1838, from New Orleans. Juan N. Seguin, *Personal Memoirs of Juan N. Seguin: from the Year 1834 to the Retreat of General Woll from the City of San Antonio in 1842*, p. 16; *Lamar Papers*, II, 14; V, 169.

force and the selection of the regimental and corps officers were left to the discretion of the Secretary of War. However, the President wrote, "I understand that the number is to be 280 rank and file." [36] A few days later, August 11, in a general order issued at Nacogdoches over the signature of Houston and his newly appointed Adjutant General, Hugh McLeod, it was emphasized that peaceful citizens on the frontier were not to be molested in the enjoyment of their rights.[37]

This emphasis was needed, for it was not always the Indians or the Mexicans who created frontier incidents. After the issuance of the general order by the President a party of Texans and Tonkawa Indians under Colonel Pinckney Caldwell departed in search of Savariego; but learning that the Mexican commander had left the frontier, the Indo-Texan party determined to seek some sort of remuneration for their alleged good intentions. After going a short distance west of Victoria, a number of the Texans, becoming aware of the intentions of certain members of the party, returned home and stated "that the object of many of said expedition was merely to plunder those who returned or would not go in consequence of being deceived. . . . [W]e are led to conclude . . . ," reported John J. Linn, foreman of the grand jury that later investigated the incident, "that when Messrs. Morehouse, Fisher and others . . . stated that the object of the Expedition had been defeated . . . instead of going on in quest of Savariego and his band of Robbers, it was the intention of those . . . to take the first horses they met." [38] Soon it was reported by Pinckney Caldwell "that certain Americans and Mexicans in and about Goliad" had seized a number of horses from the Tonkawa Indians, who had recently accompanied him to Corpus Christi Bay, and had caused them to be sold at auction, and had appropriated the proceeds of the sale to their own use. Such acts by the whites were calculated to alienate the friendly feelings of

[36] Sam Houston to Col. G. W. Hockley, Nacogdoches, Aug. 4–5, 1838, in Domestic Correspondence (Texas), 1836–1846, ms.

[37] Sam Houston, *General Order,* Nacogdoches, Texas, August 11th, 1838 [signed by:] Sam Houston [and] H. McCleod [McLeod], Adjutant General, broadside; Thomas W. Streeter, *Bibliography of Texas,* I, 243; *Writings of Sam Houston,* II, 272.

[38] John J. Linn [of the Grand Jury for the County of Victoria] to [the Secretary of State], Victoria, Sept. 22, 1838, in Domestic Correspondence (Texas), 1836–1846, ms.; see also R. A. Irion to C. Van Ness, Department of State, City of Houston, Sept. 14, 1838, in State Department (Texas), Department of State Letterbook, no. 1. Nov. 1836–Jan. 1842), ms., pp. 45–46. (Hereafter cited as State Department Letterbook, no. 1.)

these Indians as expressed in the treaty recently concluded with them.[39] "It is a matter the adjustment of which devolves exclusively on the civil authorities," wrote Secretary of State R. A. Irion, as he requested Cornelius Van Ness, the district attorney for the district in which the acts had been committed, to see that justice was done in the case. At the same time, he admonished Van Ness to use "the prudence and caution which the peculiar circumstances of the affair seem to demand. The Indians, I suppose, would be satisfied with either the restitution of the horses, or the amount of money for which they were sold." [40]

When the District Court for the county of Victoria met for its September term, Van Ness was absent, and Judge J. W. Robinson requested John D. Morris to act as the district attorney. Believing that it would be impossible to obtain a correct and impartial consideration of the case concerning the robbery of the Tonkawa Indians in Goliad County, "in as much as there were but a sufficient number of men to form a grand jury and petit jury and a large number of these were engaged in the robbery," the matter was taken, under that clause of the law in relation to depopulated counties, before the grand jury of Victoria County of which John J. Linn was the foreman. Upon investigation, the grand jury learned that after Colonel Pinckney Caldwell and the Tonkawa warriors had reached Corpus Christi Bay and found no Mexicans at the place, a party of Americans, principally from Goliad, with about twenty of the Indians separated from the main body and proceeded westward to drive off Savariego and his band who had been plundering on the frontier. Unable to locate the Mexican marauders, the Americans concluded to reap some reward for their efforts. On their way, they met a group of Mexican traders entering Texas with a large number of horses and other property. They fell upon the Mexicans, stripped them of their horses and other possessions, and claimed that they killed eight of the unfortunate traders. The Americans and Indians divided the spoils equally, and both parties separately drove their horses through the town of Goliad. It was alleged that as they passed through Goliad, four or five horses belong-

---

[39] "Treaty with Toncoway Tribe of Indians, Texas. Post of Béxar, Novr. 22d, 1837," *Proclamations of the Presidents* (Texas). Sam Houston, Nov. 1836–Dec. 1838, pp. 13–14. See also Sam Houston, *Documents on Indian Affairs, Submitted to Congress by the President, November 15, 1838.*

[40] R. A. Irion to C. Van Ness, City of Houston, Sept. 14, 1838, in State Department Letterbook, no. 1, ms., pp. 45–46.

ing to citizens of that place [41] were driven off by the Indians with the horses and mules taken from the Mexicans. The allegations seem to have been only an excuse to justify robbing the Indians, for word of the capture of the Mexican *caballada* had already preceded them, and the citizens of Goliad, under Dr. Isaac S. Tower (a member of Congress), "determined to seize upon the property and restore it, as they said, to the original owners"; [42] but, in reality, their intent was to rob the Indians and not the Americans. After the Indians passed through the town, Dr. Tower's "gang" went in pursuit of the Tonkawas, took possession of all of their horses, and returned them to Goliad. [43] "On the following day," according to Morris' report, "they put them up for sale at public auction," where all of the horses were sold, but only "a small portion of the moneys was paid in and although some of the horses were knocked down at fifty, sixty, and even seventy dollars, it was declared that no sale was quoted upon the books at more than thirty or at a much less amount than they really sold for—in other words . . . fraud had been practiced by the salesmen. They, however," continued Morris, "expressed their intention to pay over the money which was due when the proper authorities shall call for it—and seemed determined to be the judges as to the proper owners and were resolved as they said to pay it to the Mexicans." [44] Under these circumstances, the grand jury of Victoria County refused to indict the accused. The acting district attorney, upon the grand jury's recommendation, then sought to impound the money derived from the sale of the horses until the legal ownership of the horses could be determined and "those persons who were concerned with the Indians in this disgraceful outrage . . . brought to justice in order that no repetition of such shameful acts may ever occur to cause insult to our character and laws in [the] future." [45] The justice of the peace of Goliad County was requested to retain the money until he should receive orders as to whom it should be paid. The Victoria grand jury declared that it con-

[41] *Telegraph and Texas Register,* Sept. 29, 1838.

[42] John D. Morris to R. A. Irion, Secretary of State, San Antonio de Béxar, Oct. 15, 1838, Domestic Correspondence (Texas), 1836–1846, ms.

[43] No mention was made in the grand jury's report of the driving off of four or five horses belonging to the citizens of Goliad.

[44] John D. Morris to R. A. Irion, Secretary of State, San Antonio de Béxar, Oct. 15, 1838, Domestic Correspondence (Texas), 1836–1846, ms.

[45] John J. Linn, Foreman [of the Grand Jury for the County of Victoria] to [the Secretary of State], Victoria, Sept. 22, 1838, in Domestic Correspondence (Texas), 1836–1846, ms.

sidered "the Americans engaged in robbing the Mexicans . . . much the most reprehensible parties engaged in the business and that they would recommend that they be brought to justice as speedily as possible."[46]

The reaction of the Tonkawas to the conduct of the Tower's party was the commission of several murders among the whites living near the headwaters of the Lavaca. As a result of these murders, a large body of the citizens in the Goliad section were soon in arms and were said to be declaring it their intention to exterminate the remnants of the Tonkawa tribe.[47] The main body of the tribe was living at the time at the mouth of the San Antonio River and numbered about two hundred warriors.

Savariego continued to operate below the Nueces. In late September or early October 1838, a party of Texans who had crossed the Nueces met a party of Mexicans near Lipantitlán, who were driving a number of mules loaded with provisions, presumably for Savariego's men. Upon seeing the Texans, the Mexicans took flight, abandoning the mules and provisions.[48] In October Savariego and his party again entered Texas—this time from Laredo and visited Alexander's ranch, situated about twenty miles southwest of Béxar and carried away all movable articles of value, even taking the rings off of the young ladies in the house.[49] Alexander and a Mr. Bull were taken prisoners and subsequently murdered by their captors near the Nueces.

Three of the Texans captured near the Nueces earlier in the year effected their escape from the Mexican prison at Matamoros and arrived at Goliad with horrible tales of their confinement. Among these was Cairns, who had been rumored previously to have been killed at one of the small towns on the Río Grande. The escapees reported that William Brennan, the former representative from Goliad who had been captured several months past near San Patricio, was still in prison at Matamoros.[50]

Among the Texan "cow-drivers" were a number of unscrupulous men who sought easy gain. They not only drove off cattle belonging to law-abiding citizens of the Republic, but also plundered the traders on the

[46] John D. Morris to R. A. Irion, Secretary of State, San Antonio de Béxar, Oct. 15, 1838, in *ibid.*
[47] *Telegraph and Texas Register*, Sept. 29, 1838.
[48] *Ibid.*, Oct. 13 and Nov. 3, 1838.
[49] *Ibid.*, Oct. 20 and Nov. 21, 1838.
[50] *Ibid.*, Oct. 20, 1838.

frontier, often committing murder. "No doubt half of the cattle and horses that are stolen and charged upon the Indians," wrote a correspondent of the *Telegraph and Texas Register*,[51] "are taken either by white men of the vilest class, or negroes." Cattle stealing was "by far the most remunerative industry of the day; though discountenanced by the respectable class of citizens."[52] There were many clashes between the cowboys and the Mexicans, and bloody and horrible were their retaliations on each other.[53] Such forays, however, were attended often with no other effect than that of irritating the peaceable inhabitants on both sides of the river. The earnest, hardworking farmer, cattleman, and merchant was usually the victim. He constantly demanded security for his home, his property, and his life. "I greatly fear," wrote a visitor to the lower Nueces valley, "the Government is chargeable with all the waste and desolation of this garden spot of Texas," and "I may almost say with the ruin of many individuals, who have struggled for the independence of the country, and whose fortunes and support depend upon the speedy settlement and tranquility of the western frontier."[54] A garrison of fifty men stationed on the Nueces in the vicinity of San Patricio, he thought, would give pro-

[51] Dec. 4, 1840.

[52] John J. Linn, *Reminiscences of Fifty Years in Texas*, p. 310; see also John J. Linn to Sam Houston, Victoria, July 6, 1838, in Domestic Correspondence (Texas), 1836–1846, ms.

[53] Conditions had not materially changed a decade and a half later, in 1852, when Major William H. Emory visited the area as a member of the United States-Mexican Boundary Commission. Emory wrote:

Hunting the wild horses and cattle is the regular business of the inhabitants of Loredo and other towns along the river, and the practice adds much to the difficulty of maintaining a proper police on the frontier to guard against the depredation of Indians and the organization of fillibustering parties. In times of agitation and civil war on the Mexican side, parties assemble on the American side ostensibly to hunt, but in reality to take part on one side or other in the affairs of our neighbors. I heard a great deal of these wild horses, but on an examination of many hundred that had been caught, I never saw one good one. They are usually heavy in the forehead, cat-hammed, and knock-kneed. Their habits are very peculiar; they move in squads, single file, and seem to obey implicitly the direction of the leader. They evince much curiosity, always reconnoitring the camp of the traveller at full speed, and where there chances to be a loose animal, be he ever so poor and jaded, he is sure to run off with the crowd and disappear entirely.

Report on the United States and Mexican Boundary Survey, Made under the Direction of the Secretary of the Interior, I, 56–57, 61.

[54] ——— to the Editor of the *Telegraph*, Nueces River, March 6, 1839, in *Telegraph and Texas Register*, April 10, 1839.

tection against invasion by Mexicans and Indians. It had been hoped that a change in administrations would have brought more adequate protection to the frontier, but so far by March 1839, little had been done by Lamar to improve the situation; consequently, public opinion west of the Colorado was turning against the President. "Our miserable gov[ernment]t becomes more and more contemptible every year, month, day and hour," wrote Henry Austin. "Lamar is sinking like a plummet—could not be elected a constable." [55] Wrote an individual from the southwestern frontier,

We are getting into the belief that the present administration is governed by pure selfishness—that favoritism to its friends and uncompromising hostility to its enemies is the present order of the day. Let me assure you I speak the honest belief of nine-tenths of the citizens of Texas, from the Colorado westwardly and so far as I know, of every individual claiming residence in this section of the country with the *rare* exception of now and then of an officer of the Government. It is an almost miraculous revulsion in public sentiment, but nevertheless true. [56]

San Antonio, wrote Mrs. Mary A. Maverick, was a healthy and beautiful place, "as far as the gifts of nature go . . . but oh! how condemned it is by the thieves and mean wretches who inhabit it." [57] Also from San Antonio, John D. Morris wrote, "there is not a night in the year when each man here does not sleep upon his arms and when he is not subject to be[ing] roused by the allarm gun of the advance of the enemy"—be he Mexican, Indian, or bandit. "Such is the state of my country and unless some speedy assistance is afforded by the Gov[ernmen]t we will all be compelled to retire across the Guadaloupe and most probably [to] the other side of the Colorado." [58] The same was true at Victoria and at Gonzales, declared Judge Robinson from Gonzales,[59] where families were leaving for the Brazos and points east-

[55] Capt. H. Austin to J. F. Perry, Houston, March 24, 1839, in James F. Perry Papers, transcripts, ms.

[56] ———— to the Editor of the *Telegraph*, Nueces River, March 6, 1839, in *Telegraph and Texas Register*, April 10, 1839.

[57] Mary A Maverick to Agatha S. Adams, San Antonio de Béxar, Sept. 8, 1839, in Rena Maverick Green (ed.), *Samuel Maverick: Texan, 1803–1870; A Collection of Letters, Journals, and Memoirs*, pp. 88–91.

[58] John D. Morris to R. A. Irion, Secretary of State, San Antonio de Béxar, Oct. 15, 1838, in Domestic Correspondence (Texas), 1836–1846, ms.

[59] James W. Robinson to Mirabeau B. Lamar, Gonzales, Oct. 27, 1838, in *Lamar Papers*, II, 272.

ward. "We must give way," he informed Lamar, "if not immediately supported by a military force. You my friend are our hope and in you we have confidence. If your administration opens with an ample plan of defence for the frontier, and for a vigorous prosecution of the war with Mexico, I will predict, that it will not only be one of the most popular, but one of the most useful." "There is much depending here in the West as to the course which is to be pursued as to protection," wrote Andrew Neill, district attorney of the Fourth Judicial District, "but I conceive the great difficulty is the want of means . . . This country or a great portion of it will be vacated unless something is done to keep it up." [60]

Under this state of affairs, without much expectation of help from the national government, the local authorities at San Antonio took steps to ensure protection to its inhabitants from strange, irresponsible, or lawless persons who might be in the area. The city council, upon the recommendation of one of its members, Juan A. Zambrano, adopted on July 30, 1838, a resolution declaring that "all persons brought into the country by a Mexican officer and who had no visible means of support," if found either within the city or surrounding area should be obliged to depart as speedily as possible for the Republic of Mexico.[61] Two months later, October 8, at the suggestion of Zambrano, the Council unanimously agreed to order a "'general list" made out of all individuals able to bear arms, "as also of the horses and mules which each may possess, in order," said the Council, "should circumstances require . . . [that] they shall be in readiness to repel any attempt which might be made by . . . marauders to rob this city." [62] On the 11th the Council ordered the keepers of each tavern in the city to furnish the mayor daily a list of all persons staying in their houses.[63]

The law-abiding citizens of Victoria County found considerable opposition in January 1838, to their efforts to organize the county administration and to establish county and justice of the peace courts. "I must say as a man of honour," wrote John J. Linn, "that some of those who may perhaps petition for a new election do not want the laws of our country to go into effect as it would put a stop to their

[60] A. Neill to James Kerr, San Antonio de Béxar, Nov. 11, 1838, in *Lamar Papers*, II, 289–290.

[61] San Antonio, City of, "Journal A, Records of the City of San Antonio," ms., p. 29.

[62] *Ibid.*, p. 32.

[63] *Ibid.*

present mode of obtaining some property that belongs to honester persons." [64] Nine months later, Linn again wrote,

I am sorry . . . to say . . . that the frontier is and has been for some time back infested with what is usually called Cow drives but all kinds of Robbery is committed dailey. No person's property in these counties [Goliad, Refugio, and Victoria] is safe. I have to suffer along with the balance of the well disposed citizens. We are loosing our little stock constantly. This comes hard on those who had lost all in the invation of '36 for we had to buy at high prices in on[ly] one section. It is true that stock can be bought from 8 to $10 pr head in Texas Paper, but I cannot bring my mind to buy that which I know to be stolen & with marks & brands that I know as well as I do my own. We are at this time in a very bad state for all laws are trampled under foot—and those who pay any respect to the laws of the land or has any national honor is hooted at and in truth his life is not safe if he offers any resistance to the notions of the bandit that now rules. . . . The Citizens of this county have the mortification of being represented [in] this Congress by a Man who keeps the head quarters for Cow drivers & [is] by them elected to the disgrace of our country. [65]

The Third Congress in January 1839, enacted a law prohibiting the driving off by any person or persons of horses, cattle, and other domestic animals "which are not his or their legal property" from the so-called depopulated counties west of the Guadalupe River; [66] and a week later, Congress made it a felony, punishable by death, to "take, steal and carry away, any horse, mare, ass, mule or gelding, colt, foal or filly, knowing the same not to be his own," or to aid in the theft or secretion of such property. [67] It was well nigh impossible, however, for the large cattle ranchers in the western counties to keep a watch over their herds because of hostile Indians and the prevalence of banditti. "More serious in their consequences," reported a man recently from the west, "are the robberies of the cattle and horses of the Rancheros, . . . who exasperated at their losses, are ready to obtain

[64] John J. Linn to the Secretary of State, Victoria, Jan. 18, 1838, in Domestic Correspondence (Texas), 1836–1846, ms.
[65] John J. Linn to the President of the Republic of Texas, Victoria, Sept. 21, 1839, in ibid. Linn was apparently referring to Representative James Wright.
[66] "An Act to Prohibit the Driving of Cattle from that part of the Country West of the Guadaloupe," approved January 19, 1839, in Gammel (ed.), Laws of Texas, II, 53.
[67] "An Act to Provide for the Punishment of Horse Thieves," in ibid., II, 166–167.

remuneration by the same system of stealing from their neighbors, thereby keeping the whole vicinity in trouble." [68]

Both Mexico and Texas sought to suppress the gangs infesting the frontier, but with little success. Sometimes they tacitly encouraged, or tolerated, retaliatory raids upon one another. There was no peace on the frontier, and in 1840 the road from Goliad to San Antonio was still regarded as one of the most dangerous in the Republic.[69] In all, the insecurity of the frontier was quite discouraging to the average settler.

Among the lawless frontiersmen, who operated from 1838 to 1841 under the name of "Cowboy," and made it their business to steal cattle to be driven eastward for sale [70] were Captains A. T. Miles, J. C. Neill, —— Merrell, William Wells, John T. Price, Jack (V. R.) Palmer ("worthless man" [71]), —— Hull, W. J. Cairns (Scotch), John H. Yerby, James P. Ownsby, Jacob ("Jake") Hendricks (Pennsylvania Dutch), Ewen Cameron (Scotch), Samuel W. Jordan, and such lesser persons as "Tonkaway" Jones, Richard Roman, Joseph Dolan from Nacogdoches, Captain Thomas Hagler [72] of Houston, Pierre (Peter) Rouche (Frenchman), Thomas Lyons [73] (Irish), Jòhn Smith [74] (Tennessean), James Taylor, Josiah Creed, John Hefferon [75] (Irish), Mabry

[68] *Morning Star* (Houston), June 18, 1839.

[69] W. L. McCalla, *Adventures in Texas, Chiefly in the Spring and Summer of 1840; with a Discussion of Comparative Character, Political, Religious and Moral,* p. 37.

[70] "Information derived from Anson G. Neal, Laredo, May 30, 1847," in *Lamar Papers,* VI, 99, 101; see also Linn, *Reminiscences of Fifty Years in Texas,* p. 322.

[71] *Lamar Papers,* VI, 100; Hobart Huson, "Iron Men: A History of the Republic of the Río Grande and the Federalist War in Northern Mexico," ms., p. 60.

[72] Thomas Hagler, who served in the Mexican Federalist forces in 1840, was killed in a street fight at Goliad in 1846 by a man named Pool. Pool was subsequently killed on the Agua Dulce, between Corpus Christi and the Río Grande. *Lamar Papers,* VI, 127; Silvanus Hatch to Gen. M. B. Lamar, Jackson County, April 2, 1840, in Domestic Correspondence (Texas), 1836–1846, ms.

[73] Thomas Lyons was killed at China, Mexico, during the Federalist War. *Lamar Papers,* VI, 116.

[74] A man, presumed to be John Smith, was arrested early in October 1841, for stealing a horse near Rutersville, and was reported taken back to Fayette County for trial. *Telegraph and Texas Register,* Oct. 13, 1841.

[75] The name "Hefferon" has been spelled many ways by various and sundry persons too numerous to cite. The usual variations that I have found are: Hefron; Heffron; Heffenn; Heferin; Hiffin; Heffernann; Heffernan. Where the man signed his name, for instance, on a receipt for pay as a "Minute Man," he wrote it "John Hefferon."

Gray, "Big" (J? B?) Brown,[76] and others numbering not less than three or four hundred. The parties led by Brown and Gray were regarded as murderers and cutthroats, and other parties had very little to do with them because of their atrocities.[77]

Not all of the men whose names have been mentioned participated in murder or stole from their fellow citizens. It has been said that Cameron's party "committed no murders nor robbed any of the traders—they only drove off cattle," and, in that respect, only those between the Nueces and the Río Grande.[78] On the other hand, there was a man named Cox, from Bastrop, who in July 1838, declared his intention of raising an armed company to capture, plunder, and burn Laredo, and to drive off all cattle, horses, and mules that could be found. Cox's company[79] assembled and marched from Bastrop on July 17 for Béxar without the sanction of government to join with another company of Americans accompanied by seven Choctaw Indians who were on their way to the Río Grande. Being disappointed in the failure of the arrival of the Indians and the other company at the designated

John Hefferon left his wife and children to go West. He has been described by James Wilkinson, who knew him, as "a regular old Toper, but a brave old cock," and of "uncommon good nature," who was "generally kept in the rear, whilst driving [cattle or horses] that being the post of danger." He was usually taken care of by Ewen Cameron. "James Wilkinson's Account of the Cow-Boys," in *Lamar Papers*, VI, 116–117. Hefferon's hatred of the Mexican may have dated from the days of the revolution. It was reported in New Orleans in the summer of 1836 by passengers arriving from Matamoros that "previous to hearing of the defeat of Santana, some Rancheros, had murdered James Heferin, his wife and 5 children, John Heferin, his brother & John Ryan all of Sanpatrucio." Edward Hall to D. G. Burnet, New Orleans, June 20, 1836, in Binkley (ed.), *Official Correspondence of the Texan Revolution*, II, 807–808; Madray, *A History of Bee County*, p. 1. We may conclude from this report, that although John Hefferon escaped death in 1836 at the hands of the Mexicans, some of his relatives were not so fortunate.

[76] "Big" Brown, as he was known, came to Texas from Missouri. He was finally killed by Agatón Quiñones' men, having been betrayed by a Mexican in his service. *Lamar Papers*, VI, 117.

[77] *Ibid.*; Linn, *Reminiscences of Fifty Years in Texas*, p. 322.

[78] *Lamar Papers*, VI, 117.

[79] The following individuals were reported comprising Cox's company: Capt. Cox; Turner Spaulding; Hay; Gray; Hill; Burney; Edmunson; Thompson; Crockett; Hicks; Purchett; Harris; Ribingston; Herald; Alexander; Goran; William Gammel [Gamble]; Jacob Zengerle; and Louis Marble. Erasmo Seguin, J[ustice of the] P[eace] to R. A. Irion, Béxar, Aug. 7, 1838, State Department Letterbook, no. 2, ms., p. 183.

point of rendezvous, Cox, after waiting several days at San Antonio, determined to proceed on the expedition with his own company. His party left San Antonio and encamped on Tahuacano Creek,[80] where a party of Mexican traders, consisting of men, women, and five or six children from the Río Grande on their way to Béxar came up on August 2 and encamped nearby. The Mexicans indicated they wished to be on friendly terms. Mutual professions of friendship passed between the two parties, until the freebooters suddenly seized on several of the Mexicans, deprived them of their arms, shot a boy, who expired in the arms of his mother, and wounded a man. Cox's men then robbed the Mexicans of all their property (mules, horses, saddles, money, blankets, flour, sugar, leather, and every other thing of value, which the traders were carrying to Béxar to exchange for goods), leaving them neither clothing, food, nor animals, except two or three worn-out horses which they left for a woman and five or six children belonging to the Mexican party.[81] On the 3rd Erasmo Seguin, then justice of the peace of Béxar County, ordered the sheriff to arrest all suspicious characters who might have been involved in this crime and to seize the property allegedly stolen from the traders. Accordingly, William Gamble, Jacob Zengerle, and Louis Marble were arrested and a number of horses were recovered. An examining trial was held before Judge Seguin on August 4, and the Court ordered the three Americans to be held under arrest, but owing to the lack of an adequate jail and public funds, they were placed on bail.[82]

By the end of 1838 there were no less than four marauding parties of Texans west of the Nueces, engaged in plundering the Mexicans in that section. The citizens of Goliad were said to be "exceedingly exasperated on this account," believing that while this system of border pillage continued, they would be subjected to the "incursions of similar parties from the settlements on the Río Grande," who would en-

[80] The writer has been unable to identify Tahuacano Creek.

[81] "Proclamation of a Reward for the Apprehension and Delivery of one Cox, August 30, 1838," Proclamations of the Presidents (Texas), ms.; Report of Erasmo Seguin, Justice of the Peace, County of Béxar [August 7, 1838], to [the Secretary of State], Domestic Correspondence (Texas), 1836–1846, ms., Spanish.

[82] Erasmo Seguin, Justice of the Peace, County of Béxar [August 7, 1838], to [the Secretary of State], Domestic Correspondence (Texas), 1836–1846, ms. Among the Mexican traders testifying were José María Hernandez, Felipe Jaime, José Antonio Salinas, Manuel Flores, and Felix Arista.

deavor to retaliate for the injuries received from their marauding countrymen.[83]

From Live Oak Point, Refugio County, late in 1838, the citizens and residents addressed the "General Government on the subject of the dangers & embarrassments" to which they were exposed from incursions by marauding parties of Mexicans. They reported a Mexican general encamped on the Nueces, about fifteen miles from Refugio. Without giving details, they declared that he had sent "a detachment from his forces, Two Hundred Strong, well mounted and armed, . . . into our Territory nearly as far, within a few miles of Labardee [La Bahía], murdering, plundering, and making captives all in their course." The inhabitants of Live Oak Point called upon the government for protection of the frontier not only from the Mexican marauders, but also from the Karankawa Indians. They pointed out the importance of Live Oak Point as a port of entry for merchant vessels entering Aransas Bay. "We can but feel our impotency under present circumstances," they said, "and can but feel that this region of the country, abounding with fertile grounds, and this Point offering facilities to trade and commerce unsurpassed . . . are objects worthy of defence and protection." But such was not the opinion of the President, who endorsed and filed the petition with the following comment: "The object of the persons herein named was to protect the illicit trade which they were willing should be done at the expense of the Republic." The President had no means to aid the petitioners, and if he had possessed abundance the policy at the time would not have justified him.[84] Some of these "would be" traders on the frontier were soon to cast their lot with the Mexican Federalists, but the significant point here is that they did not have the confidence of the Texas government. Consequently, their petition was ignored.

[83] *Telegraph and Texas Register*, Jan. 5, 1839.
[84] Richard Pearse, R[ichard] Roman, Edward Drier, and Martin Powers, for Committee, to George W. Hockley, Secretary of War, Aransas (Live Oak Point), Refugio Co., Texas [Feb., 1839], with endorsement by Sam Houston dated Feb. 23, 1839, in Sam Houston, Unpublished Houston Correspondence, 1837–1841, vol. II, ms.

CHAPTER FOUR

Mexican Threats of a New Campaign Against Texas

ALTHOUGH THROUGHOUT THE DAYS of the Lone Star Republic Mexico threatened to invade Texas almost as often as the seasons changed, and rumors of an impending attack were frequent in Texas causing great excitement and sometimes untold hardship, the Texans, as a whole, soon came to pay little attention to such rumors. "Terrible news ! !" screamed the *Telegraph* on August 19, 1837, "Another silly rumor is afloat in New Orleans, that Bustamante and Bravo are concentrating the Mexican forces on the Río Grande above Matamoros."

Yet the repeated declarations by Mexico of her intention to renew the campaign against Texas and the very inadequate state of Texan defenses were often sufficient to alarm all but the most sanguine. On August 26 the *Brutus* and *Invincible*, after a three months' cruise along the Mexican coast, arrived before Galveston, having captured six prizes since leaving that port early in June.[1] The next day two Mexican brigs-of-war, the *Libertador* and the *Iturbide*, attacked the *Invincible* outside the harbor, forcing her to flee across the bar where she unshipped her rudder, piled upon a shoal and two days later was pounded to pieces by a severe storm. The *Brutus*, already tied up at the Navy Yard when the Mexican warships appeared, sought to go to the aid of the *Invincible* but ran aground and a few weeks later was pounded to pieces by a second storm. Without a single war vessel to protect their coast, the Texans became frantic.

Because of this naval weakness—and probably also because of the seizure and imprisonment of Colonel John A. Wharton at Matamoros upon his landing there with a detachment of Mexican prisoners to exchange for his brother William H. Wharton, Captain George W. Wheelwright, and other officers and crew of the *Independence* cap-

---

[1] *Telegraph and Texas Register* (Houston), Oct. 11, 1837; March 17, 1838; Jim Dan Hill, *The Texas Navy: in Forgotten Battles and Shirtsleeve Diplomacy*, pp. 83–92.

tured at sea off Velasco by Mexican naval units on April 17, 1837—
President Houston announced publicly on September 15, a renewal of
the policy of granting letters of marque and reprisal to prey upon
Mexican commerce:

Whereas this government proclaimed its utter abhorrence to every species
of warfare not calculated for a nation's glory and the attainment of an honorable peace, and in pursuance of that policy recalled all "Letters of Marque
and Reprisal" that had been granted under its authority; and, from time to
time released prisoners of war, without exacting the customary exchanges;
and . . . has up to the present time forborne even to execute, according to
the law of nations, *spies* heretofore taken, thereby mitigating the horrors
of war,

since Mexico does not reciprocate the kind feeling showed toward her,
Texas, he declared, has no alternative but to regard her as an enemy.[2]

Mexico must realize, wrote the editor of the Houston *Telegraph,*
that our fleet shall within six weeks commence ravaging her coasts
from Brazos Santiago to Yucatán, and unless overtures of peace have
been received from her by April next,

. . . the army of Texas will display its victorious banner *west of the Río
Grande,* and when once its conquering march shall have commenced, when
the star of Texas shall have become the guide of the Pioneers of America,
no power of Bustamante, or of Mexico shall avail, but that glorious march
shall be onward, on onward, till the roar of the Texian rifles, shall mingle
in unison with the thunders of the Pacific.[3]

The pressure of economic conditions in the United States and the
excitement of a possible campaign in Texas impelled more than one
energetic and ambitious Anglo-American youth toward Texas in the
fall of 1837. Early in October a large number of emigrants reached
Texas by way of Galveston.[4] The *Natchitoches Journal* reported that
during the month of October at least a thousand emigrants passed
through Natchitoches alone bound for Texas. "Most of them were
stout, athletic, able-bodied men, each of whom had with him the

---

[2] A Proclamation by the President of the Republic of Texas, Houston, September
15, 1837, in *Telegraph and Texas Register,* Sept. 16, 1837.
[3] *Telegraph and Texas Register,* Sept. 16, 1837.
[4] *Ibid.,* Oct. 7, 1837.

favorite weapon of the western citizen, either for the chase or more deadly strife, the unerring rifle." [5]

On September 28, President Bustamante, in a speech to the garrison of Mexico City assembled in the public square, assured the troops they would soon be called upon, along with the Army of the North, to gather new laurels on the fertile fields of Texas.[6] A short time later it was reported at Houston that a twenty-two gun brig was under construction at Baltimore [7] for the Mexican navy.

Early in November, the *Matagorda Bulletin* [8] reported General Filisola at Matamoros with 3,000 troops under his command, but Texans could only speculate on the intended objective of this force. If one read, however, the reports concerning the condition and discipline of the troops under Filisola's command, he needed have no fear of them, for they were represented as being in a most wretched condition, entirely unprovided with rations, clothing, and other necessities, "many of them nearly in a state of nudity." [9] Furthermore, there were numerous desertions daily among them, for the Mexican soldier, it was said, had "a most decided aversion to being led against Texas," and some of them were even stating openly that they could not be "prevailed upon to march against her at any price. . . . But if the Mexicans should ever again invade Texas," declared W. T. Brent, "they will as certainly get *licked,* and the Texans [will] march through Mexico as two and three make five." [10] In the meantime, the Texans took no chances of being caught by surprise. "Deaf" Smith continued to scout below the Medina in the direction of the Río Grande.[11]

Five men from Laredo reached San Antonio on November 28, 1837, and reported the Mexican government was not mustering troops, nor was there any excitement of a hostile nature perceptible, but on the contrary, they declared, "all the frontier inhabitants were well disposed towards Texas, and were most impatiently and anxiously await-

[5] Quoted in *ibid.*

[6] *Ibid.*, Dec. 2, 1837 reports this speech as made on Sept. 27, 1837, whereas under the "Chronology of Events During the Second Year of the Independence of Texas, in *ibid.*, March 17, 1838, it is reported as having been made on Sept. 28, 1837.

[7] *Ibid.*, Oct. 11, 1837.

[8] Nov. 8, 1837.

[9] *Ibid.*

[10] W. T. Brent to James H. Brent, Roseland, Va., [dated:] Velasco, Texas, Jan. 23, 1838, in Sam Houston, Unpublished Houston Correspondence, 1837–1841, vol. II, ms.

[11] *Telegraph and Texas Register*, Oct. 18, 1837.

ing the termination of the war" to commence trading with the Texans.[12] On a recent visit to the west, General Morehouse found no reason for suspecting a Mexican invasion soon,[13] and on November 4 all of the Texans who had been imprisoned at Matamoros arrived at Galveston on a vessel chartered by the Mexican government for the purpose of returning them to Texas.[14] Apparently Mexico had no intention of launching another campaign against Texas any time soon.

Yet, late in 1837, it was again rumored at Houston that a Mexican force 1,500 strong had invaded Texas and had on December 20 attacked the Alamo, which was defended by two small units under Colonels Karnes and Wells.[15] Captain Rodríquez's first-hand report on the 24th at San Felipe of the assault on San Antonio stirred great excitement. And at Houston, in a public meeting on the 26th at 12 o'clock noon, with Colonel A. S. Thurston in the chair and Francis R. Lubbock as secretary, a committee was appointed upon the motion of Dr. Ashbel Smith to draft an appropriate set of resolutions. The meeting then adjourned to 3 P.M. to await a report from its committee, consisting of General Albert Sidney Johnston, Francis Moore, Jr., B. C. Franklin, and Colonel Thurston. When the meeting reconvened, the committee introduced resolutions in favor of the appointment of a committee of vigilance "to aid and assist all who may wish to hasten immediately to the field of action, and to solicit the necessary means for procuring supplies of provisions, arms, horses," and other necessary items. In short order $2,000 was raised. The committee also recommended the creation of a committee of correspondence to keep in touch with the other towns of the Republic. Finally, since Mexico had disregarded the example of moderation and forbearance set by the Texan government in disbanding its army, the committee recommended the prosecution of "an offensive war against Mexico until the last vestige of tyranny shall have been swept from her limits." [16] Upon the motion of Colonel Andrew Neill, a resolution was added to the above recommendations urging all persons wishing to march to the aid of Karnes and Wells at Béxar to assemble in front of the capitol the next morning at 9 o'clock.

[12] C. Van Ness to R. A. Irion, Béxar Dec. 4, 1837, in State Department Letterbook, no. 2, ms., pp. 109–110.
[13] *Telegraph and Texas Register,* Nov. 11, 1837.
[14] *Ibid.*
[15] *Ibid.,* Dec. 30, 1837.
[16] *Ibid.*

After San Jacinto

General Albert Sidney Johnston, having arrived in Houston from a visit to his home, children, and relatives in Louisville, Kentucky, only a few hours before news of the Mexican seizure of San Antonio had come in,[17] was ordered by the new Secretary of War, Barnard E. Bee, to take charge of the military operations on the western frontier. He was to proceed to the frontier with troops under the expectation that Congress at its next session would meet the necessary expenses incurred in "humbling an arrogant, a cowardly and contemptible foe." "We have long been contented," declared the editor of the *Telegraph*, "with merely defying the power of Mexico; we should now teach her, that she can no longer even threaten with impunity." [18]

Johnston called out a portion of the militia and ordered it and the volunteer companies being formed in various parts of the Republic to march to the relief of Béxar. The militia and volunteers from Harris County and the east were to rendezvous at Mercer's Crossing on the Colorado.[19] By the 30th, organization of the militia was proceeding rapidly in Harris County, and sixty mounted volunteers were on the eve of making their departure for the west.[20]

On the 30th news reached Houston from New Orleans that the captain of the United States sloop-of-war *Natchez* had just returned from Matamoros with important information concerning the Mexican invasion plans. He reported the arrival at Matamoros of 600 soldiers from the interior of Mexico on November 22, and stated that a battalion of infantry consisting of some 200 men had crossed the Río Grande that day and had taken up their line of march for Texas with two pieces of artillery; and that on the following day a battalion of 350 cavalrymen had crossed the river and joined the infantrymen preparing to advance upon Texas. Four days later (November 27), a battalion of sappers crossed the Río Grande with the intention of joining the others, then advancing toward the Arroyo Colorado, where some 1,200 men were stationed.[21]

[17] William Preston Johnston, *The Life of Gen. Albert Sidney Johnston: Embracing His Services in The Armies of the United States, the Republic of Texas, and the Confederate States*, p. 86.

[18] *Telegraph and Texas Register*, Jan. 13, 1838.

[19] General Order No. 1, Head Quarters, City of Houston, Dec. 28, 1837, [signed by:] Brig.-Gen. [A. S.] Johnston, Comm[anding] Texas Army, in *ibid.*, Dec. 30, 1837.

[20] *Telegraph and Texas Register*, Dec. 30, 1837.

[21] Letter from New Orleans, dated December 24, 1837, containing data copied

Later in the day another express from San Antonio was received at Houston. It discredited the rumor of an invasion. The Alamo had not been attacked. The "scare" in that quarter was attributed to a party of some fifty Mexican marauders stealing horses. However, according to the Texan commander at Béxar, things were beginning to bear a threatening aspect in that region.[22] And to a friend, General Johnston wrote that from various sources there was reason to believe that "a heavy column [of the enemy] has already crossed the Río Grande." [23]

Consequently, Johnston left Houston on the evening of December 31 and hurried west, planning to meet two hundred mounted volunteers at the Colorado and to proceed to San Antonio for a reconnaissance.[24] When he reached Mercer's Ferry on the Colorado, however, he failed to find the force he had anticipated. The excitement had quickly subsided upon receipt of the news that the Mexican force reported to have invested San Antonio had turned out to be nothing more than a small band of marauders operating in the area.[25] Johnston found only forty men at the Colorado ready to advance. After some delay in anticipation of the arrival of additional forces, Johnston, with scarcely enough men for a single company, headed westward from the Colorado on January 18 for Béxar. He was determined to visit that frontier point to gain first-hand information. Impatient with the appeasement policy of the administration, he declared confidentially to a friend, "Our Government wants energy and prudent foresight, which those intrusted with the liberties of a people should possess." [26]

On January 20 Secretary of War Bee found it necessary to write Johnston that it would be useless to assemble troops without supplies; and a week later, fearing that Johnston might make a rash movement in the direction of the Río Grande, Bee informed him that the President was opposed to his taking up headquarters at any point beyond San Antonio.[27] Adjutant General Hugh McLeod wrote Johnston very

---

verbatim from a slip in the Exchange Reading Room, New Orleans, in *Telegraph and Texas Register*, Dec. 30, 1837.

[22] Albert Sidney Johnston to Edward D. Hobbs (of Louisville), City of Houston, Dec. 31, 1837, in Johnston, *Life of Gen. Albert Sidney Johnston*, pp. 86–87.

[23] *Ibid.*

[24] *Ibid.*

[25] Same to Same, Mercer's Ferry, Colorado River, Jan. 17, 1838, in *ibid.*, p. 87.

[26] *Ibid.*

[27] Johnston, *Life of Gen. Albert Sidney Johnston*, p. 87; Sam[uel A. Maverick] to [Mary A. Maverick], Béjar, March 13, 1838, in Rena Maverick Green (ed.),

emphatically on February 26 that "the President will *not* change the frontier line, or reinforce General Johnston with militia." [28] On the same day Bee, referring to the poverty of the nation, informed Johnston, "as we have not a dollar in the Treasury, we must be content to fold our arms." [29]

As it was, the Mexican army of invasion turned out to be nothing more than "a marauding party of fifty Mexicans from Matamoros" who were discovered in the vicinity of San Antonio, "stealing cattle . . . which they succeeded in doing," said Brent; [30] according to the United States diplomatic agent in Texas, the marauders "sought to retake some horses which the Texians had driven from the Río Grande." [31] The Mexicans surprised two men eight miles below San Antonio guarding a *caballada* of horses, took one of the men prisoner and shot the other. They even drove off some horses belonging to Colonel Henry W. Karnes.

Immediately upon receiving word of the attack, Colonel Karnes gave pursuit, but after going some eight or ten miles, he lost the trail of the marauders and returned to Béxar.[32] While Karnes considered the incident nothing more than a retaliatory raid, and possibly one by the same party that had recently visited San Patricio,[33] he thought the Mexicans were preparing for an early campaign in Texas. In this conclusion he was mistaken. The raids were retaliatory and were intended to repossess property taken by the cowboys and other Texan raiders. A small party of Texan cattle drivers below San Patricio in December 1837, captured three Mexicans, "who had written orders from General Filisola to drive in all cattle between the Nueces and the Río Grande," so troublesome had become the Texan cowboys who had been constantly engaged during the summer in stealing cattle near the Río

---

Samuel Maverick, Texan, 1803–1870; A Collection of Letters, Journals and Memoirs, pp. 63–64.

[28] Quoted in Johnston, *Life of Gen. Albert Sidney Johnston*, p. 87.

[29] Quoted in *ibid.*

[30] W. T. Brent to James H. Brent, Roseland, Va., [dated:] Velasco, Texas, Jan. 23, 1838, in Houston, Unpublished Houston Correspondence, 1837–1841, vol. II, ms.

[31] Alcée La Branche to John Forsyth, Legation of the United States, Houston, Jan. 1, 1838, in Correspondence and Reports of American Agents and Others in Texas, 1836–1845, Justin H. Smith, "Transcripts," vol. V, ms.

[32] *Telegraph and Texas Register*, Dec. 30, 1837.

[33] A marauding party visited San Patricio about December 9, 1837. *Ibid.*, Jan. 6, 1838. See p. 49 of this work.

Grande.[34] "They [the Mexicans] have mostly deserted their farms," it was reported, "and having been terribly beaten in the skirmishes with these cattle stealers," were afraid to venture out and collect their cattle unless under the protection of an escort. The mounted rancheros and the small detachments from the garrisons along the Río Grande, sent to give protection to the Mexican cattle drivers and herdsmen, thus seem to have given rise to the rumors of invading armies marching on Texas.

Karnes hurried from San Antonio to Washington, arriving there early in January 1838. From thence he proceeded to Houston, where his arrival allayed fears of an invasion: if there had been such a danger, it was presumed, Karnes would not have left Béxar.[35] In the meantime, editor Francis Moore left Houston on December 30, 1837, for Béxar to get the facts concerning the invasion. At the Colorado he learned that the reported attack upon that western outpost was a false rumor. He, however, found the western people ready and determined to defend their homes. Moore returned to Houston from the Colorado and suggested the stationing of from five hundred to a thousand troops on the Sal Colorado "as a means of destroying the commerce of Matamoros" and "causing consternation along the whole Mexican frontier of the Río Grande." [36]

General Johnston was still at San Antonio in March 1838, where it was reported he was planning to visit the Río Grande for the purpose of raising the Texas flag over Laredo.[37] On March 13 he wrote the Secretary of War that reports from all sources, however, indicated that distractions in Mexico would make it impossible for that government to launch a campaign against Texas this year. He went on to say that although the enemy would be unable "to make any serious movement against this country, we should not forget that our frontier is in a most feeble situation, and incapable of defense against even predatory parties. It is unnecessary for me to say to you," he wrote, "that on the northern frontier there is no force whatever, and on the western there

---

[34] *Telegraph and Texas Register*, Jan. 6, 1838.

[35] A. Somervell to James F. Perry, Villa de Austin, Jan. 7, 1838, in James F. Perry Papers, 1838–1839, ms. The *Telegraph and Texas Register*, Jan. 20, 1838, reported that the latest word from Béxar was that no invasion was expected according to recent information from the Río Grande.

[36] *Telegraph and Texas Register*, Jan. 6, 1838.

[37] Samuel A. Maverick to Mary A. Maverick, Béjar, March 13, 1838, in Green, *Samuel Maverick: Texan*, p. 66.

will not be a mounted man after the 3d of April." [38] Johnston strongly urged the establishment of a regiment of cavalry for frontier defense.

It was not long, however, before one of Colonel Lysander Wells' spies returned from Matamoros to report only 1,800 soldiers at that place.[39] General Perfecto Cós, he said, was at Mier with 150 men, while at Reinosa there were only 100 soldiers. In the light of such weaknesses, warlike preparations on the part of Mexico soon came to be lightly regarded in Texas. "I do not believe," wrote William H. Patton at San Antonio to the Secretary of State, "the Mexicans [will] bother us this spring. I have had two interviews with the priest of this place [who is in regular communication with Mexicans on the Río Grande] and he has given me more satisfaction than any one that I have met." [40]

The excitement was not yet over. Early in April it was reported that in a recent message to the Mexican Congress President Bustamante had declared: "With regard to the campaign of Texas, I can only say that it is the first duty of the government and of the Mexicans, and that it would be acquitting myself but poorly of my functions not to employ all my power and all my means in order to surmount those obstacles which have hitherto delayed it"; and, considering that the Executive was not entirely responsible for a Texas campaign, he reminded Congress that he relied on "the efficient aid and co-operation of the legislature." [41] On April 8 the Texan government received a report, five days from Matamoros, that a large Mexican force was headed toward San Antonio. The Secretary of War immediately sent an express rider to San Antonio with instructions to General Johnston to prepare to defend the place, and to seek the assistance of the Comanches with whom he had been holding peace talks. "Your force is so inadequate," concluded the Secretary of War, "that I can scarcely do more than say I know all that bravery can achieve will be accomplished." [42] The Mexican advance, however did not materialize,

[38] A. S. Johnston to Secretary of War, March 13, 1838, in Johnston, *Life of Gen. Albert Sidney Johnston*, p. 88.

[39] *Telegraph and Texas Register*, Jan. 13, 1838.

[40] William H. Patton to [Robert A.] Irion, Secretary of State, Houston, [dated:] City of San Antonio, Feb. 7, 1838, in Domestic Correspondence (Texas) 1836–1846, ms.

[41] Reported in *Telegraph and Texas Register*, April 18, 1838.

[42] Quoted in Johnston, *Life of Gen. Albert Sidney Johnston*, p. 90.

and in June, Johnston obtained a furlough and again returned to Kentucky.

The excitement attendant upon the threatened invasion called for a reappraisal of the defense mechanism of the country and caused the government not only to be concerned with bringing the militia to complete organization but also to try to improve its relations with the various Indian tribes. Brigadier General Edward Burleson, commanding the First Brigade, sent out instructions for the organization of the battalions and regiments of the brigade.[43] The organization of the militiamen up until then had been wholly or partially neglected in the counties of Brazoria, Fort Bend, Austin, and Washington, and in the upper and eastern portion of Matagorda County. Those portions of the counties of Brazoria, Fort Bend, and Austin, west of the Brazos River, were to form the First Regiment, with the companies from Brazoria constituting the First Battalion and those from the other two counties the Second Battalion. Those sections of Washington and Milam counties lying west of the Brazos, along with the county of Bastrop, were to form the Second Regiment, with the companies from Washington and Milam counties constituting the First Battalion and those from Bastrop the Second Battalion. The counties of Matagorda, Colorado, and Fayette were to form the Third Regiment, with the companies from Matagorda County comprising the First Battalion and those from the counties of Colorado and Fayette, the Second Battalion. The companies from the counties of Jackson, Victoria, Goliad, and Gonzales were to form the Seventh Battalion and those from Béxar County the Eighth Battalion. These two battalions were not organized into a regiment. Elections for field officers of the regiments were set for June 15 at the seat of justice of each county.

[43] Brigade Orders, Adjutant General's Office, T. M., Houston, April [blank], 1838 . . . By order of Brigadier General Edward Burleson, Commanding First Brigade [and countersigned:] H. McLeod, Adjutant General, in *Telegraph and Texas Register*, April 28, 1838.

CHAPTER FIVE

The Opening of Frontier Trade

WHILE A NUMBER OF THE TEXANS were beginning to show an interest, late in 1837, in developing a profitable trade with northern Mexico, their government was reluctant to sanction the opening of trade with the settlements along the Río Grande and beyond. Those interested in developing such a trade believed that if it were opened, the trade through the port of Matamoros, with its high customs duties, would rapidly fall into the hands of the Texans. The existing Texan policy was assisting Mexico to raise enormous revenue through the port of Matamoros, when it should be designed to cut off the trade of that port, by diverting it through Texas to the enrichment of her citizens and the coffers of her Treasury Department. In spite of the attitude of the Texan government, a profitable trade with the Mexicans on the Río Grande began to develop along the western frontier of Texas.

By June 1837, business conditions at San Antonio were reported improving rapidly, owing to an increasing number of traders arriving from the Río Grande towns.[1] Early in 1838 information was being received at Houston almost daily from the west confirming the report that a regular system of illicit trade was developing there with the Mexicans who sought to evade the French blockade of their coast, but there was interference from Texan military authorities in that quarter who sought to close the trade. The remarkable forbearance and friendly deportment of the traders, reported the *Telegraph and Texas Register*, "showed that they were desirous to renew their former intimate connections with our citizens. There was a cheering prospect that a friendly intercourse would gradually extend into the interior of Chihuahua and Tamaulipas, and eventually pave the way for a lasting peace." The fact that General Johnston sanctioned the military order was regarded as strong proof of its expediency, but, continued the editor of the *Telegraph*,

[1] *Telegraph and Texas Register* (Houston), July 8, 1837.

78

. . . this officer is evidently laboring under an egregious mistake relative to the policy of the government. He evidently imagines that his post will be soon strengthened with a body of troops from this section, which will enable him to act on the offensive. He also apprehends some offensive movements on the part of Mexico. Experience will ere long convince him that he has nothing to hope from this government and nothing to fear from Mexico. Both will remain as they have remained during the last year— entirely passive. We trust, therefore, that since it is the settled policy of this government to keep the hands of the soldiers idle, their heads will be kept also inactive, lest by being permitted to think for the citizens and to prescribe their duties, they infringe upon civil rights, which the framers of the constitution intended to place far beyond the reach of military encroachment.[2]

On the other hand, the trade on the southwestern frontier must not be permitted to jeopardize the Republic's efforts to win French friendship and recognition. The French government must not be offended, and that government was soon to be assured that the government of Texas would take the necessary steps to prevent the Mexicans evading the blockade of the Mexican ports so far as Texas was concerned. The Texas revenue cutter operating along the Texas coast would enable the Republic to have intercourse with the French blockading squadron in the gulf, and might, said Secretary of State Irion, "be of great utility to us in procuring a good understanding with the French Government."[3]

In the meantime, the Secretary of War presented to Congress the question of the advisability of the opening of trade by the Texan government between the inhabitants of San Antonio and the Mexican population beyond them to the Río Grande, in order to divert to Texas large quantities of specie passing through Mexico's northern ports to the United States. At the same time, Texas would cultivate friendship among those living on the northern frontier of Mexico.[4]

About this time, Congress, in an effort to lower the cost of living at home and to give a stimulus to trade, modified the tariff policy of the

[2] *Ibid.*, March 31, 1838; See also R. A. Irion to Sam Houston, Nacogdoches, [dated:] City of Houston, July 28, 1838, in State Department Letterbook, no. 1, ms., pp. 41–42.

[3] R. A. Irion to Sam Houston, Nacogdoches, [dated:] City of Houston, July 28, 1838, in State Department Letterbook, no. 1, ms., pp. 41–42.

[4] Report of the Secretary of War to the Senate and House of Representatives of the Republic of Texas in Congress Assembled, War Department, April 24, 1838 [signed by Barnard E. Bee], in Army Papers (Texas), ms.

nation. It removed the duties from sugar, coffee, tea, salt, flour, all furniture, cotton bagging, bale rope, books, stationery, utensils, lumber, and a few other items, but all dry goods of which cotton formed a component part were subjected to a ten per cent ad valorem tax.[5]

The attitude of Mexico toward the development of the frontier trade is revealed in an order from the Minister of the Interior to the Governor of the Department of Coahuila in April 1838, declaring that until Texas was subjugated all commercial relations between Coahuila, Sonora, and Nuevo México with the United States must be severed.[6] This order, however, did not prevent a continuation of the trade, now rapidly growing in volume.

As a result of the increasing demand for friendly trade with northern Mexico, the President of Texas on June 13, 1838, instructed the chief justices of the counties of San Patricio, Goliad, Béxar, and Victoria to permit the citizens and friends of Texas residing on the Río Grande to trade at Béxar and other parts of Texas under certain conditions designed to protect Texas from hostile acts by the Mexican government and its citizens. Twenty-four hours notice had to be given of the approaching arrival of any group of over ten persons, and upon arrival the Mexican traders were to check their arms with the chief justice of the county. No person, however, was to be allowed to trade from the settlements of Texas in the direction of the Río Grande, nor were any companies to be raised without orders from the government, except that in case of invasion the militia might be called out on the frontier. "But no company," said the President, "shall go west of the Nueces, without orders expressly from [the] Government."[7]

[5] *Telegraph and Texas Register*, Feb. 10, 1838; Asa K. Christian, "The Tariff History of the Republic of Texas." Masters' thesis.

[6] Minister of the Interior to the Governor of the Department of Coahuila, Mexico, April 28, 1838, in "Relaciones Exteriores Asuntos Varios Comercio Estados Unidos, 1825–1849," Barker Transcripts, ms.

[7] Sam Houston to the Chief Justices of the Counties of San Patricio, Goliad, Béxar, and Victoria, June 30, 1838, Documents under the Great Seal (Texas), Record Book, no. 37, ms., pp. 25–26. In Domestic Correspondence (Texas), 1836–1846, ms., the date is shown as June 13, 1838. See also [Sam Houston], *To the Chief Justice of the County of San Patricio, Houston, June 13, 1838*, broadside; Erasmo Seguin, Chief Justice, to R. A. Irion, San Antonio, Aug. 14, 1838, State Department Letterbook, no. 2, ms., p. 185. Seguin reports the posting at San Antonio of two copies of the order opening the trade and the sending of other copies to the Río Grande.

No sooner was the order issued to permit the opening of the trade than enterprising traders from the United States and elsewhere began to interest themselves in it, even if it might entail smuggling into Mexico. "The Texas-Mexican smuggling business engaged my attention most strongly," recorded Gustav Dresel, a young German businessman traveling in the New World.[8] Accordingly, Dresel left New Orleans on July 12 for Matagorda on the southwestern frontier of Texas, a desirable point from which to conduct trade with the Mexicans who came there to buy goods to smuggle into the northern states. However, in less than a month, President Houston was writing the Secretary of War from Nacogdoches "that it might be well for the Sec[retar]y of State to apprise the Commandant of the French Fleet" off Mexico concerning the smuggling going on in the vicinity of Corpus Christi, "and intimate to him that it might be judicious for him to despatch one or two small armed vessels to cruise on our coast between Copano and Brazos de St. Iago so as to detect any smuggling that may be attempted in contravention of the Blockade" of the Mexican ports. "This Government," he continued," will not connive at any infraction of National Laws, nor has it any disposition to elude the measures of France, so far as she may deem necessary to prosecute retaliating measures against Mexico." [9]

The French blockade compelled the inhabitants of the Río Grande country to look to a new quarter for their supplies. They were not only willing to trade far and risk much, but to pay well in specie for what they bought. At this time, there were only two or three mercantile establishments at San Antonio and prices there were not reduced by competition. The Mexican traders were willing to pay the prices, however, and the influx of specie excited the imagination of many, encouraging others to embark in the trade. The same was true in the other frontier communities toward the coast. Aransas was taking a sudden spurt of growth with several new families moving in, the opening of a hotel, and the erection of several buildings, "with as much apparent confidence and zeal as if this place were removed far within

[8] Max Freund (trans. and ed.), *Gustav Dresel's Houston Journal: Adventures in North America and Texas, 1837–1841*, pp. 22, 27.

[9] Sam Houston to G. W. Hockley, Nacogdoches, Aug. 4, 1838, in Domestic Correspondence (Texas), 1836–1846, ms.; *Writings of Sam Houston*, II, 266–268; see also R. A. Irion to Sam Houston, Department of State, City of Houston, July 28, 1838, in Department of State Letterbook, no. 1, ms., pp. 41–42.

the bounds of the frontier." A number of different parties of traders from Presidio del Río Grande and Laredo in June 1838 brought horses, mules, and a small quantity of flour, beans, and other eatables into San Antonio for sale. By the end of the month, however, most of these, except a few former residents of Béxar including three women, had returned to their homes in northern Mexico. But other traders soon appeared, and several traders from Béxar made profitable visits to Laredo and to the Río Grande settlements above that place. Those Mexicans who returned to San Antonio to take up residence once more in the city, reported the justice of the peace, "say nothing in particular respecting the state of public affairs in the Republic of Mexico, but one with the other agree in saying that for the present their is no talk of an expedition against Texas; and that the ports of the Republic are blockaded by the French squadron." [10]

A party of Texans ranging west from San Patricio a few miles below the Nueces in September met a small detachment of Mexicans driving a number of mules loaded with provisions, supposedly for Savariego's men. Upon seeing the Texans, the Mexicans instantly took flight, leaving their pack animals and the provisions to be seized by the Texans. [11]

During the next few months, with the opening and expansion of the frontier trade, lawlessness along the southern and western perimeter of Texas became much intensified, with every messenger from the west "bringing intelligence of new depredations committed either by lawless bands of our own citizens," declared the *Telegraph*,[12] "or by parties of Mexican marauders." In the closing days of the Houston administration a joint committee of Congress, appointed to prepare an address to the people of Texas about the frontier situation, made its report.[13] The proposed address was adopted in the House on the 12th and in the Senate on the following day. It called upon "Texians" to "unite and march to the aid and rescue" of their defenseless frontier, and declared "it is also a matter of extreme regret to us, that the Executive has wholly failed and neglected to give that aid to the frontiers which their exposed condition so imperiously demanded."

[10] Erasmo Seguin to the Secretary of State, San Antonio, June 30, 1838, in Domestic Correspondence (Texas), 1836–1846, ms.

[11] *Telegraph and Texas Register*, Oct. 13, 1838.

[12] Oct. 20, 1838.

[13] [Texas Congress, Joint Committee of], *Address of Congress to All the People of Texas*, broadside; *Telegraph and Texas Register*, Sept. 15, 1838.

 CHAPTER SIX

Lamar's Efforts to Protect the Frontier

SHORTLY AFTER BECOMING PRESIDENT on December 10, 1838, Mirabeau B. Lamar called Congress' attention to the defenseless and exposed condition of the inland frontier of the Republic. Since the victory at San Jacinto, he declared, "we have sustained but little annoyance from our principal enemy," but "our western frontier has been polluted and our citizens desquieted by small bands of Mexican brigands who war for spoil and invade only to ravage and destroy."[1] It should be our duty, he continued,

. . . to chastise these depredators and suppress their incursions. . . . I would therefore recommend a law be enacted which shall visit a just and severe retribution upon such Mexican citizens, not in the actual service of their government, as shall be found in arms, or convicted of any hostile practices within our territory. An honorable warfare we will reciprocate. But the predatory aggressions of unauthorized banditti have always received, as they justly merit the severest chastisement that an indignant community can inflict.

Lamar also made reference to the incursions of the hostile Indians along the frontier, and urged Congress to provide for security against these barbarians. He suggested, too, the need for placing the trade developing with northern Mexico on a firmer basis, with some official sanction other than the mere executive proclamation upon which it then existed. The improvement of this trade would not only help Texas to cultivate the friendship of the people of the northern Mexican states

[1] M. B. Lamar to the Senate and House of Representatives, Houston, Dec. 21, 1838, in Record of Executive Documents from the 10th Dec. 1838 to the 14th Dec. 1841, ms., pp. 14–53; Lamar Papers, II, 346–369; Lamar, Mirabeau B., Message of the President, Submitted to Both Houses, December 21, 1838. Published by order of Congress. The date of the message as published in the Journal of the House of Representatives of the Republic of Texas: Regular Session of Third Congress, Nov. 5, 1838, pp. 167–195, is shown as December 20, 1838.

83

(then in a state of revolution) but might also make it possible for the Texans to secure a more definite knowledge of the country between the Nueces and the Río Grande. The hostile Indians in the area would have to be eliminated.

"When I came into office," Lamar later informed the people of Robertson County, "I found the Country destitute of all resources necessary in cases of sudden emergency. It was without soldiers, without arms, without money, and without credit." [2] Just what could be done under these conditions to give the security at home and protection from abroad to which the inhabitants of the young Republic were entitled posed a serious problem to Lamar and his followers. On the eve of his inauguration, Lamar's cousin Gazaway B. Lamar of Savannah, Georgia, had made suggestions which he hoped might be useful to the new chief magistrate. Toward Mexico and other nations he recommended firmness, discretion, prudence, the advancement of trade and commerce, and peace. On the other hand, as far as Mexico was concerned, there was the alternative of war to force from her recognition of the independence of Texas. "By directly attracting all the dissolute and abandoned of all other nations to your standard by a proclamation of universal plunder," he said, it could be done. With

. . . such a horde more might and probably would be effected—but *cui bono?* You could not expect order and subordination from such a combination—and though they might and probably would conquer Mexico—they would require themselves to be conquered—before anything valuable could be produced of them. I would therefore recommend the use of all conciliatory measures consistent with a just respect of your own people. [3]

On the other hand, Thomas M. Bradford of Montgomery, Alabama, advised that the unsettled differences between Texas and Mexico justified aggressive measures. "Will your Congress sanction and authorize . . . [an] expedition?" he asked;

. . . and will you, Sir, go as commander in chief? If so, I assure you, from information and observation in which I cannot be mistaken, that at the first tap of the Drum for volunteers, 50,000 men (100,000 if necessary) will

[2] Mirabeau B. Lamar to the Inhabitants of Robertson County Relative to the Preparations Being Made to Relieve them from the Hostile Incursions of the Indians, Executive Department, March 13, 1839, in Records of Executive Documents from the 10th Dec. 1838 to the 14th Dec. 1841, ms., pp. 63–64.

[3] G. B. Lamar to Genl. M. B. Lamar, Savannah, Nov. 9, 1838, in *Lamar Papers*, II, 286–289.

rally under your standard and bear it triumphantly and plant it immovably on the walls of the city of Mexico! . . . The present time is peculiarly well suited to carry this project into effect. The embarrassment in all kinds of business in the U. States and the general derangement of financial matters, have thrown thousands out of business who would zealously engage in this glorious cause. The revolutionized state of some parts of Mexico show that a large portion of the inhabitants of that country would be pleased at a change of government, and hail the approach of an army of deliverance with pleasure. *It can—it must be done.* . . . This matter has engaged my attention for more than 18 months. I have consulted, confidentially with some of the heaviest capitalists in the United States.—*The Money can be had*—Now is the time.[4]

Bradford stated that he was going to Jackson, Mississippi, in a few days and hoped to hear from Lamar there.

The need for protection became more urgent by the day. Just before Christmas 1838, several carts belonging to William B. Jaques of Béxar were attacked and robbed of a considerable quantity of merchandise between the Coleto and Goliad on the Goliad-Béxar road.[5] As a result of the President's urgent request that something be done to protect the frontiers, "some of our modest heroes," wrote James H. Starr, a Lamar supporter from Nacogdoches, "recommended an appropriation to establish a line of military forts,"[6] and Congress lost no time in putting through a measure that it had had under consideration for some time—a measure which had the support and recommendation of the Secretary of War, Albert Sidney Johnston. First, on December 16, it ordered the discharge of all persons belonging to the First and Second Regiments of Permanent Volunteers, and then enacted a measure, approved by the President on December 21, to establish a line of military posts six hundred miles in length along the frontier which would provide protection and serve as bases from which war against the Indians could be carried on more vigorously. Congress provided for the creation of a regiment of 840 men, rank and file, divided into fifteen companies of fifty-six men each for the protection of the northern and western frontiers.[7] The President was given discretionary power

[4] Tho[mas] M. Bradford to M. B. Lamar, Montgomery, Ala., Nov. 15, 1838, in *ibid.*, II, 292–293.

[5] *Telegraph and Texas Register* (Houston), Jan 12, 1839.

[6] James H. Starr to Pamela O. Starr, Dec. 2, 1838, James H. Starr Papers, ms.

[7] H. P. N. Gammel (ed.), *Laws of Texas*, II, 8, 15–20; *Civilian and Galveston Gazette*, Jan. 11, 1839.

to make as many cavalry units out of these as in his opinion the public interest might require. The men were to be enrolled for three years, "unless sooner discharged," and to be paid at the rate of $16 per month. An enlistment bounty of $30 was to be paid to each man at the time of enlistment. All officers were to be appointed by the President with the advice and consent of the Senate. Congress authorized the issuance of $300,000 in promissory notes for carrying into effect the terms of this law, and gave its approval to the uniform and articles of government for the army as prescribed by the President.[8]

The regiment was to be divided into eight detachments to be stationed at the following points: 56 men at or near Red River; 168 men at or near the Three Forks of the Trinity; 112 men at or near the Brazos River; 112 men at or near the Colorado River; 56 men at or near the St. Marks (or San Marcos) River; 56 men at or near the headwaters of the Cibolo; 56 men at or near the Frio River; and 224 men at or near the Nueces River. These detachments were to constitute two battalions. Those west of the Colorado were to comprise the First Battalion and those east of the Colorado were to constitute the Second Battalion. The distance between stations was to be traversed twice a day by detachments from the stations. The troops which had been enrolled under the law of May 15, 1838, for frontier protection were to be incorporated in this regiment and immediately equipped and sent to the post on the Nueces, which post was to receive its full compliment of men from those first enlisted in the service. The detachment on the Nueces was to traverse the country between the Nueces and the Río Grande, in such manner as to give the best protection possible to that section of the country. Three auxiliary posts were to be set up within the settled area—one on the Navasota, another on the Neches, and the third near the junction of the San Gabriel and Brushy Creek. In carrying out the terms of the act, the War Department constructed additional defense works for the protection of the capital and national archives.

[8] Texas Congress, *Rules and Articles for the Government of the Armies of the Republic of Texas*. This is a reprint of "Rules and Articles" as passed by the First Congress of the Republic. Texas War Department, *Government of the Army of the Republic of Texas, printed in accordance with a Joint Resolution of Congress, approved January 23d, 1839. By order of the Secretary of War.* The Texas regulations for the government of the army follow closely the *General Regulations for the Army of the United States, City of Washington, 1835,* except for the uniform.

The law also provided for the laying out of a military road under the supervision of the colonel of the regiment and "an engineer of experience" appointed by the President. The road was to run from or near the mouth of the Kiamishua (Kiamishi) Creek on Red River to the Nueces at the intersection of the road from Béxar to the Presidio del Río Grande. The road was to be cleared and bridged to admit the passage of wagons. The colonel of the regiment was required "to select such positions on the road as will be best calculated for the erection of forts, except the post on Red River, which," declared the law, "shall be at or near the upper settlements on said river, and for the defence and protection of the country." [9]

After the site for a station had been selected, the regimental commander was to order three leagues square [10] of land to be laid off around the station. If the land were already privately owned, then certain condemnation procedures as laid down in the law were to be followed in gaining title to it. The area obtained was to be surveyed into tracts of 160 acres each. Two of the 160-acre tracts were to be reserved to the government for purposes of fortification, farming, gardening, and other uses. A tract of 160 acres was to be granted as a bounty to each soldier who fulfilled the terms of his enlistment. [11] The remaining tracts of 160 acres were to be granted in fee simple, free of expense, to such able-bodied citizens as would actually settle upon the land and cultivate it for the space of two years. The land so granted was not to be sold or transferred for a term of five years from the date of acquisition. The President was authorized, as soon as he deemed it expedient, to permit trading posts to be erected at or near each of the frontier stations to engage in the Indian trade under certain regulations.

Since the plan for establishing self-sustaining military posts and settlements along key points of the frontier was a long range development and would require some time to be fully implemented, Congress in another act, approved December 29, 1838, authorized the President to raise eight companies of mounted volunteers for the protection of the frontier against the Comanches and other Indians for a term of

[9] Gammel (ed.), *Laws of Texas*, II, 15–20.

[10] By a supplementary act passed in February 1840, Congress increased the size of the tract to be surveyed to nine square leagues of land. *Ibid.*, II, 235–236.

[11] In February 1840, the law was amended to increase the bounty to 240 acres where the land was not available near the post. *Ibid.*

six months on the same arrangement as the mounted riflemen of December 1836, had been raised. These troops were to constitute a regiment commanded by a colonel, lieutenant colonel, and major appointed by the President,[12] and were to be used "offensively or defensively" at the discretion of the President.

Less than a month later, Congress authorized the raising of a company of fifty-six rangers for three months with officers appointed by the President to range on the frontier of Gonzales County.[13] Eight days later three companies of mounted volunteers for immediate service against the hostile Indians on the Bastrop, Robertson, and Milam county frontiers were authorized on the same terms as the eight companies provided for in the preceding December.[14] The term of enlistment here, however, was to be for six months, "unless sooner discharged." [15] In the new companies the men were to elect their own officers and then the men and officers were to choose a major to command them. On January 26 an act was approved to create a ranger corps, consisting of two companies of fifty-six men each, for the protection of the counties of San Patricio, Goliad, and Refugio.[16] These two companies were to be composed of volunteers enlisted for six months, and their officers were to be appointed by the President; $15,000 was appropriated to cover the necessary costs. The pay of privates and noncommissioned officers was to be $25 per month, and the men were to furnish their own horses, arms, and equipment.

By an act approved January 24, 1839, the President was "authorized and required to discharge all officers and soldiers now in actual service, except those belonging to the regiment for the protection of the northern and western frontier,[17] and ordnance department." [18] One million dollars was now appropriated for the protection of the frontier

[12] *Ibid.*, II, 29–30. Each company was to consist of a captain, one first and one second lieutenant, three sergeants, and fifty-three privates.

[13] *Ibid.*, II, 44. This act was approved by the President on January 15, 1839.

[14] Mirabeau B. Lamar to the Inhabitants of Robertson County Relative to the Preparations Being Made to Relieve them from the Hostile Incursions of the Indians, Executive Department, March 13, 1839, in Records of Executive Documents from the 10th Dec. 1838 to the 14th Dec. 1841, ms., pp. 63–64.

[15] Gammel (ed.), *Laws of Texas*, II, 78. This law was approved by the President on January 23, 1839.

[16] *Ibid.*, II, 93.

[17] The exemption applied to the eight military posts to be established under the law approved December 21, 1838.

[18] Gammel (ed.), *Laws of Texas*, II, 84–85.

and the President was authorized to raise such forces as he might deem necessary for the defense of the country according to the law of 1836 and for more effectively carrying out the laws on frontier defense enacted by the First Session of the Third Congress. Thus, the ranger companies were to be continued in operation. The Congress made appropriations on February 3, 1840, for the support of the First Regiment of Infantry, the First Regiment of Cavalry, three additional companies of cavalry, and for horses for twelve companies.[19]

The revised Militia Act (January 24, 1839) called for the election of the major general and brigadier generals by a vote of the people. Almost immediately Felix Huston commenced his campaign for the office of major general, making numerous speeches in various parts of the country, even before Lamar issued his proclamation setting the date of the election. In March 1839, James S. Mayfield urged Lamar to issue a proclamation calling for the election of a major general, and declared: "We will make a manly defense in the East to defeat the ranting [a]mbition of Gen. F. Huston." [20] Lamar delayed until September 11 issuing his proclamation for the election to take place on the second Monday in November.[21] By the time the election rolled around there were three candidates for the office of major general: Brigadier General Felix Huston, Colonel James C. Neill, and Brigadier General Albert Sidney Johnston. Owing to the delay in reporting election results from a number of counties, the official canvass was not made until March 7, 1840, when it was announced that Huston had been elected by a majority of 1,020 votes. The vote for brigadier general of the four brigades was very close with Alexander Somervell, Edwin Morehouse, James Smith, and E. H. Tarrant being chosen brigadier generals of the First, Second, Third, and Fourth Brigades, respectively.[22]

19 *Ibid.*, II, 381–386.

20 James S. Mayfield to Mirabeau B. Lamar, Nacogdoches, March 11, 1839, in *Lamar Papers*, II, 490–491.

21 Proclamation of Mirabeau B. Lamar for the Election of Militia Officers, September 11, 1839, in *Telegraph and Texas Register*, Sept. 25, 1839.

22 *Telegraph and Texas Register*, May 1, 1839; General Order No. 5. Adjutant and Inspector General's Office, Austin, March 7, 1840 [signed by H. McLeod, Adjt. and Inspector General], in *Texas Sentinel* (Austin), March 25, 1840. In October 1841, it was being reported in the Texas newspapers that Felix Huston, who had left the country for Mississippi, had resigned the office of Major General of the Texas Militia. Apparently, he saw no opportunity to gain personal military glory under the newly elected administration in Texas. *Texas Sentinel*, Oct 28, 1841.

After San Jacinto

Colonel Edward Burleson was placed in command of the First Regiment of Regular Infantry to be formed under the law of December 1838, with headquarters at Bastrop, near where he lived. Recruiting was carried out under the over-all direction of Lieutenant Colonel William S. Fisher for the area east of the Brazos,[23] under Colonel Burleson west of the river. Fisher was to be assisted by Major P. S. Wyatt. Others who rendered assistance in recruiting from time to time were Captains B. Y. Gillan and J. M. Wiehl in New Orleans, Colonel Hugh McLeod, Captain Lawrence at Galveston, Captain W. D. Redd, Captain Adam Clendennin, Captain M. B. Skerrett, and Lieutenant H. L. Grush. Colonel Lysander Wells served on recruiting duty in the United States from October 1839, to some time in 1840.[24] Between the passage of the law and December 17, 1840, $25,348.96 were spent in recruiting and in the payment of bounties for the First Regiment of Regular Infantry. Over one-third of the expenditures were for getting volunteers from the United States.[25]

Recruitment was slow, and President Lamar found it necessary to make a requisition in March 1839, upon the counties of Harrisburg, Brazoria, Matagorda, Colorado, Liberty, and Galveston to furnish six companies of volunteers to serve for six months on the frontier. Five of the companies when organized were to rendezvous at LaGrange under the command of Colonel Burleson and one was to be stationed at Fort Milam on the Brazos River.[26]

There was not much enthusiasm in Texas for settling down to humdrum life in a military camp on the frontier; for the ambitious there were far more lucrative opportunities. But the Panic of 1837 in the

[23] H. McLeod to A. Sidney Johnston, Adjutant-General's Office, Austin, Nov. 9, 1839, in Harriet Smither (ed.), *Journals of the Fourth Congress of the Republic of Texas*, III, 81–82; List of Officer Appointments Made by the President for the First Regiment of Infantry, War Department, Jan. 30, 1839 [signed by A. Sidney Johnston, Secretary of War], in *Telegraph and Texas Register*, Feb. 6, 1839.

[24] Annual Report of Charles Mason, First Auditor, to William Sevey, Acting Secretary of the Treasury, Treasury Department, [dated:] First Auditor's Office, Dec. 15, 1840, in Texas Congress, *Journals of the House of Representatives: Fifth Congress, Appendix*, pp. 59–68.

[25] Charles Mason, First Auditor, to B. T. Archer, Secretary of War [dated:] Treasury Department, First Auditor's Office, Dec. 17, 1840, in *ibid.*, pp. 377–378. Bounties were paid through Captain D. C. Ogden, B. Y. Gillan, Colonel W. S. Fisher, Colonel Jacob Snively, Captain M. B. Lewis, J. C. P. Kennymore, Captain John Holliday, and Captain J. B. P. January.

[26] *Telegraph and Texas Register*, March 6, 1839.

90

United States had disrupted the affairs of many young men there, who by 1839 had grown quite restless and looked toward Texas, not yet in the throes of depression, as a land of hope. From Clark County, Mississippi, on July 3, 1839, William B. Trotter wrote Lamar, "There is a Parsel of able bod[i]ed active and dareing young men in this section of the country who are willing to join the Texas army as volunteers for six months provided the inducement (in pay and land) offered by the government is sufficient to Justify them to go to Texas." [27] Captain Samuel A. Plummer, on a recruiting trip to the United States to raise two companies of mounted regulars to be stationed on the lower Nueces,[28] wrote Lamar from New Orleans that, having made himself acquainted with the laws of the United States "so as to know how far I can go in recruiting men," he had made tentative arrangements with the captain of the steamer *Columbia* to transport the volunteers "as fast as I recruit at ten Dollars per head." Plummer had learned from conversation with several United States army officers that the Irish made good infantrymen and were "first rate with muskets on a charge." He believed a few companies of Irishmen might be highly useful, and that several hundred volunteers could be readily obtained if they could be assured the bounty usually paid United States soldiers—"good money" as they called it, and the issuance of two suits of coarse summer clothing, hats, and shoes upon landing and enrolling at Galveston. Only "give me a fancy uniform of Red and I can enlist first rate men," he wrote. The "dashing uniform" would be only for special occasions; in the field he would, of course, use the standard uniform.[29]

Recruiting for the First Regiment of Regular Infantry was only partially successful, and the same could be said for the eight companies of mounted volunteers which had been authorized, about the same time. "We have found it unnecessary, for reasons too apparent to mention, to establish recruiting stations within the limits of our Republic," reported the Secretary of War; and "the cost attending foreign stations, combined with the expense of transporting troops from abroad, would

[27] William B. Trotter to M. B. Lamar, Clark County, Mississippi, July 3, 1839, in *Lamar Papers*, III, 32.

[28] Regarding these two companies see endorsement by the Secretary of State on the letter of Samuel Hewes to [M. B. Lamar], City of Aransas, May 23, 1839, in *ibid.*, II, 585–586.

[29] S. A. Plummer to General [M. B. Lamar], New Orleans, April 5, 1839, in *ibid.*, II, 516–517, Same to Same, July 5, 1839, in *ibid.*, III, 33.

very greatly exceed the amount appropriated for the contemplated object." The peak enlistment in the First Regiment of Infantry was 560, rank and file. Thus, there existed a shortage of five companies, "which deficit rendered impossible the location of all points designated by Congress." [30]

A contract was made on May 29, 1839, and another on June 7, 1839, with Tryon, Son & Co. of Philadelphia to furnish 1,500 stands of muskets, with 100 being delivered monthly from the date set in the contract. Muskets manufactured in the United States were decidedly superior to those of any other manufacture because of "the excellence of workmanship, uniformity of all component parts of the arm," and "their unquestioned durability." [31] Owing, however, to the general sickness which prevailed during the ensuing summer, the contractor was unable to comply with the terms of delivery but expected to have some of the guns ready by early fall. By September a few of the guns had been received in Texas. In the meantime, in anticipation of the arms being delivered, Secretary of War Albert S. Johnston on November 8, 1839, discharged all employees in the armory, except a sufficient number to take care of the public buildings and property.[32] Colonel Lysander Wells reported in Austin about March 1, 1840, that his trip to New York in search of military stores, had been very successful. "Almost the entire equipment for two regiments, one of cavalry, and one of infantry have been procured, and are daily expected," reported the *Texas Sentinel* on March 4. By the end of 1840, 860 of the muskets had been received and paid for, and the remainder (640) were at New Orleans in storage subject to delivery whenever the government paid for them.[33]

A few of Colt's Patent Rifles were in use in Texas before November 1840, and were highly regarded since their rate of fire was five to one

[30] Branch T. Archer, Secretary of War and Navy, to the President of the Republic of Texas, War and Navy Department, City of Austin, Sept. 30, 1841, in Texas Congress, *Journal of the House of Representatives, Fifth Congress, Appendix*, pp. 115–124.

[31] George W. Hockley, Colonel of Ordnance, to Branch T. Archer, Secretary of War, Ordnance Department, September 1840, in *ibid.*, pp. 169–173; George W. Hockley to David G. Burnet, Ordnance Department, Jan. 4, 1841, in *ibid.*, pp. 400–402.

[32] George W. Hockley, Colonel of Ordnance, to Branch T. Archer, Secretary of War, Ordnance Department, September 1840, in *ibid.*, pp. 169–173.

[33] George W. Hockley to David G. Burnet, Ordnance Department, Jan. 4, 1841, in *ibid.*, pp. 400–402.

when compared with the musket then in use.[34] However, because of an unfortunate accident at Austin resulting in a death from one of the new rifles, the people called it in ridicule, "Colt's patent wheel of misfortune." [35] Mr. Jenks' rifles were also experimented with, and after some alterations agreed to by the manufacturer, 250 were ordered at a cost of $23.80 each. By the end of 1840 none of these had been received although they had all been at New Orleans in storage since August, awaiting payment by the government, which had been unable to meet its obligation.[36]

On February 18, 1840, the artillery, small arms, ammunition, and other military stores were ordered by President Lamar to be moved from Houston, the former seat of government, to Austin. They were to be shipped to Linn's Landing on Lavaca Bay and from there transported by land to the capital, but because of bad weather and the difficulty of transportation they did not reach Austin until the latter part of May.[37] Storehouses and a workshop were built at Austin to take care of the military stores, and plans were developed for the construction of a national armory, either at Austin or at some other place. A two-pound brass cannon was found near Texana, but its bore was in such bad condition from misuse that it was rebored with Brigg's horse-power machine and made into a useful four-pounder. Another Spanish brass piece, in like condition, was at the armory in Austin in September 1840, waiting to be rebored as soon as the War Department authorized the work. It was believed that this piece could be converted into a useful sixteen-pounder. The "Twin Sisters" and other cannon were in battery at the Austin garrison. By September 1840, there was only one military supply depot on the frontier, and the Ordnance Department found it impossible to keep the various posts supplied. It was urged that suitable arrangements be made at once with manufacturers in the United States for monthly, or periodic, delivery of

[34] *Telegraph and Texas Register*, Nov. 18, 1840.

[35] *Ibid.*, Dec. 9, 1840.

[36] George W. Hockley to David G. Burnet, Ordnance Department, Jan. 4, 1841, in Texas Congress, *Journal of the House of Representatives, Fifth Congress, Appendix*, pp. 400–402.

[37] George W. Hockley, Colonel of Ordnance, to Branch T. Archer, Secretary of War, Ordnance Department, September 1840, in *ibid.*, pp. 169–174; Mirabeau B. Lamar to George W. Hockley, Executive Department, Austin, Feb. 18, 1840, in Record of Executive Documents from the 10th Dec. 1838 to the 14th Dec. 1841, ms., p. 166.

powder and lead.[38] At Austin there was no lead, and the government was obliged to send to Missouri for it. The magazine at Houston was too far away to be drawn on safely by the western country if need be; there were two magazines at Austin. By September 1840, some of the guns ordered from Tryon, Son & Co. had been received; others captured from the enemy in 1835–1836 were in use in the Texan army; and 130 had been repaired during the year.[39]

Plans, with drawings, were developed during the year 1840 for the defense of Galveston,[40] San Luis,[41] Point Bolivar, Brazos Santiago, Velasco, and Aransas. Galveston's battery was regarded in September 1840 as unsafe and as needing "an immediate, complete, and thorough repair," without regard to the erection of the fort [42] recommended by Colonel George W. Hockley, head of the Ordnance Department. In April 1840, Hockley recommended and the President gave approval for the purchase of the following armament for the defense of the coast:

> For Fort Velasco
> 9 24-pounders
> For Fort Aransas
> 12 24-pounders
> 9 12-pounders
> For Fort Brazos Santiago
> 12 24-pounders
> 9 12-pounders
> 4 6-pounders
> For a Star Redoubt at the East end of Galveston Island
> 9 24-pounders
> 3 12-pounders
> "Say 15 guns, deducting 4 thirty-two pounders now there"
> For a small Triangular Redoubt at Point Bolivar
> 3 12-pounders
> For Isle San Luis
> 3 24-pounders
> 2 6-pounders
> Cannister, grape and round-shot

[38] *Ibid.* [39] *Ibid.*
[40] At the east end of Galveston Island.
[41] At the west end of Galveston Island.
[42] George W. Hockley, Colonel of Ordnance, to Branch T. Archer, Secretary of War, Ordnance Department, September 1840, in Texas Congress, *Journals of the House of Representatives, Fifth Congress, Appendix*, pp. 169–174.

5,000 flint and steel lock muskets of the best quality with all
    necessary accessories
4,0000 lbs. of lead
Sword belts, etc. for non-commissioned infantry officers [43]

By December 1840, the ordnance and advance stores purchased from N. P. Ames of Springfield, Massachusetts, had arrived safely at Galveston, and were resting in the storeroom of the customhouse pending transfer to the arsenal at Austin.[44]

The full provisions of the law of December 21, 1838, were never carried into effect. In 1840 a military road was opened between Austin and San Antonio, and a company of infantry was stationed at the headwaters of the San Marcos, midway between the two places. It was expected that by the end of the year the national (military) road connecting Red River with Austin would be completed.[45] By the time Colonel Burleson resigned command of the First Regiment of Infantry, the road north from Austin had been surveyed and marked as far as the Trinity. Burleson was succeeded in command on August 18, 1840, by Colonel William G. Cooke [46] who was to locate and establish the various posts and lay out the military road to Red River. A portion of Cooke's regiment left Austin on August 22 for Little River.

After making certain preliminary arrangements, Colonel Cooke joined the troops on September 9 on Little River, just below the junction of the Lampasas and Leon rivers, where he waited five days for the delivery of a number of mules to supplement the fifty-seven horses and fifty mules belonging to the five companies comprising his command.[47] The mules for which he waited did not arrive, and, in the

[43] Memorandum to General James Hamilton, April 22, 1840, in *ibid.*, pp. 173–174.

[44] George W. Hockley, Colonel of Ordnance, to Branch T. Archer, Secretary of War, Ordnance Department, Dec. 16, 1840, in *ibid.*, pp. 371–373.

[45] *Ibid.*

[46] E. W. Winkler, (ed.), *Secret Journals of the Senate: Republic of Texas, 1836–1845*, pp. 184, 189; *Texas Sentinel* (Austin), Aug. 22, 1840.

[47] William G. Cooke to B. T. Archer, Secretary of War, [dated:] Camp on Bois d'Arc, Nov. 14, 1840, in Texas Congress, *Journals of the House of Representatives, Fifth Congress, Appendix*, pp. 325–327; Branch T. Archer, "Annual Report of the Secretary of War to [the President], War Department, City of Austin, Sept. 30th, 1840," in *ibid., Fifth Congress, First Session*, pp. 121–122; William L. Cazneau, Acting Quartermaster General, to Branch T. Archer, Secretary of War, [dated:] Quartermaster-General's Office, Austin, Dec. 19, 1840, in *ibid., Seventh Congress, Appendix*, pp. 378–379; Texas War Department, *Report of the Secretary of War, November 1840. Printed by Order of the House of Representatives.*

meantime, the beeves escaped owing to the negligence of the guard. Deciding not to wait for the quartermaster to furnish another supply of beeves, Cooke left orders behind for Captain John Holliday to join him with the beeves whenever they were obtained and pushed on to the Brazos, arriving at the Waco Village on September 17, where he remained until the quartermaster came up with the supplies.[48]

Upon the arrival of the beeves and other necessities, Cooke proceeded with his men toward the Trinity, making slow progress of from six to eight miles a day, because of having to cross numerous creek bottoms with wagons pulled by mules in poor condition. Owing to the dryness of the season the men were forced to camp several times without water. Finding Chambers Creek dry, some ten or fifteen of the men went back upon the trail for water and, contrary to orders, without their muskets. They were ambushed by a party of Indians and five of their number killed.

That night, while the main party camped near Chambers Creek, a severe norther blew up, and the cattle stampeded and were never recovered although every exertion was made to find them. "They were probably driven away by the Indians," who prowled about Texan camps from the Brazos to the Trinity. The loss of the beeves left the troops "entirely without provisions," except for sugar and coffee, no corn having been taken upon the expedition.

From Little River to the Brazos, Cooke's men found buffalo in abundance, and also for several days after leaving Chambers Creek; but as they approached the Trinity the game became scarce, and before they could reach the main bottom of the river the men were forced to subsist for several days on dogs, mules, and horses.[49] Too far from the settlements now to turn back with the wagons and sick men, the expedition moved on toward the settlements on the Sulphur Fork of Red River, a distance of two days' ride or five days' march. Lieutenant Colonel Adam Clendennin was left on the west side of the Trinity with the wagons, some twenty horses and mules, the sick, and a guard of forty men.

Five days after leaving the Trinity, Colonel Cooke's men struck a thicket which their guide said was the headwaters of the Sabine. Five days were required to cut a path through the thicket. They then struck

[48] William G. Cooke to B. T. Archer, Secretary of War, [dated:] Camp on Bois d'Arc, Nov. 14, 1840, in Texas Congress, *Journals of the House of Representatives, Fifth Congress, Appendix*, pp. 325–327.
[49] *Ibid.*

the trail of the Chihuahua traders, which led them to the settlement on the Bois d'Arc fork of Red River, where they were able to obtain supplies from Bailey English.

Plans were now made to send back assistance to the men left at the Trinity. A company was dispatched with beeves, other supplies, and oxen to draw the wagons. Upon arrival at the Trinity on October 5, the relief party found a note from Clendennin dated the 3rd, saying that he had been starved out; that his men had eaten most of the mules and horses; and that he was compelled to leave for the settlements, but expected to return in eight or ten days.[50] At Clendennin's old campsite on the Trinity the relief party found Captain M. B. Skerrett and William D. Houghton with forty men who had followed Colonel Cooke from Austin and had reached the Trinity the day before (the 4th).

While awaiting the arrival of Skerrett and Houghton on Red River, to commence the survey and marking of the military road, Cooke selected a fine location for a post on Red River ten miles above Coffee's Station, where supplies could be obtained easily from the trading station below and where the most protection could be afforded against the Indians. This was the first of the eight military posts to be established, and Colonel Cooke was expected to plant the others as he returned along the line of defense, if Congress should provide the necessary funds.[51] This post was located on the east side of the Cross Timbers near the junction of Mineral Creek with Red River in present Grayson County northwest of Shermantown (Sherman), and was named Fort Johnson. Cooke erected a supply base (or station) near Coffee's Station, which he called Fort Preston.[52]

In early February 1841, Captain Clendennin's men, numbering about 60, were divided between the station at the falls of the Brazos and the fort on Little River, having recently returned from Waco Village where they had remained four weeks, but had erected no blockhouses,[53] for there was yet uncertainty as to whether the road should cross the Brazos at Waco Village or at the Toweash Village, above the

[50] *Ibid.*

[51] Mirabeau B. Lamar to the Senate and House of Representatives, Executive Department, Austin, Dec. 2, 1840, in Record of Executive Documents from the 10th Dec. 1838 to the 14th Dec. 1841, ms., pp. 221–222.

[52] *Texas Sentinel,* Jan. 16, 1841; William G. Cooke to Branch T. Archer, Secretary of War, Austin, Feb. 17, 1841, in *ibid.,* March 4, 1841.

[53] *Ibid.,* Feb. 11, 1841.

mouth of the Aquilla [Creek], where it was felt the line could be extended with little difficulty, directly to the mouth of the Llano.

Colonel Cooke returned to Austin about the middle of February 1841, where a grand ball was given in his honor on the evening of February 27 in the Senate Chamber, being preceded by a fine dinner presided over by Mrs. Bullock.[54] In his report to the Secretary of War he protested against Congress' determination to end the permanent military establishment, so badly needed to give protection to the frontier. He asked the Department to assume the responsibility for sustaining his regiment at a reduced size to enable completion of the military road and for giving security to the frontier settlers. He proposed to fill the company at the headwaters of the San Marcos from Major Howard's command at San Antonio, and to establish a post on the Brazos, which would make communication practicable and safe from Austin to both extremes of the frontier.[55] A bill was presented in the Fifth Congress and enacted into law, approved by Acting President Burnet on January 21, 1841, to reserve a twelve-mile strip on each side of the military road, running from Red River to the Nueces, for distribution to actual settlers who would receive 640 acres of land, if a head of family, and 320 acres, if single, on condition that they reside on it and cultivate a part of the land for a period of five years.[56] The law also prohibited any surveyor of the Republic from surveying or locating "any lands lying further north of said road than the twelve miles" as provided by the law, "or any lands lying west of the river Nueces." These lands were reserved to the future disposition of Congress.

Congress appropriated $25,000 in paper money for the construction of the military road, but the road, as well as the additional posts, failed to materialize because of the chaotic financial condition of the country. Cooke's expedition exhausted the original appropriation[57] of $300,000 and nothing further was done toward carrying on the survey or promoting a colonization program. It would have required $10,500 per quarter to maintain Cooke's force in the performance of its work. The

[54] *Ibid.*, Feb. 25 and March 4, 1841.

[55] William G. Cooke to Branch T. Archer, Secretary of War, Austin, Feb. 17, 1841, in *ibid.*, March 4, 1841.

[56] *Ibid.*, Nov. 28, 1840; Jan. 16, 1841; Gammel (ed.), *Laws of Texas*, II, 536–537.

[57] Mirabeau B. Lamar to the Senate and House of Representatives, Dec. 2, 1840, in Texas Congress, *Journals of the House of Representatives of the Republic of Texas: Fifth Congress, First Session, 1840–1841*, p. 211.

thinking behind the law was not bad, but the scheme of a system of permanent forts was too grandiose for a weak, frontier republic on the verge of bankruptcy, and the financial picture was to grow worse rather than better.

CHAPTER SEVEN

Lamar's Efforts to Promote Trade

IN HIS FIRST MESSAGE TO CONGRESS, as already noted, Lamar took up the question of frontier trade, and suggested a plan to open that trade as a means of cultivating friendship with the inhabitants of the north Mexican states, and with the added hope that it would enable the Texans to secure a more definite knowledge concerning the area lying between the Nueces and the Río Grande.[1] By a joint resolution of January 14, 1839, Congress gave its sanction to the opening of the frontier trade, which up until then had been carried on under the proclamation of Lamar's predecessor. The President was authorized to open trade with the inhabitants along the Río Grande, and on February 21 President Lamar issued instructions regarding the conduct of such trade. All Mexican traders were required to have passports from either the civil or the military authorities of the district from which they came, specifying the objects of their visit and giving a description of the merchandise and other things which they wished to dispose of. They were to enter Texas by way of Casa Blanca[2] on the lower

---

[1] M. B. Lamar to Congress, Dec. 20, 1838, *Journal of the House of Representatives, Regular Session of Third Congress*, pp. 167–195; the *Telegraph and Texas Register* (Houston), Dec. 22, 1838, mentions this message as having been transmitted at noon, Thursday, December 20, 1838, and it is printed in the *Telegraph*, Dec. 26, 1838; but in the *Lamar Papers*, VI, 346–369, it is shown with date of December 21 and it was separately published with date of December 21 as: Mirabeau B. Lamar, *Message of the President, Submitted to Both Houses, December 21, 1838. Published by Order of Congress.*

[2] Proclamation of President Mirabeau B. Lamar, February 21, 1839, *Lamar Papers*, no. 1079, ms.; H. P. N. Gammel (ed.), *Laws of Texas*, II, 117; Texas Congress, *Journal of the Senate of the Republic of Texas: First Session of the Third Congress—1838*, pp. 105–106; Record of Executive Documents from the 10th Dec. 1838 to the 14th Dec. 1841, ms., pp. 58–60. In 1807 Spain granted sixteen leagues of land, known as the Casa Blanca grant to Juan José de la Garza Montemayor. J. F. Dobie, in *Coronado's Children: Tales of Lost Mines and Buried*

Nueces, a few miles above Lipantitlán and less than forty-five miles from Corpus Christi, thus indicating that only the lower Río Grande region was to be included. Lamar had just recently acquired a league of land fronting on Copano Bay,[3] which was now expected to become a scene of considerable business activity and from which he, Samuel A. Plummer, and others hoped to profit. After presenting his passport to the commanding officer at Casa Blanca on the Nueces, the trader would then be free to proceed to either San Antonio or Goliad to dispose of his goods or items of trade and to make such purchases as he desired. Since, however, there was no military post then at Casa Blanca, the traders would, in the interim until one could be established, be permitted to proceed directly to either San Antonio de Béxar or Goliad, where, upon presentation of their passports to the highest miltary or civil authority, they would receive permits to trade. The trade was to be "free of duties or exactions of any kind" so long as similar exemptions were accorded to the citizens of Texas carrying goods into northern Mexico to trade. As for those who might enter without passports and "with horses or cattle for sale," declared the President, "such horses or cattle shall be taken by . . . [the] authorities and retain[ed] until information of their capture can be communicated to the Mexican authorities aforesaid near the Río Grande."

As a means of furthering the cause of trade and navigation generally, the Secretary of Navy was directed by Congress to have surveys made, as soon as possible, of the bars and entrances to Galveston, Velasco, Paso de Cavallo, Aransas, and the Sabine, and to mark each with "a good and sufficient buoy or buoys, in such manner that the channels

---

Treasures of the Southwest, pp. 95–96, presumes that a fort and residence was built on the land before 1807, and that an important ranch developed in the area.

The Casa Blanca mentioned here is not to be confused with the house by the same name erected by Don Erasmo Seguin before the Revolution upon his ranch between San Antonio and Floresville in what is now Wilson County. Seguin's house was "situated about four miles north-west of Floresville and one-half mile west of the highway to San Antonio." Frederick C. Chabot, *With the Makers of San Antonio,* p. 120; William Kennedy, *Texas: The Rise, Progress and Prospects of the Republic of Texas,* II, 43; Lon Tinkle, *13 Days to Glory: The Siege of the Alamo,* p. 149.

[3] Reuben H. Roberts to M. B. Lamar, Aransas [Texas], June 26, 1838 (Private), Mirabeau B. Lamar to ――― Griffith, Houston, Aug. 15, 1838; Sam[uel] A. Plummer to M. B. Lamar, on Board *Correo* [en route to New Orleans to raise money to enable Lamar to hold his townsite], Feb. 16, 1839; Same to Same, New Orleans, March 12, 1839; all in *Lamar Papers,* II, 174–175, 202–203, 452, 492, 516–517.

of the aforesaid bays may at all times be plainly indicated, together with such instructions, bearing with land marks, courses and distances as may aid the entrance of marines with all possible facility into our ports." The same was to be done for the inside bars and channels of Sabine, Galveston, Matagorda, Lavaca, Aransas, and Corpus Christi bays.[4]

Lamar had great ambitions for the future of Texas as an independent nation, not the least of which included developing and controlling her incalculable resources, and he envisioned Texas as "stretching from the Sabine to the Pacific and away to the South West as far as the enemy may render it necessary for the sword to mark the boundary." [5] The attainment of security from Indian and Mexican attacks, the promotion of internal order, the development of trade, and the stimulation of settlement of the country where important features of his policy.

On the southwestern frontier there was a gradual revival of trade between the Texans and the inhabitants of northern Mexico, although the chief justices of Goliad, Refugio, and Victoria counties at times hindered it by charging (contrary to law) a passport fee of one dollar for each member of a Mexican trading company.[6] The traders brought into San Antonio, Matagorda, Kinney's Ranch and Trading Post, and other points farther east, beans, flour, leather, *piloncillas,* shoes, saddles, and specie, which they exchanged for calico, bleached and unbleached cloth, tobacco, American hardware, and other commodities.[7]

The resumption of trade and the influx of population into the so-called "depopulated counties" caused the western frontier to be pictured as assuming the appearance of an inhabited country. A visitor to the Nueces area below San Patricio described the country as

. . . unequalled by any that my eyes ever rested upon, either in its salubrity of climate, its general features and exuberance of soil—the beautiful bottom lands that skirt the river on one side or the other, about two miles in width . . . the fine rolling pastures that swell up beyond them, with frequent hammocks of mesquite wood, all abounding with the finest and most luxuriant

[4] Gammel (ed.), *Laws of Texas,* II, 113.

[5] Inaugural Address of Mirabeau B. Lamar to Both Houses of Congress, Houston, Dec. 10, 1838, in *Lamar Papers,* II, 320.

[6] John J. Linn to the President of the Republic of Texas, Victoria, Sept. 21, 1839, in Domestic Correspondence (Texas) 1836–1846, ms.

[7] *Matagorda Bulletin,* Dec. 6, 1838; April 4, 1839.

grasses—mesquite grass, wild rye, &c. It is undoubtedly, the paradise of all sections of the country that I have yet seen.[8]

In March and April 1839, more than two hundred families arrived in the neighborhoods of Copano, Aransas,[9] and Live Oak Point and were "extending the settlements quite back into the counties of San Patricio and Refugio."[10] Many Mexican families were said to be desirous of leaving the Río Grande to settle in the western country, but were prevented from fear of Indian hostilities. The Lipans, then friendly to the Texans, were reported to have committed several murders recently in the vicinity of a place called "high timbers," just west of the Nueces, among Mexicans entering Texas.[11] The town of Calhoun was projected on January 21, 1839, when Congress directed the Secretary of the Treasury to have 640 acres on the north end of Matagorda Island surveyed as a site for a seaport.[12] Victoria, Goliad, Gonzales, and San Antonio were incorporated on January 26, 1839,[13] and Aransas City, Galveston, and Matagorda were incorporated on January 28.[14] A customhouse was located at Live Oak Point in September 1838,[15] and at Matagorda in October of the same year.[16] For nearly a year, until early June 1839, the town of Aransas served as the port of entry and as the point of customs collection for Copano Bay until the customhouse was removed by the collector of the district to the newly estab-

[8] Letter to the Editor of the *Telegraph*, Nueces River, March 6, 1839, in *Telegraph and Texas Register*, April 10, 1839.

[9] Aransas City was founded about 1837 by James Power on Live Oak Point, Refugio County (now a part of Aransas County), near the location of the old Spanish-Mexican fort of Aranzazu, which guarded the entrance to Copano Bay. *Handbook of Texas*, I, 56–57.

[10] *Morning Star* (Houston), April 27, 1839.

[11] Samuel Hewes to [M. B. Lamar], City of Aransas, May 23, 1839, in *Lamar Papers*, II, 585–586.

[12] Gammel (ed.), *Laws of Texas*, II, 61–62, 423–424, 541–542. The development of the town was delayed, however, until the survey of the coast and harbors of Texas could be completed by the navy. Lots in the town of Calhoun went on sale in June 1841, and a customhouse was established there.

[13] Gammel (ed.), *Laws of Texas*, II, 118–119. Except for Goliad these had originally been incorporated on December 14, 1837. *Ibid.*, I, 1392.

[14] *Ibid.*, II, 94–99. Matagorda was originally incorporated on December 14, 1837. *Ibid.*, I, 1392.

[15] *Lamar Papers*, II, 220–222.

[16] *Ibid.*, II, 237.

lished town of Lamar.[17] Lavaca was created a port of entry on January
23, 1839,[18] and thereafter vessels going through the Pass Cavallo were
to be sent to Lavaca Bay "in the same manner as if they were bound
for Matagorda." A year later, the frontier towns of Victoria, Gonzales,
and Goliad, which had not had enough people the year before to fill
all the county offices,[19] were reincorporated.[20]

The development of Texas, generally, was proceeding rapidly in
1838 and 1839, and the opening of the trade along the western and
southern frontiers was only one phase of that growth. "The emigration
to your Republic," wrote a friend of Karnes from Alabama, "is immense; therefore, hold on to your lands and you will realize a
fortune." [21] "The prejudices which have hitherto existed against Texas,
are fast wearing away," wrote the Texan consul at Philadelphia, "and
a spirit of migrating to that country is being awakened, particularly
among the German population." [22] It was believed that an extension
of the head-right law, then about to expire, would keep the tide of
immigration flowing into Texas. Although the Texan consuls generally
operated under the same instructions as those that governed United
States consuls,[23] as an inducement to immigration they were "prohibited from charging persons emigrating to Texas for passports or
certificates of character or intentions." The policy of the government,
declared the Secretary of State, was to encourage emigration from
other countries; and hence, "the passport system was abolished in order
to enable emigrants to avoid the inconveniences and expense which
frequently attended the procurement of passports." [24]

[17] Sam[uel] Hewes to Genl. M. B. Lamar, City of Aransas, May 1, 1839, in
ibid., II, 555; Proceedings and Resolutions of Citizens' Meeting, Aransas, Con-
demning the Removal of the Custom House to Lamar, June 15 and 17, 1839, in
ibid., III, 21–23; *Telegraph and Texas Register*, July 3, 1839; James Webb to
Editor of the *Telegraph*, [July 1839], *ibid.*, July 10, 1839.

[18] Gammel (ed.), *Laws of Texas*, II, 77.

[19] William Hunter, Chief Justice of Goliad County, to James Webb, Goliad,
March 27, 1839, in State Department Letterbook, no. 2, ms., p. 221.

[20] Gammel (ed.), *Laws of Texas*, II, 450–453.

[21] William O. Winston to Henry W. Karnes, Daniel Prairie, Greene, Ala., April
22, 1838, in Henry W. Karnes Papers, ms.

[22] Cyrus Joy to David G. Burnet, Acting Secretary of State [dated:] Texian
Consulate Office, Philadelphia, Nov. 28, 1839, Consular Correspondence (Texas),
VI, ms.

[23] *Ibid.*

[24] "Instructions to the Consuls of the Republic of Texas," issued by R. A. Irion,
Secretary of State, Department of State, City of Houston, Oct. 15, 1838, in *ibid.*

Locations were being surveyed nearly two hundred miles above Bastrop. Bastrop itself was pictured in November 1838, as growing rapidly, and LaGrange was spoken of as "going ahead" at a surprising rate.[25] By August 1839, "the most cheering accounts" were being received in some of the older settlements "of the immense emigration to the Upper Colorado and western country." [26] Yet, a year later, the country between the Guadalupe and the San Marcos, on the west, and the Colorado on the east, above a line drawn from Gonzales to LaGrange, was still a wilderness. Below this line the country was sparsely settled. Between Gonzales and Austin, on Plum Creek were two recent settlers, Isom J. Goode and John A. Neill. From Gonzales to within a few miles of LaGrange there were no settlers. There was not one between Gonzales and Bastrop, nor between Austin and San Antonio. A road from Gonzales to Austin, then in the first year of its existence had been opened in July 1839.

While thousands of emigrants were pouring into Texas in 1838–1839 from depression-ridden United States, a large proportion of them was described as

young lawyers, physicians, clerks and graduates recently from the various universities of the United States. These young men come to our shores lured by the brightest prospects and burning with high hope. They have heard Texas described as an El Dorado, where naught but golden visions cheer the bold adventurer who has but to seek her fertile prairies, and bask in the bright sunshine of uninterrupted prosperity. But alas what bitter disappointment often awaits them! They here find indeed a country unsurpassed for beauty and fertility, and abounding in agricultural wealth; but all this affords them no encouragement. They wander about from place to place, only as Arabs wander amid the fertile fields of Goshen. What is to the farmer a paradise, is to them a desert. The occupations which afford them the means of support, are here either neglected or are already overburthened and rendered sterile by competition. Often have we seen young men of this class, who have been nurtured in the lap of luxury, and who, previous to the period of their emigration, had never known the sting of want, but had been constantly fostered and sustained by wealthy and indulgent parents, here bowed by disappointment, suffering under the most abject poverty, embittered tenfold by the recollection of former and brighter days of happiness and of ease. Our country is yet quite too new and its

[25] *Matagorda Bulletin*, Nov. 15, 1838.
[26] *Colorado Gazette and Advertiser* (Matagorda), Aug. 1, 1839.

population too spare and widely diffused to afford many asylums to individuals of this description.[27]

Furthermore, all was not quiet on the southwestern frontier. An occasional Indian plundering raid or the foray of a Mexican party from the Río Grande kept the inhabitants in a state of anxiety. "For myself," wrote Samuel A. Plummer from New Orleans in July 1839, "I have no idea Mexico contemplates in the least an invasion. But that she will soon commence harassing our frontier by small body [bodies] of Cavalry and instigating the Indians to commit depredations, I have no doubt." And that it may require more men to prevent that, "then to take all their rallying points across the Río Grande is a matter that you and the Sec[re]t[ary] of War must decide."[28] The implication here was that the wisest policy for Texas would be to seize the Mexican towns immediately upon the Río Grande to prevent the crossing of the marauding parties. Plummer favored direct military action to end the Mexican threat to the Texan frontier.

Even more troublesome than either the Indian or Mexican bandit were the marauding parties of Americans. In May 1839, Assistant Secretary of War Charles Mason informed General Johnston that "Colonel Karnes gives a deplorable account of the west; and I believe thinks, of the two, the marauding parties of the Americans are worse than the Mexicans or Indians. This, of course, will be relieved by the command of Captain Ross." The "white 'land pirates,'" reported Colonel Karnes at Houston on July 6, robbed the Mexican traders from the Río Grande who were permitted by the government to come in to trade. Their robberies, he declared, were principally confined to the Mexican traders, and they were by no means particular what they took; anything in the way of plunder seemed acceptable.[29] The desolation of the depopulated counties of the southern and southwestern frontier and the ruin of many individuals who had struggled for the independence of the country was in no small degree traceable to the government's neglect of the western frontier. A small garrison on the lower Nueces would do much to ensure that protection so necessary

[27] *Telegraph and Texas Register,* Dec. 25, 1839.

[28] S. A. Plummer to M. B. Lamar, N[ew] O[rleans], July 20, 1839 (Private and Confidential), in Domestic Correspondence (Texas), 1836–1846, ms.

[29] Quoted in William Preston Johnston, *The Life of Gen. Albert Sidney Johnston: Embracing His Services in the Armies of the United States, the Republic of Texas, and the Confederate States,* p. 115; *Morning Star,* July 10, 1839.

for the peace, tranquility, settlement, and development of the lower country.[30] Following a visit to the western frontier in the summer of 1839, John Browne, second lieutenant and assistant quartermaster in the regular army of Texas, reported that he found Victoria "filled with a set of men who have given themselves the title of *a band of Brothers,*" and that he soon learned

. . . that what they said was law. They are in the cow stealing business and are scattered all over this frontier. They pretend to say that they only steal from the enemy but I am convinced, to the contrary that they steal from the Texians as well as Mexicans. I think it well to mention the names of some of the promonent persons engaged in order that the Government may be better acquainted with the character of some of its officers; Mr. [Samuel] Hughes [31] the Customs House officer for Copono headed a party not long since and drove in four hundred head of cattle. A Mr. [John T.] Price formerly a Lieut in the Army also heads a party. Mr [Cornelius] Van Ness [32] says he thinks Judge [James C.] Allen [33] at Carlos Rancho is silently connected with them. I have been told that they drove off from Carlos Rancho a caballarda belonging to Alderetta [José Miguel Aldrete] and [Juan N.] Seguin that the owners know well where their property is but dare not proceed to recover it; also that the cow stealers when on the New Aces [Nueces] the other day (some of them badly mounted) took from a party of Mexican traders all their property and killed eight of them.

While I was at Goliad one of the Gang asked me in a commanding way if I belonged to [Reuben] Ross's company [sent to maintain order on the

[30] Letter to the Editor of the *Telegraph,* Nueces River, March 6, 1839, in *Telegraph and Texas Register,* April 10, 1839.

[31] Samuel Hughes was nominated by Lamar on January 16, 1839, as collector of revenue for the Port of Aransas and was confirmed the following day by the Senate. E. W. Winkler (ed.), *Secret Journals of the Senate: Republic of Texas, 1836–1845,* pp. 127–128.

[32] Cornelius Van Ness served as district attorney for the Fourth Judicial District, December 1837–1839. *Ibid.,* 94–95; Hobart Huson, *District Judges of Refugio County,* p. 16.

[33] James C. Allen was nominated by President Houston on December 9, 1837, for Chief Justice of Refugio County, and confirmed by the Senate on November 11. On March 30, 1840, he resigned, saying that he found it no longer in his power to discharge the duties required of him. As captain of the "Buckeye Rangers" from Cincinnati, Allen landed at Galveston in June 1836. Winkler (ed.), *Secret Journals of the Senate,* pp. 87–88; William C. Binkley (ed.), *Official Correspondence of the Texan Revolution, 1835–1836,* II, 831; James C. Allan [Allen] to Secretary of State, Refugio, March 30, 1840, in Domestic Correspondence (Texas), 1836–1846, ms.

frontier] or if I was a commissioner sent to enquire into the state of the frontier. To this I said that I did not belong to Ross nor was I a Commissioner, but that I was on my way to San Antonio at the same time acquainting myself with the frontier and then [would] report to the Government. He said that he was one of the *band of Brothers,* and wished me to understand that they could defend themselves against any force the Government could send to oppose them. To this I said I would acquaint the Government of their independence and save him the trouble of setting the Nation at defiance publicly.

The Government can have no idea of the deplorable condition of the citizens of the San Antonio River. The constant dread of being murdered obliges them to receive the Rober as a friend; they dare not say a word in their defence. While I was in Goliad about twenty of this band assembled in front of a public house and declared that in three days they would visit Carlos Rancho, burn it down, kill all the Mexicans belonging to it and, as they said *make a clean turn* of every kind of cattle on the perairie. . . . I am convinced that there is not less than three or four hundred men engaged in this [cow stealing] business directly and indirectly—there are several persons of standing engaged in it silently and now about two hundred actively engaged scattered west of the San Antonio River. One of them told me they had their expresses better regulated than any Regular Army that has ever been in that country. There is some ten or a dozen now on the Atuscosa gathering up a drove of cattle belonging to citizens [of San Antonio].[34]

Lieutenant Browne also reported that Major Richard Roman of Victoria intended to make a descent upon the Río Grande and capture Matamoros. "His object is plunder," he reported. "He intends the cow drivers shall be his Troops, but [he] has no idea that his intentions are yet known." Contrary to the *Telegraph and Texas Register's* report in its issue of September 4, Major Ross had not yet reached San Antonio. He was reported still at Gonzales, and half of his horses were said to be lost.[35]

Two days later, September 15, Henry Stuart Foote, a member of the Mississippi legislature on a tour of Texas, wrote President Lamar from New La Bahía (Goliad) concerning conditions on the Texas frontier. A short while before in New Orleans on his way to Texas,

[34] John Browne to A. Sidney Johnston, Secretary of War, San Antonio, Sept. 13, 1839, in *Lamar Papers,* III, 106–107. Carlos' Rancho was located in Refugio County, twenty miles below Goliad.
[35] *Ibid.*

General Foote had informed Samuel A. Plummer, a close friend of Lamar's then on recruiting duty for the Texas army, that he was anxious to have "a full and confidential conversation" with Lamar "about matters and things in general" concerning the frontier, Mexico, and of "making the boundary with the sword." [36] A few weeks later Foote was on the Texas frontier from whence he reported to Lamar of finding a situation

. . . deeply mortifying to our feelings, and . . . [of] the most awful consequence to the Republic. It was the business of *cattle stealing*, the robbery of private property, which had become an extensive and crying evil not confined to the enemies of Texas, but going on, openly in the face of day, to the injury of many of the best citizens of the Republic; and going on under circumstances of violence and even bloodshed, which made it certain that if not staid in its progress, the whole Southwestern part of Texas must be utterly broken up and ruined.[37]

The Comanches were blamed for their wanton destruction of life and property; but, reported Foote,

I am sorry to declare it; I am grieved to be constrained, upon unquestionable evidence to state the fact, that there is a strange combination of marauders along the whole western frontier, composed in part of Mexicans, in part of Comanches and in part of men, claiming to be Texian citizens, who are allied in order to plunder and devastate indiscriminently the private property of as good citizens as any in Texas, men who have served you in war and . . . peace, and who are heart and soul devoted to the best interest of the Republic, & who would willingly die for the true glory of the nation.

Alarm, confusion, misery, and distress prevailed throughout the southwestern frontier, whose inhabitants—men, women, and children—were seriously considering abandoning it forever. "The tide of emigration is checked completely," declared Foote, "and can never begin to flow again until something is done by the Government." [38]

[36] S. A. Plummer to M. B. Lamar, N[ew] O[rleans], July 20, 1839 (Private Confidential), in Domestic Correspondence (Texas), 1836–1846, ms.

[37] Lieutenant John Browne informed the Secretary of War on September 13, 1839, that he had received information "that sixty mule loads of Powder has been delivered to the Comanchee Indians by the Mexicans high up on the Río Grande." John Browne to A. Sidney Johnston, Secretary of War, San Antonio, Sept. 13, 1839, in *Lamar Papers*, III, 106–107.

[38] H. S. Foote to M. B. Lamar, New La Bahia, Sept. 15, 1839 (Private), in *Lamar Papers*, III, 108–109.

109

The friendship and commerce developing on the southwestern frontier in 1838–1839, were soon interrupted not only by the continued activities of the "cowboys" and such Mexican brigands, as Agatón Quinoñes, but also by the Córdova-Flores incidents which brought a feeling among many in Texas that the renewed trade relations exposed them to new dangers from Mexico, by enabling Mexicans to enter Texas in the disguise of traders, when in reality they were coming for the twofold purpose of keeping the Indians in a hostile attitude toward the Texans, and of obtaining information which would be helpful to their government.[39]

In the fall of 1839 there began to appear on the frontier two marauding parties of Mexicans. One was headed by Agatón Quinoñes and the other by Manuel Leal. They were ostensibly government customs guards, but were really bandits and cutthroats, banded together for the purpose of pillaging and robbing the unguarded trader, who, according to Mexican law was a smuggler engaged in illicit traffic.

Throughout the six-year period following the revolution, there was a great deal of bitterness engendered on both sides of the Río Grande. Frequent blind alarms of Mexican invading armies, of blockading cruisers, and of devastating Indian raids, produced great excitement and confusion. "In reality," reported a newcomer to Texas in the fall of 1839, many of these alarms were "only the fear of the new immigrants, who pack up at the first suspicious rumor and take flight [from the frontier] to Houston, and even farther to New Orleans, furnishing on the way the terrible descriptions that gradually sounded as if the Turks were in the country." [40] The frequency of such rumors of a Mexican force concentrating upon the Río Grande caused the editor of the *Telegraph and Texas Register* to declare in his columns that "the rumor of another invasion by Mexico appears to be dying away, like a thousand idle rumors of a similar character, that preceded it;" [41]

---

[39] A. S. Wright to Barnard E. Bee, Mexico City, Nov. 18, 1839, Garrison (ed.), *Diplomatic Correspondence of Texas*, 1908, II, 624–630.

[40] Max Freund (trans. and ed.), *Gustav Dresel's Houston Journal: Adventures in North America and Texas, 1837–1841*, p. 57.

[41] Dec. 30, 1840; Feb. 3 and 10, 1841; *Austin City Gazette*, Feb. 19, and Oct. 21, 1840. Santa Anna's paper, the *Censor*, published at Vera Cruz on October 27, 1840, reported that the government had been authorized to borrow $2,000,000, pledging 17 per cent of the import duties as security. The money was to be used in acquiring an army and navy for the reconquest of Texas. Quoted in *Austin City Gazette*, Dec. 9, 1840. See also Joseph Eve to Daniel Webster, Galveston, Sept. 1,

but, nevertheless, such rumors too often had an adverse effect upon the development of the resources of Texas. From New York, Henry Austin wrote in July 1839, "perhaps I may effect a sale [of land] to a person I shall meet to night—but the Mexican official declaration of another invasion of Texas, renders Texas property and securities entirely unavailable [unsaleable]." [42]

For a number of years following the Texas revolution, however, Mexico, faithless, penniless, torn by internal dissensions, and imperilled by international complications, limited her efforts against Texas to the sending of spies and agents to arouse a spirit of revolt among certain discontented elements and to incite the Indians to make raids upon the scattered settlements. [43] From Béxar it was reported late in 1838 that Casemiro and Cayune, two Comanche chiefs, had lately visited Monterey. It was said that Casemiro had gone to that place to obtain the release of his brother who had been held prisoner there for several months, and that these Comanche chiefs and their followers had been escorted back to their tribe by a Mexican officer and twelve soldiers. It was also believed to have been reliably reported that the Mexican government had agreed to pay the Comanches five pesos for each Texan scalp they might take. [44] During the summer and autumn of 1838, Mexican soldiers from Savariego's command, in disguise, paid frequent visits to Houston, San Antonio, and various frontier points in Texas, and were said to be in regular correspondence with persons at these places. Jacob ("Jake") Hendrick, recently escaped from imprisonment at Matamoros, declared that the Mexican command at that place was "generally far better acquainted with the news of Houston and Béxar than with the news of Tampico and Mexico" and was "almost as well informed of the movements of the hostile Indians in Texas" as was the Texan government at Houston. It was currently reported at Matamoros that the Indians along the southern frontier of

1841, in William R. Manning (ed.), *Diplomatic Correspondence of the United States: Inter-American Affairs*, XII, 218–219.

[42] Henry Austin to Mary Austin Holley, New York, July 25, 1839, Henry Austin Papers, ms.

[43] *Matagorda Bulletin*, March 28, 1838; John Henry Brown, *History of Texas, from 1685 to 1892*, II, 143–144; H. Yoakum, *History of Texas, from its First Settlement in 1685 to its Annexation to the United States in 1846*, II, 257–264; Walter P. Webb, *The Texas Rangers*, pp. 47–50; A. K. Christian, "Mirabeau Buonaparte Lamar," *Southwestern Historical Quarterly*, XXIV (1920–1921), 43–52.

[44] *Telegraph and Texas Register*, Dec. 1, 1838.

Texas, now entirely desolate, "were acting under the direction of the Mexican government and troops which have lately been driven from Mier, Rhinosa and Comargo," by the Federalist revolt. These troops, reported Hendrick "were to have made a descent upon Béxar and Goliad, but were prevented by the intervention of the French at Vera Cruz and the insurrection of the federalists." [45]

[45] *Ibid.*, Jan. 18, 1839.

CHAPTER EIGHT

The Córdova-Flores Incident

THE IDEA OF AN Indo-Mexican alliance for a war on Texas was not new. As early as 1836 such a plan had been instituted.[1] Between 1836 and 1838 it was known in Texas that certain Cherokees on several occasions after San Jacinto had visited the Mexicans at Matamoros, where they obtained large quantities of ammunition from the authorities and discussed the possibility of a conquest of Texas. In December 1836, five Texans held prisoners at Matamoros escaped, and were pursued as far as the Nueces, where they were overtaken by a party of Cherokee Indians who brought back three of them to the Mexican authorities at Matamoros. The Cherokees, reported the U. S. Consul at Matamoros, "are no doubt in the actual service of the Mexican nation."[2] From Matamoros General Vicente Filisola,[3] commander in

[1] See extract of a letter from General Felix Huston to the Secretary of War, Headquarters, Camp Johnson, Dec. 13, 1836; extract of a letter to the Secretary of War, Camp Independence, Dec. 31, 1836, *Matagorda Bulletin,* Mar. 28, 1838, and A[nthony] Butler to Felix Huston, City of Houston, Dec. 21, 1838; Jones Douglas to William H. Wharton, Houston, Dec. 23, 1838; all in Report of the Secretary of State . . . relative to the Encroachments of the Indians of the United States upon the Territories of Mexico," Washington, Jan. 11, 1853, in United States Congress, *Senate Executive Documents,* 32 Cong., 2d sess., vol. III, no. 14, pp. 37–41; see also, report made by Col. [Moses L.] Patton in *Telegraph and Texas Register* (Houston), Dec. 1, 1838.

[2] D. W. Smith to John Forsyth, Consulate of the U. S. A., Matamoros, Jan. 6, 1837, no. 115, in Consular Dispatches (Texas), 1837–1839 (Matamoros), ms., microfilm.

[3] Vicente Filisola, an Italian by birth, served with the Spanish royalist forces during the Gachupín revolt of 1813, and as a brigadier general of the Mexican forces in Central America under the Empire. In October 1831, he obtained a contract from Mexico to settle 600 families in Texas, but had done nothing toward fulfilling his agreement before the outbreak of the Texas Revolution. He was named, in January 1833, commandant general of the eastern division of the Provincias Internas, and was second in command of the Mexican expedition under General Santa Anna to quell the rebellion in Texas in 1836. Filisola commanded

113

chief of the Mexican military forces in the north, issued instructions on stirring up the Indians in Texas; [4] and from the Nacogdoches area Vicente Córdova, styled by General Valentín Canalizo as "Commander of the Mexican forces in Texas," kept the Mexican government informed of the steps he was taking in Texas to "foster the favorable feelings which the faithful Mexicans have always entertained" toward the mother country. [5] As a part of the plan, the Indians were to be guaranteed possession of their hunting grounds in Texas and were to constitute a buffer state between the Mexican nation and the Americans of the United States.

The plan for a united attack assumed more definite form and more ambitious proportions in 1837. In the summer of 1837 the Cherokees sent a delegation to Matamoros to confer with the Mexican authorities, [6] who had nearly three thousand troops assembled there under General Filisola. [7] The plans called for the Indians to rendezvous north of the San Antonio road at some point between San Antonio and Nacogdoches, as soon as the leaves put out. When the Indians were assembled and ready, a Mexican force of five thousand men would cross the Río Grande and advance from the west to meet them. "The Texans were to be exterminated or expelled, and the Indians were to have the territory, to divide among the various bands that had participated in the war." [8] The Comanche advance to the outskirts of Matamoros late in July 1837, may have interfered with the carrying out of the plot in 1837, but it seems to have been kept alive by Filisola, his successor,

---

the Mexican troops in their withdrawal from Texas after the battle of San Jacinto. General Nicolás Bravo resigned his command on the northern frontier of Mexico, May 5, 1837, and was succeeded by Filisola who in turn was followed in command on February 7, 1839, by General Valentín Canalizo. D. W. Smith to John Forsyth, Matamoros, May 10, 1837, and Feb. 9, 1839, in *ibid.*; Proclamation of Valentín Canalizo, Feb. 7, 1839, in *El Ancla* (Matamoros), Feb. 15, 1839; Vito Alessio Robles, *Coahuila y Texas desde la consumación de la independencia hasta el tratado de paz de Guadalupe Hidalgo*, II, 197.

[4] Sam Houston, *Documents on Indian Affairs, Submitted to Congress by the President, November 15, 1838, By order of Congress*, pp. 5–11.

[5] Valentín Canalizo to Vicente Córdova, Matamoros, March 1, 1839, copy (translated by S. P. Andrews), Army Papers (Texas), ms.

[6] R. A. Irion to M. Hunt, Department of State, City of Houston, Sept. 20, 1837; Same to Same, Department of State, City of Houston, Dec. 31, 1837; in Garrison (ed.), *Diplomatic Correspondence of Texas*, 1907, I, 259–262, 277–281.

[7] *Matagorda Bulletin*, Nov. 8, 1837.

[8] Walter Prescott Webb, *The Texas Rangers*, p. 49.

The Córdova-Flores Incident

Brigadier General Valentín Canalizo,[9] and certain dissatisfied individuals around Nacogdoches, including Vicente Córdova, once prominent in the affairs of the town, Juan José Rodríquez, Juan Santos Coy, J. Vicente Micheli, Carlos Morales, Antonio Corda, Nathaniel Norris, Joshua Robertson, José Arriola, and others. In Texas history this intrigue came to be known as the Córdova incident or rebellion. The Mexican military commanders sought to stir up the discontented Mexicans around Nacogdoches, as well as Caddoes, Seminoles, Shawnees, Delawares, Biloxes, Cherokees, Choctaws, Alabamas, Kickapoos, Brazos, Tahuacanos, and other Indians to war on the Texans, causing them perpetual alarm and uneasiness. By rapid and well coordinated movements the Indians were to prevent the Texans from uniting in any large number; and, if not daily burning their homes, injuring their crops, livestock, and commerce, at least to prevent them from taking advantage of the troubles in Mexico. "This position," declared Canalizo, who had been defeated by the Federalists at Tampico on November 30, 1838, "is the most favorable for the friendly Indians (as well as for the friendly Mexicans) in order that they shall have the enemy out in front only, keeping a friendly and generous nation as Mexico *in the rear.*" [10] Tell the friendly Indians, he continued (early in 1839),

[9] Valentín Canalizo was born at Monterey about 1797; became a cadet in the Infantry Regiment of Celaya on August 31, 1811; joined the independence movement under Iturbide in 1820; and, after serving with credit in various engagements on the conservative or Centralist side, was, for his share in the death of Guerrero, promoted to the rank of general and the command of Oajaca. He succeeded General Filisola as commandant of the northern frontier in February 1839. Late in July 1840, Canalizo turned his command over to General Pedro de Ampudia, who commanded at Matamoros *ad interim,* pending the arrival of General Mariano Arista. In 1841 Canalizo was promoted to general of a division and subsequently played a conspicuous part in the *pronunciamiento* against Congress. Alberto M. Carreño (ed.), *Jefes del ejército mexicano en 1847: biografías de generales de division y de brigada y de coroneles del ejército mexicano por fines del ano de 1847,* pp. 38–40; *Boletín del Gobierno* (Mexico City), July 24, 1840; Hubert Howe Bancroft, *History of Mexico,* V, 258 n, 272–277.

[10] Valentín Canalizo to Vicente Córdova, Feb. 27, 1839, Domestic Correspondence (Texas), 1836–1846, ms. copy (translated); also quoted in H. Yoakum, *History of Texas from its First Settlement in 1685 to Its Annexation to the United States in 1846,* II, 258–259; see also Valentín Canalizo to Manuel Flores, Matamoros, Feb. 27, 1839, Army Papers (Texas), ms. copy (translated); United States Congress, *Senate Executive Documents,* 32 Cong., 2d sess., vol. III, no. 14, pp. 31–32; State Department [Texas], Department of State Letterbook, Nov. 1836–Dec. 1841, pp. 110–114, contains correspondence of Canalizo, Córdova, Flores, Juan de la Garza, Juan Baptista Soto, and Filisola.

to "expect nothing from these greedy adventurers for land, who wish even to deprive the Indians of the sun that warms and vivifies them, and who would not cease to injure them while the grass grows and the water runs." [11] Canalizo declared that Mexico, finding herself at war with France, could not at the moment reopen her operations against the revolted province of Texas, but that the friendly Indians could prevent Texas profiting from the circumstances of the moment. He advised the Indians not to approach the United States frontier, but to limit themselves to occupying the area north of a line from San Antonio de Béxar, to the junction of the San Marcos with the Guadalupe and thence along the San Marcos to its mouth. Canalizo informed the Indians that they might expect to live peacefully on the land which they had chosen within the territory of Mexico. He urged them to

Agree with the said Flores, so as to operate in such a manner as will ensure the quiet possession of your lands, and prevent any adventurer from again disturbing the peaceful repose of your families, or from trampling under foot the soil in which are deposited the remains of your ancestors; and endeavor not to deviate from the instructions which have been given to him. Proceed, relying on our generosity of which we have given so many proofs. . . . It is necessary that the success of the expedition [that is contemplated] be sudden and complete, and that those usurping adventurers shall not prosper by peace and commerce, and enjoy a repose which will secure to them an advancement truly calamitous for you.[12]

[11] Valentín Canalizo to Señor Antonio Beloxi, Captain Ignacio of the Gaupanaques, Captain Coloxe of the Caddoes, the Chief of the Seminoles, Sor. Qixg mas gefe de los Charaquies [Big Mush of the Cherokees], Captain Benito of the Kickapoos, Fama Sargento de los Brazos, Lt. Colonel Bul [Bowles] of the Cherokees, Matamoros, February 27, 1839, Army Papers (Texas), ms. copy (translated). Alcée La Branche to John Forsyth, Legation of the United States, Houston, Nov. 10, 1838, in "Report of the Secretary of State . . . relative to the Encroachments of the Indians of the United States upon the Territories of Mexico, Washington, Jan. 11, 1853," United States Congress, *Senate Executive Documents*, 32nd Cong., 2d sess., vol. III, no. 14, p. 9.

[12] Valentín Canalizo to Señor Antonio Beloxi, Captain Ignacio of the Gaupanaques, Captain Coloxe of the Caddoes, the Chief of the Seminoles, Sor. Qixg mas gefe de los Charaquies [Big Mush of the Cherokees], Captain Benito of the Kickapoos, Fama Sargento de los Brazos, and Lt. Colonel Bul [Bowles] of the Cherokees, Matamoros, February 27, 1839, Army Papers (Texas), ms. copy (translated), [endorsed:] No. 6 Circular Addressed to the Chiefs of the several tribes of Indians [taken from Flores' body].

Córdova wrote Manuel Flores, the Mexican commissioned agent among the Indians, in July 1838, that he had been ordered by Filisola to visit the Indians for the purpose of getting them to join the Mexican army being formed to invade Texas. He asked Flores to advance to him to confer with the chiefs of the Cherokees and other tribes who had promised to unite with the Mexicans in a campaign against the Texans. If, in the meantime their plans were discovered, the units under Córdova and Flores, with their Indian allies, were to commence operations at once against the hated enemy.[13]

On May 29 a Mexican by the name of Don Pedro Julian Miracle,[14] a former Federalist leader from Tamaulipas and friend of Antonio Canales, accompanied by Vicente Córdova, left Matamoros with a force of seventy-two persons, including two Indians, thirty-four soldiers from La Bahía under Savariego, twenty Cherokee and Caddo Indians, and, presumably, sixteen other citizens.[15] On the 30th they camped at Los Fresnos, where they waited four days for provisions and horses. June 3 they were joined by Juan de la Garza, who brought biscuits, sugar, coffee, and a supply of cartridges. At midday, June 3, they crossed the Arroyo Colorado and encamped on the other side at a point called Los Altos. Two days later (June 5) they camped at Los Mulatos for five days, while they sought unsuccessfully to capture wild horses. The march was resumed on the 11th. At Purgatory (Purgatoria) Hill they discovered a party of smugglers, who fled at their advance, leaving behind a valuable cargo of tobacco and fifteen horses. That night Miracle's party camped at the Borrego. During the ensuing days another effort was made to capture wild horses. On the 17th of

---

[13] Quoted in James T. DeShields, *Border Wars of Texas: being an Authentic and Popular Account, in Chronological Order, of the Long and Bitter Conflict Waged between Savage Indian Tribes and The Pioneer Settlers of Texas*, p. 268.

[14] Late in 1835 Colonel Antonio Canales had dispatched Julian Miracle to Texas to ascertain the true purpose of the Texans, who were attempting to organize an expedition against Matamoros. His report to Canales of the strong sentiment in Texas for independence rather than adherence to the constitution of 1824 apparently caused the latter, and other liberals in northern Mexico, to lose interest in the Texas movement. Hobart Huson, "Iron Men: A History of the Republic of the Río Grande and the Federalist War in Northern Mexico," typed ms., pp. 5–6.

[15] "Memorandum Book [of Pedro Julian Miracle]," in "Report of the Secretary of State . . . relative to the Encroachments of the Indians of the United States upon the Territories of Mexico, Washington, Jan. 11, 1853," United States Congress, *Senate Executive Documents*, 32nd Cong., 2d sess., vol. III, no. 14, pp. 14–17.

June they camped at the Pastel, where they killed two Irishmen, a woman and her children. The next evening the Indo-Mexican party encamped on the Arroyo Blanco. On the morning of the 19th, the Indians sought permission from Savariego, the military commander, to attack La Bahía (Goliad), and became dissatisfied when their request was not granted. Instead, spies were sent out while the main party moved on to the San Antonio River and encamped for the night. On the 20th the spies returned to report that there were twenty Americans in the vicinity of Refugio and thirty at Copano and that Villareal was at La Bahía with horses.[16]

Taking leave of Savariego on the 20th, Miracle and the Indians, now joined by Manuel Flores, crossed the San Antonio. The following day they crossed the Guadalupe and on the 24th at 1 P.M. the Colorado River. Near the Colorado they saw several Texans, but did not attack them, "at which," recorded Miracle, "the Indians were much enraged." On the 27th they crossed the Brazos, and between it and the Navasota, "in the timber," met the Kickapoo Indians, who received them kindly and accompanied them for four days toward the east, abandoning the party on July 1. The Mexican emissaries and their allies encamped on the Trinity on July 2. During the remainder of July and on into August the Mexican agents contacted the various Indian tribes—Choctaws, Cherokees (Chief Bowles), Kickapoos, Kichai,[17] Chickasaws, Caddoes, Wacos, Tahuacanos, and others, conveying to them Filisola's message and promises. A month later, about August 20, Miracle was killed near the Cross Timbers on the Red River, and upon his body were found instructions from General Filisola directed to the Mexicans and friendly Indians in Texas,[18] saying,

[16] Miracle's "Memorandum Book" is printed in *ibid.* with a comment from Anson Jones, the Texan minister at Washington in December 1838, "that many of the words are completely obliterated, and the language is also very imperfect, making it difficult to give anything like a connected or correct translation." The entry for June 19 concludes: "Advanced as far as San Antonio river, and put out spies, who returned on the 20th bringing us news of 20 men (Americans) and 30 at Copano, and that Villareal was at La Bahía with horses." I have presumed on the basis of circumstantial evidence that the 20 Americans were at Refugio or its vicinity.

[17] Sometimes spelled Keechie.

[18] Anson Jones to John Forsyth, Texian Legation, City of Washington, Dec. 31, 1838, in "Report of the Secretary of State . . . relative to the Encroachments of the Indians of the United States upon the Territories of Mexico, Washington, Jan. 11, 1853," United States Congress, *Senate Executive Documents*, 32nd Cong., 2d

The Córdova-Flores Incident

As soon as you arrive [in Texas], you will invite [the chiefs of the friendly Indians in Texas] to a meeting, and propose to them that they and their friends should take up arms in defence of the integrity of the Mexican territory in Texas. . . . Afterwards, you will invite eight or ten of each of the tribes to *smoke the pipe*, and in the name of the Supreme Government of Mexico, distribute among them powder, lead, and tobacco, in the usual manner; this being done, you will keep an account of your operations and inform me officially of the same. You will make them understand that as soon as they have agreed to taking up arms, they will be rewarded according to their merits; and that so soon as they have taken possession of the places that I have mentioned to you, you will advise me by extra-ordinary courier, giving me a detailed account of the Mexican force, and of the Indian tribes, with the plan of attack, that I may be enabled to direct the forces that are to leave from this place to the assistance of those who are to operate in that quarter. Make them understand that as soon as the campaign is over, they will be able to proceed to Mexico, to pay their respects to the Supreme Government, who will send a commissioner to give each possession of the land they are entitled to.[19]

What could be more alluring to the Indians than to think that they might come into possession of the fine hunting grounds of the Colorado, Brazos, Trinity and Red rivers.

It is thus from the instructions that he received and a diary which he kept in Spanish that we know that Miracle secretly made his way northward, visiting the Mexicans and Cherokees in the neighborhood of Nacogdoches for the purpose of inciting them to insurrection, and that he met with a degree of success, and was joined by a number of disgruntled individuals from Nacogdoches and its vicinity.[20] On August 4, 1838, while several Anglo-Texan residents of Nacogdoches,

---

sess., vol. III, no. 14, pp. 11–12; R. A. Irion to Anson Jones, Department of State, City of Houston, Nov. 28, 1838, Anson Jones to John Forsyth, Texian Legation, City of Washington, Nov. 26, 1838, in Garrison (ed)., *Diplomatic Correspondence of Texas*, 1907, I, 350–354, 358–360.

[19] "Private instructions for the captains of friendly Indians of Texas, by His Excellency the General-in-Chief Vicente Filisola," in "Report of the Secretary of State . . . relative to the Encroachments of the Indians of the United States upon the Territories of Mexico, Washington, Jan. 11, 1853," United States Congress, *Senate Executive Documents*, 32nd Cong., 2d sess., vol. III, no. 14, pp. 13–14.

[20] George Louis Crocket, *Two Centuries in East Texas: A History of San Augustine County and Surrounding Territory from 1685 to the Present Time*, p. 189; A. K. Christian, "Mirabeau Buonaparte Lamar," *Southwestern Historical Quarterly*, XXIV (1920–1921), 47–49.

who had pursued and recovered from a Mexican settlement in Nacogdoches County a number of horses stolen from them, were returning home, they were attacked and one of their number killed. They pursued their attackers a short distance, but coming into a large trail, which they recognized as having been made by Mexicans, they returned to town.[21] Three days later (August 7) Captain John Durst informed Major General Thomas J. Rusk, who commanded the militia, that at least a hundred armed Mexicans, headed by Córdova and Norris, were encamped on the Angelina River. Another report, from Captain Antonio Menchaca, who had been in the Mexican camp, gave the number as 120 Mexicans and 25 Biloxi and Ioni Indians.

Rusk immediately recruited a company of 60 volunteers and posted them at the lower fork of the Angelina River. In the meantime, he sent out a call for 200 volunteers. The enemy was then on the west side of the stream. President Houston, who was in Nacogdoches at the time, issued a proclamation on the 8th, ordering the Mexicans and Indians to disperse and to return to their homes under penalty of being declared enemies of the Republic. To this order, the leaders of the malcontents boldly and defiantly replied two days later that

. . . the citizens of Nacogdoches, being tired of the injustices and the usurpation of their rights, can do no less than state that they are embodied, with arms in hand, to sustain their rights and those of the nation to which they belong. They are ready to shed the last drop of their blood; and declare as they have heretofore done, that they do not acknowledge the existing laws, through which they are offered guaranties (by the proclamation) for their lives and property.[22]

Having made their defiant reply, the conspirators and malcontents on the 10th, under Córdova's leadership, and supported by some three hundred Indians, moved up toward the Cherokee Nation. The com-

[21] *Telegraph and Texas Register,* Sept. 29, 1838; DeShields, *Border Wars of Texas,* p. 268.

[22] Reply of Vicente Córdova *et al.* to President Houston's Proclamation [of August 8, 1838], August 10, 1838, ms., copy (translation), in Ashbel Smith Papers, ms.; DeShields, *Border Wars of Texas,* p. 294. Those signing the letter were: Vicente Córdova, Nat. Norris, Juan Arista, G. Vicente Michelle [Micheli], Juan Santos Coy, Antonio Corda, C. Morelos [Morales], Joshua Robertson, Juan José Rodríquez, José de Labome, Antonio Caderon, Julio Lasarin, James Quintly, Antonio Flores, Guadalupe Cárdenas, Napoleon de Valtz, William Dunavan, and Juan José Acosta.

mand of Major H. W. Augustine was detailed to follow their trail, while General Rusk, Major General of the Texas Militia, moved directly toward Chief Bowles' village, believing that Córdova had gone there to visit his Cherokee friends. Upon reaching the Sabine, Rusk learned that Córdova had gone hurriedly in the direction of the upper Trinity, while most of his followers had dispersed.[23] From here Córdova sent dispatches to General Filisola, dated August 29 and September 16.[24]

As the depredations on the frontier increased General Rusk called for volunteers and moved against the Mexican-Indian combination. On October 14, 1838, he arrived at Fort Houston, and learning that the enemy were in force at the Kickapoo Village (now in Anderson County), he moved in that direction. At daylight on the 16th the Indians attacked the Texan camp. After a short, but hot engagement, the Texans charged them, upon which the Indians fled precipitously and were pursued for some distance. The Indian losses were eleven killed and many wounded; whereas, Rusk had eleven men wounded and none killed.[25] During the next few months Córdova and his marauders fought several engagements with the Texas volunteer forces and militiamen sent to establish peace on the frontier. In one of these encounters General Rusk pursued a number of Caddo Indians across the United States-Texas border, without prior authority from his

[23] John Henry Brown, *Indian Wars and Pioneers of Texas*, p. 63. In a message to Congress, November 19, 1838, President Houston declared that the rebellion of the Mexicans around Nacogdoches and the calamities in East Texas were due to the Militia Law, passed over his veto in December 1837, which gave Congress, instead of the President, the right to appoint the major general in charge of the militia. It will be remembered that Congress had chosen Thomas J. Rusk for this command. Sam Houston, *A Message from the President, Relative to Indian Affairs, with Accompanying Documents; Writings of Sam Houston*, II, 299–304.

[24] Valentín Canalizo to Vicente Córdova, Commander of the Mexican forces in Texas, [dated:] Headquarters, Matamoras, March 1, 1839, in "Report of the Secretary of State . . . relative to the Encroachments of the Indians of the United States upon the Territories of Mexico, Washington, Jan. 11, 1853," United States Congress, *Senate Executive Documents*, 32nd Cong., 2d sess., vol. III, no. 14, p. 33.

[25] Colonel Hugh McLeod's detailed report of the battle will be found in Col. Hugh McLeod to Gen. M. B. Lamar, Oct. 22, 1838, in *Lamar Papers*, II, 265–267; *Telegraph and Texas Register*, Nov. 3, 1838. It is interesting to note that in reporting on the Indian-Mexican differences in East and Northeast Texas in August, September, October, November, and early December, 1838, General Rusk and Colonel McLeod, Adjutant General of the Texas Militia, by-passed President Houston and kept the Vice President and President-elect Lamar fully informed.

government,[26] and there captured and disarmed them.[27] He delivered the Caddoes to the American Indian agent at Shreveport, where the Indians made a treaty promising pacific behavior until peace should be made between Texas and the remainder of their people.[28] Back in East Texas, thirty-one of the ringleaders in the disturbances were brought to trial on charges of treason in the District Court at San Augustine, but were all acquitted except one.[29]

In the meantime, having temporarily suppressed the Indian raids into the northeastern section of Mexico and witnessed a growth in the commerce of the port of Matamoros during the French blockade and the accumulation of ample supplies for a six months' campaign, General Filisola believed that the time had arrived early in 1839 to unite all Mexicans in a war against Texas and to advance his line of operations. To this end he ordered eight hundred men under Canalizo, together with those at Mier under Severio Unda, to prepare for an attack on Béxar, while another section of the Army advanced against Goliad.[30] The Federalist revolt in Tampico interfered, and the troops earmarked for the raid on San Antonio de Béxar were used elsewhere; meanwhile, in Texas the Mexican allies anxiously awaited the promised assistance. Finally, General Canalizo, who had by this time succeeded Filisola in command at Matamoros, sent instructions to Córdova on February 27, 1839, instructions which were much the same as those

[26] Barnard E. Bee to Dr. Anson Jones, Department of State, Houston, Jan. 31, 1839; James Webb to Alcée La Branche, Department of State, Houston, March 27, 1839, in Garrison (ed.), *Diplomatic Correspondence of Texas*, 1907, I, 361–362, 379–380.

[27] John Forsyth to Alcée La Branche, Department of State, Washington, Jan. 8, 1839; Alcée La Branche to John Forsyth, Legation of the United States, Houston, Jan. 29, 1839; in "Report of the Secretary of State . . . relative to the Encroachments of the Indians of the United States upon the Territories of Mexico, Washington, Jan. 11, 1853," United States Congress, *Senate Executive Documents*, 32nd Cong., 2d sess., vol. III, no. 14, p. 17–19; "Invasion of the United States by Texas," being an extract from the *Natchitoches Herald*, Dec. 16, 1839, in *ibid.*, pp. 19–20.

[28] Thomas J. Rusk to [Albert] Sidney Johnston, Secretary of War, [dated:] Houston, Feb. 25, 1839, in "Report of the Secretary of State . . . relative to the Encroachments of the Indians of the United States upon the Territories of Mexico, Washington, Jan. 11, 1853," United States Congress, *Senate Executive Documents*, 32nd Cong., 2d sess., vol. III, no. 14, pp. 22–25; affidavit of Elias Vansickle, Nacogdoches, Jan. 23, 1839, in *ibid.*, pp. 25–26; agreement between the Caddoes and Thomas J. Rusk, dated Shreveport, Nov. 29, 1838, in *ibid.*, pp. 26–27.

[29] *Telegraph and Texas Register*, March 27, 1839.

[30] *La Brisa* (Matamoros), Sept. 6, 1839, pp. 5–6.

previously given to Manuel Flores, "detailing the manner of procedure and directing the pledges and promises to be made to the Indians." [31] Shortly after receiving this communication, Córdova, protected by fifty-three Mexicans, six Biloxi Indians including a chief, and five Negroes,[32] left his lair on the Upper Trinity River in March 1839, and sought to pass through the frontier from the headwaters of the Trinity to Matamoros to confer with Canalizo and to contact Manuel Flores. According to Burleson, his object was also to get ammunition to supply the Indians.

Córdova's trail and camp were discovered near the foot of the mountain, north of and not far from where the present city of Austin now stands, by George W. Davis and Reuben Hornsby, who were out riding on the morning of March 25. They believed they had discovered the trail of a large party of hostile Indians. The alarm was spread to the nearby Waterloo settlement (later to become Austin), to Hornsby's Bend, and to Colonel Edward Burleson at Bastrop, who received the news on March 27. Soon seventy-nine volunteers [33] were assembled at Waterloo and organized late in the afternoon of the 27th under Colonel Burleson, whose brother Jacob had recently been killed in an Indian fight on Brushy Creek, near the present town of Taylor.[34] Captains Jesse Billingsley and Micah (Mike) Andrews were each placed in charge of a company.[35] While the men were forming, spies were sent

[31] Brown, *Indian Wars and Pioneers of Texas*, p. 63.

[32] Edward Burleson to M. B. Lamar, Bastrop, April 4, 1839, in *Lamar Papers*, II, 49–50; A. Sidney Johnston to William H. Daingerfield, Houston, April 12, 1839 (Private), Army Papers (Texas), ms. The *Telegraph and Texas Register*, April 10, 1839, probably basing its report on that of the deserter Robison from Córdova's camp, gave the number of the Córdova party as 44 Mexicans and 9 Biloxi Indians. Burleson says that there were in all sixty-four.

[33] See Appendix, p. 549. Fifty-eight years later A. J. Sowell interviewed Benjamin F. Highsmith, who claimed that he had participated in this expedition under Burleson, but Burleson's muster roll shows only a "Samuel Highsmith" participating. *Benjamin F. Highsmith: One of Hays' Rangers*, pp. 9–10; A. J. Sowell, *Early Settlers and Indian Fighters of Southeast Texas*, p. 15; J. W. Wilbarger, *Indian Depredations in Texas*, pp. 151–157.

[34] Jacob Burleson was killed February 19 or 20, 1839. Brown, *Indian Wars and Pioneers of Texas*, pp. 61–62; Sowell, *Early Settlers and Indian Fighters of Southwest Texas*, p. 16; John Holmes Jenkins, III (ed.), *Recollections of Early Texas: The Memoirs of John Holland Jenkins*, pp. 56–60.

[35] Jesse Billingsley was born in Tennessee on October 10, 1818, from whence he came to Texas in 1834 and settled in the municipality of Mina (Bastrop). He participated in the capture of San Antonio from the Mexicans in 1835, and in

out. These returned late in the afternoon with information that the unknown, and presumably hostile party, had crossed the Colorado between the falls and the settlement and seemed to be headed in the direction of Seguin. Burleson at once took up the line of march. That night he camped on Bear Creek, about ten miles southwest of the Waterloo settlement. Early the next morning, before they broke camp, a runner arrived from the Hornsby's Bend settlement, saying that a large Indian trail had been discovered nearby and that the men in the expedition were wanted to protect their families. The "Córdova trail" was abandoned, and the whole party fell back rapidly toward the settlement. Arriving there, the men found that a false alarm had been given. The trail which had been discovered was the very one that Burleson had been following. Several of the men now refused to go forward once more when the pursuit was resumed. That night Burleson and his men camped again on Bear Creek. A whole day had been lost.

Around ten o'clock at night Tom Moore, often known as "Black Tom," and W. M. Robison appeared in the Texan camp and informed the men of the true character of the enemy they were pursuing.[36] Robison had been a member of the Córdova party, but for some reason of mistrust Córdova had had him court-martialed and sentenced to be shot the next day—the day that he reached Burleson's camp. While Córdova's party was preoccupied in crossing Onion Creek, Robison had effected his escape and, although Córdova had spent the whole day looking for him, he had succeeded in reaching Moore's house, and the two had set out to notify Burleson of Córdova's mission to Mexico to seek munitions of war with which to equip the Indians for their planned attack upon the Texans. Robison joined Burleson's party, but Burleson took the precaution to have him vigilantly watched then and for some time after his return from the pursuit of Córdova.

Although Burleson started early the next morning and soon found

---

the battle of San Jacinto commanded Company C of the First Regiment of Texas volunteers. In the battle his left hand was crippled for life. After the Revolution, he served as captain of a ranger company on the frontier, and in the First Congress of the Republic and in the Fifth and Eighth state legislatures. He participated in the campaign against General Adrián Woll. Kige Highsmith, "Biographical Sketch of Jesse Billingsley," in Jesse Billingsley Papers, ms.; Sam Houston Dixon and Louis Wiltz Kemp, *The Heroes of San Jacinto*, pp. 157–158.

[36] *Telegraph and Texas Register*, April 10, 1839; Col. Edward Burleson to A. Sidney Johnston, Secretary of War, Bastrop County, April 3, 1839, in *ibid.*, April 17, 1839.

the trail, but a few hours old, it was not until the following afternoon (March 28), that the Texans, who had pushed forward as fast as their horses could travel, were able to arrive within close proximity of the Mexican-Indian party. At a place on Mill Creek [37] near the Guadalupe, later called Battle Ground Prairie, about half an hour of sundown the Texan spies came in sight of Córdova's party. The men were lying around carelessly on the grass while their horses grazed with their saddles on and it was thought that Córdova had halted to rest, unaware of his pursuers. However, it was later learned from prisoners that Córdova had spies ahead spying out the situation at Seguin,[38] five miles to the west, with the object of sacking the town that night. At this time Seguin (formerly Walnut Springs) was a very small settlement of about twenty-five heads of family; including John Sowell, Asa Sowell, Ben McCulloch, Henry McCulloch, Andrew Neill, James H. Callahan, Wilson Randall, and T. N. Menter. Three prominent Mexican families lived in its vicinity. On the south side of the river lived a Manuel Flores and José M. Cárdenas, who each possessed large ranch properties, and north of town José Antonio Navarro and Luciano Navarro had ranches on San Geronimo Creek [39] in what came to be northwestern Guadalupe County. Receiving the report of his scouts, Burleson, one of those who never believed in postponing until tomorrow what could be done today, especially when it came to frontier fighting, spurred his men forward and came within sight of the enemy in an open grove of post oaks through which ran a small ravine.

In preparing to attack, Burleson divided his men, sending Captain Andrews' Company to the right and Captain Billingsley's to the left. Now for the first time Córdova was aware of impending danger, and he quickly formed his men to meet the attack. As the Texans moved into position, the line of battle assumed the form of an inverted "V".[40] The fight commenced at the head of a ravine around which the Seguin

[37] Mill Creek rises in east central Guadalupe County and flows in a southeasterly direction eleven miles to join with the Guadalupe River approximately eight miles southeast of the town of Seguin.

[38] *Telegraph and Texas Register*, May 1, 1839. From September 22, 1838, to March 1839, the town was known as Walnut Springs. A. J. Sowell, *Incidents connected with the Early History of Guadalupe County*, p. 4; Town Book of Seguin, ms. (see Appendix), p. 79; *Guadalupe Gazette-Bulletin* (Seguin), Historical Centennial Edition, April 30, 1936.

[39] Sowell, *Early Settlers and Indian Fighters of Southwest Texas*, p. 414.

[40] Wilbarger, *Indian Depredations in Texas*, pp. 154–156.

road later ran near the old Handley place.[41] Doctor James Fentress asked the informer, Robison, to point out Córdova, saying that he intended to kill him first and foremost.[42] Protected by the large trees of the forested area, Córdova's men put up a stubborn resistance. A portion of the Texans dismounted and fought from behind trees, too.[43] Seeing the enemy wavering, as the Texans inched nearer and nearer to their position, Burleson's Colorado volunteers leaped into the open and charged them. Under this first full-scale onslaught, Córdova's men broke and fled, closely pursued by the Texans. Just as twilight approached they entered the Guadalupe bottom two miles from the battlefield. As Córdova turned to flee, he was pointed out, and Doctor Fentress fired at him. Fentress was certain he had wounded him in the arm, "for he saw it fall limp at his side, but some contended it was not touched." [44] When last seen, Córdova was said to have been reeling in his saddle as if from the loss of blood.[45] His sword and hat were found about four miles from the battlefield. Doubt as to Córdova's fate was dispelled some three years later after the battle of Salado when his body was examined in death. It was found that one of his arms bore the marks of an old and severe wound.

During the chase of Córdova's men, one of the Indians became unhorse and, running back, with his gun presented, to gain the protection of a mesquite tree, came face to face with about a half dozen Texans. Doctor Fentress, one of the dismounted Texans, raised his gun, but permitted the astonished Indian to fire first, says Wilbarger; whereupon, the Indian missing his mark, the good doctor immediately fired, killing him.[46] The doctor then cut off the head of the dead Indian and carried it away with him for medical examination.[47] In the course of the fight the burning paper wads from the shotguns of some of Burleson's men fired the grass.

[41] Sowell, *Early Settlers and Indian Fighters of Southwest Texas*, p. 417.

[42] John H. Jenkins Sr., "Personal Reminiscences of Texas History Relating to Bastrop County, 1828–1847," ms., p. 91.

[43] Col. Edward Burleson to A. Sidney Johnston, Secretary of War, Bastrop County, April 3, 1839, in *Telegraph and Texas Register*, April 17, 1839; *Morning Star* (Houston), April 11, 1839; Brown, *Indian Wars and Pioneers of Texas*, pp. 63–64.

[44] Jenkins, "Reminiscences," ms., p. 92.

[45] Col. Bonnell's Report in *Telegraph and Texas Register*, April 24, 1839.

[46] Wilbarger, *Indian Depredations in Texas*, p. 156.

[47] Sowell, *Early Settlers and Indian Fighters of Southwest Texas*, p. 15.

Since further pursuit was impossible during the night, Burleson led his men up the Guadalupe valley six miles to Seguin to protect the residents there. Córdova lost thirty men killed, or nearly one half of his entire force. The bodies were found the next morning on the field of battle or in the vicinity.[48] The Texans also took several prisoners, then and later. In all, nineteen were captured. Some documents belonging to Córdova fell into the hands of the Texans and were sent by Burleson to the Secretary of War. The Texans lost none by death, but had several wounded.[49] Among the captives was a big French Negro, named Raphael, weighing about two hundred pounds, who had been left wounded on the battlefield. Colonel Burleson placed him under the custody of Thomas McKennon for safekeeping. When the Colonel returned from the chase, he found that McKennon had crossed the Negro's hands and tied them behind his back and then had tied his horse's stake rope to the captive's hands. As Burleson came up. McKennon cried out: "Colonel, I've got him fast." [50]

The Negro claimed that he had always been free and had constantly maintained a hostile attitude towards Texans, and had no intention even now of acknowledging any allegiance to the Texan government. Consequently, he was summarily court-martialed and sentenced to be shot the next day at the town of Seguin. The next morning six men were detailed to execute the sentence. They were to shoot by three's.

[48] A. Sidney Johnston to William H. Daingerfield, Houston, April 12, 1839 (Private), Army Papers (Texas), ms.; Edward Burleson to M. B. Lamar, Bastrop, April 4, 1839, in *Lamar Papers*, II, 49–50; Col. Bonnell's Report, *Telegraph and Texas Register*, April 24, 1839; DeShields, *Border Wars of Texas*, pp. 292–297; Alexander W. Terrell, "The City of Austin from 1839 to 1865," *Quarterly of the Texas State Historical Association*, XIV (1910–1911), pp. 113–128; Harold Schoen (comp.), *Monuments Erected by the State of Texas to Commemorate the Centenary of Texas Independence*, p. 143; Brown, *Indian Wars and Pioneers of Texas*, pp. 62–66. Schoen, doubtless following Brown, says that Córdova lost twenty-five men killed and that the Texans had many wounded, but none fatally. I have used the figures given by A. S. Johnston, the Texan Secretary of War, whose statements are based on Burleson's official report. On the other hand, Wilbarger, *Indian Depredations in Texas*, p. 156, basing his report of this affair on accounts given years later by several participants in the engagement, says "as near as could be ascertained by actual count" eighteen were killed. The *Telegraph and Texas Register*, April 10, 1839, reported eighteen killed.

[49] Sowell, *Early Settlers and Indian Fighters of Southwest Texas*, p. 417, says three Texans were wounded.

[50] Quoted in Wilbarger, *Indian Depredations in Texas*, p. 156.

James O. Rice, who was not among the six chosen was for some reason very anxious to shoot the Negro; so he offered to pay five dollars to anyone of the detail who would permit him to fill his place in the firing squad. One of the men among the first group to fire accepted the proposition, but much to Rice's chagrin when the order to fire was given his gun failed. Crestfallen, he exclaimed: "There my gun snapped, for the first time in my life."[51]

At this time, Captain Mathew Caldwell of Gonzales commanded in the Gonzales-Seguin area a company of six months' rangers [52] which had been formed under a law passed the previous winter. A portion of this company was stationed at Seguin under 1st Lieutenant James Campbell, and the remainder of the company was under Caldwell's direct command and located on the Guadalupe, fourteen miles above Gonzales and eighteen miles below Seguin. The night of the 29th, following Córdova's defeat, Caldwell was in Gonzales and Second Lieutenant Canah C. Colley was in charge of the camp. He immediately dispatched a messenger to Caldwell, who sent word among the local inhabitants inviting volunteers to join him at sunrise. Among those volunteering was Ben McCulloch. At daylight, Caldwell started rapidly for his camp on the Guadalupe, where, upon arrival, he found everything in readiness to take up the chase. He lost no time in uniting with Campbell. Within thirty-six hours after Córdova had been driven into the Guadalupe bottom, Caldwell had picked up his trail,[53] but one of Caldwell's spies lost his horse to Córdova's party on the 30th.[54]

Caldwell found that Córdova had considered it impracticable to ford the Guadalupe, and had during the night returned to the uplands, detoured around Seguin, and struck the river five miles above, where, at daybreak, March 30, at the edge of the bottom, he accidentally surprised and attacked a scouting party of five of Lieutenant Campbell's men, who had encamped near Young's Ford the night before. These men were James M. Day, Thomas R. Nichols, John W. Nichols, D. M. Poore, and David Reynolds. Although surprised at such an hour by men using firearms only (indicating a foe other than Indians), the five rangers fought with such determination that they were able to

[51] Quoted in *ibid.*, pp. 156–157.

[52] For a copy of the Muster Roll of Captain Mathew Caldwell's Gonzales Rangers, March 16–June 16, 1839, see Appendix.

[53] Brown, *Indian Wars and Pioneers of Texas*, p. 64.

[54] Copy of Certificate of Claim of David Reynolds for Loss, Seguin, July 14, 1839, John Henry Brown Papers, 1835–1872, ms.

beat off their assailants sufficiently to enable them to gain a dense thicket. Córdova gave up the assault and moved up the river, leaving the scouting party in a difficult situation. They had lost their horses and all belongings except their arms. All of them had received painful wounds, and James Day was in serious condition.[55] His comrades bore him to the river and secreted him under a bluff; and, while the others stayed with him, Thomas Nichols swam the river and went to Seguin for assistance. A cart was sent back under a strong guard, and Day was brought to Seguin.[56] Upon Caldwell's arrival in Seguin the next morning, the scouts were able to supply him with the latest information of the marauders' trail.

Besides those from Gonzales, Caldwell was joined at Seguin by French Smith, Ezekiel Smith, Sr., Peter D. Anderson, George W. Nichols, Sr., William Clinton, Doctor —— Henry, George H. Gray, Frederick Happle, H. G. Henderson, and possibly two or three others.[57] Caldwell's force amounted to about fifty men. He took up the pursuit, and was joined near San Antonio by Colonel Henry W. Karnes' Company. When the trail divided, the two companies parted, each following one of its branches. Burleson, in the meantime, returned toward Bastrop.

Córdova's trail crossed the Guadalupe near where New Braunfels now stands, and continued through the highlands north of and around San Antonio, and thence in a western and southwestern direction to the old Presidio del Río Grande road, where it crossed the Río Frio. When last seen by a party of Mexican traders from the Río Grande, about fifty miles below Béxar on April 5, Córdova had about twenty men in his party.[58] Caldwell broke off pursuit at the Río Frio,[59] for it was evident from the "signs" that the Texans had gained nothing in distance on the retreating foe, whom they estimated to be some thirty or forty miles in the lead.

At different points along the route the Texans discovered wounded horses abandoned by Córdova's men. One of these, found in the moun-

[55] James M. Day, Guadalupe County, to the Legislature of the State of Texas, Jan. 25, 1850, Memorials and Petitions, ms.

[56] Sowell, *Early Settlers and Indian Fighters of Southwest Texas*, pp. 417–418.

[57] The names of Peter D. Anderson, Doctor —— Henry (unless this is William N. Henry, 3rd Sergeant), George H. Gray, and H. G. Henderson do not appear on the Muster Roll of Caldwell's Company for this period. See Appendix.

[58] *Telegraph and Texas Register*, May 1, 1839.

[59] Report of Captain Andrew Neill from Béxar, April 8, 1839, in *ibid.*

tains severely wounded, attracted the experienced eye of Ben McCulloch as a valuable animal, if he could be restored to soundness. So later, when the Texans returned to San Antonio on the way home, McCulloch solicited and obtained permission from Captain Caldwell to go in search of the horse. With a single companion, McCulloch traced and found the animal and succeeded in getting it home by slow marches. The horse recovered fully and "became famous as 'Old Pike,' McCulloch's pet and favorite as long as he lived—a fast racer of rich chestnut color, sixteen hands high, faultless in disposition and one of the most sagacious horses ever known in the country." [60]

Caldwell returned to San Antonio over the serpentine route through the hills, by which he had marched out. He had started without provisions, and his men had been forced to rely upon game, which for the moment was scarce, for Córdova's party had frightened the wild animals from the line of march.[61] Caldwell's men had followed Córdova for 160 miles, and after giving up the chase they had another 110 back to San Antonio. Upon arrival at San Antonio, the Gonzales men were received with open arms. Writing some forty-eight years later, Henry E. McCulloch, who was a private in Caldwell's company during this pursuit, said: "The hospitable people of that blood-stained old town, gave us a warm reception and the best dinner possible in their then condition, over which the heroic and ever lamented Col. Henry W. Karnes presided. They also furnished supplies to meet our wants until we reached our respective encampments." [62] At San Antonio, Caldwell found nine Mexicans who had been made prisoners by a party of surveyors. They were among the unmounted portion of Córdova's men seeking to escape after the engagement with Burleson's command.[63] The prisoners were tried in the District Court at Béxar before Judge James W. Robinson and released.[64] As for Caldwell, he returned his men to Seguin, where they were disbanded on May 15 due to the expiration of their terms of enlistment.[65]

Having learned from Robison that Córdova's plans were to return

[60] Brown, *Indian Wars and Pioneers of Texas*, p. 65.
[61] *Ibid.*, pp. 64–65.
[62] Gen. Henry E. McCulloch to J. H. Brown, Aug. 24, 1887, quoted in *ibid.*
[63] *Morning Star*, April 23, 1839; *Telegraph and Texas Register*, May 15, 1839. Originally it was reported that they had been captured by Colonel Henry W. Karnes and Captain Antonio Menchaca.
[64] *Telegraph and Texas Register*, May 15, 1839.
[65] *Ibid.*, May 21, 1839.

to East Texas after his visit to the Mexican military headquarters at Matamoros, Texan authorities kept a ranging company of about twenty men [66] from Bastrop under Captain Micah (Mike) Andrews out on scouting duty to the west. Six weeks later, about mid-May, Manuel Flores, who had been active in stirring up the Indians in East Texas in 1836, and Juan Bautista Soto, accompanied by thirteen Mexicans and eleven Indians,[67] carrying arms to the conspirators in Texas, sought to pass along the frontier to contact the "Northern Indians." The second in command of this party was ensign Juan de la Garza.[68] Flores' official capacity was "commissioner" from the commander at Matamoros to the discontented Indian and Mexican elements in Texas. He had apparently been at Matamoros late in February 1839, to confer with the military commander there.[69] A passport was issued for his passage to Texas on March 9th,[70] but he did not proceed on his expedition until the latter part of April.

On May 14 Flores' party crossed the road between Seguin and San Antonio, but made the mistake of committing several murders, thereby attracting attention to their movements. A party of surveyors, who were out working between Béxar and Seguin on the morning of the 14th, hearing the report of firearms near their camp, returned to it to find the camp abandoned. They took up the trail that they found, and

[66] The Muster Roll for Captain Micah Andrews' Rangers for March 10–June 10, 1839, shows twenty-eight names. It is not likely that all of these would be on scout at the same time. See Muster Roll, Captain Micah Andrews' Rangers, March 10–June 10, 1839, in this work, Appendix.

[67] Passport issued by Valentín Canalizo, Brigadier General of the Mexican Army and Chief of the Northern Division, to Don Manuel Flores *et al.*, Matamoros, March 9, 1839, no. 7, copy, Army Papers (Republic), ms. endorsed: "translation by Mr. [S. P.] Andrews from an original found on Manuel Flores. N. Amoy C[hief] C[lerk]"; Passport issued by Vicente Flores to Manuel Flores, a Commissioner with the friendly Indians, Matamoros, Feb. 2, 1839, to carry the necessary arms for his defence, as well as all the Indians of the friendly tribes then in Matamoros, no. 8, *ibid.*

[68] Valentín Canalizo to Ensign Juan de la Garza, Matamoros, April 19, 1839, copy, *ibid.*, ms.; see also United States Congress, *Senate Executive Documents*, 32nd Cong., 2d sess., vol. III, no. 14, pp. 34–35.

[69] Valentín Canalizo to Manuel Flores, Headquarters, Matamoros, Feb. 27, 1839, United States Congress, *Senate Executive Documents*, 32nd Cong., 2d sess., vol. III, no. 14, pp. 31–32; Valentín Canalizo to Vicente Córdova, Headquarters, Matamoros, Feb. 27, 1839, in *ibid.*, pp. 33–34.

[70] Passport issued to Don Manuel Flores and Don Juan Bautista Soto by Valentín Canalizo, Headquarters, Matamoros, March 9, 1839, in *ibid.*, p. 36.

after following it about two miles found the bodies of their companions (a Mr. Ballener and three Mexicans). One of them, a Mexican from Béxar, was still breathing and regained consciousness to state that they had been attacked by a party of Mexicans and Indians who were returning from Matamoros with arms and ammunition for the hostile Indians. Upon hearing this the surveyors immediately proceeded to Béxar and gave the alarm. Cornelius Van Ness and Colonel L. B. Franks left at once to bear the word to Colonel Edward Burleson at Bastrop, reaching there on the 17th. Burleson "raised the War hoop"; and early the next morning, having received additional information concerning the hostile party, started in pursuit with some two hundred hastily assembled volunteers.[71]

In the meantime, on May 15 Flores crossed the Guadalupe at the old Nacogdoches ford, at the site now occupied by the city of New Braunfels. While on patrol south of Austin on May 15, Captain Andrews' company,[72] among whom were six civilians, probably from a surveying party that had joined the ranger group, discovered what later proved to be Flores' party returning from Mexico to East Texas.

It seems that while reconnoitering on Onion Creek near where the Old San Antonio Road crossed the creek, Lieutenant James O. Rice and B. B. Castleberry late in the afternoon of the 15th had ridden over a hill south of the creek to kill a deer for supper. They had gone but a short time before they were seen galloping back to the main body to report that they had observed in the distance a large drove of horses. However, owing to the distance and the gathering dusk, they could not say definitely whether the horses were mounted or not, but "they were satisfied part of them were [being ridden], from the fact that some of the animals were white, and there appeared to be dark looking spots on their backs,"[73] indicating that these, at least, were probably mounted.

When Rice and Castleberry discovered the yet unidentified party, it was traveling almost due north, while the rangers had been traveling almost due east. Captain Andrews now determined to intercept the unknown party at the crossing of the creek. So taking advantage of a

[71] Edward Burleson to A. Sidney Johnston, City of Austin, May 22, 1839, in *ibid.*, pp. 29–30.
[72] See Appendix for a copy of the Muster Roll of Captain Micah Andrews' Rangers, March 10–June 10, 1839.
[73] Wilbarger, *Indian Depredations in Texas*, p. 159; *Telegraph and Texas Register*, May 29, 1839.

range of hills south of the creek which obscured the unidentified party from the rangers, the patrol pushed forward as rapidly as the terrain would permit, but when the rangers arrived at the foot of the range of hills they found that the party they sought had crossed the creek and had entered the thick post oak and cedar on the north side. The Texans were now convinced that it was a party of mounted men that had been seen, and not just a herd of wild horses. The rangers took the trail and followed it a few miles; but, dark overtaking them, they halted for the night. Leaving their horses saddled, they slept on their arms. At daylight they renewed the pursuit. As they progressed, the Texans became more and more confident that it was the Córdova-Flores party returning from Mexico. Therefore, they felt the importance of overtaking them. After the rangers had pursued the trail about two miles, and just as they were entering a large cedar brake, they met the enemy face to face. The two parties suddenly came to a halt within forty or fifty yards of one another. It was evident that the enemy had been rambling around in the cedar brake all night, until, tired and worn out, he had concluded to take the back track to get his bearings.

Before coming up with the enemy, the Texans had speculated considerably among themselves as to the number and nature of the party they were pursuing. Some had contended that it was a large unit, judging from the size of the trail and the number of horses; while others had maintained that it contained not over twenty-five or thirty men. Exponents of the latter viewpoint gave a plausible argument in its support. While following the trail, they had come to a "stooping" tree, which was too low for a man to ride under on horseback. A close examination of the trail, it was recalled, had revealed that all of the horses had passed under the tree, with the exception of some twenty-five or thirty, which had gone around it. This line of reasoning afterwards proved to be correct, but at the time the Texans confronted the Mexicans in the cedar brake, the majority of them had not been convinced. So when they were face to face with the enemy, they were divided as to whether or not they should risk an attack. Although close at hand, the Mexicans were so concealed by the brush and timber that their number could not be definitely ascertained. Perceiving the hesitation of the Texans, the Mexicans sought to put up a bold front by cursing and daring the rangers to charge them. Several of the Texans who spoke Spanish retorted in that language, some of it unprintable. One of the civilians, Wayne Barton, who had gone along with the patrol, was opposed to giving battle. Turning to Captain Andrews, he

133

said, "Captain Andrews, if you take your men into that thicket it will be equivalent to leading them into a slaughter pen for they will every one be killed."[74] Captain Andrews and a number of his men, who were thinking about assaulting the unseen enemy, seemed impressed by this remark. In the meantime, while the Texans discussed the question of making an attack, the enemy moved off into the heart of the cedar brake.

In the end, Captain Andrews withdrew his men and turned his course homeward. Most of the men of his command, who were made of sterner stuff, evinced great dissatisfaction with the conduct of their captain and were soon expressing themselves in unmistakable language. The farther they got away from the enemy, the more indignant they became. After riding about three miles in the direction of home, one of the party, A. J. Adkisson, told the disaffected to hold up a little until he could ride up and ask Captain Andrews to give those who desired it permission to return and follow the enemy, for in their minds it was now beyond a doubt who they were. The men assented to this proposition. Adkisson then rode up to the Captain, informed him of the sentiment of the men, and asked permission for those who wished to do so to return and continue the pursuit. He indicated that they did not wish Captain Andrews to assume any responsibility for them, but simply to grant them permission to withdraw from his command. The Captain, we are told, hesitated a moment, and then with an oath replied: "Yes; and I'll go back, too." This was joyful news to all but six of the patrol, who continued their course homeward.

The Texans in pursuit now numbered only twenty. They cut across the country in a westerly direction with the intention of intercepting the Mexican force as it came out of the cedar brake; but when they arrived at the point where they expected to meet them, the rangers found that the enemy had already emerged from the cedar. It was now nine o'clock in the morning. The Texans started in a long gallop on the trail, but soon realized that the enemy, too, was traveling at a rapid gait. The Texans were unable to overtake them during the day. Night coming on, the rangers camped near the mountains about one mile to the north of the Colorado. During the night a heavy rain fell rendering it difficult to follow the trail the next morning. Soon after resuming the march on the morning of the 17th, Captain Andrews' horse became quite lame, and since he was a large man, of about two

[74] Quoted in Wilbarger, *Indian Depredations in Texas*, p. 160.

hundred pounds, it became necessary for him to return home. Two men, whose horses were more lame than the others, were detailed to accompany him.

With their force now reduced to seventeen, the Texans, with Lieutenant Rice in command, pushed on in pursuit, although many of their horses were quite lame. By traveling slowly and closely examining every sign, the rangers succeeded in following the dim, water-soaked trail through the mountains out into the prairie towards the San Gabriel, where the Mexicans had camped the night before. From here on the sign was fresh and plain, and could easily be followed in a gallop.

About 2 o'clock in the afternoon, they reached the south fork of the San Gabriel at a point near a celebrated spring, not far from the residence of William Johnson, wrote J. W. Wilbarger in 1889. At this point the enemy had nooned and cut down a bee tree. The bees had not yet settled when the Texans arrived, and the camp fires, four in number, were still burning. The fact that there were only four camp fires was another indication that the enemy force was not large. Realizing that the enemy could not be far ahead now, the Texans did not halt, but pushed on rapidly with renewed zeal and enthusiasm.

After going about a mile further, the rangers were signaled by their spies, Felix McCluskey and B. B. Castleberry, who were about a quarter of a mile in advance, to hold up, dismount, and cut switches. The signals were obeyed, and having provided themselves with switches, the rangers once more advanced. On coming up with the spies, they were informed that the enemy had just passed over the hill immediately beyond. The rangers now started off in a steady gallop, and within another quarter of a mile came in sight of the enemy. The Mexicans now saw them, and renewed their efforts to outdistance the Texans. Every now and then the Mexicans would make a stand as if they intended to offer battle; but the Texans never checked their speed, and as the distance between the two parties began to close, the rangers would raise the bloodcurdling Texas yell, whereupon, the Mexicans would turn and renew their flight. Each time the Mexicans stopped, their leader could be seen riding up and down the line in front of his men with sword in hand haranguing them to bolster their courage, and, as some of the Texans thought, to count the number of the oncoming foe; and then, apparently not satisfied with either, he would renew his flight. The Texans kept up the chase, however, until they had driven

135

the enemy onto a steep bluff on the banks of the North San Gabriel about twenty-five miles from the newly selected capitol site of Austin. The bluff was so steep and precipitous that it was impossible for the enemy to descend.

Finding himself now in a rather tight situation, Flores, evidently with the design of giving his men an opportunity to find a crossing, rallied a few of his companions and made a charge upon the Texans, who discovered him just in time to take advantage of a live oak grove near by. With some eight or ten men, Flores desperately charged to within fifteen or twenty paces of the Texan position, and fired a volley without effect. The Texans, who had just dismounted, did not have their horses hitched, and were, therefore, ill-prepared to receive the enemy's charge; but William Wallace, "who happened to be a little quicker than the balance, had gotten in position ready for action, and just as Flores was in the act of wheeling his horse to retreat, Wallace took good aim, fired, and at the crack of his gun, Flores rolled from his horse upon the ground, shot through the heart." [75] Two of Flores' companions were also killed. The remainder of the charging Mexicans broke and fled to join their companions who, in the meantime, had succeeded in finding a crossing. Abandoning all of their horses, except those they rode, and leaving mules, baggage, munitions of war, and other things behind, the Mexicans fled rapidly towards the mountains beyond the San Gabriel, presumably proceeding towards the Brazos to cross near the falls. Too tired to pursue them further, and feeling themselves amply rewarded for their efforts, the Texans collected 114 horses and mules and other items, including about 300 pounds of powder, a like quantity of shot, balls, and some bar lead.[76] From Flores'

[75] Wilbarger, *Indian Depredations in Texas*, pp. 163–164.

[76] A most fantastic tale to come out of the fight with Manuel Flores, judged by some well-known Texan historians as being probably "one of the most important Indian fights that ever took place in Texas," was that concerning a German by the name of Karl Steinheimer, who was said to have been a member of the Flores party. Steinheimer, it was said, had been associated with Luis Aury, the pirate, and had later mined gold in Mexico for twenty years before he learned that a woman whom he had "wooed but not won or forgotten" was still living in St. Louis. Casting his lot with Flores, he started out with ten burro-loads of gold to see her. While the Texans pressed close upon the Mexicans at the San Gabriel, the German effected his escape with the ten heavily laden burros. According to the story, he found himself in an unfriendly country infested with Indians, and is said to have buried his valuable treasure. He was later reported to have been killed by Indians, but not before he had written his lady friend a letter describing

body they took a number of papers, including several land certificates that had been taken from the surveyors killed near San Antonio [77] and a letter written at Matamoros by General Canalizo to Córdova and the chiefs of the Caddoes and Seminoles and to Big Mush and Bowles of the Cherokees.[78] Among the papers was a letter from Córdova, reported Burleson, informing Flores of Córdova's inability to accompany him on his way to the East on account of a wound he had received, presumably from his late encounter with the Texans.[79] This letter, dated April 20 at Matamoros, Burleson reported he had mislaid and could not include with the others that he was transmitting with his report of May 22 to the Secretary of War.

Everything having been collected, Rice's party [80] struck out for home, arriving at the spring on the South San Gabriel just in time to camp for the night at the same spot where the Mexicans had camped the previous night. While en route to the South San Gabriel, Rice's men

---

how he had buried his gold at a point where three creeks met, sixty feet from an oak tree, in which he had driven a large brass spike. Walter Prescott Webb, *The Texas Rangers*, p. 48; Wilbarger, *Indian Depredations in Texas*, pp. 166–167; J. Frank Dobie, *Coronado's Children: Tales of Lost Mines and Buried Treasures of the Southwest*, pp. 121–124; *Williamson County Sun* (Georgetown), Sept. 28, 1950.

[77] *Colorado Gazette and Advertiser* (Matagorda), June 6, 1839; Edward Burleson to A. Sidney Johnston, City of Austin, May 12, 1839, in "Report of the Secretary of State . . . relative to the Encroachments of the Indians of the United States upon the Territories of Mexico, Washington, Jan. 11, 1853," United States Congress, *Senate Executive Documents*, 32nd Cong., 2d sess., vol. III, no. 14, pp. 29–30.

[78] Edward Burleson to A. Sidney Johnston, Secretary of War, City of Austin, May 22, 1839, Army Papers (Texas) ms. This is Burleson's report of the engagement with the Mexicans and Indians under Flores in May 1839, on the San Gabriel fork of Little River. Yoakum, *History of Texas*, II, 260; Brown, *Indian Wars and Pioneers of Texas*, p. 65; Terrell, "The City of Austin from 1839 to 1865," *Quarterly of the Texas State Historical Association*, XIV (1910–1911), 113–128; Alcée La Branche to John Forsyth, Legation of the U. S., Houston, June 7, 1839 (vol. 1, no. 22), "Correspondence and Reports of American Agents and Others in Texas, 1836–1845," Justin H. Smith, "Transcripts," V; Alessio Robles, *Coahuila y Texas*, II, 198; United States Congress, *Senate Executive Documents*, 32nd Cong., 2d sess., vol. III, no. 14.

[79] Edward Burleson to A. Sidney Johnston, Secretary of War, City of Austin, May 22, 1839, in Smither (ed.), *Journals of the Fourth Congress of the Republic of Texas*, III, 113–114.

[80] Rice's party included: A. J. Adkisson, Jonathan Davis, S. G. Harness, and William P. Hardeman. Wilbarger, *Indian Depredations in Texas*, p. 166; Frank Brown, "Annals of Travis County and the City of Austin," Chap. VI, ms., p. 50.

were met by Captain James P. Ownsby [81] in command of some thirty six-months rangers, well-provided with provisions. They, followed by Colonel Burleson with another party, had started to the relief of the Andrews-Rice party as soon as word had come in to Austin and Bastrop by the men who had abandoned Captain Andrews' command after the cedar brake incident. It had been feared that so small a group of Texans in pursuit of a large body of Mexicans might be slain, if it should succeed in overtaking the enemy.

When Captain Ownsby's militiamen discovered a large *caballada* of horses approaching driven by a few men wearing Mexican sombreros (taken from the enemy), they believed they had intercepted the Mexican party rumored to be in that general area. Ownsby, therefore, quickly ordered his men to dismount and fire, but was prevailed upon by one of his men, who suspected that the approaching party were Texans, to cancel the order to fire. The two parties met at a point between the battleground where Flores had been defeated and the South Fork of the San Gabriel. As Rice's men came up and salutations were exchanged, some of Ownsby's men commenced talking about a division of the spoils, "one fellow laying claim to one horse, another to this one, and so on until finally Lieutenant Rice's party began to think they were in earnest about the matter, which up to this time they looked upon as a joke." [82] Perceiving that Ownsby's men were serious in making their claims to a share in the spoils, Rice's party told them that they had fought the Mexicans for the property and would fight again before they divided with the newcomers. This declaration offended Ownsby's men, who, perceiving that they were not to be permitted to share in the division of the spoils, refused to share their provisions with Rice's men, notwithstanding the fact that they had been without food for two days and nights. Furthermore, the fatigued pursuers of the country's enemies were denied the privilege of camping with those who came to their relief, and were thus compelled to mount their own guard all night to protect the horses they had captured and claimed as their own personal, rather than public, property.

Early the next morning (May 18) Rice's men started for Austin. After traveling some distance and just as they were ascending Pilot

[81] In the summer of 1839 Captain James P. Ownsby commanded a volunteer company from Austin under Colonel Edward Burleson in the Cherokee War. Brown, *Indian Wars and Pioneers of Texas,* p. 67. See Appendix for a Muster Roll of Captain J. P. Ownsby's Company, March 2–Sept. 9, 1839.

[82] Wilbarger, *Indian Depredations in Texas,* p. 165.

Knob [83] on Brushy Creek, they were met by Colonel Burleson with another relief expedition. This party generously furnished Rice's men with provisions without even asking for a share of the booty. After dinner Burleson's and Rice's forces returned to Austin, where Colonel Burleson, Samuel Highsmith,[84] and Logan Vadever [85] were selected arbitrators to determine upon the division of the spoils. It did not take them long to decide that the horses and other paraphernalia belonged to Rice's men: "to the victors belong the spoils." Rice's men then proceeded to Hornsby's Bend, nine miles below Austin, where all the captured horses were placed in a corral and divided into seventeen lots by distinterested parties. Each man drew for choice. After the division of the horses, the men proceeded to open the captured leather bags. One of these contained several letters between Córdova, Flores, and the Mexican officials at Matamoros, together with several official communications directed by the latter to the Indians in East Texas. There happened to be at the place a Mexican named Francisco, who, possessing some education, was able to make a rough translation of the documents for the Texans. This valuable information was at once turned over to Colonel Burleson, who transmitted it to the Texan government at Houston.

The captured papers convinced Lamar and his cabinet that the Cherokees were in treasonable correspondence with the Mexicans,[86] but there were no letters from Cherokee leaders to justify this conclusion. The Cherokees seem to have done little more than listen with Indian politeness to the warlike proposals of Mexican agents and conspirators in East Texas, until the inroads of land-hungry Anglo-Americans forced them to defend their homes. Whether justified or not, however, the Texans engaged in a campaign during the ensuing summer, which drove the Cherokees from Texas.[87] The Shawnees, Ala-

---

[83] *Ibid.* Pilot Knob evidently had reference to one of the elevations in the vicinity of present-day Round Rock, Texas.

[84] "Samuel Highsmith," *Handbook of Texas,* I, 809. Highsmith had had a tintype picture made of himself in Santa Anna's uniform after the battle of San Jacinto.

[85] Brown, "Annals of Travis County," chap. VI, p. 56, typed ms.

[86] D. W. Smith to John Forsyth, Matamoros, Jan. 6, 1837, Consular Dispatches (U. S.), 1837–1839, (Matamoros), ms., microfilm.

[87] More complete accounts of the expulsion of the Cherokee and allied tribes from East Texas may be found in the "Annual Report of the Secretary of War [A. Sidney Johnston], City of Austin, Nov. 1839," reprinted in Smither (ed.), *Journals of the Fourth Congress of the Republic of Texas,* III, 73–116; and in

bamas, and Coushattas were also removed, but without bloodshed, the last two tribes being given other land in Texas. Thus, more Indian land was made available to land-hungry speculators and settlers. About eighty Cherokee, Delaware, Kickapoo, and Caddo warriors made their way to Matamoros, where they were supplied with rations, arms, ammunition, clothing, and other necessities.[88]

Although Córdova was forced to flee beyond the Río Grande and Flores was killed, the effects of their activities, supplemented by the work of other agents in Texas, were felt for several years. After the opening of the land offices under the land law of December 14, 1837, the Indians needed less encouragement from the Mexican agents; for seeing the surveyors, locators, and unprincipled land-grabbers at work beyond the settlements, they were not slow in believing that the white man was taking all their hunting grounds. Consequently, in 1838–1840, and to a less extent thereafter, the whole frontier from the Arroyo Seco and Río Frio to Red River was lighted with the flames of a savage war. Red men, egged on by Mexican agents, contended against Anglo-Texans for mastery. The Indian outrages were appalling, and the whole northern frontier bled from the savage fury.

On the Southwestern frontier a similar situation existed, flavored with Mexican and Texan banditry. En route to Austin with Colonel Jacob Snively, Secretary of the Treasury, James H. Starr, in the fall of 1839, "saw a band of fifteen Texas cowboys. They carry on a predatory warfare," he recorded, "against the inoffensive inhabitants of Chihauhua on the Río Grande, murdering them, burning their houses and driving off their cattle, mules and horses to this country in violation of a law of Congress and the Proclamation of the President inviting those Mexicans to trade on friendly terms with our people and offering them protection." [89] He reported that the marauders were harboring hundreds of cattle in the vicinity [of La Grange?], and were boasting that no jury or court could be found to punish them. They "bragged that they even robbed neighbors' melon patches," he declared, confident that the blame would be put on the Tonkawa Indians.

John H. Reagan, "The Expulsion of the Cherokees from East Texas, "*Quarterly of the Texas State Historical Association* (1897–1898), 38–46.

[88] D. W. Smith to John Forsyth, Matamoros, Jan. 1, 1840, Consular Dispatches (U. S.), Jan. 1, 1840–Dec. 29, 1848 (Matamoros), ms., microfilm; *Colorado Gazette and Advertiser*, Jan. 18, 1840. The *Colorado Gazette* reported Córdova and 90 Cherokees at Matamoros early in December 1839.

[89] Private Memoranda, 1839–1840, in James H. Starr Papers, ms.

The settlers at San Antonio were informed on September 2, 1839, that the government could not at present make any force stationary at that place, but that Major Reuben Ross, with his detachment of about seventy, "well mounted and well armed," had been ordered to include that section of the country in his circuit of ranging and to afford what protection he could to its inhabitants. "The President has also written individually," the San Antonians were informed, "to John H. Moore on the Colorado to raise two hundred men to range out your way." [90]

A road was opened between Gonzales and Austin in July 1839, but as late as August 1840, there was none between Gonzales and Bastrop. Captain J. Wiehl, in company with a surveyor named Lindsay, set out from Camp Bell near Austin on October 8, 1840, to lay off a road from Austin to the springs at the headwaters of the San Marcos, as it was planned to establish a regular military post at the latter point, approximately half-way between Austin and San Antonio. [91] At first, the post on the San Marcos was garrisoned by Captain Wiehl's Company "H" of the First Regiment of Infantry commanded by Colonel William G. Cooke. [92]

[90] Thomas G. Western to Samuel A. Maverick, City of Houston, Sept. 2, 1839, in Rena Maverick Green (ed.), *Memoirs of Mary A. Maverick: arranged by Mary A. Maverick and her son George Madison Maverick*, pp. 134–135.

[91] *Texas Sentinel* (Austin), Oct. 10, 1840, quoted in *Colorado Gazette and Advertiser*, Oct. 24, 1840.

[92] The Company left Fort Skerrett, Cherokee Nation, and halted at Fort Lacy, Nacogdoches County, on July 12, 1840. From there it marched on August 6, arriving at Austin on the 29th. On October 8 Captain Wiehl and his company marched from Camp Bell, near Austin, for the San Marcos springs, arriving there on October 18, 1840. This company had been enrolled in the late summer and fall of 1839 for a three year period. Muster Roll, Capt. J. Wiehl's Co. "H" of the 1st Regt. Infty., Commanded by Col. Wm. G. Cooke, June 30–Dec. 31, 1840 [dated:] San Marcos, Jan. 1, 1841, in Militia Rolls (Texas), ms.

CHAPTER NINE

Texan Participation
in the Federalist Wars: First Phase

THE FEDERALIST REVOLUTIONARY DISTURBANCES, which broke out in northern Mexico in December 1837, gained renewed vigor following the French blockade of the Mexican coast and the capture of Vera Cruz in November 1838 and soon involved a number of Texans. While the Mexican government through its agents and spies sought to harass the young republic to the north, the Texans, on the other hand, often afforded assistance, officially and unofficially, to the revolutionists of Yucatán and the northern states of San Luis Potosí, Zacatecas, Jalisco, Nuevo León, Tamaulipas, Coahuila, Durango, Sinaloa, Chihuahua, Nuevo México, and the Californias in their struggle to overthrow the Centralist government of Anastasio Bustamante and Santa Anna.[1] On both sides of the Río Grande there were persons who believed that Texas and some of the northern states of Mexico should be formed into a North Mexican Republic, and the Mexican Congress, becoming aware of this movement on its northern frontier, passed a law declaring any overt act in that direction to be high treason, punishable as such.[2]

The real interests of the people of the northern departments of Mexico had long been neglected by the central government of their homeland. Isolated by the character of the country and the distance from the seat of political authority, confronted constantly on the frontier with a serious Indian problem, and dominated by an economic system based on farming and ranching, the inhabitants of the frontier departments had developed those qualities which made "every citizen

[1] Paul S. Taylor, An American-Mexican Frontier: Nueces County, Texas, p. 21; John Henry Brown, History of Texas, from 1685 to 1892, II, 172–177; Joseph William Schmitz, Texan Statecraft, 1836–1845, pp. 327–332; Justin H. Smith, The Annexation of Texas, p. 37; Telegraph and Texas Register (Houston), Feb. 10, 1841; Austin City Gazette, May 13, 1840.

[2] Manuel Rivera Cambas, Historia antiguas y moderna de Jalapa y de las revoluciones del estado de Vera Cruz, III, 428.

a worker, every worker a soldier, and every soldier a hero." [3] The growing dissatisfaction among the inhabitants of the departments at the indifference of the central authority to their protection [4] and the prolonged stay among the people on this frontier of the unruly army of observation against Texas, particularly since its maintenance devolved chiefly on them,[5] seemed to afford their leaders a favorable opportunity to overthrow the Centralist yoke to whose system they attributed the loss of Texas.[6] To those persons with strong republican inclinations, the decree of the national Congress ordering the ashes of the deposed emperor Iturbide exhumed and reinterred with national honors in the cathedral in Mexico City looked like a move toward the restoration of monarchy of which they cared to have no part.[7]

The discontent was not confined to the northern states, for occasionally revolts flared up in Jalisco, Oaxaca, Chiapas, Yucatán and elsewhere in the center and extreme southern portions of the republic, where large segments of the liberal masses came to fear the concentration of power in the hands of President Bustamante and the subversion of the federal plan of government. Ambitious politicians and military leaders with political ambitions too often took advantage of unrest growing out of heavy taxation and corruption in public office.

The revolt in the north broke out on December 26, 1837, under General José Urrea,[8] who, in the Texas campaign of 1836, had captured Colonel James W. Fannin and his men, and had subsequently been appointed commandant general of the Department of Sonora. He raised the standard of rebellion at Arizpe in favor of the constitution of 1824 and was "elected" and installed as governor on March 14, 1838. The Congress of Sonora made him commandant general of

---

[3] Miguel Ramos Arizpe, *Memoria sobre el estado de las provincias internas de oriente presentada a las cortes del Cádiz*, pp. 16–17.

[4] Vicente Filisola, "Commander-in-Chief [of the] Army of the North to the Justice of the Peace, Laredo," dated: Matamoros, July 30, 1838.

[5] See Juan Nepomuceno Molano á Gobernador Francisco Vital Fernández, Matamoros, Marzo 24 de 1836, in City Records (Matamoros), ms. See also *El Cosmopolita* (Mexico City), July 13, 1836.

[6] Vito Alessio Robles, *Coahuila y Texas desde la consumación de la independencia hasta el tratado de paz de Guadalupe Hidalgo*, II, 202.

[7] Hobart Huson, "Refugio: A Comprehensive History of Refugio County from Aboriginal Times to the End of World War II," vol. II, chap. 23, p. 2.

[8] José Urrea á los ciudadanos de la república, Diciembre 28 de 1837, in *El Cosmopolita*, Jan. 27, 1838; D. W. Smith to John Forsyth, Matamoros, March 16, 1838, in Consular Dispatches (U. S.), 1837–1838 (Matamoros), ms., microfilm.

the Federal army and "protector of the States of Sonora and Sinaloa." In order to give his movement some financial support, Urrea seized the customs receipts at Mazatlán in Sinaloa on September 30, 1838, amounting to an estimated $100,000.

Meanwhile it looked as if the revolt might spread; so the principal officers of the Army of the North (Filisola, Ampudia, Canalizo, Rafael Vasquez, Rómulo de la Vega, Adrián Woll, Manuel Savariego, Francisco G. Pavón, Nicolás Condelle, and Pedro de la Garza and fifteen others) appealed to their subordinates and fellow-countrymen to remain patient and firm in their loyalty to the government which, they claimed, was well aware of the sufferings they had endured from "the cruel depredations of the ferocious hordes of barbarians and the vicious gangs of rapacious volunteers from Texas." The supreme government, they promised, would soon provide the resources necessary to arm and maintain the presidial companies and to mount the cavalry units, now largely afoot, for the promotion of the peace and welfare of the frontier through the extermination of the "bloodthirsty barbarians" and the "bandits and pirates calling themselves Texan volunteers." [9] The appeal, however, seems to have fallen on deaf ears, for the frontier peoples had seen too many such promises in the past left largely unfulfilled. The flame of revolt continued to spread in Sinaloa, Durango, and Jalisco, and discontent smouldered in Tamaulipas, Nuevo León, and Coahuila. General Valentín Canalizo, a close friend of Santa Anna's, was named by Filisola to command the second division of the Army of the North, and thus, on April 3, 1838, became second in command of that army with orders to put down the Federalist uprising.[10] Urrea's initial successes in Sonora and Sinaloa ended in disaster in October 1838, and the movement was quickly suppressed in Jalisco, the principal early stronghold of the liberal movement, and in Durango, Oaxaca, and Chiapas where revolutionary disturbances had erupted.

The discontent in the north persisted, however, and suddenly on October 7, 1838, a fresh insurrection broke out at Tampico under the

---

[9] Los generales y gefes del Ejército de Norte, á sus subordinados y á todos sus conciudadanos, Cuartel General, Matamoros, Marzo 6 de 1838, in *La Concordia* (Ciudad Victoria), March 17, 1838; Vicente Filisola and others, *Los generales y gefes de Ejército del Norte, á sus subordinados y á todos sus conciudadanos*, Cuartel General en Matamoros, Marzo 6 de 1838, broadsheet.

[10] Valentín Canalizo *El gral. . . . segundo en gefe del Ejército del Norte á los indiviudos* [sic] *que componen la segunda division*, Cuartel General en Matamoros, Abril 3 de 1838, broadside.

144

leadership of Captain Longinos Montenegro. Urrea, now a fugitive from Sonora, soon arrived in the city to assume command, and the Centralist commander José de las Piedras was captured and forced to leave aboard a vessel bound for Matamoros.[11] Antonio Canales in Guerrero, Tamaulipas, issued a *pronunciamiento* on November 5 against the central government and for the federal plan of 1824. Soon declarations of a similar vein were made by the towns of Reinosa, Mier, and Laredo,[12] and by the end of November the northern Federalists were in general revolt under such leaders as General Pedro Lemus, his brother—José Lemus, General José Urrea, General José Antonio Mejía [13] (a long-time liberal leader, Texas land speculator, and organizer of the abortive Tampico Expedition of 1835), and lesser politicos, like Colonels Antonio Canales, Francisco Garay, Antonio

[11] José Urrea to Sr. Comandante principal de esta plaza, Coronel D. Longinos Montenegro, Santa Anna de Tamaulipas, Nov. 12, 1838, in *El Cosmopolita*, Nov. 28, 1838; José Urrea to Ejército Libertador, Nov. 12, 1838, in *ibid.*; Valentín Canalizo, General en gefe de la tercera division del ejército del norte a ———, Campo en la Cruz de los Caminos, Nov. 11, 1838, reprint from *El Telegrafo*, in *ibid.*; *Telegraph and Texas Register*, Nov. 28, 1838.

[12] D. W. Smith to John Forsyth, Matamoros, Dec. 10, 1838, no. 147, in Consular Dispatches (U. S.), 1837–1839 (Matamoros), ms., microfilm.

[13] José Antonio Mejía, a Cuban who immigrated to Mexico in 1823, served as secretary to the Mexican legation in Washington from about 1829 to 1831. While in the United States he became one of the incorporators of the notorious Galveston Bay and Texas Land Company; and, subsequently, with General John T. Mason, one of its agents and lobbyists. As a supporter of Santa Anna during the popular disturbances of 1832 in Mexico he led the liberal army in the capture of Matamoros, after which he came on an inspection tour of Texas to prevent the dismemberment of the province by restoring order. He supported adherence to the constitution of 1824, and after Santa Anna's election became an important man in Mexico. Later he broke with Santa Anna when the latter turned to Centralism. Mejía supported the Texans in their early protestations against Centralism, and organized and led an unsuccessful expedition from New Orleans against Tampico in November 1835, which failed because of poor discipline, and insufficient troops, ammunition, lead, provisions, money, and clothing. George L. Rives, *The United States and Mexico, 1821–1848*, I, 306; Eugene C. Barker, "The Tampico Expedition, in *Quarterly of the Texas State Historical Association*, VI (1902–1903), 169–186; José Urrea á General de brigade D. José Antonio Mejía, Cuartel-general en Tampico, Enero 4 de 1839, and José Antonio Mejía á D. José Urrea, general en gefe del ejército libertador, Tampico, Enero 4 de 1839, in *El Centinela de Tamaulipas* (Ciudad Victoria), Jan. 17, 1839; Eleuterio Méndez ál Gobernador de esta Estado D. José Antonio Fernández Yzaguierre, 3ª Division de Ejército Libertador Cuartel General en San Fernando, Enero 14 de 1839, in *ibid.*, Jan. 19, 1839; Eleuterio Méndez á Sr. Gobernador del Estado Libre y Soberano de

After San Jacinto

Tijerina (governor of Coahuila), Francisco Vidaurri y Villaseñor (a former governor of Coahuila and Texas [14]), and his son-in-law Dr. John Long, Mauricio Carrasco, Marcial Borrego, Bartolomé de Cárdenas, Colonel José María González,[15] Colonel Antonio Zapata (the owner of a large ranch east of the Río Grande), Colonel Eleuterio Méndez,[16] who appeared before Matamoros early in December with four hundred men but retired without making an attack upon the town and began concentrating his forces at Reinosa; [17] Cristobal Ramírez, Macedonio Capistrán, Basilio Benavides (alcalde of Laredo), Rafael Uribe of Guerrero, and José María J. Carbajal [18] (a former citizen of

Tamaulipas, C. Victoria, Cuartel General en los Potreras, Jan. 26, 1839, in *ibid.*, Feb. 7, 1839; Proclama de General José Urrea dado al Cuartel General del ejército libertador en Tampico, Enero 22 de 1839, in *ibid.*, Jan. 31, 1839.

[14] Francisco Vidaurri y Villaseñor served as governor from January 8 to July 23, 1834.

[15] Prior to November 1835, José María Gonzáles had been a colonel in the regular Mexican army. Eugene C. Barker, *Life of Stephen F. Austin*, p. 492; W. Roy Smith, "The Quarrel between Governor Smith ˙and the Council of the Provisional Government of the Republic," *Quarterly of the Texas State Historical Association*, V (1901–1902), 296–297; Hobart Huson, "Iron Men: A History of the Republic of the Rio Grande and Federalist War in Northern Mexico," p. 9.

[16] Eleuterio Méndez to the Inhabitants of the Northern Towns, and the City of Matamoros, City of Guerrero, Nov. 18, 1838, stating his reasons for taking up arms in behalf of Federalism, in *Telegraph and Texas Register*, Jan. 9, 1839.

[17] D. W. Smith to John Forsyth, Matamoros, Dec. 10, 1838, no. 147, in Consular Dispatches (U. S.), 1837–1839 (Matamoros), ms., microfilm; Same to Same, Matamoros, Dec. 22, 1838, no. 148, in *ibid.*

[18] José María Carbajal, a native of Béxar and surveyor in Martín de Leon's colony, had been reared and educated in the United States under the noted Rev. Alexander Campbell, founder of the Disciples of Christ. His father was José Antonio Carbajal who married Refugia, a daughter of Martín de Leon, and settled at Victoria in his father-in-law's colony, being one of the original forty-one families to settle at that place. While acting as a surveyor for the general land commissioner for Texas, J. Francisco Madero, Carbajal was arrested in February 1831, by Colonel John D. Bradburn, the commandant at Anahuac at the head of Galveston Bay. In 1836, being a member of a prominent family at Victoria, he was chosen as a delegate from that place to help frame the constitution of the Texas Republic, but failed to attend the Convention on account of the immediate approach of Santa Anna's forces which caused him to look after the safety of his family. During the Texan revolution, a vessel, the *Hannah Elizabeth*, carrying dry goods, guns, and ammunition belonging to Carbajal and Fernando de León, also a resident of Victoria, and valued at $35,000, was run ashore on the west end of Matagorda Peninsula by the *Bravo*, a Mexican vessel. The ship was boarded and

146

Victoria, Texas). These men sought to re-establish republicanism under the Mexican constitution of 1824.

The fall of Tampico greatly alarmed the Mexican authorities who, at this time, were desperately trying to ward off a full-scale French invasion and at the same time were having to contend with the growing conflagration at home.[19] Having gained access to an important gulf port, the insurrectionists could now cooperate with the French and receive military supplies more readily from abroad, and gain some financial support from the customs. The government acted quickly. It ordered General Martín Perfecto de Cós, military commandant at San Antonio de Béxar in 1835, to take command of the military forces in the states of Tamaulipas, Nuevo León, Coahuila y Téjas;[20] and in an effort to repossess Tampico dispatched General Canalizo from Matamoros, with a force which had been raised to repel the French invasion. The government troops, it was reported, were "promised the privilege of plundering the inhabitants [of the town], to encourage them, and the houses of the foreigners were pointed out to them as fittest to be pilfered."[21] Canalizo's troops, although assisted by those of General José de las Piedras and the inept General Cós and numbering upwards of two thousand men,[22] were defeated after a hard-fought

robbed of a portion of her cargo, and nine persons were taken off as prisoners. A prize crew was left on board the *Hannah Elizabeth*. Before the Mexican prize could be gotten off, Captain Hurd and S. Rhoads Fisher with a party of Texans boarded her and claimed the vessel and cargo as a prize of war. Carbajal and Fernando de León were never reimbursed for the losses. After the Texas revolution Carbajal moved with his family to Tamaulipas. There his son, José María Carbajal, Jr., married General Antonio Canales' daughter. In 1851, and again in 1862, in cooperation with a number of Anglo-Texans, Carbajal headed an unsuccessful revolt in the State of Tamaulipas, Vicente Filisola, *Memorias para la historia de la guerra de Téjas*, I, 167; V. M. Rose, *Some Historical Facts in Regard to the Settlement of Victoria, Texas: Its Progress and Present Status*, pp. iii, 154; Eugene C. Barker (ed.), *Texas History for High Schools and Colleges*, p. 259; Frank C. Pierce, *A Brief History of the Lower Río Grande Valley*, pp. 32–33; Harbert Davenport, "General José María Jesús Carbajal," in *Southwestern Historical Quarterly*, LV (1951–1952), 475–483.

[19] *Matagorda Bulletin*, Dec. 6, 1838.
[20] *Telegraph and Texas Register*, Nov. 28, 1838.
[21] *New Orleans Sun* quoted in *ibid.*, Dec. 29, 1838; see also, *ibid.*, Jan. 18 and 19, 1839; *Telégrafo de Tampico*, Dec. 5, 1838, gives an account of the battle of November 30.
[22] D. W. Smith to John Forsyth, Matamoros, Dec. 10, 1838, no. 147, in Consular Dispatches (U. S.), 1837–1839 (Matamoros), ms., microfilm.

battle at Tampico on November 30 with over five hundred casualties, and it was said that when the troops were later mustered under Nicolás Condelle they numbered only about seven hundred men.[23] Among the captives was Piedras, who was ordered to be shot on December 7.[24]

Canalizo collected his demoralized troops at Altamira, seven leagues from Tampico, and while the government planned to send a stronger expedition against Tampico under General Gabriel Valencia, it ordered Canalizo to proceed northward to take command of Matamoros from Filisola and to check the spread of the Federalist movement in the north. When he sought to move northward, he found he lacked sufficient strength; so he ordered Filisola to send him two divisions of troops to enable him to move from the vicinity of Tampico. The request was complied with, and the troops, numbering 282, were sent from Matamoros on December 27 under Colonel Francisco Garay and Pedro Lemus;[25] but they had scarcely left the city before they deserted with their men to the Federalist party recently formed under Canales.[26] In attempting to carry out his orders without assistance, Canalizo was attacked by General Fernández near Santa Teresa and beaten, but succeeded in reaching Matamoros with three hundred men.[27] Soon Canales, Méndez, and Lemus laid siege to that city with some five hundred men, consisting principally of dragoons, some musketeers, and swordsmen; and were intercepting all communications with the interior.[28] Although Filisola's garrison numbered only eight hundred, the assailants were without artillery and were unable to take the city. Later in the spring Canales informed the American consul at Matamoros that he intended to collect one-half of the internal duties on all goods destined from Matamoros to the interior of the country,[29]

[23] Hubert Howe Bancroft, *History of Mexico*, V, 209.

[24] *New Orleans Sun* quoted in *Telegraph and Texas Register*, Dec. 29, 1838.

[25] D. W. Smith to John Forsyth, Matamoros, Jan. 1, 1839, no. 150, in Consular Dispatches (U. S.), 1837–1839 (Matamoros), ms., microfilm.

[26] Carlos María Bustamante, *El gabinete mexicano, durante el segundo periodo de la administracion del Exmo. Señor Presidente D. Anastacio Bustamante, hasta le entrega del mando al Exmo. Señor Presidente Interino D. Antonio Lopez de Santa-Anna,* I, 155–156.

[27] *Telegraph and Texas Register*, Feb. 13, 1839.

[28] *Matagorda Bulletin,* Jan. 31, 1839; D. W. Smith to John Forsyth, Matamoros, Jan. 1, 1839, no. 150, in Consular Dispatches (U. S.), 1837–1839 (Matamoros), ms., microfilm.

[29] Antonio Canales to Vice-Consul of the United States at Matamoros, Reynosa, May 21, 1839, in *ibid.*

and, for a while because of their control of the hinterland around Matamoros, the Federalists were able to intercept the valuable export trade through that port, consisting of hides, horns, mules, ebony, dyewoods, and considerable quantities of specie. In the meantime, General Filisola ordered the fortifications at Brazos de Santiago, erected in 1836, demolished and the artillery spiked and thrown into the sea [30] to prevent it falling into the hands of either the French or the Federalists. The fall of San Juan de Úlloa to the French on November 28 with its attendant effect upon Vera Cruz, coupled with the Federalist military successes at Tampico, caused numerous *pronunciamientos* in favor of Federalism to be made by the towns of the north late in 1838 and early 1839.[31] Antonio Zapata defeated Francisco Pavón at Mier in late November or early December, and the latter fled to Matamoros pursued by Méndez and Zapata. As the government troops were forced out of the northern towns, many of them took refuge in Matamoros, so that by December 28 when Jacob ("Jake") Hendricks and —— Davis, Texans imprisoned at Matamoros during the past year, made their escape, fifteen hundred soldiers had congregated there, swelling the garrison to two thousand men under General Filisola. These troops were encamped in the public square which had been enclosed with pickets. Nine pieces of artillery were mounted "at each of the principal streets leading to the square." [32] Canalizo succeeded Filisola as commandant of the north on February 7, and took over command of the defenses of Matamoros.[33]

General José Antonio Mejía and Colonel Martín Peraga, from New

[30] *Tampico Telegraph*, Feb. 9, 1839, quoted in *Telegraph and Texas Register*, March 6, 1839.

[31] Declarations in favor of the constitution of 1824 were made at Ciudad Victoria (Dec. 12), Santa Barbara (Dec. 16), Burgos (Dec. 18), Mineral de San Nicolás (Dec. 18), Palmillas (Dec. 19), Bustamante (Dec. 21), Morelos (Dec. 23), Laredo (Jan. 5), Soto la Marina (Jan. 9), Monclova—where the inhabitants were dissatisfied because the capital of Coahuila continued to be located at Saltillo—(Jan. 15) and numerous other places. *El Centinela de Tamaulipas* (Ciudad Victoria), Jan. 10, 1839, Jan. 17, and Feb. 14, 1839; Alessio Robles, *Coahuila y Texas*, II, 205; Resolution passed at a Meeting of Citizens, Laredo, January 5, 1839, in Laredo Archives; José Ma. Ramón, Justice of the Peace, to the Political Chief of the Department of the North of Tamaulipas, Laredo, Jan. 5, 1839, in *ibid.*

[32] *Telegraph and Texas Register*, Jan. 18, 1839.

[33] Valentín Canalizo. El General en Gefe de la Division del Norte á los Tropas de su mando y á los habitantes, Febrero 7 de 1839, in *El Ancla* (Matamoros), Feb. 15, 1839.

Orleans where Mejía had been in exile, were landed on the last day of December, 1838, by the American schooner *Sarah Ann* at Tampico, where they discussed with Urrea, Anaya, and other prominent Federal leaders the military situation and future plans. It was determined to divide the Federal forces in the northeast into three divisions:[34] the first division, commanded by Mejía, was to advance into the interior toward Mexico City; the second division, commanded by Urrea, was to operate against San Luis Potosí, Zacatecas, and the adjoining states; and the third division was to be commanded by General Pedro Lemus, but until he could take charge, Canales was to assume the command. The third division was to advance upon Monterey and Saltillo. The three columns were to begin simultaneous operations by February 1, 1839. On January 6, 1839, Urrea and Mejía issued a joint proclamation to the Mexican people setting forth their reasons for taking up arms against the government and appealing for united support of federalism.[35]

An express was sent to the government of Texas, where it arrived in Houston on January 8 and a cabinet meeting was summoned at once. It was conjectured that the express contained "overtures from the liberal party of Mexico, for assistance from Texas in putting down the Centralists, and offering, as inducements, to unite with this Republic under a government similar to our own," declared the *Civilian and Galveston Gazette*,[36] "or to recognize our independence." The war-mongers in Texas were already active. Major General Felix Huston was said to be "endeavoring to ape Charles the Twelfth by getting up an army against Mexico."[37]

It was reported in Mexico City on February 5 that Mejía accompanied by General Urrea and Captain Ribaud, a French sea captain and friend, visited Admiral Baudin in January at San Juan de Úlloa in an effort to promote cooperation between the Federalists and the French. It was said he sought to have the fortress of San Juan de Úlloa turned over to Urrea.[38] The Centralist paper, *El Iris*, stated that Baudin agreed to supply Urrea with 200 guns if the Federalists would agree

---

[34] Huson, "'Iron Men,'" pp. 25–26.
[35] Proclamation of José Urrea and José Antonio Mejía to the Mexican People, Headquarters of the Liberating Army, Tampico, Jan. 6, 1839, in *Telegraph and Texas Register*, Jan. 30, 1839.
[36] Jan. 11, 1839.
[37] James H. Starr to Pamela O. Starr, Dec. 2, 1838, in James H. Starr Papers, ms.
[38] *El Mosquito Mexicano* (Mexico City), Feb. 5, 1839.

not to expel the French merchants and their families from Tampico and other areas that they might control.[39] It is probable that Mejía approached Admiral Baudin on the question of permitting the Federalists to pass through the French blockade of the Mexican ports.

At Monclova the Federalist uprising of January 1839, was headed by Citizen Ramón Músquiz,[40] former political chief of Béxar, and supported by Bartolomé de Cárdenas, Severo Ruiz, commanding the Federal troops, José María Cantú, José María Flores, José María de los Santos Coy, Jesús Quintero, Francisco Borrego, José María Villareal, Manuel Cárdenas, and others.[41] On January 21 the Federalists, six hundred strong under Ruiz, advanced from Monclova against Saltillo, but were defeated (Feb. 20) by the combined forces of Governor Francisco Conde and those of Colonel Domingo Ugartechea from Monterey.

Meanwhile, in pitched battles in the north on January 6 [42] and 16 [43] Colonel Eleuterio Méndez was repulsed by Colonel Ampudia on the outskirts of Matamoros,[44] falling back toward Reinosa, where Canales' forces were located. On January 12 the rebels were again defeated on the Llano del Chiltipín below Santa Teresa.[45] This gave some relief to Matamoros. Even Lemus, who commanded the Federal forces in this area, promised to return to obedience to the supreme government,

[39] *El Iris*, Feb. 9, 1839, quoted in *El Ancla*, March 8, 1839.

[40] Ramón Músquiz served as political chief of Béxar from 1827 to March 17, 1835, when he replaced Juan N. Seguin as vice governor of Coahuila y Texas, later becoming governor on June 28, 1835. Under the orders of President Santa Anna, he was at Béxar on March 6, 1836, when that place fell to the Mexican troops. Upon the withdrawal of the Mexican troops from Texas after the battle of San Jacinto, he left San Antonio de Béxar, but returned again to the city in August, 1839, a refugee from Centralism. *Handbook of Texas*, II, 253; Erasmo Seguin to the Secretary of State [of the Republic of Texas], Béxar, Sept. 6, 1839, in Domestic Correspondence (Texas), 1836–1846, ms., Spanish.

[41] *El Centinela de Tamaulipas*, Feb. 14, 1839. Many of these names were to be found later among those of Woll's division which captured San Antonio, Texas, in September 1842.

[42] Vicente Filisola al Ministerio de Guerra y Marina, Enero 8 de 1839, in *El Ancla*, Feb. 8, 1839.

[43] D. W. Smith to John Forsyth, Matamoros, Jan. 18, 1839, in Consular Dispatches (U. S.), 1837–1839 (Matamoros), ms., microfilm.

[44] Valentín Canalizo á Gobernador del Departamento de Nuevo León, Cuartel General en Villa Aldama, Agosto 26 de 1839, in *Gaceta de Tampico*, Sept. 14, 1839.

[45] Valentín Canalizo á E. S. Gobernador del departamento de N. León, Cuartel General en Villa Aldama, Agosto 19 de 1839, in Supplement to *ibid.*, Aug. 31, 1839.

"but no sooner had the colonel [Ampudia] turned his back than the latter reconsidered the situation and surprised the poorly defended Monterey" and took it.[46] Soon (May 24) Saltillo also fell into the hands of the insurgents under Lemus. A number of Texans participated in the battle of Monterey on the side of the Federalists. Among those taking part were Ewen Cameron, a cousin of Dr. John Cameron of Monclova, and about twenty-five others, including John R. Baker, George Lord, Benjamin F. Neal, John W. B. McFarlane, Alfred A. Lee, Hugh Cameron, Henry Whalen, and others who distinguished themselves.[47] Many of these were later members of the Texan Mier Expedition. The number of Texans in the Federal service was to grow with the discharge in January 1839, by the Texas government, of all men in the First and Second Regiments of Permanent Volunteers, except the troops at Galveston and San Bernard, who were to remain until they could be relieved by other troops.[48]

In the meantime, the Federalists who appeared before Matamoros to demand Filisola's surrender were pictured as numbering a thousand men, defying with cries of "Federation or Death!" the Centralist leader's demands to return to obedience to the established authorities. During the excitement attendant upon the Federalist siege of Matamoros, William Brennan, former Texas congressman, effected his escape from prison in the beleaguered city early in February and arrived in Texas to report a large Federalist force investing the place when he left.[49]

The Federalists were found to be cooperating with the French, who not only gave them arms but also permitted them to run the blockade at Tuxpan, Soto la Marina, and Tampico. The tariff was reduced to a mere fraction of the usual rates, and large quantities of goods entered the ports under Federal domination, for on February 17 the French opened to foreign vessels the upper ports on the gulf, then in the hands of the Federalists. Whether or not this helped the revolutionists' cause, it is difficult to say; "the price they [the Federalists] had to pay for

[46] Bancroft, *History of Mexico*, V, 209.
[47] Huson, "Iron Men," p. 9.
[48] A. Sidney Johnston to ———, War Department, Jan. 1, 1839, in *Matagorda Bulletin*, Jan. 31, 1839. Although dated January 1, 1839, the order seems to have been written January 29, 1839. The discharge of the First and Second Regiments was in accordance to a Joint Resolution of Congress.
[49] *Telegraph and Texas Register*, March 29, 1839; *Matagorda Bulletin*, April 4, 1839.

this advantage . . . was the one commodity they could least afford to lose: their popularity." [50] But France was not the only recognized enemy of the Mexican government from whom the Federalists sought assistance. There was Texas, proud and contemptuous of the Mexico which had steadily refused to acknowledge her independence.

Since the French blockade on April 16, 1838, had closed the Mexican ports, until some were later opened under agreements with the Federalists, the citizens of northern Mexico, whether Federalists or Centralists, welcomed the opportunity to get supplies through Texas, and a brisk trade began to develop between the two areas. The Mexican government, itself, opened the port of Matamoros to a trade in certain articles prohibited from introduction at that place under the tariff laws of the country. The old smuggling route through Corpus Christi Bay was put to extensive use. It seems that the American smuggling schooner *Lodi*, at first incorrectly reported as the *Commanche*, put into Aransas before proceeding to Corpus Christi late in August 1838, to deliver her supplies to a Mexican party from the Centralist stronghold of Matamoros. Knowing the intentions of the *Lodi*, a party of Texans (previously discussed in chapter three) set out by land to relieve the Mexicans of the goods turned over to them.[51] Most of the supplies, however, were safely conveyed to a Mexican party of about twenty-five persons, who loaded a portion of the flour, along with other items, into a light craft and headed for Matamoros, where "flour and all imported articles were selling at exorbitant prices." General Edwin Morehouse, returning from the west early in September, reported that the party of Mexicans, recently at Corpus Christi, had retired precipitantly, possibly upon the approach of a Texan foraging party, leaving on the beach about one hundred barrels of flour (some good and a portion much damaged) and a new steam engine,[52] probably intended for the mines in the interior of Mexico. This phase of the United States-Mexican trade, although involving the use of Texas soil, brought in no remuneration in the form of import duties, and neither benefited Texans nor bolstered the tottering financial structure of the young republic.

[50] Cecil Alan Hutchinson, "Valentín Gómez Farías," Ph.D. dissertation, p. 455.
[51] A gentleman from Aransas, reporting in the *Telegraph and Texas Register,* Aug. 25, 1838, declared that the supplies were "beyond the reach of any pursuing foe."
[52] *Telegraph and Texas Register,* Sept. 8 and 22, 1838.

Long before this (on April 24, 1838) the desirability of putting the trade already developing on the frontier adjacent to Mexico on a legitimate status and bringing it under regulation was pointed out by the Secretary of War, Barnard E. Bee, in his report to Congress. Bee urged Congress to give "prompt attention" to regulating the trade between the inhabitants of San Antonio and the Mexican population beyond the Río Grande. "Much of the specie which is now passing through Matamoras to the United States," he declared, "would find its way here in exchange for Tobacco, an article indispensable to their comfort, and you would thus conciliate a class of harmless inhabitants, who would imperceptibly attach themselves to our institutions, whilst you would be opening new sources of wealth to our population." [53] Another question which he posed concerned the boundary of the republic. "As we claim to the river Río Grande," he asked, "are not the inhabitants as far as that boundary . . . as subject to the jurisdiction of this Government, also [entitled] to its protection and encouragement?" He also recommended that the Mexican families who had fled from Texas during the revolutionary disturbances of 1835–1836 be permitted to return if they wished to do so, as some had already indicated.

In the meantime, trading parties of Mexicans from Laredo and other Río Grande towns were beginning to arrive daily, first, at San Antonio and, later, at Goliad, Victoria, Matagorda,[54] Lamar, San Patricio, Houston,[55] and other points, bringing in specie, horses, sugar, and flour which they exchanged for tobacco, various items of merchandise, ammunition, rifles, and firearms of every description. The trade in firearms with the country's avowed enemies did not set well with many Texans, but the merchants of Béxar and elsewhere were not averse to making a fast dollar, even if it might mean the spilling of their own or some fellow-citizen's blood at some future date. The traders arriving at Matagorda early in December 1838, were described as being of "much more general intelligence than is usually found among the straggling drovers who visit our Republic for traffic."[56] Among them was a Frenchman who had lived for several years in Mexico.

[53] Report of the Secretary of War, Barnard E. Bee, to the Senate and House of Representatives of the Republic of Texas, War Department, April 24, 1838, in Army Papers (Texas), ms.

[54] *Matagorda Bulletin,* Dec. 6, 1838.

[55] Max Freund (trans. and ed.), *Gustav Dresel's Houston Journal: Adventures in North America and Texas, 1837–1841,* p. 37.

[56] *Matagorda Bulletin,* Dec. 6, 1838.

As the traders continued to pour in from northern Coahuila and Tamaulipas, they manifested the most friendly disposition toward Texas and Texans, and by mid-December 1838, were reporting the whole country along the Río Grande as having declared in favor of Federalism,[57] as if this were a better reason than ever why they should be kindly received in Texas. "They consider that since they have almost unanimously declared in favor of federalism," reported Dr. Alsbury from San Antonio, "there no longer exists an occasion for hostilities; and as the[ir] general government can afford them no protection [having withdrawn its troops from the frontiers of Tamaulipas, Coahuila, and Chihuahua leaving the inhabitants exposed to the Comanches], they wish to make common cause with our citizens against the savages."[58]

With the spread of Federalism in the north, even Mexican citizens of the Centralist party sought refuge in the Texas frontier towns, preferring "the tranquility enjoyed even among enemies to the horrors and turmoil of civil war."[59] But a few months before, the same refugees were using every means within their control to destroy the government that now extended them its protection. Among the refugees entering Béxar were Mexicans, who during the revolutionary disturbances of 1835–1836, had fled to the Río Grande country and beyond. Nearly two hundred of these families by April 1839 had returned to Béxar. Many of them were commencing the cultivation of the ranchos near Béxar that had been abandoned since the beginning of the Texas revolution.[60] Some were opening new farms. Others were settling in the vicinity of the ranchos Calvillo and Guadalupe-Victoria.

During its early stages the trade between the Texans and Mexicans had been carried on by stealth and was little more than a system of smuggling and barter; but in December 1838, the traders began to come in openly, protected by passports from the Federal commanders, and to pay specie for their purchases. Several thousand dollars in specie, a much needed item in Texas, were brought into San Antonio in the course of a week or two, and large quantities of silver were coming in from Chihauhua. One trader arrived with $17,000 in specie, and it was estimated in May 1839 that goods valued between $100,000

[57] *Telegraph and Texas Register,* Dec. 12, 1838.
[58] *Ibid.,* Dec. 19, 1838. See also *ibid.,* Jan. 18, 1839; *Matagorda Bulletin,* Jan. 10, 1839.
[59] *Telegraph and Texas Register,* Feb. 20, 1839.
[60] *Ibid.,* May 13 and April 10, 1839.

and $150,000 could be sold immediately at Béxar for specie or bullion.[61] Prices were high, and profits were good. Business in the frontier towns experienced a short-lived boom, and there were hopes for improved business conditions; at Houston, for instance, "tradesmen of all sorts" began to arrive "on horseback from the interior of the country, among them many a Mexican smuggler." [62] The *Matagorda Bulletin* of April 4, 1839, reported a brisk demand at Matagorda for goods suitable for the Mexican market. Although its editor lamented that ten mules laden with specie, having passed through Columbus headed for Matagorda, had turned eastward upon learning that "our market was bare of goods" and that an even larger party of traders, which crossed the Colorado about forty miles above Matagorda had done likewise, he was much gratified

. . . to see specie coming into the country, let it be deposited where it may. Had we a full supply of goods of the kind suited for that trade (chiefly dry goods), we are satisfied that a heavy business could be done; and it certainly will be to the interest of our merchants to secure the business of these specie-paying traders. . . . This trade is becoming one of vast importance, and it is to be hoped that our merchants will be sufficiently awake to their own interests to make an effort to realize from it the advantages that our favorable location secures to them.

A large *caballada* left Houston on Saturday, April 20, 1839, for the west "with merchandize to the amount of ten or fifteen thousand dollars," and another arrived in town on the 21st for further supplies.[63] After the founding of Austin, Mexican traders from the Río Grande with cattle and *piloncillas* reached the new capital on December 22, 1839.[64]

Canales, one of the leaders of the Federalists in Tamaulipas against Santa Anna's Centralism in 1835 and now again prominent in Federalist circles, addressed a friendly letter early in December 1838, to President Lamar in which he reviewed the objectives and successes of the Federalist movement. "The cause of liberty must infallibly triumph," he wrote, "and those towns and yours will again very shortly be united

[61] *Ibid.*, May 29, 1839.
[62] Freund (trans. and ed.), *Gustav Dresel's Houston Journal*, p. 37.
[63] *Morning Star*, April 22, 1839.
[64] *Telegraph and Texas Register*, Jan. 1, 1840.

in bonds of former amity." [65] In conclusion, he appealed to Lamar to apprehend all persons from the Río Grande who took mules, horses, or other property into Texas for sale, unless they could produce passports, signed by him or his authorized agent. Early in January 1839, traders from the Río Grande, possessing passports from the Federalists appeared in Texas to report the successes of the liberals in northern Mexico and to announce their desire to continue a free trade with Texas, asserting, at the same time, that the Federalists were friendly disposed towards Texas. [66] When the Third Congress met the same month it took notice of the Federalist movement on the Río Grande. The House of Representatives, in secret session, requested the President to transmit to it the correspondence of the Executive with the Federal leaders and to indicate if he thought it desirable to open communications with them. [67] On forwarding on January 16 a copy of the only letter he had received to date from the Federalists relating to the substance of the House resolution, Lamar informed the House of Representatives that, "The proposition made by Genl. Canales for such steps to be taken by this Government, as may preserve harmony on the border, is cordially received by the Executive, who is ever ready to reciprocate every friendly disposition, and to adopt all honorable measures which may tend to supercede the necessity of further hostilities"; but whether the procedure suggested by Canales was best calculated to accomplish the desired object, he would leave to the judgment of Congress, although he presumed a law on the subject might be of some benefit to Texas. No matter what Congress might determine in respect to the Mexican trade, the President suggested that the nation maintain military preparedness. In view of the present condition of the Republic's relations with Mexico, he could perceive of no benefit to the nation by communicating with Canales or any other

[65] Lic. Antonio Canales to the President of the Republic of Texas [M. B. Lamar], 3d Division of the Federal Army, Reynosa, Dec. 17, 1838, Domestic Correspondence (Texas), 1836–1846, ms., translation; Garrison (ed.), *Diplomatic Correspondence of Texas*, 1908, II, 430–431; *El Ancla*, Dec. 27, 1839; *Telégrafo de Tampico*, Dec. 12, 1838, in Consular Dispatches (Tampico), ms., microfilm; *La Concordia* (Ciudad Victoria), April 27, 1839. A notice of Canales' letter will be found in *Telegraph and Texas Register*, Jan. 9, 1839.

[66] Erasmo Seguin, Justice of the Peace, to the Secretary of State [of the Republic of Texas], Béjar, Jan. 23, 1839, in Mirabeau Buonaparte Lamar Papers, ms., Spanish; copy in Domestic Correspondence (Texas), 1836–1846, ms.

[67] *Lamar Papers*, II, 419–420.

official personage representing those in revolt against their government. Lamar emphasized that he thought the opening of trade with the northern revolutionists—an unconstituted authority—would soon degenerate into plunder, robbery, and murder; but, he continued,

. . . if it be the wish of Congress that a friendly intercourse and traffic with such of the Mexicans as are disposed to neutrality, or are in a state of hostility to their own Government, should be encouraged, it will be obvious that such intercourse and traffic, if not protected by a competent force on the border would soon . . . [become] altogether subversive of the peaceful ends for which they shall be established; and instead of being productive of good, would result in disastrous consequences to our citizens on the frontier, and destroy all the hopes of negotiation to which the present amicable feelings of the liberal party in Mexico, has given rise.[68]

By joint resolution, Congress on January 26 authorized the President to open trade between western Texas and the Mexicans on the Río Grande, and on February 21 Lamar issued a proclamation [69] opening the trade. Scarcely had this policy been instituted, however, when the French lifted their blockade of the Mexican ports on March 9, ended their war with Mexico, and Mexico forthwith cancelled her decree authorizing the importation at Matamoros of certain articles prohibited under the existing tariff laws while the blockade existed.[70] The net effect was to increase discontent in the north, especially among the supporters of the government who had profited by the trade funneling through this northern port, and to intensify the smuggling between the Río Grande towns and the Texas frontier by all Mexicans regardless of political creed. After about three months another decree permitted certain articles, hitherto prohibited, to enter the port of Matamoros.[71]

[68] M. B. Lamar to the House of Representatives, *c.* Jan. 16, 1839, in *ibid.*, II, 389–391.

[69] "An Act to open the trade between the citizens of the western portion of the Republic and the Mexicans residing near the Río Grande," *Journal of the House of Representatives of the Republic of Texas: Regular Session of Third Congress, Nov. 5, 1838*, pp. 407–408; H. P. N. Gammel (ed.), *Laws of Texas*, II, 117; "Proclamation opening a trade with the Mexican citizens on the Río Grande, February 21st 1839," *Lamar Papers*, II, 457–458.

[70] "Notice to Merchants," issued at Matamoros, April 1, 1839, by Valentín Canalizo, Pedro J. de la Garza, and Manuel Pina y Cuevas, in *Telegraph and Texas Register*, May 1, 1839; D. W. Smith to J. W. Breedlove, Collector of the Customs, N. Orleans [dated:] Consulate of the U. States, Matamoros, April 3, 1839, in *ibid.*

[71] *Colorado Gazette and Advertiser* (Matagorda), July 4, 1840.

But neither the average Texan nor his government was to be stampeded into rash action. Lamar saw in the internal disorders in Mexico, and in the French invasion, an opportunity to press for recognition of the independence of Texas, and he did not wish to jeopardize his chances of success in attaining this objective by offending the Centralist government. Especially did this seem to be the opportune time, since Santa Anna, following the battle of Vera Cruz, had once more become, in the eyes of the populace, the martyred hero bleeding for his country and had taken over the direction of the government from Bustamante.[72]

It looked now as if Santa Anna might be in a position to redeem the pledges he had made in the treaties of Velasco, although Texas had long given up the idea that those pledges were binding upon the Mexican government. Several determined efforts were made by Lamar during 1839 and 1840 to come to terms with Mexico through peaceful negotiation. In March 1839, the administration sent Richard Dunlap, who had been serving as Secretary of the Treasury, to Washington to solicit the good offices of the United States in solving its differences with Mexico. From New Orleans, Dunlap wrote Lamar urging that he give the Federalists an assist in getting recruits from the United States. "The signs are this way," wrote Dunlap.

Col. [D. J.] Woodlief and Colo Morehouse, or either or both, will take 500 men from this City to Tampico to join the federalists under Genl Mexia. . . . I promised to write you on this subject as you will have to pay $10,000 for the transportation of the men who will sail under the flag of the U. Sts. and seem to be mere volunteers from this City to aid Genl Mexia, who has some friends in this City. This may embarrass Col. Bee's mission but it can be done so as not to commit the Republic. You can think of this, and if you agree to pay the passage &c, authorise Morehouse as your Consul to draw on the Gove[rnmen]t for $20,000 as this will be ample. Col. Woodlief will

---

[72] The engagement with the French forces at Vera Cruz on December 5, 1838, in which Santa Anna played a cowardly role but was so severely wounded in the left leg that subsequently it had to be amputated, is fully told in Bancroft, *History of Mexico*, V, 197–200. By decree of January 23, 1839, Santa Anna was selected provisional president to take over the helm of government while Bustamante took the field to put down the spreading revolt centered at Tampico. After being in office some four months and witnessing the success of Bustamante and others in suppression of the Federalists in the North and conscious of the great financial problem confronting the government, Santa Anna quietly withdrew from the Presidency, thus permitting the restoration of Bustamante.

resign if he goes. Write him or Morehouse. I believe that 1,000 Americans at this time would give the federal party the ascendancy.[73]

Lamar did not have the money for this purpose, and his policy was not to involve the government of Texas in the Federalist cause, although he had no objection to Texans volunteering as individuals for its support.

About the time that Dunlap was sent to Washington, Colonel Barnard E. Bee, Lamar's Secretary of State, was replaced by James Webb, and was dispatched to Mexico to negotiate for the recognition of Texas independence and to conclude a treaty of peace, amity, commerce, navigation and limits.[74]

While Bee prepared to go to Vera Cruz, the merits of the Texan policy of "watchful waiting," as it concerned the Federalist cause, were revealed by the sudden collapse of the Federalist forces in the late spring and summer of 1839. This collapse was brought on by the government's settling its score with the French in March, the lifting of the blockade of its ports, and the evacuation of San Juan de Ulloa by the French on April 7,[75] which thus released troops to suppress the

[73] James Webb to Richard Dunlap, Department of State, City of Houston, March 13, 1839, in Garrison (ed.), *Diplomatic Correspondence of Texas*, 1907, I, 368–372; R. G. Dunlap to M. B. Lamar, New Orleans, April 4, 1839, in *Lamar Papers*, II, 513–515.

[74] James Webb to Barnard E. Bee, Houston, Feb. 20, 1839, in Garrison, *Diplomatic Correspondence of Texas*, II, 433–434. For a discussion of these negotiations, see Schmitz, *Texan Statecraft*, pp. 88–89.

[75] Upon leaving Mexican waters, Rear-Admiral Charles Baudin touched at Velasco on May 5, where he, E. Maissin, and Chaucart, his aides-de-camp, in company with General Thomas Jefferson Green and Lieutenant A. Clendennin proceeded overland to Houston, while his vessels continued on to Galveston. After several days of festivities at the Texan capital with President Lamar and Dr. Ashbel Smith, the Admiral proceeded by steamboat to Galveston to rejoin his fleet. E. Maissin, *Notes et Documents et un apercu général sur l'état du Texas, avec un grand nombre de belles gravures*, pp. 522–525; Galveston City to His Excellency, the Admiral Baudin, Commander-in-Chief of his Most Christian Majesty's Blockading Squadron off the Coast of Mexico: We, the Mayor and Aldermen of the City of Galveston [etc., offering the freedom of the city "in consideration of your gallant deportment at the siege and capture of St. John de Ulloa," dated at end, May 14, 1839, and signed by John M. Allen, Mayor, eight Aldermen, including Gail Borden, Jr., and other officials] [At end:] Gladwin & Mims, Printers. [Galveston, 1839] The broadside should have been dated May 13, instead of May 14, as the festivities took place on the 13th. See Baudin to the Mayor and Aldermen of Galveston, May 13, 1839 (A. L. S., San Jacinto Museum of History), thanking the

insurrection at home; by the bringing in of munitions thereafter from the United States; [76] by President Bustamante himself taking the field against the Federalists on March 18, leaving the government in the hands of Provisional President Santa Anna; by a division within the ranks of the Federalists; and by the failure of the Federalists to win the support of the populace, who too often regarded them as little better, if as good, as the Centralists. The Centralists usually, under *these* particular circumstances, respected private property and paid for what was requisitioned. It has been said that Zapata, being forced to evacuate Soto la Marina, demanded money and goods from the citizens, and drove off horses and mules from the summer pastures, leaving cattle dead in the fields and committing many iniquities and depredations—all in the name of liberty.[77] The church of Mineral de San Nicolás was robbed of its silver and sacred vessels, and "citizens of both sex had been spoiled by rough usage." The Centralist press accused Zapata and his 260 "villianous fellows," who called themselves Federalists, of committing in the towns [78] of northern Nuevo León innumerable vexations, robberies, violences, assaults, oppressions, waste, ruin, and desolation upon honest, innocent, and peaceful citizens.[79] Zapata's actions were described as "marked by much barbarity." [80] Tales of such depredations, too often true, hurt the Federalist cause. However, on August 11 Zapata was surprised by Colonel Domingo Buiza and decisively defeated. Those of his followers who survived fled in great disorder. Zapata, himself, fled precipitantly in his shirt-sleeves.

As the reader may recall, Urrea suffered defeat in October 1838 in Sonora and was reported to have fled on foot with twelve associates through Durango headed toward Tampico, which he reached on November 8 and was there given command of the "Second Liberating Section" of the Federalist army. From San Juan de Úlloa, where he had gone with Mejía to confer with Admiral Baudin, Urrea addressed

---

people of Galveston for their courtesies. The broadside invitation and the admiral's reply were published in the *Galvestonian*, May 16, 1839.

[76] R. G. Dunlap to M. B. Lamar, New York, July 21, 1839, in Garrison (ed.), *Diplomatic Correspondence of Texas*, 1907, I, 410–414.

[77] *La Concordia*, May 25, 1839.

[78] Villa Aldama, Bustamante, Salinas, Victoria, Abasolo, San Nicolás, Hidalgo, San Francisco de Cañas, and Villa de Marín.

[79] *Gaceta de Tampico*, Aug. 31, 1839; *La Concordia*, Aug. 31, 1839.

[80] *Telegraph and Texas Register*, Aug. 7, 1839.

his troops at Tampico on February 18, urging them to remain true to the cause of liberalism and new freedom, after which he marched with the main unit of his forces into the interior.[81] En route to San Luis Potosí, where Bustamante had taken up his position, he was defeated by the Centralists under Manuel Romero,[82] but succeeded in effecting a junction with Mejía's forces on March 25 at Tuxpan. The same day General Arista,[83] leading troops from Mexico City, took Tula de Tamaulipas, and the vanguard of his command under Benito Quijano entered Ciudad Victoria on March 27.[84] Soon Linares and Santa Barbara fell, and by the end of May 1839, the state of Tamaulipas was rapidly submitting to the Central authorities.

General Cós was entrusted by Bustamante with an expedition against Tuxpan, but was routed on March 15 [85] by the Federalists under Mejía after a heated engagement of three and a half hours. In preparing now to assume the offensive, Mejía looked to Tampico for re-enforcements. Five American merchant vessels lying in the port of Tampico at the time were impressed to transport them. An agent of General Peraga [86] offered the captains of the *Andrew Jackson, Creole, Francis Amy, Tenesaw,* and *Jane* a twelve day contract each at $63.50 per diem, payable in advance, to carry munitions of war and troops to an unnamed destination. Upon their refusal to accept such an arrangement on any terms, they were given to understand distinctly that if they did not accept the offer they would be forced to do so. In order to meet the time schedule that had been set up for the movement of the Federalist troops, it was necessary to march a portion of the Tampico troops overland to Tuxpan, while the vessels on April 9 and 10, loaded with troops, arms, provisions, and other effects, proceeded along the coast.

[81] Address of José Urrea, General in Chief of the Mexican Army of Liberty, to the Federal Troops under his Command, Garrison in Ulloa, February 18 [1839], in *Telegraph and Texas Register,* March 6, 1839.

[82] *El Mosquito Mexicano,* April 26, 1839; *Telegraph and Texas Register,* March 6, 1839.

[83] "Itinerario de las campanas en Tamaulipas, Coahuila y N. León, desde 23 de Febrero de 1839 hasta hoy 28 de Marzo de 1841," in *El Ancla,* March 29, 1841.

[84] *La Concordia,* April 4, 1839.

[85] José Antonio Mejía's Report of the Battle, Tuxpan, March 15, 1839, in *Morning Star,* April 11, 1839. Cós lost all of his artillery, mules, baggage, 350 muskets, and many other items.

[86] Although the name is reported as Pedraza by Captain Meldrum, apparently the person referred to was Martin Peraga, who had only recently landed at Tampico with Mejía.

The troops were landed upon arrival at Tuxpan, but the guns and other effects were left on board without any orders as to their disposition. While awaiting further orders before Tuxpan, one of the American captains became disgusted and left the Federal service. After fourteen days in this employ, eight of which was at sea before Tuxpan without orders, "riding in an open roadstead, having parted my chain and lost my anchor," wrote the captain of the *Andrew Jackson*, whose men were showing signs of mutiny, "I left this service and set sail for Mobile," where the arms were voluntarily surrendered to the customs collector.[87] Mejía's subsequent defeat was in part attributed to his shortage of arms and munitions due to the departure of the *Andrew Jackson*.

After some delay at Tuxpan, the troops were loaded on the four remaining vessels and transported along with the supplies to the Barra de Tecolutla,[88] forty leagues from Vera Cruz, where the troops were landed on April 14, a week after the French evacuated San Juan de Úlloa,[89] and moved inland by-passing the Fortress of Perote to strike the Puebla-Vera Cruz-Mexico City road. The combined forces of Mejía and Urrea, numbering some nine hundred men, sought to advance upon Puebla, approximately seventy miles from the City of Mexico,

[87] John M. Meldrum [Captain of the *Andrew Jackson*] to the Editor of the *Mobile Register*, reproduced in the *Telegraph and Texas Register*, June 12, 1839; *Telegraph and Texas Register*, May 15, 1839; see extract of an unsigned letter, dated Tampico, April 18, 1839, in *Morning Star*, May 6, 1839.

[88] John G. McCall to John Forsyth, Tampico, April 19, 1839, in *Consular Dispatches* (Tampico), ms., microfilm; *El Mosquito Mexicano*, April 19, 1839, says the expedition landed at Tecolutla, and on May 14, quoting *La Concordia* of April 18, says the contracted vessels had sailed for Vera Cruz, but while en route two American vessels appeared and demanded that they strike the United States colors, otherwise they would be considered violating the neutrality laws of the United States. The American captains refused to haul down their colors, and it was implied that Mejía paid off at this point. The American captains, we know, were paid in advance; what is probably meant by Mejía's paying off at this point was that the troops were landed and it was presumed that the vessels were released from further service. We know that the troops were landed at Tecolutla, and it must be presumed that the United States naval units intercepted the merchantmen in that vicinity.

[89] The Mexican government concluded a treaty on March 9 ending its difficulties with the French. The treaty was ratified by Mexico on March 21 and accepted by Admiral Baudin on March 29, 1839. In compliance with the terms of the treaty, the French evacuated San Juan de Úlloa on April 7, 1839. See Charles Baudin's Order of the Day, Frigate Nereide, Port of Vera Cruz, March 29, 1839, in *Telegraph and Texas Register*, April 24, 1839; Bancroft, *History of Mexico*, V, 203–204, 210.

where many adherents stood ready to rise. At this point, Provisional President Santa Anna, with reluctant permission from the Council, seeing the Federalist threat to Puebla and Vera Cruz, which Mejía doubtless had in mind seizing upon the withdrawal of the French troops from San Juan de Ûlloa, quickly left Mexico City with a sizable force to impede Mejía's march. Santa Anna reached Puebla on April 30, and prevented it from rising to join the approaching Federalist forces. Three days later, on May 3, Mejía and Urrea were intercepted at Acajete, near Puebla on the Puebla-Vera Cruz road, by General Valencia and defeated on the plain of San Miguel.[90] Mejía was captured and executed within half an hour of his capture.[91] In the eyes of his countrymen he had been guilty of unpardonable treason in bringing foreign adventurers into the country.[92]

Urrea escaped capture and with three hundred followers fled to Tampico, which was well fortified and supported by a number of small gunboats. The commander of the gunboats, Barbarena, however, soon joined the Centralist side, thus depriving the city of supplies and exposing it to attack from its most vulnerable side. The city fell on June 6 without bloodshed to General Arista who had invested it since May 26,[93] but Urrea was able to slip out before its surrender. He fled to

[90] Proclamation of Anastasio Bustamante to the Soldiers, Ciudad-Victoria, May 10, 1839, in *Telegraph and Texas Register*, July 3, 1839; D. W. Smith to John Forsyth, Matamoros, May 17, 1839, no. 156, in Consular Dispatches (U. S.), 1837–1839 (Matamoros), ms., microfilm.

[91] Rives, *The United States and Mexico*, I, 450; Supplement to *Diario del Gobierno* (Mexico City), May 4, 1839; H. Yoakum, *History of Texas from Its First Settlement in 1685 to Its Annexation to the United States in 1846*, II, 274. Mejía was unable to effect his escape because of wounds, and was captured and executed by order of Santa Anna. It has been said, probably on insufficient authority, that Santa Anna after the battle of Acajete, on May 3, 1839, "sent Mejía a message that he was to be put to death in half an hour. 'He is very kind,' was the alleged reply, 'but if I had taken him, I would have shot him inside of five minutes.'" Rives, *The United States and Mexico*, I, 450.

[92] Manuel Rivera, *Los gobernantes de Mexico*, II, 220.

[93] The Articles of Capitulation of Tampico, June 4, 1839, are printed in the *Telegraph and Texas Register*, July 3, 1839. The surrender was effective June 6, 1839. It will be of interest to Texans to know that the Federals used the former Texan war schooner, *Independence*, captured by the Mexicans on April 17, 1837, in the defense of Tampico, but that its crew was surprised by 600 infantrymen under Arista from Altamira who arrived on the night of May 27, 1839, and captured it in a few minutes. *Telegraph and Texas Register*, June 17, 1839.

Tuxpan, which place surrendered on June 13.[94] This time, however, Urrea made an arrangement with General Paredes, whereby he was to return to service in the Mexican army and be confirmed in his position and honors as a general. Santa Anna disapproved of the agreement, and ordered Urrea into exile for six years, but on his way to Vera Cruz under guard he succeeded in escaping, and disappeared for a time. He was again taken and imprisoned in the City of Mexico, where he plotted with other revolutionists and almost succeeded in overthrowing the government in July 1840. The next year Santa Anna rewarded him for his help in overthrowing the government of Bustamante by appointing him commandant general of Sonora.[95]

Shortly after the defeat of Mejía, the Federalists suffered another serious blow, this time in the disablement of the steam packet *Pontchartrain* (formerly the *Mediterranean*), of 300 tons and mounting three 12-pound cannon, "commanded" by Colonel F. J. Ribaud,[96] a Frenchman, sea captain, and former member of the Centralist army who had sought from Lamar command of the new Texas navy being constructed at Baltimore.[97] The *Pontchartrain* had been fitted out as a man-of-war, or transport, at New Orleans. Her papers showed that she was registered and owned by an American citizen named Francisco Cowejolles, and that her crew and captain (Arthur Hughes) were Americans, with few exceptions. The *Pontchartrain* left New Orleans under American registry on May 16, 1839, for Tampico for sale to the Federalists. Three of its six boilers exploded or burnt out—one on May 22, a second on the 23rd, and the third on the 24th—as a result of the accumulation of salt in them while on their way from New Orleans to Tampico. The captain, having learned of Mejía's defeat and other signal reverses of the Federalist party before leaving New Orleans, felt compelled to put into a Texas port. Ribaud ordered the vessel's captain to direct his course for Galveston, but the distance was too great and on May 27 the *Pontchartrain* entered the port of Paso Cavallo under a crudely constructed rigging and sail of blankets and sheets sewn together, after having drifted at the mercy of winds and current for four days.

[94] *Morning Star*, July 12, 1839; *Telegraph and Texas Register*, July 19, 1839.
[95] Bancroft, *History of Mexico*, V, 238.
[96] This name was variously spelled in the press: Ribaud, Rebau, Rebec, Reibau, and Rebeau.
[97] Hill, *The Texas Navy*, p. 110; Willis Roberts to M. B. Lamar, Galveston, June 20, 1839, in *Lamar Papers*, V, 296.

It was believed in Texas, however, that the vessel could have limped into the port of Brazos de Santiago or some other Mexican port had it so desired, but would likely have fallen into the hands of the Centralists. The sheriff of Matagorda County detained the vessel as a lawful prize of war, and had her towed by the *Newcastle* from Paso Cavallo to Matagorda.[98] When informed of the presence of the Mexican vessel in a Texas port, Acting Secretary of State Burnet ordered the new naval agent, William T. Brannum, to Matagorda to make an on the spot investigation and report on the condition of the vessel, its armament, and munitions.[99] If the vessel were American property and contained no unusual amount of arms it was to be released; but if Brannum found it to be an armed Mexican vessel, then he was to retain it until he could report and receive instructions from the government. If, however, he found it to be private property "whether Mexican or not," and had no unusual quantity of arms or ammunition on board, he was "to order her immediate release, as this Government," said Burnet, "must always esteem a non-combatant enemy in distress as entitled to its hospitalities."

Brannum reported that he found no "unusual" quantity of arms and ammunition on board the *Pontchartrain*. He, therefore, ordered the vessel released, and left orders with the customs collector "to permit her to depart from that port at pleasure," [100] but, it might be said here, the *Pontchartrain* saw no further service in the Federal cause.

The loss of Tampico and Tuxpan were severe blows to the Federalists in the east, and the liberal terms under which they had surrendered to the Centralists tended to promote harmony and unity of feeling among the people. The officers, chiefs, and soldiers of the rebel party

[98] *Colorado Gazette and Advertiser* (Matagorda), June 6, 1839; Captain F. J. Reibau to President Lamar [on Board the Steamer *Pontchartrain*], Bay of Matagorda, May 27, 1839; both in State Department Letterbook, no. 2, ms., pp. 270–272; David G. Burnet, Acting Secretary of State, to Captain F. Reibau, on board the Steamer *Pontchartrain*, [dated:] Department of State, Houston, June 8, 1839, in *ibid.*, no. 1, ms., pp. 100–101; F. Reibaud to David G. Burnet, [Matagorda, n. d.], being copy of a letter left with the Collector of the Port of Matagorda, in *ibid.*, no. 2, ms., p. 272.

[99] David G. Burnet, Acting Secretary of State, to William T. Brannum, Navy Agent, Department of State, Houston, June 8, 1839, in *ibid.*, no. 1, ms., p. 100.

[100] *Telegraph and Texas Register,* June 5 and 26, 1839; William T. Brannum to David G. Burnet, Houston, June 19, 1839, in *ibid.*, June 26, 1839; William T. Brannum to [Collector of the Port of Matagorda], Matagorda, June 14, 1839, in State Department Letterbook, no. 2, ms., p. 272.

were accorded the privilege of reinstatement in the Mexican army at their former ranks or of withdrawing from the service if they so desired. Quickly the Federalist cause collapsed elsewhere, if but only temporarily. The liberal cause in the north, for many years to come, did not regain the ground it lost in the spring and summer of 1839. In Texas, the editor of the *Telegraph and Texas Register* [101] witnessed with alarm the turn of events in Mexico by the middle of 1839, and felt that as soon as the civil war there was ended Texas could look forward to a renewal of the Mexican effort to subjugate her lost colony.

After the defeat of Mejía, Lemus captured Saltillo on May 24,[102] but upon the approach of Governor Francisco García Conde, whom he had only recently caused to flee from the city, Lemus abandoned Saltillo about June 21 and moved to Monclova. Lemus' little detachment was pictured in the New Orleans *Louisianan* as "composed entirely of rancheros, a half-savage kind of people, undisciplined, not perfectly acquainted with the signification of the words *federation* and *centralism*, who have taken up arms with the sole view of avenging the horrors which they endured from the government troops in the Texian campaigns, and the various excursions which the army of Matamoros made in their province." [103] At Monclova Lemus sought to gain control of the entire Federalist forces,[104] and there was even suspicion that he would seek to dissolve the Federalists if he could not command them.

Such was the condition within the Federalist ranks when Juan Pablo Anaya, called the "Stranger," a well-known liberal from the South, appeared in the Río Grande area about August 1.[105] Accompanied by two men dressed as muleteers, Anaya reached Monclova in disguise. Here he conferred with Canales and Zapata and an intrigue was commenced to supplant Lemus in command with General Anaya.[106] Canales informed Anaya of Lemus' designs upon the army. Anaya and his co-

---

[101] July 19, 1839.
[102] Colonel Domingo Ugartechea was killed while attempting to defend the city. Bancroft, *History of Mexico*, V. 209 n.
[103] *Louisianan* (New Orleans), quoted in the *Austin City Gazette*, Nov. 6, 1839.
[104] Antonio Canales to Juan Pablo Anaya, Villa Aldama, Aug. 3, 1839, in Juan Pablo de Anaya Papers, ms.
[105] Horace V. Harrison, "Juan Pablo Anaya: Champion of Mexican Federalism," Ph.D. dissertation, p. 396.
[106] "Information derived from Dr. John Long, resident of Santa Rosa, Coahuila, Mexico," in Lamar Papers, ms.

conspirators moved the larger portion of the Federal volunteer army out of the city, leaving Lemus behind with a small garrison of regulars; but he, too, soon took his troops out and headed for Texas only to run into further difficulties.

At Villa de Aldama, Colonel Antonio Zapata, in command of the first section of the Federal army, called a meeting of the officers and men. The group drafted and signed a protest expressing a lack of confidence in Lemus' designs and leadership, ending with a declaration of support of Anaya by all the forces from the *villas* of the frontier.[107] Anaya was now given a commission by Canales on August 8, similar to the one he had received a month earlier from Manuel María de Llano, self-styled provisional president of Nuevo León,[108] naming him an emissary to Texas and the United States to solicit aid from government, associations, *empresarios,* companies, and individuals in transporting arms through Texas to the Federalists and in the recruiting of troops.[109] A week later Jesús Cárdenas, referring to himself as a representative of the people of the state of Tamaulipas, likewise commissioned Anaya.[110] Canales and Zapata both seemed anxious to be rid of Anaya whom they had just helped to elevate to the position of commander in chief. They were apparently glad for him to go abroad as the Federalist agent; and Anaya, no doubt, realizing that outside help was a *sine qua non* in achieving their ultimate objective and that whoever succeeded in bringing this help might win everlasting fame, if successful, seemed willing enough to make the attempt.

Before leaving for Texas, Anaya conferred with the top Federalist leaders, at which time it was agreed that the Texas government should be told that in return for furnishing 1,500 volunteers to the Federal cause, the Federalists would recognize the independence of Texas with its southern boundary at the San Antonio River. It was reported in the Centralist controlled newspaper, *El Gaceta del Gobierno de Zacatecas,*[111] that the Texan volunteers were each to be offered 500

---

[107] Document signed by the officers and men of the First Section of the Federal Army, Villa de Aldama, August 4, 1839, in Anaya Papers, ms. Among those signing the protest were Canales, Zapata, José González, Basilio Benavides, and others.

[108] Manuel María de Llano to Juan Pablo Anaya, Cerralvo, July 10, 1839, in Anaya Papers, ms.

[109] Antonio Canales to Juan Pablo Anaya, Aug. 8, 1839, in *ibid.*

[110] Jesús Cárdenas to Juan Pablo Anaya, Guerrero, Aug. 15, 1839, in *ibid.*

[111] Dec. 1, 1839; David Martell Vigness, "The Republic of the Río Grande: An Example of Separatism in Northern Mexico," Ph.D. dissertation, p. 140.

pesos and "free hands" in captured towns. It is inconceivable that the Federalist leadership planned to permit the Texans to loot captured towns, for to have done so would surely have turned away any prospective cooperation from the people of the areas they hoped to take over from their political opponents. It would seem likely, therefore, that this is nothing more than a specie of Centralist propaganda.

While the Federalist leaders planned for the future, their current military operations were fast approaching a *dénouement*. Recapturing Monterey, Canalizo left Colonel José María de Ortega in command while he pursued the Federalists northward.[112] On August 10 he was at Villa de Aldama. As he proceeded along the route from Monterey to Monclova,[113] Canalizo learned on August 13 that Pedro Lemus and his brother, José, had been abandoned by most of their men due to the dissension between the former and Anaya and his associates, and were preparing to flee to Texas, leaving Apolinario Morales in command of the Federalists at Monclova. Monclova fell, a few days later, to the Centralists. Lemus was defeated on August 18 by Pavón at Loma Alta, six leagues from the Lampazos road toward Laredo.[114] Pedro Lemus and approximately forty followers succeeded in effecting their escape to Guerrero, where, in the act of crossing the Río Grande, they were captured on August 21 by Lieutenant Manuel Menchaca, military commander of the Villa de Guerrero.[115] Among

[112] José María de Ortega, Coronel de Ejército y Commandante general interino de Departmento de Nuevo León á sus habitantes, Monterey, Agosto 15 de 1839, in *Gaceta de Tampico*, Sept. 7, 1839.

[113] *Gaceta de Tampico*, Sept. 7, 1839.

[114] Francisco González Pavón á [Valentín Canalizo, Commandante en gefe del Ejército del Norte] Campo sobre Loma Alta, 6 leguas del camino Lampazos hacia a Laredo, Aug. 18, 1839, in Supplement to *ibid.*, Aug. 31, 1839; *La Brisa*, Sept. 20, 1839.

[115] A copy of Lt. Don Manuel Menchaca's report to Valentín Canalizo, dated August 24, 1839, and transmitted by the latter to the Governor of the Department of Nuevo León, was published as a broadside in two columns by the Secretario de Gobierno de Nuevo León at Monterey on August 28, 1839, on the press of the *Seminario Político del Gobierno de Nuevo León* (Monterey), (an original copy is in the Thomas W. Streeter Collection); Valentín Canalizo to the Governor of Nuevo León, Aug. 19, 1839, in *Seminario Político del Gobierno de Nuevo León*, Aug. 22, 1839; *La Brisa*, Sept. 6, 1836 [1839]; Bustamante, *El gabinete mexicano*, I, 203–204; Bancroft, *History of Mexico*, V, 214 n. Bancroft says that Lemus, his brother, 18 officers, and 2 commissioners on their way to seek Texan aid were captured near Rosas at the end of August. He seems to be in error, for my account here has been based upon the official Mexican reports. Near the Island

the captives were Severo Ruiz and Mauricio Carrasco, both of whom had been commissioned by Lemus to seek aid from Texas. They were granted amnesty upon agreeing to renounce Federalism.[116]

In August, Guerrero, Nava, Morelos, San Fernando de Rosas, and Presidio del Río Grande were retaken or renounced Federalism.[117] Late in August a minor engagement between Canalizo's forces and some of the Federalists at Palo Alto resulted in the capture of seven pieces of artillery by the Centralists.[118]

So rapid was the pacification of the revolt along the northern frontier in the late summer and early fall of 1839 that Canalizo was induced to issue an address to his troops congratulating them on their untiring attention to duty and the burning patriotism exhibited in their many heroic deeds in the suppression of the rebellion and castigation of *los colonials*. After an eleven months' campaign, he declared, only a few petty rebel leaders—Canales, Anaya, and Zapata—had not surrendered, but had fled to the other side of the Río Bravo.[119] Canalizo's

---

of Lobos on October 10, 1840, Commodore E. W. Moore of the Texas navy intercepted the Mexican schooner *Conchita* bound from Tampico to Vera Cruz with a number of Federalist prisoners, among whom were Pedro Lemus, his brother (Colonel Lemus), the general's wife and six children. The general and colonel had been in prison fourteen months at Matamoros for espousing the Federal cause. Moore took the prisoners on board his vessel, the *Austin*, and landed them in the rebellious state of Yucatán, where Lemus became Minister of War and Marine. In the fall of 1842, he deserted to Centralism, and joined the forces which were soon to invade the revolting state of Yucatán under the leadership of Pedro de Ampudia, the "hero of Mier." Lemus died in the City of Mexico in April 1847, where he was serving at the time as military commandant of the city. E. W. Moore to M. B. Lamar, Austin, Dec. 20, 1847, in *Lamar Papers*, IV, pt. I, 189–190; E. W. Moore to Louis P. Cooke, Texas Sloop of War *Austin*, mouth of Tabasco River, Dec. 24, 1840, in Harriet Smither (ed.), *Journals of the Sixth Congress of the Republic of Texas*, III, 372, 375. The date shown in the foregoing *Journal* is 1841, but the letter is one of the documents included in the Report of the Chief Clerk of the Naval Bureau, Austin, Oct. 1, 1840; therefore, this must be a misprint.

[116] A copy of Canalizo's Proclamation of Amnesty, dated Villa de Aldama, Aug. 25, 1839, may be found in *La Brisa*, Sept. 20, 1839.

[117] Valentín Canalizo ál Gobernador del Departamento de Nuevo León, Cuartel General en Villa Aldama, Agosto 26 de 1839, in *Gaceta de Tampico*, Sept. 14, 1839.

[118] *La Brisa*, Aug. 30, 1839. No exact date for this engagement is given, but judging from the article, it seems to have been a recent one.

[119] Valentín Canalizo, El general en gefe de la Division del Norte á sus subordinados, Cuartel General de Matamoros y Noviembre —— de 1839. Broadside.

address seems to have been a little premature, judging by the events that were soon to transpire.

Following the restoration of order on the northern frontier, Canalizo established a garrison at Mier under Colonel Francisco Pavón and stationed other troops across the river to obstruct the passage of Texans into Mexico.[120] Manuel de la Fuente was placed in command of a small body of troops on the east bank of the Río Grande to protect Laredo. Other garrisons were stationed at Lampazos, Agua Leguas, and Villa de Aldama at the mouth of the Cañon de Sabinas. Pedro de Ampudia succeeded Arista as commandant general *ad interim* of the Department of Tamaulipas in September when the latter was named commandant general of the Departments of Coahuila and Nuevo León.[121]

[120] *La Concordia*, Oct. 12, 1839.

[121] *La Concordia*, Dec. 14, 1839; Mariano Arista to the Inhabitants of Tamaulipas, Tampico, Sept. 11, 1839, in *Gaceta de Tamaulipas*, Sept. 21, 1839, announcing his transfer and the appointment of Pedro de Ampudia as Commandant General; *La Brisa*, Oct. 4, 1839.

171

CHAPTER TEN

Mexican Federalists
Seek Support in Texas

IT WAS ONLY NATURAL that any movement in behalf of republicanism in Mexico should attract attention in Texas whose citizens less than two years before had themselves revolted against the centralizing tendencies of Santa Anna. Many of the active participants in the liberal movement in the north in the late 1830's were the same men who had shown some willingness to cooperate with the Texans in 1835–1836 until they became convinced that the objective of the Anglo-Texans was the complete separation from Mexico rather than a movement to restore the principles of the constitution of 1824. With this realization of the true objective of the "rebelled colonists," most of the liberal Mexican leaders—men like José María González, Antonio Canales, Juan Nepomuceno Molano, Pedro Lemus, José Lemus, and Julian Miracle, whom we have already noted—lost interest in the Texan revolutionary movement for they had no desire to assist in the dismemberment of their homeland, Mexico. They were at heart, first, Mexicans, interested in the preservation of the territorial integrity of the nation; and, second, believers in the principles of republicanism. This same love of country doomed their efforts in 1838–1840 to restore the republicanism of 1824 when they appealed to outsiders for help.

The reader must understand that the Federalist movement of 1838–1840 was neither the first nor the last in the first hundred years of Mexico's national history. No effort is made here to trace the history of Mexican federalism. Neither does the scope of this work justify going into all the ramifications of the Federalist disturbances of 1838–1839. This narrative is restricted to the developments occurring in the northern departments as they affected Texas-Mexican frontier relations, and is intended to show that the revolutionary movements of the Federalists were one of the causes which secured for Texas a long interval of peace after the failure of the Mexican campaign in Texas in the spring of 1836.

Federalists Seek Support in Texas

As the Federalist movement broke out in the northern departments in the winter of 1837 the Texas press carried the news of the successes and defeats of the Federalists, discussed their objectives, and speculated on the probable effects of the movement upon future Texas-Mexican relations. It was only natural that different views should be taken and expressed about the civil strife in Mexico, especially since it often involved a large section of the southern and western border of Texas and since the young nation was still technically at war with Mexico.

From the very beginning of the Mexican war, arch-Federalists sought to win support in Texas for their cause. From New Orleans, an ardent and devoted friend of Texas independence, O. de A. Santángelo,[1] a former editor of the defunct *Correo de Atlántico*, a liberal Mexican paper, outlined to Francis Moore, Jr., editor of the *Telegraph and Texas Register*, a plan for the creation of a North Mexican Republic with the aid of Texas. Santángelo, a Neopolitan by birth, had been exiled from his native land in 1821 because of his political beliefs. He resided in Spain for a brief period, and from there went to New

---

[1] A biographical sketch of O. de Santángelo will be found in *Lamar Papers*, VI, 270–271. A petition relative to a claim of Santángelo for losses sustained in behalf of the Texas Revolution was introduced in the Third Congress. "Among the ardent and devoted friends of Texas," declared the *Telegraph and Texas Register* (Houston), Nov. 21, 1838, in supporting the petition, "there have been none more efficient and disinterested than this venerable man who was among the first of foreign journalists to espouse our cause, and labored fearlessly and unremittingly during the hour of our country's suffering." One of the editors of the *Correo de Atlántico* was George Fisher, who presented in 1838 copies of the newspaper to the various departments of government of Texas. The *Correo de Atlántico*, a semiweekly newspaper, was published at Mexico City through Number 16, when its editor, O de A. Santángelo (head of a seminary in the city) was forced to flee from the country. He resumed publication of the paper at New Orleans on February 29, 1836, where it was continued until issue Number 41, dated August 15, 1836, "when in consequence of the want of patronage the Editors were compelled to suspend its publication." The "want of patronage" was due, as Santángelo explained in his petition, to his Mexican federalist friends withdrawing their financial support of the paper when he began to advocate the Texan cause of "absolute independence." "These gentlemen had taken it into their heads," declared Santángelo, "that the independence of Texas, although it was the inevitable result of unjust and ferocious aggression, and of the apathy of the other Mexican States in opposing the march of centralism, was neither more or less than a dismemberment of the Mexican territory." "Petition of O. de A. Santángelo to the Honorable Congress of the Republic of Texas, April 22, 1838," in *Lamar Papers*, II, 143–152; see also *Telegraph and Texas Register*, Aug. 23, 1836.

173

York and then to Mexico, where he offended the imperialists and was exiled, only to return after the fall of Iturbide. He later established a newspaper, called the *Correo de Atlántico*, in which he boldly defended the rights of the Texans. The result was a second expulsion from Mexico in June 1835, by order of General Santa Anna and the loss of considerable amounts of property. Santángelo then moved his newspaper to New Orleans and continued its publication for about a year. His hatred of Centralism was thus deeply rooted, and the opening of Federal activities in northern Mexico caused him to explain in March 1839, that the enemy of Texas was not Mexico but the Centralists who had destroyed the federal plan of government in Mexico. The Texans, he explained, had drawn the sword in 1835–1836 against those who sought to destroy the federal system, not against the Federal party. As long as the independence of Texas was not recognized by Mexico and the latter continued to threaten to subjugate her rebelled province, Texas would find it difficult to obtain European recognition and immigrants. The possibility of a renewal of the war by Mexico, he wrote,

. . . alone will always prove an insurmountable obstacle to every moral, industrious, and commercial improvement of [the] infant Republic. . . . War, in all the strength of the word, is still subsisting between Texas and Mexico, just as it was at the time of capture of the hero of the Alamo. The subsequent suspension of arms, has been but the effect of the actual weakness of the Mexicans and of the edifying moderation of the Texians, but it could cease on the part of either of the belligerent parties, without their having the slightest reason to complain of any want of good faith, as no convention has ever been made between them on this subject.[2] If, then, war authorize[s] hostilities and hostilities must chiefly tend to oblige the enemy to sue for peace as soon as possible, this is undoubtedly the moment to which the Texians ought to take up arms again.

Santángelo proposed the creation of an alliance between Texas and a federation composed of Tamaulipas, Jalisco, Nuevo León, San Luis Potosí, Coahuila, Zacatecas, Durango, Sinaloa, Chihuahua, Nuevo México, and the Californias. Already, he said,

the brave and enlightened Lamar by opening a commercial intercourse between Mexico and Texas, has prepared the materials for the beautiful

[2] A convention had been signed with Santa Anna, but it had, of course, not been approved by the Mexican Congress.

174

edifice to be erected; the basis of a friendship useful to both countries is laid, but they have still a common enemy to reduce to the impossibility of doing them harm, and therefore the establishment of a *political* intercourse between Texas and the federal part of Mexico is not the less important.

The defensive-offensive alliance which Santángelo advocated was to be based upon a treaty specifically acknowledging the absolute and perpetual independence of the former state of "Coahuila and Texas." [3] He regarded Texas as comprising "the whole ancient territory of Coahuila and Texas" and did not expect it to be a member of the new Mexican federation. It would have the power to treat with the federation as a sovereign state.

The troops to be furnished by Texas in defense of the contemplated federation were to be maintained at the expense of the federation while operating in its jurisdiction. "Neither . . . allied power shall ever interfere in the interior organization of each other, under any political, legislative, civil, military, or religious aspect." Furthermore, the treaty should pledge that no other Mexican state might be admitted to the new Mexican union unless it subscribe fully to the treaty then in effect between the federation and Texas. The news alone of the formation of such an alliance, he declared, would cause the "hordes of Centralists now advancing to the stroke of the whip, to fall back terrified, and their government to be struck with sudden death." If Texas, however, should elect to remain satisfied and a "cool spectator" of the present contest between Centralism and Federalism, "the latter, either conquerors or conquered, would justly and undoubtedly become enraged, and a Mexican war, truly *national*, would threaten for a long time to come, the political existence of Texas, both as a nation and as a colony.[4]

The idea of such an alliance between Texas and some of the north Mexican states was not new. Three months after the battle of San Jacinto a Zacatecan federalist appealed for *"a small assistance on the part of the Texians"* to enable the states of Tamaulipas, San Luis Potosí, Zacatecas, Nuevo León, Coahuila, Durango, Sinaloa, Chihuahua, Sonora, a part of Jalisco, and the territories of both Californias and Nuevo México to separate from the southern part of the Mexican

[3] Santángelo incorrectly assumed that Coahuila and Texas were one state, while Texas had only been a district or province attached to Coahuila for administrative purposes.
[4] O. de A. Santángelo to Francis Moore, Jr., Editor of the *Telegraph and Texas Register*, March 6, 1839, in *Telegraph and Texas Register*, April 10, 1839.

republic to recover their liberties and "secure them upon immovable bases."[5] While Santángelo's proposal was by no means identical with this earlier one, its presentation stimulated a lively discussion at public gatherings, in the press, in the halls of Congress, and in both private and official correspondence. He was answered forthwith in the press by Juan Antonio Padilla, who had served in Texas as a Spanish and, later, as a Mexican official before joining the Texan revolutionary army and serving on the General Council,[6] and who in 1839 was living in Houston.

Padilla opposed the involvement of Texas in any mutual defensive-offensive alliance with the Federalists, for it would involve her in a war now and in the future—possibly with a European power—from which she had nothing, in fact, to gain.[7] He ably pointed out that the Mexican federation with which Santángelo wanted to make a treaty of alliance, had not yet been established and could not be instituted without a war; hence, Texas could not make a treaty at this time with a federation that was nonexistent. Padilla called attention to the great disparity existing between Texas and the contemplated members of the proposed federation and referred to the grievances set forth in the Texan Declaration of Independence to prove that there could be no harmony in such an alliance.

In commenting upon Santángelo's letter, the editor of the *Telegraph and Texas Register* took the position that the author was much mistaken in supposing that the citizens of Texas could be induced to embroil themselves in the internal dissension of Mexico. Texas was luckily severed from that unhappy country, and her people and institutions, both civil and political, were entirely distinct from everything of Mexican origin. It was no longer of importance to her whether Federalism or Centralism prevailed in Mexico, except as the success of

[5] A Zacatecan Federalist to the Editor of the *Correo de Atlántico*, Zacatecas, July 28, 1836 (copy in Spanish accompanied by an English translation), in *Telegraph and Texas Register*, April 10, 1839; also *ibid.*, Oct. 5, 1836.

[6] *Handbook of Texas*, II, 323. Padilla had also served at one time as Secretary of State of the State of Coahuila y Tejas and as a member of the state legislature. He was a native of Mexico, but had for a number of years been living at Nacogdoches, where his family was residing at the time of his death in Houston, Tuesday, August 6, 1839, after a lingering illness. *Telegraph and Texas Register*, Aug. 7, 1839.

[7] J. Antonio Padilla to [Francis Moore, Jr.] Editor of the *Telegraph and Texas Register*, Houston, April 15, 1839 (copy in Spanish accompanied by an English translation), in *Telegraph and Texas Register*, April 24, 1839.

either party might affect her commercial relations with that country. The editor of the Texas newspaper felt that both Centralists and Federalists in Mexico were entitled to the confidence of Texans. Although, the leader of the present Central party was committed to aid in obtaining the recognition of Texan independence by Mexico, and the Federalists had likewise indicated their willingness to do so, both, it must be remembered, had sanctioned and abetted the massacre at Goliad. Texas, declared the *Telegraph,*

. . . detests and distrusts both alike; and such is her present situation, that she fears neither. Were the whole power of Mexico united, in the hands of the Federalists or the Centralists, Texas would bid to her enemy a stern defiance. It is in consequence of a consciousness of her own strength that Texas views the civil war now raging in Mexico with as much indifference as characterizes her sister Republic of the United States. She has but little to gain or lose by the success of either party. Her proper policy, therefore, is to remain a quiet spectator of the commotions that are thus destroying the moral and physical energies of her adversary, and husband her strength for the hour of trial, if and when it should arrive.[8]

Editor W. Donaldson of the *Colorado Gazette and Advertiser*[9] (Matagorda) declared,

There cannot be perhaps advocated a better maxim, for our country particularly in its new state and present situation, than during peace to avoid a recklessness or stagnation of national energy, and carefully . . . watch existing probabilities and be found in readiness to act with effect should the issue be war. . . . However, for ourselves we are of the opinion, that whichever way the struggle may terminate between . . . [the Centralists and the Federalists] the end will be the same to this country. We cannot doubt that both parties have alike the desire if possible to regain possession of this country.

We have no confidence in the pledges of either of the Mexican parties—both fight for power—neither for human liberties—and we look for no especial favor to our country from either.

Though the leaders of the Federal party may be disposed to act more amicably towards us than the other, yet even should they succeed, so uncertain is the tenor by which they hold the reigns of Government, that however they may wish to act, there is little hope that they will have the power to do as they wish. . . .

8 *Telegraph and Texas Register,* April 10, 1839.
9 July 4, 1839.

For ourselves we are not *spoiling* for fight, but we feel assured, that on the first intimation of an enemy's force crossing the boundaries of our country, our gallant soldiers will meet them at the threshold and dance them another reel to the tune of "Alamo and their Rifles."

In official and semiofficial circles the attitude was one of caution and noninvolvement. At Washington, D.C., the Texan diplomatic representative, Anson Jones, discussed with various friends the question of Texas and Mexico and found the general opinion to be that if Texas sought to invade Mexico, when she was tied down with the French invasion and a civil war at home, it could hardly be more than a "Chimney corner war," with Texas taking Matamoros, but finding it impossible to march to Mexico City.[10] Jones found Joel R. Poinsett in agreement with himself on "the impolicy of offensive operations against Mexico." Poinsett, reported Jones, thinks "that Mexico will not invade Texas unless, Texas invading [Mexico] should meet with a reverse. When Mexico *enheartened* would follow." [11] As it was, the north Mexican states, now in rebellion against the Centralist.controlled government, were inclined to be friendly, but, it was presumed, would "become hostile" in case their country was attacked and "give great annoyance to Texas." John Forsyth, the American Secretary of State, suggested that Texas propose peace with Mexico by agreeing to furnish her supplies through Texas to enable her to withstand the French, but Jones recorded, "I told him I thought it would not be good treatment to *Our Friends,* the French," to which Forsyth laughed and said, "no, if indeed, they are our friends." [12]

The Texan agent in Paris, J. Pinckney Henderson believed Santangelo's proposal of an alliance between Texas and the Mexican Federalists, had given the friends of Texas in France some uneasiness for they feared the entry of Texas into such a treaty would detract from the high position she had assumed. "I have assured our friends," reported Henderson, "that I believe they have nothing to fear from that quarter as I knew the Government and people of Texas would form no sort of political connexion with any Mexican authority, however specious their object might seem to be." [13] Thus the friends of

[10] Anson Jones, Memorandum Book, no. 1, Wednesday, September 19, 1838, ms.
[11] *Ibid.,* no. 1, Tuesday, November 6, 1838, ms.
[12] *Ibid.,* no. 1, Thursday, Nov. 22, 1838, ms.
[13] J. Pinckney Henderson to M. B. Lamar, Paris, April 23, 1839, in *Lamar Papers,* II, 540–541.

Texas in Paris, in the United States, and elsewhere felt that an alliance between Texas and the northern Federalists "would detract from the high position" Texas had assumed in its war of independence, and the European holders of Mexican bonds worried about a further dismemberment of Mexican territory. If the north Mexican states should separate from the southern, Jones contended in Washington, "it will be our policy to cultivate the most friendly relations but not to join them to us. On this account *Invasion* will not be advisable, if there were no other reasons. But whether they separate or not, the most friendly relations should be sedulously cultivated." [14]

The Texas government showed great sympathy for the Federalist cause, but refused to become allies in it. Officially, it pursued a hands-off policy, believing that it had very little to gain by favoring either side; besides, negotiations were pending for an acknowledgment of the independence of the country through the mediation of other powers. In the meantime, Lamar is reported to have told Canales that "at present the Federalists had nothing to hope from the Government of Texas." He further remarked, that

. . . it was for the interest of Texas, at present, to pursue a pacific policy; the country had been subjected to heavy expenses in expelling the Cherokees, and could ill afford to incur further expenditure, unless absolutely necessary to secure internal quiet. Its citizens were enjoying the blessings of security, and were prosperously and peaceably pursuing their respective occupations in every section of the Republic. It was his duty to permit them to remain so, provided this could be done without endangering the public security. If, hereafter, Mexico should continue to threaten an invasion, and to encourage the Indians to continue hostilities, he would cheerfully avail himself of any honorable means of crippling the power of the Mexican Government; and if he could do this more effectually by aiding the Federal party, he would grant the aid required. [15]

The President declined the opportunity of joining with the Federalists in the internecine war in Mexico, "which . . . could have been made greatly advantageous to Texas." To have done otherwise would have so unsettled the Texan national character in Europe and in the United States "that such a course with the apparent signs of peace might have proved very deleterious in the present crisis." Instead, upon the break-

[14] Jones, Memorandum Book, no. 1, Thursday, November 22, 1838, ms.
[15] Quoted in *Telegraph and Texas Register*, June 24, 1840.

179

ing out of the Federalist revolt, Lamar had determined, as we have noted, to take advantage of the internal situation in Mexico to send his Secretary of State, Colonel Barnard E. Bee, to Mexico and Richard G. Dunlap to the United States in an effort to bring about a peaceful solution of the difficulties between Texas and Mexico either by direct negotiation or through the mediation of outside powers.[16]

The new Texan minister at Washington was instructed in March 1839, to approach the government of the United States with a view to invoking the mediatorial aid of that government in bringing about a negotiation for the settlement of the differences between Mexico and Texas. He was instructed to emphasize the forbearance shown by Texas after the battle of San Jacinto in not pushing aggressively the advantages which the battle had given her over a prostrate foe; and particularly the magnanimity Texas had since displayed in a suspension of hostilities while Mexico labored under the embarrassments of the French invasion and rebellion at home.[17] The next day, upon the receipt of news which seemed to indicate that the "Federal Party" was likely to succeed over the "Central" government of Mexico, Dunlap was advised that his chances of working out an arrangement for bringing to an end the present difficulties with Texas were improving, for as he was informed, "the liberal or Federal party in Mexico have always professed to entertain the most friendly sentiments towards this Government," and that some of their influential men had already opened a correspondence with President Lamar, addressing him as "President of the Republic of Texas." Wrote Webb,

They speak of the *justice of this Government,* and propose to reciprocate friendly offices in protecting the property of the citizens of either, which may be stolen by evil disposed persons, and carried from one to the other. Indeed, Santa Anna himself, stands committed by his solemn obligation and promise to this Government, to use all of his influence to procure an acknowledgment, by Mexico, of the Independence of Texas; and these obligations and promises may be rendered very available in your efforts to bring about a negotiation, if it be true, that he is now at the head of the Mexican Government [even if he headed the "Central" or Government party of Mexico].

[16] R. G. Dunlap to J. Pinckney Henderson, Washington [D. C.], May 24, 1839, in Garrison (ed.), *Diplomatic Correspondence of Texas,* 1907, I, 394–396.

[17] James Webb to Richard G. Dunlap, Department of State, City of Houston, March 13, 1839; and R. G. Dunlap to J. Pinckney Henderson, Paris [dated:] Washington [D. C.], May 24, 1839, in *ibid.,* I, 368–372, 394–396.

But whether the revolution has succeeded or not, the President believes that the recognition of our Independence may be accellerated by sending a minister directly to Mexico, with plenary power to negotiate a treaty with that Govt having for its objects, the acknowledgment of the Independence of Texas, and a reciprocal trade and intercourse between the two countries.[18]

For this purpose Barnard E. Bee was commissioned minister plenipotentiary of the Republic of Texas to Mexico.

As a means of promoting an amicable solution of the difficulties between Mexico and her former colony, the idea of purchasing the area lying between the Nueces and the Río Grande, once discussed in "Cabinet Council" in Texas, was interjected into the discussions in Washington, and Secretary of State John Forsyth privately hinted to Dunlap, "that perhaps the Mexican Minister [at Washington] believed, that this would be a favorable crisis in the affairs of Mexico to get a little money" and thus facilitate a speedy adjustment of the difficulties between Texas and Mexico. There was even some thought that the boundary might be run westward to the Pacific so as to include California. "This may seem too grasping, but if we can get it, ought we not to take it and pay for it. Texas is *the* rising sun of the day," declared Dunlap.[19] As for mediation by the United States, Dunlap was informed by Forsyth, "You will perceive that a mediation is not to be offered unless invited by Mexico." [20]

Bee's efforts to open negotiations in Mexico failed, no doubt owing to the improvement of the Centralist position; and he left Vera Cruz for New Orleans via Havana on June 1, but not before receiving overtures from Juan Vitalba, a secret agent of Santa Anna, which seemed to indicate that Mexico was desirous of proceeding with some sort of negotiation, provided it was deeply shrouded in secrecy. After considerable correspondence between Bee, Vitalba, James Hamilton, James Treat, James Morgan, Lamar, and his Secretary of State, the Texas government concluded to make another effort to open negotia-

[18] James Webb to Richard G. Dunlap, Department of State, Houston, March 14, 1839; and Same to Same, Department of State, Houston, March 14, 1839 (both letters of same date), in *ibid.*, I, 372–375.

[19] R. G. Dunlap to [M. B. Lamar], Washington [D. C.], May 16, 1839 (Private), and Same to Col. Barnard E. Bee, Washington [D. C.], May 17, 1839, in *ibid.*, I, 383–385, 388–389.

[20] Nath[anie]l Amory to A. S. Lipscomb, Legation of Texas, Washington, May 8, 1840, in *ibid.*, I, 452. The original of John Forsyth to Genl. R. G. Dunlap, July 17, 1839, has not been located.

tions with Mexico through Treat, who had spent many years in South America and had lived in Mexico for seven years where he had made the acquaintance of Santa Anna and other Mexican leaders. This time Lamar had the assurances of Bee and the British minister to Mexico, Richard Pakenham, that Mexico would receive an agent should one be sent. Treat was then commissioned a private or confidential agent of the government and handed instructions at Austin on August 9 similar to those given Colonel Bee previously.

Meanwhile, as the Federalist resistance collapsed in the north and peace seemed to be returning to the nation, a howl was set up by some of Santa Anna's supporters for a renewal of the Texas campaign, probably with nothing more in mind than to embarrass Bustamante, the regularly elected President. However, an appeal for the subjugation of Texas—an object which enlisted their national pride as well as their religious hatred, it was said—was one way of readily uniting the whole Mexican nation. Too, it gave an opportunity for many of the late rebels to demonstrate their loyalty by appearing to be enthusiastic for a renewal of the Texas war. On June 18, 1839, the Minister of War, José María Tornel, in the name of the Provisional President, Santa Anna, submitted to the Chamber of Deputies a project for the reconquest of Texas. The President, said Tornel, is "resolved to propose another expedition, which shall offer to the Texians peace, or war— indulgence, or punishment." He wishes to be authorized "to incur the necessary expenses until the pacification of the 'Department of Texas,' is fully accomplished, and to dictate all measures which may be considered necessary for the attainment of this end." [21] It was stated in the *True American* of Saturday, July 6, that the Mexican troops were to approach the western settlements of Texas in small detachments, simultaneously, and to rendezvous on the Brazos until their forces numbered 8,000 or more. They would then commence a war of extermination, giving no quarter, destroying all houses, and pursuing a policy of universal pillage.[22]

The American consul at Mexico City, W. D. Jones, believed that the

[21] José María Tornel to their Excellencies the Secretaries and Deputies, Mexico, June 18, 1839, in *Telegraph and Texas Register*, July 24, 1839; also quoted by W. D. Jones to John Forsyth, Consulate of the U. S. A., Mexico, June 22, 1839, vol. 7, no. 274, Consular Letters (Mexico), 1833–1847, in Justin H. Smith, "Transcripts," IV, ms.

[22] *True American* (New Orleans), July 6, 1839, reported in *Morning Star* (Houston), July 12, 1839.

object of this project for the reconquest of Texas was "merely to divert the attention of the people, and get rid of General Bustamante, [by] investing him with the chief command of the invading army," [23] with the belief that the Texans would never permit him to return to Mexico, or if he survived the campaign that he would be compelled to flee the republic, covered with the odium and disgrace of repeated failure. It was even hinted that should Bustamante encounter defeat in Texas, Santa Anna had promised to come to his assistance at the head of 10,000 men. "It has long been surmised," declared the editor of the *Telegraph and Texas Register,*[24] "that Mexico would, after subjugating the Federalists, turn her arms in the direction of Texas. . . . The campaign, it is said, will begin in September." Jones' appraisal of the situation, however, seems to have been more correct.

The New Orleans *True American* was of the same general opinion as Consul Jones, but emphasized that Santa Anna, "forbidden by his own promises to the Texans, which policy only induces him to keep, . . . will never invade in person the revolted territory. . . . Another contest between Mexico and the new Anglo-Saxon republic will prove fatal to the future peace of the Mexican provinces, and in our humble opinion," continued its editor, "all Santa Anna's dreams of despotic power are destined to be dissipated." [25] The editor of a Texas paper, however, was not convinced that Santa Anna would not relish the opportunity to lead the invading army himself, in spite of his promise.[26] However,

For ourselves, we do not apprehend any attempt on the part of the Mexicans to make war against us at present. Still we are inclined to deny the propriety of preparing for the worse so that we may not be taken by surprise. But we consider the idea of an invasion of Mexico by Texas, at this time, when we are without a dollar in the world, and with only a handful of men, as preposterous in the extreme. The scheme is so visionary that it seems strange that any one should entertain it for a moment,

for Texas would do well, in its present financial state, to defend itself

---

[23] W. D. Jones to John Forsyth, Consulate of the U. S. A., Mexico, June 22, 1839, vol. 7, no. 274, Consular Letters (Mexico), 1833–1847, in Justin H. Smith, "Transcripts," IV, ms.; R. G. Dunlap to M. B. Lamar, New York, July 21, 1839, in Garrison, (ed.), *Diplomatic Correspondence of Texas,* 1907, I, 410–414.

[24] July 19, 1839.

[25] *True American* quoted in *Telegraph and Texas Register,* June 12, 1839.

[26] *Telegraph and Texas Register,* June 12, 1839.

against both Indians and Mexicans.[27] While the inhuman treatment of Mejía seems to have produced great indignation in the United States, Americans generally approved of Lamar's policy of not meddling in Mexican affairs. But, reported R. G. Dunlap from Philadelphia, where he had gone to hear a speech by Dr. Breckinridge "on the condition and prospects of Texas,"

if the Mexicans shall again put their bloody and poluted feet on our consecrated soil, Delenda est Carthago, is the motto that will bring to your standard thousands of gallant spirits, from the United States, with the good wishes of the whole country for your success. Such an event, will be but the birth days, of new spirits of chivalry, who will enter into the cause of a nation['s] liberty with as much devotion, as the soldiers of the cross, ever moved in the Crusades against the delusive power of the cressant.[28]

As to whether the Mexicans really intended to invade Texas, one thing was sure: no one in Texas knew. "Conjecture is on stilts, and opinions stagger among us—no three men agreeing on their thoughts. But happily," declared the *Telegraph*, "all agree in one thing—that if they do come, our western prairies will receive a copious manuring." [29]

While Mexican officialdom threatened war, enterprising and adventuresome Texans carried on their own private war along the Mexican frontier. Their reward was the loot they obtained or the satisfaction gained in the annihilation of a rival Mexican banditti party. The increased volume of trade, stimulated and abetted by the recent wars, and the gradual encroachment of settlers into the so-called no man's land, made their work all the more attractive. While officially the Mexican authorities attempted to prevent the trade, they often winked at the violation of the law and too many times were suspected of participating in the profits. In August 1839 several groups of Texans advanced to the Mexican settlements just north of the Río Grande, near Matamoros, and captured a number of horses and cattle, causing the prefect of the northern district of Tamaulipas to call upon the commandant general for additional protection for Matamoros. He claimed that the Texans were becoming progressively bolder and larger in

[27] The question of the removal of the Cherokees came to a head after the discovery of the Mexican-Indian conspiracy from the papers taken from the body of Manuel Flores. In July the Cherokees were expelled from east Texas.

[28] R. G. Dunlap to M. B. Lamar, Philadelphia, June 2, 1839, in Garrison (ed.), *Diplomatic Correspondence of Texas*, 1907, I, 401–403.

[29] *Telegraph and Texas Register*, June 19, 1839.

numbers, and that it was impossible for the local inhabitants to devote all of their time to defense, it being necessary for them to make a living.[30] The *Brisa* (Matamoros) pointed out in September that the Texans, supported by citizens (Mexicans) from La Bahía del Espíritu Santo [Goliad] frequently raided the ranches on the north bank of the Río Grande, driving off large numbers of all specie of livestock; they also dealt in contraband, including tobacco and other merchandise.[31]

At Matamoros, a number of volunteers and a few regulars were organized into a company, known as the "Volunteers of La Bahía," [32] to follow the Texan marauders with tenacity. From time to time, they recovered considerable quantities of tobacco and quite a few horses. Captain Manuel Savariego in one of his expeditions approached the San Antonio River, where he defeated a party of "colonists," capturing some and killing others. General Filisola sent five hundred men under Colonel Rafael Vasquez, who reached the Nueces River, and succeeded in recovering "a great quantity of livestock which the Texans had collected there belonging to the inhabitants" of the Río Grande towns.[33]

While one of the Texan raiding parties was endeavoring to return to the settled area of Texas, it was overtaken and defeated on August 14 by Captain José María Villareal, in command of twenty-one regular cavalry and seventy-five rancheros, in the *rodeo*[34] just below the Carricitos.[35] Five of the party of thirteen Texans were killed, three made prisoners, and the others escaped on foot and without arms through the dense woods. The Mexican losses were reported as only two horses wounded. The Mexicans effected the release of 280 head of cattle, 75 wild mules and horses, 24 burros, 19 tame horses, and 3 tame mules, all of which they claimed had been taken from the frontier ranches. The 19 or 20 horses belonging to the Texans, their saddles,

[30] *La Brisa* (Matamoros), Aug. 30, 1839.

[31] *Ibid.*, Sept. 6, 1839.

[32] Quite a number of the volunteers came from the area of La Bahía del Espíritu Santo (Goliad), who remained loyal to Mexico during the Texas Revolution and found it necessary to get out of Texas when the Mexican troops were withdrawn, or who because of threats, discriminations, and appropriation of their property by greedy, designing, and unscrupulous Anglo-Americans sought safety beyond the Río Grande.

[33] *La Brisa*, Sept. 6, 1839; *Colorado Gazette and Advertiser*, Aug. 1, 1839.

[34] As employed in this sense, the term "rodeo" was a corral used for catching wild horses and cattle.

[35] *La Brisa*, Aug. 30, 1839.

and arms were also captured and distributed among the rancheros, and "those horses which had been stolen by their Texan riders were released to their rightful owners." [36]

On August 23 a Mexican force of approximately one hundred men left Matamoros upon the receipt of information that at the junction of the Arroyo Santa Rosa with the Bahía Road, fifty to one hundred Texans were rendezvousing to make a foray upon the northern frontier. The intention of the Mexican expedition, it was said, was defensive and for the protection of the settlements on the east side of the Río Grande from depredations by marauding companies. It could not be imagined how Mexico in her present disorganized and crippled situation could possibly seriously entertain the idea of carrying on an offensive war. "It is with great regularity," reported Prefect José Antonio Chapa, "that the Colonists are coming to ruin our frontier notwithstanding the defeats that they have received, for many of them are criminal adventurers . . . who not having anything to live on, launch themselves unhesitatingly into some enterprise to rob the fruits of labor of some poor Mexican as may be in misery from their depredations." [37]

While continued publicity was being given to the Federalist cause in Texas, and some Texas newspapers speculated upon the concentration of Centralist troops upon the frontier of the Republic for the purpose of resuming hostilities against the undefended western frontier,[38] the revolutionists in northern Mexico sought to contact the Texas government for assistance. One of their agents, Francisco Vidaurri y Villaseñor, a former governor of Coahuila y Texas,[39] appeared in San Antonio in July 1839, where it was reported he advertised for support for the liberal cause. Representing that all of the north Mexican states adhered to the Federal party, he proposed that Texas form with Coahuila, Tamaulipas, Nuevo León, Chihuahua, Nuevo México, Durango, and the Californias an alliance and that they separate from the rest of Mexico. He contended that the people in the northern states were more intelligent and desirous of liberty than those of the south, who were ignorant and factious and could be governed only by a despotism.

[36] José Antonio Chapa á el Secretario del Gobierno de este Departamento, Prefectura del Norte del Departamento de Tamaulipas, Matamoros, Agosto 23 de 1839, in *Gaceta de Tampico*, Sept. 7, 1839.
[37] *Ibid.*; *Colorado Gazette and Advertiser*, Aug. 1, 1839.
[38] *Matagorda Bulletin*, June 28, 1839.
[39] Vito Alessio Robles, *Coahuila y Texas, desde la consumación de la independencia hasta el tratado de paz de Guadalupe Hidalgo*, II, 438.

Even if Texas refused to enter into such an arrangement, the northern states, he said, would declare their independence, and he had little doubt concerning their success in achieving it.⁴⁰ The Texan government took no official notice of Vidaurri's proposal, although there were some individuals in the Republic who favored the establishment of such a federation. However, the majority opinion concerning his proposal was probably most ably expressed by one of the Houston newspapers. Wrote the editor,

It is not our policy to unite with those people [the Federalists]. They would now outvote us, and we do not want to place ourselves in a situation in which it would be possible to fall under the control of even the best portion of the Mexican people. But we wish them success, and although we refuse to become parties to the controversy, we feel an interest in every struggle which is calculated to advance human liberty.⁴¹

Later, learning that the Federal emissaries in Texas were offering army commissions to some of the Texans to enlist in their service, and promising that if their plans were successful to give Texas any kind of treaty she wished, the *Telegraph and Texas Register* again stated what it thought was the attitude of Texas and most Texans. "We cannot but wish them success, and have but little doubt of their ability to maintain the ground they have assumed. . . . We have no objection to acknowledg[ing] their independence as soon as they establish a good government, and show to the world their ability to maintain it; but we cannot involve ourselves in their difficulties.⁴²

After the defeat and capture of their leaders in a ten months campaign, Canales, González, and Zapata, accompanied by their attendants, Cristobal Ramírez, José María Carbajal,⁴³ Cameron's men, and a small group of rancheros and Carrizo Indians⁴⁴ armed with lances

⁴⁰ *Telegraph and Texas Register*, Aug. 14, 1839; see also, *La Concordia* (Ciudad Victoria), April 27, 1839, in respect to this mission.
⁴¹ *Telegraph and Texas Register*, Aug. 14, 1839.
⁴² *Ibid.*, Aug. 28, 1839.
⁴³ José Vicente Miñon, Comandante general del Coahuila y Tejas, ál Ministro de Guerra y Marina, Saltillo, Sept. 13, 1839, in *La Concordia* (Ciudad Victoria), Oct. 12, 1839.
⁴⁴ The Carrizo Indians, whose name was sometimes spelled "Caris," "Care," and "Caresse," lived between Camargo and Matamoros and along the gulf coast in northeast Tamaulipas, Mexico. They were known to the Kiowas and Tonkawa tribes as the "shoeless people," because they wore sandals instead of moccasins.

187

badly constructed, rendezvoused in late June and early July at Cala-
vasos, on the east side of the Río Grande near Mier, and from there
retreated to Lipantitlán, on the Nueces, having previously sent a few
prisoners to San Antonio for safekeeping.[45] As they withdrew on to
the Texas side of the river, a portion of the Federalists under Canales
met a party of thirty to forty cowboys under Captain Cairns near the
Agua Dulce. Seeing the Mexicans approach, the Texans prepared for
battle, but, says Benjamin F. Neal, Carbajal advanced under a flag of
truce to make known their object and plans, stating that they had no
enmity toward Texas and Texans. The cowboys readily accepted the
invitation to join the Federalist cause and together they proceeded to
the Nueces.[46]

From thence, Canales, a Montereyan, border ruffian, conspirator, and
now, in fact, commander of the Federalist forces, accompanied by
Carlos Lazo from San Fernando de Rosas in Coahuila, proceeded to
San Antonio early in August 1839, with a force of about thirty to thirty-
five, where his men were furnished clothing and provisions. Lazo, the
father-in-law of Philip Dimitt,[47] carried papers from José María
Carbajal and Luciano Navarro. Among the papers from Navarro that
Carbajal had forwarded to Lazo was "one from his Excellency the
President of this Republic," reported Erasmo Seguin, chief justice at
San Antonio, "which contains the same business made known to
Navarro," [48] presumably granting them personal protection but no
official recognition whatsoever. Lazo informed the Texans at San Antonio that six hundred Comanche warriors ("bucks") were encamped
between the Río Frio and the Leona above the Presidio del Río Grande
road about thirty leagues from San Antonio with orders from the military commander at Matamoros to intercept all commerce between
Texas and the Río Grande settlements. With the Comanches were a

---

Frederick Webb Hodge (ed.), *Handbook of American Indians North of Mexico,*
I, 209.

[45] Hobart Huson, "Iron Men: A History of The Republic of The Río Grande
and The Federalist Wars in Northern Mexico," pp. 36–37. Some of the Federalists'
prisoners effected their escape from San Antonio, and the others, no doubt, were
transferred to the Federalist camp on the Nueces.

[46] Huson, "Refugio: A Comprehensive History of Refugio County from Aboriginal Times to the End of World War II," vol. II, chap. 23, p. 3.

[47] *Ibid.,* II, 3.

[48] Erasmo Seguin to the Secretary of State [of Texas], Béxar, Aug. 8, 1839, in
Domestic Correspondence (Texas), 1836–1846, ms.

few Caddo Indians and some half dozen Mexican Centralist soldiers, acting perhaps as observers. Casemiro, one of the Comanche chiefs, was reported to be ravaging Laredo and its vicinity with some two hundred warriors.[49] It was reported that Lazo was forced to recognize the independence of Texas before he could remain at Béxar, which he did; and he also declared that Mexico would recognize it if the federal system was re-established.[50]

Before the arrival of the Federalist leaders at Béxar, the Texan military commander at that place had been instructed by Lamar's administration to inform Canales "that personal protection was all that he could expect from us." The Texas government, wrote Secretary of State, Abner S. Lipscomb, would not recognize him in any official character whatever; if there were an invasion it would not permit any other flag than its own on this side of the Río Grande; and in that event, if he and his dispersed followers took part against the invaders, it must be under the Texas flag, and under the orders of Texan officers.[51]

At Béxar, Carbajal contacted General Luciano Navarro and solicited his assistance in the Federalist cause, which for the next year or so came to be confined principally to the departments of Tamaulipas, Nuevo León, and Coahuila. Navarro, availing himself of the opportunity to use Colonel Karnes as an emissary, passed Carbajal's "confidential communication" on to President Lamar at Houston "for whatever purposes may be suitable to the Republic." Wrote Navarro, "Karnes will be able to give you a more detailed explanation of their contents." [52] Karnes, who commanded a regiment of volunteers on the frontier, reached Houston on August 21 with news that the Mexican states adjacent to Texas had declared themselves independent of the central government, so it was reported, but the President, declared Ashbel Smith that evening, "has not been apprised of it." [53]

Karnes' object in going to Houston was to gain permission to in-

[49] *Ibid.; El Ancla* (Matamoros), June 12, 1840.

[50] Reports of Mexicans at San Antonio. *El Ancla*, June 12, 1840.

[51] Abner S. Lipscomb to Gen. James Hamilton, in Europe, [dated:] Galveston, Jan. 6, 1840, in Texas Congress, *Journal of the House of Representatives, Fifth Congress, Appendix*, pp. 281–283.

[52] Luciano Navarro to Mirabeau B. Lamar, Béjar, Aug. 9, 1839, in *Lamar Papers*, V, 304.

[53] Ashbel Smith to Col. Barnard E. Bee, City of Houston, Aug. 21, 1839, in Ashbel Smith Papers, ms.

crease the size of his command in order to conduct a campaign against the Indians and to give more effective protection to the southwestern frontier; he also wanted to confer with the administration on the policy to be pursued toward the Federalists, who had sent letters to San Antonio, including one to Karnes, soliciting assistance and whose emissaries were already appearing at that frontier city.[54] A company of eighty volunteers raised at Galveston for Karnes' command reached Houston during the week of September 11.[55] On September 2 Karnes' regiment consisted of three companies commanded respectively by Captain J. P. Ownsby, Captain Bartlett Sims, and Captain M. B. Lewis. D. J. Woodlief served as lieutenant colonel, and Matthew P. Woodhouse was first lieutenant of Captain Ownsby's Company.[56]

As soon as Canales' proclamation calling for volunteers came to Lamar's attention, Adjutant General Hugh McLeod was instructed to contact José Ramos, alcalde of Laredo, by letter for information concerning the Mexican filibustering expedition being organized on the Texas frontier and the number of troops. Wrote McLeod,

President Lamar especially desires to know if there are any considerable number of Texans in the expedition, the names of the leaders, both of Mexicans and Americans. I am not sure that I understand what it proposes to accomplish. The President regards such an expedition, at this time, unfortunate for Texas, as it will tend to further excite envy and hatred among the Mexicans who have recently given assurance of a better understanding of our people and our government.[57]

From San Antonio Canales went to Austin with five men to solicit the aid of the Texas government, leaving the rest of his men at the old Río Grande crossing of the Medina under the command of Francisco Vidaurri, and Juan Lom, who had about two hundred men supplemented by a number of armed colonials (Texans) under Colonel

[54] *Telegraph and Texas Register*, Aug. 14 and 21, 1839; *Colorado Gazette and Advertiser*, Sept. 22, 1839.

[55] *Colorado Gazette and Advertiser*, Sept. 22, 1839, *Telegraph and Texas Register*, Sept. 11, 1839.

[56] See Paymaster General J. Snively's Certification of Payments made at the City of Austin, Oct. 10, 1839, to Col. Karnes' Regt. Volunteers, in Militia Rolls (Texas), ms.

[57] Sam Houston Dixon, *Romance and Tragedy of Texas History: being a Record of many thrilling Events in Texas History under Spanish, Mexican and Anglo-Saxon Rule*, I, 258, quotes from McLeod's letter to José Ramos.

Reuben Ross camped at the mission of Espada. However, it was reported on the Río Grande that some of the Mexicans were deserting for lack of supplies—corn and other items. Others drifting into San Antonio included an old familiar face—Ramón Músquiz—former political chief of Texas, stationed at Béxar from 1827 to 1835, who had returned to San Antonio with the invading army of '36.[58] Now, on August 29, 1839, he again appeared, this time as a refugee from Centralism.

But these were not all of the Federalist agents to enter Texas in the fall of 1839. The ablest and best known of them all, Juan Pablo de Anaya, or simply Juan Pablo Anaya,[59] crossed the Río Grande at Laredo, leaving his four hundred men there under the command of Colonel Macedonio Capistrán.[60] He reached San Antonio August 26, and like those whom he had been commissioned to represent, but who

[58] Erasmo Seguin al Secrta de Estado, Béxar, 6 Septiembre de 1839, in Domestic Correspondence (Texas), 1836–1846, ms., Spanish; *Telegraph and Texas Register*, Sept. 11, 1839.

[59] Juan Pablo Anaya was born June 24, 1792, in Lagos in the present state of Jalisco. He attended the College of Guadalajara; studied law; fought in the revolution with Hidalgo; and was sent to the United States in August 1814 to seek aid in men, arms, and munitions in behalf of the independence movement in Mexico. He reached New Orleans on September 6, 1814, where he connived with pirates and adventurers to get aid for Mexico. While in the vicinity of New Orleans, Anaya fought with Andrew Jackson in 1814 in the battles of December 23 and 28, and of January 8, 1815. Anaya represented Guadalajara in the First Congress of the Mexican Republic, and was one of the principal leaders in an effort to overthrow Iturbide in 1822, for which he suffered a short term of imprisonment. From 1825 to 1828 he was commandant general of Chiapas with the rank of brigadier general. For a while he was a supporter of Santa Anna; served as *ad interim* Secretary of War, Jan. 7–Jan. 26, 1833; later supported Vice-President Valentín Gómez Farías, the Federalist; was imprisoned for desertion from the army about April 1835–Sept. 1836 for opposing Santa Anna's Plan of Cuernavaca; became one of the outstanding leaders of Mexican federalism; was defeated in Chiapas in May 1841; was exiled to Cuba, 1842–1844; but upon being pardoned by Santa Anna, returned to Mexico; fought against the United States in the Mexican War; and died rather unexpectedly at Lagos, August 24, 1850, of cholera. Horace V. Harrison, "Juan Pablo Anaya: Champion of Mexican Federalism," Ph.D. dissertation, *passim*; *Telegraph and Texas Register*, Sept. 11, 1839.

[60] Erasmo Seguin al Secretario de Estado [de Téjas], Béjar, Agosto 30 de 1839, in Domestic Correspondence (Texas), 1836–1846, ms., Spanish; Same to Same, Béjar, Aug. 8, 1839, in Lamar Papers, ms. Spanish; Alessio Robles, *Coahuila y Texas*, II, 206; *La Concordia* (Ciudad Victoria), April 27, 1839, *El Ancla*, Dec. 27, 1839.

After San Jacinto

had been forced to flee so suddenly that they had preceded him, he arrived full of excitement and fear of the Centralists' plans to destroy the Liberals in northern Mexico and to invade Texas. He did not tarry long at San Antonio, but accompanied by José María González, Juan Rafael Garza, Agapito Galban, and Sergeant Juan Ramos, Anaya proceeded with Colonel Andrew Neill from San Antonio to Houston,[61] reaching there on September 11, where the *Telegraph and Texas Register*,[62] on the very day of his arrival, gave him a good buildup. The very next day, however, the *Morning Star*[63] warned that the Texan authorities should exercise "particular caution" in dealing with the Federal emissary.

At Houston Anaya informed Lamar that the opening of trade across the Río Grande had assisted the Federalist cause, and because of this beginning in friendly relations, he now sought an agreement between Texas and the revolutionary states of the north, by which the federation would agree to acknowledge the absolute independence of Texas from Coahuila in return for military support and the privilege of recruiting volunteers in Texas, and transporting troops and supplies across Texas to northern Mexico.

Anaya's plan for the restoration of the constitution of 1824 contained ten articles.[64] It was clearly emphasized in the plan that the "present

[61] In his doctoral dissertation on "The Republic of the Río Grande," p. 141, David M. Vigness says Anaya went from San Antonio to Austin where he conferred with President Lamar. I have been unable to substantiate this statement. The site for the City of Austin was not selected until April 13, 1839, and the construction of the government buildings did not get under way until May 1839. The first town lots were surveyed and offered for sale on August 1. The archives of the government reached Austin on October 9, at about which time the government officials began to arrive from Houston and the new government offices were opened. See Claudia Hazelwood, "Austin, Texas," in *Handbook of Texas*, I, 85–86; *Telegraph and Texas Register*, Sept. 18, Oct. 9, 16, and 23, 1839.

[62] Sept. 11, 1839.

[63] Sept. 12, 1839.

[64] "Plan proyectado por los federalistas mexicanas para el restablecimiento de las instituciones de 1824." Ms. copy, unsigned and without title, dated Houston, December 14, 1839, is found in the Anaya Papers, ms. Manuel Rivera Cambas, *Historia antigua y moderna de Jalapa y de las revoluciones del Estado de Vera Cruz*, III, says the plan was published in both Mexico and the United States. It is highly probable that the ideas in this plan were not fully developed until near the date shown on it. Anaya's plan was published over his signature in *Le Courrier* (New Orleans), Jan. 15, 1840; and on March 20, 1840, *Le Courrier* published an article in both French and Spanish and signed by Juan Pablo Anaya, which is a

192

fight against the Central government was not for the purpose of dividing the Mexican Republic, but for the re-establishment of the constitution of 1824 with such changes as the experience and . . . knowledge of the century make necessary for a free people." Among the delegates to the convention were to be certain "foreigners, who by their services, integrity, adhesion to the country, knowledge and virtues, recommend them as representatives of the nation." Pending the establishment of a permanent government a provisional one was to be established as soon as a secure and appropriate place was found, and in the new government there was to be "one or two foreigners of integrity and ability."

Since foreign capital was essential to the development of the abundant resources of Mexico, all laws prohibiting foreigners from acquiring rural and urban lands or mines were to be repealed. All existing foreign and domestic debts were to be paid, and liberal provision was to be made, in addition to their regular pay, for all persons who rendered military service in behalf of the Federal cause. Those individuals who contributed money or effects to the Federal cause would likewise be rewarded. All financial obligations owed to the military and others, as a result of the present crisis, were to be met out of available funds; "if not, the amounts will be carried and all amounts paid in full upon the completion of victory. . . . Foreigners who give services in behalf of and in support of the Mexican nation in the present fight," it was stipulated, "shall enjoy the privileges and rights of the Mexicans." Those "foreigners who enter into the service of the Mexican nation shall submit to the regular order and military discipline and all the laws of the country."

There must have been some misunderstanding of the ultimate objective of revolutionary activities which Anaya supported. The first impression in the Texas press was that of a separatist movement, and it was announced in the *Telegraph and Texas Register* on September 18 that Anaya was seeking assistance in the establishment of a stable government over six or seven of the northern Mexican states (departments), which would assume and pay their proportionate share of the existing national debt of Mexico. Either there was a misunderstanding of what he told certain important Texans; or, if he were reported correctly, he felt it impolitic to publicize the fact at this stage, for it would

---

spirited defense of the Mexican Federalists against certain allegations of the Centralists.

most likely cause the Federalists to lose considerable support among their fellow Mexicans. It seems to the writer that Anaya was first a Mexican, interested in the preservation of the national territory, and secondly a liberal at heart. He was quick to deny any idea of establishing a separate government in northern Mexico, even one dedicated to the federal principles of 1824; and it is a fact that a few weeks later when he left Texas for New Orleans, he lost interest in the Federalist cause in the north where the separatists seemed to be gaining the ascendancy and went to Yucatán which had once more risen in rebellion in behalf of the federal principles of 1824. In Article IV of his *plan proyectado,*[65] Anaya declared that "the idea of dividing the present Mexican territory into two republics, as some have opined lightly, cannot be accepted," owing to an indebtedness, both foreign and domestic, in excess of ten million dollars for which the whole of Mexico was responsible to England and certain other creditors, who would be disturbed at any effort to prorate it between "the pretended republic of the north" and that of the south.

In the latter is the greater population, the territory more cultivated, although smaller, and many of the national possessions. In the northern part there is much less population, less wealth, less culture, less industry, and greater territory. For both parts there are works not only of mutual usefulness for them, but for all nations. Besides, there are no suitable and natural boundaries that are fixed by the topographical state of the country; it would remain an absolutely uncertain line, and would be in sure and inexcusable dispute.

The general opinion in Mexico, he felt, was decidedly in favor of the re-establishment of the federal system, for they knew that "this beautiful form of government efficaciously provides the necessities of all parts. For this reason the Federalists exist in greater number through all the expanse of the republic, and if it is attempted to form a republic of the north, the Federalists elsewhere would be opposed to such a measure."[66]

In a letter to the editor of the *Telegraph and Texas Register*, Anaya declared that separatism was not contemplated for the northern de-

[65] The revolutionists in Yucatán declared the province independent of Mexico "until the federal system should be re-established." Hubert Howe Bancroft, *History of Mexico*, V, 218.
[66] "Plan por los federalistas mexicanas para el restablecimiento de las instituciones de 1824, Houston, December 14, 1839," in Anaya Papers, ms.

partments. "It is more than evident to me," he wrote, "that the wish of the Mexican Nation, very explicitly and generally expressed, is to re-establish the Federal constitution of 1824, and by means of a convention make such reforms in it as the experience and information of the present age have demonstrated to be necessary for a free people." He refused to say whether he had been well or badly received in Texas, but did state that President Lamar had treated him "with the greatest urbanity" and had manifested to him "the kindest sentiments . . . in favor of the Federal cause in Mexico." [67] He denied that he had ever thought of appealing over Lamar and his cabinet to the Texas Congress. At the proper time and when he considered it suitable, he declared, he would be glad to explain his views "not only to the Congress, but to the people of Texas, and to all the liberals of the world." This he did in the plan above referred to, which was drawn up and signed on December 14, 1839.

On the question of independence of Texas from Mexico, Anaya had not been too clear, and, of course, the Texans had long given up the idea of desiring statehood in the Mexican federation. The *Morning Star* [68] (Houston) suggested that the Texas government give very careful consideration to such factors as the difference in language, race, and concepts of what constitutes a liberal system of government before entering into any sort of formal alliance with the Federalists; although, "We wish our neighbors well," said the editor, "and should rejoice to see their efforts crowned with the most complete success," and be "the first to advocate a recognition of their independence, we are not willing to hazard the existence of our own government, and perhaps the downfall of both." The editor went even further on September 17, asserting that the government's decision not to permit the free use of the Texas ports for the introduction and transportation through the Republic of articles needed by the Federalists and to prohibit the recruitment of volunteers on the soil of Texas was correct. While Texas should assist neither directly nor indirectly the Federal cause, the editor declared that the government's refusal to aid should not be too "comprehensive." [69] Have our leaders, he asked, in the short space of three years forgotten "the hour when we, trembling and weak, stood begging for assistance of another nation? . . . It looks as if our own

[67] Juan Pablo Anaya to the Editor of the *Telegraph and Texas Register*, Sept. 20, 1839, in *Telegraph and Texas Register*, Sept. 25, 1839.
[68] Sept. 12, 1839.
[69] *Morning Star*, Sept. 17, 1839.

success and prosperity has made us haughty and unmindful of others in their adversity."

On the other hand, men like George Fisher, a Serbian by birth and former citizen of Mexico before his expulsion with José Antonio Mejía in 1835 for their liberal political views,[70] which he disseminated through his newspaper, *El Mercurio del Puerto de Matamoros,* worked actively in behalf of the Federalist cause in Texas. Having recently received a divorce from his first wife [71] and remarried, he was anxious to escape the harassment of three suits for debt in the October 1840 term of court by finding some sort of employment, perhaps filling the vacancy in the chief justiceship of Harris County, or serving as an agent to either the Mexican government or to the Federalists on the Río Grande, or going on a diplomatic mission to Spain or on a trip to California or Santa Fé in behalf of the Texas government. "I need an excitement under my present oppressed state of mind," he wrote a member of Congress, "which can only be had by travelling and I wish to do so, with honor to myself and profit to my country. The compensation is no object to me. I must have a diversion." [72] In the Federalist cause he saw the opportunity for that diversion.

Although Fisher saw many reasons why Texas should remain aloof from the civil war in Mexico, he saw in the efforts to re-establish the constitution of 1824 in Mexico a chance for Texas to win the blessing of the Federal party in case that party were successful. Texas' co-operation in the Federalist cause could scarcely make the Centralists any more the enemy of Texas than they already claimed to be. Later, when the Federalists sponsored the idea of an independent republic of the Río Grande, Fisher pointed out the great commercial, manufacturing, and agricultural advantages to Texas that might accrue from friendly relations with the new nation, which would possess only one seaport of significance, Matamoros, situated thirty miles from the mouth of the Río Grande. The Federalists, he said, have no

. . . shipping for their imports and exports, nor have they any machinery, factories, breweries, distilleries, foundries, glassworks, saw mills, tanneries,

[70] Eugene C. Barker, "The Tampico Expedition," in *Quarterly of the Texas State Historical Association,* VI (1902–1903), 170. For a biographical sketch of George Fisher, see *Handbook of Texas,* I, 600–601; Mary Fisher Parmenter, *The Life of George Fisher, 1795–1873, and the History of the Fisher Family in Mississippi.*
[71] H. P. N. Gammel (ed.), *Laws of Texas,* II, 72.
[72] G[eorge] F[isher] to Gov. Henry Smith, Houston, Oct. 29, 1840, in Domestic Correspondence (Texas), 1836–1846, ms.

&c., and . . . Texas, in a few years more, will be able to supply them with the goods and produce of all kinds, and by direct importations from Europe. Therefore, the success of the independence and the final establishment of the Republic of the Río Grande, is much to be desired by every friend of Texas, and cherished by every Texian.[73]

From Mexico City, an unidentified writer wrote a letter on August 13, 1839, which was published in the *Louisianian* (New Orleans) and found its way into Texas. The writer urged careful consideration in Texas of the propositions which he presumed Anaya was making in reference to the recognition of the independence of Texas and the conclusion of treaties of commerce and amity. He contended that if Texas would furnish and equip twelve to fifteen hundred volunteers to the Federalist cause that they could so deal with the Mexican army as to make Texas safe from any reinvasion by Mexico. He believed that the success of the Federalist cause would be assured.[74] Even the newspaper, *La Enseña* (Mexico City), urged that the independence of Texas be acknowledged, and "a great number of Mexicans, recognizing that reconquest was impossible, were in favor of this recognition."[75]

However, it was believed that any Mexican Federalist who operated under the Texas flag should be considered a traitor to his country. The mere fact that one rose in arms against his government apparently was not enough to constitute treason; for in Mexico of that day, rebellion seems to have been the normal thing. The Mexican attitude is further reflected in the reports of an informer in Mexico.

As respects the feelings of this people, [wrote A. S. Wright,][76] it is hostile

[73] George Fisher to the Editor of the *Morning Star*, Feb. 29, 1840, in the *Morning Star*, March 3, 1840.

[74] *Louisianian* (New Orleans), quoted in *Austin City Gazette*, Nov. 6, 1839.

[75] Alessio Robles, *Coahuila y Texas*, II, 206 n. It must be noted here that the United States diplomatic agent in Texas reported that Anaya had pledged that if the Federal party triumphed in Mexico, the independence of Texas would be immediately recognized. Alcée La Branche to John Forsyth, Legation of the United States, Houston, Oct. 25, 1839, in "Correspondence and Reports of American Agents and Others in Texas, 1836–1845," Justin H. Smith, "Transcripts," V, ms.

[76] A native of the United States, educated at St. Mary's College near Baltimore, A. S. Wright lived many years in Spain, became a trader in Mexico, claimed Texas citizenship, was employed by the Texan government in 1838 to furnish information regarding the frontier Indians, became the secret agent of Barnard E. Bee in Mexico in 1839, and continued to give information to the Texan

to Texas, but there are some of the leading characters of the Federal party who pretend to be friends with Texas, not openly, but from a private source (and in confidence) have I learned the same. But I would not have you lay too much confidence upon the friendship proposed by those who skirt the Río Grande, and [Texas] nearly to the Río Nueces. Some of those, I have learned, have made propositions to the Government of Texas; be *Alert*, be aware of treachery; the same proposals have been made to the Centrals (who are now in power) by the same individuals, proposing to lay aside their national quarrel for the present, and join as a patriotic body in the expulsion of a foreign enemy. Beware of CANALES. He has called on the Mexican Govrmt. for assistance to drive the Texians from their post on the Río Nueces (Casa Blanca or White House). *He no doubt has called on Texas in the same way.*[77]

Again Wright wrote: "As respects El Sr. Canales . . . it is supposed by some here that he has thrown himself upon that Country. As before mentioned, he proposed by letter to Genl. Canaliso of Matamoros to join against Texas; the Genl. was suspicious, but proposed to a higher source, that it would be well to secure Canales for a time, until the truth of his loyalty or villainy was determined."[78] Information concerning the duplicity of Generals Arista, Vasquez, Reyes, and Colonel Rodríquez was also conveyed to President Lamar in a letter from one of the Texans aiding Canales. He, too, warned of the Mexican plans to invade Texas.[79]

Officially, Texas refrained from participating in the intestine war, and refused to aid the Federalists in any way, except to grant them political asylum and to permit Texans to trade with them. Neverthe-

---

government as late as 1841. Barnard E. Bee to James Webb, Merchants Bank, New Orleans, July 9, 1839; A. S. Wright to Barnard E. Bee, July 1 [1840]; Same to M. B. Lamar, City of New Orleans, March 18, 1841, in Garrison (ed.), *Diplomatic Correspondence of Texas*, 1908, II, 460–462, 657–662, 731–732; *The Red-Lander* (San Augustine), Sept. 29, 1842; *Telegraph and Texas Register*, June 12, 1839.

[77] A. S. Wright to Barnard E. Bee, Mexico City, Nov. 10, 1839, in Garrison (ed.), *Diplomatic Correspondence of Texas*, 1908, II, 618–620.

[78] Same to Same, Head Department, Mexico City, Nov. 1839, in *ibid.*, 1908, II, 620–624.

[79] J. N. Seguin to His Excellency the President of the Republic of Texas, Austin, Feb. 26, 1840, in *Telegraph and Texas Register*, Feb. 3, 1841; William Bryan, Consul, to Secretary of State, Consulate of Texas, New Orleans, Feb. 11, 1840, in Consular Correspondence (Texas), 1838–1875, ms., forwarding letters from A. S. Wright dated Nov. 21, Dec. 7, 25, and 27, 1839.

less, because of the activities of certain Texans occupying positions of influence and trust and because of the threats of Lamar to take offensive operations against Mexico unless she recognized the independence of the Republic, the Texan government was blamed by Mexican officialdom for the rebellion, always anxious to bolster support at home by declaring for a reduction "of Texas, *that Texas* which is the head quarters of the Anarchists, and the nursery of Revolutions." [80] The Mexican government apparently believed that the government of Texas had an active part in the invasion of Mexico and prepared to "strain every nerve to retake that colony." [81]

I am sorry, very sorry, [wrote A. S. Wright in Mexico] that Texas ever made any conditions with the Federals or Anglo-Mexicans; you will find [them] in the end a curse. . . . They will never remain loyal to strangers, treachery will ever be found in their ranks; they . . . aspire to reign over Mexico and should they gain their point, would turn upon Texas with as much fury as the present enemy. I say be careful. I like not the movement. Texas was growing strong. Texas was crowding out the Mexicans, and [there was] no need of bringing on them this terable and ferocious war. Had it not been for this present movement with the federal [party] in Texas Mexico would have slept until next summer during which time Texas would have augmented her power and means and Mexico fighting one with the other would have been spending her little strength.[82]

It was sheer folly to threaten Mexico, for "whenever a campaign is set on foot it will be disastrous," recorded Anson Jones.[83]

[80] Speaker of the House of the Mexican Congress quoted by James Treat to M. B. Lamar, Mexico, July 4, 1840 (Private), in Garrison (ed.), *Diplomatic Correspondence of Texas*, 1908, II, 663–664; A. S. Wright to William Bryan, Mexico City, Dec. 25, 1839, *ibid.*, 1908, II, 518–520; Same to Same, Mexico City, Nov. 21, 1839, *ibid.*, 1908, II, 496–499.

[81] A. S. Wright to William Bryan, Mexico City, Dec. 25, 1839, in *ibid.*, 1908, II, 518.

[82] A. S. Wright to William Bryan, City of Mexico, Dec. 7, 1839, in *ibid.*, 1908, II, 503–504. Bryan, a prominent New Orleans merchant, was one-time United States vice-consul at Pernambuco. During the Texas revolution, he served as "General Agent for Texas" in New Orleans in the recruitment of men, supplies, and money for the Texas cause. On May 24, 1836, David G. Burnet replaced the Bryan agency with Toby and Brother Company, but on December 26, 1838, Lamar appointed him again Texan consul in New Orleans, which position he held until February 7, 1842. After a brief interval he was reappointed in August 1842. Eugene C. Barker (ed.), *The Austin Papers*, III, 303–304; *Handbook of Texas*, I, 234.

[83] Anson Jones, Memorandum Book, no. 2, Wednesday, Aug. 14, 1839, ms.

By its very attitude the Lamar administration seems to have given some encouragement, whether intentionally or not, to the unofficial participation of Texans in the Federal cause on an individual basis; however, the government could ill-afford to jeopardize Hamilton's negotiations for a loan in London by carrying on offensive war against Mexico and blockading her ports, or to throw stumbling blocks into its efforts to obtain French and English recognition,[84] or, by a blockade of Mexico ports, to antagonize the United States who had offered its services as mediator in Texan-Mexican affairs, or to defeat the efforts of its secret agent, James Treat, to obtain from Mexico recognition of Texas independence and a satisfactory boundary adjustment, followed, if possible, by a treaty of peace, amity, and commerce.[85] The government position was not wholeheartedly supported by all citizens. Wrote an opponent of the policy,

When we view the causes of this determination on the part of our Government, we cannot but believe that jealousy and the fear of the advancement of others has prevailed over the more rational opinion of some of the Cabinet and that they as citizens would pursue a course different from that which they as ministers will allow others to do. The paltry excuse or reason for refusing a cooperation with the federal forces at present being the opinion entertained that England and the United States will sooner or later . . . endeavor to effect a compromise between us and the present government or central party of Mexico.[86]

[84] A treaty of commerce and friendship was concluded with France on September 25, 1839, and ratified on February 14, 1840. British recognition was obtained in a series of treaties concluded in November 1840, but not ratified until June 28, 1842. The war between France and Mexico probably hastened French recognition.

[85] James Hamilton to Mirabeau B. Lamar, New York, Aug. 1, 1839, in Garrison (ed.), *Diplomatic Correspondence of Texas,* 1908, II, 468–469; David G. Burnet to James Treat, Department of State, Houston, Aug. 9, 1839, in *ibid.,* 1908, II, 470–472; Same to Same, Houston, Aug. 19, 1839, in *ibid.,* 1908, II, 476–477; R. G. Dunlap to David G. Burnet, New York, June 28, 1839, in *ibid.,* 1907, I, 406–408. Eugene C. Barker (ed.), *Texas History for High Schools and Colleges,* pp. 360–362.

[86] One sheet of one and a half pages of manuscript, unsigned and undated, but commencing: "The negociation of General Anaya on behalf of the federal forces of Mexico and our Government has closed unfavorably to him . . ." in Domestic Correspondence (Texas), undated, ms.

CHAPTER ELEVEN

Texan Participation
in the Federalist Wars: Second Phase

THE ROLE OF TEXAS in the Federal War was thoroughly and vehemently discussed by many a veteran of the Texas revolution who frequented the City of Houston seeking pay in military scrip and bounty lands because the Republic possessed no cash. These veterans often made up for the long-sustained privations by patronizing Henry Kessler's Arcade on the west side of Travis Street, between Preston and Prairie, where they pawned their land certificates with this native Silesian and Kentucky volunteer of the Texas revolution, for brandy cocktails, gin toddies, claret punches, and cherry-brandy *de la foret noire*,[1] while discussing the whimsicalness of Mexican politics and the advantages to Texas and *themselves* of taking sides in the Mexican civil war. Another famous meeting place was the City Hall. Houston was full of restless men eager for lucrative employment and adventure. The weather in May was discouraging and business was slow. The editor of one of the local papers described the climate as "dry, hot and oppressive. Streets dusty and disagreeable," and money was "scarce, and getting scarcer. Business dull, and growing duller, Loafers have increased, are increasing, and ought to be diminished. District Court in session—crimes and criminals are undergoing its scrutiny—hope it will have some effect upon the loafers." [2] When fall came and the northers set in, there were only three stoves in the whole of Houston, and fires were lighted in front of the saloon in the evenings and the inhabitants stood around them and enjoyed—"not excepting the President—hot

---

[1] Max Freund (trans. and ed.), *Gustav Dresel's Houston Journal: Adventures in North America and Texas, 1837–1841*, p. 32.

[2] *Morning Star* (Houston), May 11, 1839.

drinks with merry speeches."[3] At this time, there were probably fifteen hundred to two thousand persons, mostly men, living in Houston "in the most dissimilar manner. The President, the whole personnel of the government, many lawyers who found ample means of support in those new regions, a large number of gamblers, tradesmen, artisans, former soldiers, adventurers, curious travelers from the United States, about a hundred Mexican prisoners who made suitable servants," and a considerable number of Indians who came to trade. "Crimes, the desire for adventure, unfortunate circumstances of all sorts, love of freedom, and the fair prospect of gain had formed this quaint gathering," wrote a foreign observer in 1839. "It was everyone's wish to be somebody in the general company, and therefore everyone threw the veil of oblivion over past deeds. Everyone stood on his own merit."[4] Houston at the time had only a few cabins, numerous tents, and many camps of recently arrived immigrants.

It was under these conditions that, upon the arrival of Anaya and other Federalist leaders in Houston, a series of public meetings was held from September 21 to September 23, 1839, in favor of the Federalist cause. In a public meeting of September 21 the policy of the Texas government in respect to the Federalist cause was criticized. It was said that the administration refused to cooperate with the federal forces in the hope that England and the United States would take up the Texas question and seek to effect a compromise between Texas and the Central party in Mexico, "who are in fact usurpers of the rights of their people . . . and who may be overturned by their enemies ere the compromise could be taken advantage of and leave us then to treat with those who are now rejected by us."[5] It was proposed that individuals who wished to aid the Federalists should be permitted to do so. The meeting then adjourned until the next day, when the discussion about aiding the revolutionists continued. At this time the meeting was addressed by Juan Nepomuceno Margain. Resolutions were adopted for appointing a committee to receive volunteers and donations. Those who volunteered their assistance in recruiting included the following: Andrew Neill, John Weston, J. C. Deartrioe, Ephriam M. Haines, Edward C. Woodruff, J. W. Hays, J. D. Watkins, John B. Couteany, Daniel Stanby, Henry Blood, John Chenoweth, and

[3] Freund (trans. and ed.), *Gustav Dresel's Houston Journal*, p. 36.
[4] *Ibid.*, p. 33.
[5] [Unsigned Draft of an Address delivered before a Meeting at Houston, September 21–23, 1839, in favor of the Federalists], in Juan Pablo Anaya Papers, ms.

G. A. Mull.[6] M. T. Rodger offered to subscribe $5,000 to the cause, paying $500 on the spot.[7]

On September 23 Margain submitted a report of the situation at Matamoros and the strength of the Centralists. An agreement was presented and approved concerning the terms of service and pay of those Texans who might be willing to volunteer. In this agreement, signed by Anaya and Andrew Neill, it was stipulated that the Texan volunteer cavalrymen in the Federalist service were to be governed by the same laws as if they were serving under the government of Texas. All spoils of war that might be taken—and spoils were to be taken only from the Centralist troops—were to be appraised and distributed equally among the officers and soldiers of the forces occupied or employed in taking it, except the arms, munitions, and other items of military significance which would be retained for the use of the Federalist forces generally. The term of enlistment was left indefinite, but it was stated that the Texans could withdraw from the Federal service whenever a majority of them desired to do so. As for pay, both officers and soldiers were to receive the same rate of pay as if they had been in the Texas army. Their pay would commence from the day of their arrival in the Federalist camp near the Nueces or at any other point where Mexican Federalist troops might be stationed.[8] Anaya appointed Andrew Neill a provisional colonel in the cavalry of the Texan Auxiliary,[9] and authorized him to issue temporary commissions

[6] [Portion of a document dealing with the Mustering of the Auxiliary (Texan) Forces, dated: Houston, September 23, 1839, and signed by Juan N. Margain], in Domestic Correspondence (Texas), 1836–1846, ms.

[7] "Subscriptions for the Western Expedition, Houston, September 23d, 1839," unsigned, in *ibid.*, ms.

[8] Los que subscriben en conferencia del dia de hoy sobre los voluntario auxiliar que de Texas marchan a los poblaciones de Mexico pa. ayudar la hecha del restablecimiento del Gob[ier]no federal bajo la constitution de 1824, acordamos los articulos siguientes [signed by:] Juan Pablo [Anaya] [and] A. Neill, Houston, Septe 28 de 1839, in *ibid.*, ms.; Minutes of Meeting to Adopt Means for Rendering Aid to the Federalists, Houston, Sept. 21, 1839, D. S., English, 1 p.; Minutes of Meeting to Adopt Means for Rendering Aid to Federalists, Houston, Sept. 22, 1839; Minutes of a Meeting to Adopt Means for Rendering Aid to the Federalists, Houston, Sept. 23, 1839; Report [of Margain as to Matamoros and the strength of the Federalists], Sept. 23, 1839, Spanish; also a Spanish version of the same unsigned, all in *ibid.*, ms.; copies in Anaya Papers, ms.; Vicente Riva Palacio, *Mexico á través de los siglos*, IV, 449.

[9] Despacho provisional de coronel de caball[a] de auxiliary de Texas á favor del Ciud. Andrew Neill, [signed by:] Juan Pablo de Anaya, General de Division de

to other officers who might serve under his command.[10] Neill was to establish a rendezvous point for the Texan volunteers.

Andrew Neill,[11] who came to Texas in 1836 as captain of a company of volunteers under General Felix Huston, was deeply interested in the Federalist cause. His resignation from the Texas military service had been accepted on August 21, 1838,[12] and he felt free to plan military operations with Anaya. He represented the Anglo-Americans in dealing with Anaya, and signed with the latter the agreement under which the "Texan volunteers" were to participate in the Federal service. Neill had been for some time in touch with some of the Federalists and, in May 1839, had been informed that Reuben Ross and Thomas J. Golightly were in Houston, "both well and doing nothing," and that Samuel G. Powell, "an old citizen" who "has been through a great deal of Mexico," and Al[l]en Johnston, both "good fellows and No. 1 in any case of immergency," were being given letters of introduction to him.[13]

With no expectation of direct help from the Texas government, Anaya determined to go on to the United States to seek aid for his cause, but his departure for New Orleans was delayed at Houston by illness.[14] By November 27 his health was reported to be improving,

---

la Republica Mexicana y en Gefe del ejército federal, Houston, 28 de Sept. 1839, in Domestic Correspondence (Texas), 1836–1846, ms.

[10] Juan Pablo de Anaya, General en Gefe de Ejército federal á Sr. Don Andrew Neill, Comand[an]te de los voluntario auxiliares de Texas, Houston, Sept. 28 de 1839, in *ibid.*, ms.

[11] Andrew Neill was born at Lough Fergus Farm, County of Ayr [or Ayrshire] in southwest Scotland. In his youth he immigrated to western Virginia, where he studied law. In 1836 he was living in Mississippi and serving as a probate judge when he volunteered for service in the Texas revolution. He was one of the founders of Seguin, Texas, in 1838. *Handbook of Texas*, II, 268.

[12] George W. Hockley to Capt. A. Neill, Department of War, Aug. 21, 1838, in Army Papers (Texas), ms.

[13] Major James Izod to A[ndrew] Neill [at San Antonio], Houston, May 28, 1839, in Domestic Correspondence (Texas), 1836–1846, ms. Thomas J. Golightly was a candidate from Harris County of the House of Representatives, Third Congress, in September 1838. Out of seven candidates in the race, he tied for sixth place, polling only 12 out of 717 votes cast. *Telegraph and Texas Register* (Houston), Sept. 8, 1838.

[14] *Telegraph and Texas Register*, Jan. 1, 1840; Sam G. Powell to Andrew Neill, San Antonio, [dated:] Houston, Nov. 27, 1839, in Domestic Correspondence (Texas), 1836–1846, ms. Powell wrote: "You would be surprised to hear how many persons have died here."

and he left Houston during the last week of December for New Orleans by way of Galveston. In New Orleans, Anaya frequented the French Café at the corner of Market Square, but soon lost interest in the political leadership of the northern Federalists and their separatist tendency and turned his attention to giving aid to the revolutionists of Yucatán, even going so far as to draft a constitution for the contemplated new nation.[15]

In the meantime, the other members of Anaya's delegation in Texas proceeded by way of Texana, Victoria, and Refugio to the Federalist camp on the Nueces, recruiting men and supplies at each of the places through which they passed. Taking up position at Lipantitlán, near desirable landing places for sea communication, Canales issued a proclamation inviting the Texans to join him, promising an equal division of the spoils, twenty-five dollars per month, and a half league of land to such as would serve during the war. He then proceeded to recruit, on soil claimed by Texas, a force composed of Mexicans from the Río Grande, a number of poorly armed Carrizo Indians,[16] and more

[15] Freund (trans. and ed.), *Gustav Dresel's Houston Journal*, p. 100. Later, in three Texan and three Yucatec vessels, Anaya launched an invasion of Tabasco in November 1840, where he served as governor from November 17 to December 6, 1840. Being defeated, however, he fled to Yucatán. In 1841 he was defeated at Comitán in Chiapas, after which the inhabitants of Tabasco and Campeche turned away from him. He now gave up his ideas of revolution. In 1847 he was acting President of Mexico for a brief period, but was defeated in the battle of Mexico City. Hubert Howe Bancroft. *History of Mexico*, V, 215 n, 219; "Information derived from Dr. John Long, Resident of Santa Rosa, Coahuila, Mexico," in *Lamar Papers*, VI, 157. H. Yoakum in his *History of Texas from its First Settlement in 1685 to its Annexation to the United States in 1846*, p. 274, makes the mistake of saying that Anaya was captured and put to death at Tampico.

[16] On hearing that the Carrizo (Cane) Indians living about Reinosa were about to join the Federalists, the Centralist authorities arrested and imprisoned those of the tribe who were at Matamoros. There the Indians lay in jail for some time until their chief proposed to the Commandant of the town

to let his men come out and take exercise, which their health required. The commandant consented; and the Indians were brought out naked. They propose[d] a favorite game of kicking the Ball. Bets were made for and against their kicking the Ball from Monterey [Matamoros] to Rinoso a distance of sixty miles. Guards mounted on good horses were ordered to follow. . . . If they kicked the ball to Rinoso, [the story goes] they won; if not they lost. . . . The game was opened—the ball was tossed and all pursued it to give it a kick. They kept it rolling onward until the horsemen appointed to guard them broke down—and were not able to keep up. The ball was kicked [to] Rinoso, where the Indians made their escape and joined Canales.

Lamar Papers, VI, 105–106.

than two hundred Texans. Spies were sent regularly to Camargo, Reinosa, Guerrero, and other points on the Río Grande to report on conditions there.[17]

San Antonio proved a haven of succor and comfort to the Federalists. The frontier traders, Samuel A. Maverick, mayor of the city, John W. Smith, Leandro Arriola, the Menchacas, Navarros, Seguins, and others were quite active in the support of the Federal cause. O'Driscoll's Tavern, at Refugio, was also the scene of considerable activity, serving both as headquarters and refueling station for some of the Texan units. Vidaurri obtained a loan of upwards of $3,000 from Samuel G. Powell, long time resident of Texas, of which Andrew Neill was fully cognizant.[18]

Supplies were assembled at various Texas and United States ports, particularly at New Orleans, and sent by the schooners *Louisiana* and *Olynthus*, the latter under the command of Captain Philip Black. Both vessels were owned by the mercantile establishment of Black & Schoolfield of Austin.[19] Colonel James Power, mayor of the city of Aransas and justice of the peace of Refugio County,[20] and Colonel Henry L. Kinney, "who were at the time associated together in the mercantile business and the promotion of a townsite at Live Oak Point," saw in the Federalist movement an opportunity for profitable commercial enterprise. In September 1839, Kinney transferred his business to Corpus Christi to be nearer the scene of operations, and thereafter for a number of years from his ranch became the purveyor of supplies and information to armed bands and ranger troops, spy companies, and "armies," both Mexican and Texan, operating in that area. At one time enthusiastic about the cause of Mexican federalism, Kinney's interests now deviated to the making of a quick dollar in a lucrative contraband trade. Even Memucan Hunt, the Texan representative on the Joint United States-Texas Boundary Commission, "determined to commence a trade with the northern States of Mexico" at some point

[17] *El Ancla* (Matamoros), June 12, 1840.

[18] A[ndrew] Neill to Francisco Vidaurri y Villasenor en Santa Rosa, San Fernando, Oct. 3, 184[2], in Domestic Correspondence (Texas), 1836–1846, ms. Vidaurri's note to Powell was dated November 5, 1839.

[19] John P. Black and Charles Schoolfield. Hobart Huson, "Iron Men: A History of the Republic of the Río Grande and the Federalist War in Northern Mexico," p. 58.

[20] N. Amory, Chief Clerk, to James C. Allen, Chief Justice, Refugio County, Department of State, Houston, June 26, 1839, in State Department (Texas), Department of State Letterbook, Nov. 1836–Dec. 1841, ms., p. 106.

on the Texan side of the Río Grande in order to recoup his fortune; and he inquired of Lamar in January 1840, if he could "expect any protection to the enterprise from the Gov[ernmen]t troops." "If the Cavalry is organized, will not a part of the Corps be appropriated to the protection of western population and trade?" [21] he asked. The Federalist war brought increased trade activity at other Texas ports, like Copano, Lamar, Aransas City, Live Oak Point, Black Point [22] at the place where the Aransas River emptied into Copano Bay, and at other places, even as far away as Houston and Galveston.

The impetuous Texans who joined the Mexican Federalists were venturesome spirits discontented with the dull monotony of peaceful every day life. They were as fearless as they were reckless. They saw in the Federalist cause opportunities for service, a chance for adventure, or for gain, and, as one recent writer so aptly expressed it, there were some who "simply went for the ride; to match wits with the weather, and one kind of brutality with another, and power with guile." [23] "We have noticed a number of genteel vagrants lounging about the different boarding houses of this city," reported the editor of the *Telegraph* (Houston), "who have no ostensible means of gaining a livelihood and have for some time past neglected to pay their board bill and wash women." [24] These individuals the Federalists sought to attract to their cause. "We would say to those not engaged in business at home," reported two Texans from the Federal army, "Mexico presents a fair field on which with your services you may reap both honor and profit." [25] "Texas," wrote an astute observer at Brazoria in August 1839, "is overwhelmed with Army & Navy officers—there are enough for Russia—& poor Texas is without means to support them on many weeks longer." [26] Thus it is likely that many of these men looked upon the Federalist movement in Mexico as an oppor-

[21] Memucan Hunt to M. B. Lamar, Galveston City, Jan. 4, 1840, in *Lamar Papers*, III, 299–300.
[22] The community of Bayside now occupies this old site. Hobart Huson, "Refugio: A Comprehensive History of Refugio County from Aboriginal Times to the End of World War II," vol. II, chap. 21, p. 2; *Handbook of Texas*, I, 169–170. Philip Dimitt had his trading post here in 1839.
[23] Paul Horgan, *Great River: The Río Grande in North American History*, II, 561.
[24] *Telegraph and Texas Register*, Sept. 15, 1839.
[25] John F. C. Henderson and Thomas Jamison to [the Editor of the *Colorado Gazette and Advertiser*], Jan. 8, 1840, in *Colorado Gazette and Advertiser* (Matagorda), Jan. 18, 1840.
[26] Anson Jones, Memorandum Book, no. 2, Thursday, Aug. 15, 1839, ms.

tunity for profitable employment as well as a chance to add additional glory to their names. The Seminole War in Florida was ending,[27] and no doubt some of the volunteer adventurers, now unemployed, made their way to Texas to participate in further military campaigns. Furthermore, the Cherokee war in east Texas had suddenly terminated during the last week in July, freeing several hundred restless men whose appetite for military glory had only been whetted by the late easy-going campaign.[28]

Considering the condition of the rest of the world in the fall of 1839, as a result of the Panic of 1837, Texas, according to Dr. Ashbel Smith, was "in a flourishing—*very* flourishing state." [29] The number of emigrants entering the country was great. In March the City of Houston was described as having over five hundred men, mostly new arrivals, seeking or eligible for jobs. Many immigrants were arriving from the United States, where the effects of the panic were first felt. During the first ten days of April three steam packets and several sailing vessels landed quite a number of immigrants in Texas.[30] One can assume that most of the immigrants pouring in from the United States found employment in the commercial and agricultural life of the nation, but undoubtedly a few of these from time to time found employment in the Federalist enterprises or the ranger service of the Republic, or both. Even a smaller number joined the hell-raising, plundering cowboys on the southern frontier, where the economic outlook was not as rosy as Dr. Smith pictured conditions in Texas. In the west credit was gone and the collection of debts was at a stand-still with "little prospect of change for the better." [31] "There is *no kind* of currency afloat among us," wrote W. Pinkney Hill from Bastrop in July 1839, "not even shinplasters, sufficient to meet the ordinary transactions of marketing, for *table use* even." [32]

At Houston, as early as May, it was rumored that General Felix Huston, long an advocate of a stern policy towards Mexico, was selling out his property in Mississippi preparatory to emigrating permanently

---

[27] *Telegraph and Texas Register*, May 15, 1839.

[28] *Ibid.*, Aug. 14, 1839; "Cherokee War," *Handbook of Texas*, I, 334–335.

[29] Ashbel Smith to [Westar] Pennock, City of Galveston, Texas, Oct. 21, 1839, in Ashbel Smith Papers, ms.

[30] Same to Gen. [M. B.] Lamar, Houston, Dec. 31, 1839, in *ibid.*, ms.

[31] Bartlett Sims to Austin Bryant, San Felipe or Brazoria, Texas [dated:] Bastrop, Nov. 26, 1838, in James F. Perry Papers (transcripts), ms.

[32] W. Pinkney Hill to J. F. Perry, Bastrop, July 8, 1839, in *ibid.*, ms.

to Galveston with his family.[33] General Huston was in Houston by Saturday, August 19, and on the following Monday evening addressed a large gathering of citizens in the Senate chamber. "We did not hear his speech," declared the editor of the *Telegraph*, "but we understand from those who were present, that it was received with great applause, . . . and that his views with regard to the present and future military operations of the country were very interesting." [34] Huston then set out on a tour of the country to campaign for the post of major general of the militia to succeed Thomas J. Rusk. At Washington-on-the-Brazos he declared in a public speech that he had abandoned for the present all idea of offensive operation against Mexico, and stated that if he were elected, he would devote his whole attention to the protection of the frontier and would endeavor to bring to a speedy termination the country's Indian difficulties.[35]

Having made his campaign in Texas, Huston went to Mississippi, where his return to Texas was delayed by repeated attacks of the ague and fever. By early December, however, his health had so improved that he wrote Lamar he expected to start for Texas before January 1. When he did come, he would proceed immediately to Washington, to await the orders of the government, believing, as he said, by the incomplete election returns he had seen reported, that he had been elected major general. "I shall be prepared for action," he declared, "and contemplate spending most of my time on the frontier." He hoped that Congress, then in session, would enact such legislation in respect to the militia as would "render that arm of defence prompt and efficient." [36]

Colonel Ross,[37] a Virginian and late aide to General Felix Huston,

[33] Major James Izod to A[ndrew] Neill [at San Antonio], Houston, May 28, 1839, in Domestic Correspondence (Texas) 1836–1846, ms.

[34] *Telegraph and Texas Register*, Aug. 21, 1839.

[35] *Colorado Gazette and Advertiser*, Sept. 22, 1839.

[36] Felix Huston to Mirabeau B. Lamar, Natches, Dec. 9, 1839, in *Lamar Papers*, V, 332.

[37] Colonel Reuben Ross, a native of Virginia, was the nephew of the Reuben Ross who fought in Texas against Spanish authority as a member of the Bernardo Gutiérrez and Augustus Magee expedition of 1812–1813, and who was eventually elected a major under Magee. As a result of barbarous treatment accorded a group of prisoners captured at San Antonio, Ross abandoned the cause with others and fled the country. He later received a grant of land from the Mexican government, but was murdered shortly afterwards in the State of Tamaulipas. His grant was then cancelled by the government and assigned to Dr. John Cameron on

209

sought and obtained from the Texan government permission to raise a volunteer company for the protection of the southwestern frontier. His was the first company formed in the west for that purpose, and he was hailed as a "brave and gallant" officer, "possessing that discretion so peculiarly necessary in the performance of his particular duty." By the end of June he had recruited seventy-five or more rangers.[38] It was understood that Ross' company was to be mounted and was to render protection and assistance to the civil authorities of the counties of San Patricio, Refugio, and Victoria "against a banditti composed of Americans, Mexicans, and Indians who have," declared one of the Houston newspapers, "for some time committed the most desperate outrages upon the Río Grande traders," who conduct their business in accordance to a law laid down by the last session of Congress.[39] In permitting Ross to organize a company for frontier service, the Texas administration was seeking to carry out its slowly developing plans to provide a respectable and permanent corps for the western frontier.

Colonel Ross' company was not the only group being organized for this purpose. "We learn," reported the editor of the *Morning Star*,[40] "that a company is about being raised [under Colonel Henry W. Karnes] to proceed to the West, to preserve the citizens and traders from further violence." Early in September volunteers reached Galveston on the steamboat *Rufus Putnam*, destined for service on the frontier under Colonel Karnes, who had been authorized to receive

---

September 19, 1828. John Henry Brown, *History of Texas from 1685 to 1892*, I, 57; Dudley G. Wooten, *A Comprehensive History of Texas, 1625 to 1897*, I, 79, 82; Curtis Bishop and Bascom Giles, *Lots of Land*, p. 88; Walter F. McCaleb, "The First Period in the Gutiérrez-Magee Expedition," *Quarterly of the Texas State Historical Association*, IV (1900–1901), 218–219; "Information derived from Major Roman," *Lamar Papers*, VI, 137; J. R. Lewis to David G. Burnet, Natchez, March 26, 1836, in Executive Department Journals, Mar. 1836–Sept. 1836, p. 187, ms. The younger Ross, a lawyer by profession, came to Texas in 1836 with General John A. Quitman's Mississippi volunteer regiment and entered the regular army of Texas. In 1837 he served as an aide-de-camp to General Felix Huston. In 1838 he was made captain of a ranger company on the western frontier, and in the following year was promoted to the rank of major.

[38] James Izod to Capt. A. Neill, San Antonio, [dated:] Houston, June 25, 1839, in Domestic Correspondence (Texas), 1836–1846, ms., [endorsed:] Received July 4th.

[39] *Telegraph and Texas Register*, July 17 and 31, 1839.

[40] July 10, 1839.

350 volunteers in addition to those already under his command.[41] A week later the *Alexander* brought from the United States thirty more recruits for the army. "We have not heard," declared the *Galvestonian,* "whether they were recruited out of the charity hospital or the calaboose—perhaps neither"; yet, the *Telegraph and Texas Register* [42] was quick to defend them, declaring that it had "not seen a finer set of troops in Texas."

Heading west from Houston around July 3 with his company, Ross received at the Navidad reports from San Antonio that a force of Mexicans and Indians was concentrating between the Nueces and the Río Grande; the reports expressed fear that this force might descend upon Béxar. Ross promptly advanced toward San Antonio reaching that city late in August with sixty-five men.[43] He was at Gonzales the first week in September, and from there apparently went to Goliad. Claiming now that he had been given discretionary powers, he interpreted his orders liberally, and assumed that the best way to protect the western frontier was to cross the Río Grande and levy war upon the authority responsible for the banditti raids upon Texas.[44] Therefore, he proceeded to cast his lot with Canales, meeting him at the Agua Dulce, near San Patricio, sixty miles southwest of La Bahía.

Several days after Ross left Houston, Colonel Henry W. Karnes arrived in the city on Saturday, July 6, from San Antonio [45] to see to the recruiting of his frontier regiment. Captain William F. Wilson raised a company of Mounted Volunteers at Galveston for Karnes' regiment.[46] The fiitting out of Ross' company and the enlistment of volunteers to strengthen Karnes' unit must have given some consolation at Houston to the permanent and more stable residents of the place, for at the end of the year we find Dr. Ashbel Smith, an important speculator in Texas real estate, writing that "Business is become very brisk in Houston, and is much greater than any previous year. The

---

[41] *Telegraph and Texas Register,* Sept. 18, 1839.
[42] Sept. 25, 1839.
[43] *Telegraph and Texas Register,* Sept. 4 and 11, 1839.
[44] Peter H. Bell to Branch T. Archer, Oct. 30, 1839, in Army Papers (Texas), ms.
[45] *Morning Star,* July 10, 1839.
[46] Muster Roll of Captain William F. Wilson's Company of Galveston Mounted Volunteers commanded by Col. H. W. Karnes, Militia Rolls (Texas), ms. The roll contains sixty names. Among them were William Dunbar, orderly sergeant; Ephraim McLane, private; Francis White, private; and William H. Emory, private. The men went on active duty, September 8, 1839.

town presents a different appearance from what it did formerly: chiefly from the disappearance of the large class of gentlemen loafers and blackguard loafers who infested it," [47] some of whom, no doubt, were attracted by the spirit of adventure and the opportunities afforded by participation in the Federalist campaigns. During the latter part of July the Houston town council, re-enforced by a joint resolution passed by the Texas Congress in January 1839, effective March 1, 1839, providing for the arrest of vagrants and their punishment by imprisonment or whipping,[48] was "busily engaged, . . . in disposing of the gamblers and loafers." Through the exertions of the peace officers and the co-operation of the good citizens, the council's efforts were attended with great success.[49] No doubt, the ravages of yellow fever caused many to leave and reduced the number of those who remained. In late August 1839, the streets of Houston were deserted; all shops were closed; the city seemed dead. "The water of the bayou looked so lazy and dark-green, and the air was so oppressively sultry and ghastly," reported Gustav Dresel,[50] that surely the Federal ranks benefited some from this local situation.

Present at the meeting between Ross and Canales at Victoria were

[47] Ashbel Smith to Gen. [M. B.] Lamar, Houston, Dec. 31, 1839, in Ashbel Smith Papers, ms. Reported the *Morning Star* of July 11, 1839,
  Our town is apparently quiet again, after the late disturbances. The city authorities have been well rewarded for their energy and vigilance, by complete success in restoring the city to order. . . . The proceedings of the last few days, in this city, may afford a lesson to those of the States who have looked upon our country as merely a place of refuge for crime, and a den of dishonor and licentiousness, and may force upon them the conviction, that although here, as in every other town of the known world, we are troubled with a certain proportion of bad and vagrant characters, there is sufficient dignity among our citizens to know what is their due, and sufficient energy to enforce its being paid.
[48] "A Joint Resolution for the Punishment of Vagrants," approved January 10, 1839, H. P. N. Gammel (ed.), *Laws of Texas*, II, 39–40. The law on vagrancy required all justices of the peace and other civil officers after March 1, 1839, "to arrest all vagrants and idle persons living within their respective jurisdictions, and examine into their mode and manner of living, and where no visible means" could be shown for their support or "no proper exertions" made by the party concerned "to obtain an honest livelihood, they shall be judged to work for the public, thirty days for the first offence, sixty days for the second, and one year for the third offence, or receive thirty-nine lashes on his bare back."
[49] *Telegraph and Texas Register*, Aug. 7, 1839; Freund (trans. and ed.), *Gustav Dresel's Houston Journal*, pp 37, 78.
[50] Freund (trans. and ed.), *Gustav Dresel's Houston Journal*, p. 78.

Samuel W. Jordan, late a captain in the Texas service in charge of a company for the protection of the frontier near San Antonio, and more recently from the Cherokee campaign in which he had been severely wounded,[51] Captain John T. Price, Ewen Cameron [52] of Price's Company, and Samuel A. Plummer, an intimate friend and business associate of President Lamar.[53] At the meeting with the leaders of the Mexican Federalists, it was determined the expedition would march under the Texas flag. The Texan force was to operate as a separate unit under its own officers, but with Canales in command of all the Federalist forces; Colonel Carbajal was to serve as his chief of staff; Lieutenant Colonel Jordan was to be corps staff officer; and Dr. Shields Booker, corps surgeon. The terms under which the Texans served in the Federal army were signed in Houston by Anaya and Neill a week after the Texans began their march from the Nueces toward the Río Grande. Canales offered the Anglo-Texans who would join him twenty-two dollars a month for their services and an equal portion of all spoils taken.[54]

The wily Canales was not a military man by profession, but a lawyer with considerable education and culture. He had been a member of the legislature of Tamaulipas in 1832, where he had served as presi-

[51] A. S. Johnston, Secretary of War, to M. B. Lamar, Dec. 23, 1838, in *Lamar Papers*, II, 371–372; S. W. Jordan, Captain Commanding Post Béxar, to William G. Cooke, Acting Quartermaster General, Post Béxar, April 22, 1839, in W. P. Webb Collection, Texas Rangers, ms.; E. Morehead, Adjutant-General and Colonel Commanding to Captain [S. W.] Jourdan, Head Quarters of the Army, Camp Chambers, Oct. 7, 1837 (General Order No. 11), Army Papers (Texas), ms.; John Henry Brown, *Indian Wars and Pioneers of Texas*, p. 68. Jordan resigned from the 1st Regiment of Infantry on September 2, 1839. *Texas Sentinel* (Austin), May 16, 1840.

[52] Ewen Cameron, whose education was limited to elementary reading and writing, was one of the first of the cowboys to fight with the Federalists. In April 1839, in the second battle of Saltillo, Cameron and the twenty-five Americans under him aided Pedro Lemus in defeating the Centralists under Ugartechea and Arredondo. Dr. John Long, a resident of Santa Rosa, Coahuila, declared that Cameron did "more execution in the fight at Saltillo than any other man." And Brown says that "he was a prudent and sagacious man of few words, careful of the lives of his men, who idolized him, and never hesitated to follow where he led." *Lamar Papers*, VI, 157, 313; Brown, *History of Texas*, II, 216.

[53] Huson, "Refugio," chap. XXIII, 11.

[54] John F. O. Henderson and Thomas Jamison to [Editor of the *Colorado Gazette and Advertiser*], Jan. 8, 1840, in *Colorado Gazette and Advertiser*, Jan 18, 1840.

dent of the Chamber of Deputies.[55] As one writer expressed it, he was "the most persistent and unconquerable leader of Federalism in Northern Mexico," [56] and it might be added he pursued his political ideal with everything but talent. Canales was a small man of brown complexion, whose eyes, reported a German businessman who met him in Houston, were "as false as those of a mustang." [57] Another person described him as being approximately thirty-five years of age, "with a mild and intelligent expression of countenance and a high forehead denoting intellect." [58] It is said that he usually did not strike one favorably at first, but that upon acquaintance it was impossible to remain uninterested in him and his cause. Although he possessed a rather magnetic personality, his skill in military leadership, upon which Mexican politics too often depended, was very limited. As a military man he proved to be incompetent and timorous. He believed in divination, and on all hazardous occasions would have his horoscope cast, and govern his actions accordingly.

The Federalist army was composed of two divisions—one of Mexicans and the other of Texans. The Texans, numbering 226 strong, proceeded to organize. They chose as their commander, Ross, who was given the title of "Colonel." [59] Richard Roman,[60]—a Keutuckian who

---

[55] *Gaceta Constitucional* (Monterey), Sept. 13, 1832. Canales served as *ad interim* governor of Tamaulipas for a few months in 1851. Gabriel Saldivar, *Historia compendiada de Tamaulipas*, p. 311.

[56] Huson, "Iron Men," p. 62.

[57] Freund (trans. and ed.), *Gustav Dresel's Houston Journal*, p. 101.

[58] W. F. O. to W. D. Wallach, Bastrop, May 5, 1840, in *Colorado Gazette and Advertiser*, May 23, 1840.

[59] "Information from Capt. Benj. Hill," in *Lamar Papers*, VI, 134–135; Huson, "Iron Men," pp. 75–76; *Handbook of Texas*, II, 500.

[60] Richard Roman, son of William Roman, was born in Fayette County, Kentucky, in 1811. He attended the medical school of Transylvania University, 1830–1831, but did not graduate. He participated in the Black Hawk War in 1832. In January 1836, he landed at Velasco, Texas, and enrolled as first lieutenant in Captain John Hart's Company, and a few weeks later, February 13, became captain of the company. He fought in the battle of San Jacinto, but afterwards resigned from the regular army and settled at Victoria where he was elected to the First Congress. In 1838 or 1839 Roman moved to Refugio and on April 25, 1839, was elected clerk to the Board of Land Commissioners. In 1839 he represented Refugio County in the Third Congress. After the first Federalist campaign from Texas, he moved to Victoria and was elected county clerk in 1841. He represented Victoria, Jackson, and Calhoun counties in the Ninth Congress. During the Mexican War Roman served as a Ranger under Colonel John C. Hays. For a

had come to Texas in 1836, had fought in the battle of San Jacinto, had been an aide-de-camp to General Thomas J. Rusk and subsequently a congressman from Victoria—was elected lieutenant colonel; James Dolan of Nacogdoches, major; Captain Benjamin Hill,[61] adjutant of the command; and Dr. Edmund J. Felder,[62] assistant surgeon. Jordan had no command, but, as we have already seen, was accorded a place on Canales' staff as a Lieutenant Colonel. Among the captains were Thomas Allen of Houston, who succeeded to the command of the company of about thirty men recruited by Ross in Houston when Ross was elected commander of the Texan division; Wiley B. [?] Merrell, Alonzo B. Sweitzer, Thomas Pratt,[63] John T. Price (largest company), Jacob Eberly (eighteen men), and Thomas Hagler of North Carolina and Houston (forty men). Other participants in the expedition who were prominent men at the time, or later became so, were John R. Baker, John W. B. McFarlane (a cousin of the Camerons), Henry Ryals, James Fox, Michael Fox, Alfred S. Thurmond, Willard Richardson, William St. John, Henry Whalen, Michael Whalen, and others, not to forget Alonzo B. Sweitzer, already mentioned as a captain, who had a government contract in the spring of 1839 to furnish provisions for the Texan troops at Post Béxar, but had taken no steps whatsoever to comply with his contract.[64] The Anglo-Americans enlisted for no set period.

---

full biographical sketch of Richard Roman, see Brown, *Indian Wars and Pioneers of Texas*, p. 142; *Biographical Directory of the Texan Conventions and Congresses*, pp. 162–163.

[61] Benjamin F. Hill served as clerk of the Eighth Congress of the Republic of Texas, and was later a member of the 1st State Legislature. During the Mexican War he served as a captain in the United States Army, and for a time occupied the position of Adjutant-General of the State of Texas. He was killed at Victoria in 1866. Huson, "Iron Men," pp. 76–77.

[62] Dr. Edmond J. Felder, a citizen of Harris County, was appointed on July 2, 1839, assistant surgeon in the Texan Army. He reported for duty to Captain Reuben Ross and "proceeded with his command from Houston to Gonzales and thence by way of San Antonio to the Nueces near San Patricio, where he went with the Federalists to the Rio Grande," Harriet Smither (ed.), *Journals of the Sixth Congress of the Republic of Texas*, II, 8 n.

[63] Thomas Pratt made application on July 23, 1838, for a captaincy in the cavalry of the Republic, but was rejected on the grounds that he was "unworthy" the position. Thomas Pratt to M. B. Lamar, Houston, April 17, 1838; Same to Same, Richmond, Jan. 7, 1840, in *Lamar Papers*, V, 274–275, 398–399; Yoakum, *History of Texas*, II, 274 n; *Telegraph and Texas Register*, Oct. 30, 1839.

[64] S. W. Jordan, Capt. Comg. Post Béxar, to William G. Cooke, Actg Quarter

The Federalist division was made up of a regiment of infantry under Colonel Luis Lopez and two cavalry units commanded by Colonel José María González and Antonio Zapata,[65] respectively. The Mexicans numbered about nine hundred men, but the command was without artillery.[66] Down in Mexico, the states of Durango, Chihuahua, and Coahuila were reported to be "scratching together ways and means to assist Tamaulipas to drive the Texians off the Nueces."[67]

In preparation for the forward movement of the main Federalist army, Zapata advanced from his position on the Río Blanco below the Nueces, to which place he had retreated upon the defeat of the Federalists, toward Guerrero, the first point to be attacked. At Guerrero his unit of 150 men was to be met by Canales and a combined attack would then be launched against the place. When the main body left

---

Master Gen¹., Post Béxar, April 22, 1839, Office of the Adjutant General, Texas, in W. P. Webb Collection, Texas Rangers, ms.

[65] Antonio Zapata, known among the Indians as "Sombrero de Manteca" because his hat usually shone with perspiration and oil from his hair mixed with the dust and dirt which settled upon it, was one of the ablest and bravest of the Mexican military leaders. Born in Guerrero of poor parents, he became a sheepherder in his early youth, and eventually a ranchero, specializing in sheep raising. He married an orphan girl, and one of his daughters in 1839 married Budd Edmondson, a Texan. Zapata's ranching operations proved very successful and he gradually accumulated a fortune in sheep and land. At one time it is said that he drove 90,000 head of sheep to Mexico City in one drive, from which he made a large profit and established himself as a merchant in Guerrero. At the beginning of the Texas revolution, he was considered one of the wealthiest men of northern Mexico, but during the war the Mexican armies ravaged his flocks, carried away his property, and caused the foreign merchants to close their trading houses in northern Mexico. Their liquidation hurt Zapata, who was unexpectedly called upon to pay debts which he owed these foreign businessmen. Since he was a man of great personal honor and integrity, this meant bankruptcy for him and his family. It is reported that he paid the foreign merchants $70,000. In politics, Zapata was a staunch republican, adhering to and vigorously supporting, even to death, the principles of the constitution of 1824, which, after 1834, for many years was seldom adhered to by the ruling authorities of Mexico. Virgil N. Lott and Mercurio Martinez, *Kingdom of Zapata*, p. 51; Huson, "Iron Men," p. 66–67.

[66] "From Capt. Benj. Hill," in *Lamar Papers*, VI, 134–135; *Telegraph and Texas Register*, Oct. 30, 1839.

[67] A. S. Wright to Barnard E. Bee, City of Mexico, Nov. 10, 1839; see also, Same to William Bryan, Mexico City, Nov. 22, 1839, in Garrison (ed.), *Diplomatic Correspondence of Texas*, 1908, II, 618–620, 497.

216

the Nueces on September 20 to join Zapata, the Indians were on foot, "the rest mounted, without tents, bread or money, not one man in the company having $5.00." [68] Ten days later, numbering some 600 [69] effective men, including the Texans, the Federalists reached the Río Grande opposite Guerrero, where they were joined by the 150 men under Zapata. At this point Canales determined that the expedition should no longer continue under the Texas flag, and over the protest of Colonel Ross, the "Lone Star" flag was abandoned. [70]

With the main force of Federal Mexicans, Ross and Roman crossed the Río Grande at Carrizo (now Zapata) below the Salado on the night of September 30, and took up a position southeast of Guerrero on the road to Mier. Jordan and Zapata were to cross their troops at a point above the Salado. Canales and his men, mostly Mexicans and Indian allies lingered behind. On October 1, after encountering some delay in crossing the river, probably caused by a limited number of boats, [71] the Federalists, about 100 in number evenly divided under Lieutenant Colonel Jordan [72] and Zapata, crossed the Salado above its

[68] "Information from Major [Richard] Roman," in *Lamar Papers*, VI, 136.

[69] Arista reported the force being fitted out on the Nueces as consisting of 830 persons. Mariano Arista, "Proceso institutido contra los extranjeros Victor Lupín y Benito Watman acusados de haber tomado armas contra el Gobierno de la Republica, March 26, 1840," Exp. Núm. 1360, Legájo Núm. 34 (1839–1842); the U. S. Consul at Matamoros says that 300 Texans participated in the attack on Mier on November 1, 1839. D. W. Smith to John Forsyth, Matamoros, Nov. 10, 1839, no. 160, in Consular Dispatches (U. S.), 1837–1839 (Matamoros), ms., microfilm. "A gentleman just from the Río Grande" reported early in November that on October 26 he had encountered encamped near the river 3,000 Federalists and 300 Texans, who intended to march against Mier to repossess several pieces of artillery which the Centralists had taken from the Federalists. *Colorado Gazette and Advertiser*, Nov. 2, 1839.

[70] "Information from Major [Richard] Roman," in *Lamar Papers*, VI, 136. The American consul at Matamoros reported that the Texan flag was displayed triumphantly over the walls of Mier. This rumor, however, was explicitly denied by Canales. D. W. Smith to John Forsyth, Matamoros, Nov. 10 and Dec. 24, 1839, in Consular Dispatches (U. S.), 1837–1839 (Matamoros), ms., microfilm.

[71] In the dry season, when the river was not in flood, the Indians frequently swam the Río Grande, transporting their belongings across on rafts made of buffalo hides, with one between four of them holding to the raft with one hand and swimming with the other.

[72] *La Brisa* (Matamoros), Nov. 8, 1839. Hill declared that no Mexicans participated in the taking of Guerrero—that they were all in the lower division with Ross. He also recalled the garrison as numbering 320 strong; whereas, Major

mouth a little before day and entered Guerrero between daylight and sunrise, following a spirited fight with the garrison comprising 200 [73] men under José Bernardo Maximiliano Gutiérrez de Lara,[74] one of the early independence leaders in New Spain and ex-governor of the State of Tamaulipas who had been appointed to the command only three or four days before to succeed Captain Pedro Rodríquez. The Centralists fled toward the Salado. Ross crossed below the mouth of the Salado and entered Guerrero after the dispersal of the garrison. Gutiérrez, who had two sons in Canales' command, attempted to ford the river when one of the Texans, seeing him cried out: " 'Look! There is the priest! Seize him!' " The old man, realizing that he was about to be captured, turned back, and as he stepped out of the water, "drawing himself up with quiet dignity," announced,

"I am no priest; I am Bernardo Gutiérrez. I desire to see the American commander."

A call went up for Col. Ross, which was heard by the venerable prisoner. When Ross reached the place, Gutiérrez inquired,

"Are you related to the Major Reuben Ross who was my compatriot in 1812 and 1813?"

Ross replied, "I am his nephew."

Roman reported the force as 150. "Information from Capt. Benj. Hill," in *Lamar Papers*, VI, 134–135; "Information from Major Richard Roman," in *Lamar Papers*, VI, 136.

[73] The number is given as 100 men in the *Colorado Gazette and Advertiser*, Jan. 4, 1840.

[74] "Information from Major [Richard] Roman," *Lamar Papers*, VI, 136; "Information from Captain Benjamin Hill," *ibid.*, VI, 134; "Information from Juan Ramos," *ibid.*, VI, 117; Huson, "Iron Men," pp. 2–7. For a sketch of the renowned José Bernardo M. Gutiérrez de Lara see Kathryn Garrett, *Green Flag over Texas: a Story of the Last Years of Spain in Texas*; Harris G. Warren, *The Sword Was Their Passport: A History of American Filibustering in the Mexican Revolution*; Vito Alessio Robles, *Coahuila y Texas desde la consumación de la independencia hasta el tratado de paz de Guadalupe Hidalgo*, I; Rie Jarrett, *Gutiérrez de Lara, Mexican Texan: The Story of a Creole Hero*; Bancroft, *History of Texas and the North Mexican States*, II; McCaleb, "The First Period of the Gutiérrez-Magee Expedition," *Quarterly of the Texas State Historical Association*, IV (1900–1901), 218–229; *Handbook of Texas*, I, 749–751; "Dr. Willard's 'Tour' from Council Bluffs, Missouri to Santa Fé, New Mexico, thence down the general course of the Río del Norte to its mouth, comprising a distance of 2,000 miles," in "Patties' Personal Narrative," in R. G. Thwaites (ed.), *Early Western Travels, 1748–1846*, XVIII, 362–364.

Federalist Wars: Second Phase

"I am Bernardo Gutiérrez," said the captive simply. "Knowing the character of the uncle, I doubt not that I will be treated with humanity by the nephew." [75]

After shaking hands with the distinguished captive, Ross ordered that he be treated kindly, and rode off to direct the work of bringing in the fugitive garrison. In the meantime, Gutiérrez seated himself on a pile of baggage to await the pleasure of his captors. Later in the afternoon, Canales, with a detachment of Indians and Mexicans, entered Ross' camp.

Seeing Gutiérrez there, the Federalist chief strode toward him exclaiming, "Ha! I see the traitor! You shall not escape your deserts!" With this he lunged at the captive with his sword, while his followers fell upon the aged and defenseless hero and tore off his clothing [and buttons]. Gutiérrez's two sons, who were in the victorious army, appealed to Colonel Ross to save their father's life. Ross immediately came to the scene and stopped the maltreatment of the prisoner, and curtly rebuked Canales.

After that, the stories vary. Some accounts say that Ross immediately granted the old man his freedom; whereas, others say he was freed after the battle of Alcantro (Alamo). However, in spite of this kind treatment, on October 22 Gutiérrez wrote Zapata in reference to the obstinate recklessness of the Federalists in continuing their revolutionary designs, and asserted that in obtaining the services of foreign auxiliaries, the Federalists were "transforming themselves by such a horrible step, from residents [citizens] to traitors." He declared that in spite of his age (65) and bad health he had accepted the military command of Guerrero with a sworn statement not to put down his arms until death or the salvation of the national honor and integrity of the nation's territory.[76]

In the capture of Guerrero, the Federalists lost none of their men, but the Centralists not only lost a quantity of baggage, arms, ammunition, but also had twenty men killed and many more drowned in

[75] Huson, "Iron Men," pp. 88–89; Jarrett, *Gutiérrez de Lara; Mexican Texan*, p. 67.
[76] José Bernardo Gutiérrez de Lara to Antonio Zapata, Oct. 22, 1839, reprinted from *Alcance al Seminario Politico*, Oct. 31, 1839, in *Gaceta de Tampico*, Nov. 23, 1839. This letter was transmitted to Zapata by Cárdenas, mutual friend of both. See also, "Information derived from Major [Richard] Roman, in *Lamar Papers*, VI, 136–138.

the Río Grande and the Salado.[77] Some fled to Mier with the terrifying news of defeat, and the loyal press and officialdom sought to arouse the people to the dangers of an invasion by "colonials," assisted and abetted by disgruntled groups at home. They attributed the success of the Federalists to their Texan allies, and the usual invectives against Texas and Texans in the press and among the public were multiplied.[78] The editor of *El Diario del Gobierno* (Mexico City) declared that "the Mexicans were less fortunate than the [people] of the most unlucky country of the world. There are among us, I am forced to say, men so vile, so destitute of modesty, lastly, so traitorous, that they have no hesitancy in making common cause with the enemies of [our] territorial integrity and . . . independence." [79] The union of Canales with Ross, declared *El Ancla*,[80] "constitutes treason; it is the lack of loyalty to the sovereign Mexican nation."

It was the opinion of the loyal citizens and frontier officials that the incursion of Ross was authorized by the Texan government and that his unit was the vanguard of a much larger force to be dispatched to the assistance of the Federalists. Consequently, dispatches were sent in great haste by the Centralist frontier commanders to the City of Mexico calling for assistance.[81]

In the meantime, at Matamoros, Canalizo declared as traitors Anaya, Canales, Zapata, and the other Federal leaders, for seeking the aid of the "rebellious" Texans—for the horrible crime of making common cause with the Texans at the risk of "menacing Mexican independence and liberty." [82] This was followed on December 9 by President Bustamante's sending to Congress a proposal to make it treason against the state for anyone "to write, act, or speak in favour of the views and intentions of the Texans; or in favour of the views of any foreign

---

[77] "Information from Juan Ramos," in *Lamar Papers*, VI, 112–114; "Information derived from Anson G. Neal, Laredo, May 30, 1847," in *ibid.*, VI, 100; Yoakum, *History of Texas*, II, 274; *Colorado Gazette and Advertiser*, Jan. 4, 1840, says the Centralists lost 6–8 men.

[78] James Treat to David G. Burnet, City of Vera Cruz, Nov. 29, 1839 (Confidential) and Same to James Hamilton, Mexico, Dec. 16, 1839, in Garrison (ed.), *Diplomatic Correspondence of Texas*, 1908, II, 501–503, 507–512.

[79] Quoted in *El Ancla*, Dec. 20, 1839.

[80] Dec. 27, 1839.

[81] *Telegraph and Texas Register*, Dec. 18, 1839; *New Orleans Bulletin* quoted by the *Colorado Gazette and Advertiser*, Dec. 21, 1839.

[82] *La Brisa*, Nov. 7, 1839.

power having for its object to dismember the territory of Mexico." [83]
Congress was called upon to give the President special powers to levy
taxes to support the war against Texas and to reunite that department
to the union.[84]

The recent defeat of Centralist forces does not decrease the courage
of the Mexican army, declared *La Brisa*, nor does it diminish the enthusiasm of the Mexicans. The absurdity of the current civil war is
that while Mexicans fight among themselves over such issues as to
whether or not the government should be one of Federalism or Centralism, or assemblies called "congresses" or "juntas," and the provinces
called "states" or "departments," the independence of the nation is
threatened by invading hordes of foreigners. Let all unite, cried the
editor, and cooperate with General Canalizo in defense of the honor
and integrity of our country and in meting out punishment to the
traitors among us and to the perverse adventurers who come to insult
us.[85] After expelling the invader, the army should enter Texas to remove from that beautiful province the usurped domination of those
pirates who occupy it. The Texans aiding the Federalist cause, declared
the editor of *La Brisa*,[86] are not sincere, for their only pretense is "to
enrich themselves with the spoilation of our properties. Our lands, our
livestock, our equipment and all we possess will undoubtedly capture
their greediness." With the present inhabitants driven from the country or reduced to the most degraded slavery, our land, unless we rally
to the support of the government, will shortly be occupied by a foreign
people, different in religion, customs, and language; and the miserable
Mexican who might survive such a disgrace, will become a stranger
in his own land.

The Texan infantry commander while at Camargo, reported the
editor of *El Ancla*,[87] "saw a lady whose graces he insisted upon to
propagate his specie, and prompted by only this reason, he said before
all bystanders that there was 'the woman I desire,' and without more,
nor less, took her by the hand, and in broad daylight, and in the

---

[83] James Treat to James Hamilton, Dec. 16, 1839, in Garrison (ed.), *Diplomatic Correspondence of Texas*, 1908, II, 518–520.

[84] *Ibid.*; *El Ancla*, Dec. 20, 1839; A. S. Wright to William Bryan, Mexico City, Dec. 25, 1839, in Garrison (ed.), *Diplomatic Correspondence of Texas*, 1908, II, 518–520.

[85] *La Brisa*, Aug. 30, 1839 and Nov. 8, 1839.

[86] November 15, 1839.

[87] Jan. 3, 1840.

presence of all who were there," threatening the Mexican infantry commander with a charge of the bayonet if he interfered, he shamefully mistreated her in the presence of her husband.

The unhappy woman, full of shame, resisted with all her strength; while the men were without means other than to say "that he should leave her alone, that in this country such acts were very reserved and were [performed only] with the full consent of the parties; and that to the contrary was punished severely; that this was a married woman, and that her husband was present. . . . To which the Spanish-fly Anglo-American replied, "I desire a married woman, this one is good for me." While such unheard of happenings were transpiring, one of those present determined to relate the whole to General Canales . . . who instructed "that no one interfere with that man, because he had paid 4,000 pesos into the treasury for the aid of independence of this frontier; he had rendered many services and was very enthusiastic in the cause that he defended."

Owing to the unhappy transaction [at Mier and Guerrero between the Federalist-Texans and Mexicans] which took place lately on the Rio Grand[e] [reported A. S. Wright, the secret agent of Texas in Mexico], must be attributed this precipitate and unlooked for . . . [declaration of war by] the Mexican Government. I was aware that an expedition was fitting out for that Country [Texas] for the coming spring and that an invasion would be the Result if another internal revolution did not prevent it. . . . But owing to the awful fact that their Frontiers upon the R. Grand[e] now swarms with enemies of foreign blood presents a scene of such magnified danger to the country that every consideration of minor importance has been laid aside and the country with all its towns will be left to the mercy of the Bandit hord[e] who may deluge the republic and the revolting foe. [The] Government under present circumstances cannot stay the depredations of the robber; she alone is able to call upon the people in patriotic strains to lay down their domestic quarles . . . to crush the rebel Texian foe and grind to powder the more accursed traitors of their own blood attached to that hateful flag.[88]

In Mexico City the Texans were reported on the Río Grande with several schooners of war. It was said that the people of the United States were indirectly aiding Texas with means to carry on the war, and that some of the old friends of Texas in the United States had

[88] A. S. Wright to William Bryan, Mexico City, Nov. 21, 1839, in Garrison (ed.), *Diplomatic Correspondence of Texas*, 1908, II, 496–497.

awakened "to a new era of speculation even beyond the Río Grand[e]. The clustering stars upon the American flag have had their song of joy in hopes of an additional star," it was said, "even that of Texas being added to their number." [89] What does Texas have to fear? asked Wright. He then proceeded to give a description of the Mexican troops being assembled for the Texas campaign. Assume, he said, that you are standing on some

. . . towering height near Monterey or Durango where the various divisions that compose this campaign will meet. Look to the S. W. [and] behold that numerious throng that crowd the highways. These are the troops from Mexico, Pueblo and other central districts of Mexico. They are the best clothed of any you see, but they are in rags. Many are without hats and many are even without sandals; how slow they move; what an awful spectacle of human misery, their vivacity has fled for want of the necessaries of life; a little further on are hundreds of poor females following their husbands barefooted with their children upon their backs—still further on you may see in the way they come a continual Hospital of dead and dying. To the North you behold a crowd advancing more like burned pilgrims dressed in tatters than people going to war. You may see a similar scene to the South, perhaps a little better conditioned but bereft I perceive of a heroic spirit. Do they not remind you of the Philistians going to take Sampson? [90]

At Ciudad Victoria, José Antonio Quintero called upon the people of Tamaulipas to rise in defense of their country against the "bankrupt Texians" whose "horrible cry" has reached "our ears from the towns of the North. Our territory," he said, "has been violated by hordes of savages and adventurers, who unfurl a flag that is not ours and selecting our fertile fields and vast plains, call us to war. . . . From bankrupts, they have become conquistadores thanks to the Mexicans who have succumbed to the seduction," but "the brilliant columns of our veteran army" will "return the sword to the adventurers" who will flee to the woods of Texas, and will later be lanced from them near the Sabine.[91] The *Gaceta de Tampico* and the *Voto publica* denounced the allies and protégés of the Texans and called upon all Mexicans to unite in the preservation of their independence and national unity. "Our territory," declared *El Voto publica*,[92] "will not be violated with im-

[89] Same to Same, Nov. 22, 1839, in *ibid.*, 1908, II, 497–498.
[90] Same to Same, [Mexico City], Nov. 26, 1839, in *ibid.*, 1908, II, 498–499.
[91] José Antonio Quintero to the Inhabitants of Tamaulipas, Ciudad Victoria, Nov. 15, 1839, in *Gaceta de Tampico*, Nov. 23, 1839.
[92] *El Voto publica* quoted in *Gaceta de Tampico*, Dec. 7, 1839.

punity if we all cooperate to repel a perfidous and ungrateful enemy." General Mariano Arista and General Isidro Reyes appealed to the people in the most patriotic strains to rally to the support of the government and army to save the country from pillage and destruction.[93]

Many Mexicans and their officers were convinced that the Texans' ambitions were not limited to the attainment of independence for themselves, but also for Nuevo León, Nuevo México, Coahuila, and San Luis Potosí.[94] Such, it was said, has been their desire since 1836 and now late in 1839, in spite of their "odious flag," they seek to persuade the multitude to believe that those who captured Mier were not Texans, but only Federals. This, it was said, is an utter falsehood. Whatever support the liberal cause in northern Mexico may have had up to this time, it began to wane as the Centralist press sought more and more to exploit "nationalism." A revolutionist was one thing. An ally of the hated, revolted Texans was something else. The cooperation of Texans and Federalists injured the Federal cause tremendously. Yet, on the other hand, the Mexican government was "thunder struck at the poor turn out of the patriots and the slow augmentation of the army" destined for frontier service.[95]

While the Mexican government sought to bolster the morale of its loyal citizens and stave off further humiliating defeats, the Federalists lost no time in pushing on toward Mier. Zapata and Ross hastened to join Canales, who commenced his march rapidly toward Mier about 3 o'clock in the afternoon following the capture of Guerrero.[96] Upon the receipt of the news at Matamoros of the fall of Guerrero, the commandant there immediately dispatched a "respectable section" of troops to re-enforce the convoy of supplies he had earlier started toward Mier; [97] while, on the other hand, from Reinosa the alcalde, Manuel de la Fuente and his associate, Pablo Ansaldua, confederates of Canales, hastened to join the Mexican-Indian-Texan army.[98]

At 2 o'clock the next morning the Federalists arrived within four miles of Mier and encamped. Their spies soon reported that Colonel

[93] A. S. Wright to William Bryan, City of Mexico, Dec. 27, 1839, in Garrison (ed.), *Diplomatic Correspondence of Texas*, 1908, II, 520–527.
[94] *El Diario del Gobierno* quoted in *El Ancla*, Dec. 20, 1839.
[95] A. S. Wright to William Bryan, City of Mexico, Dec. 27, 1839, in Garrison (ed.), *Diplomatic Correspondence of Texas*, 1908, II, 520–522.
[96] *Telegraph and Texas Register*, Oct. 30, 1839.
[97] *Gaceta de Tampico*, Nov. 23, 1839.
[98] *El Ancla*, Jan 3, 1840.

Francisco González Pavón,[99] in command of the First Regiment of Cavalry at Mier, was making hasty preparations to abandon the town. The Federals determined to push on immediately, having rested two hours. They entered Mier half an hour after sunrise without meeting resistance, Pavón having fled toward Monterey only a short time before with five hundred regulars and four pieces of artillery—one long nine-pounder, two six-pounders, and a seven inch howitzer.[100] Within an hour the Federalist troops were filing through the city in pursuit. The Texans, it was reported, displayed their lone star flag triumphantly over the town,[101] but Canales later explicitly denied that the Texan flag had ever been raised at Mier or elsewhere in the northern towns.

The Federalists, with Ross' 231 Texans out in front, pursued and overtook Pavón at the Alamo, twelve miles southwest of Mier on the old road between Mier and Paras,[102] where on an eminence in the rolling, rough country Pavón had drawn up his forces to await the Federalist assault on October 3. Pavón's cannons were mounted on top of a knoll to protect his infantry and cavalry, which were stationed at a short distance down the hill.[103]

As the Federalists came up about 11 o'clock in the morning, the

[99] Francisco González Pavón, native of San Salvador el Verde, Department of Puebla, entered service as a soldier in the Regimiento del Comercio de Puebla on March 30, 1809; in 1834 he was commander-in-chief of Puebla, and later commanded a brigade in the Army Corps of the North which he surrendered in October 1839, to a combined Federal-Texan army. For the surrender he was court-martialed by his government and sentenced to six months in prison. From 1853–1855 he served as commandant general of Zacatecas. Alberto M. Carreño (ed.), *Jefes del ejército mexicano en 1847: biográfias de generals de division y de coronels del ejército mexicano por fines del año de 1847*, p. 217.

[100] *Colorado Gazette and Advertiser*, Jan. 4, 1840. The *Gazette* reported that the Centralists evacuated Mier at 8 A.M., and that the Federalists began filing through the streets in pursuit an hour later. In Matamoros it was said that Pavón had about 600 troops under his command. D. W. Smith to John Forsyth, Matamoros, Nov. 10, 1839, no. 160, in Consular Dispatches (U. S.), 1837–1839, (Matamoros), ms., microfilm. The *Colorado Gazette and Advertiser*, Jan. 4, 1840, reporting what is described as an authentic account of the engagement with Pavón gave the size of his force as 780 men.

[101] D. W. Smith to John Forsyth, Matamoros, Nov. 10, 1839, no. 160, in Consular Dispatches (U. S.), 1837–1839 (Matamoros), ms., microfilm; Same to Same, Matamoros, Dec. 24, 1839, no. 161, in *ibid.*

[102] The rock house at this point, which served as Pavón's hospital and asylum following his defeat, still stands.

[103] *Colorado Gazette and Advertiser*, Jan. 4, 1840.

Americans and Carrizo Indians dismounted, hitched their horses and fell in a ravine, known as the Alto Limpia, and, taking cover behind the mesquite bushes immediately to their left, quietly crept along until they had taken up position behind a number of large rocks in that part of the arroyo nearest the enemy. The Mexican Federalists did not come up. They paraded some distance off, out of reach of the enemy cannon. Zapata did all he could to lead them up, but they refused obedience. Pavón, perceiving that he was not to be attacked by the main force of the enemy, turned upon the Americans, who he thought had halted behind the timber to await the coming up of the main body. The Centralist infantry, supported by cavalry, extended itself down the hill to a line of straggling trees which bordered the arroyo and thus unwittingly took a position within eighty yards of the Texan rifles. The Texans permitted the Centralist infantry to form, and the first intelligence that Pavón's men had of the proximity of their neighbors was from a well directed fire which they withstood for five or ten minutes, before they retreated precipitantly under cover of their artillery.

Thinking to use his artillery to advantage to annihilate the enemy in the ravine, Pavón now directed his four pieces of artillery upon the Texan position and kept up a cannonade for four hours, until satisfied by the silence of the Americans that he had slain them all (actually, they had been resting and some of them even sleeping). Convinced that the Texans surely must have been slaughtered by now, Pavón moved with his whole force against their position; but when the Centralists arrived within easy gunshot of the ravine, at a point about as near as their infantry had reached at the first onset, Cameron rose up and fired upon the drummer, who fell dead.[104] This was the signal for a general fight, the first real opportunity afforded the Texans to use their rifles effectively. The whole company now arose to pour a destructive fire upon Pavón and to charge his entire line. By this time, the main Federalist force came up and charged the enemy's right flank "without making an impression, though they suffered severely for their temerity."[105] Falling back they formed behind their Anglo-American friends. The Centralists withstood the fire of their opponents for five

---

[104] *Ibid.*; "Information derived from Anson G. Neal, Laredo, May 30, 1847," in *Lamar Papers*, VI, 100–101. Neal was a participant in the battle of the Alamo River, commonly referred to in many of the early accounts as the battle of Alcantro or El Cántaro.

[105] *Colorado Gazette and Advertiser*, Jan. 4, 1840.

or ten minutes, then fell back once more under the protection of their artillery. Jones of Lavaca was the only Texan killed in resisting the Centralist charge.[106]

The second charge soon made by the Mexican infantry was likewise repulsed with considerable loss to the Centralists, and again they retreated to safety behind their artillery, which played on the arroyo for some time without injuring anyone. Ross is alleged, at this point in the fight, to have sent a courier to Canales, saying that he could not hold his position much longer under the punishing artillery fire of the enemy. The courier returned to report that Canales would move soon to the Texans' relief, but as it turned out he remained inactive.[107] Growing tired of waiting. Ross now dispatched an officer to urge Canales to come forward, but to no avail.

Perceiving the continued lack of cooperation among his opponents, Pavón launched a third and what was intended to be an all-out attack upon the Texan line. With their cavalry in the lead, Pavón's men charged with great intrepidity. While the battle raged, Zapata, becoming disgusted with his cowardly chief, led twenty-five Mexicans under his immediate command into the ravine to aid the Texans, and was followed by a few men under Carbajal and by the Carrizo Indians, who fought bravely. Except for the few men under Zapata and Carbajal, (whose left arm was broken by a bullet during the engagement), a majority of the Mexican troops at the rear under the leadership of Canales remained idle spectators of the scene, having rejected the repeated appeals of Ross and Zapata for help. During the Centralist assault, "Canales sounded his horn and galloped about in the chaparals about ½ mile from the enemy." [108] Between the hours of 3 and 4 o'clock in the afternoon the Centralist cavalry charged the Texans in the ravine, but hastily withdrew when its commander was killed by Private Bowen of Price's Company, who leaped to his feet, crying out, "Boys, by God, I have knocked him over, and now let us charge them." [109] A general shout now resounded down the Texan line, and the Anglo-Saxons who had grown restless from inactivity charged from the arroyo in wild zest and, being joined by a portion of the main body of Federalists, dashed up the hill after the retreating Mexican column as it wavered under the concentrated fire of Ross' men. Thereafter, a

106 *Ibid.*
107 Huson, "Iron Men," p. 91.
108 "Information from Major [Richard] Roman," in *Lamar Papers,* VI, 137.
109 Quoted by Captain Benjamin Hill, in *ibid.,* VI, 135.

bitter hand to hand fight ensued which lasted until near sunset. "The impetuosity of the Texans broke through all restraint, and completely deranged and destroyed the plan of battle." [110] The Texans, however, were checked within ten to fifteen steps of the enemy's artillery and were forced to seek the cover of the ravine. Part of the Texan difficulty resulted from a conflict in orders. Great confusion ensued when, in the charge upon Pavón, Hagler called for a retreat.[111] Ross, Jordan, and other officers exerted themselves in vain to enforce order among their men; but the Indians and a few of the Texans could not be checked and "every man was an officer and a host within himself, and fought on his own account." In the assault, the Federalists had two killed, both Texans, and sixteen wounded.[112]

No sooner had the Texans gained the protection of the ravine than the Centralists blew a charge, but their men could not be brought to the attack. Their artillery continued to play upon the Texan position until near dark, when both parties drew off for the night—the Federalists to the water on the right and the Centralists half a mile farther up the hill. The fire of the artillery gradually subsided; the sun went down; the heavy and reverberated report of cannon came at longer and more uncertain intervals; finally, it was hushed; a profound and painful silence descended, and the cold, deepening shadows of evening crept silently over the field. The two armies were still there, and were still regarding each other face to face, awaiting the coming of day to renew the struggle.

That night the two armies lay camped in close juxtaposition, about two miles apart; but an hour or two before day, before their movements were known, the Centralists were on the march. The mounted Texans, however, were soon in quick pursuit, leaving the Federalist infantry to overtake the enemy's rear guard and baggage. Pavón sent a white flag to the Federalists at 8 A.M. as a ruse to hold them in check while his artillery and infantry moved towards water, his forces having been without water all night. Perceiving the object of his opponent, Canales sent forward a battalion of cavalry (about 160 men) and the whole body of Texans to head him off. Thus, on the morning of October 4, finding himself cut off from water and perceiving the Texans out in front, Pavón surrendered at discretion after a brief, but spirited

[110] Yoakum, *History of Texas*, II, 275.
[111] "Capt. Newcomb's Recollections," in *Lamar Papers*, VI, 123.
[112] *Colorado Gazette and Advertiser*, Jan. 4, 1840. Jacob ("Jake") Hendricks and —— Hammons of Lavaca were the two Texans killed in the charge and repulse.

engagement. Handing his sword to Benjamin Hill, instead of to Canales, who demanded it, Pavón boldly declared: "I do not surrender, Sir, to such a cowardly recreant as you but I yield to those brave Americans." [113] The Mexican flag was handed to Major Joseph Dolan of the Texan forces.[114] After the enemy had stacked their arms, Pavón's sword was restored to him.

When Pavón hoisted the white flag, a large section of his command bolted. Abandoning their ammunition, artillery, and camp equipage, they fled to the protection of a cattle pen at a *ranchería*, about five miles distant, where they meekly surrendered to the some fifty Anglo-Texans who had pursued them. On the battlefield of the Alamo the Texans lost two killed and a number wounded, five of whom subsequently died of their injuries.[115] The priest of Mier, although professing

[113] Quoted in "Information derived from Anson G. Neal," in *Lamar Papers*, VI, 101. Bustamante refers to the Federalist victory over Pavón as a "triumph of perfidy." He claims that on November 1, 1839 [wrong date], the Centralists completely defeated Canales, who on the following day signed an agreement offering to place himself at the disposition of the government. Relying upon this commitment, Pavón's troops relaxed their guard and were attacked and routed by the Federalists. Bustamante, *El gabinete mexicano*, I, 213. Bustamante's account was probably based on a report made by Pavón to the Secretary of War, dated Monterey, November 7, 1839, in which he claimed a victory over Canales' forces on November [?] 1 and asserted that his surrender the next day was caused by an unexpected attack by Canales after the two had agreed upon a truce. Francisco G. Pavón, [Account of the revolutionary activities of the Texans], San Luis Potosí, Noviembre 30 de 1839, published as a 5 p. double column *Suplemento a la Gaceta*, numero 101, San Luis Potosí, Diciembre 3 de 1839. From the account given in the present work, based upon original source materials, it may be readily seen that not only are Bustamante's dates of the battle incorrect but his account of Pavón's surrender is at variance with those of the actual participants in the battle.

[114] Yoakum, *History of Texas*, II, 276.

[115] Among those Texans who lost their lives were Jacob ("Jake") Hendricks, late of Pennsylvania and formerly a merchant in the frontier trade and a cowboy, who had recently spent some time in a Matamoros prison; "Tonkaway" Jones (so-called because of his association with the Tonkawa Indians) of Lavaca and Gonzales, who was a blacksmith by trade; John Aikins; ——— Quail of Goliad; ———Hammons of Lavaca; and two others. Among the wounded was a man named ——— Black. Captain Benjamin Hill says the Texans lost five killed and fourteen wounded. Jones and Hendricks were among the cowboys engaged in cattle stealing. While in the process of stealing a drove of cattle near San Patricio, a group of Texans had been surprised in 1837 by a party of Mexicans. "They all fled with the exception of Hendricks, who, in trying to get off with the cattle, was taken prisoner, and carried to Matamoros where he remained one year and

to be a Federalist, refused to permit the Texans to bury their dead in the local churchyard, claiming that they were heretics (*i. e.*, not Roman Catholics). The Centralist losses consisted of 85 killed on the ground and numerous wounded. In all, the Centralist losses were about 150. Pavón was suspected of treachery by his government and was subsequently court-martialed and sentenced to six months in a fort.[116]

The 350 captives now joined the victors; their leader (Pavón) and his officers, however, were paroled. News of Pavón's defeat went down the river to Matamoros and inland to Monterey, causing consternation and dismay. At Matamoros, the first alcalde, Jorgé López de Lara, issued a proclamation on November 8, calling upon the local citizenry in high sounding phrases to rise up and place themselves under the commander of the Army of the North to repel the invading Texan horde and recover that fair land for the mother country.[117]

Following the surrender, the Federalists remained on the battlefield all that day and the next, and then marched back to Mier. As October and a part of November passed away, the frontier town of Mier "glistened and rang with the colors and music and chatter of the autumn fair with its carnival." Meanwhile the government forces down

---

one month before he escaped. Carnes [Cairns], who was sick at San Patricio, was also taken, and carried to Matamoros with Hendricks. When they returned to Texas they resumed their old trade of driving off cattle." *Lamar Papers*, VI, 99–105, 134–135; *Colorado Gazette and Advertiser*, Jan. 4, 1840; *Telegraph and Texas Register*, Oct. 20, 1838. Richard Roman later reported 18 to 20 of the Texan Federalists and Indians killed. *Lamar Papers*, VI, 136–137. *La Brisa*, Nov. 15, 1839, reported Colonel Ross wounded.

[116] Carreño, *Jefes de ejército mexicano en 1847*, p. 217 n. Later, however, in 1841 in an effort to clear his name of the charge of treachery, Pavón issued a *Manifiesto*, published as a Supplement to Number 37 of the *Mosquito Mexicano* in which there is an account of the Battle of Alcantro [Alamo] by Canales that shows that Pavón's forces, being without water and food after the first day's engagement, Pavón asked for a truce and when it was granted sought to escape, but was captured. While the latter account tends to clear Pavón of the charge of treason, it shows that he made a false claim in 1839 of his victory the first day of his encounter with the Federalists and that he had misstated facts relative to Canales' conduct in respect to the truce. Francisco G. Pavón, *Manifestación que hace de su conducta milita, a la nación, el coronel del 1er Regimiento de Caballeria*, Mexico, 1841.

[117] Jorgé López de Lara, *El Ciudadano Jorgé López de Lara, Alcalde 1o Constitucional de Esta Ciudad á Sus Habitantes*, Matamoros, Noviembre 8 de 1839, broadside.

river and inland caught their breath and had time to prepare their defenses, and the Texans fumed at inactivity; some of them went home.[118]

The Federalists rested at Mier forty days,[119] augmented their forces, and finally took up the line of march for Matamoros via Camargo and Reinosa, leaving Dr. Felder behind to administer to the Texan wounded until they could be removed with safety to Matamoros. Upon rejoining the army before Matamoros, Dr. Felder procured a guard of seventeen men and proceeded with the wounded to the settlements on the Guadalupe.[120] From thence, Felder reported, he went to Austin early in January 1840, to make his report to the adjutant general. At Austin he learned that he, and the whole of Ross' Company had been stricken from the service rolls, and their names published in every paper throughout the Republic as deserters;[121] nevertheless, "scores of hardy riflemen" were said to be hurrying westward to join the Federalists on the Río Grande and to assist in seizing Matamoros, which for so long had been the ambition of many Texans.[122] The *Telegraph* at Houston pictured the Texan adventurers as the nucleus around which the Federal Mexicans were rallying,

. . . with a confidence not unlike that with which the Tlascalans formerly rallied around the adventurous band of Cortéz; and a panic like that which preceded him wherever he turned his citorious standard, now spreads in the van of the Federal army. . . . Scores of hardy riflemen are hurrying to join them; and it is not improbable that this now apparently rash and imprudent expedition may eventually terminate in the downfall of the present Mexican dynasty.[123]

[118] Horgan, *Great River*, II, 563.
[119] Alessio Robles, *Coahuila y Texas*, II, 216.
[120] Petition of Dr. Felder, Military Affairs Committee, Dec. 30 [1840], in Memorials and Petitions (Texas), ms.; Smither (ed.), *Journals of the Sixth Congress of the Republic of Texas*, II, 8 n.
[121] In January 1842, a Joint Resolution passed Congress requiring the Secretary of War to give E. J. Felder an honorable discharge from the muster roll of the Texas Volunteer Service, without receiving any pay for his services. President Houston permitted this resolution to become a law without his signature. There was no general law enacted to cover Ross' men in the same way. *Ibid.*, III, 476; II, 197, 197 n.
[122] *Telegraph and Texas Register* quoted in *Colorado Gazette and Advertiser*, Dec. 7, 1839.
[123] *Ibid.*

At Camargo the Federalists tried to rally the inhabitants of the frontier states of Tamaulipas, Nuevo León, and Coahuila, while Canalizo at Matamoros on November 7 sought to rally the loyal Mexicans of the north, and particularly those of Matamoros, to the defense of the country.[124]

Arriving within two or three miles [125] of Matamoros at the beginning of December, the Federalists, numbering about 1,700 [126] men, entrenched themselves on December 12. During the next two days the Federalist cavalry made several attacks on the enemy's outpost, driving the pickets up to the fortifications. The following day (December 15) Canales sent in a small party of cavalry—sixteen Mexicans and seventeen Texans—under Zapata to decoy the Centralists out from behind the entrenchments in the city. Zapata's cavalry rode up to the vicinity of the town, dismounted and charged one of the principal outposts, consisting of a battery of three artillery pieces manned and defended by one hundred men. After a spirited engagement of fifteen minutes, the Federalist decoy party, perceiving a strong re-enforcement joining the enemy fell back to their horses without the loss of a man, leaving thirteen of the enemy dead and seven wounded; but Canalizo, commander in chief of the northern division, with fifteen hundred soldiers and eighteen cannon at his disposal in the city, refused the invitation. Instead, he immediately withdrew all his outposts into the city, and redoubled his efforts to fortify the town. The thirteen Anglo-Federals, who were held prisoners in Matamoros, were employed from daylight to dark in work on the fortifications.[127] Rumors were afloat that Anaya

[124] El Gral. en Gefe de la Division del Norte [Valentín Canalizo] á los habitantes de sus departamentos, Cuartel General en Matamoros, Noviembre 7 de 1839, in *La Brisa*, Nov. 7, 1839.

[125] An informant told the editor of the *Telegraph and Texas Register*, Dec. 18, 1839, that 2,500 Federalists had arrived within nine miles of the Matamoros fortifications and were preparing to assault the place the next day, that being the day after he left.

[126] D. W. Smith to John Forsyth, Matamoros, Dec. 24, 1839, no. 161 in Consular Dispatches (U. S.), 1837–1839, (Matamoros), ms., microfilm; John F. C. Henderson and Thomas Jamison to [Editor of the *Colorado Gazette and Advertiser*], Jan. 8, 1840, in *Colorado Gazette and Advertiser*, Jan. 18, 1840, says the Federalist force under Canales numbered 1,400 strong, including 200 Anglo-Americans and 1,200 Mexican Federalists supported by the four pieces of artillery taken from Pavón.

[127] Alessio Robles, *Coahuila y Texas*, II, 216; John F. C. Henderson and Thomas Jamison to [Editor of the *Colorado Gazette and Advertiser*], Jan. 8, 1840, in *Colorado Gazette and Advertiser*, Jan. 18, 1840. Henderson and Jamison, it was

was on his way with three hundred Texans to assist in an assault upon the city.[128]

Upon regaining their horses, Zapata's men remounted and rode around the town in plain view of the enemy for about an hour, until the Centralist cavalry put in a tardy appearance, causing the Federalists to retreat to their own lines.

All intercourse between Matamoros and the Northern departments was effectively suspended and business of every description was completely paralyzed by the military operations in the north. For his support, Canales exacted one half of the import duty on goods and specie to and from the interior by placing small detachments of troops at various points on the roads.

After encamping four days before Matamoros and making several fruitless attempts to draw the Centralists out from behind their entrenchments, Canales became alarmed, alleging that superior Centralist re-enforcements were coming to the relief of the city's garrison. Doubtless he was aware of the government's concentration of troops in northern Mexico. On December 7 the *Gaceta de Tampico* reported the occupation of Saltillo by General Isidro Reyes, the arrival of General Mariano Arista at San Luis Potosí with a second body of troops, the presence of Manuel Romero in Tula with his lancers, and the landing of troops from Vera Cruz at Tampico. Besides, there were garrisons at Monterey and Matamoros. So in a council of war, Canales declared that since the Centralists would not come out to do battle, he did not think it wise to attack them in the city and, therefore, he intended to abandon the siege.

The failure of Canales to take Matamoros, reported "an officer in the Federal Army" in a letter published in the Houston *Morning Star*,[129] was due first, to the re-enforcements that had reached the Centralist garrison at Matamoros before Canales' arrival; second, to the inadequate supplies of ammunition possessed by the Federalists for a long siege; third, to the superiority of the Centralist artillery (they possessing eighteen pieces of artillery to the four belonging to the Federalists); and, fourth, to the desire to draw the Centralists out of Matamoros by lifting the siege.

---

said, had gone to Mexico to look for their Negro slaves, who had gone off with the Mexican army when it withdrew from Texas.
[128] *La Brisa*, Nov. 15, 1839.
[129] March 31, 1840; Alessio Robles, *Coahuila y Texas*, II, 216.

Other factors that may have caused Canales to decide against launching a full-scale attack upon Matamoros were the malfunctioning of his horoscope and his undue suspicion of treachery. Since he believed so strongly in divination, it was believed by some that he had had his horoscope cast, or had played a little game, as he often did before making major decisions. He would take a piece of paper, dividing it into four sections, upon which he painted a lion, an eagle, a sheep, and a dove, respectively, and then blindfolded he would prick the sheet of paper with a pin. "If the warlike bird or animal was pricked," reported Neal, "he argued favorably; if the lamb or dove, he argued otherwise." [130] Canales was always suspicious and, as the Texans were beginning to learn, a coward. While encamped before Matamoros, a baker appeared in the Federalist camp with a wheelbarrow of bread for sale. Suspecting that the bread might be poisoned, Canales ordered the baker to eat three loaves before, he said, he would permit it to be sold in camp. The baker did not object to eating some bread to satisfy the test, but he did object to the quantity that he was ordered to eat. However, he was forced to comply with Canales' demand, and after he had eaten enough bread to kill an ordinary man, reported Neal, Canales refused "to let men purchase the bread, because he thought the poison was of a slow nature, and time would not allow him to make a fair test of it." [131]

Seeing that Canales intended to abandon the siege of Matamoros, the Texans offered to storm the city by themselves, but Canales rejected their offer.[132] Suddenly on the 16th of December Canales stampeded, taking the road toward Monterey without launching an attack upon the city,[133] although the authorities in Mexico City the next day received an express saying that Matamoros had fallen to the Fed-

---

[130] "Information derived from Anson G. Neal, Laredo, May 30, 1847," in *Lamar Papers*, VI, 101–102.

[131] *Ibid.*

[132] Horgan, *Great River*, II, 563; Bancroft, *History of Texas and the North Mexican States*, II, 328.

[133] Huson, "Iron Men," p. 98, quotes John Hughes of Atlanta, Georgia, who, he says, was a visitor at the American consulate in Matamoros at the time, to the effect that Canalizo was defeated. There was no battle. See D. W. Smith to John Forsyth, Matamoros, Dec. 24, 1839, in Consular Dispatches (U. S.), 1837–1839, (Matamoros), ms., microfilm; Agnes S. Menefee to John S. Menefee [of] Austin, Texas [dated:] Jan. 3, 1840, in John S. Menefee Papers, ms.

erals.[134] The rancheros who had been called by Canalizo to defend the city, now returned home, leaving only six hundred Centralist troops to hold Matamoros[135]

Canales' timorousness proved disgusting to more than one Texan, including Ross, who had other cause, too, for dissatisfaction. Disgruntled by Canales' procrastination on launching an attack upon Matamoros and repudiated by his own men who elected Jordan to command them, Ross returned home accompanied by Sweitzer,[136]

[134] James Treat to Col. James Love, [Mexico City, Dec. 17, 1839], in Garrison (ed.), *Diplomatic Correspondence of Texas*, 1908, II, 512; A. S. Wright to William Bryan, Mexico City, Dec. 25, 1839, in *ibid.*, 1908, II, 518.

[135] Report of Reuben Ross and Alonzo B. Sweitzer upon their arrival in Austin. *Telegraph and Texas Register*, Dec. 25, 1839.

[136] Alonzo B. Sweitzer, an Ohio physician of considerable literary ability, arrived in Texas after the battle of San Jacinto; served as a captain in the Texan army from May 15 to December 17, 1836, and thereafter until July 31, 1837, as a lieutenant colonel in the 1st Regiment, Permanent Volunteers. While stationed on Galveston Island in 1836, Captain Sweitzer forcibly, through the seizure of the fort and the training of its cannon upon the ships in the harbor, prevented the Secretary of War and the Army Quartermaster from transferring to Velasco for the use of the main army recently arrived supplies of clothing, provisions, and other items until his men first had been properly supplied.

In 1837 Sweitzer was sent by General Felix Huston to destroy the fortifications at Béxar, but was prevented from doing so by Colonel Juan N. Seguin. From August 24, 1837, to June 24, 1838, he was a special agent to treat with the Comanche Indians. From Novembr 6, 1838, to January 24, 1839, he represented Gonzales in the Third Congress; and in the campaign for re-election he accused Ben McCulloch of being a moral coward for his refusal to debate him in the campaign; McCulloch won the election by a large vote. In the pursuit of the Comanches following their raid on Linnville in August 1840, Sweitzer accused Ben McCulloch of trying to lead the Texans off the trail of the Indians for which McCulloch challenged him to a duel and again later on the Blanco River after the pursuit of the Indians, but Sweitzer backed down. Later, at Gonzales, reported Captain Benjamin Hill, Reuben Ross bore a challenge to Benjamin McCulloch from Sweitzer, "a d——d mean man, . . . although unworthy of the friendship of Ross," whom he tried to supplant in the command at Matamoros. "Ross took the place of his friend [when McCulloch refused to meet Sweitzer] and wounded McCulloch at their meeting" at Gonzales September 19, 1840, in the right arm. Ross was a gentleman and offered the services of his own surgeon, which were received. "This [fight] rankled in the breast of the McColoughs [McCullochs]," reports Hill; "and one of them, Henry McColough, subsequently [at a Christmas party the same year] at Gonzales sought an occasion whilst Ross was drunk, to provoke a controversy, and shoot him." Mortally wounded, Ross died early in January 1841. Sweitzer was finally killed by Major R. S. Neighbors while Neighbors was performing his duties as quartermaster. "Information from Capt. Benj.

Roman, Hill, and others, numbering approximately fifty. Ross and Sweitzer, having left the army before the raising of the siege, reached Austin on December 15, but received a cool reception from the Texas authorities, whose official attitude in the internecine war in Mexico was that of strict neutrality, and who were inclined to believe that Ross and his men had deserted when they joined the Federalists and were entitled to less consideration than if they had been dishonorably discharged from the public service. The government refused to sanction any of Ross' acts, or to pay any of his soldiers.[137] After all, this "wild adventure" of a handful of reckless characters could easily result in the concentration of a strong Mexican force on the northern frontier which would make it necessary to maintain a corresponding body of Texans near at hand to watch their movements and to protect the exposed border. The public interest could be very definitely affected by its citizens' privately levying war beyond the boundaries of the Republic.

The effects of Ross' action was clearly presented by the *New Orleans Commercial Bulletin*:

It is expected that the [Mexican] government will immediately concentrate its whole disposable military force upon Matamoros. The terror of the Texian flag waving on the West bank of the Río del Norte, will arouse the energies of the whole nation. Under the circumstances, it would not be surprising if the wild adventure of Colonel Ross should bring about very important results. The Mexicans may regard the denial of having authorized the proceedings of Col. Ross as an artifice or stratagem to hide their actual participation in, or instigation of the outrage. In this event, actual hostilities between the two countries will be resumed—war will be waged in earnest, and the struggle so long pending be brought to a speedy issue.

Hill," in *Lamar Papers*, VI, 135; Huson, "Iron men," 73; *Biographical Directory of the Texan Conventions and Congresses*, 178; *Colorado Gazette and Advertiser*, Jan. 11, 1840; Edward J. Wilson and G. L. Postlethwaite to the Public [Lexington, Ky.], quoted from the *Lexington Intelligencer* in the *Telegraph and Texas Register*, Nov. 12, 1836; see also comment by the editor of the *Telegraph* on the Wilson-Postlethwaite letter in *ibid.*

[137] Quoted in *Colorado Gazette and Advertiser*, Dec. 21, 1839. For additional information on Sweitzer and Ross, see *Telegraph and Texas Register*, Dec. 25, 1839; "Recollections of Capt. Newcomb," in *Lamar Papers*, VI, 123; Yoakum, *History of Texas*, II, 274; Victor M. Rose, *The Life and Services of Gen. Ben McCulloch*, pp. 50–54. Captain Benjamin Hill claimed that he, Ross, and Roman had been dispatched as emissaries to Texas to raise new recruits.

Any semblance of cooperation by Texas with the enemies of the Mexican government would be impolitic in view of the negotiations of James Treat, who had reached Vera Cruz on November 28, about the time the Federalists and their erstwhile Texan allies were clamoring at the gates of Matamoros.

Treat found that the excitement growing out of Texans' participating in the Federalist revolution interfered with his plans. Because of that participation, two measures were introduced in the Mexican Congress in the middle of December. One requested of Congress special powers to levy taxes to support a war against Texas with the object of reuniting that department to the national union, and the other, emanating from the Secretary of War, Juan N. Almonte, proposed to make it treasonable for anyone "to *write, act* or *speak* in favour of the views and intentions of the *Texans.*" [138] Nevertheless, during the course of the next few weeks, Treat seems to have gained the impression that the Mexican government really had no intention of conducting a campaign against Texas. He informed Lamar on January 7,

The Govmt. *Still* appear to adhere to their *apparent* old plan of preparing an Expedition, *nominally* against Texas, but *not* with a View of ever carrying the new invasion into effect. Their *real plan* . . . , I *am induced to believe* . . . [is to] obtain the means and authorization from Congress to raise an army of 10,000 Men (they have only about 5,000 *now, all told*) to place . . . on, or near, the frontiers, and *then* negotiate as they think to greater advantage. . . . This is the *real object* tho' it will only be avowed to *some*, while *others* will be made to believe that the Govmt. *are in earnest* in their Views of *Restoring Texas* to the National Union.

The leading officials and all who were enlightened on the subject were fully aware that Texas could never be reconquered; but the government "being weak and tottering" (and stood to be even more so if Canales succeeded in capturing Matamoros or Monterey) sought to gain strength by assuming "The Texas expedition as their *real object,* when it is only the *pretext,* and the *best,* if not the *only one,* they can now adopt to produce the desired effect on the Chambers" of Congress.[139] During the ensuing weeks and months, however, Treat was

[138] James Treat to James Hamilton, Mexico, Dec. 16, 1839 (Private and Entirely Confidential), Garrison (ed.), *Diplomatic Correspondence of Texas,* 1908, II, 507–512.

[139] James Treat to M. B. Lamar, Mexico, Jan. 7, 1840 (Private), in *ibid.,* 1908, II, 527–529.

to learn how he had ben strung along by the Mexican authorities until they had the situation well in hand on the northern frontier. In the meantime, he was unable to secure an audience with Cañedo, the Mexican Secretary of Foreign Affairs, before February 1, 1840, because of the belief, later dispelled in part by Lamar's proclamation, that the Texas government was in alliance with the Federalists in the north.[140]

Furthermore, the conduct of its pugnacious citizens caused the Texan government other embarrassments on the diplomatic front. The success of James Hamilton's negotiations for a loan in Europe "depended, to some extent, upon keeping Texas removed from all situations which might affect the market for the bonds." [141] Wrote General Hamilton to the Texan Secretary of State,

I cannot conceal from you that we have great difficulties to contend with, which have been continued, without any intermission in the face of a universally accredited rumor, that *Arista* was about to invade and overrun Texas, burn your capital and destroy your army; then came the report of your having murdered forty Comanche chiefs, in cold blood [at San Antonio in March 1840], whom you . . . invited to a friendly council to treat for peace and the surrender of prisoners; next came the President's proclamation, ordering all free persons of color out of the territorial limits of Texas,[142] which has been put down on this side of the water as a barbarity equal to that of the revocation of the edict of Nantes; and lastly, the *Great Western* brings the intelligence of the still further depreciation of your treasury notes. Against these adverse currents we had been endeavoring to make headway. . . . I think I may say we are making steady progress towards the final consummation of our object. . . . But our success depends entirely on your measures at home; if you should join the Federalists, unite in an invasion

---

[140] J[ames] Treat to M. B. Lamar, Mexico, Jan. 31–Feb. 1, 1840 (Confidential), in *ibid.*, 1908, II, 533–542; Joseph William Schmitz, *Texan Statecraft, 1836–1845*, p. 113.

[141] Schmitz, *Texan Statecraft*, p. 103.

[142] By the terms of a law of February 5, 1840, setting forth the free Negro policy of the Republic, immigration of free Negroes was prohibited and Negro residents were required to remove themselves from Texas within two years on penalty of sale into slavery. Gammel (ed.), *Laws of Texas*, II, 325–326. The President was instructed by Congress to order all free persons of color then in Texas to remove themselves before January 1, 1842. President Houston, however, issued a proclamation on February 5, 1842, extending to free Negroes of good character the privilege of remaining another twelve months. *Writings of Sam Houston*, II, 476–477.

of Mexico . . . we could not borrow one dollar for you—not for love or money.[143]

This warning was hardly necessary, for Lamar was well aware of the possible consequences of the Texans' joining the Federalist forces. As early as December 21, 1839, he had issued a proclamation in which he referred to those Texans who had crossed the established boundary (the Río Grande) of Texas and had associated themselves with one of the belligerent parties in Mexico as acting without any authorization from the government of Texas. He warned and admonished "all citizens of Texas to abstain from all attempts to invade the territory of Mexico" and also from participation in "marauding incursions and other acts of hostility . . . except in defense of our territory." He considered it "incompatible with the true interest and honor of Texas" to meddle in the internal affairs of Mexico.[144] Citizens violating the proclamation were to be considered without the protection of the government of Texas, which disclaimed all participation in their conduct and would not sanction any hostile act molesting the inhabitants of Mexico. In this manner, the members of Ross' command "were published in every paper throughout the Republic as deserters," and when Doctor Edmund J. Felder[145] petitioned Congress for compensation for his services in Ross' command, the House Committee on Military Affairs reported that, in their opinion, he was "not entitled to any consideration for his service having abandoned the service of his country and joined the Federal Mexicans, under Col. Ross."[146] The Committee went on to say that it had "no inclination to censure his course; his errors have been the common errors of many others," but it was the opinion of the Committee "that Texas ought not to pay for services rendered to the Federal Mexicans."

[143] Gen. James Hamilton, Commissioner of Republic in Europe, to Abner S. Lipscomb, Secretary of State, [dated:] Hague, July 28, 1840, in Texas Congress, *Journal of the House of Representatives, Fifth Congress, Appendix,* pp. 289–290.
[144] "Proclamation Warning and Admonishing Citizens of the Republic Taking up Arms Against the Mexican Government, City of Austin, December 21, 1839," in Documents under the Great Seal (Texas), Record Book, ms., p. 50; *Colorado Gazette and Advertiser,* Jan. 11, 1840; *Austin City Gazette,* Jan. 1, 1840; Yoakum, *History of Texas,* II, 288.
[145] Petition of Dr. Edmund J. Felder (endorsed: "18/ Petition of Dr. Felder / Military Affairs / Dec. 30"), Memorials and Petitions (Texas), ms.
[146] *Ibid.*; "Report of the Committee on Military Affairs," Texas Congress, *Journals of the House of Representatives, Fifth Congress, Appendix,* p. 293.

Even before the issuance of Lamar's proclamation Lieutenant Colonel Benjamin H. Johnson, assistant adjutant general of the army, was dispatched by the President to the Río Grande and beyond, if necessary, so that "by his presence the delusion under which some of our citizens were laboring might be dispelled, and the policy of the President not compromited, by their misguided and imprudent zeal in taking part against what they supposed to be the common enemy." [147] He was also to inform Ross of his dismissal from the service of Texas. Johnson went down the Río Grande to Reinosa, where he arrived on November 15 and informed the Texans of their government's attitude. It is said that he did not see Ross who had left a few days before. At this point four Texans—William G. Small, Irving W. Redfield, W. H. Wyatt, and ———— Clements deserted Johnson's command and remained with their countrymen in the Mexican Federal Army.[148] Having performed his mission, Johnson and his party of eight, comprising two Mexican servants and six Texans, left Camargo on December 11, and, after crossing the Río Grande at Mier on their way home, were intercepted and attacked by a party of Caddo Indians and several Mexicans,[149] probably Córdova's *partida*. The six Texans were killed,

[147] Abner S. Lipscomb, Secretary of State to Barnard E. Bee, City of Austin, Feb. 6, 1840, in Garrison (ed.), *Diplomatic Correspondence of Texas*, 1908, II, 545–546; *Colorado Gazette and Advertiser*, Jan. 11, 1840.

[148] R. B. T. to the Editor of the *Colorado Gazette*, Victoria, April 8, 1840, in *Colorado Gazette and Advertiser*, April 18, 1840.

[149] Abner S. Lipscomb, Secretary of State to Barnard E. Bee, City of Austin, Feb. 6, 1840, in Garrison (ed.), *Diplomatic Correspondence of Texas*, 1908, II, 545–546; *Telegraph and Texas Register*, May 11, 1842; *Colorado Gazette and Advertiser*, Jan. 18, 1840; *Texas Sentinel*, Feb. 1, 1840; D. W. Smith to John Forsyth, Matamoros, Jan. 1, 1840, in Consular Dispatches (U. S.), (Matamoros), 1840–1848, ms., microfilm. D. W. Smith reported the Indians as belonging to the group of some eighty Cherokee, Kickapoo, Delaware, and Caddo Indians who fled Texas earlier in the year. The *Colorado Gazette and Advertiser*, Jan. 11, 1840, reported that forty Cherokees left Matamoros about the first week in December 1839, and it was believed they killed Colonel Littleberry Hawkins and also six Mexicans "who were massacred a few miles below Reinoso by a band of 40 or 50 strange Indians." Hawkins was well known both in the United States and Texas, and was at the time of his murder serving in the Federalist forces. He started on the morning of October 29 a little ahead of the army in company with Carbajal, Canales' private secretary, and other officers. At 11 A.M. as the main Federalist army passed a thicket he was discovered lying under a tree, permitting his horse to graze. As he did not come up that night, on the next morning a detachment was sent back to look for him; after searching about for some time they returned without bringing tidings of him. On the return of the army from the battle of Mier, a

stripped of their clothing and effects, and their bodies left hanging from a tree. The two servants, one of whom had been wounded with seven rifle balls, succeeded in making their way to the settlements on the Río Grande, where they were captured and taken as prisoners to Matamoros. In time, this whole incident was carefully reported abroad by the Texan diplomatic corps as evidence of the intention of the Texan government to avoid meddling in the internal affairs of Mexico,[150] and care was taken to see that the Mexican government was made aware of the true conduct of the Texas government in relation to the Mexican Federalists.

As long as there was no peace on the frontier, the defenses of the country came under careful consideration. By November, Lamar was lamenting to Congress,

It is with much regret and mortification that I refer to the distracted condition of our Southwestern frontier. Believing that a friendly commercial intercourse between our citizens and the peaceful inhabitants on the West of the Río Grande would be eminently advantageous to us, I issued a proclamation inviting and authorizing such intercourse under restrictions which were deemed expedient. The trade for some time progressed with entire harmony and mutual advantage. Under its successful operations several thousand horses have been introduced into our country abundantly supplying its domestic and military wants. But I am informed, on good authority, that recently a number of persons of desperate character and fortunes have congregated on that frontier and have committed many atrocious depredations upon those who were participating in the trade. The Brigands, whether composed of our own citizens, or refugees from the justices of other countries, or of hostile Mexicans, ought to be promptly and effectually suppressed.[151]

Mexican living in the neighborhood exhibited a hat, bridle and holsters, which were recognized by the Anglo-Federalists as having belonged to Hawkins; he said that he found them by a mangled body. It was supposed that he had been murdered by the Cherokees.

[150] B. E. Bee to John Forsyth, Legation of Texas, Washington, April 5, 1840; R. G. Dunlap to Abner S. Lipscomb, Legation of Texas, Washington, March 27, 1840; and Barnard E. Bee to Abner S. Lipscomb, Washington, April 21, 1840, in Garrison (ed.), *Diplomatic Correspondence of Texas*, 1907, I, 444–448, 451–452.

[151] Mirabeau B. Lamar to Fellow Citizens of the Senate and of the House of Representatives, Executive Depart., City of Austin, Nov. 12, 1839, in Harriet Smither (ed.), *Journals of the Fourth Congress of the Republic of Texas*, I, 6–31; *Austin City Gazette*, Nov. 20, 1839; Record of Executive Documents from the 10th Dec. 1836 to the 14th Dec. 1841, ms., pp. 96–135.

In the same message to Congress, on November 12, 1839, Lamar declared that one of the best safeguards to the frontier was a well organized militia. "Its entire disorganization when I came into office and the difficulties experienced in organizing it since," he complained, "owing in some degree to the sparseness of our population, but mainly to the general repugnance which is felt to the performance of militia duty unless an immediate call to the field is intended have rendered that most important arm of National defence in great degree, unavailable." He found sufficient patriotism among the citizens of the country to cause them to rush to the battlefield whenever the enemy put in his appearance, but this was not enough. The country needed a well organized and well disciplined military establishment, but, in the end, he said, the chief reliance against sudden invasion must be placed upon the militia. In attempting to conform to the law enacted by the last Congress [152] for the organization of the militia, the President stated,

I have most ardently endeavoured to make it a bulwark indeed, and . . . every measure has been adopted, which it has been thought might be conducive to that end. But although these efforts have not resulted as satisfactorily as was desired yet the work is now progressing with an energy which assures us that it will in a short time be accomplished to as great an extent as the scattered condition and the habits of our population will admit. Complete success however, may not be expected so long as a law leaves it optional with individuals to conform to its requirements or not, as it may chance to comport with their feelings or conveniences.

By November 1839, the organization of the militia had progressed through the formation of companies in twenty-four counties. In seven counties the companies were still incomplete.[153] Of the twenty-four counties in which the militia had been organized, muster rolls had been forwarded to the Adjutant General's Department, representing 4,620 men organized into 111 companies.

Not only was there the problem of organizing an effective militia, but there was also the problem of raising the regular force contemplated by the law of the last Congress. In raising the latter force,

[152] Third Congress. See Gammel (ed.), *Laws of Texas*, II, 88.
[153] H. McLeod to A. Sidney Johnston, Adjutant-General's Office, Austin, November 9, 1839, in Smither (ed.), *Journals of the Fourth Congress of the Republic of Texas*, III, 81–82; printed separately under title: [Texas Adjutant General] *Report of the Adjutant-General, November, 1839. Printed by order of Congress.*

declared Lamar, difficulties had been encountered resulting from the depreciation of the currency and the high cost of labor, but he believed that, now under an able officer, the recruiting service was being conducted with such success that a sufficient force would be obtained during the winter to enable the administration early in the spring "to carry out the law for establishing a line of military posts upon the frontier . . . a measure which is considered . . . essential to the peace and safety of our people, and one which no efforts will be spared to accomplish as speedily as possible."

Accompanying the President's message was the annual report of the Secretary of War [154] in which he outlined what had been accomplished under the law of the preceding December for the organization of fifteen companies for the protection of the frontier. The officers for the organization had been promptly appointed and recruiting stations established at various points in the Republic, under the supervision of the field officers of the regiment and the general supervision of Lieutenant Colonel William S. Fisher. However, the number of recruits proved too few to justify the expense of maintaining the recruiting stations and they were soon discontinued. The principal excuse for failure was the timeworn statement: "We cannot calculate on better success in recruiting at home, while the inducements to remain in the walks of civil life," he declared, "continue so much greater than those to enter the military service for a term of years." Recruiting was resumed later in the year, reported the Secretary, and, although it met with a greater degree of success, there was a need for funds to raise recruits elsewhere, no doubt in the United States. The regular army at the end of October 1839, numbered 359, rank and file, plus an additional 16 on the general staff, medical staff, and the paymaster and purchasing departments.[155]

Much effort was made at home and abroad to raise the eight companies of mounted riflemen authorized by the act of December 29, 1838, to be employed on the frontier, but success here was limited by the inability of those who would have volunteered to equip themselves. Only three companies were raised, and two of these had been mounted

[154] Texas War Department, *Annual Report of the Secretary of War, November, 1839. Printed by order of Congress*; reprinted in Smither (ed.), *Journals of the Fourth Congress of the Republic of Texas*, III, 73–116.

[155] H. McLeod to A. Sidney Johnston, Adjutant-General's Office, Austin, Nov. 9, 1839, in Smither (ed.), *Journals of the Sixth Congress of the Republic of Texas*, III, 81–87.

and equipped at public expense. These were attached to the regular force under Colonel Burleson. During the past year, it had become necessary to enroll companies of citizens in some area for local defense, and these were taken into the service of the Republic as rangers.[156]

After some consideration in both houses of Congress of the problem of frontier protection and the inadequacy of the existing services, the Senate called upon the Secretary of War on December 10 to propose a plan for the protection of the northern, western, and southwestern frontiers.[157] The plan submitted was very similar to that provided by the law of December 21, 1838, except in the number and distribution of the forces and in the location of the various posts, together with the addition of a line of auxiliary posts. Johnston recommended the establishment of nine front line posts and three auxiliary ones. Of the front line posts, he recommended that a post be established at or near each of the following locations: (1) the Basin Springs, on the great Mineral Bayou, fifteen miles southwest of Coffee's Trading Post on Red River; (2) the west fork of the Trinity, in the Cross Timbers, about forty miles from the Basin Springs; [158] (3) the junction of the Bosque and the Brazos rivers; (4) the junction of Pecan Bayou and the Colorado River on the east bank; (5) the source of the San Marcos River; (6) the upper fork of the Cibolo; (7) the Frio River, above the San Antonio road to Laredo; (8) the ford where the road from San Antonio to Laredo crossed the Nueces River; and (9) a site near San Patricio on the Nueces. This line of posts, he declared, was selected "in such a manner as to embrace the settlements already established, and to cover those districts which need only protection, to induce their immediate settlement."

The three auxiliary posts were to be located, respectively, one at the junction of the San Gabriel and Brushy Creek, to be designated

---

[156] *Ibid.* For further details concerning the raising and employment of the regular army, see pp. 85–99 of this work.

[157] A. Sidney Johnston to the Senate of the Republic of Texas, War Department, City of Austin, Dec. 18, 1839, Army Papers (Texas), ms.; printed in Smither (ed.), *Journals of the Fourth Congress of the Republic of Texas*, I, 156–159; Texas War Department, *Reply of the Secretary of War to a Resolution of the Senate, Passed Dec. 10, 1839, Instructing Him to Report a Plan for the Defence of Our Northern and South-Western Frontiers.* The resolution making the request passed the Senate on December 9, but Johnston's opening sentence in his report refers to "Your resolution of the 10th instant." Smither (ed.), *Journals of the Fourth Congress of the Republic of Texas*, I, 93, 118.

[158] Approximately the site of present Ft. Worth, Texas.

No. 10; one at or near the Neches, above where the Comanche Trace to Nacogdoches crossed that stream, to be known as No. 12; and the third to be established "at or near where a right line from the post on the Neches to the post on the San Gabriel would intersect the Navosoto River" and to be designated No. 11. The auxiliary posts were intended to give support and greater effect to the general plan and at the same time provide local defense and protection to those settlements which lay too remote from the primary chain of forts to be effectively protected by them.

In making his recommendations as to the size of the force needed to garrison the posts due consideration was given to economy and to the nature of the principal enemy—the Indian. The size and nature of the force recommended was as follows:

Post No.	No. of Inf. Cos.	No. of Mounted Inf. Cos.	No. of Cavalry Cos.	No. of Unmounted Cavalry Cos.
1	1			
2	2	2		
3	2	2		
4	2	2		
5			1	
6			1	
7			1	
8			2	1
9			1	1
10	1			
11	1			
12	1			
	10	6	6	2

Together the companies would form two regiments—a frontier regiment of infantry and a frontier regiment of cavalry.

The Secretary of War felt that there was no need of a road to connect one fort with another, for he believed that the smallness of the garrisons and the great distance between the posts precluded any active support being given by one fort to another, in time of emergency. Rather, he thought, that if roads were to be constructed, they should tie the forts to the settlements from which re-enforcements and supplies must come. Such roads would also contribute greatly to the convenience and benefit of settlers residing on or near the frontier.

In the meantime, while the Texan government planned its defenses, Zapata and Jordan, against their better judgment, set out with Canales for Monterey. The Federalists hastily withdrew from before Matamoros westward through Norias and Cayetano toward the Zacate Pass on the Río de San Juan (now called the Pesquería), remaining at the pass several days. From thence they went up the valley of the eastern tributary of the San Juan River, now known by that name, through China toward Cadereyta. The delay of the Federalists at the Zacate Pass proved of great benefit to General Mariano Arista who had been sent hurriedly north from Mexico City on November 17 with a small escort to organize and command an Auxiliary Division of the North.[159] Arista reached San Luis Potosí on November 26, and while he tarried to permit his men and horses some respite from their arduous march north from the capital, he collected re-enforcements. On the 1st of December he resumed his march and reached Saltillo on the 11th, where he was joined by the First Brigade of the Army of the North under General Isidro Reyes. Here on the 12th Arista issued a proclamation to the inhabitants of the Departments of Tamaulipas, Coahuila, and Nuevo León in which he levied a vigorous attack upon the "traitor Canales," declaring him and his followers not Federalists, but robbers, barbarians, criminals, and worse. Arista called urgently upon the loyal citizens in the northern departments to rally to the support of the troops under his command to suppress the revolt along the Río Grande and expel the foreign revolutionists.[160] Nine days later, while he was still at Saltillo, the Second Brigade under Colonel José C. Montoya joined him. The following day, December 22, Arista and the First Brigade left for Monterey; they spent the night of the 23rd at Rinconada and reached Monterey on the 24th, where the Second Brigade joined them two days later. Arista found that the defenses of the city had been well arranged by Colonel José María Ortega.

In the meantime, Cadereyta was occupied by the Federalists on December 22, where the Texans and Mexicans secured provisions and each soldier was paid five dollars out of the resources of the community. The next day Canales pushed on at a leisurely pace toward Monterey, twenty-five miles away, crossing the Sierra de la Silla to the village of Guadalupe, where he halted, claiming that he had learned that the

[159] "Itinerario de las campañas en Tamaulipas, Coahuila y N. León, desde 23 de Febrero de 1839 hasta hoy 28 de Marzo de 1841," in *El Ancla*, March 29, 1841.

[160] Mariano Arista, *General en gefe de la Division Auxiliar del Norte, á los habitantes de los departamentos de Tamaulipas, Coahuila y Nuevo León*, Cuartel General en el Saltillo, Diciembre 12 de 1839, broadside.

garrison at Monterey had been re-enforced by sixteen hundred men. As a matter of fact, Arista did not reach Monterey until the day after Canales' arrival at Guadalupe, and even then not in full strength. If Canales had pushed on rapidly from Cadereyta it is possible that even in spite of the delay at the Zacate Pass he might have been able to enter Monterey without much difficulty. After a report from his scouts and upon the insistence of the trigger-happy Texans, Canales advanced to El Rancho de los Talayotes, two leagues beyond Guadalupe and slightly less than one from Monterey, where his army, variously estimated at from 1,000 to 1,250 men supported by four pieces of artillery, halted and hastily threw up a breastwork, expecting a close engagement from General Arista's troops who were rumored to be approaching.[161]

With Arista's arrival at Monterey, a brief exchange of correspondence ensued between the two leaders of the contending forces, but failing to convince Canales of the errors of his ways, Arista decided to show his strength.[162] Believing himself sufficiently strengthened by the arrival on the 26th of the Second Brigade, he prepared to attack the Federalist forces. Leaving behind three hundred regulars and two hundred *defensores* under Reyes, the governor of Coahuila, to protect the city, he left Monterey with Ortega in the afternoon of the 29th with a thousand men and four pieces of artillery. As he advanced toward Guadalupe, he encountered on December 30 a portion of the Federal army in a narrow well-concealed defile near Talayotes, three miles from Monterey. He charged them with his cavalry and put them to flight. After fleeing some distance in order to draw Arista further from the city, the Federalists formed in a cane field, where, entrenched, they opened fire with their cannon upon the pursuing Centralists, who came to a sudden halt and fell back out of the range of fire. The Federal entrenchments were manned by four hundred infantrymen, supported by the four field pieces which had been taken from Pavón. The remainder of the Federalist troops were deployed slightly to the rear at the foot of a hillock eager to join the affray. Arista dared not

161 *Ibid.*; Alessio Robles, *Coahuila y Texas*, II, 217 n.; D. W. Smith to John Forsyth, Matamoros, Jan. 17, 1840, in Consular Dispatches (Matamoros), microfilm, ms.; *El Ancla*, Feb. 28, 1840; *El Diario del Gobierno* (Mexico City), Jan. 12, 1840.

162 Mariano Arista, El Comandante general de Tamaulipas y en gefe del Division auxiliar del Norte, á Ministro de la guerra y marina, Dec. 28, 1839, in *El Ancla*, Feb. 28, 1840.

attack, but held his men formed for battle. That night the two armies camped near each other, and maintained careful vigilance.

Throughout the next day an intermittent cannonade was kept up between the two sides, but Arista showed little desire to come to grips with the revolutionists. A small hill separated the two contending forces. Late in the afternoon a few of the Texas cavalry spied out the location and number of the enemy, after which the four pieces of Federalist artillery [163] were moved to the top of the hill. With the enemy now in full view, the Texans intensified their cannonade. Their fire proved so effective that the enemy became discomfited. The artillery duel ceased at dark, and during the night Arista retreated to Monterey, pursued by the Federalists, who took up a position in an unfinished church (Bishop's Palace on Independence Hill at the western edge of the city) and trained their cannon upon the city. Arista's official version of this episode was that during the night Canales sought to impose himself between Arista's position and the city, thus causing Arista to withdraw his army hurriedly toward Monterey on the 31st to protect the city.[164] The fact remains, however, the Federalists succeeded in establishing themselves in a suburb of the city, and during the night and most of the next day an ineffective cannonade was kept up on both sides, the Centralists using a seven-inch mortar which they had placed during the night on the roof of a house.

About 4 P.M. the enemy cavalry and a portion of his infantry sallied forth from the city. The Texans were anxious to leave their positions to give them battle, but Canales, ever suspicious, superstitious, and cowardly, forbad an attack, claiming that the enemy had extensive reserves and was only attempting to decoy him from his stronghold. Canales, related Anson G. Neal, "was not disposed, personally to leave his place of safety, and wanted the Americans to remain with him." [165] Instead, he sent Zapata out with a detachment of cavalry to reconnoiter. Upon coming in contact with the Centralist cavalry, Zapata charged fiercely, and found no great difficulty in putting them to flight.[166] "His

[163] One nine-pounder, two six-pounders, and one nine-inch mortar. *Lamar Papers*, VI, 102.

[164] Alessio Robles, *Coahuila y Texas*, II, 217 n.

[165] "Information derived from Anson G. Neal, May 30, 1847," in *Lamar Papers*, VI, 103; *El Ancla*, March 13, 1840.

[166] "Itinerario de las campañas en Tamaulipas, Coahuila y N. León, desde 23 de Febrero de 1839 hasta hoy 28 de Marzo de 1841," in *El Ancla*, March 29, 1841, says the Centralist cavalry defeated the enemy.

name was sufficient to do this," declared Neal. The enemy infantry, perceiving the retreat and confusion of their cavalry, instead of rendering assistance fled in disorder toward the city. This brief, but decisive victory was marred by the refusal of nearly one-fourth to one-third of Zapata's men under Colonel José María González to charge and by the flight of one or two of the Federalist cavalry companies, which took advantage of the excitement to desert to the enemy. "The gestures were all fierce—the spirit, if not frivolous, then preoccupied. The Texans again were scandalized."[167]

While this brief battle was being enacted without the city, some of Pavón's infantrymen deserted into the town and informed Arista of the number and condition of the Federalist forces. "An officer in the Federal Army," reported later that a colonel of infantry was bribed as well as a Major General López, "the best skilled officer in the force."[168] With the aid of the deserters, Arista planned to encourage the remainder of the Pavón men to betray their new-found friends, "to steal the ammunition; and when he . . . should give the appointed signal to turn upon the Federalists & slaughter them," narrates Neal. On the night of the 1st Arista sent agents among the Federalist bivouacs. "The plan was all arranged—and . . . [might] have succeeded, but that a Letter was rec[eive]d by Canalis, late at night, from a friend in the City, apprising him fully of the treachery." Early the next morning, Canales assembled his troops and prepared to retreat. "The treacherous soldiers of Parbone [Pavón], suspecting that their designs were detected, broke precipitately from the garrison & made for the City."[169] Finding his ranks suddenly reduced to approximately four hundred men by treachery, desertion, and bribery, Canales fled hurriedly in the direction of Marín twenty-five miles to the north.[170] Canales, himself, proceeded in advance "with a company of Life Guards commanded by the notorious Dr. [Horatio Alexander] Alsbury of San Antonio—Zapata brought up the rear, with Captain Price."[171]

[167] Horgan, *Great River*, vol. II, p. 564.

[168] *Morning Star*, March 31, 1840.

[169] "Information from Anson G. Neal, May 30, 1847," in *Lamar Papers*, VI, 103–104; Bustamante, *El gabinete mexicano*, II, 39–40; Supplement to *El Diario del Gobierno*, Jan. 12, 1840, gives Arista's report of the battle.

[170] The literature of the time often uses the word *"Marino"* and *"Marín"* interchangeably.

[171] "Information from Anson G. Neal, May 30, 1847," in *Lamar Papers*, VI, 103–105; Petition of Juana Navarro Alsbury to the Legislature of the State of

The superior Centralist force quickly followed in pursuit with nine hundred men and three pieces of artillery. A forced march, characterized by great confusion, resulted. Canales was terrified, and "not knowing what to do, permitted his men to fall into the utmost disorder and confusion. His life-guard fled and never returned. . . . Men were strewed in confusion for ten or twelve miles, with their ammunition stampeded on mules, they knew not where . . . Zapata, in the meantime, keeping in the rear, wou[l]d occasionally turn upon the purs[u]ing army, and hold them in check." The Centralists, snapping at the heels of the Federalists like coyotes, dared not risk an attack, but fell back each time Zapata stopped. This continued until Marín was reached. Just as the last of Zapata's men crossed the San Juan (Pesquería) River at Marín, the Centralists appeared on the opposite side. Several Texans who had lingered in Marín to purchase bread, drink, and other items while the main body had gone forward, came near being caught. The Centralists broke off the pursuit at the narrow pass of Sabinas, near Marín, on January 3,[172] but the frightened Canales continued in great haste across the Río Meteros until he reached a mountain thirty miles from Marín, where he encamped, thus ending a continuous march of sixty miles from Monterey. The life guard, commanded by Dr. Alsbury, which had deserted, "encamped five miles beyond the army," [173] resuming its march toward the settled area of Texas the next day. Becoming convinced that the Federalists had dispersed, Arista returned to Monterey on January 4, and remained four days; following which, he advanced to Sabinas, where he encamped six days, and then moved to Marín and thence to Cadereyta on the 18th of January, where he established his headquarters for thirty-nine days.

Texas, San Antonio, Texas, Nov. 1, 1857, in Memorials and Petitions (Texas), ms. The petitioner stated that she was in the Alamo at the time of its fall, and that she was the widow of Dr. Alexander Alsbury who was taken prisoner by General Adrián Woll and imprisoned at Perote, 1843–1844. Alsbury accompanied the American army to Mexico in 1846 and was killed by the Mexicans near the Río Grande in 1847. The legislature granted Mrs. Alsbury a pension of $100.00 per year during her life. Sam Houston Dixon and Louis Wiltz Kemp, *The Heroes of San Jacinto*, pp. 308–309.

[172] "Itinerario de las campañas en Tamaulipas, Coahuila y N. León, desde 23 de Febrero de 1839 hasta hoy 28 de Marzo de 1841," in *El Ancla*, March 29, 1841.

[173] "Information derived from Anson G. Neal, May 30, 1847," in *Lamar Papers*, VI, 104.

The Canales and Zapata forces now separated briefly. Zapata marched directly to Guerrero, his home; whereas, Canales on January 7 crossed the Río Grande at Mier (where he had previously engaged in the practice of law) and proceeded up the east side of the river toward Guerrero. There the Federalist forces were soon reunited. As soon as the Río Grande was crossed, forty-five of the Texans, including Neill, Cairnes and John C. Hays, dissatisfied with the incompetence of Canales, took their leave and returned home. Ten or twelve of the Texans reached Victoria early in February.[174] The number of Federalists under arms east of the Río Grande was reported at approximately 250 Mexicans and 50 Americans.[175]

Upon arrival at Guerrero, Zapata found two of his men, a *gachupín* by the name of Jeffreys, whose life he had saved from a Centralist lancer when Jeffreys had lingered behind at Marín, and a Mexican by the name of Mandeole, who had deserted a day of two before. Both men were exacting a money contribution from the inhabitants of the town; and when questioned about their conduct, declared that they had been sent there by Canales to collect funds for the army. Zapata, however, placed them under arrest until he left the place.[176]

While Canales was in the vicinity of Mier laying his plans for the future, the Federalist leader Francisco Vidaurri was defeated near Peyotes [Pellotes] in Coahuila by a force of presidials under Juan José Galán, supported by ranchero cavalry commanded by Captains Pedro Rodríquez and Elguézabal. The Federalists fled into Peyotes, fortifying themselves in its houses, and while Galán was preparing to lay siege to the place, Vidaurri and his men escaped from the eastern edge of the town. The Centralists pursued them to the bridge of the Mole.[177] Finally, on January 7, 1840, at Villa de Gigedo Vidaurri's forces were soundly defeated by 275 Centralists under Captain Galán, and Vidaurri fled to the Río Grande to join Canales.[178]

[174] *Colorado Gazette and Advertiser*, Feb. 8, 1840.
[175] *Ibid.*
[176] *Ibid.*
[177] Alessio Robles, *Coahuila y Texas*, II, 217.
[178] José María de Ortega to the Governor of Nuevo León, Jan. 14, 1840, in *Seminario Politico del Gobierno de Nuevo León*, Jan. 16, 1840.

CHAPTER TWELVE

Formation of the Republic
of the Río Grande

AFTER CROSSING THE RÍO GRANDE on the 7th of January, Canales, with the remaining Texans under Jordan, proceeded up the east bank of the river from Mier about six miles and issued a call for a convention of delegates to organize the "Republic of the Río Grande," comprising the states of Tamaulipas, Nuevo León, Coahuila, and that portion of Texas lying west of the Nueces River. With their forces at their lowest ebb in numbers, Canales and his cohorts chose this time to proclaim to the world the purpose of their recent, scattered and fruitless campaign.

On January 18 the delegates met at Canales' headquarters on the east bank of the Río Grande, opposite Guerrero, at the Oreveña Ranch in the neighborhood of present day Zapata (formerly Carrizo),[1] and organized a provisional government based on the long-lamented Mexican constitution of 1824, and chose Jesús Cárdenas, a lawyer of Reinosa and former political chief of the northern district of Tamaulipas, President; Manuel Nina, quartermaster general;[2] Francisco Vidaurri y Villaseñor, former governor of Coahuila y Texas, Vice President; Canales, commander in chief of the army; and Juan Francisco Farías, secretary *ad interim*. A council consisting of five regular and three supplementary members was established. The regular seats went to the President, Vice President, and one representative from each of the three departments included in the new republic. Juan Nepomuceno Molano, former alcalde of Matamoros and ex-lieutenant governor of Tamaulipas, was to represent Tamaulipas; Manuel María de Llano, former governor of Nuevo León, to represent his native state of Nuevo

---

[1] "From Jesús Bar[r]era," *Lamar Papers*, VI, 130–132; Virgil N. Lott and Mecurio Martinez, *Kingdom of Zapata*, p. 105. Barrera claims he was with Zapata.

[2] *Lamar Papers*, VI, 120.

León; and Francisco Vidaurri, to represent Coahuila. José María Carbajal was named secretary of the general council; he, Canales, the military chief, and Anaya, then in the United States seeking aid, were to be supplementary members of the council.[3] Hobart Huson says, "a presidential guard, composed entirely of Texans, 60 in number, was organized, and placed under the command of Captain Jack Palmer. It was the duty of this guard to protect the President and civil officers of the provisional government." [4]

Laredo, within the claimed boundary of Texas, was proclaimed the seat of government, but it was determined that for the present the government would remain at Guerrero, since a printing press was available at that place.[5] The new government tendered José Antonio Navarro of San Antonio the appointment of agent "to establish relations of amity and commerce with the Government of your Country [Texas]." [6] Cárdenas unblushingly admitted that the successes which the Federalists hoped to enjoy would rest not only upon their own efforts, but "upon the succors which we ought to expect to receive from the Government of Texas." Navarro, however, rejected the appointment, believing, he said, that Texas wanted no part in the internal affairs of Mexico.[7] The new government established an official newspaper called the *Correo del Río Bravo del Norte,* replacing the old *Tamaulipeco,* and its prospectus was issued at Guerrero under date of Wednesday, February 2, 1840.[8] The government press was in charge of José María González Cuéllar. In recruiting troops, the Federalist government promised to grant larger land bounties than had any government before it, and to appropriate the property of the convents and churches, including the large landed estates, in order to pay the volunteers.[9]

[3] George Fisher to the Editor of the *Morning Star,* Feb. 29, 1840, *Morning Star* (Houston), March 3, 1840.

[4] Hobart Huson, "Iron Men: A History of the Republic of the Río Grande and the Federalist War in Northern Mexico," p. 109.

[5] At Matamoros, *El Ancla,* Jan. 17, 1840, reported that the name of Guerrero had been changed to Ciudad Canales, which it presumed would be the future metropolis of the new republic.

[6] Jesús Cárdenas to [José] Antonio Navarro, Laredo, Feb. 29, 1840, in *Austin City Gazette,* May 13, 1840.

[7] José Antonio Navarro to the President of the Free Frontier States of the Mexican Republic, Béxar, March 15, 1840, in *ibid.*

[8] "Prospectus of the Correo del Río Bravo del Norte," *Lamar Papers,* V, 403.

[9] George Fisher to the Editor of the *Morning Star,* Feb. 29, 1840, *Morning Star,* March 3, 1840.

After San Jacinto

The convention specified the boundary of the new republic as including all of Tamaulipas and Coahuila as far north as the Nueces and Medina rivers, respectively, and extending south to the Sierra Madre, including also Nuevo León, Zacatecas, Durango, Chihuahua, and Nuevo Mexico.[10] On January 23, 1840, the provisional government, described as "elected by the People," issued a decree known as the "Organic Law of the Republic," declaring it did not represent any legitimate authority belonging to the present Mexican government against which it intended to war until overthrown. It called for the convening of a convention of delegates of all the states of the new Mexican Republic on May 28, or sooner, to provide a permanent government.[11] The convention finished its work on January 28 and the President, council, and army proceeded to the city of Guerrero, where the President-elect and Vice President-elect were joyfully inaugurated the next day, January 29,[12] amid whatever pomp and ceremony the little river town of adobe and rock houses, willow-edged *acequias*, and jacals of brush and wattles, could furnish. Canales had taken care to supply his troops with ample rations and mescal before crossing the river, and by the time they had reached Guerrero to unite with Zapata's troops they were in the proper mood for a grand, if simple, celebration. A federal flag was planted in the center of the plaza and the "soldiers . . . marched under it,[13] kissing it as they passed; which was considered an oath of allegiance to the new Govt. A great Ball was given at the House of Zapata, and all were welcome who chose to attend; many, however, were unable to go for want of suitable clothes; they were literally naked. After the party each soldier rec[eive]d $2.00 in part pay[men]t for past service." [14] So far the adventure had not netted the Texans much in the way of remuneration. Those who still remained

10 *Ibid.*
11 Huson, "Iron Men," p. 108.
12 "Dispatch of Jesús Cárdenas to all the Officers of Government in the Northern States of the United Mexican States, City of Guerrero, Jan. 30, 1840," translation in *Colorado Gazette and Advertiser* (Matagorda), March 28, 1840.
13 Canales was said to have planted on an Indian hut (jacal) at Puentecitos a flag with three stars, signifying the departments of Coahuila, Nuevo León, and Tamaulipas. *El Ancla* (Matamoros), Sept. 14, 1840.
14 *Lamar Papers*, VI, 104; A. Canales to [the troops under his command], Guerrero, Feb. 8, 1840, in *ibid.*, III, 330–331; same document, but slightly different translation, *ibid.*, V, 403–404; H. Yoakum, *History of Texas, from Its First Settlement in 1685 to Its Annexation to the United States in 1846*, II, 289.

254

active in the Federalist cause were beginning to become disillusioned with an enterprise that left them so poor.

The very day that the convention finished its work Canales opened negotiations with Arista with the object of ending the war. From Mier he wrote Arista on January 28:

My very dear Sir. I have had the pleasure of talking to my Uncle D. Francisco yesterday, who has assured me of the good faith with which you discuss soothing our differences for the sake of our country sufficiently unhappy now with such aberrations of its government. I am disposed to end a war, the longer it lasts, the more terrible are the symptoms it presents. Only you and I can agree upon the method of ending it. We will discuss in private the means of attaining so noble an object. . . . I desire to speak with you and to acquaint you of the real character of our revolution. We are not really fanatics; as it is of little importance to the villages what kind of government the Republic has.

The Federalists, he continued, wanted respect, protection, and security to persons and property, which the government of Cuernavaca did not give. Canales proposed a truce pending conferences with Arista to acquaint him with the character of the revolution.[15]

To Canales' invitation to negotiate, Arista replied from Cadereyta most emphatically, "no." "Each paragraph of your letter of the 28th . . . ends," he said, with "an insult to a legitimate government which by debt and opinion I respect and defend. Never have you used a style so caustic, mixing it with ideas of compromise." Canales' sincerity was made suspect by the fact that he showed neither meekness nor a desire to make some sacrifice to gain peace; his only anxiety was for the towns of desolate Tamaulipas and Nuevo León. This attitude, combined with Canales' conduct in uniting gangs and forcing those now tired of the fight to continue piling up corpses, was too much for Arista to understand.

Your style of writing and your actions have given me to understand that what you wish is to impose laws upon a legitimate government, recognized and respected by all nations. . . . I have permitted you some acquittals in your former letters because I know the surprises to self-esteem by making

15 Lic. Canales to Gen. D. Mariano Arista, Mier, Jan. 28, 1840, in *El Ancla*, Feb. 28, 1840.

a sacrifice to give up attractive plans formed by a light hearted imagination; but now that we are drawing nearer to an end [of this war], you must be meek, polite, and governed by reason. . . . If in good faith, I repeat, you wish peace, you will know that in treating with a government which sees only the misguided subject, that submission to the law is guarantee of one's true conduct. Give these proofs and then you will be heard.

Arista concluded by blaming Canales for the misery suffered by the frontier—the desolation, the killing of husbands and sons, the fighting of presidial troops, the entrance of the barbarians, the driving off of cattle. In particular he blamed him for allying himself with the Texans, and asserted that arms would decide his fate. No peace could be had, he said, until Canales separated himself from the hated "colonials." [16]

Unwilling to accept these conditions, especially in the absence of any guarantee of personal safety for himself and his men, Canales determined to fight and yet stand ready to accept any reasonable offer of amnesty. Returning to Guerrero on February 8, Canales, as "General in Chief of the Conventional Army," addressed the troops under his command.

Soldiers of the People, To-day you have entered into the solemn obligation of sustaining at hazards the Provisional Government of these States, and I doubt not but you will be willing to sacrifice yourselves to do so. Our enemies are filled with dismay at seeing it [this Government] established in the midst of all their forces, and will use all their endeavors to destroy it. But they can have no success when in our favor the opinions of the age march in our vanguard and the sympathies of all the world in our rear-guard. The march of time cannot be impeded, and tyranny shall remain far behind.

He then proceeded to denounce those classes, represented by the Centralists, who wished to restore the old order of nobility and of privilege to the detriment of liberty and equality. He denounced their neglect of frontier defense and their efforts to divide the people by seeking "to provoke war against strangers [Texans], to excite animosities among them," to the end of protecting the privileged classes and extinguishing patriotism among the Mexicans. "Citizens!" he concluded,

[16] Mariano Arista to Antonio Canales, Cadereyta, Jan. 31, 1840, in *ibid.*, Feb. 28, 1840.

"the hour is come. . . . The liberty and felicity of this Republic [of the Río Grande] are nigh at hand. Let one part be organized quickly and the others will follow its example." [17]

Canales remained at Guerrero until February 18, when it was reported that Arista was advancing from Cadereyta toward that place. He then headed up the river to Presidio del Río Grande, which place he entered on March 3 without opposition. The inhabitants of Coahuila and Durango, farther to the west, did not rally to his standard in great numbers as he had expected, but instead gave evidence of succumbing to the frantic appeals of Generals Arista and Reyes, couched in the most patriotic strains, "to rally to the standard of war, in order to save the country from the traitors, pirates, rebels and savages whose sole aim," they said, "are to rob you of your wives, your children, lay waste your Farms, burn and destroy your property, change your laws, in fine enslave you like they would the black man." [18]

At Presidio the seventy-four Texans in the Federalist army proposed that Canales establish his headquarters on the Nueces where there would be a better opportunity to recruit Texans, who had definitely proven themselves the heroes in the battle of the Alamo (Alcantro, El Cántaro). When Canales refused to agree to this proposition, sixty of the Texans under the command of Colonel Jordan returned home, taking different routes and suffering much on the way. After Jordan's departure, Canales sent Zapata's small force of thirty men of the Guerrero Squadron, including 12 Anglo-Texans, on detached duty to Santa Rita de Morelos to gather money, corn, and other effects,[19]

[17] Lic. [Antonio] Canales, General in Chief of the Conventional Army, to the Troops under his Command, City of Guerrero, Feb. 8, 1840, in *Colorado Gazette and Advertiser*, March 28, 1840.

[18] Quoted in A. S. Wright to William Bryan, City of Mexico, Dec. 27, 1839, in George P. Garrison (ed.), *Diplomatic Correspondence of Texas, in Annual Report of the American Historical Association*, 1908, II, 520–522.

[19] There is some indication that the real reason for the division of the Federalist force at this point was a quarrel between Zapata and Canales. Their differences must not have been serious, however, for Canales soon went to the relief of Zapata. "Information derived from [Augustin] Soto [Alcalde of Laredo], in *Lamar Papers*, VI, 116, 121; Lic. A. Canales to His Excellency, the President of the Provisional Government of the Northern Frontier of the Mexican Republic, Conventional Army, General-in-Chief, Río Grande, near Fernando, March 26, 1840. in *Texas Sentinel* (Austin), May 9, 1840 (trans. by José María J. Carbajal of the Federal Army). Canales says Zapata's force numbered 39 men.

while he took up his position at the presidio of San Fernando de Rosas, having left Presidio del Río Grande on March 15. Morelos was one and a half leagues from San Fernando.[20] According to Captain Allen, Canales intended to make a feint towards Monclova, so as to divert Arista's attention to enable the Federalists to countermarch to Guerrero, "in order to afford their friends on the Río Grande an opportunity of leaving and crossing with them to the Nueces."

As General Arista advanced up the left bank of the Río Grande in pursuit of the remnant Federalist army, "President" Cárdenas, accompanied by one hundred Mexican rancheros and a few Texans,[21] moved the seat of government from Guerrero to Laredo. From there Cárdenas commissioned Captain John T. Price on March 1 "to proceed to . . . the Republic [of Texas] . . . to solicit volunteers."[22] The Texas volunteers were to be recruited under the following terms: each volunteer must agree to serve for a period of from six to nine months, subject to a renewal of the enlistment if the government should need his services; however, if the services of the volunteers were not needed, they might, at the end of three months, be returned home or be permitted, at their pleasure, to settle on the frontier; the pay of the men and officers was to be the same as that then enjoyed by the volunteers serving in the Conventional (formerly Federal) Army, *i.e.*, twenty-five dollars per month for privates, and was to commence from the time they were organized and began their march for Laredo; "the government," it was said, could not

. . . at present offer any more assistance than that which circumstances may permit; but in support of its credit, it pledges the property and rents of the nation, and promises that so soon as any port or town of importance

[20] "Facts of the Overthrow of Canales derived from Captain Allen of the Federal Army," from the *Richmond Telescope*, April 18, 1840, in *Telegraph and Texas Register* (Houston), April 29, 1840; Mariano Arista to Gobernador del Departamento de Nuevo-León, Cuartel General en la Villa de Morelos, Marzo 26 de 1840, in *Alcance del Ancla*, April 3, 1840.

[21] Captain Jack Palmer commanded the "Life Guard" of the President. Bacilio Benavides, a former alcalde of Laredo, has described Palmer as "a good-natured man, but not great fighter." *Lamar Papers*, VI, 133; Mariano Arista al Ministro de la Guerra, Cuartel general en Sta. Rita de Morelos, Marzo 26 de 1840, in *El Ancla*, April 24, 1840; *Telegraph and Texas Register*, April 29, 1840.

[22] Jesús Cárdenas to Capt. John T. Price, Mexican Republic, Frontier of the North, Provisional Government, Laredo, March 1, 1840, in *Colorado Gazette and Advertiser*, March 28, 1840.

shall be taken the volunteers shall be paid their dues. . . . All booty that may be taken from the troops of the centralists shall be valued and distributed among the troops occupied or employed on each particular occasion; except the arms, munitions, and other things relating to the military service.[23]

Captain Price reached Victoria on or just before March 24 and commenced his recruiting operations. It was expected that he would be ready to start for the Río Grande around the 7th or 8th of April with one hundred volunteers.[24] Already, however, probably with the idea of forestalling further desertion from the Texan military units either for the purpose of joining in an expedition against northern Mexico or of simply abandoning the Texan service, Lamar had issued an "Address to the Soldiers of the Army" on March 14, 1840, in which he emphasized that "A soldier's duty should be a soldier's pride" and that fidelity to one's country was "the first great principle of all duty." Desertion, he declared, is "the highest of all crimes which a soldier can commit and most deserving the punishment of death." He warned that the severity of the law should be meted out to future deserters, but offered a pardon to all persons now classed as deserters if they should voluntarily return to duty.[25]

Meanwhile, as Arista continued to advance after reaching Guerrero, Cárdenas fled through the chaparral towards the Nueces, taking up his position at Lake Espantosa [26] on the Nueces, ultimately moving to Casa Blanca, on the lower Nueces which had been designated by Lamar as a check-point for Mexican traders.

Arista's First Brigade was commanded by General Isidro Reyes, second in command of the Army of the North, re-enforced by a section under Captain Juan Galán and two pieces of artillery. Reyes' unit

---

[23] *Ibid.*

[24] ———— to W. D. Wallach, Victoria, March 24, 1840, in *Colorado Gazette and Advertiser*, March 28, 1840, W. D. Wallach was a civil engineer at Matagorda and editor of the *Gazette*.

[25] Mirabeau B. Lamar's "Address to the Soldiers of the Army," March 14, 1840, Executive Department, Austin, March 14, 1840, in Record of Executive Documents from the 10th December, 1838, to the 14th December, 1841, ms.; [Address to the army on the subject of desertion, dated:] Executive Department, Austin, March 14, 1840. [Text begins:] Soldiers: I am constrained by feelings of deep regret and mortification, to address you in the language of admonition . . . , broadside.

[26] *Telegraph and Texas Register*, April 8, 1840.

numbered 650 men, and formed the vanguard of Arista's advance.[27] On March 15 Arista left Guerrero and four days later was at Laredo, where he was joined by Captain Galán with 150 presidials. It was reported that when Arista crossed the river to Laredo, on the Texas side of the doubtful boundary, he remarked, "O famous Río Bravo del Norte, God only knows whether after this campaign in Texas, I shall recross you." [28] Learning on the 20th that Canales was at San Fernando de Rosas, Reyes' brigade immediately advanced in that direction. On the road Reyes learned that Zapata was at Santa Rita de Morelos; so he dispatched eighty-eight of his best horsemen from the presidials of Río Grande and Lampazos to apprehend him. At two leagues from Morelos, Captain Galán was ordered to advance to the attack on March 24.

According to his instructions, Zapata was to have been absent one day from the main Federalist force; but, contrary to orders, he remained five days, apparently in anticipation of a Comanche Indian attack upon Morelos which had been rumored. Jesús Barrera, who was with Zapata at the time, tells how Zapata was tricked by the Centralists of Morelos, posing as ardent Federalists, into remaining at Morelos longer than he intended. As Zapata's men were saddling their mounts early in the morning to return to San Fernando to join Canales, the principal citizens of Morelos assembled around Zapata, expressing great surprise and hurt feelings that he intended to leave so soon his friends who were so anxious to serve him. After offering him every hospitality, they proposed to kill a beef for his men. "He yielded to their kindness, and ordered his men to dismount, saying that he would spend the day in Morelos. His horses were given to the care of those who had invited him to remain; and by them immediately delivered up to some soldiers, who until then had not made their appearance and whose being there, Zapata knew nothing of." [29] Their supposed friends no sooner secured possession of the Federalists' horses than they opened fire upon Zapata and his men. Their shots missed Zapata, who took refuge in an adjoining house, where he was soon joined by as

[27] *El Ancla*, Suplemento al num. 14, April 3, 1840.
[28] Quoted in an extract of a letter of C. Van Ness to Adjutant and Inspector General [Hugh] McLeod, San Antonio, April 7, 1840, *Telegraph and Texas Register*, April 22, 1840; *Texas Sentinel*, April 15, 1840.
[29] Jesus Bar[r]era's Account of the Battle of Morelos, in *Lamar Papers*, IV, 131–132.

many of his men as could make their way to him through the hail of shots Galán's soldiers concentrated upon the house from three directions. The surprise attack commenced about noon of the 24th. Zapata and his men resisted tenaciously, and fought to their last cartridge. By special messenger Galán informed Reyes that Canales might advance from San Fernando, one and a half leagues away, to the relief of his coconspirator. Consequently, Reyes marched quickly with the 11th Infantry Regiment and Squadron 1 of his cavalry. Even after Reyes reached the plaza of Morelos, the Centralist-Federalist fight continued for a brief spell. Finally, Zapata's men flung open the doors to the house which had been "pierced by hundreds of ounce balls" and surrendered.[30] In surrendering Zapata broke his sword in the face of the victors.[31] Of the thirty men in Zapata's command, six were killed, twenty-three taken prisoner,[32] and one—Martin K. Snell,[33] a Texan—

[30] Samuel A. Maverick Diary, Oct. 7, 1842, in Samuel A. Maverick Papers, 1825–1888, ms.; Rena Maverick Green (ed.), *Samuel Maverick, Texan, 1803–1870: A Collection of Letters, Journals and Memoirs*, pp. 177–178.

[31] *Lamar Papers*, IV, pt. I, 251.

[32] Isidro Reyes, "Informe de Isidro Reyes G[ene]ral de Brigada del Ejército Méjicano 2d en Jefe de la Division Auxiliar del Norte y Com[andan]te General Inspector del Departamento de Coahuila y Téjas, Abril 10 de 1840," Archivo de la Secretaría de Gobierno, Saltillo, Coahuila, Vol. XLI, Exp. Núm. 1360, Legájo Núm. 34 (1839–1842), ms., transcript; Mariano Arista á Governador del Departamento de Nuevo León, Cuartel General en la Villa de Morelos, Marzo 26 de 1840, in *El Ancla*, Abril 3, 1840 (Supplement to No. 14); Isidro Reyes al General en Gefe D. Mariano Arista, Morelos, Marzo 24 de 1840, in *ibid.*, April 24, 1840. Reyes reported 3 of Zapata's men killed and 4 gravely wounded; and that he himself had two chiefs from the Río Grande cavalry lightly wounded. *El Ancla*, April 3, 1840, reports 7 of Zapata's men killed and 23 captured, but probably did not know of Snell's escape. Jesús Barrera who participated in the fight on the Federalist side later stated that 4 men were killed inside and 3 outside of the house. Jesús Bar[r]era's Account of the Battle of Morelos is in the *Lamar Papers*, VI, 131–132. The Texan volunteers killed or captured (and later executed) were: ——— Clements, W. H. Wyatt, Irving W. Redfield, William Spooner, Bennett McNelly, ——— Francis, P. H. ("Budd") Edmondson, Dr. ——— Emett, and Colonel (Major) Luis Lopez. The first four were deserters from Colonel Johnson's command, which had been sent by the Texas government to recall Ross and his men and to reclaim the public property carried off by them when they left the Texas service. R. B. T. to the Editor of the *Colorado Gazette*, Victoria, April 8, 1840, in *Colorado Gazette and Advertiser*, April 18, 1840.

[33] Martin K. Snell served as a private in one of the New Orleans companies

succeeded in escaping. He was pursued and overtaken by a Mexican who had known him at San Antonio and was his friend. He was secreted by his friend. Arista ordered a careful search of Morelos for him, but "the women took him and hid him under some canes." [34] Zapata and his son-in-law-to-be, P. H. ("Budd") Edmondson,[35] a Texan, were among the captured. The Centralist casualties consisted of two minor officers of the Río Grande Cavalry who were slightly wounded.

At the time of the attack on Zapata, Canales was at San Fernando, about five miles distant, and learning of the former's capture about 3 P.M., he immediately dispatched Colonel López to his aid with forty infantrymen, fifty dragoons, and one field piece. Canales himself prepared to advance his whole force in an effort to liberate Zapata by attacking Reyes during the night. In the meantime, at Morelos, Reyes, who had delayed his advance against Canales at San Fernando in order to feed his horses, received information late in the afternoon of the approach of Canales' vanguard with cannon. Reyes hurriedly prepared for the expected attack. At 4:30 P.M. López advanced to the outskirts of the town and Reyes opened fire. The initial assault of the

---

that participated in the San Antonio campaign of 1835. He was promoted on December 24, 1835, to First Lieutenant, and a year later, December 11, to the rank of Captain of an infantry company. While commanding a company of regulars at Velasco in March 1837, Snell killed a Lt. J. T. Sprowl, apparently in self-defense, following an argument concerning the latter's absence from the post. On March 24 Snell, with two or three soldiers, went to arrest Sprowl, "who being a powerful man resisted violently, striking Capt. Snell to the ground and wresting his sword from him." Snell quickly drew his pistol and shot Lt. Sprowl through the head. Snell was exonerated, but years later, after several unfortunate difficulties, he was killed at Hempstead. Francis R. Lubbock, *Six Decades in Texas: or Memoirs of Francis Richard Lubbock*, p. 35; Comptroller's Military Service Records (Texas), ms.; *Telegraph and Texas Register*, April 4, 1837. Snell recruited, between Sept. 19–Oct. 5, 1838, a small company composed of the following men: John Noble, James B. Reavis, James White, William Clements, John Hare, Harrison Simpson, and William Felton. Capt. Martin K. Snell's Muster Roll (Sept. 19–Oct. 5, 1838), Militia Rolls (Texas), ms.

[34] "Information derived from Anson G. Neal, May 30, 1847," in *Lamar Papers*, VI, 105.

[35] Among those executed was P. H. ("Budd") Edmondson, who was reported to be engaged to Zapata's daughter. *Lamar Papers*, VI, 111; R. B. T. to the Editor of the *Colorado Gazette*, Victoria, April 8, 1840, in *Colorado Gazette and Advertiser*, April 18, 1840.

Federalists was easily repulsed, and as Reyes awaited the coming of the moon to launch his own attack, he hastily dashed off a note to Arista, fourteen leagues away, saying that he had complete confidence in victory and that his spies were out to warn him if the enemy should attempt to flee during the night.[36]

Canales' force had been diminished a few days before when he sent two squadrons of cavalry in pursuit of a marauding band of Comanches; so when he finally arrived upon the scene, about 7 P.M., with the remainder of his force, he only had 280 men in all, supported by three cannon. During the night both sides held their positions. A few shots were exchanged between the pickets. At daybreak, the 25th, the cannonading commenced.

Arista had hoped to surprise Canales at San Fernando, the last portion of the country in that vast area populated by Mexicans. At 7 P.M., March 24, Arista reached the village of Peyotes [Pellotes], seven leagues from Morelos. General Ampudia commanded the Third Brigade under Arista, and Colonel José Stavoli, the Second Brigade, which protected the convoy of supplies conveyed by four hundred mules. Learning of Canales' advance to Morelos and his attack upon Reyes, Arista, known in Mexico as *el tigre del Norte*, started at an early hour on March 25 [37] to the relief of his subordinate, arriving in the vicinity of Morelos at 10 A.M.

While Arista prepared to attack, the officer guarding Zapata reported that Zapata wished to talk to the commander in chief, believing that Canales would surrender if he (Zapata) sent him a message. Having failed so far to prevent the shedding of blood and the looting of the frontier, Arista seized the opportunity to conclude his mission without the further expenditure of lives and property. He, therefore, agreed to talk to Zapata, who assured him that his signature would cause Canales to surrender. Zapata hastily scribbled a note to Canales and a prisoner was released to carry it, with instructions to inform Canales that Arista

[36] Isidro Reyes al General en Gefe D. Mariano Arista, Morelos, Marzo 24 de 1840, a la diez de la noche, in *El Ancla*, April 24, 1840.

[37] Yoakum, *History of Texas*, II, 289, and Bancroft, *History of Texas and the North Mexican States*, II, 239, mistakenly gives the date of the battle of Morelos as March 15, and Alessio Robles, *Coahuila y Texas desde la consumación de la independencia hasta el tratado de paz de Guadalupe Hidalgo*, II, 218–219, incorrectly reports Zapata's capture as March 15 and Canales' defeat as taking place not long thereafter.

would wait a half hour, with his watch in hand, for the surrender. If it did not take place within that time, he would attack until he had destroyed him.

The messenger was sent; the half hour and a quarter more passed, then Arista gave the signal to attack. The attacking force consisted of three columns of cavalry; the center force made up of two columns of 150 men each under Brevet Lieutenant Colonel José Tato and Captain Juan José Galán, and another of 100 from the 7th Regiment under its commander Cayetano Montero, with the artillery, composed of two six-pounders and one four-pounder. On the right were 120 infantrymen of the 4th Regiment under Captain Antonio Gonzáles Davila, and on the left 100 men from the veteran cavalry from Tampico under Captain Juan Beneneli. The entire force was commanded by General Ampudia, and was assigned to attack the enemy's center.

The reserve on the left was composed of the 7th Cavalry commanded by Arista, himself, and on the right was the 11th Infantry of 200 men commanded by General Reyes. The remaining forces of General Reyes guarded Zapata and the other prisoners. Captain Allen reported that Arista's force amounted to 1,300 men; whereas, Canales had only 400 men.[38]

Canales' troops were in front of the town of Morelos, protected by a grove of chaparral and two *acequias* that cut across the field. He had drawn his men together in the shape of a small triangle, defended by his three pieces of artillery which were under the direction of Captain Tomás Bonilla, Captain Orisanto Misa, and Lieutenant Gustave. At 11:30 A.M. the attack began with the two wings of the Centralist force moving quickly to their assignments. The Federalists fought bravely, although hopelessly outnumbered. Planting themselves around their three pieces of artillery, they held their fire until the enemy approached within thirty yards, when they opened a heavy discharge of cannister and grape, cutting down the Centralists in scores. In consequence, it became necessary for Arista after an hour of firing to send in the 7th Cavalry. At about 1:30 in the afternoon the Federalist ranks broke in complete rout. Quarter was neither asked nor offered.

[38] "Facts of the Overthrow of Canales derived from Captain Allen of the Federal Army," from the *Richmond Telescope*, April 18, 1840, in *Telegraph and Texas Register*, April 29, 1840; W. F. O. to W. D. Wallach, Bastrop, May 5, 1840, in *Colorado Gazette and Advertiser*, May 23, 1840, says Canales' force at Morelos numbered only 180, which figure seems to be exceedingly low.

The three pieces of artillery, an eight-pounder and two four-pounders, all the *parque,* equippage, flags, and other property of the rebels was captured. Canales and a few of his followers sought safety in flight.[39] They were pursued for three leagues. During the pursuit Canales was overtaken by a small body of Centralist cavalry, whose officer asked him to surrender. Turning in his saddle, Canales demanded: " 'To whom?' " "The officer," we are told, "recognized in Canales the features of one to whom he was but recently a prisoner, and to whose magnanimity he was indebted for his life and liberty. Turning back to his men, he observed, 'Let him go, he is nothing but a Ranchero,' which (he being disguised as such) was readily believed, and Canales made good his escape."[40]

By the first reports, 157 Federalist dead were counted, including some American adventurers from Texas and 20 Carrizo (Carece) Indians, and it was believed that the number would eventually reach 200;[41] 21 were reported to be gravely wounded. The Carrizo Indians in the Federalist organization were almost entirely wiped out as they fought bitterly to the last,[42] while Canales and many of his Mexican friends sought safety in flight. Out of some 320 Federalists involved in the engagements during the two days of March 24 and 25, 176,

[39] Mariano Arista á Gobernador del Departamento de Nuevo-León, Cuartel-general en la Villa de Morelos, Marzo 26 de 1840, in *El Ancla,* April 3, 1840 (Supplement to No. 14); Mariano Arista al Ministro de la Guerra, Cuartel-general en Sta. Rita de Morelos, Marzo 26 de 1840 ("Battle Account"), in *ibid.,* April 24, 1840; an English translation of Arista's report will be found in the *Telegraph and Texas Register,* April 29, 1840; Antonio Canales to President of the Provisional Government of the Northern Frontier of the Republic of Mexico, March 26, 1840, in *Austin City Gazette,* May 6, 1840.

[40] "Facts of the Overthrow of Canales derived from Captain Allen of the Federal Army," from the *Richmond Telescope,* April 18, 1840, in *Telegraph and Texas Register,* April 29, 1840; R. B. T. to the Editor of the *Colorado Gazette,* Victoria, April 8, 1840, in *Colorado Gazette and Advertiser,* April 18, 1840.

[41] Arista, "Itinerario . . . ," in *El Ancla,* March 29, 1841. Under date of March 25, 1840 (which apparently included the entry for the 26th), Arista listed 215 Federalists killed and 181 taken prisoner.

[42] *Telegraph and Texas Register,* July 13, 1842, says, "Several of these [Carrizo or Cerece] Indians accompanied Jourdan's men in the 'Canales war.' They were, however, so cowardly that they could not be induced to engage in a fight, and were only serviceable as spies and for stealing horses." Manuel Reducindo Barragan to D. Mariano Arista, Morelos, March 25, 1840, in *El Ancla,* April 24, 1840, reported more than 20 Carrizo Indians killed.

including two Texans, were taken prisoners—the Texans being in addition to those already taken by Reyes. Among the prisoners were Colonel Antonio Zapata, Brevet Lieutenant Colonel Captain Manuel Barberena, Captain Cesario Guajardo,[43] Second Lieutenant Diego Ungaray, Mauricio Carrasco, Colonel Torres, Colonel Luis López, and 69 wounded.[44] Arista declared that his losses were "sensible," and that they consisted of 20 killed "of the character of troops," 40 wounded in the hospital, and others less gravely wounded.[45] Canales, however, claimed that the Centralists lost 600 men and that he lost 81 killed.

Supposing that this was the end of the war, Arista was resolved to make the last act, like that of a regular drama, the most bloody and horrible. Zapata and his followers had been captured with arms in hand forcibly resisting the troops of the supreme government and having enlisted Texans, enemies of the country, to fight on their side. Accordingly, on March 28 Zapata, along with the 22 who had been taken prisoner with him, both Texans and Mexicans, were tried by a hastily summoned court-martial and convicted of treason against the Republic of Mexico. The next day at 10 A.M. they were executed at Morelos, and Zapata's head was cut off, "placed in a cask of brandy,"[46]

---

[43] Arista gives the name as Captain Cesario Delgado. (Mariano Arista ál Ministro de la Guerra, Cuartel-General en St. Rita de Morelos, Marzo 26 de 1840, in *El Ancla*, April 24, 1840), but Manuel Reducindo Barragan ál general-en-gefe de la division auxiliar del Norte D. Mariano Arista, Morelos, Marzo 25 de 1840, in *El Ancla*, April 24, 1840, gives it as Guajardo.

[44] *El Ancla*, April 3 (Supplement to No. 14) and 24, 1840; Manuel Reducindo Barragan ál general-en-gefe de la division auxiliar del Norte D. Mariano Arista, Morelos, Marzo 25 de 1840, in *ibid.*, April 24, 1840; El General de Brigada Mariano Arista á la Division de su Mando, Cuartel general en Morelos, Marzo 27 de 1840, in *ibid.*, May 8, 1840, contains Arista's proclamation to his troops on the victory of March 24–25, 1840; D. W. Smith to John Forsyth, Matamoros, April 4, 1840, in Consular Dispatches (Matamoros), 1840–1848, ms., microfilm.

[45] Captain Allen reported 500 Centralists killed and nearly as many wounded, which to the writer seems to be an extreme exaggeration. See *Richmond Telescope*, April 18, 1840, quoted in *Telegraph and Texas Register*, April 29, 1840. Francisco de la Garza, a sargeant in the Centralist army, later reported Canales' losses as 300 dead and 60 wounded; and those of Arista as 150 killed and wounded. *Lamar Papers*, III, 598–599.

[46] Probably *vino de mescal*. Alessio Robles, *Coahuila y Texas*, II, 219, says that Zapata and four Anglo-Americans were court-martialed and executed in the plaza of Monclova. This is an error. Mariano Arista á Gobernador del Departamento de Nuevo-León, Monclova, Abril 8 de 1840, in *El Ancla*, May 8, 1840.

and taken by Ampudia to Guerrero," "theater of his iniquities," and stuck on a pole opposite Zapata's house, where it remained for three days as a warning to his wife, children, and the people who worshipped him." [47]

[47] *El Ancla*, April 10, 1840, reports the court-martial trial of Zapata. See also El General Mariano Arista en gefe de la Division Auxiliar del Norte á los habitantes de las villas del Norte, Cuartel general en Santa Rita de Morelos, Marzo 29 de 1840, in *ibid.*, May 8, 1840; this is Arista's proclamation to the people of Guerrero upon the erection of Zapata's head there. For other accounts, see "Information derived from Anson G. Neal," *Lamar Papers*, VI, 104; "Information derived from Mr. [Augustin] Soto [Alcalde de Laredo], in *ibid.*, VI, 116; Samuel A. Maverick Diary, Oct. 7, 1842, in Maverick Papers, ms. Ampudia commanded the Mexican artillery during the attack on the Alamo in 1836. Carlos E. Castañeda (trans.), *The Mexican Side of the Texan Revolution [1836]: By the Chief Mexican Participants . . .*, pp. 72, 99, 103. The severing of the head of a rebel leader and placing it on a pole at the scene of the crime or before his home as a warning to others of the fate that would be theirs should they imitate him was not uncommon. Juan Bautista de las Casas, the commander of the presidio at San Antonio de Béxar and leader of a revolt there in 1811 against Spanish authority, was captured, sent to Monclova, shot, and his head placed in a box and returned to San Antonio where it was hung on a pole in the middle of the plaza. Antonio Menchaca, *Memoirs*, Yanaguana Society *Publications*, II, [13]. Jesús Barrera, who was with Zapata and was captured, says the prisoners taken with Zapata were marched in chains under heavy guard via Monterey, Saltillo, and San Luis Potosí, where they were imprisoned a year until released. [Jesús Barrera's account of the Battle of Morelos], in *Lamar Papers*, VI, 131–132. Barrera seems to be in error. No other account that the author has found corroborates his statement.

CHAPTER THIRTEEN

The Republic of the Río Grande
on the Frontier of Texas

THE REMNANT OF THE FEDERAL ARMY was completely dispersed with its rout before Morelos. Out of some 400 Federalists, only Canales and about 150 of his loyal followers escaped across the Río Grande. At the water hole of Los Sauces the shattered Federalist Army picked up the officials of the Republic of the Río Grande and the refugee government protected by 35 men from the squadrons of Teran and Moctezuma proceeded once more toward the lower Nueces.[1] The others accompanied Canales toward the Presidio crossing of the Medina River. A small contingent of Federalists under Carlos Lazo, the father-in-law of Philip Dimitt and a kinsman of Martin de León, the *empresario*, was reported at the latter's Aunt Calvilla's ranch.[2] The victory of the Centralists at Peyotes over Vidaurri, the retreat of Canales from before Monterey, and his crushing defeat at Morelos could be expected to inspire the victors with the bold idea of invading Texas, the home of the filibusters, or at least of penetrating into Texas as far as San Antonio where they might "triumph with ease and reap heavy booty. . . . I trust," wrote Navarro earlier in the year upon receipt of Canales' failures at Monterey, "that the Government will take immediate steps to relieve us from our threatened and dangerous position.[3]

On leaving the Río Grande the members of the provisional government of the Republic of the Río Grande appointed the Lake of Espantosa, on the Nueces River,[4] as the seat of government for the new

[1] Hobart Huson, "Refugio: A Comprehensive History of Refugio County from Aboriginal Times to the End of World War II," vol. II, chap. 23, p. 13.

[2] *El Ancla* (Matamoros), June 12, 1840.

[3] José Antonio Navarro to [M. B. Lamar], Béxar, Jan. 29, 1840, in *Lamar Papers*, III, 321; see also Joseph William Schmitz, *Texan Statecraft, 1836–1845*, p. 104.

[4] Espantosa [Haunted] Lake was nearly 100 miles below Camp Wood (formerly

268

republic. The establishment of the Federalist headquarters over a hundred miles north of the Río Grande, together with the presence of Mexican troops—even Federalists—on the soil of Texas, aroused a strong feeling in Texas that this was "too bold and daring an invasion of the territory of Texas to be passed by without animadversion from our government." [5] The establishment of an alien government within the boundary claimed by Texas was a clear indication that the Federal party considered the area between the Nueces and the Río Grande as falling within the boundaries of Tamaulipas. It is, pointed out the editor of the Houston *Morning Star,*

. . . the first step towards actual possession, and is a most gross and glaring invasion, which to submit to, would be courting insult and injury. . . . The fact, that the principles professed by the Federalists are more liberal than those of their opponents, is no reason why we should silently suffer them to dispossess us of our territory, and occupy with their seat of government the delightful part of our country. Were they worthy of the enjoyment of freedom and liberal institutions (which, by the way, we very much doubt), they would find some other means of acquiring them, than the invasion and possession of a soil friendly to their cause. . . . If the miserable Mexican soldier under Canales possessed a tythe of the spirit which nerves a free-man's arm—when striking for his rights, Matamoros, Tampico, Monterey, and all the towns this side of the mountains would have been in their power long before this. They are too imbecile, indolent, and cowardly, even to make good their independence even against such opponents as they have to contend with; and instead of calling for aid, as they are continually doing, they should be taught that the gods help those only who are willing to help themselves.[6]

Cornelius Van Ness, congressman from San Antonio, thought otherwise.

Mission San Lorenzo de la Santa Cruz; *i.e.,* El Cañon). It now lies between Crystal City and Carrizo Springs on the border of Dimmit and Zavala counties. It was fed by numerous small streams, and possibly at one time even by the Nueces River. It was a famous camping spot for the Indians traversing the vicinity. The *camino real* between Presidio del Río Grande and San Antonio used to skirt the lower end of the Lake. Cyrus Tilloson, "Espantosa Lake," in *Frontier Times,* XXVI, (1948–1949), 132–135; J. Frank Dobie, *Coronado's Children: Tales of Lost Mines and Buried Treasures of the Southwest,* pp. 62, 68.

[5] *Telegraph and Texas Register* (Houston), April 8, 1840.
[6] From the *Morning Star* (Houston), in *Telegraph and Texas Register,* April 8, 1840.

They [the Federalists] certainly are entitled to our warmest sympathies, for at times, when in possession of the frontier, our citizens (and several American merchants have visited them) have been allowed free ingress and egress, and have received every friendship and protection. The Centralists have never failed, when an opportunity offered, to despoil, and incarcerate, and generally conclude by murdering. In fact, the federalists for the last eighteen months, have served as a barrier between us and the enemy. They have been fighting our battles, and alone and unaided, almost repudiated by us, have been doing what we should have done. We want and need no better protection on the western line, than the possession of that frontier by them.

Van Ness did not believe that the Federalists were violating the territory of Texas. Is it, he asked,

. . . no violation for our open, sworn and ruthless foe to occupy and garrison Laredo, to send in Quinto, alias Manuel de la Luña, a renegade Mexican from this town [San Antonio], with 300 men on the lower road to scour as far as he can safely do it, and to despatch marauding and robbing parties of Indians and Mexicans on the other routes for the same purpose?

He estimated that the Federalist force in Texas on April 19 numbered about eight hundred men.

I hope (and believe we agreed, in opinion, when we last conversed on this subject), that the government will leave them free to operate. It is not an open and avowed coalition they desire, but simply the privilege of acting, preparing and providing in óur territory. . . . The federalists acknowledge our rights to all territory this side of the Río Grande. Now let us permit them to make as good a fight as they can upon the other side, and we will be safe on that frontier.[7]

In an effort to dispel any apprehension that the Texans might have for their own territorial integrity, Vice President Francisco Vidaurri upon re-entering Texas quickly informed the Texans that his government had no intention of claiming jurisdiction north and east of the Río Grande.[8] This being the case, asked George Fisher,

[7] Extract of a letter from C. Van Ness to a gentleman in Austin [M. B. Lamar?], San Antonio, April 19, 1840, in *Texas Sentinel* (Austin), April 29, 1840.

[8] *Telegraph and Texas Register*, April 15, 1840; see also letter written to the Editors of the *Texas Sentinel* at the request of Vidaurri, reproduced in *Texas Sentinel*, April 1, 1840.

Why did they hold their convention, organizing the Provisional Government at "Casa Blanca?" and why is it dated "done at Casa Blanca, in the STATE OF TAMAULIPAS," where is Casa Blanca? *east* or *west* of the Río Grande? is it in the State of Tamaulipas, or in the Republic of Texas? Again, have they ever had possession, and exercised, or do they now exercise Civil and Military Jurisdiction in the Town of Laredo? and make the citizens of that town tributary of their authority, by compelling them to perform military services, and exacting from them contributions? Is Laredo *east* or *west* of the Río Grande? [9]

"A word to the wise" should be sufficient.

At San Antonio, Mayor John W. Smith accurately summed up the situation when he reported, "my opinion is that the Centralists under Arista can only move against the Federalists with a view to break them up and give no time for them to form in a body. I am fully of the opinion that we stand in more danger from the Comanches at this time [after the Council House Fight, March 19, 1840], than from any other enemy." [10] However, there was great uneasiness at San Antonio following the receipt of news of Canales' disastrous defeat and his flight east of the Río Grande with possible pursuit by General Arista. On Friday morning, April 3, Lieutenant Colonel William S. Fisher, commanding a detachment of the First Infantry at the Mission of San José near San Antonio dispatched a messenger in "hot haste" to the Secretary of War at Austin concerning the presence of the Federalists in Texas and the policy to be pursued towards them. The messenger reached Austin at midnight of the same day, bringing news of the defeat of the Federalists in the bloody engagement at Morelos. Fisher was told that if General Canales or anyone else, representing himself as a commander of Federal armed forces, should present himself at San Antonio, he was to inform him that he would not be permitted to organize or recruit a force within the limits of Texas for prosecuting war against the Mexican government, or "with any party within the border of his own country." Should Canales or any other Federal military officer seek asylum in Texas, it would be granted, but not for the purpose of

[9] George Fisher to the Editor of the *Morning Star*, Houston, April 14, 1840, reprinted in the *Telegraph and Texas Register*, April 15, 1840; *Texas Sentinel*, April 1, 1840.
[10] John W. Smith to [Secretary of War?], San Antonio, June 5, 1840, in Walter Prescott Webb Collection. "I presume," wrote Smith, "that Capt. Howard has forwarded a report or information received, as to the movements of Genl. Arista and that the same was received two days ere this will reach you."

enabling him to prosecute the war in Texas or to prepare to renew it elsewhere. The Federal troops were to be permitted to avail themselves of the limits of Texas for their immediate safety and protection, and for their sustenance to purchase supplies but to do no more, unless Texas was invaded by the Centralists. In the event that the Federalist troops were pursued into Texas, Texas was bound to expel the pursuers; and, for this purpose would expect the services of the Federal army to aid in repelling the invasion; but with the clear understanding that although commanded directly by their own officers they would operate under orders from the Texas government, the flag of Texas, and the commanding officer of the Texan troops. Canales and his officers were to be accorded those courtesies due to them as gentlemen. In conclusion, Fisher was advised by the War Department that re-enforcements would be sent immediately to post San Antonio.[11]

While Fisher's force at the old Mission San José consisted of only approximately 160 men, organized into three companies (they had been dispatched there to afford protection to the commissioners sent to negotiate with the Comanches), it was believed that these, with the cooperation of the local inhabitants could check the enemy's advance until the 300 troops in the Austin area under Colonel Edward Burleson, and volunteers from everywhere, could rush to their support. At Austin, Colonel Burleson's proposed march against the Indians was delayed. Captain Pierce of the Pitkin Guards from Houston was immediately ordered from Austin to San Antonio to strengthen Fisher's command. The Guards were, however, delayed briefly in getting off on account of the high waters of the Colorado, owing to the heavy rains of the last few days.

On April 7, Cornelius Van Ness at San Antonio reported Canales with "about 130 followers[12] within fifteen miles of San Antonio, and the balance of his forces, estimated at 200 on this side of the Nueces on the lower road with the 'Government'."[13] Canales was expected to enter San Antonio on April 8, but apparently did not, for Fisher that

[11] H. McLeod, Adjutant and Inspector General, to Lt. Col. Wm. S. Fisher, Austin, April 4, 1840, Special Order No. 26, Army Papers (Texas), ms.; *Telegraph and Texas Register*, April 15, 1840; *Texas Sentinel*, April 8, 1840.

[12] *El Ancla*, June 12, 1840, reported a citizen from Guerrero who had been to San Antonio as giving the size of Canales' force as thirty to thirty-five men.

[13] Extract of a letter of C. Van Ness to the Adjutant and Inspector General [Hugh McLeod], San Antonio, April 7, 1840, in *Telegraph and Texas Register*, April 22, 1840; see also *ibid.*, April 15, 1840.

day reported him on the Medina with 150 men in the utmost disorder,[14] and another party of Federalists under Jesús Cárdenas as having crossed lower down, on the route to Goliad. Apprehensive that Canales might be followed by General Arista or Ampudia as far as San Antonio for the purpose of robbing Béxar, Live Oak Point, Lamar, Goliad, and other small towns in the extreme west, Fisher dispatched a message to Canales, "informing him of the terms upon which he would be allowed to remain in Texas."

The acting head of the Mexican legation in Washington leaked information on March 26 that his government "was secretly organizing an army for the invasion of Texas, and spoke of the conquest with much confidence." [15] His purpose in leaking this information was probably to strengthen the antiannexationists in the United States and to harass the Texans with the thought of an invasion.

From below the Río Grande on March 26 Arista, in conformance to instructions from his government, issued a declaration that all "foreigners who should disembark in any port of the Republic or penetrate by land into it, armed and with the object of attacking our territory," would be "treated and punished as Pirates." [16] To aid in curtailing the possible infiltration of Texans and others into Mexican territory, the Minister of Foreign Affairs issued a circular on April 25 to the governor of each of the departments ordering them to list all foreigners in their departments and to see that each foreigner possessed "letters of security" which were necessary for legal residence in Mexico.[17]

About the time Arista issued his proclamation, referred to above, he informed the Mexican consul at New Orleans that all the revolutionists who had repented and submitted to the authority of the supreme government had been pardoned in accordance with the instructions that had been given to him, and that peace now reigned in

---

[14] Lt. Col. Commanding Detachment First Infantry William S. Fisher to Col. Hugh McLeod, Adjt. & Inspector General, H. Q., Dept. 1st Infantry, Mission San José, April 8, 1840, in *ibid.*, April 22, 1840; *Texas Sentinel*, April 15, 1840.

[15] R. G. Dunlap to Abner S. Lipscomb, Legation of Texas, Washington, March 27, 1840, in Garrison (ed.), *Diplomatic Correspondence of Texas*, 1907, I, 444–446.

[16] See Expediente Núm. 1360. División Auxiliar del Norte. Año 1840. Legajo Núm. 34, 1839–1842. Archivo de la Secretaría de Gobierno, Saltillo, Coahuila, XLI, p. 120; D. W. Smith to John Forsyth, Matamoros, May 26, 1840, no. 166, in Consular Dispatches (Matamoros), ms., microfilm.

[17] *El Ancla*, May 29, 1840; see Circular of Jesús Garza González, Secretaría de Gobierno del Departamento de Nuevo León, Monterey, May 9, 1840, in *ibid.*

northern Mexico. However, he hastened to say that he had two thousand troops, rested and without employment, ready

. . . to hurl against the first [Texans] who dare to cross the frontier. Matamoros is garrisoned with 1,400 veterans and Tampico with 1,000. This imposing position in which we find ourselves will be terrible to the Texans who will not enjoy much longer the land which they have stolen. In short, in the position in which we find ourselves, I wish that that perverse man, the traitor Anaya, may come, with the adventurers whom he succeeds in deluding, to receive the pay which the law owes him for his crimes.[18]

This unfortunate one, reported Arista, has committed many crimes, but "the most terrible, the unpardonable one to the Nation was the betraying of the Country by attracting foreigners; he allied himself with the Texians and in union with them fought Mexican troops."[19] Nevertheless, when it came to dealing with Zapata, Arista is said to have treated him with the "utmost politeness" and to have offered him a commission of colonel in the regular Mexican army,[20] but when this offer was proudly rejected by the defiant Zapata, he was promptly court-martialed and executed.

In concluding his letter to the Mexican consul at New Orleans, Arista requested the consul to inform him if the whereabouts of Canales and Cárdenas, who have plunged themselves among the guileless ones of Texas, should ever become known to him. A few weeks later at Saltillo, in the name of the President, Arista published notice of a general amnesty to all of the Federalists "who may become convinced of their errors . . . [especially] since the battle of Morelos" and who might wish to avail themselves of the clemency of a "paternal government." The terms on which the pardon would be granted were: (1) the individual must report in person to the civil authority of the department in which they reside for one month; (2) he must agree not to venture more than twenty leagues beyond the department without previously obtaining permission from competent authority; and (3) those who had served as officers or chiefs in the rebel forces must

[18] Mariano Arista al Consul Mexicano en N. Orleans, Cuartel General, Saltillo, Mayo 14 de 1840, in W. B. Stephens, "Collection," ms.
[19] Mariano Arista to the Governor of the Department of Nuevo León, Monclova, April 8, 1840, in *El Ancla*, May 8, 1840.
[20] Extract of a letter from C. Van Ness to the Adjutant and Inspector General [Hugh] McLeod, San Antonio, April 7, 1840, in *Telegraph and Texas Register*, April 22, 1840.

give security to the authorities for good behavior.[21] Thus we see that the policy of the Mexican government continued to be one of conciliation backed by a stern hand.

Arista's manner of settling the difficulties in the northern states of Mexico, wrote Van Ness from San Antonio,

. . . is prudent and politic, and unquestionably will be most successful in the accomplishment of his views. Instead of arresting or persecuting in any way such as have aided the Federalists, he is forgiving and forgetting. In his march he does not insult or offend, nor does he touch an article for his men without paying for it. Different from their usual practice of sacrificing lives and property, he says he has come to relieve and to save, and not to finish the ruin of an already suffering and impoverished people and country.[22]

In Texas it was reported that the Centralists were "settling down along the Río Grande, and taking civil, military, and domestic possession of the whole country."[23] All Río Grande trade with Victoria and San Antonio was cut off, and at the former place, where large stocks of merchandise had been accumulating for some time for a lucrative traffic with the Mexicans, business was "dull even to stagnation and the hope of better times . . . [was] faint and faltering."[24] At Victoria the businessmen saw little hope of improvement until Arista's roving troops, especially Córdova's party, they said, could be expelled from the trans-Nueces country, even from the banks of the Río Grande. Their apprehensions were further stimulated by a Mexican cavalry unit of six hundred men, accompanied by a number of Cherokee and Caddo Indians, which penetrated within the asserted boundary of Texas as far as the Nueces in an effort to capture the Federalist government. Arista and Canalizo were expected to cross from Guerrero and Matamoros with several thousand troops.[25] The cavalry unit, however, did not cross the Nueces; but its appearance on the frontier caused the Texans in the vicinity of Victoria to organize a small spy com-

[21] Notice issued by General Arista at Saltillo, April 30, 1840, reprinted in English translation in the *Telegraph and Texas Register*, July 29, 1840.

[22] Extract of a letter of C. Van Ness to the Adjutant and Inspector General [Hugh] McLeod, San Antonio, April 7, 1840, in *Telegraph and Texas Register*, April 22, 1840.

[23] *Telegraph and Texas Register*, April 29, 1840.

[24] *Ibid.*

[25] Letter to W. D. Wallach, Victoria, March 14, 1840, in *Colorado Gazette and Advertiser* (Matagorda), March 28, 1840.

275

pany of twenty men to patrol along the Nueces as a precautionary measure.[26]

The Lamar administration promptly ordered General Edwin Morehouse to intercept Arista if he should seek to enter Texas. Morehouse reached Houston on April 21 from Austin with instructions from the Secretary of War to enroll one-third of the militia regiment of the area and to hold his men in readiness to take the field immediately,[27] and Lamar planned "to march a force to be commanded by Col. Karnes to occupy a position near or upon the banks of the Río Grande." [28] This action was not dictated by any anxious apprehension of danger, but only as a necessary precaution against surprise, in view of the concentration of some 1,500 to 2,000 Mexican troops upon the western frontier, if not within the territory claimed by Texas. While few Texans seriously believed they would have to repel an invading army, many were of the opinion that in case a "tug of war" should come, "the Río Grande will no longer be our southwestern boundary—we prefer the mountains beyond Monterey," wrote editor Francis Moore.[29]

At Galveston James Love was expatiating on the virtues of sending the navy to sea to patrol the gulf and capture Mexican vessels. No additional expense would be involved, he argued, and

. . . if Mexico was merely amusing us with prospects of negotiation it will have the effect to make them think seriously of it. If they are in earnest it will make them hasten their action. If they seriously intend an invasion it will necessarily be the means of dividing their force, because they will naturally suppose we intend making a descent on the gulf shore. A large land force thrown across the Río del Norte would produce the idea abroad, that we were fighting for conquest and enlarged territory, and would of course lessen the confidence in the stability of our Government, and our credit, but whilst we adhere strictly to the public declarations of your Excellency, that we do not seek for Territory beyond our limits, the action of our fleet on the gulf will only be evidence of our wish to *enforce* peace and secure the boundary we claim.[30]

[26] Samuel A. Plummer to M. B. Lamar, Victoria, April 25, 1840, in *Lamar Papers*, III, 381–383.

[27] *Telegraph and Texas Register*, April 21, 1840.

[28] Memucan Hunt to Gen. Mirabeau B. Lamar, Galveston, May 3, 1842, in Lamar Papers, ms.

[29] *Telegraph and Texas Register*, April 21, 1840.

[30] James Love to Gen. [M. B.] Lamar, Galveston, March 15, 1840, in *Lamar Papers*, III, 353–354.

And well might Love look with hope to the navy to render effective
service against Mexico. In less than two years Texas had built up its
second navy and that organization was attracting attention in Mexico.
At the time of the arrival of the French fleet off Vera Cruz, in 1838,
the Texan Secretary of the Navy W. M. Shepherd had breathed a
sigh of relief; "and in accordance with Houston's pressure for economy, disbanded the naval personnel down to the skeletonized crew
that manned the unseaworthy 'receiving ship'—Potomac."[31] Plans,
however, were already under way to create a new Texas navy; and
by the time the French fleet sailed from Mexican waters in April 1839,
leaving on the Mexican coast only one uncaptured schooner, and taking off to France the remaining Mexican vessels, the S. S. Charleston,
a steam side-wheeler, had been purchased and converted into a man-
of-war, and brought into Galveston harbor in March 1839, where she
was promptly rechristened the Zavala in honor of the first Texan Vice
President. At the time of Admiral Baudin's visit at Galveston in May
the Texan navy was practically nonexistent. It consisted of the receiving ship Potomac, which was never completely seaworthy, and the
steamer Zavala. A secret resolution passed unanimously by the Texan
Senate on January 16, 1839, urged that Texas purchase the recently
captured Mexican fleet from the French[32] in addition to the ships contracted for and under construction in the United States. The French,
however, were not ready to give up their prize collection, consisting
of the twenty-four–gun Iguala, three beautiful brigs, and two schooners.

During the summer and early fall other Texan naval units came off
the shipways and hastened to fill the gap left by the withdrawal of
the French fleet.[33] In June, the schooner San Jacinto, with four medium
twelve-pounders and a long nine-pound brass cannon mounted on a
pivot, reached Galveston. Her sister ship, the San Antonio, arrived in
August, and the San Bernard, identical in armament with the San
Jacinto, reached Galveston in September. The 400-ton gun brig Colorado (later rechristened Wharton), with sixteen medium eighteen-
pounders, was delivered in October. Two months later, the flagship
Austin entered Galveston Bay, a 600-ton ship mounting at the time
eighteen medium twenty-four-pounders and two medium eighteen-

[31] Jim Dan Hill, The Texas Navy: in Forgotten Battles and Shirtsleeve
Diplomacy, p. 108.
[32] Ibid., pp. 113–114.
[33] R. G. Dunlap to M. B. Lamar, New York, July 21, 1839, in Garrison (ed.),
Diplomatic Correspondence of Texas, 1907, I, 410–414.

pounders. The brig *Galveston* (later named *Archer*) was delivered in April 1840, but never went to sea on a major cruise.[34]

As soon as the new vessels were acquired for the Texas navy, Lamar sent them to sea under the command of Commodore Edwin Moore to patrol off Matamoros, Tampico, Vera Cruz, and the coast of Yucatán. They were without authority to capture Mexican vessels or bombard Mexican ports, pending the outcome of treaty negotiations in Mexico. The effect, nevertheless, soon proved disastrous to Mexican commerce. The editor of the *Jalapa Conciliador* of October 18, 1840, lamented that Mexican trade and commerce were being discouraged by the presence of the Texan vessels off the Mexican coast, and on October 22, 1840, the Vera Cruz *Censor* complained that Mexican commerce was being tied up by the mere presence of the Texan warships, even though the Texans had made no actual captures. The editor of *El Censor* was already quite alarmed by what was happening. Texas, he declared, was no longer a mere boy; it was becoming "more robust each day. . . . Supreme Government, awake! . . . . a little longer and it will be too late." [35]

This then was the navy in which Love placed such confidence. In addition to sending the navy out, he suggested ordering a draft of militiamen from each county *"to be ready* for service." "It is wise," he said, "to provide against contingencies in time. If the necessity should not exist, it costs nothing."

By April 25 a volunteer company had been enrolled at Galveston and was ready to march at a moment's notice to protect the frontier.[36] At the same time, but from a different quarter, came assurance of aid from the United States. From Mississippi, Henry S. Foote, then in the process of writing his history of Texas, upon receiving news of the Federalist disaster at Morelos, wrote Lamar immediately to inform him that should Texas need military aid from Mississippi he would "immediately raise a body of volunteers of the right sort to be of service to you." "I now assure you," he continued, "that if you really desire aid from this quarter; or if events should at [any] time make such aid desirable, I will immediately turn out and, with the assistance

[34] Alex Dienst, "The Navy of the Republic of Texas," *Texas State Historical Association Quarterly*, XIII (1909–1910), 9.
[35] Sept. 7, 1840.
[36] R[euben] H. Roberts to Mirabeau B. Lamar, Galveston, April 24, 1840, in Lamar Papers, ms.; James Love to M. B. Lamar, Galveston, April 25, 1840, in *Lamar Papers*, III, 380–381.

of Judge [James Coffield] Mitchell, Judge Caswell R. Clifton, and other generous right-minded men" raise "instantly from one to two thousand men in a few counties of our State bordering on this central county." [37]

Prior to leaving Laredo, as the reader will remember, "President" Cárdenas had sought to open negotiations with the government of Texas by contacting José Antonio Navarro, a prominent leader of the San Antonio Mexicans. [38] He had informed Navarro of the establishment of the provisional government of the so-called Republic of the Río Grande, and requested him to be the agent of the new government in Texas with full powers to "establish relations of amity and commerce with the government of your country," upon whose assistance the success of the Federalist enterprise unmistakably rests. [39] Like José Luciano Navarro, his brother, with whom Carbajal had corresponded the year before, Navarro politely refused the offer and informed Cárdenas of what seemed to him to be the continued official attitude of Texas.

Your Excellency will be pleased to excuse me for remarking, that the opinion of the Government of this Republic being so clearly manifest, ever since the conference held with General Juan Pablo Anaya, it appears to me, it will be very difficult for the agent of the people of your States, whatever his influence might be with this Government, to induce it to change its policy, which is guided by the force of public exigencies . . . not to intermeddle officially with the domestic quarrels of the Mexicans, with which country it has its own difficulties . . . involving its future existence.

Although the government of Texas was hopeful of triumphing in its quarrel with Mexico, he continued, "I believe it desires to be justified

[37] Henry S. Foote to M. B. Lamar, Raymond [Miss.], April 25, 1840, in *Lamar Papers*, III, 378–379. James Coffield Mitchell was a former Congressman from Tennessee (1825–1829) and judge of the eleventh circuit of Tennessee (1830–1836). In 1837 he settled near Jackson, Hinds County, Mississippi, where later he was an unsuccessful candidate on the Whig ticket for governor of Mississippi and for the Mississippi state House of Representatives. He died at Jackson, Mississippi, August 7, 1843. *Biographical Directory of the American Congress, 1774–1927*, pp. 1819–1820.

[38] José Antonio Navarro was one of the signers of the Texas Declaration of Independence, and a representative of Béxar County in the Third Congress, 1838–1839. He was re-elected to the Fourth Congress, but resigned because of ill health.

[39] Jesús Cárdenas to José Antonio Navarro, Laredo, Feb. 29, 1840, in *Austin City Gazette*, May 13, 1840.

279

in the sight of the whole world, and will omit no means, decorous and compatible with its independence, to obtain the settlement of its differences on friendly terms." [40]

The sudden turn of military events along the Río Grande frontier within a few weeks caused the Federalist leaders themselves to seek asylum in Texas, thus enabling them to conduct their negotiations directly with the Texan government. From Victoria on April 8 Cárdenas wrote directly to President Lamar, stating that "the government of the northern frontier of the Mexican republic has always recognized in Texas . . . a land of refuge in the event of an unfortunate occurrence," and such an event having taken place at Morelos on the 25th of last month, the government was now in Victoria, trusting that it might be permitted to stay until it could arrange its affairs. "These affairs are the establishment of peace," he said, "and commercial relations, and the negotiation with your government for aid in order that this government may resume the war against the government of Mexico." [41] To this end, Cárdenas on the 8th appointed José María J. Carbajal to represent his government at the Texas capital. Cárdenas' communication was apparently carried to Austin by Carbajal, accompanied by Juan Molano, bearing a letter of introduction from Philip Dimitt, who described Molano as "a long devoted and true friend of our Country and her cause." [42] Two months earlier, Dimitt had written to Lamar:

The President of the Govt. who sent those Gentle[men] Com[mission]ers has shown & manifested a political character, that bears truth & frankness, and a moral attitude of integrity. His moral, and political opinions, since, in this section are most emphatically identified with the general interest & policy of Texas, if, public opinion, and national investigation support what he says and wishes to effectuate with the Govt. of Texas. [43]

[40] José Antonio Navarro to President of the Free Frontier States of the Mexican Republic, March 15, 1840, in *ibid.*, May 13, 1840.

[41] Jesús Cárdenas to the President of the Republic of Texas, Mirabeau B. Lamar, Villa de Victoria, April 8, 1840, in *Lamar Papers*, III, 364–365.

[42] Phil[ip] Dimitt to M. B. La Mar, Villa de los Jacales, [April 12, 1840], in *ibid.*, III, 369; V, 416. Dimitt described Molano as "the defender and protector of those 28 prisoners, that was sent to Matamoros and ordered to be shot by St. Ana in 1836."

[43] Phil[ip] Dimitt to [M. B. Lamar], La Villa de los Jacales, [Feby. 1840], in *ibid.*, III, 345–346.

Leaving his troops at the pass where the old San Antonio-Presidio Road crossed the Medina under Francisco Vidaurri and Juan Lom, Canales entered San Antonio, where he was reported on April 8 endeavoring to raise volunteers.[44] He asked Juan N. Seguin, senator from Béxar, to aid him in this enterprise, but Seguin, whose interpreter during the late session of Congress had been the ardent Federalist supporter George Fisher,[45] suggested that he first obtain the permission of President Lamar.[46] So Canales, bearing letters of introduction from Cornelius Van Ness and Seguin,[47] hastened to Austin with Colonels López, Molano, and González to confer with Lamar.[48] Van Ness, who was interested in promoting trade with northern Mexico, praised him as an efficient gentleman of "high intelligence and character" whose "generous & liberal conduct towards our frontier citizens & traders will entitle him to your friendly attention." Seguin, on the other hand, being a more experienced and astute judge of Mexican character, merely informed Lamar, "you will be satisfied that he is an individual in whom many [good qualities] are united." [49] Canales reached Austin, Friday, April 24, and Lamar received and treated him kindly, but declined to commit the government of Texas to the Federalist cause, having no confidence in the Federalist leadership; neither could Canales be counted upon to support Texan independence, a question on which he avoided committing himself. He merely said, "Very soon, when the ties that now unite us [the north Mexican states] to proud Mexico shall have been torn asunder, we shall have [oc]casion to prove to your Excellency and to all [the in]habitants of this Republic,

---

[44] *Colorado Gazette and Advertiser*, April 8, 1840; *El Ancla*, June 12, 1840. The editor of *El Ancla* reported some 200 regular Texan troops at this time under arms at Mission Espada, near San Antonio.

[45] Max Freund (trans. and ed.), *Gustav Dresel's Houston Journal: Adventures in North America and Texas, 1837–1841*, p. 36.

[46] Juan N. Seguin, *Personal Memoirs of Juan N. Seguin, from the year 1834 to the Retreat of General Woll from the City of San Antonio in 1842*, p. 19.

[47] C. Van Ness to M. B. Lamar, San Antonio, March 20, 1840 [April 20, 1840?]; Juan N. Seguin to M. B. Lamar, San Antonio, April 20, 1840; both in *Lamar Papers*, III, 375; V, 413, 418.

[48] *Austin City Gazette*, April 29, 1840. *El Ancla*, June 12, 1840, reported Canales to be proceeding to Austin accompanied by five men, and the *Texas Sentinel*, April 29, 1840, reported General Canales and Colonels Molano, López, and González reaching Austin a few days before.

[49] Juan N. Seguin to M. B. Lamar, San Antonio, April 20, 1840, in *Lamar Papers*, III, 375; V, 418.

that those of [the] Río Bravo know how to appreciate and comply [with] the duties imposed by gratitude." [50] On other and sundry occasions while in Texas, Canales "often stated that he would never consent to yield up the territory west of the Nueces. He was willing to yield up all claim to the old territory of Texas proper," reported the editor of the *Telegraph and Texas Register*, "but would not yield an inch of Tamaulipas or Chihuahua." [51] By agreeing to accept the Río Grande as the boundary of Texas, he would have offended many Mexicans below the Nueces and on both sides of the Río Grande. Before leaving Austin on May 2 for Houston, Canales addressed a letter to Lamar, thanking him for the many favors shown him, and declaring that the warm and generous reception with which the Federalists were received in Texas, would "never be effaced from the hearts of the Mexicans of the Northern frontier." [52]

Although Lamar withheld recognition, it was not because he did not wish to see the movement to set up the Republic of the Río Grande succeed; but because Texas was, at the time, seeking British mediation to secure Mexican recognition of her independence, and the government itself, through James Treat, had commenced negotiations in Mexico. Canales was told that the defeated Federalists would be accorded personal protection in Texas, but that the fugitives could not be recognized as belonging to any government, nor would any flag but that of Texas be permitted within the territory claimed by the Republic.

There seems to be little doubt, however, that the Texan officials made use of the idea that unless the Mexican government made a satisfactory, peaceful settlement with Texas aid would be given to the Federalists. Prior to leaving for Europe to dispose of bonds of the Republic and to seek treaties of recognition with the various powers, General James Hamilton of South Carolina, who had long been interested in the affairs of Texas and who had already acted as a Texan financial agent abroad, had been given full authority to negotiate with Mexico. Hamilton's scheme for obtaining Mexican recognition of the independence of Texas and a boundary settlement at the Río Grande was regarded as a "desperate one," but *"desperate diseases require*

---

[50] Antonio Canales to Genl. M. B. Lamar, City of Austin, April 29, 1840, in *ibid.*, V, 424.

[51] *Telegraph and Texas Register*, July 27, 1842.

[52] Antonio Canales to Genl. M. B. Lamar, City of Austin, April 29, 1840, in *Lamar Papers*, V, 424.

desperate remedies," recorded Anson Jones.[53] It differed from that of Bee, who had been sent by Lamar to Mexico in the late spring of 1839 while Santa Anna was serving as provisional president for the purpose of negotiating for the recognition of Texas independence and the fixing of the boundary between the two countries. For a boundary at the Río Grande, Bee was authorized to pay up to $5,000,000. Although Bee landed at Vera Cruz on May 8, the Mexican government refused to open negotiations with him as long as recognition was sought; and on June 1 Bee sailed for New Orleans via Havana. Hamilton's plan was that instead of the $5,000,000 being paid to the Mexican government, the money should go directly to the British Mexican bondholders to whom the Mexican government had given a lien on territory located beyond the Río Grande which Texas regarded as her own soil. The English bondholders would then release to the Republic of Texas the land already allocated to them by the Mexican government. It was through this proposition that Hamilton hoped to get England to use her influence to bring about peace between Texas and Mexico, with the Río Grande as the boundary.[54]

Hamilton's commission to deal with Mexico for peace through British assistance did not mean that Texas was no longer interested in Treat's plan. Both had full authority to negotiate. Hamilton opened correspondence from New Orleans with Pakenham in Mexico. He described Texas as holding her citizens in check for the present, and as evidence of this policy enclosed a copy of Lamar's proclamation enjoining restraint on the part of Texans in the Federalist activities. However, he believed that, should Mexico refuse to negotiate, "the rein would be loosened and Texas citizens permitted to cross the border and revolutionize the adjacent provinces of Mexico." [55] Hamilton then proceeded to Europe, while the negotiations in Mexico under Treat, supported by the British minister, proceeded with many exasperating delays.

We have "forbid and used the best influence of the Government to prevent volunteers from Texas joining the Federal party," wrote Lipscomb, Secretary of State, to the secret agent of Texas in Mexico. "We have given then no more countenance, nor protection than would

[53] Anson Jones, *Memorandum Book* No. 2, January 1, 1840, ms.

[54] E. D. Adams, *British Interests and Activities in Texas, 1838–1846,* p. 37; Schmitz, *Texan Statecraft,* pp. 106–107; E. W. Winkler (ed.), *Secret Journals of the Senate: Republic of Texas, 1836–1845,* pp. 162–164.

[55] Adams, *British Interests and Activities in Texas,* p. 40.

have been afforded to fugitives under such circumstances by a government on the most friendly footing with Mexico." [56] How has the Mexican government reacted? he asked. It has fomented Indian raids in Texas, sent small parties from the Río Grande to ravage our frontiers, and General Arista is "unremitting in fulminating his threats of invasion and universal extermination of our people. . . . Our forbearance is nearly exhausted, the patience of the people will not much longer submit to a procrastination from which they can perceive no adequate advantage, and the administration will be forced to return War for War." The President, he continued, suggests that,

It would perhaps be well for you to urge upon Mexico the moderation of this Government in not co-operating (thus far) with the federalists on the Río Grande, as she has been strongly urged to do, and might have done with great benefit to herself and detriment to Mexico, that it is a forbearance we cannot practice much longer, lest we lose all the advantages which such a co-operation would give us, without gaining anything from the Central government of Mexico. The Federalists are still sanguine of success, and unremitting in their overtures to us, to make a common cause in making war on the Centralists, and in return, would grant every thing we could reasonably ask of them.

On another occasion, Lipscomb wrote that the administration had been

. . . compelled to submit patiently to continued and violent abuses of its inactivity and apathy, in not resorting to active offensive measures to extort peace, and we have found it difficult to keep our navy in port without losing all of our officers; they are impatient of what appears to them strange and unaccountable inactivity on the part of the Government. The people at large cannot understand the President's position, and policy forbids all such explanations as would be comprehensible to them; we are, therefore, compelled patiently to submit to a temporary depreciation of popularity. This state of things, however, cannot be long sustained; if something definite is not done soon, we shall be forced to change our position, and to commence active offensive operations,

not for the acquisition of territory across the Río Grande but to compel Mexico to recognize Texas independence and to stop the marauders, whether Centralists or Federalists.[57]

[56] Abner S. Lipscomb, Secretary of State, to James Treat, Galveston City, June 13, 1840, in Garrison (ed.), *Diplomatic Correspondence of Texas*, 1908, II, 642–645.
[57] Abner S. Lipscomb to Gen. James Hamilton, April 18, 1840, Texas Congress,

"The Mexican officials," wrote Philip Young in his *History of Mexico* in 1847, "are admirable diplomatists, they can spin out a negotiation and involve an unsuspicious envoy in so many difficulties, that he needs the thread of Ariadne to make his escape from the mazes of the political labyrinth into which they have entangled him." [58]

As the months passed, it became apparent that neither President Bustamante nor his Secretary of Foreign Affairs, Juan de Dios Cañedo, would be willing to recognize the independence of Texas, much less accept the boundary at the Río Grande.[59] It became evident that Mexico was only indulging in a shrewd diplomatic game at the expense of Texas, playing for time to keep the Texan government from allying itself with the revolutionists in Mexico. The defeat of the Federalists at Morelos and the almost complete dispersion of the rebels in the north, declared Treat, "will serve to strengthen the present Ministry." [60] The Mexican government was pictured as *"timid* or *bold* just in proportion to its *weakness* or *Strength."*

While Federalism seemed to be dying in the north, it was breaking out in the south. Early in June 1840 a rebellion broke out in Yucatán, and the government continued to play for time, hoping to gain strength at home before acting on the Texan propositions. Although most members of the Mexican Congress and a number of other governmental officials, believed Treat, knew that Texas was irrevocably lost to Mexico and that it would undoubtedly be advantageous to settle her difficulties with her former province by concluding a treaty, "they were afraid to act because such a measure would certainly be unpopular, so unpopular, in fact, that the Cabinet might be broken up as a result and the men lose their portfolios." [61]

By early summer it was apparent to Lamar and his Secretary of State that Mexico had no intention of coming to terms with Texas,

---

Journal of the House of Representatives of the Republic of Texas, Fifth Congress, Appendix, p. 279.

[58] Philip Young, *History of Mexico: Her Civil Wars, and Colonial and Revolutionary Annals, from the Period of the Spanish Conquest, 1520, to the Present Time, 1847; including an Account of the War with the United States,* pp. 265–266.

[59] James Treat to M. B. Lamar, City of Mexico, Dec. 31, 1839; Same to Same, Mexico, Jan. 7, 1840, in Garrison (ed.), *Diplomatic Correspondence of Texas,* 1908, II, 523–529; Schmitz, *Texan Statecraft,* pp. 110–111.

[60] James Treat to M. B. Lamar, Mexico, April 10, 1840 (confidential), in Garrison (ed.), *Diplomatic Correspondence of Texas,* 1908, II, 601–605.

[61] Schmitz, *Texan Statecraft,* p. 111.

but was only dangling the hope of reconciliation before Texan eyes until she could strengthen her position at home, possibly with the hope of renewing the Texan campaign. Up until now Texas had remained aloof from the internal dissensions in Mexico, but if Mexico were trifling with Treat, maybe it was time to threaten an alliance with Yucatán. Already diplomatic procrastination in Mexico had permitted the opportune time to pass for making an alliance with Canales and the northern Federalists. If the Mexican policy of procrastination were allowed to continue, Bustamante's government might also prevent an alliance being made between Texas and Yucatán and either crush the revolt in the south or arrange a compromise with Yucatán. Under these circumstances, Treat was now instructed to inform the Mexican government that while Texas earnestly desired peace and friendship, its forbearance was tested almost to the limit by the lack of definite action on the part of Mexico. He was to make one further effort to conclude a treaty of peace, and if there seemed to be no hopes for its successful conclusion within a reasonable time, he was to return home. Before departing, however, he was to propose an armistice for three or four years with the Río Grande as the demarcation line.[62]

A week later, Commodore Moore of the Texas navy was told that if Treat broke off negotiations, he was to begin seizure of Mexican ships and a blockade of Mexican ports. He was authorized to repel force with force. In the meantime, he was to contact the Federalists in Yucatán, Tabasco, and Campeche to ascertain their attitude toward Texas and to make a show of strength by the Texan navy to let them know that Texas had the ability to serve them as a friend, if they were friendly; if otherwise, to despoil them as an enemy.[63]

By September 1840, Treat concluded that his efforts were futile, and made plans to withdraw. Before doing so, he proposed to the Mexican Minister of Foreign Affairs an armistice to continue for three or four years, subject to termination by either party giving six months advance notice of wishing to put an end to it. In the preliminary memorandum for an armistice, Treat proposed that,

If any Mexican troops shall be found on the left side of the Río Bravo del Norte, they shall forthwith return to the right side of Said River; and,

[62] Abner S. Lipscomb to James Treat, Republic of Texas, Galveston City, June 13, 1840, in Garrison (ed.), *Diplomatic Correspondence of Texas*, 1908, II, 642–645.
[63] Mirabeau B. Lamar to Commodore E. W. Moore, Galveston, June 20, 1840, in *ibid.*, 1908, II, 651–652; Mirabeau B. Lamar to Fellow Citizens of the Senate

if any Texian Troops shall be found on the right Side of Said River, to return forthwith to the left side; and it is further hereby agreed, that the Troops of neither of the Contracting parties shall repass the Said Río Bravo during the continuance of the present Armistice.[64]

The proposition for a truce was submitted to Cañedo by Pakenham, and Cañedo rejected it on the grounds that it did not have the previous sanction of the Texan government. Pakenham was informed that even if an armistice were possible that the line of separation would have to be not the Río Grande but a line farther to the east. In no case, he was told, could the Mexican government agree "to a provisional line of demarcation to the Southward, or on this side, of the River at San Antonio." [65] Whereupon, Treat at once discontinued his negotiations with the Mexican officials, "without having been able to present officially, or *formally*," the propositions he had been instructed to make, and left the country.[66] Before leaving, however, he informed Pakenham, in accordance with instructions from his government, that should Texas "be constrained to change its position, and Commence offensive operations, it will not be with a view of extending its Territory beyond the Río Grande; and any occupation or Military movement, west of that River, will be temporary, and solely with the view of forcing the enemy to make peace." [67]

While Texans generally approved their government's policy in respect to Mexico and the Federalists, there was some feeling that individuals and private parties could do as they pleased in respect to aiding the Federalists. "Though we heartily approve of . . . [the] line of government policy which restrains our present administration from interfering in the internal affairs of Mexico," declared the *Colorado Gazette*, "yet we believe that no power on earth can or should prevent

---

and House of Representatives, Executive Department, Austin, Nov. 1, 1840, in *Lamar Papers*, III, 464–470.

[64] "Preliminary Memorandum, for the Arrangement of an Armistice between Mexico and Texas, Mexico, Septr 25th, 1840"; James Treat to A. S. Lipscomb, Mexico, Sept. 29, 1840; both in Garrison (ed.), *Diplomatic Correspondence of Texas*, 1908, II, 708 and II, 704–706.

[65] R. Pakenham to James Treat, Mexico, Oct. 15, 1840, in *ibid.*, 1908, II, 726–727.

[66] "Memorandum, Mexico, September 21st, 1840"; James Treat to A. S. Lipscomb, Mexico, Oct. 17, 1840; both in *ibid.*, 1908, II, 706–707, 711; Adams, *British Interests and Activities in Texas*, pp. 47–48.

[67] J. Treat to Richard Pakenham, City of Mexico, Oct. 14, 1840, in Garrison

our people from individually aiding these neighboring farmers and herdsmen in ridding themselves of the yoke imposed on them by a corrupt soldiery and an abandoned priesthood." [68] In Mexico, the policy of the Texas government in respect to the Federalists came to be recognized and brought relief; yet, it was not applauded, and various leaders and papers continued to rant against Texas. Declared the editor of the Matamoros *Ancla,*

We know beyond doubt that the improvised Government of Texas has suggested to the Federalists passing to the other side of the Río Bravo, for it could not consent to the territory of Texas, whose limits are that same Río Bravo, being the theater of discord and war. With that, one may say that nothing has been accomplished by Canales having planted on a *jacal* [69] of Puentecitos his flag of three stars representing the Departments of Coahuila, N. León, and Tamaulipas. [70]

Meanwhile, the Federalist cause received considerable attention on the southern frontier. Juan N. Seguin, writing in 1858 as an imbittered ex-citizen of Texas, says Lamar gave permission to ˙Canales to raise troops in Texas and to obtain arms from the armories of Texas. [71] The writer has found nothing to substantiate this accusation. It is true that Texans, contrary to the publicly announced policy of their government's neutrality, joined the Federalists and some of them undoubtedly took into the Federal service whatever public arms they had in their possession at the time or could lay their hands on. Seguin, himself, claimed that in an interview with President Lamar, the latter not only authorized him to raise volunteers to cooperate with the Federalists, but ordered that he should be supplied with arms from the government's stores. [72] In yielding to Seguin's request for permission to raise a company of men for the Federal service, Seguin asserted, Lamar declared "that any movement against the tyrannical government then existing in Mexico would be promotive of the independence of Texas." Seguin

---

(ed.), *Diplomatic Correspondence of Texas,* 1908, II, 722–723; Adams, *British Interests and Activities in Texas,* p. 49.

[68] *Colorado Gazette and Advertiser,* April 18, 1840.

[69] Indian hut.

[70] *El Ancla,* Sept. 14, 1840; R. G. Dunlap to [M. B. Lamar], Washington [D. C.], Oct. 23, 1839, in *Lamar Papers,* III, 142–143.

[71] Seguin, *Memoirs,* p. 19.

[72] *Ibid.,* p. 20.

raised a company at San Antonio and marched to the Río Grande, but had gone no farther than Laredo by the time Canales surrendered. While Canales was in Austin, Cárdenas proceeded to Victoria, accompanied by Colonel Juan N. Margain (a staff officer), Don Manuel Nina [73] (quartermaster general), and other officers of the army of the new republic, arriving there on the evening of April 7. At Victoria public sentiment in favor of the Federalist cause was "as warm as it is possible for it to be," wrote an observer; [74] and over at Matagorda, the editor of the *Colorado Gazette and Advertiser* expressed confidence in the final triumph of the Federalists, "for they have the sympathy of all Texas to back them and in less than six months they will have the cooperation of 1,000 American riflemen, who will soon shake Bustamante's unholy tottering throne to its centre." [75] Prior to crossing the Guadalupe at the Paso del Gobernador, a short distance above town, the Mexicans sent across a request for permission to enter Victoria, having done the same at La Bahía (Goliad) before passing through that place. At Victoria the whole population of the community went down to the river, and the local officials and a body of horsemen escorted the Federalists to quarters provided for them in the town. Reported an eye-witness,

The scene at the crossing was most interesting and extremely beautiful— Their recognition of members who had recently returned from the Federal army and had been preparing to join them, was affecting and mutually affectionate—the beautiful banks of this bounding river need no accessories but the files of men and horses fording above, the officers and attendants crossing in boats below, the costumes, Mexican accoutrements and trappings, pack mules and lead horses, and above all the associations connected with the idea of a young and chivalrous government retreating from despotism, to recruit and sojourn in a foreign country, formed an event long to be remembered by the spectator—few marks of depression were shown, and if any, it was rather with the Americans who accompanied them than those who were preparing to return to the frontier; the Mexicans were soon

[73] *Telegraph and Texas Register*, April 29, 1840, reports the name as Don Manuel Varia.
[74] Samuel A. Plummer to M. B. Lamar, Victoria, April 25, 1840, in *Lamar Papers*, III, 381–383; R. B. T. to the Editor of the *Colorado Gazette*, April 8, 1840, in *Colorado Gazette and Advertiser*, April 18, 1840.
[75] *Colorado Gazette and Advertiser*, April 18, 1840; see also W. A. Croffut (ed.), *Fifty Years in Camp and Field: Diary of Major General Ethan Allen Hitchcock*, pp. 193–194.

smoking their corn-shuck cigars and mingling in the amusements of the place with cheerfulness and familiarity and a confident reliance on their American comrades.[76]

The Federalist camp was established between La Bahía and Victoria on the Coleto, eight miles from Victoria. Three companies of Federalist troops were stationed at or south of the Nueces. One company early in April was reported to be at the Nueces, below San Patricio; another was collecting cattle in the vicinity of the Río Grande; and the third was reputed in pursuit of a group of Comanches and Cherokees who had collected "an immense number of horses," so eagerly desired by the Anglo-Americans around Victoria.

About three weeks before, eighteen persons, describing themselves as merchants of Victoria carrying on an extensive trade through Lavaca Bay, petitioned Lamar to consider "the propriety of affording protection to the Mexican Trade and of enforcing respect to the laws of the land." Their imports from which the government derived considerable revenue were almost exclusively for the Mexican trade. They explained that there

. . . still exists in our adjacent frontier bodies of Armed Americans who rob and otherwise molest the traders to an extent that none, or very few, are able to reach the settlement, and lately their outrages have been so daring the trade is almost wholly stopped. . . . Formerly these American parties contented themselves with pressing a few horses and other necessaries for Cow driving . . . notwithstand[ing] which the traders continued to come in with their money and trade; but since there is not only a risk of property but of life to the adventuring traders their trade has almost ceased.

The petitioners implied they could not mention the names of those who had committed the outrages "in defiance of Law and common decency," for the motto among these armed thugs was *"Dead men tell no tales"* and it was likely that their names were only known to the perpetrators of the evil deeds. For example, "a few days since an examination was had before a Justice of the Peace of this town," they said.

An individual who headed a party of those Americans was arrested. Two

[76] R. B. T. to the Editor of the *Colorado Gazette*, Victoria, April 8, 1840, in *Colorado Gazette and Advertiser*, April 18, 1840.

Americans of Credibility were sworn as witnesses. From their testimony it appeared that about four weeks since a company of traders were attacked on this side of the Nueces not far from San Patricio by a company of Americans who severely wounded one of their number. The Mexicans were scarcely quit of the Company who first attacked them than another company of Americans overhauled them and pressed their horses for the use of the Federal Mexicans (alias cow driving) Service. The matter is still before the examining court but we are fully satisfied the law will avail nothing; they are able at all times to exculpate themselves by means of pliant witnesses.[77]

The situation was no better at Goliad. At that place there was "a great stir about stolen horses," and upon his arrival there, one evening in the spring of 1840, narrated Rev. W. L. McCalla,

. . . while I was telling my hospitable, pious and intelligent host that I apprehended danger of horse-thieves, and therefore felt anxious to secure my pony in a good inclosure, the animal and its beautiful lariat disappeared and we saw them no more. At the same time my [Mexican] companion was missing, and several other horses disappeared. I concluded that on the Guadalupe and the San Antonio the name of Camanchees was a very convenient cloak for Mexican murderers and horse-thieves.[78]

By the time the petition from Victoria reached Austin, the administration had a more pressing and immediate problem to contend with. The efforts to sign a peace treaty with the Comanches had blown up in the Council House fight at San Antonio on March 19,[79] and the

[77] James D. Owen and Others to M. B. Lamar, Victoria, March 13, 1840, in *Lamar Papers*, III, 350–351.
[78] W. L. McCalla, *Adventures in Texas, Chiefly in the Spring and Summer of 1840: with a Discussion of Comparative Character, Religious and Moral*, pp. 42–43.
[79] The various Comanche tribes had been invited to send representatives to a council in San Antonio on March 19 to discuss peace terms with agents of the Texas government. The Indians had been told to bring in all of their white prisoners, but only one girl, Matilda Lockhart, who had been held captive some two years, was brought in. The Texan delegation, supported by three companies of troops under Colonel William S. Fisher, determined to hold the twelve chiefs, the Indian women, and children prisoners until the other white captives were brought in. Texan troops guarded the doors to the Council House and were posted inside. The chiefs were informed that it was known they had other captives and that until these were surrendered they could consider themselves prisoners. A bloody fight ensued in which thirty-five Indians were killed and eight wounded, and twenty-seven Indian women and children and two old men were captured.

massacre of their chiefs could be expected to light the torch along the whole western frontier. The Mexican Federalists on the frontier also posed a problem. Consequently, Lamar determined to make a special investigation of conditions on the San Patricio-Victoria-Goliad frontier, and for this purpose he sent Colonel Samuel A. Plummer, a close friend, from Austin as an agent of the government to the southwestern frontier. Plummer was in Victoria at the time of the arrival of Cárdenas. His purpose, declared a correspondent of the *Colorado Gazette*,[80] was to raise volunteers "to sweep the country between the Nueces and the Río Grande, catch Córdova, and be ready to cross the Río Grande if Mexico does not acknowledge" the independence of Texas. Actually, there seems to be no justification for concluding, as did the correspondent of the *Gazette*, that Plummer's ultimate objective was to wring from Mexico a recognition of the independence of Texas. His mission was to recommend measures for the protection of the Republic's frontier and to clean out the banditti. His immediate objective was to get the cooperation of the cowboys, "between whom and the American portion of the Federal army there is a great affinity."[81] In the meantime, a number of self-constituted companies were formed on the frontier to maintain order or, more often, for the purpose of plundering.

Shortly after the arrival of the Federalists on the evening of April 7, a public meeting was called by Plummer at which some 350 persons, including President Cárdenas, assembled at the courthouse, where they were addressed by Colonel Plummer. Plummer explained the "propositions" of the Texas government and "declared his intentions." After he had finished his talk, the meeting was adjourned at the request of Cárdenas until the next evening to permit him to consult with his officers on the question of cooperation with Plummer, whose objectives "seemed to coincide with his."

The next day (April 8) a public meeting was held by the citizens of the town, and it was reported Plummer had a satisfactory conference with Cárdenas.[82] At this meeting it was resolved to give Cár-

---

Seven Texans were killed and eight wounded. John Henry Brown, *History of Texas, from 1685 to 1892*, II, 175–177.

[80] R. B. T. to the Editor of the *Colorado Gazette*, Victoria, April 8, 1840, in *Colorado Gazette and Advertiser*, April 18, 1840.

[81] *Ibid.*

[82] Philip Young in his *History of Mexico*, published in 1847, says that a secret treaty was made between the Federalists and the authorities of Texas at Laredo,

denas and his suite a public dinner as a manifestation of the local sentiment in favor of those engaged in "the holy cause of liberty." Many of those attending the meeting were merchants whose business was suffering from the re-establishment of Centralist control in the north Mexican states and the elimination of the French blockade. A committee composed of J. J. H. Gramment, H. J. Moore, J. T. O'Reilly, merchant, and Captain John T. Price, from the Federal army, was appointed to officially welcome and to extend to "His Excellency" the freedom of the city and to invite him and his staff to a public dinner at a time most convenient to the refugees.[83] The dinner was apparently scheduled for the 9th, but was later postponed a day "for the purpose of receiving further expected intelligence." On the 8th Canales was reported to be at Béxar and was expected to reach Victoria on the 10th.[84] It seems likely that the hope of having Canales also present at the dinner was the principal cause for its postponement.

In the meantime, Cárdenas addressed a letter on the 8th to Lamar, "President of the Republic of Texas," requesting asylum, peace, commercial relations, and aid from the Texas government in the resumption of the Federalist war against Mexico.[85] He informed Lamar that he

---

presumably in December 1839. If any such agreement was made, it must have been in March or April 1840, but it certainly was not made with any authorized agent of the Texas government. Young gives the terms of the treaty as follows:

> The President of the Republic of the Río Grande pledges himself to declare and establish the Federal Constitution of 1824, as soon as he shall have established his headquarters within the territory claimed by the said Republic.
> That the Republic of the Río Grande, shall immediately after said declaration of independence, recognize the independence of Texas.
> The Republic of Texas pledges herself to aid the Federalists of the Río Grande in their struggle for independence, as soon as her own independence is recognized by the Republic of the Río Grande.

In fulfillment of this treaty, Young declares that a volunteer force was raised at Béxar and marched under Colonel Jordan to join the Federal army. No formal treaty was ever made by the Texan government with the Federalists. See Winkler (ed.), *Secret Journals of the Senate: Republic of Texas, 1836–1845.*

[83] Account of the Reception given to the Leaders of the New Government of the Río Grande by the Citizens of Victoria, April 13 [*sic*], 1840, in *Telegraph and Texas Register*, April 29, 1840; J. J. H. Gramment and Others to Jesús Cárdenas, President of the Federal Government, of the Frontier of the Río del Norte, and Officers of the same, Victoria, April 8, 1840, in *ibid.*; Jesús Cárdenas to J. J. H. Gramment and Others, [April 8, 1840], in *ibid.*

[84] R. B. T. to the Editor of the *Colorado Gazette,* Victoria, April 8, 1840, in *Colorado Gazette and Advertiser,* April 18, 1840.

[85] Jesús Cárdenas to M. B. Lamar, Villa de Victoria, April 8, 1840, in *Lamar*

had appointed an agent to represent "the government of the northern frontier of the Mexican republic" in the Texas capital. This communication, as previously noted, was apparently carried to Austin by that agent, Colonel José María J. Carbajal, and Juan Molano, bearing a letter of introduction from Philip Dimitt.[86]

The large, well-attended dinner, prepared by Mr. James, was held at 3 P.M. on Friday, April 10,[87] under the shade of the venerable post oaks on Diamond Hill with Colonel T. H. Poage presiding, assisted by Major James D. Owen, merchant and mayor, and Judge David Murphree. After the tables were cleared, the honorable guest, Jesús Cárdenas, a handsome, noble-looking man of about thirty-four or thirty-five years of age, clear-headed, mild, and collected, briefly addressed the gathering.

Eighteen months ago, the Eastern States of the Mexican Republic, being no longer able to endure the onerous and ignominious yoke of a government, consisting of the continued power of the Military and Clergy, such as now exists in Mexico, commenced a struggle . . . [for] the establishment of the Federal system, with the improvements which the experience and intelligence of the age require. [Last January] all the citizens of said states who were not completely overpowered by the oppression, established a provisional government . . . .

He then proceeded to mention the recent disaster suffered by the Federalists at Morelos and their flight to safety in Texas,

where they have not hesitated to come to solicit aid that they may return and operate again against the tyrannical government of Mexico. . . . The sympathy which has always existed between Texas and the people of the northern frontier of the Mexican Republic, the uniformity of the interests of the inhabitants of both countries, the identity of the cause which they support, the general good feeling which this Republic has for the new Government of the frontier, is a sure presage that that government will soon return to its own territory, with the aid which it has repaired here to solicit of the friends of liberty. The enemy of the liberal party of Mexico, are the implacable enemies of Texas—they are the same who shed the blood of

Papers, III, 364; H. Yoakum, *History of Texas from Its First Settlement in 1685 to Its Annexation to the United States in 1846*, II, 288.

[86] Phil[ip] Dimitt to M. B. La Mar, Villa de los Jacales, April 12 (?), 1840, *Lamar Papers*, III, 369; V, 416.

[87] R. B. T. to the Editor of the *Colorado Gazette*, Victoria, April 8, 1840, in

Texians in the Alamo and at Labahía—they are the same who now wish to re-enact these scenes of horror and barbarity—can there be a doubt that Texas will afford auxiliaries against such enemies? No, gentlemen, the new government which has been received with such generosity in this town . . . hope not without reason, that there are men here who are willing to aid them. To ask assistance is their motive for appearing among you, and to obtain it they excite the sympathies and the love which all here present cherish for the cause of liberty.[88]

The address was followed by a lively conversation and the drinking of numerous toasts, accompanied by "cheers of the citizens and the roaring of the old twelve pounder." Besides the usual toasts offered to "liberty" and to the "distinguished guests," the following are suggestive of the thoughts of the people at that time: "The Lone Star of Texas—unless arrested by the hands of peace, shall be unfurled to the mountain breeze of Mexico"; "The new Government of the Northern Frontier of Mexico—the blood of her brave soldiers shed on the plains of Morelos has sealed her independence forever"; "General Don Antonio Canales—the soldier, the patriot, and the statesman—too honest to be bought, and too brave to be daunted by misfortune"; "Our fellow citizens who fell at Mier and Morales—worthy of the cause in which they died"; and "The tri-colored flag—like the fair of Victoria, by whose hands it was made, will never need the support of the enemies of freedom." [89]

"I never saw any thing," reported Plummer, "go off with more enthusiasm, or [be] better conducted. The crowd was so great that many had no room for seats—I for one. But the loss of the dinner was made up in side bar drinking—and that too of very fine champaign." [90]

As an excuse to raise a force to aid the Federalists and, possibly at the same time protect the frontier trade, the citizens of Victoria sought to get up a company of about 125 volunteers to go in search of Córdova, "who it will be remembered," declared one of the Texas newspapers,[91] "is the leader of a small band of motley race, form and

---

Colorado Gazette and Advertiser, April 18, 1840; Same to Same, Victoria, April 11, 1840, in *ibid.,* April 25, 1840.

[88] Address of Jesús Cárdenas, President of the Federal Government of Mexico, to the Citizens of Victoria, Texas, March 8 [April 10?] 1840, in *ibid.,* April 25, 1840.

[89] *Telegraph and Texas Register,* April 29, 1840.

[90] Samuel A. Plummer to Gen. [M. B. Lamar], Victoria, April 25, 1840 (Private), *Lamar Papers,* III, 381–383.

[91] *Telegraph and Texas Register,* April 29, 1840.

feature," who escaped annihilation on the Texas frontier a few months ago. Córdova's band of some fifty to a hundred men, "chiefly Indians," supported by a number of "mixed up Mexicans, mulattos, negroes, and desperate renegade Americans," for the last six months, it was said, had "been committing murders, depredations, and robberies along the Río Grande, and between that river and the Nueces." He was said "to have immense droves of cattle, horses, and mules, stolen from the ranchos and from the Mexican traders, besides large quantities of other plunder. The prospect of a rich harvest of spoils," declared the editor of a leading newspaper,[92] "will doubtless allure into an expedition against Córdova many whom the desire to rid the frontier from this scourage, and protect the Mexican trade from ruin, would fail to call out." A correspondent of the *Colorado Gazette* reported on the 11th of April that there was "force enough now [at Victoria] to occupy the disputed territory between the Nueces and the Río Grande—peace or war. Why should a people care about their independence being 'acknowledged'," he asked, "when Nature assists them so much in acquiring territory and enables them to hold it?"[93]

With these objects in mind, during Court Week when there were many persons in town from various parts of the Republic, "a large and respectable meeting of [the citizens] of Western Texas" was held in the courthouse at Victoria on Thursday evening, April 23. On the motion of Colonel Plummer, Judge John Hemphill was elected chairman of the meeting; and on motion of John D. Morris, Andrew Neill, the district attorney, was appointed secretary. Other prominent persons in attendance were: Judge James W. Robinson, French Strother Gray, E. L. Holmes, Major James Kerr,[94] and John J. Linn. Representatives from the surrounding counties were present. Judge Robinson explained that the object of the meeting was to petition the government for the protection of the people on this exposed frontier. Colonel Plummer

[92] *Ibid.*, *Brazos Courier* (Brazoria), March 10, 1840.

[93] R. B. T. to the Editor of the *Colorado Gazette*, Victoria, April 11, 1840, in *Colorado Gazette and Advertiser*, April 25, 1840.

[94] In the John Henry Brown Papers, ms., there is a handwritten copy of a letter in Spanish from Santiago Kerr por orden del Comdte de Division federal de Texas, á Guilermo O'Dorharty, San Patricio, 5 Noviembre de 1838 las 8 de la mañana. While the salutation of this letter shows the name O'Dorharty, it is addressed to "Al Commandante / Div Nicholas Rodríquez / En / Le Pantitlan." The letter offers the services of "a good surgeon and doctor" for the enemy wounded in the engagement of November 4. Kerr, who returned to San Patricio on the 5th, also

observed that it was impossible "to o[b]tain men or to carry out the
views of the executive by ra[i]sing tr[oop]s for six months but that
an expedition against Córdova and [his] allies would meet the views
of the public," and suggested that the government be petitioned to
permit the raising of a volunteer company to afford protection to
the frontier. A special committee was then authorized and appointed
by Judge Hemphill to draft suitable resolutions. Assuming that the
Indians and Centralists were making preparations for an attack upon
the Texas frontier, the Committee drafted and the meeting adopted
unanimously a series of resolutions requesting the President of Texas
to grant permission to an individual to enroll volunteers "to [the]
number that may be offered who shall report themselves at this place
[Victoria] and organize, with the distinct understanding that they will
look to the liberality of some future Congress for the remuneration to
which their services may entitle them." [95] In particular, they wanted
the government to place the mounted cannon, ammunition, and arms
of every description at Victoria and neighboring towns [96] at their disposal "for the purpose of arming and equiping such as are disposed
to volu[n]teer in the service of the Country and unable to arm
the[m]selves." They requested permission to organize and pursue Córdova and his Indian allies and to "make such terms and conditions . . .
with the Federal Mexicans as may secure their friendship not com-
promitting the Honor and character of the Texian Government."

After the meeting, Plummer privately informed Lamar that upon
strict inquiry he found the citizens of that section of the country willing
to "turn out almost to a man for a single dash to the Río Grande to
break up Córdova and his Indian allies." He thought it would be
almost impossible to raise sufficient men for six months service to accomplish the desired object, not to mention the terrible expenses to
the government; but, he declared, there were thousands of adventurers in the

---

stated that the priest was free to attend the wounded and the burial of the dead.
This letter is significant in that it connects James Kerr with the early Federalist
movement.
[95] "Proceedings of a Public Meeting Held at Victoria, April 23, 1840, Judge
[John] Hemphill, Chairman," in Lamar Papers, ms. The Committee consisted of
James W. Robinson, Chairman; F. S. Gray; E. L. Holmes; John J. Linn; S. A.
Plummer; James Kerr; and John D. Morris.
[96] At Linnville were large quantities of "Powder &c and Cannon." Samuel A.
Plummer to M. B. Lamar, Victoria, April 25, 1840, in *Lamar Papers*, III, 381–383.

. . . U. States and this country . . . [who] have seen and heard of their [Mexico's] beautiful fields and gold mines and they are like the Lion at the feast—"we will take this for our share." . . . So now in relation to the Federalist you may just as well tell them to go—for go they will and that pretty soon, peace or no peace. This feeling arises, part[ly] from sympathy, part[ly] for gain, part[ly] from the hard times and the largest part for the want of something to do. Now I wish this done, first—drive out Córdova and his Indians and then if necessary join the Feds—break up that infernal hole Matamoros, that must ever in her presen[t] situation, sit on our frontier like an incubus—instigating Hostile Indians to all sorts of violence and furnishing them wit[h] arms and ammunition.[97]

Plummer found strong sympathy along the southwestern frontier for the Federalist cause, but the news concerning the civil war in Mexico he found to be quite contradictory; and, he reported, "judging from all accounts put together" the Federalists "are in a hell of a box." By joining with the Federalists now the Texans could help them out of an awkward situation. He argued for the formation of an alliance between Texas and the Mexican Federalists.

Once join the Federalists, and Texas will never stand in need of hereafter spending one dollar in fighting Mexicans. Americans will flock there by thousands and join the Federal Cause. We will get clear of a large number of useless population—we can loose no wealth. We make a warm friend of a neighbour and you put down all Centralism in Mexico at the very first advance in the Federal Cause. . . . I again assure you we are for fight here— and for driving out the Indians and *joining in with the Federalist[s]. I know not of a single exception.*

Plummer suggested that if the President should grant the petitioners their request that he make his instructions "as loose as possible, no positive order to go or not to go across the Río Grande—but to break up Córdova and catch him." Others contended that nothing could be lost by cooperating with the Federalists, for, it was said,

. . . we . . . owe nothing to the forbearance of the Mexican government that *we* would forbear in turn. Had they the power equal to the will to work us harm we should soon experience a repetition of the sanguinary scenes which have damned them already in the eyes of the civilized world. . . . One bold stroke now would not only be advancing the cause of liberty

[97] Samuel A. Plummer to M. B. Lamar, Victoria, April 25, 1840, in *ibid.*

but would give us peace and all the blessings following in her train. Canales only asks to be allowed to recruit men and get supplies through us, and even this pitiful boon is denied by the powers that be, with the Van Buren noncommittal cold-heartedness. Our beautiful little navy, instead of lying up in inglorious idleness, could put them in possession of Matamoros—the first step in the certain success of their cause.[98]

As for the editor of the *Colorado Gazette and Advertiser* [99] who seemingly represented the prevailing attitude of the settlers along the Matagorda-Victoria-Goliad-San Patricio frontier, he not only wished the Mexican Federalists every success but declared that he intended aiding them in the future with all the means at his command irrespective of government policy.

The conduct of the citizens of Victoria in exhibiting such exuberance for the Federalist cause was not considered beyond reproach by other Texans. "If these officers of the new government were received and treated as private foreign citizens in distress, no question could be raised as to the propriety of the . . . [public dinner]; but they are received as the officers of the government of the Río Grande," commented the editor of the *Telegraph and Texas Register*.[100]

We cannot approve of it, because we bear too fresh in mind that this new government was organized *in our own territory,* and went into operation and exercised jurisdiction there—thus, in fact, invading Texas, and bringing disturbance, war and confusion into the borders of a country inclined to be friendly to their cause, though much doubting their ability to maintain it. We rejoice that our government has kept aloof from either of the belligerents, and had all our citizens, been wise enough to do the same, they would have been spared from much sacrifice and suffering, and our government from much expense and annoyance.

Along the same general line, the *Austin City Gazette,*[101] edited by C. K. Teulon, disagreed with an anonymous Béxar correspondent who, signing his name "San Antonio," advocated sending an expedition against Mexico in 1840.

We entirely disagree with the policy advocated by "San Antonio." It is the policy of Texas to act on the defensive, and not on the offensive,—we are

[98] W. F. O. to W. D. Wallach, Bastrop, May 5, 1840, in *Colorado Gazette and Advertiser,* May 23, 1840.
[99] April 18, 1840.   [100] April 29, 1840.   [101] Nov. 18, 1840.

able to defend ourselves against all invaders, but we are not in a condition to become aggressors, the people of Texas live by the sweat of their brows—they have lands to tend, families to support, and their homes to defend against the Indians; they, therefore, have but little time to spend for any Quixotic expeditions. The Government of Texas have neither the means or credit to enable them to carry on an offensive war. "San Antonio" may be assured, that let a Texian army plant the single star on the western bank of the Río Grande, and Centralists and Federalists will forget their own private differences, and unite to expel the *"heretics"* from out their borders. But suppose we were to join the Federalists, could we depend on them. We cannot. For most assuredly, if they are base enough to betray each other, they would not suffer many scruples of conscience in betraying those whom they have ever been taught to regard as heretics and enemies, they would rather think, that in betraying Texians, they were performing a service, alike acceptable to God and beneficial to Mexico.

On the other hand, Benjamin F. Neal, the Chief Justice of Refugio County, wanted to know what to do about "persons calling themselves Federals" traversing the county. In the absence of Lamar from the capital, Acting Secretary of State Joseph Waples replied, "I can at present only advise you to enjoin . . . upon all civil officers . . . strict vigilance in preventing depredations from being committed and as soon as the President and Secretary of State return home (and we are daily expecting them), your letter shall be laid before them." [102] The problem became even more complicated when several of the county officers of Refugio County and elsewhere joined the Federal cause and sought to retain their offices under Texas law and have the duties of those offices exercised by deputies until their return or until the termination of the war. Their action, it was reported, was creating "considerable dissatisfaction among the citizens." Complained Chief Justice Neal,

Your Excellency are doubtless aware of the recent organization of this county and the difficulties we are now laboring under on account of our frontier position, having a foreign Army on our southwestern boundary line and bands of Mexicans traversing different parts of our County with weapons of war, our Citizens know not when their lives and property are

[102] Joseph Waples to B. F. Neill, Department of State, Austin, July 29, 1840, State Department Letterbook, no. 1, ms., pp. 183–184. Benjamin F. Neal to Secretary of State, Mission Refugio, Jan. 11, 1842, in Domestic Correspondence (Texas), 1836–1846, ms.

in safety. In fact, reports are daily in circulation of the loss of property that individual[s] have sustained by these marauding parties of Mexicans. The Mexican character is so well known to the American that we never know when to trust them, those parties roam through the country calling themselves Federals. We know nothing of the truth of these statements and yet the citizens of our County has [sic] to suffer for the depredations committed by these parties. If your excellency could advise any means whereby the authorities of this County could demand of those parties some showing where they belong and what business leads them here so they might travel the County as our Citizens, certainly our county would feel herself guarded from those apprehensions of danger that daily occur.[103]

When the question of the status of county civil officers who joined the Federal army or accepted commissions from the government of the Republic of the Río Grande came up, the Attorney General of Texas ruled that the government of Texas would not recognize as an officer any man who left his position as such, or received a commission from any foreign power.[104] The Acting Secretary of State, Joseph Waples, ordered all vacancies created under such circumstances to be filled according to law.

In view of the strong sentiment for the Federalist cause among the inhabitants of the lower Nueces frontier, Cárdenas lost no time in enlisting Texan volunteers for the new Federalist army, and Plummer, himself, organized a spy company to operate along the lower Nueces to give warning of any Centralist advance in that direction. John McDaniel, a lieutenant in the Federal army, appealed in an open letter "to the young and the brave," saying,

You now have the most favorable of opportunities for displaying your chivalry and generosity and crowning yourselves with that glory for which the youth of Texas so eagerly pant, by shouldering your rifles and marching beyond the Río Grande, and relieving the oppressed, who are now strug-

[103] Benjamin F. Neal to Mirabeau B. Lamar, Refugio, Refugio County, Texas, July 1, 1840, in *ibid.*

[104] Joseph Waples, Acting Secretary of State, to B. F. Neill [Neal], Department of State, Austin, July 29, 1840, State Department Letterbook, no. 1, ms., pp. 183–184; Benj. F. Neal, Chief Justice, R[efugio] C[ounty] to Mirabeau B. Lamar, Refugio, Refugio County, Texas, July 1, 1840, Domestic Correspondence (Texas), 1836–1846, ms. Benjamin F. Neal was Chief Justice of Refugio County. He resigned this office on January 11, 1842. See Benj. F. Neal to Secretary of State, Mission Refugio, Jan. 11, 184[2], *ibid.*, ms.

gling for the liberty which we, in times past, obtained by arresting the power of that same despotism which now rules that unfortunate people with an iron rod.

You must remember, he continued, the Mexican Federalists

. . . have come into our country humbly and imploringly soliciting our aid in the achieving of their Independence—in the rescuing of their Liberty from the iron grasp of Priestcraft and Despotism—and in return for our aid in the glorious cause, they offer to give us all in their power to bestow, *or that would be demanded by a Texian, to wit: their lands, their silver and their gold.* The people of Texas are too philanthropic to refuse granting the prayer of the unfortunate. . . . The Texian youth will surely take "the tide at its flood" and triumphantly ride to glory, honor, and fortune.

All those who might be interested in wresting from the "worst of slavery" that unhappy people now "inhabiting the most fertile portion of the Western Continent," were requested to rendezvous at either San Patricio or Live Oak Point by June 20 to join with the Federal army, consisting, at this time, of about six hundred Texan volunteers and fifteen hundred Mexicans, he said.[105] It was reported that the "provisional government" *intended* offering a bounty of half a league of land and it was said that the spoils were to belong exclusively to the Americans.[106] The Texans who had been in northern Mexico described the country about Monterey in glowing terms—"snow on the mountains—clustering and luscious fruits in the valleys—abundance spreading around, and a people, to judge by specimens and descriptions, far superior than accounts from other parts of Mexico have led us to suppose. Can better prospects with less amount of risk be pointed out?" they asked. "No portion of the world presents a fairer field for enterprise, enthusiasm, enjoyment, eventual wealth and happiness."[107]

Not only did civil officers in the frontier counties often join the Federalists, but desertions from the Texan military post at San Antonio de Béxar became so great during the ensuing weeks that the utmost vigilance had to be used to apprehend the deserters, and even then very few were ever caught. "It is highly probable," wrote George W.

[105] John McDaniel "To the Young and the Brave," Matagorda, June 5, 1840, in *Colorado Gazette and Advertiser*, June 6, 1840.
[106] R. B. T. to the Editor of the *Colorado Gazette*, Victoria, April 8, 1840, in *ibid.*, April 18, 1840.
[107] *Ibid.*

Hockley, Acting Adjutant and Inspector General, "that the greater part of the men are endeavoring to join the federal army." [108] So bad had the situation become, even before the appearance of Cárdenas at Victoria, that President Lamar found it necessary to issue a proclamation warning of the penalty for desertion, and assuring a pardon to all deserters who would voluntarily return to duty; but, he declared, "the recreant who shall hereafter abandon the standard which he has pledged to maintain may read his destiny in the stern arbitrament of the law." [109] It would, however, have taken more than proclamations to stop the desertions.

"Gen[era]ls Canales & Carbajal have been and still are," wrote George W. Hockley, twice Secretary of War under Houston, "a curse to our country. They are the primary cause of our late mutinies at Béxar (now fortunately quelled) and their agents [are] doubtless still at work. They should have been allowed time to recruit their horses, and leave the Republic. They are Mexicans and they are enemies. Time will show that I am right. The fact is now being developed." [110]

Many other men, not in the Texan service, joined the Federalists for the want of something else to do. Texas currency was circulating at sixteen cents on the dollar, and times were "extremely hard," although probably not as bad as in the United States. "All business is much depressed," wrote Ashbel Smith, "unless an exception be made to Law," there being twelve hundred cases on the docket of Harris County alone.[111] In reference to a projected business deal, James

[108] Geo[rge] W. Hockley, Act. Adjt. & Inspector General, to Capt. A. Clendenin [Commanding Post San Antonio], July 30, 1840, Army Papers (Texas), ms., copy.

[109] Mirabeau B. Lamar's "Address to the Soldiers of the Army, March 14, 1840, Executive Department, Austin, March 14, 1840," in Record of Executive Documents, from the 10th December 1838 to the 14th December 1841, ms.; *Lamar Papers*, III, 352–353; also published as a broadside, Mirabeau B. Lamar, [Address to the army on the subject of desertion], together with General Order No. 6, Adjutant and Inspector General's Office, Austin, March 14, 1840.

[110] Geo[rge] W. Hockley to Ashbel Smith, Austin, June 1, 1840, in Ashbel Smith Papers, ms. In regard to the desertions at Béxar, Hockley reported that two deserters had been shot,
. . . which I think will have a salutary effect—the five ring leaders of the late mutiny, who had been confined in the Calaboose at Béxar and escaped, have returned and surrendered themselves all save one who was drowned in crossing the river—he "packed" the lead &c—and could not swim—they were evidently assisted in their escape—but prudence and duty enjoin silence upon this subject. I give you that which has become public.

[111] Ashbel Smith to Col. Barnard E. Bee, May 22, 1840; Same to Ralph Hubbard

Morgan wrote his friend Samuel Swartwout, "I will go ahead in this matter & do all that I can do and if times were not so d——nable here you should not want. I cannot sell a foot of land—no money in the County. We'r perfectly drained & times awfully hard indeed in the money way—property valued two yrs. ago . . . at $55,000 in the town of Houston sold lately under the hammer at Sheriffs sale for $800!!" [112]

On May 2 Canales, after promising to reward Lamar for the kindness shown him and his troops,[113] left Austin in company with Carbajal, López, González, and Molano, for Houston and Galveston to procure clothing, provisions, and supplies for another expedition. En route, Canales and his suite stopped for one day at Bastrop upon the invitation of Colonel Jacob Eberly and other citizens to make known his views. In the evening a ball was given in his honor. Canales addressed the company in a short and eloquent speech, delivered in Spanish, which was then translated by Colonel Carbajal, who spoke English fluently, "being free from any offensive idiom or provincialism in accent or expression." [114] The Federalist commander expressed appreciation for the sympathy and attention that had been shown him by the citizens of Texas, and gave a brief outline of his military operations and future intentions. He denied that his party had committed any aggression upon the territory claimed by Texas. He said,

We are not anxious about boundaries but are willing to allow Texas any line she may choose; we are fighting for liberty, both civil and religious, the principles of which are the same everywhere; we are now following in the footsteps of Texas, and wish to establish a government of our own in-

---

[Houston, April 1840]; Same to James Hamilton, Houston, July 26, 1840, in *ibid.*

[112] James Morgan to Samuel Swartwout, July 6, 1840, in James Morgan Papers, ms., quoted in Stanley Siegel, *A Political History of the Texas Republic, 1836–1845,* p. 145.

[113] Lic. Canales to M. B. Lamar, Austin, Texas, April 29, 1840, in *Lamar Papers,* III, 386; V, 424.

[114] W. F. O. to W. D. Wallach, Bastrop, May 5, 1840, in *Colorado Gazette and Advertiser,* May 23, 1840. José María J. Carbajal, brother-in-law of Luciano Navarro and cousin of José Antonio Navarro, attended school in Lexington, Kentucky. He married Manuela Canales, daughter of Colonel Antonio Canales. Huson, "Refugio," chap. XXIII, 3; Huson, "Iron Men: A History of the Republic of the Río Grande and the Federalist War in Northern Mexico," pp. 42–44; Harbert Davenport, "General José María Carabajal," in *Southwestern Historical Quarterly,* LV (1951–1952), 475–483. Davenport mistakenly adds an extra "a" in the spelling of "Carbajal."

304

dependent of Mexico, and modelled after your own. To you we offer the hand of friendship, and whether accepted or not feel ourselves under a weight of obligation for your ready sympathy and individual assistance already rendered to us. And our course, although obscured by the clouds of misfortune at the present moment, never was more prosperous, and we feel that we *must* and *shall* succeed.[115]

Following the speech, dancing commenced in which the General and his staff joined in great good humor. Although the Anglo-American reels and cotillions were new to them, the native grace of their country carried them through with much éclat. After the company departed, a guitar was handed to Canales, who took it and accompanied his companions in singing some of their beautiful songs.

The romance of the scene, [wrote a witness from Bastrop] you can readily imagine, and I could not help contrasting it with the dire conflict from which they had so recently escaped. For the moment they were again at home, carroling their national airs with all the buoyancy of a gay spirit, forgetting that they were exiles from home and among a people so recently their enemy. Canales and his compatriots are all educated men, very intelligent, and gentlemanly in manners, and must make a favorable impression wherever they go.[116]

At Galveston the Federalists received considerable aid, "purchasing whatever they could obtain upon credit, whether it was useful to their purpose or not." Their purchases were not confined "to munitions of war and military supplies, but [they] bought women's dresses, parasols and every other thing they could get." A steamboat, the *Constitution*, was procured to take the goods and supplies to San Patricio, on the Nueces. John P. Kelsey, a native of New York, had arrived in Galveston in December 1839, and had set himself up as a merchant and speculator. In company with Paul Bremond, a successful general merchant of Houston, he took a stock of arms, munitions, and other supplies to Corpus Christi for sale and delivery to Canales; and when Canales marched to the Río Grande, Kelsey and Bremond accompanied the expedition. Some of the Texan traders and their Federalist cohorts saw in the revolutionary disturbances in the north, declared the historian John Henry Brown, "a clever subtifuge to cross into Mexico a

[115] Quoted in W. F. O. to W. D. Wallach, Bastrop, May 5, 1840, in *Colorado Gazette and Advertiser*, May 23, 1840.
[116] *Ibid.*

lot of merchandise and munitions free of duty."[117] The Mexican press reported considerable smuggling being carried on through Reinosa, then under the control of the Centralist authorities. "The civil authorities," it was reported by *El Ancla*, "happen to be the most deeply engaged in this illicit trade. The Texans are permitted to bring in goods without paying duty, and they afterwards openly sell, chiefly on account of the government officers."[118] It was believed that the traitor Canales still held a secret influence over the people of that section of the country, who would not swear against smugglers when apprehended.

From the southwestern frontier it was reported that things were beginning to boom in the vicinity of Copano Bay, and many respectable persons visited in that section of the country "desirous of getting a foot holt there." "The encouragement the Govmt. of Texas had extended to the Federalist[s] has given a new impulse to every thing here," wrote Plummer to Lamar from Victoria.[119] "The Federalist[s]," he said, "will be able to raise enough men, not only to whip the Centralist]s[but the whole Country across the Río Grande if they desire it. . . . The Feds that I have seen are so well pleased with you, I would not be surprised you were invited over there to take a term as President after your term of service here. The administration now is as popular as it can be."

The *Constitution*, bearing Canales, sailed from Galveston on May 30,[120] for Linn's Landing, without the Federalist leader having had a further interview with Lamar as he had desired; but he wrote that he would return shortly, and begged that, in the meantime, his cause be not forgotten. Other vessels in the Federal service were two schooners, the *Cornelia* and the *Abispa* (*Wasp*) and the steamship *Pontchartrain*, still too disabled for further use.[121] The *Constitution* on its return to Galveston without cargo was wrecked on the beach within fifteen miles of Pass Caballo and lost. The *Cornelia* and *Abispa* were used in con-

[117] John Henry Brown, *Indian Wars and Pioneers of Texas*, pp. 759–760.
[118] Reported in *Telegraph and Texas Register*, July 29, 1840.
[119] Samuel A. Plummer to M. B. Lamar, Victoria, May 17, 1840 (Private), in *Lamar Papers*, III, 392.
[120] "Information derived from Anson G. Neal, Laredo, May 30, 1847," in *ibid.*, VI, 105; Antonio Canales to Gen. Mirabeau Lamar, Galveston, May 30, 1840, and [Antonio] Canales to Mirabeau Lamar, Galveston, May 31, 1840, in *ibid.*, V, 427; III, 397; *Brazos Courier*, June 9 and 30, 1840.
[121] [Antonio] Canales to Gen. Mariano Arista, Camp Los Olmitos, on the left bank of the Río Bravo, Nov. 2, 1840, in *Telegraph and Texas Register*, Sept. 14, 1842.

I. SAM HOUSTON.   Courtesy Barker Texas History Center, The University of Texas.

2. MIRABEAU B. LAMAR.   Courtesy Barker Texas History Center,
The University of Texas.

3. DAVID G. BURNET.   Courtesy Barker Texas History Center, The University of Texas.

4. ALBERT SIDNEY JOHNSTON.   Courtesy Barker Texas History
Center, The University of Texas.

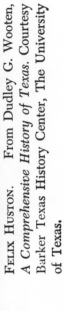

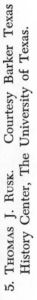

Felix Huston. From Dudley G. Wooten, *A Comprehensive History of Texas.* Courtesy Barker Texas History Center, The University of Texas.

5. Thomas J. Rusk. Courtesy Barker Texas History Center, The University of Texas.

6. THE CAPITOL AT HOUSTON.   Courtesy Barker Texas History Center, The University of Texas.

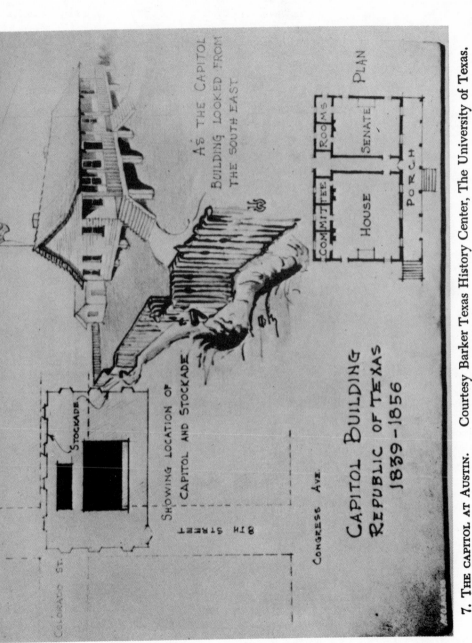

COLORADO ST.

STOCKADE

8TH STREET

SHOWING LOCATION OF
CAPITOL AND STOCKADE

CONGRESS AVE.

AS THE CAPITOL
BUILDING LOOKED FROM
THE SOUTH EAST

COMMITTEE ROOMS

HOUSE | SENATE

PORCH

PLAN

CAPITOL BUILDING
REPUBLIC OF TEXAS
1839-1856

7. THE CAPITOL AT AUSTIN.   Courtesy Barker Texas History Center, The University of Texas.

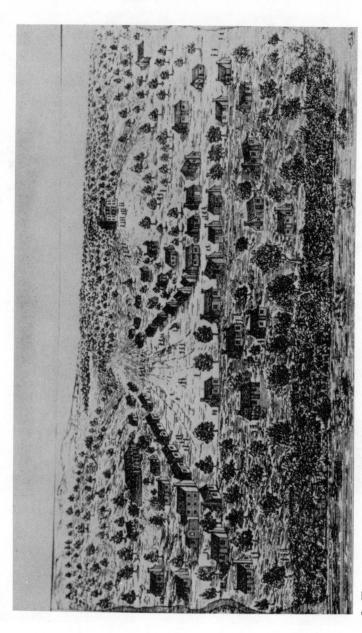

8. The city of Austin in 1840.   Courtesy Barker Texas History Center, The University of Texas.

9. ANASTASIO BUSTAMANTE.   Courtesy the Latin-
American Collection, The University of Texas
Library.

10. MARIANO ARISTA. From Manuel Rivera Cambas, *Los gobernantes de México*. Courtesy the Latin-American Collection, The University of Texas Library.

11. Nicolás Bravo.   From Manuel Rivera Cambas, *Los gobernantes de México*. Courtesy the Latin-American Collection, The University of Texas Library.

12. Vicente Filisola.   From C. L. Prudhomme (ed.), *Album méjicano*. Courtesy the Latin-American Collection, The University of Texas Library.

Grãl de Div CANALIZO

13. VALENTÍN CANALIZO. From C. L. Prudhomme (ed.), *Album méjicano*. Courtesy the Latin-American Collection, The University of Texas Library

14. View of Matamoros.   From Thorpe Thomas Bangs, *Our Army on the Rio Grande*. Courtesy Barker Texas History Center, The University of Texas.

15. VIEW OF MARÍN.   From Samuel C. Reid, *The Scouting Expeditions of McCulloch's Texas Rangers*. Courtesy Barker Texas History Center, The University of Texas.

16. MONTEREY FROM THE BISHOP'S PALACE. From Samuel E. Chamberlain, *My Confession*. Courtesy Harper and Brothers.

centrating men and supplies on the lower Nueces and were scheduled to aid in the proposed attack on Matamoros. However, when Canales marched to the Río Grande, the *Pontchartrain* remained at Matagorda and the *Cornelia*, mounting one of the twelve-pound cannons taken from her, lay at Corpus Christi undergoing repairs from an accident.[122]

Canales was again in Galveston on June 16, where he no doubt saw Lamar [123] and received a communication from Lipscomb, the Texan Secretary of State, pertaining to two deserters from the Texan navy who had joined the Federalist forces. Canales denied any intention whatsoever of permitting those under his orders to conceal deserters from the Texan service, and declared that the company alluded to by Lipscomb as harboring the deserters was not enlisted in the Federal service. He said that he had been informed "that Cap[tain] Stone, who commands the citizens alluded to, will with pleasure accompany Lieut. Williamson or any other officer in examining all the men that accompany him, and should such deserters be recognized among them, far from admitting or concealing them he will do everything in his power to have them apprehended." [124]

After a brief stay at Galveston, Canales again returned to his troops on the Texas frontier, and by proclamation transferred his headquarters to San Patricio. He called for more volunteers, and it was rumored that General Albert Sidney Johnston, who had resigned as Secretary of War in February 1840, had been offered the command of the Federal army.[125] In spite of Lamar's proclamation, a number of adventuresome young men rallied to the Federalist cause. "Many young men are leaving Houston and Galveston for the Federal army," reported the *Brazos Courier*. "They had better stay at home." It is "Humbug—To call the Federalists patriots; and maintain that they are fighting in a

---

122 Two 12-pound cannon still remained mounted on the *Pontchartrain*.

123 Lamar was in Galveston from May 31 to July 27, 1840.

124 Lic. Antonio Canales to Abner S. Lipscomb, Secretary of State of the Republic of Texas [dated:] Galveston City, June 17, 1840, Domestic Correspondence (Texas), 1836–1846, ms.

125 Geo[rge] W. Hockley to Ashbel Smith, Austin, June 1, 1840, in Ashbel Smith Papers, ms. "General Johnston will not go to the States so long as a probability exists of invasion," wrote James Love from Galveston in April 1840. "We intend him for our Capt[ain]." James Love to Gen. M. B. Lamar, Galveston, April 14, 1840, in *Lamar Papers*, III, 371–372. Love's statement no doubt had reference to a company of men to be raised at Galveston for protection of the frontier. This company had been enrolled by April 25 as already noted.

holy cause." [126] By the time Canales reached San Patricio, the army contained 520 recruits—300 Mexican rancheros, 80 Carrizo Indians from Mexico, a few runaway slaves from Texas, and 140 Anglo-Texans. The army lacked provisions, munitions, horses, and even adequate clothing. Once more Canales wrote President Lamar not to forget the Federalist cause, reminding him that *now* is the time for success to crown their combined efforts for the liberty of Texas and the Federalists. [127] Carbajal, at Galveston, was instructed to inform Lamar verbally that Canales would be ready to begin his campaign by August 15. In the Federalist camp there were already one hundred kegs of powder, and Carbajal informed Lamar of his intention of taking one hundred more men, two hundred kegs of powder, and additional small arms to the Nueces before that date. He only needed, he said, some artillery with round shot. The Texan officer in charge of the artillery piece at Texana, he complained, refused to deliver it up. "We have shells 7½ inch and shott for that size Howitzer," he declared, "but no piece." In conclusion, Carbajal reported that General Anaya had written from Yucatán that he was coming with one thousand infantry, and he expressed Canales' desire that McLeod and Karnes would join him on the Nueces. [128]

About the 10th of July several companies of volunteers sailed from Galveston to Aransas to join the Federal forces on the Nueces. Later

[126] *Brazos Courier*, June 9, 1840; see Silvanus Hatch to M. B. Lamar, Jackson County, April 2, 1840, in Domestic Correspondence (Texas), 1836–1846, ms., and Same to Same, Jackson County [Texas], May 5, 1840, in *Lamar Papers*, V, 426, concerning "Nancy," belonging to Silvanus Hatch, and another runaway slave that was sought. The figures given here on the size of the Federalist force are estimates made by Anson G. Neal, a member of Jordan's Company. *Lamar Papers*, VI, 105. Lamar's private secretary reported on June 21 that the Federalists near San Patricio had about 200 Americans and 600 Mexicans under arms. [Henry J.] Jewett to M. B. Lamar, Austin, June 21, 1840, in *ibid.*, III, 413–414. A report from the West on July 6 said that Canales' force at San Patricio amounted to about 1,000 Mexicans and 250 Americans. Many Americans, not then with the Federal troops, were said to be prepared to join their standard whenever the campaign should open. *Telegraph and Texas Register*, July 29, 1840. D. W. Smith to John Forsyth, Matamoros, June 30, 1840, no. 168, in Consular Dispatches (Matamoros), ms., microfilm.

[127] Lic. Canales to Mirabeau B. Lamar, San Patricio, Texas, July 21, 1840, in Lamar Papers, ms.

[128] José M. J. Carbajal to [M. B.] Lamar, July 27, 1840, Galveston, Texas, in *ibid.*, ms.

in the month Canales and other Mexican officers of the Federal army embarked at Galveston on the schooner *Cornelia* for Live Oak Point.[129] The steamer *Zavala*, bearing dispatches from Colonel Canales to General Anaya in Yucatán, left Galveston on July 22 for Sisal,[130] and was soon followed by the *Austin* and the *San Bernard*.

Colonel James Power reported on July 31 that at Lipantitlán there were about 230 foreigners (Anglo-Texans and Americans) with some Mexicans under Canales.[131] The editor of the *Ancla* at Matamoros declared, probably as of late August, that the forces under Canales and Molano consisted of 700 men, of which 500 were foreigners and the rest Indians and Mexicans.[132]

Meanwhile roving bands, represented as Federals by the newspapers loyal to the Centralist authority, but just as likely highwaymen obligated only to self, were described as plundering the frontier settlements and driving off horses to Texas. It was reported in May that Romualdo Martínez, with Manuel Flores and others from the scattered Federals, had robbed Pantaleon Treviño at the Capazon Rancho of horses which were allegedly to be taken to Texas.[133] Also in May Eusebio Guajardo (*alias* Novedad) with four armed men from the dispersed Federalists entered Reinosa and had gone thence to the Mesa with the intent to plunder, and, perhaps because they were Federalists, had not been reported even a few weeks later, either by the subprefect, the alcalde, the priest, or the clerk of Reinosa.[134] Several hundred Centralist cavalry in mid-July were ranging east of the Río Grande between Laredo and Camargo, endeavoring to prevent the Federalists from driving cattle and horses from the vicinity of the Río Grande settlements for the use of their army on the Nueces, and to intercept Mexican traders from the Río Grande.[135]

A writer, under the name of "El Gato" ("The Cat") in *El Tigre* spoke of the accursed tactics pursued by the "gangs of thugs" under Canales and other Federal leaders who, secreting themselves in the woods, refused to come out in the open and fight, thus proving that they were the "guerrilla geniuses" born to change the present system

[129] *Colorado Gazette and Advertiser*, Aug. 1, 1840.
[130] Jim Dan Hill, *The Texas Navy: in Forgotten Battles and Shirtsleeve Diplomacy*, pp. 126–128.
[131] *Telegraph and Texas Register*, Aug. 26, 1840.
[132] *El Ancla*, Sept. 28, 1840.   [133] *Ibid.*, May 8, 1840.   [134] *Ibid.*
[135] José M. J. Carbajal to M. B. Lamar, Galveston, July 27, 1840, in *Lamar Papers*, III, 424–425.

and to assure the future happiness of the country. Their ritual, he said, forbids them wearing trousers with their shirts, and they carry no provisions for they have made as their patrimony the property of the towns wherever they go. "In each house they find a free storehouse. They replace horses at discretion and consume cattle from the *hacienda* of Uñate. In short, they take all as a measure of their desires, without taking the trouble of buying it or of carrying it [off]. Thus it is that they move with the greatest speed and place themselves beyond danger," and pass for brave men among *"exaggerated patriots."* [136]

"Can it be," asked the editor of the *Ancla*, "that men would be so obsessed or so stupid as to serve in any army under the orders of Canales and Cárdenas to divide our republic, to accept orders from those who vilified them, who have humiliated them to the last extreme, delivering their own possessions, their own wives, their own sons into the hands of a foreign enemy." [137]

Apparently, however, the marauding bands made no distinction between Centralist and Federalist ownership of property and were even completely indifferent as to whether it was Mexican or Texan. Furthermore, little seems to have been done during the last few months towards breaking them up. Wrote Judge John Hemphill of the Fourth Judicial District to his fellow judges of Texas,

Since the dispersion of the Federal Army, marauding parties have dispersed themselves throughout the country between the Guadalupe and the Río Grande, and robberies and other outrages have been committed to a considerable extent on the Río Grande. About the time of the expiration of the courts in my district, large droves of cattle arrived from the Río Grande, . . . which had been stolen from ranches on this side of the Río Grande. Murder of the Rancheros were also charged on some of these plundering bands. From circumstances which will at once suggest themselves to your reflection, I find great difficulty in suppressing these most pernicious evils in some sections of the Western country. To accomplish this object I rely greatly on the co-operation of my brother judges of the interior. If they will arrest and have prosecuted the purchasers or the original robbers who drive the cattle into the interior counties, those enormous violations of law and the rights of property and life must cease. I understand that a large drove or droves of cattle will reach Houston in some short time from the West. I have no doubt these are stolen cattle, and I have as little doubt that after the droves arrive in Houston, the evidence of the larceny or that they were

[136] Quoted from *El Ancla,* March 13, 1840.
[137] Sept. 14, 1840.

310

driven from the other side of the Guadaloupe in violation of law—and that the purchasers knew of their being stolen at the time they were bought can be obtained from the drivers themselves. There would doubtless be abundant evidence at Victoria, but that could not be obtained without difficulty. To suggest this matter to you is sufficient I know to insure your efficient co-operation. Many of the cattle that were driven in belonged to the President and other gentlemen high in office in the new Republic of Río Grande, and were brought through New La Bahía before the facts [were fully ascertained] and at the defiance as it were of these gentlemen.[138]

While the Federalists were completing their preparations for renewing the campaign in northern Mexico, General José Urrea, a state prisoner in the old Inquisition Prison, was freed between 1 and 2 A.M., July 15, 1840, by friends led by Gómez Pedraza, who surprised the guard, and joining with others took the National Palace without the firing of a shot. At daylight President Bustamante was arrested in his quarters.[139] The government and its friends displayed greater energy and activity than the insurgents had expected, and within a few days freed Bustamante. Santa Anna, in the meantime, having collected a large number of troops, headed for the capital to aid in suppressing the revolt; and Bustamante, fearing that Santa Anna would not only gain credit for restoring order but would use it to extend his influence, accepted a capitulation of the Federalist leaders in the capital, assuring the revolutionists the undisturbed enjoyment of their property and their positions under the government, and granting them a pardon for their past offenses. Thus, by late July the Federalist revolt at the center ended, and Canales and his cohorts on the lower Nueces were without a strong diversion so necessary if their forthcoming military maneuvers were to stand much chance of succeeding.

With Plummer's report in hand and fully aware that something needed to be done to protect the southwestern frontier, Lamar hesitated to take any action which might jeopardize his efforts to settle the issues between Mexico and Texas by negotiation. Before the end of May he left the capital for Houston and Galveston, spending nearly

138 John Hemphill to A. B. Shelby, Judge 1st Judicial District, Washington, Texas, May 30, 1840, in *Telegraph and Texas Register*, July 8, 1840. John Hemphill was elected judge of the Fourth Judicial District, January 20, 1840, and automatically, thereby, became an Associate Justice of the Supreme Court. March 19, 1840, he was in the Council House Fight with the Comanches.

139 John Black to John Forsyth, Consulate of the U. S. A., Mexico, Aug. 22, 1840, vol. 8, no. 307, Justin H. Smith, "Transcripts," IV, ms.

two months at the island, "where he attracted very little attention indeed for a President." [140] During the months of May, June, and July the pressure on the administration for direct participation in the Federalist cause increased. The country was kept in a state of continual excitement by rumors that great preparations were being made in Mexico to drive the Federalists off the Nueces and to invade Texas. Rumors were received late in May that the Mexican commander at Matamoros was endeavoring to promote a large-scale Indian attack upon the frontier settlements.

At Houston on May 28 Lamar spoke at a public dinner given in his honor. The speech was in defense of his administration and was also aimed at bolstering the secret negotiations going on in Mexico. In referring to the negotiations being carried on by Treat in Mexico, he said,

. . . we shall expect a definite answer in a reasonable time, and when that shall be rendered, we shall do and do promptly what remains to be done. If the response shall be war! our gallant Navy will take up the war cry with alacrity, and send its loudest reverberations throughout the shores of Mexico. And our armies will march to the aid of a neighboring people who are striving after our example to cast off the yoke of oppression.[141]

It was at this time that the rumor was going around that Albert Sidney Johnston, then on a visit to the United States, would probably command the Federal army.[142]

In view of the rumored Mexican-Indian assault to be launched against the frontier and while the steadying hand of Lamar was away from the seat of government, his "quite unpopular" Secretary of War Doctor Branch T. Archer,[143] after consultation with the cabinet and Vice President Burnet, on June 6 ordered out the militia of fourteen counties west and south of the Trinity, the Gulf counties excepted, to meet the anticipated danger.[144] Archer declared that General Arista

140 Ashbel Smith to Col. B. E. Bee, [Galveston? Aug.–Sept. 1840], in Ashbel Smith Papers, ms. Lamar was at Houston by May 28, where he spoke at a dinner in his honor, and at Galveston from May 31–July 27, 1840.

141 "Lamar's Speech in Defense of His Administration, Houston, May 28, 1840," in *Lamar Papers*, III, 393–397.

142 George W. Hockley to Ashbel Smith, Austin, June 1, 1840, in Ashbel Smith Papers, ms.

143 Ashbel Smith to Col. B. E. Bee, [Galveston? Aug.–Sept. 1840], in *ibid.*

144 Texas War Department, [Proclamation beginning:] War Department, City

was believed to be approaching San Patricio with a considerable force, and that the Cherokees, Comanches, and other Indians were concentrating a large number of their braves on the upper Brazos "with a view doubtless of attacking our towns and settlements."

Most of the members of the cabinet warmly supported the idea of calling out the First and Second Brigades of the Militia. No sooner was Albert Sidney Johnston, Archer's predecessor in the War Office, apprised of the order calling out the militia *en masse* from the districts comprising the first two brigades, than he hurried back to Texas, where from Galveston on August 6 he informed Lamar that at the suggestion of a mutual friend (probably James Love) he had been told that "his services in a military capacity would probably be required." Consequently, he had returned immediately to Texas, and if Lamar contemplated a movement against Mexico, he would be much gratified to contribute to its success.[145] General Felix Huston, major general of the Texas Militia, was at Bastrop on June 21 "ready to obey any orders." It was not long after the order had been issued before the militia was beginning to turn out, and it was expected to do so in considerable number.

Reflecting persons of more mature judgment within the administration and among the opposition, however, believed that Archer's call upon the militia was premature and unwise, and that the information upon which the decision had been made was both meager and unreliable. "We all know," wrote Ashbel Smith, that Doctor Archer's "talents are not imminently practical."[146] Colonel Burleson, who com-

---

of Austin, June 6, 1840: Fellow Citizens: Information has been received by the Department of such a nature as to render necessary an appeal to arms." [Proclamation signed by B. T. Archer, Secretary of War, publishing:] General Order, No. 24. Adjutant and Insp'r Gen's Office, Austin, June 5th, 1840. The Brigadier Generals of the First and Second Brigades are required to immediately bring into the field, the full militia of the counties named below . . . By Order of the Sec'y of War. Geo. W. Hockley, Acting Adj't and Insp'r Gen'l, broadside. See also *Colorado Gazette and Advertiser*, Aug. 8, 1840; and Annual Report of B. T. Archer to the President of the Republic of Texas, War Department, City of Austin, Sept. 30, 1840, in Texas Congress, *Journals of the House of Representatives of the Republic of Texas, Fifth Congress, Appendix*, pp. 115–124.

[145] A. Sidney Johnston to M. B. Lamar, Galveston Bay, Aug. 6, 1840, in *Lamar Papers*, III, 427.

[146] Ashbel Smith to Col. B. E. Bee, [Galveston? Aug.–Sept. 1840], in Ashbel Smith Papers, ms. The *Texas Sentinel* defended the calling out of the militia. The editor declared: "the secretary of war and the cabinet would have been

manded the First Regiment of Infantry, resigned from his command. "It will require great prudence as well as energy to make the 'movement' result creditably to the Administration," wrote Lamar's private secretary. He suggested to Lamar, who was then in Galveston, that he give *"specific directions,* with a plan of operation," in case he did not return to Austin in season to direct measures in person. The heavy expense of maintaining the militia in the field made it imperative that the troops do "something more than marching out, and then marching home again."[147] "The 'corn campaign' of 1840, under Major General Felix Huston," declared President Houston a year and a half later after the collapse of the Mier expedition, "cost the government upward of a hundred thousand dollars, and resulted in nothing but the purchase and waste of property."[148]

While there were a number of ambitious young men who might relish a campaign against Mexico and see in the call of the militia a step toward getting the ball rolling while the Federalists were preparing to renew their campaign from the soil of Texas, more sensible persons, including the President, considered the call quite unnecessary and encompassing many dangers. "The fool orders calling out the militia came out yesterday," June 6, recorded Anson Jones in his *Diary.* "A crazy administration have nearly ruined the country. One year more the wretched work will be complete."[149]

After some delay Lamar made up his mind as to what to do about frontier defense. He issued orders on June 23 to raise a frontier regiment of volunteers, and a few days later took steps to halt the calling out of the militia. "On the most mature consideration," he wrote the Secretary of War on June 29, "I feel constrained to differ with you on the necessity or policy of calling out the Militia." Believing the late rumors of an impending invasion to be much like those thrown into

highly culpable to the nation, had no steps been taken to guard against an invasion, which is most certainly contemplated and which every circumstance seemed to indicate was then about to be made." *Texas Sentinel,* quoted in *Colorado Gazette and Advertiser,* Aug. 8, 1840.

[147] Henry J. Jewett to M. B. Lamar, Austin, June 21, 1840, in *Lamar Papers,* III, 412–414.

[148] Sam Houston to the House of Representatives, Executive Department, Washington, Jan. 14, 1843, in *Writings of Sam Houston,* III, 292–297.

[149] Anson Jones, Memorandum Book, No. 3, Sunday, June 7, 1840, ms. Jones vigorously opposed the confirmation of Archer's appointment as Secretary of War. Anson Jones to B. T. Archer, City of Austin, Dec. 9, 1840, in Anson Jones, *Memoranda and Official Correspondence Relating to the Republic of Texas, Its History*

circulation during the last six or eight months "fabricated by the Federalists or their friends for the purpose of drawing an army to the West, in hopes that when there it would be an easy matter to induce the men to cross the Río Grande and commence offensive operations against the Centralists," Lamar declared, "it is therefore my desire (unless you have some positive knowledge of the fact that the Country is invaded by a formidable force) that your call on the Militia be countermanded, and that such of the militia as have assembled, at your order, be discharged." [150] Even if the rumor should be in part true, the President felt that he had rather rely upon raising volunteers adequate to the threat, rather than calling out the militia *en masse*, "a measure which I never like to resort except in cases of the greatest emergency," he said.

I think however we have nothing to apprehend, from any immediate invasion, of a serious character. And if a portion of the enemy should make their appearance on this side of the Río Grande the number must necessarily be small in as much as they have no strong force collected now nor [are] likely to assemble one on the borders very soon. It is impossible for the central party to organize and march a large body of troops into the neighborhood of the Río Grande unresisted by the Federalists and without our being apprised of it in due time to make ample preparations to meet them, if they should attempt to cross the Río Grande.[151]

Lamar then proceeded to inform Archer that he had authorized Colonel Henry W. Karnes to raise a volunteer force "under certain conditions not calculated to embarrass the Government." "This force," he said, "when thrown into that section will I hope be sufficient for all the emergencies, which are likely to arise very shortly, and will supercede for the present the necessity of any further military operation in the West." It is "for the purpose of extending our jurisdiction to the Río Grande, chastizing the Indians in that section—repelling such marauding parties as may be committing these depredations, this side of the River; and affording to the West that protection to which it is entitled but has not hitherto enjoyed."

---

and Annexation: Including a Brief Autobiography of the Author, pp. 158–159.

[150] Mirabeau B. Lamar to Branch T. Archer, Galveston City, June 29, 1840, in Record of Executive Documents, from the 10th December 1838 to the 14th December 1841, ms.

[151] *Ibid.*

 CHAPTER FOURTEEN

Texan Participation
in the Federalist Wars: Final Phase

IN COMPANY WITH Captain Howard and Lieutenant Houghton, Colonel Henry Karnes arrived in Austin on June 13, conferred with the Secretary of War, and hurried on to Houston to confer with Lamar concerning increased Indian depredations in the vicinity of Béxar, partly brought on by Centralist agents operating among the Comanches. His conference with Lamar resulted in the order to raise a regiment of volunteers "to operate immediately upon the extreme western frontier, with the view of establishing permanently the national jurisdiction to the Río Bravo, and securing the territory of Texas from any further violation, by an enemy who are now stationed in considerable force within our borders, at Laredo." [1] Karnes was told that in the event regular troops were called into service to operate in the same area jointly with him, under an officer of equal grade as his, the command would devolve upon the colonel of the regular service until a brigadier general should be appointed to take charge of the combined force. The President hoped that an adequate number of volunteers could be raised without the necessity of having to use any of the regulars, "whose services will be wanted in another direction." [2]

The selection of Karnes for this most delicate task was a credit to Lamar's administrative ability. Not only would the choice instill confidence in the average westerner, but Karnes could be depended upon to support the policy of the government without becoming embroiled in Federalist machinations. Born in Tennessee on September 8, 1812, Henry Wax Karnes came to Texas from Arkansas in 1835 and joined the Texan revolutionary volunteers at Mission Concepcion and par-

[1] H. W. Karnes' Call for Volunteers, Houston, June 24, 1840, in *Telegraph and Texas Register* (Houston), July 1, 1840; *Brazos Courier* (Brazoria), June 30, 1840.
[2] Mirabeau B. Lamar to Col. [Henry W.] Karnes, Galveston, June 23, 1840, in Record of Executive Documents, from the 10th December 1838 to the 14th December, 1841, ms., p. 196.

316

ticipated in the siege of Béxar. In March of the next year he organized
a company of cavalry at Goliad and was elected its captain. He fought
in the battle of San Jacinto, and in 1836 was a member of the Texas
delegation sent to Matamoros to effect an exchange of prisoners. There
he was thrown in jail by the Mexicans, but soon effected his escape,
after which he lived at San Antonio where he became known as an
able frontier Indian fighter. On August 10, 1838, Karnes' company of
twenty-one men was attacked on the Arroyo Seco by a party of two
hundred Comanche warriors, and defeated them. None of Karnes' men
were injured. Karnes, however, received a slight wound from a rifle
bullet which grazed his temple.

In October 1838, he left Houston for New Orleans to make plans for
raising troops and supplies for a force needed for a campaign against
the Indians on the western frontier. In December of that year he was
authorized to raise eight companies of volunteers to carry out a campaign against the Comanches. The following year, hearing reports of
Comanches lurking about San Antonio, Karnes went out to look to the
safety of a *caballada* of horses that he had in the vicinity. Seeing
someone lying in the road, he rode up and asked who he was. Whereupon, an Indian wrapped in a blanket sprang to his feet and shot
Karnes with an arrow in the hip, severely wounding him.[3] He never
fully recovered from this wound; yet, in the summer of 1840, he agreed
to raise a force of sufficient strength to protect the territorial integrity
of the Republic.

Karnes was short of stature and weighed approximately 160 pounds.[4]
According to Brown, he was one of the "most unselfish and bravest
of men who fought for Texas at any time between 1821 and 1846."[5]
Mrs. Maverick knew him as "a short, thick-set man with bright red
hair." Although uneducated, "he was modest, generous and devoted
to his friends." [6] He was brave, untiring, and a terror to the Indians,
who spoke of him as "Captain Colorado" ("Red Captain") because of

---

[3] *Lamar Papers*, IV, pt. I, 232; Sam Houston Dixon and Louis Wiltz Kemp,
The Heroes of San Jacinto, pp. 307–308; *Telegraph and Texas Register*, Sept. 1
and Oct. 20, 1838; Anna Muckleroy, "The Indian Policy of the Republic of Texas,"
Southwestern Historical Quarterly, XXVI (1922–1923), p. 14.

[4] H. Yoakum, *History of Texas from Its First Settlement in 1685 to Its Annexation to the United States in 1846*, I, 373 n.

[5] John Henry Brown, *Indian Wars and Pioneers of Texas*, pp. 50–51.

[6] Rena Maverick Green (ed.), *Memoirs of Mrs. Mary A. Maverick: Arranged
by Mary A. Maverick and Her Son George Madison Maverick*, p. 41.

his red hair and referred to him as "muy wapo" ("very brave"). Once, while he was a prisoner of the Comanches, the squaws so admired his red hair that they felt it, and washed it (almost drowning him in the process) to see if the "dye" would come out, but when they found that the color was fast nothing would satisfy them but that they each should have a lock of his hair.[7]

The increasing boldness of the Comanches depredating along the western frontier, coupled with the Mexican threat to Texan sovereignty to the region between the Nueces and the Río Grande and the likelihood that the southwestern portion of the Republic might become a battleground between two rival foreign political factions, made it necessary for Texas to strengthen its defenses in that area. As for the Comanches, Major General Felix Huston received orders in June to take command of the regular troops at Nashville in preparation for an Indian campaign up the Brazos. There were regular troops stationed also at San Antonio, but their dependability was in serious question. This fact was, no doubt, one reason for the raising of the new military unit. In May 1840, a serious mutiny had developed among the troops at San Antonio. "The mutineers," reported the *Texas Sentinel* (Austin), "are mostly recruits from abroad. They have recently come among us, and cannot be supposed to have been imbued with a very deep sense of patriotism toward the country in whose service they have been enlisted"; but there was no apology for "this want of subordination to the laws, and none for their insolent attempt at dictation to the government in whose service they had engaged." [8]

But other reasons for raising the new force were afloat, and these were unofficially associated with the Federalist activities on the frontier and the fitting out of their last expedition from the soil claimed by Texas.[9] Nothing had been said about the Federalists occupying a position far deeper within the claimed boundary than the Centralists stationed at Laredo. Not only would the stationing of a Texan military force on or near the Río Grande give encouragement to the Federalists in Chihuahua, Coahuila, Tamaulipas, and adjoining states, but it would enable the people of northern Mexico to engage in trade with Texans, by compelling the Centralist armies to fall back to Monterey and Matamoros. Should this be done, the marauding parties that frequented the region between Laredo and San Antonio would soon be dispersed

[7] *Ibid.*
[8] *Texas Sentinel* (Austin), May 16 and 23, July 4, 1840.
[9] *Colorado Gazette and Advertiser* (Matagorda), Aug. 8, 1840.

by the Texas rangers. "The merchants of those states," declared the *Telegraph*, "would therefore be enabled to resort to the markets of Béxar, Aransas, and other western towns in perfect security, and procure foreign manufactures, which have been almost prohibited in those states by the high duties" imposed on their importation.

As the population in those states is three or four times greater than that of Texas, doubtless in a few months the receipts of the custom houses of the western ports would exceed those of all the others in the republic, and be more than sufficient to defray the expenses of the troops requisite to protect the trade. Thus, we should be carrying out the maxim of Napoleon, by causing the enemy to support our army,

declared the editor of the *Telegraph*. Should the trade be freed from the various restrictions now impeding its development, it would increase rapidly,

. . . and prove so lucrative that the current of emigration would soon set so strongly in that direction that the western frontier would, in one or two years, present a line of defense settlements, which would prove an impregnable rampart to Mexico. There would be another advantage derived from this measure. The presence of a considerable force of Texians in that section, would encourage the Federalists to take up arms, and hundreds of our young men who are now idle and useless in the country, would readily join their standard, and possibly enable this party to regain and maintain the ascendancy in those States. As our navy has complete command of the Gulf, should it at any time be deemed expedient, Matamoras could be captured, and a port of entry be established at Brazos Santiago.[10]

At Houston on June 24, Karnes issued a call for volunteers "well mounted and armed" and for four to six companies of infantry. The volunteers were to rendezvous within thirty days at San Antonio, where they would be mustered into service for six months and from whence they would commence their march to some point on the frontier. The horses, equipment, and arms furnished by the volunteers would be appraised in par money and "stand as a charge against the government in the event of their being lost in the public service," to be paid for whenever it could be done with convenience to the government.[11] Thus

[10] *Telegraph and Texas Register*, July 1, 1840.
[11] H. W. Karnes' Call for Volunteers, Houston, June 24, 1840, in *ibid.*, July 1, 1840.

reimbursement was quite uncertain, especially in view of the fact that Congress had not authorized the administration to raise such a force, and could scarcely be expected to vote an appropriation without being well satisfied of the necessity for raising the troops now called for. The volunteers, however, were to defray their own expenses to the point of rendezvous.[12]

Company officers were to be elected by the volunteers, but field officers were to be appointed by the President. Karnes announced that he would adhere at all times "most strictly to the orders of the government, [and] in order to secure the honorable accomplishment of the objects in view and that the expedition may result beneficially to the country and with glory to itself," he would "upon all times require and exact the most perfect subordination and obedience to orders." The importance of the establishment of this force was forcefully pointed out. "The west and south-west have long been involved in disorder, and prey to wanton and marauding parties," declared Karnes. "The Indians, Mexicans, and other lawless banditti, have broken up the trade established between this Republic and friendly states beyond the Río Grande, have plundered the population, murdered many of our people, and have prevented the settlement of that interesting section of the country, by destroying all security for property or life." Karnes had good reason to know how insecure was the life and property of a frontier trader, for he, in company with a young man recently from the United States, and several Mexican servants, while en route from Copano to San Antonio on July 20, 1838, had been attacked twenty miles from Goliad by a band of Mexican smugglers.[13] Karnes was wounded and taken prisoner, but soon effected his escape.

Karnes was apparently very successful in his recruiting efforts. By the middle of July it was reported five hundred men from Washington County would soon join him, and that another one or two hundred from Fayette and adjoining counties were prepared to turn out.[14] The planters in the west seemed to be quite enthusiastic about the fitting out of an expedition; and since many of them had secured their crops and were at leisure for the season, they looked forward to "the expedition as a pleasing and useful relaxation from the toils of agriculture." By engaging in it they would not only render valuable service to the

[12] *Colorado Gazette and Advertiser*, Aug. 8, 1840.

[13] Dixon and Kemp, *The Heroes of San Jacinto*, 308.

[14] *Morning Star* (Houston) quoted in *Telegraph and Texas Register*, July 15, 1840, and in the *Colorado Gazette and Advertiser*, Aug. 1, 1840.

Republic "with but little sacrifice or hazard on their part," but would "also be furnished with an excellent opportunity of exploring a section of Texas, that . . . [had] hitherto been but little known," and would become more fully acquainted with the character and disposition of the citizens of the adjoining states of Mexico.[15]

In order to forestall the crisis likely to develop in friendly capitals because of this sudden outburst of military activity on the part of the Texan government, Secretary of State Lipscomb, in July, finding "so many rumors . . . afloat, and so many imprudent and erroneous newspaper publications, of invasions from the Mexicans, and of Texian armaments for offensive operations," thought it advisable to state the present position of his government in respect to the Mexican Federalists in a letter to the special agents of Texas abroad.

We have been in . . . receipt almost every week, for the last six or seven months, of rumors of an invasion from Mexico, headed by Arista, and the rumors have come to us with all the appearances of being authentic, when at the same time, we have been fully advised of the total inability of the Mexican Government to cross the Río Grande, in any force that could give us any trouble. These rumors have been generally traced to the Federalists and their friends, fabricated with the evident object in view of drawing an army to the west, knowing that from the restless disposition of our people, and their innate love of enterprise, they could not be restrained from crossing the western boundary in great numbers, and joining them against the Centralists. The President had baffled all these attempts to be drawn into offensive measures, and succeeded in preventing any excitement or calls upon our people for a force to repel such threatened invasion. But a short time after he left the Seat of Government for this place [Galveston], a similar rumor reached there—that of an invasion, with an extensive coalition of savages, in conjunction with the Mexicans. This rumor seemed to have had so much the appearance of authenticity, that it effected a call from the War Department of a levy, *en masse*, of our militia west of the Trinity, with the exception of the Gulf counties. This was a source of much uneasiness to the President, as he believed the rumor was another phantom from the same fruitful source, that had already proved as prolific as *Bancos*. He counteracted its efforts as far as practicable, and the militia have been disbanded before much inconvenience or expense had been incurred. We are now satisfied that this conjecture was correct.

The Federalist leaders, declared Lipscomb, are "unremitting in their

15 *Ibid.*

321

efforts to induce our Government to aid them. To effect this, they are ready to grant whatever we would ask; we have rejected all their overtures." [16]

Karnes returned to San Antonio near the time of the scheduled rendezvous of his troops, but was soon stricken with typhoid fever, which he had evidently contracted while at Houston. During his illness soldiers from nearby Camp Cooke cut the corn from his *labor*.[17] In the meantime, other volunteer companies were being formed, and Canales' agents, also engaged in recruiting activities in Texas for the Federalist army down on the Nueces, seemed anxious to effect some sort of understanding and working arrangement, if not an alliance, with Karnes' regiment being organized at San Antonio. Although Canales was aware of the policy of the Texas government with respect to a foreign flag within the claimed boundaries of the Republic and of Karnes' determination to adhere to that policy, he hoped to win Karnes to his side and to his use. Karnes, however, was not another Ross. He was more loyal to his superiors and the trust they placed in him. Although uneducated, he was modest, generous, brave, fearless, and determined to defend the boundary of Texas against all parties. Canales, however, was determined to make one last effort to win Karnes' support. About the middle of July, he wrote Colonel Seguin at San Antonio a friendly letter announcing his return to the Federalist headquarters on the Nueces, and in it requested Seguin to effect a reconciliation between himself and Karnes.[18] A few days after Seguin showed the letter to Karnes, the latter wrote Canales, saying Colonel Seguin had shown him

your esteemed letter . . . soliciting a change of sentiments between us; I embrace the opportunity with pleasure, inasmuch as it evolves the means of securing the good issue of our wishes or separate efforts. . . . The volunteers under my command will be here in a few days from this date, and at their arrival I shall make all the necessary preparations for a rapid march

[16] Abner S. Lipscomb to James Hamilton and A. T. Burnley, Galveston City, July 7, 1840, in Texas Congress, *Journals of the House of Representatives of the Republic of Texas, Fifth Congress, Appendix*, pp. 281–284.

[17] R. S. Neighbors, Quarter Master, T. A., to Capt. [A.] Clendenin, Comdg. Camp Cooke [dated:] Quarter Master Office, San Antonio, Aug. 4, 1840, in Army Papers (Texas), ms. A *labor* was 177 acres of land given by the Spanish government to the head of a family for farming purposes.

[18] H. W. Karnes to General Antonio Canales, Béxar, July 26, 1840, in *Telegraph and Texas Register*, Aug. 31, 1842.

to Laredo. I shall wait here only the general orders of the Government. Meantime the pretentions of the Federalists to the territory between the Nueces and the Río Grande have wounded the feelings of the President and have also excited the indignation of the people. The line of demarcation having been established by the first Congress of Texas, the President considers the preservation of the said boundary as one of his constitutional duties, and with the view of preserving the said law inviolate, he has ordered a large regular force thereto, under the command of Col. Cooke. Should this difficulty not be arranged before taking up the line of my march, I shall proceed to Laredo and thence along the Río Grande to its mouth, and plant the standard of Texas on its eastern bank. But should the boundary line be recognized as defined, then the Government of Texas will give you all the succor which may be in its power for the glorious cause you defend. Having been a defender of liberty from my youth up to this day, you may with certainty infer that all my sympathies are united in your favor, and if I am not found battling by your side, it is not because your cause is less pleasing to me, but because I prefer that of my own country. In a word, my friend, some guarantee must be given before an union is formed, or before we enter into any mutual combination.

Should you coincide with me in sentiments, and be willing to enter into stipulations with my Government, and should you think convenient to propose to the President to invest one with plenary powers to settle the matter, I would proceed to any place you may point out on the Río Grande, and I should be much pleased to act the part of a peacemaker in this important crisis. Our united efforts this time, in my humble opinion, will place your liberties upon a permanent basis, while disunion may lead it to dissolution and death.

In conclusion, Karnes stated that in a few days he would be in need of beef for the troops that were to assemble at San Antonio, and since many of the Mexican ranchers around Béxar were Centralists, he asked Canales if he could furnish him with 150 to 200 beeves. He was authorized to pay for them by drafts on the Treasury Department, "but should you not be able to furnish them, I shall be compelled," he wrote, "to take them from the citizens *by consent or by force."* He also requested of Canales eight or ten good horses for gathering cattle.[19]

Canales was indignant that Karnes should presume he had so little honor,[20] and hastily informed him that the Federalists had

[19] *Ibid.*
[20] Lic. [Antonio] Canales to Col. H. W. Karnes, Lipantitlán, Aug. 4, 1840, in *ibid.*, Aug. 31, 1842. Translation by George Fisher. It is most doubtful that

. . . not taken up arms to sell, or to cede, or to deliver up our territory to strange persons. Our object, [he allegedly wrote] was nothing less than to establish a frank, enlightened and phylanthropic Government, which would make for the happiness of our country. Such noble objects moved us to abandon our family and our interests, exposing our existence to establish these principles. And after so many s[a]crifices, so much hard labor, suffering and miseries of all kinds to which our destiny had reduced us, do you wish, sir, to propose us in recompence that we should commit treason to our country? Could you sir, have believed us to be capable of committing such villany? No doubt you have made a mistake, measuring all Mexicans with one and the same strockle [sic].

I shall never suffer that the flag of Texas should be displayed without the ancient limits of the old province of Texas. To effect it, it will be necessary to pass over our corpses and those of all other Mexicans; for upon this subject there exists no division among us. If you advance upon Laredo, you will have to fight with the detachment I have ordered thither to occupy it, with the express order not to permit you to enter it. I wish you, sir, to understand that if you do not desist from the object which carries you to Laredo, as you say, I shall have to call to my assistance the central troops. This is the only case in which I can yield of being a Federalist, because the national honor and the integrity of her territory is above all.[21]

Canales declared he had no horses or cattle for Karnes' men, "if it be for the object you solicit them." "Should any of your forces be willing to come subject to my orders, and for the pay when it can be had, they shall be well received, and shall be furnished with horses and provisions; on the contrary, they will be the first enemy with whom I shall be compelled to fight."

Nowhere in his letter does Canales mention the Republic of the Río

---

Canales ever sent such a letter, and it is even more certain that had its contents been known among the Americans in his command, they would have withdrawn, if they did not force him beyond the Río Grande. The Catholic priest at San Antonio refused to permit the tolling of the bells of San Fernando church at the funeral of Colonel Henry W. Karnes. "Resolutions adopted at a Public Meeting, San Antonio, August 17, 1840, in Memory of Henry W. Karnes," in *Texas Sentinel*, Aug. 29, 1840. We are not asking for benefit of scriptures, say the resolutions, but for the tolling of the bell, "which in a frontier village, has ever been used indiscriminately for evil and spiritual purposes" and should be tolled on an occasion of a "national grief."

[21] Lic. [Antonio] Canales to Col. H. W. Karnes, Lipantitlán, Aug. 4, 1840, in *Telegraph and Texas Register*, Aug. 31, 1842.

Grande or "the government of the northern frontier of the Mexican republic," or in any way imply that he was engaged in a movement to dismember the nation. He does not mention the new Federalist flag. If orders had been issued to the detachment sent to Laredo in July, it is quite certain that Jordan and his fellow Texans, who comprised one-third of that force, did not know about them. And, then, one wonders why a person who was fighting the established government of Mexico and seeking to establish a new republic in the north, should suddenly become so concerned about preservation of "the national honor and the integrity of her [Mexico's] territory." Besides, Canales had been repeatedly told that Texas considered her boundary to be at the Río Grande, and that no flag but that of Texas was to be unfurled east of that river.

Karnes' letter and Canales' reply thereto were not made public until after the latter's surrender, two and a half months after Karnes' death. It seems probable that Canales' reply was never actually sent, but was prepared as a part of his plan for a return to the Centralist fold. Certainly, it is doubtful if any of the Texans cooperating with the Federalists would ever have consented to accept the boundary of the Republic of Texas at the Nueces. Canales would not have dared to make known his reply if he expected the assistance from the Texans which he was striving so hard to obtain at the time the letter was supposed to have been written. If the letter had been received by Karnes, Canales would not have expected that it would not be made public.

In the meantime, Karnes' health improved and believing it necessary for him to go to Houston to see Lamar in respect to his forthcoming military operation, he started out, contrary to his doctor's advice, for Houston in a light wagon. The first day out from San Antonio he suffered a relapse and was taken back to the city. He died on August 16. He was succeeded in command by Captain George T. Howard, who was promoted to the rank of major, and in the fall led an expedition against the Comanches by way of Uvalde Canyon.

Shortly after his return to the Nueces in July, Canales detached Colonel Jordan, who had again enlisted under the Federalist banner, with fifty Anglo-Texans, and Colonel Luis López with one hundred Mexican rancheros to be sent in advance of the main body. They were to clear the country of Centralists between Camargo and Laredo, and to get the six or eight thousand pounds of lead the Federalists had hidden at Laredo.[22] The movement toward the Río Grande was not unexpected in Mexico, for as early as June a report was afloat at Matamoros that the Federalists were expected to be on the river some time in July.[23]

Among those serving under Jordan were Captain John T. Price and Ewen Cameron. In the excitement attending the preparations to move against Laredo, Cameron's horse was lost at the camp on the Nueces, but was later found in possession of a Mexican. Cameron seized the horse and a heated argument developed. Hearing the altercation, Canales intervened, ordering Cameron to surrender the horse to the Mexican. Drawing his pistol, Cameron refused to deliver up the horse, declaring in broad Scotch that he would shoot the first man who should lay hands on his property. Whereupon, for disobedience of orders, Canales ordered Cameron tried by a court-martial presided over by Captain Thomas Pratt as judge advocate. The court acquitted Cameron, and ordered the horse restored to him.[24] Canales never forgot this incident.

About the middle of July, Jordan and López began their march for Laredo, and by the late evening of the 24th they were within thirty miles of the place. A forced night march brought them to the town, where their scouts met them and reported the enemy forces, mostly in the town on the east side of the river, as numbering 140 to 150 men under, as López reported later, "the vile prostituted Captain Rodríquez, *alias* Chicharron." By leaving the road and taking to the chaparral, Jordan's men succeeded in eluding the Mexican sentinels placed on the road in anticipation of the Federalist advance. About one half mile from Laredo the Texans hid their horses in a corral, and silently entered the town on foot, secreting themselves in some weeds and bushes along the banks of the river, within a hundred yards or less of the public square.[25] An hour later it began to dawn, and an elderly woman, making

[22] José María J. Carbajal to M. B. Lamar, Galveston, July 27, 1840, in *Lamar Papers*, III, 424–425.

[23] D. W. Smith to John Forsyth, Matamoros, June 30, 1840, in Consular Dispatches, Matamoros, 1840–1848, ms., microfilm.

[24] Yoakum, *History of Texas*, II, 377; Maude Wallis Traylor, "Those Men of the Mier Expedition," in *Frontier Times*, XVI (1938–1939), 307.

[25] "Information derived from Anson G. Neal," in *Lamar Papers*, VI, 106; Luis López to Lic. A. Canales, Conventional Army, 1st Section of Operations, Laredo, July 26, 1840 (translated by George Fisher), in *Telegraph and Texas Register*, Aug. 26, 1840, being López's report of the Laredo campaign.

her way to the river for water, discovered them and sounded the alarm. The Texans immediately leaped up and dashed for the plaza, Jordan entering it at one point and Price at another. Taken by surprise, the garrison became panic-stricken and fled from its barracks and the town, after offering only slight resistance. The fleeing Centralists effected their escape either by swimming the river or taking cover in the timber along its bank. The enemy losses included four killed, six wounded, and seventeen taken prisoners, including Ramón Botello and Mathías Sartuche, Centralist spies, who were apprehended in flight. The two spies were immediately court-martialed, sentenced to death, and executed the next day. There were no losses among the Texans. One volunteer (Mexican or Texan—López's report does not say) was wounded.[26] López reported that Rodríquez "escaped, naked, although I am assured," he told Canales, "that he is severely wounded." The captured property included several muskets, lances, saddles, mules, horses, and other articles.

Reported Neal,

When the fight was over, and the town taken, the Mexicans under López, who had remained without the town, under the impression that they could be more useful there in intercepting the Centralists in their flight when they should be routed by the American, . . . came charging into town, with loud huzaz and firing off their guns in great Jubilee. It happened, however, that though they remained out of town to intercept the flying foe, they did not encounter them, for whilst the foe fled in one direction, López with his men entered in another.[27]

The Federalists now proceeded to plunder Laredo—"friends and foes."[28]

[26] One of Jordan's men was killed during the morning by the accidental firing of a pistol. "Information derived from Anson G. Neal," in *Lamar Papers*, VI, 106.
[27] *Ibid.*
[28] "It is said the Federalists plundered Laredo when they took it—friends and foes." Hugh McLeod, Adjutant-General, to Gen. M. B. Lamar, Béxar, Aug. 28, 1840, in *ibid.*, III, 439. However, López reported to Canales on the day of the taking of Laredo that the inhabitants of the town were "in perfect liberty and security, for the volunteers [Texans], as well as the Mexican soldiers have deported themselves during the fight in the town in such a manner as will always reflect honor upon them." Luis Lopez to Lic. A. Canales, General in Chief of the Conventional Army, Laredo, July 26, 1840 (translated by George Fisher), in *Telegraph and Texas Register*, Aug. 26, 1840.

After a few days rest at Laredo, during which time a Federalist controlled government was installed, Jordan and López returned to the Nueces with their prisoners. They found Canales at Lipantitlán, three miles above San Patricio. While these events were in progress, the Comanches in great number, infuriated at the treatment they had received at San Antonio the previous spring, slipped through the frontier late in July all the way to the coast, causing severe destruction and loss of life. They attacked Victoria and burned Linnville on August 8. During the absence of Jordan and López, the Anglo-Texan contingent of the Federalist force had been increased. Captain John T. Price, as we have already noted in the Laredo campaign, and Captain Thomas Newcomb joined again, but Roman, Felder, and others, while still sympathetic, declined having any further active part under the Federalist leadership. Joe Wells, sometime cowboy, accepted a majority.[29] In the vicinity of Lipantitlán were assembled approximately two hundred Texans under Colonels Juan N. Seguin [30] (100) and S. W. Jordan [31] (110), the latter having their headquarters at Kinney's ranch. Whether Lamar ever gave written permission for Seguin to raise troops in Texas for the Federalist cause, is not known; but Seguin may have believed from his conversations with Lamar that he did have such permission, as he later claimed in his memoirs.[32] Certainly there is no indication that Lamar ever disapproved of Seguin's or any other private citizen's conduct in the Federalist wars. J. M. Menchaca of San Fernando de Rosas, then only nineteen years old and a relative of the Menchacas in Béxar, assisted Captain Antonio Pérez in raising a volunteer company, it was said, of fifty Mexicans and thirty Americans in Austin and San Antonio. Leandro Arriola of Béxar likewise raised a

[29] Hobart Huson, "Refugio: A Comprehensive History of Refugio County from Aboriginal Times to the End of World War II," vol. II, chap. 23, p. 15.

[30] Juan N. Seguin resigned his seat as senator in the adjourned Fourth Congress prior to his march to Laredo. John S. Simpson, Chief Justice of Béxar County, to Secretary of State, San Antonio, Monday morning 8 o'clock, Oct. 26, 1840, in Domestic Correspondence (Texas), 1836–1846, ms. In Seguin's company was Benjamin F. Highsmith. A. J. Sowell, *Early Settlers and Indian Fighters of Southwest Texas*, p. 13.

[31] The number of men under Jordan's command has been variously stated. Anson G. Neal says it was 90 (*Lamar Papers*, VI, 106); John Henry Brown, *History of Texas, from 1685 to 1892*, II, 173, gives it as 112; and Yoakum, *History of Texas*, II, 290, says 110.

[32] Juan N. Seguin, *Personal Memoirs of Juan N. Seguin, from the year 1834 to the Retreat of General Woll from the City of San Antonio in 1842.*

company, and a third company was made up of Americans from Austin. No list of these various volunteer units has been found, but apparently many of those who may have enrolled did not serve, or if they did, probably served under one of the other commands, possibly under Colonel Fisher. The three companies under Seguin, it was reported, comprised one hundred men.[33]

Meanwhile, for Texan frontier defense, the Border Guards and Pitkin Guards (named after John W. Pitkin of Houston, who organized them) were enrolled and stationed at San Antonio as a part of Karnes' unit being assembled at that point; but, according to Adjutant General Hugh McLeod, they "were worthless and complaining"[34] and it became necessary for McLeod to discharge them. "They have done and would *do nothing*. . . . They are now out [of] service," McLeod wrote on August 21, "without a weapon of any sort for defence on their return" home. It is possible that some of Seguin's men were drawn from the discharged "Border" and "Pitkin" Guards.

At Tenoxtitlán, on the west bank of the Brazos twelve miles above the Béxar-Nacogdoches Road, Lieutenant Colonel William S. Fisher, who had served on the staff of the First Infantry under Colonel Edward Burleson since January 23, 1839, and commanded companies "A," "C," and "I," on the southwestern frontier, organized a command of two hundred men and joined with Canales' forces by August 19.[35] Fisher's conduct seems to have brought about a general reorganization of the Texan frontier forces. Fisher was dropped (indicating that he did not resign) from the rolls of the army on August 18, 1840. At the same time Colonel Burleson resigned from the army and Colonel William G. Cooke was placed in command of the First Infantry, and George T. Howard was promoted to command a detachment of the First Infantry at San Antonio. W. D. Houghton, adjutant, was transferred to the command of "G" Company, Infantry, by promotion on August 18. P. S. Wyatt, who had been appointed Major of the Frontier Regiment on January 23, 1839, also resigned on August 18.[36]

[33] "Information derived from J. M. Monchaca [Menchaca?], San Fernando," in *Lamar Papers*, IV, pt. II, 70–71.

[34] H. McLeod to M. B. Lamar, San Antonio, Aug. 21, 1840, and Same to Same, San Antonio, Aug. 28, 1840, in *Lamar Papers*, III, 437, 439.

[35] "Information derived from Anson G. Neal," *Lamar Papers*, VI, 106.

[36] E. W. Winkler (ed.), *Secret Journals of the Senate: Republic of Texas, 1836–1845*, pp. 128–129; General Order No. 39, quoted in Semi-Annual Roll of Field & Staff of 1st Inf. from 30th June to 31st December 1840, Militia Rolls

Besides the Texans, Canales' force on the Nueces also included approximately three hundred Mexican rancheros and seventy to eighty Carrizo Indians.[37] With this force Canales prepared for his third expedition—the second launched from Texas—against the Centralists. Jordan's success at Laredo inspired the army, and the men were anxious to descend to the Río Grande.

Jordan was now ordered to scour the Río Grande country between Guerrero and Reinosa with his company aided by a number of Mexicans under López. Canales and Fisher were to follow later with a single piece of artillery—a four-pounder which the Texans had found spiked at Victoria, but had been able to unspike.

As for Arista, having defeated and dispersed the Federalists at Morelos, he began on March 30 to march the main body of his troops by way of Monclova to Saltillo, which he reached, after a leisurely march, on April 21, anniversary of the battle of San Jacinto. After resting his troops there for twenty-eight days, he headed northward on May 20 for Monterey, reaching there on the 22nd. Tarrying a month at the capital of Nuevo León, he departed for Ciudad Victoria, Tamaulipas, leaving the Second Division of the Army Corps of the North at Monterey, under General Rafael Vasquez. In the meantime, on July 2, Arista was placed in command of the Mexican Army of the North, replacing General Canalizo who announced that he was going to the nation's capital to re-establish his health.[38] From Linares, where he announced his assumption of command of the army on July 2, Arista headed toward Victoria. At Villagran he detached Colonel Ampudia to proceed to Matamoros to assume command of the some nine hundred troops there,[39] for word had been received that the Federalists on the Nueces were about to take up the line of march for the Río

---

(Texas), ms. Ashbel Smith to Col. B. E. Bee, [Galveston?, Aug.–Sept. 1840] in Ashbel Smith Papers, ms.

[37] The Centralists estimated the Federalist force at seven hundred, including five hundred foreigners and the rest Indians and Mexicans. *El Ancla* (Matamoros), Sept. 28, 1840. The number of foreigners involved seems to have been overestimated.

[38] Mariano Arista, general en gefe del egército del Norte á los Compañeros en armas, Cuartel general en Linares, Julio 2 de 1840, in *El Ancla*, Aug. 7, 1840; General Valentín Canalizo á sus subordinados, Matamoros, Julio 19 de 1840, in *ibid.*, July 24, 1840.

[39] *Austin City Gazette*, Aug. 5, 1840; *Boletin del Gobierno* (Mexico City), July 24, 1840; José M. J. Carvajal to M. B. Lamar, Galveston, July 27, 1840, in *Lamar Papers*, III, 424–425.

Grande and that their main objective was to take Matamoros.[40] Canalizo continued to command at Matamoros until relieved to report at Mexico City.

Ampudia reached Matamoros on July 10 [41] from the San Fernando campaign against Canales, and found there great excitement brought on by reports of a combined Texan-Mexican Federalist-Indian force of two thousand men about to descend upon the city from their encampment on the frontier of Texas. It was reported at Matamoros that Generals Woll, Conde, and Bradburn had refused to serve under Ampudia and had left there for the City of Mexico.[42]

In the meantime, Arista continued to Victoria, where he arrived on July 6 [43] and two days later proceeded toward Tampico, reaching there on July 13. On July 22 he learned of the revolution in Mexico City on July 15 in which General Urrea and a few supporters had seized President Bustamante in his apartments. An incipient revolution broke out in Tampico on July 24, but was quickly suppressed by General Arista. By August 1 the revolution at Mexico City had failed, and Arista came forth in an address to his troops praising Santa Anna and the return to peace and happiness at the center, and viciously attacking "the perfidious usurpers of Texas, united with some denaturalized Mexicans, [who] march toward our frontiers led by the perverse Canales. Let us fly," he said, "to inflict on them an exemplary punishment, to give them another lesson even more severe than that of March 25 at Morelos." [44] Declared the editor of the *Ancla*,[45]

Very soon, they [the Texans] will substitute for Canales a Texan leader, who will take care of . . . the stupid Mexicans who although they remain united to our enemies, the foreigners in the end will make themselves own-

[40] *Telegraph and Texas Register*, Aug. 12, 1840.

[41] *El Ancla*, July 17, 1840.

[42] See report from an unnamed correspondent of the New Orleans *Commercial Bulletin* from Puertes Verdes (near Matamoros), July 10, 1840, in *Telegraph and Texas Register*, Aug. 12, 1840, and of July 30, 1840, quoted in *ibid.*, Aug. 26, 1840.

[43] Arista was said to have had 1,500 troops under his command at Victoria. *Telegraph and Texas Register*, Aug. 12, 1840.

[44] Mariano Arista, El General en Gefe de los tropas de los Departamentos de Oriente, á sus subordinados, Cuartel General en Tampico, Agosto 1 de 1840; Mariano Arista, El General en Gefe del Cuerpo del Norte, á sus subordinados, Cuartel General en Tampico, Agosto 1 de 1840, Supplement to No. 31 of *El Ancla*, Aug. 7, 1840.

[45] Sept. 28, 1840.

ers of the land; . . . [and they] will treat us as slaves. Our women, our properties, the precious land of our fathers will be prey to their greedy and ravenous covetousness, and then you will know [it], if well out of season. . . . But no, it will not succeed! Long live God! Let us all die before we suffer such infamy, let us clutch the avenging sword, let us repel without a doubt the aggression.

Arista hastened north from Tampico on August 4 with troops to strengthen the defenses of Matamoros and other frontier towns expected to be the points of the anticipated Federalist attacks. In an effort to distract the Texans at home, Arista, upon leaving Tampico, issued a proclamation, calling upon the Cherokees, Shawnees, Wacoes, Kickapoos, Conchates [Coushatti?], and other tribes to put into execution their plans for attacking the Texas settlements.

I have received, with much pleasure, the news that you have united yourselves on the height of the Brazos . . . with the object of making war on the Texians, unjustly your enemies. These robbers have taken from you the land which Mexico gave you; and they are the same lands which she [Mexico] offers to you now. . . . It is necessary that you make common cause with the Mexicans [to recover them].[46]

On the 16th Arista was at Matamoros, and on the 27th [47] of August he crossed the Río Bravo with eleven hundred men and five pieces of artillery, with the intention of marching through the desert to surprise the revolutionists in their lurking place.[48] Eight hundred men remained as a garrison at Matamoros under General Pedro de Ampudia while Arista marched north into "no man's land," for a short distance. The first night out of Matamoros Arista camped at Los Fresnos. Nine infantrymen died from the excessive heat and forty became ill. The second night he camped on the Arroyo Colorado fifteen leagues from Matamoros, where he received a report that several Texan vessels were approaching Brazos Santiago, near the mouth of the Río Grande. Only too glad for the excuse to turn back, he returned at once to Matamoros, reaching there on September 1.[49] The next day, General Ampudia,

[46] Proclamation of Arista, Aug. 6, 1840, translated in *Austin City Gazette*, Nov. 4, 1840.

[47] Itinerario de las campañas en Tamaulipas, Coahuila y N. León, desde 23 Febrero de 1839 hasta hoy 28 Marzo de 1841, in *El Ancla*, March 29, 1841.

[48] *El Ancla*, Aug. 31, 1840, says Arista crossed the Río Bravo with 1,000 men.

[49] A report in the *Austin City Gazette*, Sept. 16, 1840, based on intelligence received from Brigadier General Edwin Morehouse of the Texas Militia, declared

commanding the First Division of the Second Brigade, was sent out with five hundred men and two pieces of artillery to investigate. Ampudia was instructed to reconnoiter the coast from the Isle of Balli on the north to the bar of San José on the south.[50] He remained at the mouth of the Río Grande until September 11, when he returned to the city to report that the Texan vessels had all retired.[51]

All this excitement seems to have been caused by the Texan Commodore E. W. Moore, who never lost an opportunity to worry the Mexican government. Moore had stationed three of his ships, the *Austin*, the *San Bernard*, and the *San Jacinto* off the coast of Vera Cruz within a few miles of the Castle of San Juan de Úlloa hoping to learn whether the Texan diplomatic agent, James Treat, sent under a United States passport to Mexico, was having any success in his negotiations for the recognition of Texas independence. Hearing a rumor from Tampico that Canales was advancing toward Matamoros at the head of two thousand troops,[52] seven hundred of whom were Texans, Moore, left the *San Bernard* off Vera Cruz to maintain contact with Treat and sailed north in the *Austin*, accompanied by the *San Jacinto*. The latter he sent on to Galveston with communications for the Texan State Department, while with his flagship, the *Austin*, he laid off the mouth of the Río Grande for a number of days by way of making a demonstration against Matamoros. Even if there may not have been a preconcerted plan to cooperate with the Mexican Federalists, then preparing to advance from the Nueces, the presence of the Texan vessels

---

that owing to a large proportion of his men declaring for federalism, Arista appeared to follow their example and persuaded them to stack their arms. No sooner was this accomplished than they were immediately made prisoners by those who remained loyal and Arista again declared boldly in favor of the Centralists. About this time an express from Matamoros reached his camp with intelligence that the citizens had joined with the troops in declaring in favor of Federalism. This caused Arista's hasty return to the city. The writer has found no reliable data to corroborate these conclusions. It is highly improbable that the citizens of Matamoros would declare for Federalism at this late date when that cause was becoming increasingly unpopular in northern Mexico.

[50] *El Ancla*, Sept. 21, 1840; Mariano Arista, *El general en gefe del cuerpo de Ejército del Norte, á la 1ª division*, Cuartel general en Arroyo Colorado, Agosto 30 de 1840, broadside.

[51] Itinerario de las campañas en Tamaulipas, Coahuila y N. León, desde 23 Febrero de 1839 hasta hoy 28 Marzo de 1841, in *El Ancla*, March 29, 1841.

[52] E. W. Moore to Louis P. Cooke, Texan Sloop of War Austin, Mouth of Tabacco River, Dec. 24, 1841 [1840?], in Harriet Smither (ed.), *Journals of the Sixth Congress of the Republic of Texas*, III, 373.

caused a change in Centralist military plans. Arista judged the sudden appearance of the Texan flagship at this point as indicative of a joint naval and military offensive operation against Matamoros in conjunction with Canales.[53] Arista's conclusion seemed to be supported by a report at Matagorda on October 10, that Commander Ribaud of the southern Mexican Federalists had been "a few days since in Corpus Christi Bay concerting action with Canales." [54]

It was not long before reports began to reach Matamoros that the advance units of Canales' forces had commenced their march for the Río Grande. Arista, accordingly, left Matamoros on September 16 with seven hundred cavalry, a strong division of infantry (numbering in all one thousand men), and four pieces of artillery to protect the Villas del Norte.[55] He moved in the direction of Mier. Colonel Mendoza was ordered to San Fernando de Rosas with a respectable force, and General Reyes, who had been at Mier with the Second Division (nine hundred men)[56] since September 7 left there on September 20 in pursuit of Molano. On the 21st Arista was at Reinosa Viejo, on the 22nd at Camargo, and on the 23rd was reported at the Arroyo San Pedro, five days journey from Monterey toward which place he was directing himself at forced marches to intercept Canales, who had crossed the Río Grande and the San Juan, and was advancing toward China, now pursued by General Reyes. The area between Presidio del Río Grande and Laredo was protected by the cavalry of Lieutenant Colonel Galán, commander of the frontier presidial companies (three hundred men).[57] The heavy rains of mid-September impeded military operations. On the 28th [58] Arista reached Concepción, approximately midway between Cadereyta and China on the north bank of the San Juan River, where on the 29th he was joined by the forces under Reyes and Vasquez,

[53] Jim Dan Hill, *The Texas Navy: in Forgotten Battles and Shirtsleeve Diplomacy*, pp. 129–130; [Mariano Arista] General in Chief of the First Division, Aug. 30, 1840, in *Seminario Politico del Gobierno de Nuevo León*, Sept. 10, 1840. James Treat to Abner S. Lipscomb, City of Mexico, Oct. 25, 1840, in Garrison (ed.), *Diplomatic Correspondence of Texas*, 1908, II, 711–713.

[54] *Colorado Gazette and Advertiser*, Oct. 10, 1840.

[55] *El Ancla*, Sept. 21, 1840.

[56] *Ibid.*, Sept. 14 and 21, 1840; this same paper on Oct. 12, 1840, reported that on Oct. 6 Reyes had six hundred cavalry. He probably had no infantry at that time under his command.

[57] *Ibid.*, Sept. 14, 21, and 28, 1840.

[58] *Itinerario de las campañas en Tamaulipas, Coahuila y N. León, desde 23 Febrero de 1839 hasta hoy 28 Marzo de 1841*, in *El Ancla*, March 29, 1841.

comprising the Second Division. Here plans were laid for intercepting and defeating the Federalists and their "unspeakable" foreign auxiliaries. It was agreed that Reyes, in command of the 650 cavalrymen of the Second Division should pursue Canales who was reported advancing toward China; that Arista should advance to the relief of Victoria with the First Brigade of the First Division of 700 men and four pieces of artillery; and that Vasquez, with the Second Brigade of 300 men and three pieces of artillery should remain to accord protection to Monterey and Saltillo.

In the meantime the Federalists were on the move. While en route to the Río Grande, Jordan was overtaken by a small force of Federalists under Colonel Juan N. Molano, brother-in-law of Canales,[59] with orders to advance as far as China, on the San Juan, to get horses. The López-Molano-Jordan force crossed the Río Grande near Clay Davis' rancho on September 7, reported Molano,[60] with 350 men, of whom 120 were "strangers," meaning "foreigners" or "Texans." The *Ancla* at Matamoros, however, reported that this force numbered 400 "bandits," 300 of whom were foreigners;[61] actually, it numbered only some 110 Anglo-Americans comprising Jordan's company and about 150 Mexicans under López and Molano. Near the Río Grande they caught two Centralist spies, whom they carried ultimately to China, tried by court-martial and shot. Although mistrustful of their wily comrades, the reckless Texans moved on, capturing Guerrero, Mier, Camargo, and China on the Río San Juan. By striking southward from the Río Grande settlements thay hoped that new companies might be recruited and arms, ammunition, and money collected. At China they found no horses. Molano caused Jordan to believe that the inhabitants had run them off at the approach of the Federalists, and that they could be found in a town close by. Thus the Texans were lured on from place to place, following first one dimly marked trail and then another in their search for horses. Often they found the trails ran away into infinity to be lost southward in mountain passes of naked rock, hot by day and cold by night. Near one of the towns the Texans forced a small detachment

[59] "Information derived from Anson G. Neal," in *Lamar Papers,* VI, 107.
[60] Juan Nepomuceno Molano a Señores Editores del *Ancla,* Matamoros, Marzo lo de 1841, in *El Ancla,* March 15, 1841; "Statement of P. F. Bowman, Buffalo, N. Y.," in *Lamar Papers,* IV, pt. I, 239.
[61] Sept. 28, 1840. October 12, 1840, *El Ancla* printed a report from one of Arista's officers saying that Molano's force at Victoria numbered 400 men, including 150 "colonials" (Texans).

under a Mexican colonel, collecting horses and arms for the Centralists at Monterey, to surrender without resistance. Jordan's men took possession of the three hundred muskets and large quantity of cartridges the Centralist foragers had taken up. The colonel was made a prisoner, and his men joined the Federal cause and now marched under its banner.[62] Finally, the next day, "at a small dirty town [De Grande] or ranch at the foot of the mountains. . . . we found a number of good horses," recorded Neal, and supplying themselves with what they needed (about ninety), they rested two days and a night. At this point, a captain of a small company of Mexicans from San Antonio, Antonio Pérez, "a man well known in San Antonio, Texas, and not a coward," warned Jordan that Molano intended treachery. Jordan failed to heed Pérez; whereupon, the latter "abandoned the enterprise, stole a large Cavayard [caballada] of horses [at De Grande] and left for Texas."[63] Later Pérez, who had seen service as a frontier spy employed by the Texas government, committed a number of murders and robberies and left Texas for San Fernando, where he became known as a notorious highwayman.

All was not at ease, however, among the Texans. They protested against advancing farther into the heart of the enemy's country unless the whole Anglo-Texan force was along. Now that they were well mounted they wished to return. López and Molano, nevertheless, continued to urge that if they would proceed on to Victoria, sixty miles away, they should be paid off. There was nothing some of the adventurers would have liked better than a little money. So Jordan and his men, with their Mexican brethren, pushed on rapidly toward Ciudad Victoria, capital of the Department of Tamaulipas, capturing Montemorelos, San Cristobal, Linares, Villagran, and Hidalgo en route. It was a long tedious march in the burning sun. At Villagran, Molano later wrote, his difficulties commenced, for the Texans, he said, were not satisfied with the lenity he observed toward the people of the towns through which they marched. They demanded the "spoils of war" that they said they had been promised when enlisting in the Federal service. Molano informed them that the "spoils of war" consisted only of what might be taken from the troops sent to fight them,

[62] "Information derived from Anson G. Neal, Laredo, May 30, 1847," in *Lamar Papers*, VI, 107.

[63] "Information derived from Anson G. Neal," in *Lamar Papers*, VI, 107; "Capt. Newcombe's Recollections," in *ibid.*, VI, 121–123. Newcombe was a member of Jordan's party.

and since they had encountered no troops there were no "spoils of war." But the Texans, he continued, insisted that all those who had not taken up arms for the Federation were Centralists and that they must sack the towns, haciendas, and ranches and distribute to themselves what was captured.[64] To this Molano is alleged to have replied that he did not come to make war against his own country; that he had never offered them such spoils; and that he had rather lose his life first than consent to such infamous conduct as they wished to follow, which would be extremely prejudicial to the cause which the Federalists were defending, "for our depredations," he said, "would form a contrast before the eyes of the people with the severe discipline maintained by the troops of General Arista and his constant system of respecting the persons and goods of all peaceful inhabitants." [65] The reaction to the Federalist seizures of property and mistreatment of the inhabitants was daily becoming more evident as "an insuperable barrier to the progress of the revolution."

In view of this attitude, the Texans held a council and agreed to separate from Molano's command and not to continue forward; but as "they observed my cheerful compliance," reported Molano, they sent a commission to me "to tell me that they had changed their opinion [mind] and were determined to follow under my orders." Thus the Mexicans and Texans continued to operate as a combined unit; but, Molano later seeking to justify his betrayal of the Texans and make a secure place for himself in Mexico, declared, "vengeance lodged in their hearts" and the Texans intended to separate from us "at the best opportunity." In the meantime, he said, they introduced discord among the Mexicans and conspired against his person, "under the pretext that I did not have the necessary energy to provide myself resources." Since the threatening reply of Colonel Karnes to Canales, discussed earlier, he said, he had opposed the use of foreign troops, being "convinced of their ambition and perfidious intentions" and had concluded that the Federalists must choose between the extremes of having a country badly governed, or of "losing it forever and bending . . . beneath a strange and ominous yoke."

Thus from the time of the incident at Villagran, Molano determined to put an end to the horrors of war, especially as he saw no hope of

---

[64] Juan Nepomuceno Molano á Señores Editores del *Ancla,* Matamoros, Marzo 1º de 1841, in *El Ancla,* March 15, 1841.
[65] *Ibid.*

any advantage to the northern towns by continuing the war. The failure of the Federalist cause in the North he attributed to the excesses of the Texans, rather than to the superiority of the Centralist forces in the field, the policy of moderation pursued by Arista, the separatist policy of the Federalists, and the bankrupt financial condition of the revolutionists.

Finally, on September 29 Victoria was entered without resistance by a force of 250 men, including 115 Texans.[66] As soon as the Federalists took possession of the plaza, they raised their flag of rebellion and began proclaiming, with repeated "vivas," the federal system.[67] The flight of the governor of Tamaulipas, with the small garrison, from the city three hours before had been accelerated by rumors spread by a Mexican, named Martinez, "who represented the Americans as perfect cannibals & devils, and advised the Governor [José Antonio Quintero y Barberena] to take time by the forelock and fly whilst he might." [68] Molano recommended to the prefect of the District of Ciudad Victoria, Luiz Pérez, that a junta be convened in the city composed of any and all respectable inhabitants who might wish to take part in the deliberation and speak for or against the subjects to be taken up. He then stated that the purpose of this junta was to study the question of returning to the federal constitution of 1824 or of continuing adherence to the Centralist government based on the Plan of Cuernavaca.[69] The junta was called on September 30 to meet on October 1 in the consistorial room. It included not only the men of the Ayuntamiento but also a large portion of the "most respectable" citizens of the town,[70] and was presided over by Prefect Don Luiz Pérez. Pérez read the letter he had received from Molano urging the calling of the junta

[66] Quoting from *La Concordia* (Ciudad Victoria), *El Ancla*, Oct. 19, 1840, says the town of Victoria was surprised by a Federalist force of 250 men, including 115 colonials and the rest Mexicans from the northern towns under Juan Molano. A week earlier *El Ancla* reported 150 colonials (Texans) in the Federalist force at Victoria. See note 61 above.

[67] *Gaceta del Gobierno de Tamaulipas* (Ciudad Victoria), Oct. 13, 1840.

[68] "Information derived from Anson G. Neal," in *Lamar Papers*, VI, 107 n; Yoakum, *History of Texas*, II, 288; *La Concordia*, quoted in *El Ancla*, Oct. 19, 1840.

[69] Juan Nepomuceno Molano á Sr. Prefecto del Distrito de esta C[iudad] D. Luis Pérez, Victoria, setiembre 30 de 1840, in *Gaceta del Gobierno de Tamaulipas*, Oct. 13, 1840.

[70] The *Gaceta del Gobierno de Tamaulipas*, Oct. 13, 1840, contains a list of those who attended the Federalist junta on October 1, 1840, at Victoria, Tamaulipas, to elect a governor and a vice governor.

and pointed out the need of a provisional civil government to maintain order and tranquility, since the governor and the garrison had abandoned the city to its fate. After a brief discussion, a vote was taken on the question of adherence to the Federal system and the constitution of 1824, or to Centralism as it then existed in Mexico City. The vote was unanimously in favor of Federalism. The second proposition submitted by Molano—for a civil government—was approved by a vote of 76 without any discussion. A provisional government for the "Free and Sovereign State of Tamaulipas" was instituted,[71] with Don José Nuñez de Caceres being elected Governor and Don Eleno de Vargas, Lieutenant Governor. Pérez and Secretary Geronimo Olivera were removed from office. The new officers were forthwith sworn into office, after which the junta adjourned.

The inhabitants of Victoria received the Texans with open arms and "the merchants threw open their stores to the credit of our men," wrote Neal. They could scarcely afford to do otherwise. Victoria yielded only $1,100 in gold and silver, which, when distributed among the command, left each man a very "trifling sum."[72] According to Molano's account, the money was "only divided among the strangers, which caused extraordinary disgust to the Mexicans, and aggravated [in that] manner my situation."[73] At Victoria and other places Molano and López had seized cigars which now amounted, in all, to the value of some $15,000.[74] With these López expected to pay off his soldiers, but when they refused to take them in payment, he ordered the cigars burned later at Jaumave.[75] During their stay at Victoria, the Federalists were accused of invading private properties "without pity" and of removing all the tame horses they could find from the ranchos and summer pastures in the vicinity. They levied requisitions for money, cattle, and provisions, it was said; they outraged honorable citizens, casting many into prisons when they did not promptly turn over to them the resources they demanded; they ravished the unfortunate

[71] Minutes of the Ayuntamiento of Ciudad Victoria, Oct. 1, 1840, in *ibid.;* Luis Pérez á Gobernador de Tamaulipas, Octubre 2 de 1840; Jose Nuñez de Caceres al D. Luis Pérez, Victoria, Octubre 3 de 1840, in *ibid.*
[72] "Further Information from Captain Newcombe," in *Lamar Papers,* VI, 124.
[73] Juan Nepomuceno Molano á Señores Editores del *Ancla,* Matamoros, Marzo lo de 1841, in *El Ancla,* March 15, 1841.
[74] The value of the cigars taken at Victoria was reported as 10,700 pesos. *Ibid.,* Oct. 19, 1840; *Gaceta del Gobierno de Tamaulipas,* Oct. 13, 1840.
[75] *Lamar Papers,* VI, 108, 114.

women whom they encountered, "threatening them with dagger and pistol to force them to succumb to their brutal desires." [76]

The Federalists tarried at Victoria a week awaiting the advance of Canales. During that time they afforded protection to the newly installed Federalist regime under Licenciado José Nuñez de Caceres the Old.[77] Finally, despairing of aid from Canales, whose forward march was reported cut off by General Arista's advance from Matamoros, the Federalists discussed the question of abandoning Victoria. Molano reported the receipt of intelligence of the approach of a large hostile force of some five or six hundred under Arista,[78] which was expected to reach Victoria within a few hours. On October 6 Arista was encamped at the hacienda de la Gavia, near San Carlos, with eight hundred infantrymen and six pieces of artillery.[79] A council of Federalist leaders was hastily assembled and Molano urged that the city of Victoria be evacuated at once and that the Federalists head for Saltillo, where, he said, it would be possible "to sack the city and pay ourselves." [80] His proposal was quickly adopted, and the Federalists retired to the mountains to the west of the city on October 6, but because of strong opposition from the Texans, the entire force halted at Aguayo, about three miles from Ciudad Victoria, so as to control the pass of the mountains at which point they hoped to give the enemy battle. Upon the withdrawal from Victoria, a few of the Texans loitered behind, "got drunk and surrendered themselves to scandalous license," but certainly not "nearly all" of the Texans, as represented by Molano, sank to such degradation.[81] Jordan dispatched Captain Price to bring them out. Price found James Wait from La Bahía, Texas, who desired to obtain some tobacco before leaving. An argument ensued, during which Captain Price drew his pistol and shot Wait, who died the next day in the home of a rich *gachupín* woman. Before his death Wait is reported to have told the woman that he had been shot for disobedience of orders, and because of "a grudge which the Capt. had against

[76] *El Ancla,* Oct. 19, 1840.

[77] *Lamar Papers,* VI, 114. *El Ancla,* Oct. 12, 1842, says the new governor's name was spelled "Casares."

[78] S. W. Jordan to Gen. Lic. Canales, Laredo, Nov. 2, 1840, typed copy in John S. Ford, "Memoirs," II, 238–241, ms., this being Jordan's field report of his regiment after the battle of Saltillo.

[79] *El Ancla,* Oct. 12, 1840.

[80] *Lamar Papers,* VI, 108.

[81] Juan Nepomuceno Molano á Señores Editores del *Ancla,* Matamoros, Marzo 1o de 1841, in *El Ancla,* March 15, 1841.

me growing out of the murder of a Mexican at Victory [Victoria] in Texas."[82] Molano's report six months later of the evacuation of Victoria makes it appear that it was "necessary for him to lance the Texans by force from the city and to kill one of them in order to dissuade the others by this example from the unheard-of excesses that they were commiting."[83]

The Federalists remained at Aguayo several days without the enemy putting in his appearance. At this point, about 3 o'clock on the morning of the 8th, Molano sent Jordan word that it would be necessary to go farther on to unite with Captains García and Montenegros who were encamped beyond in the pass and there await the enemy. Accordingly, Jordan resumed the march and about daylight joined García. Here he was informed that the beeves he had ordered for the subsistence of the troops had not been procured, and that their only recourse for provisions was to cross the mountains. Therefore, on the 10th the Federalists renewed their march southwestward towards Jaumave, situated on a buttress of the Sierra de Tamaulipas, and General Arista coming by way of Santa Eduvige on the 10th, occupied Victoria on the 11th.[84]

On the 8th the Federalist governor, José Nuñez de Caceres, "knowing with full certainty that they [the Federalists] have crossed the mountains," addressed a letter[85] to the former prefect, Luiz Pérez, resigning his position and turning the powers of government over to the Centralists. On the 10th Arista suggested that Pérez convene the junta which had voted adherence to the Federalist cause and have

[82] "Information derived from Anson G. Neal," in *Lamar Papers*, VI, 108.

[83] Juan Nepomuceno Molano á Señores Editores del *Ancla*, Matamoros, March 1, 1841, in *El Ancla*, March 15, 1841.

[84] *Gaceta del Gobierno de Tamaulipas*, Oct. 13, 1840, says Arista entered *"antes de ayer"*—"day before yesterday"; *El Ancla*, Oct. 19, 1840; Vito Alessio Robles, *Coahuila y Texas desde la Consumación de la independencia hasta el tratado de paz de Guadalupe Hidalgo*, II, 220; Mariano Arista, El General en Gefe del Cuerpo de Ejército de Norte á los Habitantes de los Departamentos de Tamaulipas, Nuevo León y Coahuila, Cuartel General en Victoria de Tamaulipas a 13 de Octubre de 1840, in *El Ancla*, Oct. 19, 1840; also issued separately as a broadside, printed probably at Victoria in 1840—see Thomas W. Streeter, *Bibliography of Texas*, III, 212–213.

[85] José Nuñez de Caceres al Prefecto del Distrito de esta capital D. Luis Pérez, Victoria a 8 de Octubre de 1840, in *Gaceta del Gobierno de Tamaulipas*, Oct. 13, 1840, Matamoros Archives, photostat in University of Texas Archives; *El Ancla*, Oct. 19, 1840; Luis Pérez and Geromino Olivera, Secretario, to D. Mariano Arista, general en gefe del ejército del Norte, Ciudad Victoria, Oct. 11, 1840, in *ibid*.

341

that act, which he conceded was the work of a minority, repealed.[86] The junta accordingly met on the 11th, and, except for a few who were too ill to attend or who had fled, unanimously repealed the acts establishing the provisional government, which, after all, they claimed, had been set up temporarily to meet a situation of anarchy.

It was rumored that the Centralist governor of Tamaulipas had taken up his position at Jaumave, a small mining community fifteen leagues from Victoria; but when the Federalists entered the place on October 16, they found that the enemy, the town officials, and a large proportion of the better class of people had fled, leaving behind most of their property, a few peons and decrepit citizens to take care of themselves. The Federals proceeded to invest one of the peons with the dignity and power of an alcalde. "At first . . . he entered timidly upon the discharge of his high functions," but "as his principal duties, however, consisted in responding to the requisitions of the federal army, he soon learned how to discharge them" to the satisfaction of his superiors and his own rapacity. "When a requisition was made for a beef, or a mutton, or a fowl, he took care to order a like supply for himself, being fully persuaded that the entire blame could be laid upon 'los diablos Tejanos!' Thus the federal army, with the new *alcalde* and his brother-peons, lived sumptuously in the town of Jaumave," [87] known to the Texans as "Deadman's Town."[88]

Before leaving Victoria, a Mexican ranchero from San Antonio informed a Texan soldier named Long that on the preceding night he and a friend, while bathing in the stream near the town, had heard footsteps approaching, and not desiring to be seen had remained concealed in the water. Three men, whom they identified as Molano, López, and a person who had brought them dispatches that day, came down to the stream and seated themselves on the bank. The dispatch bearer then proceeded to inform the two colonels "that he was authorized, on behalf of the Governor and leading centralists, to offer, and guarantee the payment of a large sum of money to them, provided they would desert the Federal cause; and an additional sum, if they would

[86] Mariano Arista al Sr. Prefecto de Centro de Tamaulipas [Luis Pérez], Ciudad Victoria, [dated:] Cuartel General en Santa Edubige, Octubre 10 de 1840, in *Gaceta del Gobierno de Tamaulipas*, Oct. 13, 1840, Matamoros Archives, photostat in University of Texas Archives.
[87] Yoakum, *History of Texas*, II, 291–292.
[88] "Capt. Newcomb's Recollections," in *Lamar Papers*, VI, 121; "Information derived from Anson G. Neal, Laredo, May 30, 1847," in *ibid.*, VI, 108.

dispose of the Texas soldiers, under their command, that they might be massacred." [89] The agent is reported to have offered 100,000 pesos upon compliance with the proposals. Molano and López agreed to the scheme, and declared that compliance would be made at Saltillo. They then laid plans with the agent for stationing the contending forces at Saltillo. When Long reported the "plot" to Jordan and another Texan officer, the two officers refused to believe the intrigue and vowed that "the caluminator should be punished for attempting to incite insubordination." When the name of his informant was demanded, Long refused to reveal it.

Molano and López went forward with their plans to make peace with the Centralists and to betray the Texans. Prior to his arrival at Victoria, Arista received an emissary from Molano, by the name of Blas Cabazos, informing him of their desire to recognize the government of Mexico. Upon occupying Victoria, Arista wrote Molano on the 11th, saying that he had been informed by Blas Cabazos of his and López's desire to break the strange alliance which made the Federalist leaders "so odious in the eyes of their own countrymen." Arista declared that he would be happy to help wash away that stain. With a letter from each of the Mexican Federalist leaders or a single message from both of them, he declared an end could be put to this unhappy situation, and as evidence of his moderation he was willing to assure the Mexicans all sorts of guarantees. "Reflect that you are lost," he continued; "Canales has been dispersed by Gen. Reyes, who pursues the remnants [of his army] to the Río Bravo; my numerous forces cover all the passes, and no recourse remains to you but death, or performing the service of abandoning to their fate those adventurers, as Cabazos proposes to me in the name of all the Mexican commanders. I await with anxiety your reply, and I place my faith in you." [90]

Arista's communication was received by Juan N. Molano at Palmillas at 6 P.M., October 12, and after a hasty consultation with López and Manuel Molano, he "determined from that moment," he said, "to accede to it as the most effective and opportune means of saving the country [and] restoring it to peace." So immediately, October 12, Juan N. Molano replied from Pamillas, announcing that he was disposed

[89] John C. Reid, *Reid's Tramp: or a Journal of . . . Travel Through Texas, New Mexico, Arizona, Sonora, and California*, pp. 73–74.

[90] General [M.] Arista al S[r] D[on] Juan Nepomuceno Molano, Ciudad Victoria, Octubre 11 de 1840, in *El Ancla*, Dec. 7, 1840.

to end his revolt under certain conditions.[91] Molano and López fully agreed that the Federalists' greatest sin had been in uniting with the "odious Texians," whom, they said, they hated and would always hate. In view of the court-martial and execution of Federalists, including one of their great leaders, at Santa Rita de Morelos, Molano said he and his men were very apprehensive of what might be in store for themselves if they surrendered; but, "if you, as we hope you will, shall act with good faith in this affair, we promise on our word of honor, as Mexican citizens, and in the name of our idolized and unfortunate country, that from this moment not a single shot shall be fired by this division at a Mexican citizen, unless we see ourselves persecuted tenaciously by our own brothers or see the lack of good faith" in carrying out the surrender agreement. Molano then proposed that the terms of capitulation include a general amnesty for all who had participated in the present rebellion under the leadership of Canales; that his men each be given "letters of security" signed by General Arista and the "other respectable chiefs, with a promise to comply with and sustain their tenor"; that the Mexicans in his command should be permitted to march to the neighboring town and the men be permitted to retain "such of their arms, horses, and equipage," as may be necessary for their defense on the frontier; "that payment for the march be made to each person according to his rank"; and, finally, that the Federalists and Centralists both pledge themselves not to solicit or accept assistance from the Texians, the country's enemies.[92] As for himself, Molano was willing to rely upon Arista's word, and the terms he asked, he said, were solely for the security of those who accompanied him. The Federalists, he promised, would then be willing to serve in a campaign against Texas. In the meantime, Molano informed Arista, he would continue his march toward Matehuala, and hoped en route to hear from Arista.

In reply to the offer of the two Federalist leaders to surrender, Arista declared that the sentiments expressed by such "true patriots and worthy Mexicans," gave him great pleasure; yet, in the eyes of the nation, the unfortunate tie with the foreigners (Texans) made it

[91] Alessio Robles, *Coahuila y Texas*, II, 221. The correspondence exchanged between Arista and Molano was published in a Supplement to Number 90 of the *Seminario del Gobierno de Nuevo León*, Thursday, Nov. 19, 1840, and reproduced in *El Ancla*, Dec. 7, 1840.

[92] Juan Nepomuceno Molano and Luis López to D. Mariano Arista, Palmillas, Oct. 12, 1840, in *El Ancla*, Dec. 7, 1840.

difficult to accept these expressions of loyalty. However, Arista countered with the demand that the Federalists swear never to rebel again against the supreme government or ever recognize the independence of Texas; that the Texan adventurers be abandoned to their fate; and that the Federalists prove their loyalty and sincerity by assisting in a renewal of the Texas campaign.[93] By way of showing Molano how foolhardy it was to continue the campaign, Arista again supplied him with information concerning Canales. He declared that Canales had been overtaken after a tenacious pursuit of eight days, and that after a brief skirmish in the Bosque de Gallo his forces had been dispersed in the direction of the Río Grande. Colonel Mendoza, he continued, had been dispatched from Matamoros to Camargo to intercept their crossing of the Río Grande and had already destroyed all canoes, chalanas, and rafts, and that no one could now pass the river in that vicinity except by swimming. To Arista, it seemed rather foolish to continue the war in view of the ability of the Centralists to concentrate their forces against Molano and López. The available Centralist forces for such an effort consisted of six hundred cavalry under General Reyes, Arista's own division, a brigade under Rafael Vasquez, and the sections under Colonel Ampudia and under Romero.

The following terms upon which Arista would accept the Federalist surrender accompanied his letter of October 14 to Molano:

Conditions under which the Mexicans under the command of Don Juan Molano submit to the Supreme Government of the nation:

Knowing that all Mexicans have not a knowledge of the situation or risk that have caused us to admit the aid of strangers for the advancement of our project, we give this as a public testimony of our patriotism and fealty to our country, declaring:

1st. That we are Mexicans, decided lovers of our countrymen, that we have never thought to rebel against the nation, nor much less acknowledge the independence of Texas.

2d. That we hate the occupiers of that fertile department; and, in proof of this, offer our persons to combat them—this offer being made in full

[93] Mariano Arista á D. Juan N. Molano, Victoria, Octubre 14 de 1840, in *El Ancla*, Dec. 14, 1840. The editor of *El Ancla* reported the letter was not received by Molano until after the battle of Saltillo because the courier entrusted with its delivery was unable to overtake Molano, due to the deficiency of horses and the fear of the battle. The terms that Arista proposed in the document accompanying his letter of October 14 were substantially the same as those ultimately agreed upon. *Ibid.*

security of the good faith of the general in chief of the army of the North, Don Mariano Arista, we offer

Firstly, All Mexicans under the command of Don Juan Molano will separate from and abandon to their fate the adventurous strangers (Texians) at present among them, and immediately place themselves at the obedience of the Supreme Government, under the following guarantees, which will be secured with all the requisites necessary.

Secondly, All who sign this document and all soldiers included in the accompanying list, remain perfectly guaranteed, not to be molested for any of their acts during the present revolution.

Thirdly, All other individuals engaged in the same revolution will remain equally guaranteed, provided they abandon it before the passing of two months.

Fourthly, We pledge to march in any rank that may be deemed fit, for the object of making a campaign against the ungrateful colonists of Texas, to verify with our blood that we have never been traitors to our country.

Fifthly, While the above campaign is getting ready we will retire to our homes—Gen. Arista giving us the necessary aid to do so—permitting those who live on the frontier to retain their arms as a defence against the barbarians (Indians).

Sixthly, The aforesaid Gen. Arista will name the commissioners to come and sign with us this contract after we have separated ourselves from the strangers.

These conditions will do honor to you before your compatriots, and will save you from inevitable disgrace.

It is necessary not to lose time, as all depends upon the contest.

Head quarters, in the City of Victoria, 14th Oct. 1840.

Mariano Arista [94]

At the same time the ex-Federalist governor, José Nuñez de Caceres, wrote Molano, saying that he was in full accord with the sentiments expressed by General Arista, whose heart, he found, was "full of generosity and nobleness." He said, "I have seen with my own eyes and I have read in him the great interest that he has for you, Sr. López and all Mexicans who accompany you." [95] Now is the time to save yourselves and cast into everlasting oblivion past misconduct, and give to your country a day of happiness and returning joy. "I believe firmly in the word of Sr. Arista," but you must act quickly for "there is no time to be lost."

[94] *Telegraph and Texas Register*, Dec. 16, 1840.
[95] J. Nuñez de Caceres al Sr. D. Juan N. Molano, Victoria a 14 de Octubre de 1840, in *El Ancla*, Dec. 14, 1840.

In the meantime, Arista issued a proclamation at Victoria on October 13 in which he referred to the Texans as "Pirates," led by that Mexican traitor and criminal Canales.

These naked bandits, full of misery and crime, [he declared, come from Texas] to rob the most industrious towns of N[uevo] León and Tamaulipas. . . . There is nothing to equal the immorality of those highwaymen; with their rifles in hand they insult our countrymen, saying they wish to discharge it into a *Mexican Comanche Indian*, as they call us. They have violated our women in front of their husbands. They kill whom they please and upon the body of their opponent falling to the ground, raise their pistol and say firmly: "good gun, it never fails!"

Fortunately, concluded Arista, most of the people of the northern towns do not adhere to them.[96]

Returning to Jordan and his Federalist cohorts, we find that after a few days at Jaumave, a council of war was held in which it was determined to proceed to Saltillo as planned and to avail themselves of the resources needed, for Jordan's men were nearly naked. The Mexican conspirators also held out the hope of uniting with Canales there, although Molano and López both knew that he was in retreat toward the Río Grande.[97] After they had gone seven or eight miles, the Anglo-Americans discovered that the Mexican Federalists were taking them on the road to San Luis Potosí. The Texans now became suspicious of Molano's and López's integrity, especially when they realized that in the small towns and ranchos through which they had passed since leaving Victoria, Molano had repeatedly refused to accept volunteers who wished to join his small army. Captain Newcomb halted his men, and speaking the sentiment of most of the Texans declared that he would go no farther in that direction. Upon Jordan's inquiry as to what he proposed to do, he replied he intended to return to Texas if the march toward San Luis Potosí was continued. Many of the Mexican soldiers likewise remonstrated against going to San Luis, claiming that there were too many government troops there. Molano,

[96] [Mariano Arista] *El general en gefe del cuerpo de Egército del Norte á los habitantes de los departamentos de Tamaulipas, Nuevo León y Coahuila,* Cuartel General en Victoria de Tamaulipas a 13 de Octubre de 1840, broadside. See also, Pedro de Ampudia, Cuerpo de ejército del Norte. 1ª Division, 2ª Brigada. Orden del dia 3 de Octubre de 1840, in *El Ancla,* Oct. 5, 1840.

[97] S. W. Jordan to Gen. Lic. Canales, Laredo, Nov. 2, 1840, in John S. Ford, "Memoirs," II, 238–241, ms.

however, despite the statements by other Mexicans who knew the route, insisted that they were on the right road to Saltillo, although he knew himself that this was not the road to Saltillo.[98] After some argument, he finally admitted that he was in error, having taken the wrong road from his ignorance of the country. By this act he lost the confidence of most of the Texans, but not of Jordan. The Federalists now retraced their steps, and the Texans, and probably a part of the Mexicans, spent the night of October 11 at Jaumave, while Molano and a few of the others stopped at Palmillas, nearby. In the meantime, Molano and López displayed great energy in "calming the torrent," said Molano, "that had no other object than to deprive me of command, perhaps assassinating me," and taking control of this contingent of Federalist troops.[99] It was at Pamillas, on the following day, that Molano received Arista's appeal of October 11 from Victoria to end the war, and it was from this time on, declared Molano, that "all my efforts were directed toward separating the Mexicans from the strangers."[100]

At 3 o'clock on the morning of October 12 Molano ordered the tobacco which had been brought from Victoria burned in the public square of Jaumave, and three hours later, after having encamped in the Jaumave area one night, the Federalists headed northwestward toward Saltillo, the capital of Coahuila. On the fourth day after leaving Jaumave, a youthful ranchero from San Antonio named Martinez[101] informed one of the Texan officers "that López and Molano were conducting their forces to a deep mountain gorge, wherein the Texans were to be butchered."[102] Jordan ordered a halt, and the Texans demanded an explanation. Molano and López were horrified. How could

[98] Molano later wrote in reference to his withdrawal from Victoria: "Later they [the Texans] noticed that my movement was not for Saltillo, city which they had chosen as victim for their ravenous prey." Juan Nepomuceno Molano á Señores Editores del *Ancla*, Matamoros, Marzo 1º de 1841, in *El Ancla*, March 15, 1841.

[99] *Ibid.*

[100] *Ibid.*; "Notes taken from a conversation with [José María] Gonzáles," in *Lamar Papers*, VI, 114.

[101] Yoakum, *History of Texas*, II, 292, says that Captain Peña of the mounted rancheros was the informant; and Virgil N. Lott and Mercurio Martinez in the *Kingdom of Zapata*, p. 112, in a garbled, confused version of Jordan's march from Victoria and of Arista's movements, mention the name of Captain Raul Peña of Guerrero as the informant. They say that Peña retired to Texas with Jordan and died in San Antonio in 1850.

[102] "Information derived from Augustin Soto," in *Lamar Papers*, VI, 115; Reid, *Reid's Tramp*, p. 74.

he (Jordan) even think of such a thing of them? They declared that his informer must be a personal enemy of theirs who wished to ruin them. The two Mexican colonels asserted most positively that they were on the most direct route to Saltillo and that there was no gorge in their direction. They declared, with hurt pride, that their intentions were honorable. Nevertheless, the course was changed, and the Texans, with their allies, crossed the Sierra del Cuauhchichil, passed through the small farm known as La Hedionda, and approached Saltillo from the south-southeast without further incident, except that within one day's march of Saltillo, Molano stated that the road ahead was fortified and that it would be necessary to diverge from the main route. A circuitous route was pursued until midnight when the Federalists halted at la ranchería de la Potosí the 22nd of October. The ranch abounded in forage and provisions. Here, in the vicinity of Buena Vista, made memorable a few years later in the war between the United States and Mexico, the Federalists remained until eight o'clock the next morning, within six miles of Saltillo. Doctor Shields Booker came in during the evening bearing an express from Canales with orders to take possession of the country and collect contributions from the enemy.[103] After much insistence on the part of Jordan, Molano now reluctantly ordered the boxes containing the captured guns to be opened and the muskets to be distributed to those whose arms were in poor condition. Ammunition was also distributed, but in such small quantities as to give general dissatisfaction.

Once more Jordan was warned against impending treachery. A Mexican soldier who had been detained sick at Victoria de Tamaulipas arrived in the Texan camp at la hacienda de la Potosí before Saltillo, bearing dispatches from an unknown person, who warned that the Mexican colonels were in correspondence with the Centralists. For some time the Texans had realized that Molano and López were in receipt of letters daily, and that the Texan officers never received any. Strong suspicions developed that Jordan's mail was being intercepted and destroyed. As a result Jordan protested, and thereafter "forged letters were prepared & delivered to him to allay his suspicions."[104] The new rumor of a "plot" deepened and greatly excited the suspicions of

[103] "Statement of Mr. P. F. Bowman, Buffalo, N. Y.," in *Lamar Papers*, IV, Part I, 238. Bowman was a member of Jordan's company.
[104] "Capt. Newcombe's Recollections," in *ibid.*, VI, 121; Bancroft, *History of Texas and the North Mexican States*, II, 329–331; Brown, *History of Texas*, II, 172–173.

the Texans. A hurried consultation among them resulted in a solemn determination that "if sold," their "delivery" should not be made with their consent. After checking their arms and moulding a few more bullets, the Texans laid the letter before Molano and López, who, "though wonderfully disconcerted, expressed themselves as feeling mortified that their fidelity should be questioned; and emphatically branded the charge as false—the author as a slanderer, and [a] Centralist, whose motive was to create a division in the Federal Army." [105]

The interview with the Mexican officers once more tended to allay the suspicions of a majority of the Texans, but not for long. Late the next night the friend of the San Antonio ranchero who had been bathing in the stream at Victoria at the time the Centralist agent had plotted with Molano and López, overtook the Texans before Saltillo, where he contacted Long. Long again warned Jordan of impending danger, and Jordan ordered that the new informer be brought before him for questioning. As a result of the interview, Jordan became apprehensive for the safety of his men, and charged them to be on the alert for treachery.

From his camp at Buena Vista Molano dispatched a messenger toward Saltillo, soliciting a conference with General Montoya. [106] At 9 o'clock on the morning of October 23, being prepared for battle, the Federalist forces began to move nearer to Saltillo. Reaching its vicinity at 1 P.M., at the hacienda del Refugio (now called Guerreadero, in memory of this action), some three miles to the south of Saltillo, they encountered the Centralists, reported Jordan, consisting of 400 infantrymen, 400 cavalry, and two pieces of artillery under General Montoya entrenched on a small hill. The Federalists possessed themselves of another eminence six hundred yards away and separated from the former by a barranca. The Federalists numbered 355 of whom 111 were Texans. [107] For the first time the Texans now became aware of

---

[105] Reid, *Reid's Tramp*, p. 75; Yoakum, *History of Texas*, II, 293. Some time later James Wilkinson told Lamar that Jordan only remonstrated with Molano, "but did nothing else." "The real fact," he said, "was that he [Jordan] had got to drinking, & had been drunk 3 or 4 days." *Lamar Papers*, VI, 130. The writer has found nothing in the numerous accounts given of the affair at Saltillo to collaborate the contention made by Wilkinson that Jordan was drunk on the eve of the battle.

[106] Juan Nepomuceno Molano á Señores Editores del *Ancla*, Matamoros, March 1, 1841, in *El Ancla*, March 15, 1841.

[107] Jordan reported, "Our whole force consisted of 231 men, 111 were Americans, 4 of whom, however, were sick, thus reducing my command to 107 men, rank and

a greatly superior enemy force, numbering 1,000 men including those left behind in the city and two 9-pounders under Generals Vasquez and Montoya. Unbeknown to them another Centralist army of about 1,000 men under General Juan Morales had taken up its position at Agua Nueva, seventeen miles out on the Saltillo road toward San Luis Potosí.[108] Arista had advanced from Victoria to Linares, where since the 21st he had been guarding "las salidas de la Sierra." [109]

Nevertheless, the Federalists quickly formed for battle, Jordan urged an immediate attack, "but Molano and López judged it best to send a communication to the enemy, offering him terms of capitulation," [110] but did not tell Jordan that they had already sent in an emissary to the enemy. At this point, a white flag was seen approaching from the lines of the enemy, no doubt in response to Molano's solicitation for a conference. Molano's "valor suddenly evaporated," and, instead of warning it away, he sent out a white flag of his own to demand what message the enemy's courier brought. The two emissaries met between the lines, and the Centralist messenger reported that the town was willing to meet any reasonable requisition if the Federal troops would not enter. The Centralist courier was now escorted within the Federalists' lines, where he was received. He stated that General Montoya wished to confer with Molano, who immediately left the Federalist lines, under an escort of several soldiers, none of whom were Americans, and passed over to the enemy's lines.[111]

In the ensuing conference with Montoya, Vasquez, and Licentiate Don Juan Ramos, Molano explained that he had been in correspondence with General Arista and produced letters and copies of letters to prove it. He declared that his "irrevocable decision" was to subject

---

file." S. W. Jordan to Gen. Lic. Canales, Laredo, Nov. 2, 1840, *Telegraph and Texas Register*, Dec. 16, 1840; typed copy in John S. Ford, "Memoirs," II, 238–241, typed ms. Samuel A. Maverick, reporting in general terms two years later, placed Jordan's battleground at Buena Vista, eight miles from Saltillo. Rena Maverick Green, *Samuel Maverick: Texan, 1803–1870: A Collection of Letters, Journals and Memoirs*, p. 181.

[108] Alessio Robles, *Coahuila y Texas*, II, 220.

[109] Itinerario de las campañas en Tamaulipas, Coahuila y N. León, desde 23 Febrero de 1839 hasta hoy 28 Marzo de 1841, in *El Ancla*, March 29, 1841.

[110] S. W. Jordan to Gen. Lic. Canales, Laredo, Nov. 2, 1840, in *Telegraph and Texas Register*, Dec. 16, 1840; typed copy in John S. Ford, "Memoirs," II, 238–241, typed ms.

[111] *Ibid.*; *Lamar Papers*, VI, 109; Mariano Arista to Pedro de Ampudia, Oct. 27, 1840, in *El Ancla*, Nov. 2, 1840.

himself to the authority of the supreme government with or without guarantees, "because I preferred to be immediately shot by my countrymen to continuing united to foreigners," he declared later. He demanded the fulfillment of the promises that had been made to the Mexicans who would lay down their arms, and "in respect to the foreigners," he reported, "I asked that they might be permitted to remain in the country to which they wished to belong peacefully, permitting those who desired to leave." [112] These terms, and others, being agreed upon, Molano says he asked permission to return to his camp for the purpose of putting the agreement into execution, but was not permitted to do so. It is doubtful if Molano was forced to go to General Montoya's headquarters as he implied later.

While Molano was away, Martinez "informed Col. Jordan, that a short distance to the right, in sight, was the gorge which it had been the purpose of the Mexican commander to march through." [113] Several times during the consultation between Molano and the Centralist leaders, the San Antonio ranchero, previously referred to, who had gone with Molano,

. . . returned with messages from Molano to López, and during each visit he slyly whispered to Long. López reported to Jordan that Molano had received a proposal from the enemy to pay into the Federal military chest $200,000 [114] and five days' rations to each man, provided the Federalists would not enter Saltillo; that M[olano] expected $250,000 and, that the negotiations were being continued. . . . Long's report . . . [based on that of the ranchero] to Jordan, differed from this; it being that Molano and the officers of the Central Army had agreed upon the amount which he and López should obtain for their intended desertion and instrumentality in having the Texans massacred; also, that they had agreed, that the best position in which the Texans could be stationed was in the mountain gorge; that M[olano]'s return was delayed till expected re-inforcements would arrive; and that on his return the attack would be made. [115]

There is little doubt that López was kept informed of Molano's negotiations and was well aware of his plans to separate the Mexicans from the Texans, and to annihilate the latter, if possible.

[112] Juan Nepomuceno Molano á Señores Editores del *Ancla*, Matamoros, Marzo 1o de 1841, in *El Ancla*, March 15, 1841.
[113] Reid, *Reid's Tramp*, p. 76.
[114] Anson G. Neal reported that Molano had been offered $50,000 not to sack the city. *Lamar Papers*, VI, 109.
[115] Reid, *Reid's Tramp*. p. 76.

Having concluded his arrangements with Molano, Montoya, now full of confidence of impending victory, hastily dashed off a note to General Arista, declaring, "the foreigners against whom I have directed all my means, must perish today; *you will tell me whether I shall shoot all, or only those who come last"* [116] to surrender.

When it was announced, or assumed, in the Federalist camp that Molano was being retained as a prisoner, López "cried out for . . . [his] rescue and urged Jordan to charge upon the foe." Jordan declared that he did not care to act hastily, but would like to know more about the strength, position, and design of the enemy before going into battle. He called in his scouts, and moved to a point where he could get a better view of the whole force of his opponent. With López, he chose a position for battle, and awaited the advance of the Centralists, but they did not move. Each side waited for the other to advance. As the day wore on Molano sent messengers at regular intervals reporting alternately progress and delay in the negotiations. About 2 o'clock in the afternoon a considerable re-enforcement belonging to General Montoya's command was received by the Centralists, and preparations were immediately made for an attack upon the Federal lines. The Centralists, besides possessing two cannons, now numbered over 1,000 men, of whom 400 were cavalry; whereas the Federal army had dropped to 150 mounted rancheros, 75 Mexican infantrymen, and 110 Texans, mounted, numbering in all less than a third of their opponents.[117]

Under these circumstances López now proposed that the Texans and Mexicans fight separately, and said "that he would move around the hill and attack the Enemy in the rear whilst Jordan charged him in front." The movements were to be carried out simultaneously, López pressing upon the rear and Jordan pushing upon them in front. The fire of the guns was to be the signal for Jordan to attack. López then formed the Federal troops in double column, the Texans in the rear, and ordered them to march to the right. The Mexican Federalist cavalry was to attack the enemy's right, while the Americans, as infantry, reported Jordan, were to advance to the enemy's left.[118]

At 2:30 P.M. the Federalists began their advance. The head of the

[116] Quoted in *Telegraph and Texas Register*, Dec. 16, 1840.
[117] Yoakum, *History of Texas*, II, 294.
[118] S. W. Jordan to Gen. Lic. Canales, Laredo, Nov. 2, 1840, in *Telegraph and Texas Register*, Dec. 16, 1840; typed copy in John S. Ford, "Memoirs," II, 238–241, ms.

Texan column was directed toward the place already indicated for the slaughter of the Texans. Captain Allen, suspecting treachery, "rode rapidly to Colonel Jordan and exclaimed: 'Where in the name of God, Sir, are you leading us? If you take us to yonder gorge, the enemy will not leave a man to tell our fate.'" [119] Hastily surveying the field, Jordan inquired if water was to be had on the right, and when he was told that there was none, he determined to follow López, who was making a left flanking movement. On went the front columns. Soon López's men began to round the hill, and when they had gone some distance, he halted and spoke to his men: he told his men that they were in eminent danger; that escape was impossible; and that if a battle ensued their destruction was inevitable. He declared that the only alternative was to "go over to the enemy." Colonel José María González [120] of Laredo "abhorred the sentiment, and urged the men to stick to their integrity." To this López turned a deaf ear and renewed the advance with his cavalry as if intending to bring on a fight with the enemy, now appearing numerous in the distance. As soon as he had approached to within three-quarters of a mile of the Centralists, López fired his guns into the air and shouted, "Long live the Republic of Mexico, kill the Texans," [121] and dashed off towards the enemy lines, followed by Captain García from Mier and many other members of the cavalry unit, discharging their guns into the air and shouting "death to the Americans." "The shout rang through his lines, and . . . most of the force followed their perfidious and dastardly leader," whose unit was soon blended with the enemy forces. González, still scorning the part of a traitor, "collected the few who adhered to his counsels, and told them that matters were rendered desperate by this treasonable act of Molano and López, and that they must now look to their own safety," for if they remained they could not save the Texans and their courage would only result in the destruction of all. The foe was too strong to be resisted, and flight became indispensable as well as right in their estimation. They must seek safety in escape through the mountains. González and his men appeared to follow

[119] Yoakum, *History of Texas*, II, 294.
[120] For González's account of what happened at Victoria and Saltillo, see *Lamar Papers*, VI, 132–133.
[121] Jordan reported that he yelled: "Death to Texas and [long] Live Mexico; follow me soldiers, and save yourselves." S. W. Jordan to Gen. Lic. Canales, Laredo, Nov. 2, 1840, in *Telegraph and Texas Register*, Dec. 16, 1840.

López for a short distance, and then "broke over the mountains" and were soon out of sight.[122]

The Anglo-Texans, assisted by a few Carrizo warriors,[123] were now left to their fate, betrayed by one party and abandoned by the other, with a large proportion of the already short supply of munitions having been carried away by the absconding groups. Hastily surveying the situation, Jordan "ordered his men, 'about face—to the left wheel,' and with a quick step marched them [along the bed of an arroyo to] . . . an old *hacienda* [known as El Oja del Agua], beyond the range of the enemy's ordnance." [124] Still undaunted, the Texans quickly prepared to defend themselves. But as the enemy were tardy in coming, Jordan became impatient from the inactivity. Finally, he decided to do what he could to bring on a fight, saying "dam them we can whip [them], as few as we are, and I will meet them half way." [125] So saying, he left his horses and a small guard at the corral of the hacienda and moved forward about half a mile. On perceiving this movement, the enemy sought to cut the Texans off from their horses by secretly falling into a deep ravine which Jordan's men had just crossed and which lay between them and their horses. Captain Newcomb, who had been left with a few men to guard the crossing of the ravine, discovered the design of the Centralist command, and gave the alarm in sufficient time for the Texans to fly back along the ravine to their horses. In avoiding interception by the enemy cavalry in the ravine, the Texans passed within 150 yards of the Centralist infantry. In their retreat, they

[122] "Further Information from Capt. Newcombe," in *Lamar Papers*, VI, 125–126; *Austin City Gazette*, Dec. 2, 1840. Jordan reported that the Federalist cavalry remained firm, many firing at López as he passed. The Centralist cavalry, he said, immediately attacked the Federalist cavalry, but the latter, deprived of their leader in whom they had put implicit confidence, offered but a feeble resistance, and in a few minutes retired to the mountains. They were not pursued by the enemy, who knew that they could not unite with the Texans under Jordan. S. W. Jordan to Gen. Lic. Canales, Laredo, Nov. 2, 1840, in *Telegraph and Texas Register*, Dec. 16, 1840. The governor of Coahuila informed the Minister of War that the Texans under Molano's command were defeated and that the Mexican troops under Molano joined General Vasquez's command. Nota del Gobernador de Coahuila Ignacio de Arizpe ál Ministro de la Guerra, Saltillo, 5 de Noviembre de 1840, in Archivo de la Secretaría de la Defensa Nacional, *Operaciones Militares*, 1840.

[123] *Telegraph and Texas Register*, July 13, 1842.

[124] Reid, *Reid's Tramp*, p. 78; Huson, "Refugio," vol. II, chap. 23, p. 18.

[125] "Further Information from Capt. Newcombe," in *Lamar Papers*, VI, 125–126.

were followed by a "great many peons . . . who hallowed at us," said P. F. Bowman, later a member of the Mier Expedition, "calling us robbers. Cameron fired at them and broke the leg of a peone, which was the first gun fired." [126]

The Centralist horde, variously estimated up to 7,500,[127] now moved forward from their entrenchment, and occupied three sides of the Texan position, the other side being protected by the mountains. In this manner, fortified by liquor and confident in their numbers, they slowly advanced under cover of their two nine-pound cannon and repeated volleys of musketry. Jordan ordered his men to withhold their fire until the enemy approached within easy range. Accordingly, "they lay snugly ensconced behind the old [stone] walls and an *adobe* fence, forming a half-moon" about a peach orchard, and, conserving their small quantity of ammunition, did not fire a shot until about 4 o'clock in the afternoon. In the meantime, the Mexicans kept up an intense and prolonged cannonade until 4 o'clock, when General Montoya, supposing from the extent of his own fighting that most of the Texans had fallen, ordered a general assault upon the hacienda. When the assailants came within thirty yards of the walls, the Texans gave them a shout of defiance, followed by a fearful volley from their rifles. The Texans fought desperately, but the enemy also fought well, being "cheered from the hill in their rear by the thousands of men, women, and children, who had come out to see *los Tejanos* taken. At that distance, the [Texan] rifle-bullets went on no foolish errand, but nearly all took effect. Column after column of the Centralists advanced, faltered, and fell under the murderous fire" of their opponents who fought like Tartars. Sometimes the little band of Texans succeeded in turning the enemy back only after he had gained within a few feet of their position.[128] Outnumbered ten to one, Jordan's little band, aided only by a Captain Lari and a Mexican bugler, beat off the repeated

[126] *Ibid.*, VI, 238; Brown, *History of Texas*, II, 174–175. P. F. Bowman was from Buffalo, New York.
[127] This figure probably includes a good many sight-seers from Saltillo. In his November 2, 1840, report of the battle, Jordan says the Centralist force numbered eight hundred cheered on by five hundred *"pelados."* S. W. Jordan to Gen. Lic. Canales, Laredo, Nov. 2, 1840, in *Telegraph and Texas Register*, Dec. 16, 1840; typed copy in John S. Ford, "Memoirs," II, 238–241, typed ms.
[128] Yoakum, *History of Texas*, II, 295–296. D. W. Smith to John Forsyth, Matamoros, Nov. 12, 1840, (no. 173) in Consular Dispatches (Matamoros), ms., microfilm.

charges of the men under Vasquez and Montoya, until at length toward dusk the ranks of the Centralists became disordered; a panic followed; and the enemy fled. "Soldiers, citizens, women, and children, all took the road to Saltillo, and in such confusion as though the Texans were in close pursuit at their heels!" [129] The enemy, reported Jordan, broke and fled in every direction, but as they retreated "their artillery commenced a severe fire with grape and canister," holding the Texans in check.[130] Seeing that the enemy were rallying and surrounding him in every direction as night approached, Jordan now decided to give up the Federalist cause and return to Texas.

The shooting seems to have been quite contrary to Montoya's expectations. In the bloody repulse, the Centralists had 408 killed and wounded and lost a great quantity of muskets and munitions, whereas, the Texan losses were 3 killed and 9 wounded, two of the latter mortally; [131] yet, Arista in his report of the battle, according to the

[129] *Ibid.* The late Vito Alessio Robles, one of the leading historians of Mexico, declared in 1946 that he had known for many years from the very old inhabitants of Saltillo that the Centralist troops, after having made the Texans flee, entered triumphantly the capital city of Coahuila. He recognized that there were different versions of the Centralist-Federalist battle circulating among the very old inhabitants of Saltillo. Vito Alessio Robles, *Saltillo en la historia y en la leyenda* pp. 231–234; Alessio Robles, *Coahuila y Texas*, II, 222 n.

[130] S. W. Jordan to Gen. Lic. Canales, Laredo, Nov. 2, 1840, in *Telegraph and Texas Register*, Dec. 16, 1840.

[131] In reporting on the battle, Jordan says the Centralists left upwards of three hundred killed and wounded on the field. The Texan losses, says Alessio Robles, following Jordan's account, were five killed and seven wounded. *Ibid.*; Alessio Robles, *Coahuila y Texas*, II, 222. Jordan listed as killed before Saltillo: Lt. James Gallagher, O. S. Stultz, Private ——— Woodruff; and as wounded: Captain ——— Allen, severely; Captain Still [Martin K. Snell]; Private ——— Bratt, mortally; ——— Wiggins, severely and left; ——— Beckham, slight; Sergt. ——— Blood; Private ——— Hull; ——— Blannerhasset/t/; Captain ——— Donnelly, died at Laredo. Missing at the time Jordan made his report at Laredo were: ——— Byrom, ——— Alsbroke, ——— Kelsenger, and Mustard Walsh. Jordan's report coincides with that later given by Anson G. Neal in regards to the Texan losses, except that Neal does not mention Stultz, Wiggins, Blood, Hull, or Donnelly, but does add that the Mexican bugler was killed. Two of the missing are probably accounted for, in part, by Arista's statement that "two prisoners were taken from those who escaped from Saltillo." Mariano Arista al Jesús Cárdenas, Cadereyta, Nov. 7, 1840, in *El Ancla*, Nov. de 23, 1840. Neal says Snell got separated from the command in crossing the mountains at Saltillo, remained in the country and taught school at Monterey. "Information derived from Anson G. Neal," *Lamar Papers*, VI, 111. The American consul at Matamoros

Telegraph and Texas Register,[132] represented "that the whole of the *foreigners* (Texians) were slain!" Such was "the sacrifice and slaughter of our misguided citizens," wrote James Love of Galveston, "who were rash enough to put faith in a misguided Mexican."[133]

Night descended. All was now so calm. Indeed, hardly a sound could be heard, save the cries of the wounded and the occasional dismal flapping of the wings of the fierce *zapalotes*,[134] now hovering over the Pass, or the distant and almost human yell of the hungry wolves, answered by others away in the gloomy recesses of the surrounding mountains. They were already beginning to gather in their horrible repast.

During the night the little band of Texans gathered up what personal gear they could take with them, destroyed the remainder,[135] collected their nine wounded, gathered arms and munitions from the enemy dead, mounted their horses and sought to escape through a pass in the mountains. As they entered the pass, the Texans found the Mexican cavalry and infantrymen planting a cannon there. The Centralists made a desperate charge, but once more fled under a hot and galling fire from the Texans, which caused many to fall, including their commander. Jordan's men turned and ascended a mountain ordinarily deemed impassable. Volunteer enemy troops from Saltillo, consisting of men, women, and children, according to one eye-witness account, stationed on the brow of the mountain rolled stones down upon the Texans[136] and received the "gringos" with a concentrated fire of muskets, but one well-directed fire from Jordan's men felled

reported to Washington that the Texan losses were six or eight killed and wounded. D. W. Smith to John Forsyth, Matamoros, Nov. 12, 1840, in Consular Dispatches (Matamoros), 1840–1848, ms., microfilm; José Cayetano de Montoya, *Comandancia militar de Saltillo. Á Señor Goneral [sic] en Gefe D. Mariano Arista*, Saltillo, Octubre 30 de 1840.

[132] Dec. 23, 1840. It was reported here that Jordan's command numbered 114.

[133] James Love to Dr. Anson Jones, New Orleans, Nov. 30, 1840, in Anson Jones, *Memoranda and Official Correspondence Relating to the Republic of Texas, Its History and Annexation: Including a Brief Autobiography of the Author*, pp. 156–157.

[134] The *zapalote* (za-pa-lo-te) is a specie of vulture with black body and wings. The head, tail, and tips of the wings are white. They fly by night as well as by day, and are very fierce.

[135] The *Austin City Gazette*, Dec. 2, 1840.

[136] "Statement of Mr. P. F. Bowman, Buffalo, N. Y.," in *Lamar Papers*, IV, Pt. I, 238.

many and put the remainder to flight. During the brief engagement, P. F. Bowman stopped to fix his gun, during which time a concealed Mexican snapped his gun at him three times, before a man named St. Clair [137] from Houston shot the Mexican in the head. The passage was now open to them and the Texans succeeded in crossing the mountain during the night, but in the dark and without a guide they got lost. They reached a valley where they found several boys herding sheep, but could gain no satisfactory information from them. A short time later while passing through a corn field, they heard the enemy cavalry approaching. As the popping of the cornstalks grew louder with the enemy's approach, Jordan's men dismounted and waited until they came within twenty paces before their captain ordered them to fire. Forty Mexicans fell, killed and wounded, and the remaining enemy cavalry fled hastily from the field. One Texan was killed.

Early the next morning the Texan vanguard learned at a rancho that they had been wandering circuitously and were only seven miles from Saltillo. They obtained accurate information from persons at the rancho, and pushed on as rapidly as possible, with the Mexicans following in their rear.[138] When the Mexican cavalry came in sight a man by the name of Mustard Walsh dismounted and fled to the mountains never to be heard from afterwards. As the Mexicans continued to draw closer, Grisenger, a German tailor from Austin, whose horse gave out, took off the bridle and saddle of the animal and shouldering them sought to follow his comrades on foot. He was advised to throw the equipment away as it would impede his travel, but he refused to do so. Soon he was taken captive by the Mexicans, and eventually taken to Arista's headquarters, where he was interrogated and, after being warned not to come to Mexico again to fight, was given ten dollars and told to go home.[139]

The next day the Texans succeeded in reaching the Monclova road under the guidance of a peon whom they had captured after leaving the rancho. Upon reaching the Monclova road, they found three of González's men, who had been left hidden in the chaparral along the road to assist those who might escape from the battlefield below Saltillo.

[137] Bowman gives the name as "Sinclair." *Ibid.*
[138] *Ibid.*; S. W. Jordan to Gen. Lic. Canales, Laredo, Nov. 2, 1840, in *Telegraph and Texas Register*, Dec. 16, 1840.
[139] "Statement of Mr. P. F. Bowman, Buffalo, N. Y.," in *Lamar Papers*, IV, Pt. I, 238.

After San Jacinto

The Centralists pursued closely, and it was no easy matter for the Texans to fight their way out of Mexico. However, warding off enemy cavalry attacks, they followed the Monclova road for some distance, and then turned eastward toward Candela, and thence northward through Santiago, La Presa, and Lampazos to Laredo. During the retreat they unexpectedly came upon 1,200 Centralist troops headed for Saltillo, who did not attack them but doggedly pursued them to Candela.[140] At Candela the Texans were joined on the 28th by González, who accompanied them to Laredo, where he resided. The enemy pursued them as far as Lampazos, a small town between two mountains,[141] seventy-two miles below Laredo; thereafter, without further molestation the Texans reached the Río Grande on the 31st and crossed to Laredo—their escape was an achievement which has been likened to that of Xenophon. At some forty miles below Laredo, Jordan's men were met by two small companies under Antonio Pérez and J. M. Menchaca, totalling some thirty or forty in number,[142] which in name may have been "a regiment," but in numbers was far from it. Pérez and Menchaca were sent from Laredo by Seguin, who had arrived on the frontier at that point, where word had been received of the betrayal of the Texans and of their flight.[143] In the retreat through the mountains of northern Mexico, Captain Lari of Zacatecas and Ewen Cameron led the way, and, "becoming separated from the command, never rejoined it." Cameron succeeded in reaching home safely to fight again against Mexico, but the fate of Lari is unknown.[144]

[140] "Information derived from Anson G. Neal, Laredo, May 30, 1847," in *Lamar Papers*, VI, 110–111.
[141] These mountains were plainly visible from the Río Grande.
[142] "Statement of P. F. Bowman, Buffalo, N. Y.," in *Lamar Papers*, IV, Pt. I, 239; Huson, "Refugio," vol. II, chap. 23, p. 14. Bowman reported Seguin with one hundred Americans at Laredo.
[143] "Information derived from J. M. Monchaca [Menchaca?], San Fernando," in *Lamar Papers*, IV, Pt. II, 70–71; Seguin, *Memoirs*, 20.
[144] "Captain Newcombe's Recollections," in *Lamar Papers*, VI, 127. "Capt. Lari, from Zaccateccas, followed us thro' the first campaign," said Neal, "and after the defeat of Canalis near San Fernando, went to Mexico; made fair weather with the Govt. but returned again, and joined us on the Nueces, went with Jordan thro' the whole campaign but was too terrified at Saltillo to fight. He was afraid to desert with Lopez, because he had once adjured the cause & had been forgiven by the govt. and he knew very well, if retaken he would find no quarters. He could neither desert nor fight. He remained hid during the battle, and whilst crossing the mountain with Jordan, he fled and has not been heard of since." *Ibid.*, VI, 111.

At Laredo the premeditated treachery of Molano and López was revealed to Jordan in no uncertain terms. Molano's pack mules had been left at Saltillo in the corral with Jordan's horses and other packs. When Jordan retreated, the mules with the trunks were taken along, and "in this way Malino' [Molano's] trunks fell into the hands of Jordan who brought them to Laredo. . . . When the Trunks were opened, the Correspondence between Molano and the Centralist Commandant at Saltillo was found; and by this means Jordan came to a full knowledge of the manner in which he had been betrayed and sold to the enemy. The whole was disclosed in the letters." [145] At Laredo Jordan and González quarrelled over the distribution of Molano's clothes. González claimed them, but Jordan would not give them up. From Laredo on November 2 Jordan wrote a report of his exploits.[146]

At Laredo Seguin informed Jordan he had received word that an agreement had been made between the Centralist and Federalist forces at Camargo, in which it was stated the Federalist officers were to be confirmed in the commands bestowed upon them by Canales, and that the Federals, both Mexicans and Texans, were to be given the option of joining the Centralists or receiving the pay promised by Canales and returning home.[147] Canales was reported to have informed Seguin that "he and all the Federalist leaders had resolved to join the Centralists on the terms proposed, which included a stipulation to join in an invasion of Texas now getting up." Seguin and Jordan proceeded to unite their forces, and two days after Jordan's men had arrived at Laredo [148] started down the east bank of the Río Grande toward Camargo to receive their pay, having no desire to become affiliated with the Centralists. On their way down they met Cárdenas at San Ygnacio, "who was going up to Laredo on some important business, . . . he said, but did not explain it." [149] Seguin and Jordan

---

[145] "Information from James Wilkinson," in *ibid.*, VI, 130. James A. Wilkinson was General M. B. Lamar's interpreter in Laredo, 1846–1847, and upon the organization of Webb County in 1848 was elected first chief justice of the county.

[146] The report was in the form of a letter from S. W. Jordan to Gen. Lic. Canales, Laredo, Nov. 2, 1840. A copy of this letter appeared in the *Telegraph and Texas Register*, Dec. 16, 1840, and is reproduced in John S. Ford, "Memoirs," II, 238–241, ms.

[147] *Telegraph and Texas Register*, Dec. 16, 1840.

[148] "Statement of P. F. Bowman, Buffalo, N. Y.," in *Lamar Papers*, IV, Pt. I, 239.

[149] "Information derived from J. M. Monchaca [Menchaca?], San Fernando," in *ibid.*, IV, Pt. II, 70–71.

continued their march, but in the woods off the road at el rancho Laja, near the Río Grande, they intercepted a courier, whom their men chased and captured. After a careful search of him, they "found in the sole of one of his shoes, a letter from Canalis . . . to Molano."[150] Upon opening and reading the letter, Jordan learned of Canales' plans to surrender to the Centralists. Canales, apparently not yet aware of the incident at Saltillo when he wrote, is reported to have written Molano that all was going well and that he was in the process of concluding a secret treaty with the enemy by which the Americans were to return home and the Centralists and Federalists were to end the war and once more become brothers.[151]

Jordan now dispatched Arriola and Menchaca with fifty men to hasten to Camargo to request Canales to remain there until he and Seguin could join him. They were ordered "to apprehend and hang him" [Canales], if he should attempt to leave, reported Menchaca.[152] When Arriola and Menchaca arrived before Camargo, they found that Canales had crossed the river, disbanded his Mexican troops, and had gone to Mier to confer with General Reyes. The two captains wished to pursue Canales and carry out the orders that they had received but Colonel Fisher objected, saying that Canales had stipulated in the treaty for the payment of the American soldiers and others before they were disbanded. This was the most that could be hoped for under existing circumstances, although it was becoming clearer all the time that Canales was a traitor to the cause he espoused and to the volunteers he had enlisted in Texas. Arriola and Menchaca gave up the idea of carrying out their plan to attempt a capture of Canales.

While Jordan had been marching toward Saltillo, Canales with about two hundred Mexicans and one hundred Texans led by Joe Wells,[153] a Houston bricklayer, and approximately eighty Indians advanced upon Marín, with the intent of pushing on to Victoria to join Jordan and Molano. Fisher did not accompany Canales in his march towards the interior, but remained behind at Camargo sick with the smallpox. Finding a large body of Centralists under Generals Isidro Reyes and Arista near Marín blocking his advance, Canales, after a brief skirmish in the Bosque de Gallo, retreated toward Camargo with Reyes'

---

[150] *Ibid.*   [151] *Ibid.*   [152] *Ibid.*

[153] *Lamar Papers*, VI, 117, 127; *El Ancla*, Sept. 28, 1840, says Canales had 200 Texans, 20 Indians, and about 80 countrymen; *ibid.*, Oct. 12, 1840, says Canales had 200 colonists, 80 Indians, and 30 Mexicans, and that Molano had 400 men, including 150 colonists.

cavalry, followed by Arista's infantry, "at his heels all the way. The Americans were anxious to halt and give Ariste battle, but Canalis always said," narrated Captain Newcomb who was not present, "that Ariste was too strong—it seems that it was not Ariste's desire to attack Canalis on his retreat, but to force him out of the Country without a fight. Every morning the buglers of Ariste . . . [were] heard in Canalis' Camp." [154]

Abandoning to Reyes and Arista his cannons, some provisions, some freight, and a part of the remount, Canales fell back toward the Río Grande without firing a gun, except in the Bosque de Gallo. During the retreat, Reyes' troops killed two of Canales' men and took four prisoners. Finally, Canales recrossed the Río Grande at El Rancho Clareño (five leagues from Guerrero) on October 17, in precipitate flight, having covered the distance from Marín to Clareño in six days, with General Reyes only three hours behind, alleging he could never catch up with the hasty retreat of the Federalist leader. [155]

Once more General Arista, "offering new guarantees," invited Canales to put an end to the war. [156] In the meantime, Arista halted at Montemorelos on November 1, where he remained three days due to the illness of eleven officers and one-fifth of his men who were suffering from intermittent fever. [157] Canales remained inactive on the east bank of the Río Grande and ultimately surrendered, largely as the result of a special appeal made by his cousin, José María Carrasco, and Padre Rafael de Lira of Candela. Padre Lira wrote Canales that if the Texans saw the Mexicans

shedding each other's blood in torrents, they will gladly lend us a helping hand; and if you, yourself, and all those that accompany you, were to perish in carrying out the plans you have proposed, they will dance for joy; for they wish not only to appropriate to themselves the beautiful and fertile lands of Texas, but to rob us of as much more of our beloved Republic as they can. . . . You ought no longer to reckon on your former friends; First, because they are only solitary spectators, or feeble enthusiasts.

[154] *Ibid.*, VI, 122.
[155] *El Ancla,* Nov. 2, 1840; Mariano Arista General en Gefe Cuerpo de Ejército del Norte á General D. Pedro Ampudia, Cuartel general en Linares, Octubre 27 de 1840, num. 43, in *ibid.*
[156] Itinerario de las campañas en Tamaulipas, Coahuila y N. León, desde 23 Febrero de 1839 hasta hoy 28 Marzo de 1841, in *El Ancla,* March 29, 1841.
[157] *Ibid.*

Secondly, because they reprobate your conduct, in the strongest terms, for uniting yourself with those Texian infidels. And thirdly, and lastly, because we can never forget the robberies, murders, and outrages which they have perpetrated on the persons of the best and most respectable citizens of our towns; so that even your own followers disapprove your conduct, except the few who surround you.[158]

Menaced by a superior Centralist force and deprived of the opportunity of finding another asylum in Texas by the treatment of his Texan allies at Saltillo, Canales sought to extricate himself from an unpleasant situation. From his camp at Los Olmitos, on the left bank of the Río Bravo, he wrote General Reyes on October 31 expressing fear of vengeance from the Americans after the way they had been betrayed at Saltillo and indicating his willingness to abandon the Republic of the Río Grande if given time "to arrange all matters" in regard to the surrender.[159] In response to Canales' appeal, General Reyes dispatched to Canales' camp late in the evening of the same day, Lieutenant Colonel José M. Carrasco, a cousin of Canales and a friend of Jesús Cárdenas, to call upon the Federalist leaders to surrender, to offer in return forgiveness for past actions, and to grant them a truce for eight days.[160] In reporting upon his conference with Canales and Cárdenas, Carrasco informed Arista:

They have confided in me their misfortunes, and the well known causes which forced them to recruit adventurers; but they have shown me clearly by written documents, and I have read in their hearts that they have never been traitors. They recruited soldiers in Texas, an enemy's country, that was their crime, but neither the Texian flag nor officers of that Government

[158] Rafael de Lira to Seignor Licentiate Don Antonio Canales, Mier, Oct. 12 [1840], in *Austin City Gazette*, Dec. 2, 1840; *Telegraph and Texas Register*, Dec. 16, 1840. For Carrasco's part in effecting the reconciliation, see *Austin City Gazette*, Dec. 30, 1840.

[159] *Telegraph and Texas Register*, Jan. 31, 1841; Antonio Canales to Isidro Reyes, Los Olmitos, Oct. 31, 1840, in *Gaceta del Gobierno* (Ciudad Victoria), Nov. 14, 1840, and *El Ancla*, Nov. 9, 1840.

[160] The terms of the Armistice which are dated November 1, as well as much of the correspondence concerning its drafting and transmittal, are printed in *El Ancla*, Nov. 16, 1840; *Telegraph and Texas Register*, Jan. 13, 1841; and in a six-page double column supplement to *El Seminario del Gobierno de Nuevo León*, no. 88, del Jueves 4 de Noviembre de 1840, which is headed: "Paz de la frontera de los Departamentos de Coahuila y Tamaulipas, y feliz union de los mejicanos para combatir a los usurpadores de Téjas," and published at Monterey, 1840.

directed their forces. This recruiting which might bring upon the nation immense evils, has produced general peace, and taught the Mexicans of the frontier that in vain they seek for brothers beyond their own country; and that foreign sympathies are those of interest, and are as abstract as the word.

The inhabitants of the Frontier saw and became acquainted with that horde of savages who are called a nation, without nationality, without origin, with laws written in the mouth of the pistol; arrogant and feeble, because they have not that point of union, that common sentiment which is country, and which is nothing else but the same origin and the land of our ancestry.[161]

The day after Carrasco's arrival in the Federalist camp, Canales penned a warm letter of acceptance to Reyes at Mier and outlined a plan for effecting the surrender. In offering "obstinate resistance" to party persecution, Canales revealed that he had "prepared so many means" that it was necessary for him to consult Reyes on "how to destroy them successfully."

I speak to you candidly, because it is incumbent upon one thus to speak to a friend. You are aware of the position which I occupy, and the motives which impelled me to take a determination which the greatest difficulties could not overcome. It only remains for you to know the number of . . . men at this time under my command, in order that with . . . your advice and experience, I may with ease extricate myself from my position without jeopardizing the life of any Mexican, or the munitions, arms, and other tren and baggage, which were over [last?] night at five leagues distance from this place [Los Olmitos]. I have in one camp 161 men, of whom 93 are foreigners. With [Rafael] Quintero are coming 258, of whom 43 only are Mexicans. With Juan Seguin are coming 213, of whom 43 are from Béxar and La Bahía.[162] The tren and baggage is coming with Quintero, also one piece of artillery, a 4-pounder. This is my force; I reveal it to you, because

---

[161] Quoted in *Telegraph and Texas Register*, Jan. 31, 1841. The *Seminario del Gobierno de Nuevo León* (Monterey) in its extra numbers of November 4 and 12, 1840, contains much of the correspondence between Arista, Reyes, Canales, and Cárdenas ending the Federal War.

[162] No doubt included in Seguin's count were Jordan's men. Thus the Federalist forces, as shown by Canales' statistics on November 1, numbered in all some 632 men:

	Foreigners	Mexicans	Total
Canales	93	68	161
Quintero	215	43	258
Seguin	170	43	213
	478	124	632

. . . you may thus be better able to advise me how to save everything. I have ordered Quintero to halt; on tomorrow he will begin to forward the supplies gradually to the river, and to cross them immediately at the ford of Carnestolendas [the Carnival]. To do it with more dispatch, it will be necessary for you to assist me with 20 or 25 pack mules on tomorrow

in order to lighten the burden of those carrying arms, as most of them are "loaded with three packs and are much fatigued." A similar number of mules had been requested from Camargo, but Canales was not sure that these would be available in time. "It will also be well," he continued, "that as many inhabitants as can be mounted should come on both sides of the river," in order that "we may with greater facility purloin everything from the view of the Americans," who, not counting Seguin's contingent which was not near, outnumbered the Mexicans in Canales' command three to one. In the meantime, special precautions were to be taken not to mention to the Texans in Canales' command "the occurrence at Saltillo." [163] "You may rely upon all on this side of the river" proceeding "with me on tomorrow to conduct the first loads. The inhabitants of this village who go to the ford of Carnestolendas will go from there in my company. If the Americans resist, it will be necessary to fight them; but I do not wish that they should do so, at least until the artillery and arms are in our possession." In conclusion, the Mexican colonel declared, "I hope to God that we shall soon have the Texians in a situation, that they will not be able to maintain even the territory of which they have robbed us, and that they shall know how much the Mexicans are worth when united." [164] Canales enclosed in his dispatch to Reyes a letter to General Arista, which he left open for the former's perusal, in which he declared

. . . our difficulties are at an end, peace has been restored, and confidence cemented, when we least expected it. On my part I assure you, that I have it at present in such a degree, that even without the necessity of a treaty, or guarantees I am disposed to surrender to you and to Gen. Reyes. The conduct of my auxiliaries [Texans] has caused me to dispair; and the occurrence at Saltillo has corroborated this determination; not on account of

[163] Apparently, as late as November 1, the Texans under Canales were unaware of the Mexican double cross at Saltillo.

[164] Lic. Canales to General Reyes, Camp at Los Olmitos, Nov. 1, 1840, in *Telegraph and Texas Register*, Sept. 7, 1842, and *Civilian and Galveston City Gazette*, Oct. 5, 1842.

what it may be worth in regard to my forces, but to prevent the atrocious vengeance which the Americans would take on the Mexicans who from henceforth may fall into their hands, and on the unfortunate settlers of this frontier, whose happiness, and nothing else, has been the object of my sufferings. Our war would have . . . ended since August last, had not the Texians intended to plant their standard along the whole northern bank of the Río Bravo, and in which case I should have ceased to be not only a Federalist, but a Christian, if you please, had I permitted this new insult to our country, and particularly to us Mexicans on the Nueces.[165]

Whereupon, Canales enclosed a copy of Captain Karnes' letter of July 26 and a copy of his own reply of August 4. He described Karnes as "the arrogant chief of Béxar," simply because Karnes had indicated that the President of the Republic of Texas was displeased with the pretensions of Canales that the boundary of Texas on the south was the Nueces and *not* the Río Grande as claimed by Texas.[166] It is believed that the letter was never actually transmitted to Karnes,[167] but Canales undoubtedly was glad to have Karnes' letter and a copy (or so-called copy) of his vigorous denunciation of it and Karnes to keep him from sharing Zapata's fate if his ambitious enterprise failed. Wrote Canales,

Karnes' letter is nearly destroyed from wearing it so long in my pocket, where I kept it with the view that had I perished in any battle, an evidence of my fidelity to my country should be found upon my body, to which I have been wrongfully and upon appearances only, denounced as a Traitor. A horrible baseness which I never will commit, not even against my most inveterate enemies, and no doubt much less against my country, to which I owe my most constant services! From this day, then, my friend, I am at your command; my friends shall be your friends; and all the forces of the villages of the frontier are united to you, to co-operate in the salvation of the frontier, and to avenge the national honor.

To Karnes' request that the Federalist leadership recognize the Texas boundary as being at the Río Grande, Canales, in making his peace with Arista, represented himself as having replied indignantly.[168] To

165 Lic. [Antonio] Canales to General Mariano Arista, Camp Olmitos, Nov. 2, 1840, in *Telegraph and Texas Register*, Jan. 13, 1841; Sept. 15, 1842.

166 Col. H. W. Karnes to Gen. Canales, Béxar, July 26, 1840; Antonio Canales to H. W. Karnes, Lipantitlán, Aug. 4, 1840, in *ibid.*, Aug. 31, 1842.

167 For the views of Karnes and Canales, see pp. 322–325 of this work.

168 *Ibid.*

Reyes, however, Canales admitted having permitted the Texas flag "once to be hoisted in the desert," south of the Nueces, for the purpose of securing the Texans "more effectually under the national flag," under which they were "to render their services." [169] His righteous indignation at Karnes' demand for recognition of the southern boundary of Texas at the Río Grande has a hollow ring when Canales, himself, at the very time Karnes' letter was supposed to have been written, was seeking a dismemberment of his own country and the creation of a northern republic.

Canales' hatred of the Texans, whom the Mexicans often called Americans, persisted, as is evident from a manifesto he issued as a general officer in the Mexican army, on April 4, 1847, urging "reprisals" against Americans and requiring his citizens "to give no quarter to Americans, whether armed or unarmed." [170]

Cárdenas, too, on November 2, the anniversary of Colonel Pavón's defeat, indicated his desire to terminate the war and to resume the one against Texas, having gained important information about that country during his recent visit.[171] Once more the specter of dismemberment of the Mexican nation had risen as in 1835 to cool the enthusiasm of the Mexican Federalists in their cooperation with the Texans. In 1835 the increasing number of outspoken demands for independence in Texas and for annexation to the United States had caused a number of ardent Federalists, opposed to the dictatorship of Santa Anna, to abandon temporarily their political views in the interest of maintaining the territorial integrity of the nation. Among them had been General José Antonio Méxia and Antonio Canales. Although the General Council in Texas had printed and issued on December 11, 1835, a statement that the object of the Texans was not independence, as the Centralists under Santa Anna were asserting, but the restoration of the federal constitution of 1824, and although the Council had appealed to the Mexican republicans for cooperation, Canales' agent, Captain Julian Miracle, who had gone to Texas, had apparently caught and reported the undercurrent of the sentiment among certain elements in Texas for independence and annexation to the United States.[172] The

---

[169] Lic. Canales to General Reyes, Camp at Los Olmitos, Nov. 1, 1840, in *Civilian and Galveston City Gazette*, Oct. 5, 1842.

[170] Quoted in Huson, "Iron Men," p. 56.

[171] Jesús Cárdenas to Mariano Arista, Nov. 2, 1840, in *Gaceta del Gobierno de Tamaulipas*, Nov. 28, 1840.

[172] Huson, "Iron Men," p. 6; Eugene C. Barker, *The Life of Stephen F. Austin*,

result was that most of the Federalists of northern Mexico either joined Santa Anna in his efforts to prevent a dismemberment of the Republic or remained neutral in the conflict which followed.

Upon the receipt of Canales' letter, Arista declared, "the barrier which was dividing us, in a manner, almost eternal, was destroyed, so soon as I had read Karnes' letter, and your worthy and patriotic answer. These documents are, no doubt, your vindication before your fellow-countrymen." Since, however, "I fear much for you," continued Arista, "and am uneasy, because I know the ferocity of these colonists [Texans], and the occurrences that have taken place in Saltillo, have inclined them secretly to a cruel vengeance," I am dispatching today "for your own security . . . General Vasquez . . . with 500 men and 3 pieces of artillery to be stationed where it may best appear to Gen. Reyes and to you" to facilitate the surrender and save the supplies and the Mexicans;[173] however, Canales was repeatedly cautioned not to expose himself "to become a victim of those cannibals, from whom your treating with us cannot be concealed. . . . Unite with the troops of the Supreme Government, [and] we will take from them much more than they can carry with them at this time." To Cárdenas the next day General Arista wrote: "I am solicitous for Sr. Canales. I have data from two prisoners who were taken from those who escaped from Saltillo of the vengeance they prepare in retribution for the conduct of Molano and López the 23rd of the past month."[174] In the meantime, the *Seminario del Gobierno* at Monterey, in a special number, heralded the return of peace to the frontiers of Coahuila and Tamaulipas and "the auspicious union of the Mexicans to combat the usurpers of Texas."[175]

On November 5 Canales dispatched three emissaries—Colonel Juan Nepomuceno Margain, Manuel de la Viña (in charge of the Commissary), and Rafael Quintero—to the right bank of the river to meet

pp. 422–426; Stanley Siegel, *A Political History of the Texas Republic, 1836–1845*, p. 26; Eugene C. Barker (ed.), "The Tampico Expedition," *Quarterly of the Texas State Historical Association*, VI (1902–1903), 169–186.

[173] Mariano Arista to Antonio Canales, Caderaeta [Cadereyta], Nov. 6, 1840, in *Telegraph and Texas Register*, Sept. 14, 1842; *El Ancla*, Nov. 23, 1840; *Seminario del Gobierno de Nuevo León*, Nov. 12, 1840.

[174] Mariano Arista to Jesús Cárdenas, Caderaeta, Nov. 7, 1840, in *El Ancla*, Nov. 23, 1840.

[175] *Seminario del Gobierno de Nuevo León*, Nov. 4, 1840, quoted in *Telegraph and Texas Register*, Jan. 13, 1841.

a similar number—Colonel Cayetano Montero, Lieutenant Colonel José María Carrasco, and Captain Francisco Schiafino—representing General Reyes, then at Mier, to arrange the terms of surrender. A convention was concluded and signed at 2 o'clock on the morning of November 6 on the right bank of the Río Bravo opposite Camargo, and was ratified by both Canales (in El Campo en el Rodeo) and Reyes,[176] and sent by the latter under special courier at 10 o'clock that night to General Arista at Cadereyta for his approval.[177] At the same time Carrasco sent word to Arista that "My Cousin Canales, I am sure, will be in these towns [of the North] your best friend and in my opinion your most active collaborator." Cárdenas, who had marched to Laredo, he said, had sent several agents to say that he was willing to quit. "This friend is frank; he is grateful to you," Carrasco wrote Arista, "and will never fail you because he is a gentleman." [178]

Meanwhile, on November 7, Arista gave approval of the armistice concluded between Reyes, commander of the Second Division of the Army Corps of the North (cavalry), and Canales.[179] Upon the arrival of the Convention on the 8th at Cadereyta, Arista quickly approved it, with a few minor reservations (it was said that he hoped, by his approval, to gain local influence and Canales' support for his own contemplated revolution).[180] To Cárdenas, "the philosopher," Arista wrote that by his surrender of arms a "real service" had been rendered to the frontier and to the whole nation; first, by bringing about peace and permitting the nation to defend itself from the barbarians; and,

[176] An English translation of the Convention is to be found in the *Telegraph and Texas Register*, Sept. 21, 1842; *Civilian and Galveston City Gazette*, Oct. 5, 1842; the armistice terms in Spanish are found in *El Ancla*, Nov. 16, 1840; the first news of the Convention being reached between Reyes and Canales was published in *ibid.*, Nov. 6, 1840; José María Carrasco to Gen. Mariano Arista, Camargo, Nov. 6, 1840, in *ibid.*, Nov. 23, 1840.

[177] Isidro Reyes á Mariano Arista, Cuartel General en Mier, Noviembre 6 de 1840, a las diez de la noche, in *ibid.*; see also, Antonio Canales to Gen. Mariano Arista, Camargo, Nov. 6, 1840, in *ibid.*

[178] José María Carrasco al Gen. Mariano Arista, Camargo, Noviembre 6 de 1840, in *El Ancla*, Nov. 23, 1840.

[179] Mariano Arista to Isidro Reyes, Cuartel General en Cadereyta Jimenez, Nov. 7, 1840, in *ibid.*

[180] *El Cosmopolita*, Jan. 23, 1841; Mariano Arista to Lt.-Col. D. José María Carrasco, Cadereyta, Nov. 7, 1840, in *El Ancla*, Nov. 23, 1840. The reservations will be found in the *Telegraph and Texas Register*, Sept. 21, 1842. Arista's approval of the Convention was dated Cadereyta, November 6, 1840, which seems to be a mistake.

second, by permitting preparations to be made for "the glorious march of the Mexicans to wash their transgression on the fields of Texas. . . . I shall have no peace," he said, "until I see this [war] terminated and all Mexicans secure! With what pleasure we shall fire our balls, with the conviction that they do not kill except those who are the enemy of the Nation and of our fellow countrymen." [181]

The Convention put an end to the civil war in the north. In Article I of the Convention it was stated that the Federalists, in the interest of promoting "the security of the frontier" and of all Mexicans from "the instant danger of exposure to the vengeance of the foreigners [Texans] who menace them," were sacrificing "their former pretensions, with a view of helping sustain the national dignity and decorum." By the terms of the Convention, the lives, liberty, and property of all who surrendered were guaranteed; prisoners taken by both sides were to be liberated immediately; and all officers and soldiers who formerly belonged to the regular army of Mexico were to be permitted to re-enter the regular service at their former rank, or, if they preferred, to receive their discharges.[182] The Centralist government was to receive and assume the liability for paying the vendors, often Texan or American traders, for two hundred rifles, five hundred muskets and bayonets, with accoutrements, and one hundred kegs of fine gunpowder "contracted by what was called the Provisional Government" of the Río Grande.[183] The Federalists agreed to surrender immediately one four-pound fieldpiece, with carriage and train, two hundred muskets with bayonets, fifty kegs of fine gunpowder, all equipment for sappers, engineers, and field armorers, and other equipment. Arista agreed to "receive into the national service and complete the payment of the steamer *Mediterranean* or *Ponchartrain* (at Matagorda) of 300 tons, armed with three pieces of large caliber, which," said the Convention, "is already paid for, and requires only fifteen hundred dollars for its repairs and demurrage; the *Loro* of 100 tons, for which a part is

[181] Mariano Arista al Jesús Cárdenas, Cadereyta, Noviembre 7 de 1840, in *El Ancla*, Nov. 23, 1840.

[182] In giving his approval to the Convention, Arista explained "That the regiment of the six villages of the North mentioned in the 4th Article, is considered to be organized in companies, with the title of 'The Defender of the Frontier,' according to the plan established in the departments under my command, with the approbation of the Supreme Government." *Telegraph and Texas Register,* September 21, 1842.

[183] See the Amendment to Article 8 imposed by Arista. *Telegraph and Texas Register*, Sept. 21, 1842.

paid; and two schooners, the *Cornelia,* loaded with supplies and equipment, and the *Abispa* (*Wasp*) the first manned with three guns, and the last with two, for which also a part is paid." These vessels were reported to be in Corpus Christi Bay under the command of Ribaud and Thompson. It was further agreed that the Texans were to be permitted to return unmolested to their country; and as there were among them a few Europeans who had sought a home among the Mexicans, Arista was authorized to permit them to remain in Mexico, "if he should deem it expedient."

In proclaiming the cessation of civil war as "the work of reason and of conviction," Arista announced that "hence forward united we will combat those savage and cruel enemies of our common country, to wrest from their impure hands the fertile territory of Texas which they have usurped. . . . This is a real day of glory!" [184]

The approved armistice reached Mier at 4 P.M., November 7, and Reyes at once sent it off in the care of Carrasco to Camargo with orders to remove all the effects of the Federalists to the opposite bank of the Río Bravo.[185] Reyes was instructed by Arista that if the "foreigners," when informed that they might retire, wished to argue about the matter, he was to unite his forces with those of Canales and force their withdrawal.[186] The supplies, munitions, and other effects of the Federalists were crossed over without damage; however, an artillery piece with troops was left on the other side of the river to protect against any hostile act from the discontented Americans, who were reported to have just marched towards the Nueces. Late the following day, November 8, Canales with the remainder of the Mexican troops who accompanied him reported to Reyes at Mier, "leaving only at the bank of the river a party of observation," the Texan adventurers having just departed. Accompanied by a great many officers, Canales entered Mier at night with all the train and the four-pounder. "The rejoicing," he informed Arista, "was of such a general nature that it

184 "Proclamation of Mariano Arista, Commander in Chief of the Northern Army Corps, to the troops of his command, Head Quarters at Cadereyta Jimenez, Nov. 8, 1840," in *Civilian and Galveston Gazette,* Oct. 5, 1842; *Telegraph and Texas Register,* Sept. 21, 1842; *El Ancla,* Nov. 23, 1840.

185 Isidro Reyes to Mariano Arista, Army Corps of the North, 2nd in Command, Division of Cavalry, Mier, Nov. 7, 1840, no. 69, in *El Ancla,* Nov. 23, 1840.

186 Mariano Arista to Gen. D. Isidro Reyes, Cuartel General en Cadereita Jiminez, Noviembre 8 de 1840, num. 63, in *ibid.*

seems that we should never have been divided," [187] and, declared Arista a short time later, in a proclamation to the inhabitants of Tamaulipas, Coahuila, and Nuevo León, we can all now turn our attention towards the "barbarous Indians" and Texan usurpers. "Peace! Peace! eternal peace among Mexicans! war, war, eternal war against Texans and the barbarous Comanches!" [188]

Waiting until he was securely protected in Mier by the Centralist troops, Canales just before setting out for Arista's headquarters on the 10th penned a brief note to Colonel Jordan and enclosed a copy of the convention he had signed with Arista ending hostilities.

By it, our persons and property, and the debts contracted by the provisional government, and by me, as commander of the forces, are guaranteed [assumed]. I have nothing more to desire, and the war we have been waging is now completely terminated. Therefore, the auxiliary Texian troops will retire to their homes, within three days after the date of this. The creditors only will remain and receive their dues. Any disobedience of this will be considered an act of hostility, and will be immediately resented.[189]

Having abruptly dismissed his Texan allies, Canales headed for Cadereyta on the 10th to give Arista a "close embrace" and to receive a twenty-one cannon salute; and before the end of another year had been named councilman for Nuevo León.[190] Together Arista and Canales proceeded to Monterey where a triumphal entry was made and the solemn *Te Deum* was entoned in the cathedral; and, in the presence of the august Dean, the two "comic chiefs" washed their hands and were blessed [191]—the one a traitor, who in the hour of defeat when his back was to the wall, was forgiven by the other, his opponent, who thought only of acquiring local influence for promoting his own revolution at some favorable time. "If the government does not seriously consider trusting the command of this frontier to another

[187] Lic. Canales to Mariano Arista, Mier, Nov. 9, 1840, in *ibid.*

[188] Mariano Arista, *El general en gefe del cuerpo de Egército del Norte, á los habitantes de los departamentos de Tamaulipas, Coahuila y Nuevo León,* Cuartel General en Monterey, Enero 3 de 1841, broadside, photostat.

[189] Lic. Canales to Col. Jordan, Mier, Nov. 10, 1840, in *Telegraph and Texas Register,* Dec. 16, 1840.

[190] *El Cosmopolita,* Nov. 3, 1841.

[191] "El Patriota" to the Editors of the *Censor* (Vera Cruz), Matamoros, Dec. 1, 1840, quoted in *El Cosmopolita,* Jan. 23, 1841.

general of better judgment, of greater skill, and of better intentions, this important territory," declared a writer under the name of "El Patriota" at Matamoros, "will disappear from the map of Mexico."[192] Yesterday Arista called Canales a "traitor" and a "criminal," but today in his letters he calls him his "good friend." Such was Mexican politics about which most Texans were so naive.

In the meantime, Cárdenas, acting under instructions from Canales, marched his men to Laredo, the erstwhile capital[193] of the soon-to-be-defunct Republic of the Río Grande, where the Mexicans laid down their arms and the Anglo-Americans retired to Texas, leaving much of the munitions in the hands of the Mexicans. As for the Texans, they had no desire to place themselves in the hands of General Arista, who had only recently characterized them as "those blood-thirsty enemies of our country," who are recruited from "the most filthy scum of the demoralized people of that country!"[194] Already many of the Anglo-Texans were restless and dissatisfied with the conduct of their Mexican friends, whom they had learned by bitter experience were Mexicans first and Federalists second. They feared further treachery. At the same time, the Mexicans had no desire to provoke another slaughter as had occurred at Saltillo. Consequently, the Texans were exempted from the capitulation and were accorded the privilege of either joining the Centralists or of receiving their pay and returning home, supposedly without molestation. Fisher and the Texans temporarily joined the Centralists "for the purpose of obtaining safety and protection until they . . . [could] find an opportunity of rejoining their countrymen."[195] They, however, retained their arms and separate organization, and their adhesion to the Centralist cause was entirely nominal and opportune. Canales made no provision for the Carrizo Indians, who had suffered so much in the seemingly endless struggle between Centralism and Federalism.

The Texans waited a few days around Camargo for their pay and

[192] *Ibid.*
[193] Paul Horgan, *Great River: The Río Grande in North American History*, II, 568, describes the capital as a "two-room adobe and stone . . . building on the high north bank of the river at Laredo."
[194] Mariano Arista, *El general en jefe del cuerpo de Ejército del Norte á los habitantes de los departamentos de Tamaulipas, Nuevo León y Coahuila*, Cuartel General en Vitoria de Tamaulipas, a 13 de Octubre de 1840, broadside. See also, "Proclamation of Mariano Arista, Head Quarters in Victoria de Tamaulipas, October 13, 1840, in *Austin City Gazette*, Dec. 2, 1840.
[195] *Telegraph and Texas Register*, Dec. 16, 1840.

for horses on which to return home.[196] During this time Colonel Fisher and several other Texans sent word by Dr. James Murphy, one of the first to return to Texas, that the Mexicans, who had been so loudly proclaiming their intent of castigating the "usurper," would not trouble Texas, as plans were being laid by five states to revolt shortly and form a separate government in northern Mexico.[197] Murphy reported one thousand to twelve hundred troops east of the Río Grande, mostly above Laredo, where they had gone to chastise the Comanches and repel their incursions. He estimated, in January 1841, that there were five hundred troops at Matamoros and a few at Saltillo, making, in all, a grand total of nearly two thousand men on this side of the mountains. Eventually, within about two weeks time, most of the Texans under Fisher's command had started for home, disappointed that their efforts had met with so little success and even less reward. A few tarried to see if they could not obtain payment for the supplies they had furnished. Among these was John P. Kelsey, who failing to accomplish his object, struck up an acquaintance with Don Mateas Ramírez, "a wealthy and influential Spanish gentleman" through whom he met General Arista. No doubt the two men developed an understanding in respect to the frontier trade, for Kelsey was in New Orleans in March 1841, acquiring an assorted stock of merchandise for a trading station at Corpus Christi, which he operated until September 1842, when he temporarily abandoned it.[198]

When Jordan and Seguin arrived opposite Camargo, they found the troops under Canales and Arista glaring "peacefully" at each other. Seguin advised his men to proceed immediately to the Nueces, as Canales had deserted the cause. As for himself, he would cross the river and seek to obtain their pay from Canales as provided for in the Convention, but his followers declared that they were willing to forfeit it, rather than that their leader should run the risk of being arrested. Seguin insisted on going, for he had personally expended

---

[196] During the stay at Camargo, Jack Palmer was murdered by a Mexican servant. *Lamar Papers*, VI, 111.

[197] Captain James D. Owen to Patrick Usher, Victoria, Jan. 26, 1841, in *Telegraph and Texas Register*, Feb. 10, 1841. Patrick Usher was nominated by President Houston for Chief Justice of Jackson County, and Senate confirmation was accorded on December 20, 1836. He later represented Jackson County in the Fifth Congress. Winkler (ed.), *Secret Journals of the Senate: Republic of Texas*, p. 34; Brown, *History of Texas*, II, 187.

[198] Brown, *Indian Wars and Pioneers of Texas*, pp. 759–760.

$4,000 in fitting out the volunteers in his command and the debts con-
tracted in the fitting out of the auxiliaries, according to the Convention,
were to be honored by the Centralist government which would obtain
possession of the Federalist property. Seguin had his way, and with
his interpreter crossed the river and proceeded to Mier,[199] where he
expected to find Generals Arista and Reyes. At Mier he found only
Reyes; but he was well received by him, and during his stay of three
or four days there he saw Vasquez come in with seven hundred men
and three pieces of artillery and heard frequent conversations relative
to an approaching campaign against Texas. The chiefs, officers, and
soldiers all seemed enthusiastic about such a campaign and anxiously
awaited the moment to begin the march.[200]

From Mier Seguin proceeded to Monterey to see Canales and to
have an audience with Arista about the pay of his men for which the
Convention made by Canales had called. During the course of his
discussion with Arista, the latter mentioned to Seguin his forthcoming
campaign against Texas. Seguin encouraged the conversation, as he
later said, for the purpose of gaining as much valuable information as
possible, and it was soon being reported from Monterey that Don
Juan Seguin, the "commander of a party of Strangers [Texans] and
Bejarenos," who had come to join Canales, had presented himself to
General Arista, making known to him his decision in favor of the
cause of the fatherland and "the most profound aversion to the usurpers
of our territory" against whom he now offered his good services.[201]
Seguin had several conversations with Arista until the latter realized
that Seguin did not contemplate entering the Mexican service and
withdrew from further conversation on the campaign.[202] As for paying

[199] Why Seguin would need an interpreter in dealing with the Mexican officials
is difficult to say. Maybe he felt he would come in contact with Anglo-Americans
or Englishmen. Some of the Americans crossed the river into Mexico after the
surrender. Seguin's proficiency in English was very limited. When he represented
Béxar County in the Senate of the Fourth Congress, he found it necessary to have
an interpreter. That person was William P. Lewis, and later in the session, George
Fisher. Harriet Smither (ed.), *Journals of the Fourth Congress of the Republic of
Texas*, I, 37, 71.

[200] J. N. Seguin to the President of the Republic of Texas [Lamar], Austin, Dec.
26, 1840 (translation), Domestic Correspondence (Texas), 1836–1846, ms.;
Telegraph and Texas Register, Feb. 3, 1841.

[201] *El Ancla*, Dec. 7, 1840.

[202] J. N. Seguin to the President of the Republic of Texas [Lamar], Austin,
Dec. 26, 1840 (translation), Domestic Correspondence (Texas), 1836–1846, ms.

Seguin's men, Arista flatly refused to make any payments, saying he had to seek advice in Mexico City. Losing hope of securing any remuneration for himself and the services of his men, Seguin returned to Texas in December.[203]

In the meantime, Canales sought to prevail upon Jordan to bring his men across the river to receive their pay, which seemed to be no more than a ruse to get them on the Mexican side of the Río Grande, but Jordan unhesitatingly declared that he had been betrayed once and if he should be betrayed a second time, it would be his own fault. He left it optional with his men whether they wished to cross or not. A few crossed, but Jordan and a majority of those under him returned to Texas.[204] Jordan proceeded to Austin which place he reached on Saturday, December 11, where he was, unlike Ross the year before, accorded a hero's reception.[205] Those who crossed the river were imprisoned by Arista for two months, first at Camargo and afterward at Matamoros, and then turned loose without pay to return home by way of New Orleans.[206] Thus ended the so-called Republic of the Río Grande, but the idea continued to haunt Colonel Fisher and others of the disbanded "filibusteros" whose tastes for civil pursuits had been destroyed by their revolutionary activities and occasional forays into Mexico.

[203] Seguin, *Memoirs*, p. 20; *Telegraph and Texas Register*, Jan. 6, 1841.

[204] [Capt.] James D. Owen to Patrick Usher, Victoria, Jan. 26, 1841, in *Telegraph and Texas Register*, Feb. 10, 1841.

[205] *Telegraph and Texas Register*, Dec. 16, 1840, gives a report of Jordan's arrival at Austin. See also, *El Ancla*, Jan. 25, 1841; *Texas Sentinel*, Dec. 12, 1840.

[206] *Lamar Papers*, VI, 111–112; Capt. James D. Owen to Patrick Usher, Victoria, Jan. 26, 1841, in *Telegraph and Texas Register*, Feb. 10, 1841.

CHAPTER FIFTEEN

Invasion Excitement

IN HIS ANNUAL MESSAGE to Congress on November 4 Lamar took a dim view of the negotiations going on in Mexico.

Resentful of any indignities that may be offered our Country [he declared] I should be strongly tempted as an individual to adopt a course, in common with the feelings of many, which would be calculated to accelerate the movements of our foe; but as a public functionary looking with an exclusive eye to what I conceive to be the true interest of the Country, I am constrained to admit that there are considerations of a cogent nature, why we should persevere for a while longer in our pacific policy, rather than resort at the present crisis, to any active and vigorous measures against our enemy.

The "considerations of a cogent nature" were the insuperable obstacles of a depreciated currency and an already heavy debt, which, if increased would impose so heavy a burden upon the people as to crush their prosperity for many years to come.[1]

While Lamar was convinced, at least for the time being, of the futility of aggressive military action against Mexico, there lurked in official circles in Mexico in 1840–1841 a hope of invading Texas. The Federalist forces had been disbanded, and the wily Canales had joined the Centralists with the rank of major general in the Army of Mexico. Arista proceeded to reorganize and revitalize the system of frontier defense. As early as December 15, in a circular letter to the governors of the eastern departments, he announced that, the civil war being over, it was time to prepare for an all out campaign against the In-

[1] Mirabeau B. Lamar to Fellow Citizens of the Senate and House of Representatives, Executive Department, Austin, Nov. 1, 1840, in *Lamar Papers*, III, 464–470. Although dated November 1 in the *Lamar Papers*, and in the Record of Executive Documents from the 10th Dec. 1838 to the 14th Dec. 1841 (Pres. Mirabeau Buonaparte Lamar), ms., pp. 204–218, this message was presented to Congress on November 4. See Texas Congress, *Journal of the House of Representatives of the Republic of Texas: Fifth Congress, First Session, 1840–1841*, pp. 15–16.

dians. He reported that the settlements in Tamaulipas on both sides of the Río Grande, known as the "villas del Norte," had generously offered to provide seven hundred mounted men, armed and provisioned for one month in the field. Three weeks later he again referred to the opportunity afforded by peace at home to carry on a war against the Indians and for a campaign against Texas, too.[2] He ordered the formation of squadrons of *defensores* for the frontier.[3] In the principal northern towns four squadrons and one company were to be formed under the name of "Defensores de la Frontera." Each squadron was to be under the command of a "commandant" and an "assistant commandant" or "adjutant," and to be composed of two companies, each consisting of a captain, one lieutenant, two ensigns, one first sergeant, four second sergeants, six corporals, two buglers, and forty-two privates. A squadron was to be formed in each of the towns of Guerrero, Mier, Camargo, and Reinosa; and a company was to be organized at Laredo, a town within the boundary claimed by Texas. The chiefs and officers of each company were to be appointed by Arista, and the sergeants and corporals were to be named by the captains. Those who participated in these organizations would be exempt from service as couriers and *cordilleras* (rangers), and their horses would be exempt from seizure for auxiliaries or transportation. The *defensores* would be subject to the orders of the military commandant of the town when he should find it necessary to make war against the Indians or the colonials (Texans).[4]

At this time, as usual when there were not too many other pressing distractions confronting the government of Mexico, there was some talk of renewing the Texas campaign. A circular, dated October 10, 1840, called upon the governors of the various departments, prefects in the towns, and diocesean leaders to urge support of the government's campaign to restore Texas to the union.[5] Talk of a Texas cam-

[2] Mariano Arista, *El general en gefe del cuerpo de Ejército del Norte á los habitantes de los departmentos de Tamaulipas, Coahuila y Nuevo León*, Cuartel General en Monterey, Enero 3 de 1841, broadside, photostat.

[3] Mariano Arista, *General en gefe del cuerpo de Ejército del Norte, á Exmo. Sr. Gobernador del departamento de* ———, Cuartel general en el Saltillo, Diciembre 15 de 1840, broadside.

[4] Mariano Arista, "Cuerpo de Ejército de Norte, General en gefe [Mariano Arista], Monterey, Enero 23 de 1841," in *Gaceta del Gobierno de Tamaulipas*, March 13, 1841, circular, photostat.

[5] *Colección de leyes y decretos, publicados en el año de 1839* [and 1840], pp. 791–793.

379

paign usually served as a good excuse to raise money and troops to bolster the administration and at the same time as a way to avoid any appearance of desiring seriously to negotiate a peaceful settlement which would in any way seem to approve what had happened in Texas.

In the meantime, while Arista was effecting a reorganization of the frontier forces, the suspicions of the Texans were once more aroused by the prospects of a Mexican invasion.

Captain William Thompson of the schooner *Wasp* left Corpus Christi on December 2, 1840, for San Luis, where he reported an attack was hourly expected upon Aubrey & Kinney's rancho by three hundred men under Rodríquez, who, it was said, were being sent to destroy the rancho. If such were the intentions of Rodríquez, declared Thompson, a party of twenty-five men at the rancho, with one twelve-pounder, plenty of small arms and ammunition, and some picketing for fortification was determined to defend the property and their homes.[6]

About midnight, December 1, 1840, a party of some fifty Mexicans under the command of González,[7] supposedly from Brazos de Santiago, entered Corpus Christi Bay in a large boat and attempted to capture or steal the sloop *Phoenix* belonging to the firm of Aubrey & Kinney. Boarding the vessel, they ordered her crew to remain below deck, while they shipped the anchor, hoisted sail, and sought to take the vessel out of the harbor. While attempting to tack, they ran the *Phoenix* ashore; whereupon, the Mexicans ordered the crew on deck and without allowing the men time to clothe themselves, took them prisoners aboard their own vessel, destroyed the sails of the sloop, and headed for the open gulf, presumably bound for home. The two Texans who were taken captive were John Allen of San Luis, Texas, and James Gibson of Galveston. The mate, Mr. Hurd, remained secreted below deck on the *Phoenix*,[8] and thus avoided capture. Captain Litting, of the sloop, was on shore at the time and also avoided capture. When this incident came to the attention of General Arista, he declared that González was not in the government service, and upon the latter's return to Mexico, had him arrested by General Ampudia and held in close confinement at Matamoros, where he was reported

[6] *Telegraph and Texas Register* (Houston), Dec. 16, 1840.
[7] *Ibid.*, Jan. 20 and 27, 1841.
[8] *Ibid.*, Dec. 16, 1840. One of the Texans, I do not know which one, was reported to have been murdered by González. *Ibid.*, Jan. 27, 1841.

later to have been brought to trial and condemned to execution by a firing squad.[9]

A Mexican party of between fifty and sixty soldiers under Rodríquez [10] left Matamoros on December 14 with orders from Arista to take the property left at Corpus Christi by Canales. This was apparently the party to which Captain Thompson had reference. When the party reached Corpus Christi it did not find the property it had been sent to take possession of, for that had already been appropriated by sundry private parties; so Rodríquez left without disturbing or destroying anything at the rancho.[11]

Two days after Rodríquez left Matamoros, Juan Ignacio started from there, too, for Texas. He brought word that a large expedition was being prepared for a renewal of the Texas campaign. James Campbell informed Burnet, Acting President, that he had talked to Ignacio, upon whose statements reliance could be placed. Ignacio reported about six thousand troops on this side of the mountains, and said that he had heard that others were on their way to make up an invading force of twenty thousand men, but believed that not more than fifteen thousand men could be brought into the field against Texas. The Mexican government had already obtained a loan of two or three million dollars, and General Adrián Woll had recently been to New Orleans to obtain supplies. Ignacio declared that four hundred men had left Matamoros for San Patricio on December 12 and that another eight hundred were on the way from Mier. Campbell further said reports arriving at San Patricio confirmed Ignacio's statements.[12] In preparation for the invasion, all the cattle this side of the Río Grande had been collected "low down by Matamoros," where they were being guarded by two hundred troops. The number of cattle was estimated at 100,000 head. Most likely, these cattle were concentrated near Matamoros to protect them from the Texas cowboys.[13]

[9] *Ibid.*, Jan. 20 and 27, 1841; *Civilian and Galveston Gazette*, Jan. 25, 1841.

[10] *Telegraph and Texas Register*, Dec. 16, 1840.

[11] *Ibid.*, Jan. 27, 1841; *Colorado Gazette and Advertiser* (Matagorda), Feb. 6, 1841.

[12] James Campbell to David G. Burnet, Austin, Dec. 28, 1840, in Domestic Correspondence (Texas), 1836–1846, ms.

[13] "No doubt half of the cattle and horses that are stolen and charged upon the Indians, are taken either by white men of the vilest class, or negroes," reported a visitor to the frontier in a letter to the editor of the *Telegraph and Texas Register*, dated Dec. 4, 1840, and printed in the *Telegraph and Texas Register*, Dec. 16, 1840.

Colonel Jordan, fresh from his campaign in northern Mexico, appeared in Austin on December 5, and what he reported caused the Austin *Sentinel* to run out "another Extra, flaming, for the one thousandth time, with Mexican invasion, fire and thunder." The Mexicans were made out to be six thousand strong "carrying or to carry horrors in their train," laughed the editor of the Houston *Telegraph,* "when the truth is that all the troops under Arista, could be enclosed in a *wolf-pen*—but perhaps this fact will not quiet the fears of the major," George W. Bonnell, publisher of the *Texas Sentinel.*[14] The Houston *Morning Star* commented: "Another Mexican invasion is frightening the *editors,* women, and children of Austin."[15]

The renewal of the invasion threats by the Mexican consul at New Orleans[16] and by Arista on the Río Grande stirred Texans to action. Congress was in session; a bitter debate over the Cherokee land bill. was in progress, and the people of Austin were pictured as "quite full of fight."[17] Amid the excitement, tempers were short. Colonel Jordan and General Houston had bitter words the night of December 8, "which ended in Jordan striking Houston with a stick."[18] The next day the two patched up their differences, but the excitement over a possible invasion continued to increase.

A dispatch from Major George T. Howard,[19] commander of the Texan forces at San Antonio de Béxar, reached the War Department in Austin on December 10, stating that he expected an immediate attack to be made on San Antonio by a Mexican army from the Río Grande,[20] numbering some seventeen hundred men.[21] According to

[14] *Telegraph and Texas Register,* Dec. 16, 1840.
[15] Quoted in *ibid.,* Dec. 30, 1840. [16] *Ibid.,* Dec. 30, 1840.
[17] K—— to the Editor of the *Colorado Gazette,* Austin, Dec. 9, 1840, in *Colorado Gazette and Advertiser,* Dec. 19, 1840.
[18] *Ibid.* Jordan reached Austin on December 5. Adolphus Sterne recorded in his diary under date of December 10 that Jordan would have attacked Houston with an ax if it had not been for his (Sterne's) interference. Harriet Smither (ed.), "Diary of Adolphus Sterne," *Southwestern Historical Quarterly,* XXXI, (1927–1928), 80.
[19] George T. Howard was commissioned sheriff of Béxar County in April or May 1840. Joseph Waples to John S. Simpson, Chief Justice [of] Béxar County, Department of State, Austin, May 4, 1840, State Department Letterbook, no. 1, ms., p. 174, enclosing commission for Howard as sheriff of Béxar County.
[20] George H. Flood to John Forsyth, Legation of the U. S. A., City of Austin, Dec. 11, 1840 (vol. 1, no. 10), in "Correspondence and Reports of American Agents and Others in Texas 1836–1845," Justin H. Smith, "Transcripts," V, ms.
[21] *Telegraph and Texas Register,* Jan. 27, 1841.

some reports the troops were already on the march for the Nueces; whereas, other reports said they were awaiting the orders of Arista. A larger force was said to be on the march north from the interior of Mexico.[22]

Upon the receipt of the dispatch from San Antonio, Secretary of War Archer immediately ordered Major Howard to maintain scouts to the west and particularly to watch the crossings of the rivers to the west of San Antonio and to keep the War Department informed.[23]

Although anxious to comply with the instructions he had received, Howard complained from his headquarters at the Alamo that the horses at Post San Antonio were in such a poor condition that he could only carry out the orders very slowly. Besides, he had only one keg of musket powder on hand. His situation was expected to be somewhat improved with the arrival of Lieutenant Lewis' detachment the next day (December 17). Major Howard recommended that all communications between San Antonio and the Río Grande by traders be intercepted, "for I am certain," he said, "that the majority of them are Centralists, and our enemies." [24] Some envelopes which he had found, "of letters carried in by them, addressed to suspicious individuals of this place, convinces me," he continued, "that the sooner the trade is stopped the better." He went on to say that he had received information that on the night of December 14 "a courier had arrived in town in great haste" from the Río Grande, and since then it had been rumored that Captain Arriola, Captain Antonio Pérez, and Colonel Seguin, all of Béxar, had accepted commissions in the Centralist service.[25] In conclusion, Howard suggested the purchase of three or four good American horses to be used by the Texan spies. Such horses, he believed, could be obtained at San Antonio for $150–$200 in par money. The War Department however, had not one dollar at its command, and could not, the Secretary informed the President "extend to

---

[22] *Ibid.*

[23] This particular order has not been found, and the statements in this paragraph are based on information gleaned from the references listed in footnotes 24–26 of this chapter.

[24] George T. Howard to Branch T. Archer, Post San Antonio, Dec. 16, 1840, Army Papers (Texas), ms.; also printed in Texas Congress *Journals of the House of Representatives, Fifth Congress, Appendix*, pp. 374–375; David G. Burnet to the Senate and House of Representatives, Executive Department, Austin, Dec. 21, 1840, in *ibid.*, p. 322.

[25] *Ibid.*, p. 322.

the troops at Béxar the munitions of war necessary for their defence." Even though the necessary powder and lead were available in the arsenal at Austin there were no means to pay for its transportation.[26] A few days later Congress upon urging of the Executive, made provision for transporting certain necessary items to San Antonio.[27]

In the midst of this crisis, Lamar on December 12 asked for and was granted a leave of absence by Congress to go to the United States for treatment for an intestinal disorder. Vice President David G. Burnet then became Acting President "under the most dark and inauspicious circumstances," [28] and continued in that capacity until Lamar's return to the capital on March 5, 1841,[29] after Congress had adjourned. What Lamar and Samuel A. Plummer, who was in New Orleans at the same time on personal business and recruiting activity for Texas, may have plotted in respect to a Mexican campaign has not been resolved. Lamar, no doubt, took the opportunity to explore with leading persons in New Orleans the idea of an expedition to Santa Fé, New Mexico.

Congress on December 14 called for a report on the status of the First Regiment of Infantry since its organization in January 1839, and Colonel Hugh McLeod, Adjutant and Inspector General of the Texas Army, reported on December 17 that out of 674 men recruited, 169 had deserted, of whom only 61 had been apprehended; honorable discharges had been issued to 48 and dishonorable ones to 7; 24 had died; 13 had been killed; and 3 executed by order of a General Court-Martial. Thus 465 still remained in active service.[30] Obviously, such a

[26] B. T. Archer, Secretary of War, to David G. Burnet, War Department, City of Austin, Dec. 19, 1840, in *ibid.*, pp. 374–375.

[27] H. P. N. Gammel (ed.), *Laws of Texas*, II, 474–476.

[28] *Telegraph and Texas Register*, Dec. 23, 1840; Mirabeau B. Lamar to the Senate and House of Representatives, Executive Department, Dec. 12, 1840, in Record of Executive Documents from the 10th Dec. 1838 to the 14th Dec. 1841, ms., pp. 222–223. Lamar went to New Orleans for medical treatment. E. W. Winkler (ed.), *Secret Journals of the Senate: Republic of Texas, 1836–1845*, p. 190 n; Herbert Pickens Gambrell, *Mirabeau Buonaparte Lamar: Troubadour and Crusader*, p. 261; Sam Houston Dixon and Louis Wiltz Kemp, *The Heroes of San Jacinto*, p. 301.

[29] J. S. Mayfield to David G. Burnet, Department of State, Austin, March 5, 1841, in State Department Letterbook, no. 1, ms., p. 213.

[30] "Statement of the First Regiment of Infantry since its Organization, Jan., 1839, as required by a resolution of the Hon. Congress, adopted 14th Dec., 1840, Adjutant and Inspector-General's Office, Austin, Dec. 17, 1840, and signed: H. McLeod, Adj. & Insp.-Gen., Texas Army, Texas Congress, *Journals of the House of Representatives, Fifth Congress, Appendix*, p. 376.

force was wholly inadequate for carrying on offensive war against a nation of eight million people.

Four days after assuming the presidency, Burnet, in a "wild message" to Congress, based on intelligence received the evening before from the west that Mexico was "again marshalling her forces for the invasion of Texas," declared that a resort to the sword cancelled all previous pledges and opened the way to a new adjustment. He recommended that Texas take immediate action to end for all times its controversy with Mexico. "Let the decision be prompt and final." "Texas proper," he declared, "is bounded by the Río Grande—Texas as defined by the sword may comprehend the Sierra del Madre. Let the sword do its proper work"; [31] whereupon, he transmitted to Congress a project submitted to him by Major General Felix Huston of the Texas Militia for an offensive campaign against Mexico and "cordially" recommended its adoption.[32] Huston proposed that one regiment be drafted from each militia brigade to serve for a six months period, if not sooner discharged. He suggested that a regiment from the First Brigade be called into immediate service and stationed at Gonzales, and that the regiments from the other brigades be placed in readiness for action whenever called out. Huston also recommended that a volunteer company of artillery be recruited for twelve months' service and stationed at Gonzales under such officers as the President might name. He also suggested the appointment of an officer to recruit as many men as could be enrolled at Victoria and west thereof to serve for six months. For the appointment, he recommended Captain S. W. Jordan (to be given the rank of major) as the best qualified by frontier experience.[33] "There is a smell of saltpetre about this," commented the editor of the *Telegraph*.[34]

Burnet's message and recommendations were presented in the House of Representatives on December 17, where they were referred to the

[31] David G. Burnet to Congress, Executive Department, Austin, Dec. 16, 1840, in Texas Congress, *Journals of the House of Representatives of the Republic of Texas: Fifth Congress, First Session, 1840–1841*, pp. 292–293; David G. Burnet, *Message of the President, on the Subject of Our Mexican Relations*; *Telegraph and Texas Register*, Jan. 6, 1841.

[32] Huston's report, submitted to the President on December 16, 1840, was printed in David G. Burnet, *Message of the President, on the Subject of Our Mexican Relations*; *Telegraph and Texas Register*, Jan. 6, 1841.

[33] Felix Huston to David G. Burnet, President of Texas, Austin, Dec. 16, 1840, *ibid.*; *Telegraph and Texas Register*, Jan. 6, 1841.

[34] *Telegraph and Texas Register*, Dec. 30, 1840.

joint committee of Congress which had already under consideration the Republic's relations with Mexico. On the 18th the committee reported that it was in full agreement with the Executive in the urgent necessity of placing the frontier of the Republic "most exposed to Mexican invasion in the best possible condition of defence." It felt, however, that Mexico, knowing that her former province was "forever and irretrievably lost," merely intended to harass Texas. The tone of the report urged caution, preparedness, and a firm determination to repel any attack.[35]

Meanwhile, in Mexico City the negotiations of James Treat had come to an end. Discouraged and ill, Treat left Mexico for Texas. While on his way home on the Texan schooner of war, *San Antonio*, he died of consumption on November 30, 1840. His body was brought back to Texas for burial at Galveston. With colors at half mast and the firing of minute guns, the *San Antonio* announced its sorrowful message as it sailed into Galveston harbor on December 9.[36]

In notifying Congress on the 19th of the death of Treat, Burnet said he was satisfied to know from Treat's own hand that the overtures of peace which he had borne to Mexico had been rejected.

We should now address ourselves with promptitude and energy to the only alternative which a gallant people can meditate. When our enemies reject "proposals for an armistice," which is only a temporary qualified peace, we ought certainly in all good conscience and prudence, to consider of the means of prosecuting the war. The ultimate purpose of war, is peace, and the more rigorously it is conducted, the more certain and proximate is the attainment of its object.[37]

Further apprehension concerning an invasion was stimulated by Juan N. Seguin's report. Returning to San Antonio from his recent participation in the Federalist campaign,[38] Seguin is alleged to have reported that the Mexican "officers, troops and all classes of citizens speak incessantly of the war against Texas" that is to be waged. It

[35] Texas Congress, *Journals of the House of Representatives of the Republic of Texas: Fifth Congress, First Session, 1840–1841*, pp. 300–301.
[36] *Telegraph and Texas Register*, Dec. 16, 1840.
[37] David G. Burnet to the Senate and House of Representatives, Executive Department, Austin, Dec. 19, 1840, in Texas Congress, *Journals of the House of Representatives of the Republic of Texas: Fifth Congress, First Session, 1840–1841*, p. 315.
[38] *Telegraph and Texas Register*, Jan. 6, 1841.

Invasion Excitement

was said that he learned in a private conversation with General Arista
that two Americans, incognito, had been sent into Texas "to offer
guarantees to the old settlers for their persons and property, offering
them trial by jury—their own Legislature and Executive—[and]
freedom of their ports, provided they became dependent on the Government of Mexico." If the promises made by the two emissaries were
not accepted, it was intimated, the campaign for the reconquest of
Texas would commence and continue until the rebelled province was
subdued. The campaign, he reported, was certain and could be expected to commence by the month of April.[39]

A few days later, on December 25, while upon a visit to Austin
where he had gone in company with Van Ness to report to the President, Seguin was requested by Burnet to make a written report of the
impressions he had gained from his recent visit with Arista and other
Mexican military leaders. Seguin made his report [40] the next day. In
it he declared that during the three or four days he had spent at Reyes'
headquarters at Mier, he had heard frequent conversations about the
approaching campaign against Texas. Reyes made "many inquiries"
of him relating to "the feeling of the old colonists, and their disposition
to return to their former state of obedience to the Mexican government, under certain guaranteed privileges. Having gone to Mier in the
hope of seeing Canales, but finding that he had proceeded to Monterey
to see Arista, Seguin also had gone to that place. Upon arrival there,
Seguin, with a number of his former friends, visited Arista, who stated
he wished to converse with him alone. In the private conversation that
ensued, Arista is said to have asserted:

It is impossible that these men [Texans] can continue much longer as a
nation or republic, without means to meet the public expenses; without
credit abroad; their paper worth only eighteen cents per dollar; and even
their agent in England has been unable to borrow any money. *My Government* has obtained a loan of three millions, one third of which has been
appropriated for the purchase of steam vessels of war, and the balance is
for the forces destined to operate by land against Texas. I have received
from the house of Rubios an order on Tampico for 80,000 dollars, and their
agent in Matamoros has placed at my command, in New York and New

[39] *Ibid.*
[40] J. N. Seguin to President of the Republic, Austin, Dec. 26, 1840, in *Colorado
Gazette and Advertiser,* Jan. 23, 1841; *Telegraph and Texas Register,* Feb. 3,
1841; translated copy in Domestic Correspondence (Texas), 1836–1846, ms.
Seguin and Van Ness reached Austin, Thursday, December 24, 1840.

387

Orleans, each, 60,000 dollars. With these means, and with six thousand men, now ready to move at my order, out of fifteen thousand, which the Government has destined for the campaign, I shall march upon my return from Saltillo, to take possession of San Antonio and Goliad, from which places I shall offer the following terms to the old colonists: Land to all who have not obtained it; their ports free for ten or fifteen years; and a state legislature and government. Should these propositions have no effect, I will continue the war until the country is *subdued*. I have already given orders to my light troops to advance and commence hostile operations on the frontier.

Believing that Seguin was willing to throw in with the Mexicans against the Texans, and using "every means in his power to induce him to do so," [41] Arista went on to give pertinent information about the distribution of his troops and the plans of the campaign that he had in mind. When suddenly he realized that Seguin did not contemplate entering the Mexican service he withdrew from further conversation on the campaign. Seguin reported the distribution of the Mexican forces in the North as follows: 500 cavalry, 250 infantry, and 4 pieces of artillery under General Rafael Vasquez east of the Río Grande on the road to San Patricio with orders to take that place immediately; [42] General John D. Bradburn, from Matamoros, was to join Vasquez with 400 infantry at San Patricio; General Arista was at Monterey with 350 infantrymen, 150 cavalrymen, 4 eight-pounders, 2 culverins of four-pounds, and 2 eighteen-inch mortars; General Eredia [Ampudia?] was at Cadereyta with 500 infantry; 300 infantry and 200 cavalry were at Presidio del Río Grande; at Matamoros there were other troops and some sixty pieces of artillery, of all sizes, ready for the field; and General Juan José Andrade was moving up from San Luis Potosí to the northern frontier with 6,000 troops. Already it was said, Colonel Rodríquez had visited San Patricio with 80 horses. The

[41] Quoted in *Telegraph and Texas Register*, Jan. 6, 1841.

[42] Major James D. Cooke supplied the Houston *Morning Star* with a letter "from the most respectable source in Austin, dated the 23rd December" 1840, and based on information received at Austin on December 22 from San Antonio. The letter handed the *Star* is probably one written by Van Ness or a copy (possibly the original) of Seguin's letter to Van Ness. Seguin wrote Burnet on the 26th, "Your Excellency may have seen, in the note I handed to Mr. Van Ness . . ." *The Morning Star* quoted in the *Telegraph and Texas Register*, Jan. 6, 1841; J. N. Seguin to President of the Republic, Austin, Dec. 26, 1840, in *ibid.*, Feb. 3, 1841; Mary A. Maverick to Agatha S. Adams, San Antonio de Béjar, Feb. 21, 1841, in Rena Maverick Green (ed.), *Samuel Maverick: Texan, 1803–1870: A Collection of Letters, Journals, and Memoirs*, pp. 138–140.

Mexicans could muster immediately between 5,000 and 6,000 armed men, counting citizens of the frontier villages.

With such reports pouring in to the seat of government, certain members of Congress began to demand that effective and sanguinary measures be instituted at once; others only proposed placing the country in a state of defense. A law hastily passed and approved December 26 authorized the raising of three spy companies to range the northern and western frontiers.[43] In the House of Representatives a resolution was introduced advocating an invasion of Mexico, and was thought by those on the southern and western frontier to be the most popular measure of any that had occupied the attention of the present session of Congress.[44] Such grandiose plans seemed rather ridiculous in view of the deplorable condition of Post San Antonio. "The importance of maintaining that interesting post is too obvious to require discussion," Burnet chided Congress on December 22. "The fact that the Department of War is without the means of transporting the small supply of munitions at present required," he declared, "will assuredly convince an enlightened Congress of the necessity of a prompt action in this behalf." By the 24th it was reported that $4,000 had been spent or had been authorized to be spent for transporting ammunition to San Antonio and for obtaining horses to be used in scouting.[45]

Those who favored carrying the war into Mexico claimed that an army of eight thousand if subsisted by the Republic until it could cross the Río Grande, could easily "march to the walls of Mexico—living on the enemy—and make their own terms of peace, quietude, and conquest." Such an invasion, it was claimed, would "attract the attention of men of the first respectability in point of intellectual acquirements, wealth, political standing, and love of liberty in the Southern states, many of whom have heretofore lost their relatives and friends by the inhuman mode of warfare carried on by Mexico against Texas."[46] The United States' diplomatic agent in Texas, George H.

43 See below, p. 399.
44 Letter addressed to Hon. James W. Byrne, Senator in Congress, dated Matagorda, Dec. 14, 1840, copy in *Colorado Gazette and Advertiser,* Dec. 19, 1840.
45 David G. Burnet to the Senate and House of Representatives, Executive Department, Austin, Dec. 21, 1840, in Texas Congress, *Journals of the House of Representatives of the Republic of Texas: Fifth Congress, First Session, 1840–1841,* p. 322; Gammel (ed.), *Laws of Texas,* II, 474–476.
46 David G. Burnet to the Senate and House of Representatives, Executive Department, Austin, Dec. 21, 1840, in Texas Congress, *Journals of the House of*

Flood, too, while conceding the poverty of the Texan government, was confident that such an expedition could succeed.[47] Even the editor of the *Telegraph and Texas Register* now took up the cry to send an invading army into Mexico.

Col. Jourdan in his recent campaign with his little band of heroes ascertained the real weakness of that country and . . . has pointed out to his admiring countrymen the path to a rich harvest of wealth and glory. It appears the famous army of Arista, that has been so long hovering in imagination like a tremendous thunder cloud, ready to pour desolation over our western counties, is but a mere handful of miserable, cowardly, half armed, half starved creatures that tremble at the very name of Texian. About sixteen hundred of the wretches have been huddled into encampments on the Río Grande,[48] and the Mexican government pretends that they are to invade Texas! The militia of the Guadalupe and La Baca [Lavaca] could alone repel this army of poltroons. Mexico, however, is well aware of their imbecility. She knows full well that the day for the invasion of Texas has long passed and she wishes to vent her spleen and malice by these threats, which she hopes will retard the immigration to the country and injure it more effectually than the arms of her miserable soldiers. It is time that she should be made to feel that she cannot even threaten with impunity. If a few of her frontier towns are laid waste, and one or two of her sea ports are blockaded in return for this threat, she will hereafter be more cautious. . . . But in order to effect this object, nothing should be done to disturb the tranquility of our republic. Not a single farmer should be called from his plow nor a mechanic from his work. The militia should be permitted to remain undisturbed. If it should be found necessary to chastise this cowardly people there are volunteers enough to effect the object. These alone, therefore, should be led into the field and permitted to carry on the invasion when they shall have once crossed the Río Grande, the path of conquest will open wide before them and the rich cities of the enemy shall furnish the means of their own subjugation.[49]

Representatives of the Republic of Texas: Fifth Congress, First Session, 1840–1841, p. 332.

[47] George H. Flood to John Forsyth, Legation of the United States, City of Austin, Dec. 28, 1840 (vol. 1, no. 11), "Correspondence and Reports of American Agents and Others in Texas, 1836–1845," J. H. Smith, "Transcripts," ms.

[48] In his *History of Jalapa*, Rivera Cambas states that early in 1841 the Mexican forces on the Texas frontier amounted to about 2,200 men, not counting the troops at Matamoros and San Luis Potosí, and that they were provided with artillery. Manuel Rivera Cambas, *Historia antigua y moderna de Jalapa y de la revoluciones del estado de Vera Cruz*, III, 515–516, 526.

[49] *Telegraph and Texas Register*, Dec. 30, 1840.

In like vein the editor of the *Morning Star* [50] declared that

. . . the question whether a Mexican army is advancing or not has but little to do with the policy we advocate. We should not wait for any demonstration from the enemy—*we must carry the war into CARTHAGE.* It can be done by volunteers with the most triumphant and brilliant success. Let the tocsin be sounded, and let the call be made upon the generous, the brave and the daring to rush to the conquest of a paradise held by dastards—offer the terms proposed by the bill lately passed the House of Representatives—the plunder of the enemy and one league of land beyond the Río Grande to each soldier—and the low state of our finances would no longer be an obstacle to the raising and subsistence of as noble and gallant an army as ever made the earth tremble beneath its tread. Five thousand volunteers raised on this plan would be amply sufficient, with the coöperation of the navy, to conquer the country to Monterey, and to maintain such conquest; [and] with the accessions which would constantly arrive from the United States, we might calculate with safety upon a volunteer army of 7000 men, armed to the teeth, and dependent upon their own resources, and upon those of the enemy for support and reward.

Others were not so enthusiastic about volunteers from the United States. "I Shall," wrote John Henry Brown, "allways—[oppose] another volunteer army from the U.S. entering Texas or having any thing to do with such a body. . . . If it becomes necessary to porsecute the War we can best do it with our Navy by blockadeing Mexican ports, &c. &c. and make reprisals without any expense to go[v]t." [51]

Aware of the failure of Treat's mission, Samuel A. Plummer wrote Burnet from New Orleans that "if England does not settle the question between the two countries soon the whole country should rise and end the war with the sword. A small flogging would not hurt . . . [the Mexicans] pending the negociation" particularly if they had entered the territory of Texas as is rumored.[52] Treat's failure to reach some sort of peaceful adjustment with Mexico, whether of a permanent or temporary nature was disheartening to most Texans; and his death made the denouement of his efforts most distressing.

In response to the sentiment for action, General Huston now switched

---

[50] Quoted in *ibid.*, Jan. 6, 1841.

[51] Extract of a letter from John Henry Brown to Thomas M. Duke, Matagorda, July 12, 1841, in John Henry Brown Papers, ms.

[52] Sam[ue]l A. Plummer to Judge [David G. Burnet], New Orleans, Jan. 20, 1841 (Private), in Domestic Correspondence (Texas), 1836–1846, ms.

from the defensive to the offensive and proposed to the Secretary of War that, in spite of the trade developing with that area,[53] an expedition against Chihuahua be organized to start about April 1, 1841, from northeastern Texas. He believed that one thousand men could be raised for that purpose, and could "be thrown to a point that would greatly embarrass an invading Army and compel them to abandon any fortifications they may take this side of the Río Grande." [54]

As a more permanent program, however, Huston suggested a plan for colonizing the area adjacent to the Río Grande. He pointed out that in case of an invasion from Mexico, Texas would need foreign aid. This could, he believed, be obtained by establishing a military colony near the Río Grande. Texas could issue $600,000 in bonds to outfit the colonists, who would settle there on condition of rendering military service for two years without other remuneration than the lands to be assigned to them, together with one-half of all money that might be added to the military funds as a result of their activities.[55] The remaining portion of such money was to be used to bring in colonists and to help them to settle on the lands after the war that he presumed was now unfolding. In this way, Huston estimated that from three to six thousand men with himself as leader, could be thrown into the west at an expense to the government of not more than $600,000 plus the lands to be appropriated. The latter were already in possession of the government.

A week later, Acting President Burnet, in submitting Huston's trans-Nueces colonization plan to Congress, commented:

The establishment of a colony of brave and active yeomanry upon the inland frontier, with suitable precautions which shall guarantee the certain and uninterrupted jurisdiction of the government, would greatly contribute to the protection of our borders from the Indian tomahawk; as it will also operate to restrain the inherent animosities of our Mexican neighbors, who will not fail in years to come, to indulge the most sinister jealousies of our growing Republic. . . . But I submit the accompany[ing] propositions relative to this subject, presented by Major Gen. Huston, more for the purpose of eliciting the mature judgment of their propriety and usefulness,

[53] *El Ancla*, Jan. 25, 1841.
[54] Felix Huston to Branch T. Archer, Dec. 23, 1840, in Army Papers (Texas), ms.
[55] *Ibid.*; William C. Binkley, *The Expansionist Movement in Texas, 1836–1850*, p. 52; H. Yoakum, *History of Texas from Its First Settlement in 1685 to Its Annexation to the United States in 1846*, II, 302; *Writings of Sam Houston*, I, 515–516, 516 n.

if found practicable. Much may be said in favor of it whereas there are some serious objections to the project. . . . That the early occupation of the territory adjacent to the Río Grande, will be a matter of great moment, in the event of a treaty with Mexico, is most evident; and it is a question worthy of enquiry, whether the ordinary ingress of population will accomplish that object in a convenient season. A superinduced population, to be planted there, would more certainly effectuate it.[56]

In presenting the Huston colonization proposal to Congress, Burnet toned down the idea of an offensive campaign against Mexico. He pointed out the lack of prosperity in the land, the slow growth of population, the distressing financial situation of the government, and the great deficiency in the essential materials of war.

Our supply of ammunition is limited, and inadequate to a protracted campaign. We are destitute of horses for cavalry purposes, and the enemy will doubtless muster largely of this active and efficient force. Our field artillery is at a point where it is, and will be, perfectly inutile; and we are without the means of transporting it to the probable theatre of action. Provisions, camp equipages, and many articles which are necessary to the comfort of soldiers in the tented field, are wanting, and we have no means for their procurement. These [he declared] are unpropitious circumstances to a people threatened with formidable invasion.[57]

The President's message was referred to a select joint committee of the House of Representatives and Senate, which made its report on January 12. The committee fully concurred in the views and opinions of the Executive on the problem of frontier defense, and declared it was prepared to urge upon Congress "the propriety and necessity of carrying those views into practical operation." It would go further; it would suggest inquiring into "the expediency of adopting the most effective measures whereby Mexico could be forced to concede us those rights which have been so long and so unjustly withheld by her," and declared that Texas "has the perfect right to wrest from Mexico her possessions and property of every kind and description," if necessary to force Mexico to acknowledge the independence of Texas. The committee was convinced "that an invasion of the enemy's territory,

[56] David G. Burnet to Congress, Dec. 30, 1840, in Texas Congress, *Journals of the House of Representatives of the Republic of Texas: Fifth Congress, First Session, 1840–1841*, pp. 388–390.
[57] *Ibid.*

393

with all the concomitant circumstances that must necessarily attend such an event, would be the most certain and legitimate mode of attaining that end." But as to whether it was "the true policy of Texas to carry her arms into Mexico, and retaliate in part, the horrors that have been enacted, upon her citizens; or wait, in a state of armed neutrality and inactivity, such as is recommended by the Executive" it was unable to say. The committee's conclusion was that Texas had neither money nor credit at home or abroad to sustain an army in the field for any length of time for defensive operations; but it believed that an army could be supported for offensive operations out of "the coffers of the enemy, wrested from him with a strong hand." In its opinion, "it would be much easier to sustain an army beyond the Río Grand[e]," than within its own territory. There the war would be made to support the war, and the proceeds from the captures and contributions, in accordance with the law of nations and the usages of war, would, if well managed, defray all the expenses entailed in operating the army in the enemy's country.

Considering, however, the dangers of the Indian frontier, the weak financial position of the Republic, the lack of a self-sufficient economy at home, and the nation's obligation to treaty stipulations and the proposed mediation of England, the committee hesitated to recommend offensive operations at the present time against Mexico; but in the end urged "the immediate appropriation of every legitimate means to place the resources of the country in such a condition as to be most available and efficient, to maintain the integrity of our soil, repel the threatened invasion and avert the horrors of war within our settlements." [58]

Huston's colonization plan was not taken up in Congress, for on the day the select joint committee reported favorably upon it, a bill was presented in the House by Sam Houston for the incorporation and establishment of the Franco-Texienne Company for the purpose of introducing eight thousand Frenchmen into Texas as colonists. [59]

[58] Report of the Joint Select Committee of Congress to the Hon. David S. Kaufman, Speaker of the House of Representatives, Committee Room, Jan. 12, 1841, in Texas Congress, *Journals of the House of Representatives, Fifth Congress, First Session*, pp. 473–480. This report is signed by James S. Mayfield, Chairman of Select Committee, W. Henry Daingerfield, Chairman of the Joint Committee on the part of the Senate, and W. N. Porter, Chairman of the Joint Committee on the part of the House.
[59] See hereinafter, pp. 499–500.

Huston, however, was not willing to abandon his use of "scare psychology." He now proceeded to address the people of Texas through the columns of the *Texas Sentinel,* warning them that great efforts would be made by some individuals to discredit the reports of a Mexican invasion in the spring. "Many of the most intelligent men in the country," he declared, "believe that a Mexican invasion will take place, and that every effort should be made to meet it as far to the west as possible. . . . It is my sincere advice to every Texian to plant corn early, and be prepared in every respect, to meet a large Mexican force to the west, and Indian depredations to the North." [60] From New Orleans, whence he had gone on personal business and to recruit for the First Regiment of Infantry, Samuel A. Plummer wrote Burnet he had conversed with a man just from Matamoros who reported that "the day before he left" six hundred rancheros and one hundred Mexican regulars "were fitted out for Live Oak Point on a robbing expedition." [61] Scarcely had the joint committee report been made than a letter from Philip Dimitt, dated January 9, reached the President at Austin on the 13th with information supplied him by a Captain Sewell, that Arista was preparing to attack Texas with four thousand men. He was reported to be already on the Texan side of the Río Grande. Dimitt appealed to the President to act without delay in expelling the four to five thousand enemy troops now on the Texas side of the Río Grande, and "not suffer the whole frontier to fall a victim to the Mexican Guellatine and expose your Country to eminent danger." [62] This report was immediately transmitted to Congress by President Burnet in exciting language: "Intelligence of the movements of the enemy crowds upon us, and I feel it my duty to impart it to the representatives of the people." Dimitt, he declared, is an "intelligent citizen residing at La Villa de los Jacales," and his letter seems to add strong confirmation to the many rumors that have preceded it in regard to a new invasion by the enemy.[63]

[60] Felix Huston to the People of Texas, *Texas Sentinel* (Austin), Saturday, Jan. 23, 1841.

[61] Samuel A. Plummer to Judge [David G. Burnet], New Orleans, Jan. 20, 1841 (Private), in Domestic Correspondence (Texas), 1836–1846, ms.

[62] P. Dimitt to [President Lamar], Ten o'clock, Jan. 9, 1841, in Texas Congress, *Journals of the House of Representatives, Fifth Congress, Appendix,* pp. 399–400; also in Domestic Correspondence (Texas), 1836–1846, ms.

[63] David G. Burnet to the Senate and House of Representatives, Executive Department, Austin, Jan. 13, 1841, Texas Congress, *Journals of the House of Representatives, Fifth Congress, First Session,* pp. 494–499.

A more reliable report, however, concerning the intentions of the Mexicans was that of January 26 by Dr. James Murphy, fresh from Camargo where he left "Many of the Texian federalists waiting for their pay, and for horses to return on." He reported everything as quiet; and that although some of the Texans on the border for a while had believed the Mexicans contemplated an invasion, there was not now the slightest prospect of such an occurrence.[64] Murphy reported that after he had mounted his horse ready to return home, Colonel Fisher and several others told him to say to their friends in Texas that the Mexicans would not trouble them. They said they were at liberty to tell him, as he would not speak with anyone on the subject until he reached Victoria, that five states would shortly revolt and form a separate government.

The Texan government, however, did take one precautionary measure against a possible Mexican raiding party penetrating into the settled area of the Republic. Shortly before the receipt of the Convention with Great Britain, Acting President Burnet ordered Major General Huston of the Texas Militia to raise a force of 350 to 400 volunteers from the counties adjacent to the Colorado "for the purpose of dislodging and driving back a detachment of the Mexican army, consisting of about seven hundred men," who were supposedly encamped some leagues on the Texan side of the Río Grande.[65] The arrival of the British treaty with its clauses for mediation of the issues between Texas and Mexico and its ready ratification by the Senate, caused Burnet shortly afterwards to countermand his order to General Huston relative to the raising of a force to expel the Mexican troops from the territory claimed by Texas, pending the efforts at mediation which were expected to follow.

Owing to increased political and financial difficulties at home and to renewed Comanche depredations, the Mexican government found no time to prepare for a Texas campaign,[66] and as their threatened

[64] Capt. James D. Owen to Patrick Usher, Victoria, Jan. 26, 1841, in *Telegraph and Texas Register*, Feb. 10, 1841.

[65] Vice President Burnet to the Senate, Saturday morning, Dec. 4, 1841, in Harriet Smither (ed.), *Journals of the Sixth Congress of the Republic of Texas*, I, 92–97; *Telegraph and Texas Register*, Dec. 29, 1841; *Morning Star*, Dec. 25 and 28, 1841.

[66] *El Cosmopolita* (Mexico City), July 28, 1841; Jesús Cárdenas, P. E. D. S., á Antonio Salazar, Sr. Srio. de Gobierno del Departamento, Ciudad Victoria [dated:] Matamoros, Julio 16 de 1841, in *Gaceta del Gobierno de Tamaulipas* (Cuidad

invasion failed to materialize, the business of organizing an expedition in Texas was directed toward another point—Santa Fé. The Fifth Congress contented itself with the enactment of several measures for frontier protection, but declined to make provision for taking a census of the population. The majority of the House Committee on the State of the Republic to which had been referred a bill providing for the taking of a census (none having been taken in the past) declared "it would be very impolitic, at present, to pass the bill, . . . because it would, in their opinion, be a useless expense for little or no profit; in fact they are of opinion," declared their report, "that much greater injury to the public interest would result from the measure than advantage." [67] Their report refrained from "stating . . . the reasons which operate" in reaching their conclusion, but we "will leave that to be stated verbally when the subject comes before the House," they said. A minority report was also filed, declaring that "it is proper and politic that the census should be taken."

It is a well-established fact that many counties, possessed of great wealth and numerous inhabitants, stand in the councils of the nation with no more influence or voice, than districts with a sparse population and little wealth. No one, at this time of the world, will deny that representation and taxation are and should be synonymous; that the majority should govern, and that, in a free government, men should be allowed to impose their own taxes, and adopt the laws by which their liberties and lives are to be protected. If a minority have an equal voice in the Congress of the country, are not the rights which a republican government guaranties to her citizens violated? . . . Your Committee [meaning the minority members] cannot be influenced by the feelings which a majority express, that if the census is taken, Texas will prove that she is but small in population, and too weak to be admitted among the nations of the earth; that if the census is taken, the United States and foreign powers will discover that the estimates of the number of our inhabitants have been false and unfounded. [68]

Among many western members of Congress, there was considerable

---

Victoria), July 31, 1841; Mary A. Maverick to Agatha S. Adams, San Antonio de Béjar, Feb. 21, 1841, in Green, *Samuel A. Maverick: Texan*, pp. 138–140.

[67] Report of the Majority of the Committee on the State of the Republic . . . William Menefee, Chairman, in Texas Congress, *Journals of the House of Representatives, Fifth Congress*, Appendix, pp. 320–321.

[68] "Counter Report of a Minority of the Committee on the State of the Republic . . . [signed:] James S. Mayfield [and] Thomas B. Huling," *ibid.*, Appendix, pp. 321–322.

apprehension over the loss of representation to the benefit of the eastern section of the country, but more especially were they concerned with the effects the publication of accurate population statistics might have in causing the Mexicans to make bolder efforts to subjugate the country. Consequently, when the question of taking a census came up for a vote in the House of Representatives on December 7, the motion for engrossment was defeated by a vote of 19–19.[69] Every member west of the Brazos voted against it. When presented again in the Sixth Congress, the census bill was once more defeated in the House.[70]

Among the several measures enacted during this Congress for frontier protection, the first, approved by Burnet on December 24, provided for the transportation of ammunition to the ranger post at San Antonio and for the "purchase of three Spy Horses" at that place.[71] At San Antonio, Major Howard commanded three companies of regulars (150), and Colonel Samuel W. Jordan was authorized to raise a battalion of three hundred volunteers to be stationed on the western frontier to watch Arista's movements on the Río Grande and to act only on the defensive.[72] Jordan raised a company of men and kept them on the frontier for a while in the Victoria area. It has been impossible to determine the number of men raised and the length of their service.[73] It was said that Jordan was eager "to redress his wrongs and to snatch payment from a people who had rec[eive]d his services and then betrayed and insulted him." [74] While in the midst of raising

[69] "From our Austin Correspondent, Austin, Dec. 10, 1840," *Telegraph and Texas Register*, Dec. 23, 1840; Texas Congress, *Journals of the House of Representatives of the Republic of Texas: Fifth Congress, First Session, 1840–1841*, p. 214.

[70] Smither (ed.), *Journals of the Sixth Congress of the Republic of Texas*, II, 194–195.

[71] Gammel (ed.), *Laws of Texas*, II, 474–476.

[72] *Colorado Gazette and Advertiser*, Jan. 23, 1841.

[73] During part of the time the men were in service, they were encamped on land in Victoria County belonging to Captain John F. Kemper, who "sustained considerable loss by the depredations committed on his stock by the company of men raised by Colo. Jourdan." Petition of John F. Kemper for Redress, Oct. 30, 1841, accompanied by affidavits of (1) John T. Price, (2) H. Ledbetter, and (3) P. Wright, Richard Roman, T. Francis Brewer, James Ingram, etc. testifying to his losses. See John F. Kemper, in Memorials and Petitions (Texas), ms.; Smither (ed.), *Journals of the Sixth Congress of the Republic of Texas*, II, 77 n. A law approved January 29, 1842, provided $132.44 to be paid J. T. O'Reilly for supplies furnished to the companies commanded by Captains J. M. [S. W.] Jordan and J. T. Price. *Ibid.*, III, 493.

[74] "Capt. Newcombe's Recollections," in *Lamar Papers*, VI, 123.

his force, he was invited by General Arista, through Colonel H. L. Kinney, to visit him. Jordan accepted the invitation and went to Mexico. After his conference with Arista, Jordan returned to Texas, and was in New Orleans in June 1841, enlisting volunteers for the support of the rebellion in Yucatán; when the boat for Yucatán sailed without him and the men he had enlisted, "Jordan in a fit of depression committed suicide by taking an overdose of laudanum on June 22, 1841." [75]

A second law, approved on December 26, authorized the President to appoint and commission three persons to raise fifteen men each to serve as spies on the northern and western frontiers for the space of four months, unless sooner discharged by the President.[76] The companies were already recruited and functioning at the time of the passage of the law.[77] On the same day as the enactment of this law, Captain John T. Price was instructed to raise a small company to scout toward Corpus Christi to keep an eye on the movements of Canales, Vasquez, and Villareal, who were operating in the area below the Nueces.[78] The other companies were raised by John C. Hays and Eli Chandler of Robertson County.[79] As already noted a joint select committee of Congress on the President's message of December 30 advised on January 12 against offensive war against Mexico owing to the poverty of the Republic. At the same time, however, it recommended that the country be placed in a state of defense against invasion.[80]

By an act of January 18, 1841, Congress abolished the office of Secretary of Navy and transferred the duties of that office to the Secretary of War.[81] Although Congress sought to curtail expenses in ad-

[75] *Handbook of Texas*, I, 929; *Telegraph and Texas Register*, June 30, 1841.
[76] Gammel (ed.), *Laws of Texas*, II, 474–476; *Telegraph and Texas Register*, Feb. 10, 1840.
[77] *Telegraph and Texas Register*, Jan. 6, 1841.
[78] Walter Prescott Webb, *The Texas Rangers*, p. 32, says the three companies were probably commanded by John T. Price, Henry W. Karnes, and John C. Hays. However, Karnes died August 16, 1840, and therefore could not have commanded under the law of December 26, 1840.
[79] *Telegraph and Texas Register*, Jan. 6, 1841.
[80] Texas Congress, *Journals of the House of Representatives of the Republic of Texas: Fifth Congress, First Session, 1840–1841*, p. 473.
[81] At this time the War Department's name was changed to "The Department of War and Navy" and later to "The Department of War and Marine." Within this Department on January 21, 1841, there was created the Naval Bureau headed

ministration, the two houses failed to agree on the appropriation bill for the regular army, as provided for by the act of December 21, 1838, and thus this arm of defense soon came to an end. In his valedictory to the Senate on Saturday morning, December 4, 1841, Vice President and presiding officer of the Senate, Burnet, defended his disbandment of the army while acting as President. "The late Congress," he said, "having adjourned without making any provision for the support of the regular army, and the hon. House of Representatives having adopted and transmitted to me, a resolution recommending the disbandment of that army, I was left without a choice of policy; and the army was promptly disbanded." [82] With the disbandment of the army, reliance was placed on the militia as the principal means of defense.

With this in view, a new law concerning the organization of the militia was enacted and approved by Acting President Burnet on January 18.[83] The new law called for immediate completion of the militia organization to full complement. It was specifically declared that the militia of each "beat" were to choose their own company officers, but if they failed to do so the commanding officers of the regiment were authorized and required to appoint them. The major general, brigadier generals, and colonels were to be selected according to the law of December 1837, and to have authority "to appoint the necessary staff officers appertaining to their respective grades, in accordance with law." The law called for the organization of three brigades; the First Brigade to comprise the area lying west of the Brazos "and all those portions of the county of Brazoria, Fort Bend, Austin and Washington, east of the Brazos"; the Second Brigade to consist of the counties lying between the Brazos (except those portions mentioned above) and Trinity rivers, including the county of Liberty; [84] and the Third Brigade

by a chief clerk. "To Abolish Certain Offices therein named, and to fix the Military and Naval Establishment of the Republic," Approved January 18, 1841, by David G. Burnet, in *Laws of the Republic of Texas, Passed at the Session of the Fifth Congress,* pp. 105–107; Gammel (ed.), *Laws of Texas,* II, 569–571.

[82] Message of David G. Burnet to the Senate, Dec. 4, 1841, in Smither (ed.), *Journals of the Sixth Congress of the Republic of Texas,* I, 93.

[83] Gammel (ed.), *Laws of Texas,* II, 497–498.

[84] A year later, Congress provided for the organization of the militia of Robertson and Brazos counties into one regiment to be attached to the Second Brigade. The militia of Robertson County was to constitute the First Battalion of said regiment and that of Brazos County the Second Battalion. "An Act for Organizing the Militia of the Counties of Robertson and Brazos," Approved Jan. 16, 1842, in *ibid.,* II, 865–866.

was to include all counties between the Trinity and Sabine rivers, including Harrison County, "and the counties of Bowie, Red River, Lamar, Fannin and Harrison" were each to "constitute one regiment." Regimental boundaries and company beats were subject to determination by the respective brigadier generals and company commanders, as the increase or diminution of the population from time to time might require.

Should it become necessary for the President to issue a call, by draft, on the militia, he was authorized to receive volunteers in lieu of drafted men. The volunteers were extended the privilege of electing their own officers, and reporting themselves by companies, battalions, or regiments, as the case might be. When mixed troops, part volunteers and part drafted men, were called out, and should apply to the commander in chief, or the commandant of the expedition so ordered out, they were to be permitted to elect their own officers, and "any companies which shall be called into service, and not enough to form a battalion, the commandant of the expedition shall have power to attach them to any other battalion or regiment." [85] Congress' decided hostility toward offensive warfare is shown by the insertion into the militia laws of the specific stipulation "that nothing in this act shall be so construed as to authorize the President to call out, either militia or volunteers, except to suppress insurrection or repel invasion." [86]

By another law, approved on February 4, 1841, the frontier counties of Fannin, Lamar, Red River, Bowie, Paschal, Panola, Harrison, Nacogdoches, Houston, Robertson, Milam, Travis, Béxar, Gonzales, Goliad, Victoria, Refugio, San Patricio, Montgomery, and Bastrop were authorized to raise volunteer companies of mounted Minute Men of not less than twenty nor more than fifty-six, rank and file "for the purpose of affording a ready and active protection to the frontier

---

[85] *Ibid.*; *Telegraph and Texas Register*, May 11, 1842.

[86] Section 16 of the Militia Law of December 6, 1836, stipulated "that the president for the time being, when he deems it necessary, shall call forth into the service of this republic, such a number of militia as he shall deem expedient," but by the supplementary Militia Act of January 18, 1841, this was changed by Section 11 to read: "That nothing in this act shall be construed as to authorize the president to call out, either militia or volunteers, except to suppress insurrection or repel invasion." "An Act to Provide for the National Defense by Organizing the Militia," Approved Dec. 6, 1836, in Gammel (ed.), *Laws of Texas*, I, 1114–1128; "An Act to Complete the Organization of the Militia," Approved Jan. 18, 1841, in *ibid.*, I, 497–498, and again printed on pp. 579–580 of this same volume.

settlements." [87] Only one such company was to be organized in each county, and it was to choose its own officers. The sole judge of the necessity of a "tour of duty" was to be the individual captain.[88] The members of the companies so raised were at all times to be "prepared with a good substantial horse, bridle, and saddle, with other necessary accoutrements, together with a good gun, and one hundred rounds of ammunition; and in addition to this, when called into service, such number of rations as the captain may direct." Persons enrolled in such companies were to be exempt from "any kind of militia duty, from working on roads or public highways, for paying a state, county, or corporation poll tax, and the tax assessed by law upon one horse." The captain of a company could detail from his company any number of spies, not exceeding five, to act upon the frontier. For active service as a spy or as a member of a company the government would pay one dollar a day, subject to the limitation, however, that no one was to receive pay on any one expedition for a longer period than fifteen days, nor for an aggregate of more than four months in a year, except the spies.[89] Congress appropriated $75,000 for the payment of spies and volunteers in the frontier service.[90]

Having instituted plans for the reorganization of the militia and the creation of volunteer companies of Mounted Minute Men, the House of Representatives of the Fifth Congress, motivated by the idea of retrenchment, pushed through a measure on January 28, 1841, to disband the regular army.[91] The Senate, however, refused to concur in the measure. Whereupon, the House then refused to make any appropriation for the support of the army and thus accomplished its destruction, for the President, finding that no provision had been made for

[87] "An Act to Encourage Frontier Protection," Approved Feb. 4, 1841, in *ibid.*, II, 646–648; George B. Erath, "Sketches on Milam and Robertson County," in *Lamar Papers*, IV, pt. 1, 34. Captain George M. Dolson organized a company of "Minute Men" at Austin on March 28, 1841, and Captain Eli Chandler did the same for Robertson County (Franklin), March 29, 1841, and the latter was functioning, June 19, 1841. Captain George B. Erath formed a similar company for Milam County.
[88] George W. Hockley to Sam Houston, Department of War and Navy, Austin, Jan. 25, 1842 in Army Papers (Texas), ms.
[89] "An Act to Encourage Frontier Protection, Approved Feb. 4, 1841," in Gammel (ed.), *Laws of Texas*, II, 646–648.
[90] *Ibid.*, II, 107–111.
[91] Texas Congress, *Journals of the House of Representatives of the Republic of Texas: Fifth Congress, First Session, 1840–1841*, p. 631.

financing the regular army, instructed the Secretary of War to order Colonel Cooke of the First Regiment of Infantry to disband, as soon as practicable the troops on Red River, on the Trinity, those stationed between the Trinity and Austin, and those stationed on the San Marcos, at San Antonio, and at Galveston. The troops at San Antonio, except for those who wished to reside there, and at San Marcos were to be marched to Austin before being discharged.[92] Lamar instructed the comptroller on March 24 to open an account on his books for the disbanding of the army.[93] Although a complete staff had been set up under the law of December 1838, and great effort had been exerted to enlist enough men to bring the army to efficiency, the army of regulars never attained the strength intended, and at the time of its discharge numbered about 540 rank and file.[94] Thus with the disbandment of the First Regiment of Infantry, the responsibility for frontier defense was taken out of the hands of the Executive and placed in the hands and under the direction of the chief justices of the frontier counties. Below the Río Grande there was great rejoicing, when it became evident that no invading force might be expected from Texas,[95] despite the braggadocio and idle palaver on both sides.

With the disbandment of the troops, the work on the military road now came to an end. Under the direction of William H. Hunt, the engineer for that project, the route for a wagon road had been surveyed from the Brazos to Red River. The route lay through "a fertile, well watered and timber country," which before many years was expected to be thickly populated.[96] "Should the road be opened any

[92] B. T. Archer, Secy of War and Navy, to Col. Wm. G. Cooke, War Department, Austin, March 2, 1841, Special Order No. [blank], Army Papers (Texas), ms., copy.

[93] Yoakum, *History of Texas*, II, 323 n.

[94] Branch T. Archer, Secretary of War and Navy to the President of the Republic of Texas, War and Navy Department, City of Austin, Sept. 30, 1841, in Texas Congress, *Journals of the House of Representatives, Fifth Congress, Appendix*, pp. 115–124; Smither (ed.), *Journals of the Sixth Congress of the Republic of Texas*, III, 357; Texas War Department, *Report of the Secretary of War, September 1841*. The original is in the Texas State Archives, Austin, and is endorsed: Report of the Secretary of War & Navy to the 6th Annual Congress Read and referred to Committee on Military Affairs.

[95] *Telegraph and Texas Register*, March 10, 1841.

[96] William H. Hunt to B. T. Archer, Austin, June 1, 1841, in Smither (ed.), *Journals of the Sixth Congress of the Republic of Texas*, III, 437, transmitting a map of the Military Road from Red River to Austin. The map is not with the

lower down," declared Engineer Hunt, "it will pass through an extensive Prairie Country, which in summer is almost destitute of water." Red River was navigable as far up as Fort Johnson, and the government of the United States was reported, at this time, to be erecting a fort nearly opposite Fort Johnson. "If," reported Hunt, "there could be a small force established at the crossing on the Trinity; another at the Toweash Village on the Brazos, the Road would soon be opened by the citizens of Fannin and Red River Counties, and by emigrants from the United States."

The survey of the coast and harbors of the Republic, provided for under a law approved January 26, 1839, had begun; and by October 1, 1841, the bar and pass of Sabine had been surveyed, the surveying of the bar and anchorage at Galveston was nearly complete, and the coast had been surveyed as far west as Paso Cavallo, with the depth of the water upon the bars recorded and "sailing directions for entering the Harbors" prepared.[97]

---

original letter in the Army Papers, but is in the General Land Office, Austin; for clarification see *ibid.*, III, 360 n.

[97] Augustus Seeger, Chief Clerk of the Naval Bureau, to B. T. Archer, Secretary of War and Navy, Naval Bureau, Austin, Oct. 1, 1841, enclosed in B. T. Archer to President of the Republic of Texas, War and Navy Department, City of Austin, Sept. 30, 1841, in Smither (ed.), *Journals of the Sixth Congress of the Republic of Texas*, III, 364–367.

CHAPTER SIXTEEN

The Southwestern Frontier:
Late 1840-1841

THE LATE WINTER and early spring months of 1840-1841 saw considerable activity on the southwestern frontier. Raising a small company of men on January 3, 1841,[1] in accordance to instructions from the War Department of December 26, Captain Price proceeded west from Victoria on the 4th and reached the Nueces on the 9th,[2] where he met Captain Hays, who had scouted from the mouth of the Frio along the Nueces. Hays reported he had found no evidence of the enemy having passed above. From the point of rendezvous, Price proceeded to Kinney's rancho on Corpus Christi Bay, forty miles below San Patricio, where he "learned from an authentic source, that about the first of the month Col. Variel [Villareal], in command of three hundred cavalry, had been in the immediate vicinity of that place." Captain Enrique Villareal approached to within a short distance of the ranch on January 6, and at his request Colonel Kinney met him about nine miles from the ranch. Kinney's version of what took place is at variance with the reports made by others. He claimed he had a force of forty men at his ranch when the Mexicans appeared in the vicinity, but that the superiority of the Mexican force caused a desertion of all of these men except eight. With this small force he sought to keep up a deception re-enforced by his efforts to impress upon "the Mexicans that he had buried bombs and other secret means of destroying them" should

---

[1] See Appendix, for a copy of the Muster Roll of Captain John T. Price's Company of Spies, January 3–May 2, 1841.

[2] John T. Price, Capt. of Spies, to Branch T. Archer, Secretary of War [dated:] Victoria, Jan. 23, 1841, in David G. Burnet to Senate and House of Representatives, Austin, Jan. 28, 1841, in Texas Congress, *Journals of the House of Representatives of the Republic of Texas, Fifth Congress, First Session, 1840–1841*, p. 636; *ibid., Fifth Congress, Appendix*, pp. 444–446; Harriet Smither (ed.), *Journals of the Sixth Congress of the Republic of Texas*, II, 206, 206 n; *Texas Sentinel* (Austin), Jan. 30, 1841.

they seek to take possession of his trading post.³ If this be true, then it might be asked why did Kinney, who was apprehensive of the intentions of the Mexicans, proceed nine miles to their camp? Was he convinced that their protestations of friendship were sincere? Why did not Kinney have Villareal himself with a limited number of his men come to the ranch for the interview?

The facts are that Kinney and Aubrey were carrying on a clandestine trade in violation of the laws of both countries, and since the Texas government could not afford them protection, it was up to them to get along with the Mexicans. Upon meeting Kinney, Villareal informed him that he had come with no hostile intentions, but merely for the purpose of procuring the cannons, arms, and powder left at Corpus Christi by the Federalist forces of the defunct Republic of the Río Grande.⁴ The Mexican officers, reported Philip Dimitt (one of Kinney's rivals in the frontier trade) brought two letters to Kinney, one from General Arista and the other from General Canales, offering protection to Kinney during the attack Arista expected to make on Texas with four thousand men. This information was supplied by Captain Sewell. The points of attack, wrote Dimitt, were to be Live Oak Point, Victoria, and La Villa de los Jacales, where Dimitt resided. Arista intended to subject these places to repeated attacks until "he could provoke the Texians to pass west of the Nueces," where the Mexicans would concentrate all of their forces against them. Villareal wanted to know if Kinney claimed the land he occupied under title from the Texan government, or "with the expectation of purchasing it from him—being a tract granted him (V.) by the Mexican Government. Mr. Kinney," it was said, "assured Col. V[illareal] that he intended to procure title from him, and accordingly made the purchase." ⁵ The Rincon del Oso grant was made to Enríque Villareal in 1810 by the

³ "Information from Col. Kinney, Corpus Christi, 184—?" *Lamar Papers,* IV, pt. I, 213–214.

⁴ *Ibid.*; Villareal's statement is substantiated by a report made in the *Colorado Gazette and Advertiser* (Matagorda), Feb. 6, 1841. The *Gazette* wryly poked fun at the Austin *Sentinel's* "oft threatened invasion" from Mexico which had more the ring of politics than realism.

⁵ P. Dimitt to [Secretary of War], 10 o'clock, Jan. 9, 1841, Army Papers (Texas), ms., copy. Dimitt's letter is endorsed: "Executive Dept., Jan. 13, 1841," and was carried to Austin by Captain Wells. See also, Coleman McCampbell, *Saga of a Frontier Seaport,* pp. 6–7; *Corpus Christi: A History and Guide,* p. 55; "Information from Col. Kinney, Corpus Christi, 184—?" *Lamar Papers,* IV, pt. I, 213–214; *Colorado Gazette and Advertiser,* Feb. 6, 1841.

The Southwestern Frontier

Spanish king (later confirmed by the Mexican government) and included the present city of Corpus Christi.[6] Villareal, who was asked by Kinney to carry back letters to Arista and Canales, "professed to know nothing of an intention of his government to invade Texas," but, reported Price, who investigated the situation, "assured Mr. Kinney, if an invasion did occur, that his person and (property) effects should be scrupulously respected." Price wrote the Secretary of War,

I deem it my duty to inform you that from the best information I could obtain, Mr. Kinney intends to avail himself of the proffered protection. From the fact of Mr. K's ranch being convenient and accessible by vessels of considerable draft, I feel confident he could be of much service to the enemy in case they were to invade this country. *I also have assurance that Kinney has promised his assistance to the enemy.* There is a twelve pound cannon (iron) at Kinney's, mounted on two wheels, with all the appurtenances requisite for service. It was left by Gen. Canales last summer. I would respectfully suggest the propriety of its removal as soon as possible; and also that some means be adopted by the Government to render ineffectual, if possible, the treasonable designs of Mr. Kinney.[7]

James Gourlay made substantially the same statements under oath six months later concerning Colonel Kinney's relations with the Mexicans. Gourlay says he was asked by Kinney to translate the letters that he had received from Canales and Arista, and that the one from the latter informed Colonel Kinney that he "was perfectly willing that he [Kinney] should remain tranquil and undisturbed at his *rancho* in Corpus Christi, and pursue his commercial business by paying to the Mexican government the duties on the goods he received, the same as he had heretofore done to Gen. Canales, and also request[ed] of Col. Kinney to keep him advised from time to time of the movements of Texas."[8] The letter from Canales had simply stated that he had talked to General Arista in regard to his remaining in the Corpus

6 Virginia H. Taylor, *The Spanish Archives of the General Land Office of Texas,* p. 88.

7 John T. Price, Capt. of Spies, to Branch T. Archer, Secretary of War [dated:] Victoria, Jan. 23, 1841, in David Burnet to Senate and House of Representatives, Austin, Jan. 28, 1841, in Texas Congress, *Journals of the House of Representatives of the Republic of Texas, Fifth Congress, First Session, 1840–1841* p. 636; *ibid., Fifth Congress, Appendix,* pp. 444–446.

8 Affidavit of James Gourlay of Lamar, Refugio County, given at [Victoria], Victoria County, Republic of Texas, July 17, 1841, in *Telegraph and Texas Register* (Houston), Aug. 11, 1841.

Christi area and that General Arista was favorable to him doing so and would write to Kinney. A few months later it was reported that Kinney had been to Arista's headquarters, where he had received assurances that he would not be molested in his operation at Corpus Christi.[9]

Meanwhile, General Arista was reported on the Texas side of the Río Grande with four or five thousand men prepared to make an immediate attack upon the lower frontier settlements. On the 7th and 8th of January several Mexicans came in to La Villa de los Jacales, but the information Dimitt obtained from them was so contradictory that he advised Colonel Jordan to arrest them as spies.[10]

With his command, Price returned from Corpus Christi to Victoria on Saturday evening, January 23, "in consequence of the weather and the muddy and almost impassable state of the prairies." Furthermore, his horses had been "hastily selected and were rendered almost useless by the recent inclemency of the weather." He was badly in need of three or four good horses, "suited for extraordinary service." He reported that he had learned from two Mexicans directly from Reinosa that Vasquez was still in camp opposite Mier, about fifteen miles east of the Río Grande, with a cavalry force estimated at eight hundred; that on the Texas side of the river opposite Matamoros there were three thousand infantry and other small detachments at the various crossings between Laredo and Matamoros; and that Arista was advancing from Saltillo with a large force and "a call had been made by the Mexican Government on the three states east of the mountains for two thousand troops each for the invasion of Texas."[11] The writer has found no evidence to substantiate the statement that the Mexicans had at this time troops in such numbers on their northern frontier or had committed the numbers given to build up their military strength on that frontier. It seems likely that the two Mexicans who had been intercepted near Kinney's rancho and questioned by Price were not

[9] *Telegraph and Texas Register,* June 9, 1841.
[10] P. Dimitt to [President of the Republic of Texas], 10 o'clock, Jan. 9, 1841, Army Papers (Texas), ms., copy. Dimitt says that he wrote the President on January 8, 1841, also; but this letter has not been found.
[11] John T. Price, Capt. of Spies, to Branch T. Archer, Secretary of War [dated:] Victoria, Jan. 23, 1841, in David Burnet to Senate and House of Representatives, Austin, Jan. 28, 1841, in Texas Congress, *Journals of the House of Representatives of the Republic of Texas: Fifth Congress, First Session, 1840–1841,* p. 636; *ibid.,* *Fifth Congress, Appendix,* pp. 444–446.

ordinary Mexicans; in view of their professed knowledge of the distribution of troops and the military plans of their government, they may well have been sent by the Mexican authorities to deceive the Texans.

Price planned to remain at Victoria eight or ten days to recruit his horses before proceeding west "as far as practicable." In the meantime, he requested information concerning the length of time his command was to be enrolled and the means of procuring provisions, ammunition, and other supplies.

From San Antonio, at the other end of the line on the southwestern frontier, it was reported in January 1841, that a party of forty Mexicans, supposedly of General Vasquez's command, had appeared at Seguin's and adjoining ranches and driven off some two hundred head of cattle. They were thought to be encamped on the Terdeo, a small stream between the San Antonio and Nueces rivers. Major George T. Howard, accompanied by Colonel Juan N. Seguin and a few citizens of Béxar, was reported to have gone in pursuit of the raiders with a detachment of troops from the command at Béxar. Actually, since the fall of 1839 marauding gangs, commanded by Agatón Quiñoñes (formerly a resident of Béxar), with thirty men, and Manuel Leal, and more recently one under Ignacio García, with twenty-five men, had made their appearance on the Nueces frontier, "ostensibly as government customs guards." According to ranger Ford, they were "really unauthorized bandits and cut-throats, banded together for the purpose of pillaging and robbing the unguarded trader." [12] Arista, of late, it was reported at San Antonio, had given a severe check to the commerce in that region, "by granting roving commissions to certain parties of marauders, who are authorized by him to plunder all traders whom they meet coming from Texas." [13] It was probably one of these roving bands which raided Seguin's ranch.

[12] John S. Ford, "Memoirs," I, 243–247. It is interesting to note that Manuel Leal, who commanded the district around Presidio del Río Grande before the Americans took over during the war between the United States and Mexico, petitioned the American commander of the area, a Texan, in February 1848, for "protection against the Mexicans! with many protestations of friendship for 'los Americanos' declaring that he had never robbed any one but *Mexicans* during his official existence." John A. Veatch to Gen. M. B. Lamar, Presidio de Río Grande, Feb. 23, 1848, in *Lamar Papers*, IV, pt. I, 193–194.

[13] R[euben] M[armaduke] P[otter] to the Editor of the *Morning Star*, San Antonio de Béxar, May 15, 1841, reproduced in *Telegraph and Texas Register*, June 9, 1841.

At the time of the raid Captain Hays' party was out on a scout.[14] Having contacted Price on the lower Nueces, Hays went in the direction of Laredo to see what he could learn about the assembling of Mexican troops for an invasion. Finding but a few soldiers at Laredo, who, not wishing to engage the Texans, crossed to the other side of the river, Hays boldly entered the town. The Texans appropriated a number of horses in the city and drove them to their encampment. The next morning the horses were returned to the inhabitants of the town with a note that the Texans were willing to fight enemy troops but not to rob peaceful citizens.[15] The explanation offered for the seizure of the horses was, reported Hays, "merely to let the Mexicans know that if we chose to retaliate the robbing which had been committed on the Americans," we "were fully able to do it."

Early in 1841 Antonio Herrera and Francisco Ganado [16] and their associates left San Antonio with several mules loaded with important cargoes. They were attacked near Laredo by a band of freebooters under Agatón. The unfortunate traders hastily returned to San Antonio to report their losses. Becoming concerned with the increasing interference with their trade, some of the leading merchants [17] hastily dispatched a request to Lamar at Austin for permission to raise a company of rangers for the protection of the frontier trade. The President referred the matter to Congress, and in the meantime authorized the raising of a company for immediate service. As soon as Chief Justice John S. Simpson received this authorization at Béxar, Captain Hays, who was out on patrol in conformance with orders from the War Department, was notified; and he immediately set out on the 15th of March [18] in pursuit of the marauders.[19] His company comprised twelve

[14] Benjamin G. Gillan, Capt. of 1st Inf., Secd Com^dr of the Post, to Col. Hugh McLeod, Adjt. and Insp. Gen., T[exas] A[rmy], Alamo, San Antonio, Jan. 10, 1841, Army Papers (Texas), ms.; Ford, "Memoirs," II, 243–247.
[15] *Lamar Papers,* IV, pt. I, 232. The date here is incorrectly given as 1840.
[16] Francisco Ganado was elected a member of the City Council on July 16, 1842. San Antonio, City of, "Journal A, Records of the City of San Antonio," p. 120, ms.
[17] John S. Ford names these merchants: [James W.] Robertson [Robinson?], [Henry Clay] Davis, William Elliot, and Nat Lewis. Ford, "Memoirs," II, 243–247.
[18] *Ibid.*
[19] John S. Ford, who was a member of this company, gave the names of the men as follows: Mat Jett, Stephen Jett, Michael Chevallie, John Hancock, Robert Patton, Jim Hudson, Joshua Thredgill, James Dunn, Nat Herbert, J. N. Fisk, John C. Hays, and himself. *Ibid.* The Muster Roll for John C. Hays' Spy Company,

Americans, including himself, and thirteen Mexicans under Captain Antonio Parez, who was chosen second in command.[20] Parez was a daring Indian fighter and citizen of San Antonio, who had not yet learned how to write his own name.

On the way toward Laredo, where it was presumed the bandits would be falling back to, Hays' Company stopped at Antonio Navarro's ranch for one day to bury two Mexicans killed by the Comanches a day or two before. Although Hays had taken every precaution to conceal his intended movements, his plans had become known to Francisco Flores at San Antonio, whose loyalty to Texas was doubtful. After Hays' party left San Antonio, Flores sent an express under two men to his son, Eduardo Flores, at Laredo, informing him of Hays' intentions. On the third day out from Navarro's ranch, the express carriers passed Hays' encampment post-haste in the night carrying the news to Laredo that the Texans were coming. As a result, García, who had only reached Laredo the day before Hays' appearance in the vicinity, now led out his party of twenty-five men supported by fifteen regular cavalry to capture or drive off the "gringos."[21] In the meantime, since the enemy would now undoubtedly have advance information of the Texans' approach, Hays pushed forward more rapidly, disregarding all attempts at secrecy but exercising greater precaution against surprise.

About ten miles from Laredo the Texans were intercepted by the Mexicans on April 7. The Texan spies, P. L. Burger, and Matias Díaz, who were riding in advance, were the first to observe the approach

---

Jan. 10–May 10, 1841, lists the names as follows: John C. Hays, Captain; Privates: P. S. Buquier, M. Chevalier [Chevallie], E. H. Davis, William Escew, A[rchibald] Fitzgerald, Peter Fahr, N[athaniel] Harbert, Thomas Hancock, Stephen Jett, James M. Jett, W. B. Small, W. H. Attwell, and James Trueheart. Muster Rolls, 1830–1860 (Rangers), ms.

20 Ford lists the Parez party as being composed of Francisco Longavilla, Damacio Galban, Manuel Montalvo, Matias Curbier, Euzevio [Ensano] Farías, Matias Díaz, Antonio García, Antonio Sánchez, Margil Salinas, Francisco Granado, Antonio Coy, [Crisanto] Casanavo, and Antonio Parez. A Receipt Roll for Captain Antonio Parez's Spy Company, Jan. 20–May 20, 1841, Militia Rolls (Republic), ms., shows the following names: Antonio Parez, Captain; Privates: C[risanto] Casanavo, Louis [Luis] Castano, Antonio Coy, Ensano Farías, Leandro Garza, Matias García, Raphael García, Francisco Granado, Francisco García, Canato Parez, Pablo Parez, Margil Salinas, Antonio Sánchez, M[elchor] Travena [Travias?], and J. O. Truehart [Trueheart].

21 J. D. Affleck, "History of John C. Hays," pt. I, p. 148.

411

of the Mexicans. As the Texans halted, the Mexicans likewise halted at a distance, and demanded repeatedly that the Texans surrender or be overwhelmed by superior forces. When the Texans gave no indication of laying down their arms, the challengers sounded their bugle and launched an attack, but owing to the distance their *escopetas* did no harm. The Texans returned their fire, killing one Mexican ranchero and wounding another. The enemy now rode off a short distance and endeavored to surround the Texans and to create the impression that his force was much larger than it really was. The Mexicans filed off to the left of a small knoll and through the brush circled the hill and appeared from the opposite direction in an attempt to give a false impression as to their actual numbers. They opened fire on the Texans, while proceeding to a hill in the Texan rear with the object of cutting off any effort of the Texans to retreat. Being somewhat confused as to the number of the Mexicans and seeing themselves about to be surrounded, and the Mexicans occupying at their rear a strong position upon an eminence, where some of their number were already dismounting, the Mexican-Texan volunteers seemed on the verge of panic, when Captain Parez assured them he was well aware of the material comprising the enemy force, and declared that with ten men selected from the rangers he could put the enemy to flight. As a result of this little speech, the confidence of the Texans was restored and they prepared to fight. Hays' men now crossed a deep ravine to their left, dismounted within two hundred yards of the enemy, and tied their horses in a mott of Spanish persimmons (*chapotes*), which they left under guard of five men, while the remainder of their group deployed left and right through a thick underbrush in the direction of the enemy. Upon coming within six yards of the enemy, the Texans commenced firing. Since most of the Anglo-Americans carried Kentucky rifles and Colt's "Patent Rifles," whose rate of fire was five to one for the old guns,[22] their fire was not only more intense but their shots were accurate. Five Mexicans were killed and several were wounded at the

[22] *Telegraph and Texas Register*, Nov. 18, 1840; John C. Hays to T. B. [*sic*] Archer, Secretary of War, [dated:] San Antonio, April 14, 1841, in *ibid.*, April 28, 1841; Smither (ed.), *Journals of the Sixth Congress of the Republic of Texas*, III, 411–412; *Texas Sentinel*, April 22, 1841; Affleck, "John C. Hays," I, 448–455; H. Yoakum, *History of Texas from Its First Settlement in 1685 to Its Annexation to the United States in 1846*, II, 320–321. P. L. Burger's report of the engagement is said to have been published in the *Floresville Chronicle*. It was later reproduced in Ford, "Memoirs," II, 243–247.

first fire. The Texans continued to advance as they reloaded and fired again and again. The Mexicans, in the meantime, had also dismounted and were firing from behind their horses, but both their guns and their marksmanship were inferior to those of the Texans. They became demoralized, and began to fall back on foot. About this time, Hays directed two of his men to ascend a hill nearby to see if any more of the enemy could be discovered. Learning that the whole Mexican force was in front of them and seeing the enemy begin to give way, the Texans charged furiously, seized some of the abandoned horses, and gave pursuit, discharging their rifles and pistols as they pursued the fleeing enemy. After fleeing several hundred yards, the Mexicans made one further attempt to rally. They again dismounted to make a stand. Coming up to within one hundred yards of them, the Texans likewise dismounted as the enemy's bullets whistled around them. As soon as they had dismounted, the Texans charged furiously upon the enemy, drove him from his position and captured his remaining horses. The Mexicans, with the exception of their captain and three who had remained mounted, soon surrendered, while their mounted brethren sought safety in flight. At this point, the Mexicans had two of their number killed on the field. The Texans vaulted into the saddles of the enemy and continued the pursuit. Upon being overtaken, the remaining Mexicans threw down their arms and called for quarter. Only one of the enemy horsemen succeeded in effecting his escape, and he was their leader—Captain Ignacio García—"who carried off a bullet in his left cheek from Captain Burger's rifle." [23]

During the fight, Mike Chevallie was thrown from his horse, some distance from the main body of the Texans, and was pursued by several Mexican lancers while endeavoring to get back to his comrades. Witnessing the race, Hays turned in his saddle and shot the foremost lancer dead; whereupon, the others retreated, much to the relief of Chevallie.[24]

The Mexicans from Laredo lost nine [25] killed and three severely

[23] Affleck, "John C. Hays," I, 154; *Lamar Papers,* IV, pt. I, 232–233.

[24] James T. Shields, "Jack Hays: Famous Texas Ranger," in *The American Home Journal,* June 1906.

[25] P. L. Burger reported, and John S. Ford seems to confirm his statement, that nine Mexicans were killed. Both men participated in the fight. The official report, made by Hays, gives the number as three Mexicans killed, three severely wounded, and says that several other Mexicans, wounded early in the fight, were carried off. It is possible that some of those who were carried off may have died later. Hays'

wounded; twenty-five were taken prisoners, among whom was Eduardo Flores. Hays reported that several other Mexicans were wounded early in the fight and carried off. The Texans lost not a single man killed and only one or two wounded. They captured twenty-eight horses with saddles and bridles.

Captain García quickly carried the news of his defeat to Laredo with the result that great excitement prevailed and many of the residents "jumped the river." A deputation headed by the alcalde came out with a white flag to beg the Texans to spare the town and promised to accede to any demand for a requisition that might be made. Hays informed them that all the Texans wished was for Agatón and Leal to be delivered to them, and for assurances to be given that protection would be accorded to the traders going to and from San Antonio. The alcalde assured him most positively that these conditions would be met. After questioning several of the prisoners, including Eduardo Flores, a man of intelligence, the Texans released the captives.

About a month later, a Mexican force was reported to be near the point where the Presidio del Río Grande road crossed the Nueces, within sixty miles of San Antonio. This force was under Calixto Bravo, frontier commander, who it was said, had left Presidio del Río Grande to pursue Antonio Parez's party from San Antonio, which was rumored to be ranging the frontier. Bravo united his men with the forces of Captains Menchaca, Rodríquez, and Agatón Quinoñes.[26] The combined Mexican force was estimated by the Texans to number between one hundred and two hundred men.

The merchants of San Antonio felt that this opportunity to punish the marauders should not be lost. Again the local merchants furnished the necessary supplies to outfit a punitive expedition.[27] Although the men who had recently pursued García had completed the terms of their enlistment, they once more agreed to take the field. A few others joined them, and on May 9 the volunteers, numbering forty men, marched westward under Captain Hays. They sought to overtake a small convoy

---

report of the "first charge" of the Texans makes no comment on the Mexican losses, but he does mention the losses of the enemy at the "first repulse" and the "second charge." Yet, the main fight was at the "second charge." Ford, "Memoirs," II, 243–247; John C. Hays to T. B. [*sic*] Archer, Secretary of War [dated:] San Antonio, April 14, 1841, in *Telegraph and Texas Register*, April 28, 1841.

[26] *El Ancla*, June 7, 1841.

[27] R[euben] M[armaduke] P[otter] to the Editor of the *Morning Star*, San Antonio de Béxar, May 15, 1841, reproduced in *Telegraph and Texas Register*, June 9, 1841.

of traders that had left Béxar a few days before in the direction of the Río Grande, to give it protection, but they were too late. The "bandits," as they were called in Texas, had intercepted the convoy and robbed all of them except one, who, it is said, had a license from Arista.[28] The captors distributed among themselves the tobacco and other effects taken from the traders, and the twenty-three *contrabandistas,* it was reported, were sentenced according to the decree of April 14 to ten years in the presidial companies.[29]

The robbers had fled in the direction of the Río Grande before the arrival of the Texans. Although the latter sought to overtake them, they failed to do so. It is doubtful if they had succeeded in catching up with them that they could have attacked them with success, for it was reported that the Mexican party numbered three hundred, about two-thirds of whom were regular troops.[30]

Shortly after this, a party of nine men from the Río Grande brought in a remittance to a merchant at San Antonio, and an order for more goods, which were sent. Thus apparently, the Mexicans were determined to hang on to the trade, in spite of their government and the dangers of the trail. The trade of Béxar continued "quite brisk, notwithstanding the threats of the banditti of the Río Grande." [31] Many traders were reported arriving from the Mexican settlements with quantities of specie. Fifty-seven merchants from Chihuahua arrived at Austin with 50,000 pesos to engage in trade between the United States and the inhabitants of the north Mexican states.[32] The improvement of the trade was attributed in part to the energetic efforts being made by the Texan government to disperse the marauders infesting the frontier, but these efforts were sporadic and often ineffectual. Another factor which no doubt accounted for some improvement in the trade was the cessation of the revolutionary disturbances in the north. But regardless of who controlled the crossings of the Río Grande, the Nueces, the San Antonio, the Medina, or the Guadalupe, smuggling flourished and the civil authorities of Mexico were "the most deeply engaged" in the illicit trade with the Texans, who brought their goods into the Reinosa markets without the payment of duties and openly sold their wares there, even though the Centralists were

28 *Ibid.*; Affleck, "John C. Hays," I, 146.
29 *El Ancla,* June 7, 1841.
30 *Telegraph and Texas Register,* May 22, 1841.
31 *Ibid.*, May 19, 1841.
32 *El Ancla,* Jan. 25, 1841.

in control of the town.[33] By the end of March, after the rumor of an impending invasion began to die out, "like a thousand idle rumors of a similar character that proceeded it,"[34] a considerable trade had sprung up at San Antonio with the Mexicans on the Río Grande. Large flocks of sheep were driven into the western counties from the Río Grande.[35] Competition filled the market, and according to one account, large amounts of specie were being brought into the city. Within two weeks time two sizable shipments of specie had reached Austin by way of San Antonio on their way east to buy goods in New Orleans for the Mexican trade.[36]

While much has been written concerning the influx of specie into Texas and the prosperity of the western trade, little has been said "whether the dollars were realized at a profit or loss, and it is no doubt from miscalculations of this kind," reported Reuben M. Potter,[37] "that the trade of Béxar has been overrated and overdone." Since its opening the trade had become more competitive; prices were depressed, being in May 1841, about half what they were the year before. "Merchandise is, indeed, cheaper here at present," wrote Potter, "than in any part of Texas, which leaves little chance of profit where the expense and risk of transportation are so great, and the stock on hand is sufficient for many months. The trade, however, was only with the small towns on or near the Río Grande, and not yet extended to any of the larger cities beyond the frontier and could not be expected to do so until there was a "treaty or truce with Mexico, or with the western part of it in case of a new insurrection."

Depressed market conditions at San Antonio, due to overstocking,[38] reflected not only increased competition among traders in that quarter, but the growth of the trade carried on with northern Mexico from other frontier settlements, especially those located along or near the Texas coast, which had ready connections with New Orleans, Mobile, Pensacola, and other United States ports. The inland towns on the frontier were at a disadvantage in transportation, in that it was not only more expensive, but was also more dangerous owing to the

[33] *El Ancla,* quoted in *Telegraph and Texas Register,* July 29, 1840.
[34] *Telegraph and Texas Register,* Feb. 3, 1841.
[35] *Ibid.,* Jan. 5, 1841.
[36] *Ibid.,* April 7, 1841.
[37] R[euben] M[armaduke] P[otter] to the Editor of the *Morning Star,* San Antonio de Béxar, May 15, 1841, reproduced in *Telegraph and Texas Register,* June 9, 1841.
[38] *Telegraph and Texas Register,* June 16, 1841.

marauders and occasional hostility of the Indians. Typical of the increased activity of the seaports is the industriousness of W. B. Goodman, who arrived at Live Oak Point, on Aransas Bay, on March 28, with a cargo of goods which he carried down the bay to Corpus Christi, where they were sold.[39] From thence he returned to New Orleans for another cargo, which he landed at Corpus Christi on the following July 4.

The life of the traders, however, was a precarious one, for before November 1840 Canales with his gangs of Federalist politicians and cohorts, and after that date the Centralists, often captured them and made the flow of commerce very uncertain. "Communications with the interior [of Mexico]," reported the American consul at Matamoros, "is frequently interrupted by numerous banditti, who infest the roads, committing robberies and assassinations with impunity. Great efforts have been made by the local authorities of this place to bring the offenders to justice, but hitherto without success. So formidable are these outlaws that they have recently," he said, "defeated two separate detachments of troops in attempting to arrest them." [40] The Mexican authorities were not always unsuccessful, for we find that Adolphus Sterne was able to record in his diary under date of July 24, 1841, the news that "50 Cow Thieves have been overhawled by the mexicans and all Killed—good." [41] Yet, on the other hand, there can be but little doubt that some of the Mexican gangs were commissioned by such frontier commanders as Arista, Canales, and others for the purpose of breaking up the existing trade, if not at times turning it to their own personal advantage.[42]

Not all of the difficulties of the frontier trader can, or should be attributed to the Mexicans, whether operating as banditti or under the cloak of governmental authorization; nor were the Mexican raids upon the Texas frontier always without provocation. The cattle raids eventually led to the interference with frontier trade and the conduct of other types of legitimate business in the west. The collapse of the

[39] W. B. Goodman, "A Statement of Facts, Washington, Feb. 10, 1843," in W. D. Miller Papers, 1833–1860, ms.

[40] D. W. Smith to John Forsyth, Matamoros, May 13, 1841, Consular Dispatches (Matamoros), ms., microfilm.

[41] Harriet Smither (ed.), "Diary of Adolphus Sterne," *Southwestern Historical Quarterly* XXXII (1928–1929), 166.

[42] Hubert Howe Bancroft, *History of Mexico*, V, 262 n; *Telegraph and Texas Register*, June 9, 1841.

projected Republic of the Río Grande and the cessation of the Federalist activities did not put an end to the gangs of desperadoes on the frontier, who continued "perfectly regardless of the rights of any one, robbing indiscriminately and not wishing to know or *hear* of any Orders to the contrary." [43] "We find ourselves in a continuous hostility," reported *El Ancla* at Matamoros. Various parties of Texans and Indians, "seduced and commanded" by the Texans, have come to hostilize the frontier to divert the troops that protect it, while their expedition proceeds to Santa Fé.[44] On a visit to Austin late in May 1841, Captain Hays reported "wandering parties of Mexicans and squads of Texian cow-thieves . . . materially interrupting the Mexican trade. They embody between the Río Grande and the Nueces and seize everything they can get hold of in the way of plunder." The editor of the *Texas Sentinel* of May 27, like the editor of the *Austin City Gazette*, wondered if some plan could not be devised "by which a dozen or two of these cow-boys could be caught and punished."

Representing Matagorda County in the Texas state constitutional convention at Austin in 1845, Albert C. Horton asked what protection, if any, had Texas ever given to the people residing between the Nueces and the Río Grande? "What is their peculiar situation?" he queried.

When the Americans have gone there they have preyed upon them; they have been necessarily compelled, by force or otherwise, to give up such property as they had. So *vice versa*, when the Mexicans have come in, they have been necessarily compelled to furnish them the means of support. . . . Since 1837 they have been preyed upon by our countrymen. I am ashamed to say it, but I speak the truth before high heaven, bands of robbers have driven off their cattle by hundreds and thousands, to this portion of the country, to the Brazos and further east. The cry is that they have taken up arms against this country. Against who have they taken up arms? Against a set of robbers, sir. . . . Not only have they been despoiled of their property, but, I am ashamed to repeat it, such violations as have been committed upon females there, fix a blot upon the American character.[45]

Traders, like Aubrey and Kinney, continued to request protection from interference by such lawless bands, alleging that if the present

[43] Aubrey & Kinney to M. B. Lamar, Corpus Christi, Aug. 15, 1841 (Confidential), in *Lamar Papers*, III, 562–563.

[44] *El Ancla* quoted in *El Cosmopolita* (Mexico City), Aug. 14, 1841. A small party of Indians attacked a man on July 31, 1841, near Mier. *Ibid.*, Aug. 28, 1841.

[45] William F. Weeks, *Debates of the Texas Convention*, pp. 408–410.

rate of losses continued, they would soon have to withdraw from the frontier trade.[46] Wrote Chief Justice Ferguson of San Patricio County to the Secretary of State,

I find myself placed in a very difficult and unpleasant, unsafe & critical situation. I have no control at all over some 50 or 75 men who have come out here expecting to derive advantage from the order of the Hon[orable] Sec[retary] of War. The civil law is entirely unnoticed & useless. Unless I can have some power or authority here I do assure (candidly) that it is useless and even dangerous to remain here. . . . We have been overflooded with men from all the western counties, most of whom are perfectly reckless. It is absolutely necessary that something should be done. Now the strongest rules, and I cannot tell or even imagine what may happen.[47]

In the interest of greater security, the City Council of San Antonio, at the suggestion of Doctor Launcelot Smithers, one of its members, enacted an ordinance on September 9, 1841, requiring any person, not an inhabitant of the Republic of Texas, entering the city in the future to present himself or herself immediately upon arrival before the mayor of the city, upon penalty, for failure to do so, of being fined at the discretion of the mayor.[48] It was further ordained "that any citizen harboring any person of suspicious character in his or her house" in the city, upon conviction before the mayor, would be fined not more than $100, nor less than $25 at the discretion of the mayor.

[46] Aubrey & Kinney to M. B. Lamar, Corpus Christi, Aug. 15, 1841 (Confidential), in *Lamar Papers*, III, 562–563.
[47] A. Ferguson to the Secretary of State, San Patricio, Aug. 26, 1841, in Domestic Correspondence (Texas), 1836–1846, ms.
[48] San Antonio, City of, "Journal A, Records of the City of San Antonio," Sept. 9, 1841, ms., copy.

CHAPTER SEVENTEEN

Rumors of Invasion

LAMAR RETURNED TO TAKE OVER the duties of President on March 5. About two weeks later, one of the late participants in the Federal army, Doctor Shields Booker, reached Austin fresh from Arista's headquarters to report that the Centralist commander had an army of four thousand troops already assembled for a campaign against Texas, and was daily expecting to be re-enforced by five thousand more, who "were said to be on their march from the mountains." [1] Booker also stated that Arista's army was furnished with a park of artillery consisting of eighteen mounted guns and that it had five hundred mule packs of provisions deposited at one of the crossings of the Río Grande. Declared Lamar in a circular letter to the militia colonels throughout the Republic,

The avowed object of assembling this force by the Mexicans is an expedition against the Indians; but Doctor Booker feels perfectly satisfied that their real intention is to make a descent on Texas, and to take us by surprise. That such is the design of Arista . . . is rendered plausible and probable by the additional consideration that an army of nine thousand men and so large a park of artillery is altogether unsuited to the character and habits of the enemy which they pretend to move against. It is so inconsistent with the nature of Indian warfare as to leave but little doubt that the force has been organized for some other purpose than the avowed one. What that secret purpose may be remains to be developed; but we have sufficient grounds to believe that an attack upon this place or some other portion of our country is intended. It behooves us therefore to be on the alert and fully prepared to meet them. . . . It is not my intention to create any alarm; or to call out the militia unless it becomes absolutely necessary to repel a

[1] Letter Addressed [by Mirabeau B. Lamar] to the Militia Colonels throughout the Republic, relative to Information received by Doc[to]r Booker of preparations for invasion by the Mexicans, Executive Department, City of Austin, March 22, 1841, Record of Executive Documents, from the 10th Dec. 1836 to the 14th Dec. 1841, ms.

420

direct invasion; I shall, therefore, issue no proclamation until it is believed there is an absolute necessity for immediate and active operations, when I confidently hope the call will be responded to with energy and promptness.

One spy company was already out with instructions to watch the enemy's movements, and Lamar was preparing to dispatch forthwith one or two other companies to different parts of the country for the same purpose. In the meantime, he urged that the militia officers bring their various commands up to full quota without delay and that they be prepared "to move at one hour's notice." [2] The chief justices of the various counties were instructed to see that the militia was well organized. A month later, Chief Justice Thomas H. Poage of Victoria County reported that his county had been laid off into three "Captain's Beats," one of which had been previously organized, and that A. S. McDonald, a resident of the county who had been elected colonel during the past summer, was proceeding with the organization of the militia. The volunteer company recently organized in the county, having elected its officers, was preparing to move to San Patricio to make that place its headquarters to protect the inhabitants of that county and, as far as possible, those along the southwestern frontier.[3]

For the purpose of facilitating the work of the volunteer company and of establishing a suitable organ for communicating with the administration, Poage urged Lamar to appoint a chief justice for San Patricio County. For that position, he recommended Colonel Alanson Ferguson, "at present of Victoria, but who is now associated with the number destined for that county." [4] Andrew Neill, the district attorney for the Fourth Judicial District, likewise pointed out the need of a chief justice for the county of San Patricio, owing to the rapid increase in the population of the whole valley of the Guadalupe.[5] In another

[2] *Ibid.*
[3] Thomas H. Poage to President [Lamar], Victoria County, April 28, 1841, in Domestic Correspondence (Texas), 1836–1846, ms.
[4] *Ibid.*
[5] A Neill to D. G. Burnet, Austin City [dated:] Victoria, April 28, 1841, in Domestic Correspondence (Texas), 1836–1846, ms. The increase in population was due principally to heavy emigration from the United States early in 1841 and was not wholly confined to the west. "There has been a large emigration to our country this year," wrote E. A. Pease from Brazoria, "and it is thought that our recognition by Great Britain and the prospect of our Independence being acknowledged by Mexico in the course of this year, will give us a larger emigration next year." E. A. Pease to Mrs. Eliza C. Barrett, Brazoria, Texas, Feb. 16, 1841, in Don Carlos Barrett Papers, 1800–1897, ms.

421

year Neill felt the district court would be required to go to San Patricio. He, too, recommended the appointment of Alanson Ferguson to be chief justice of San Patricio County, and the citizens of the county concerned also approved of that choice.[6] As a result, Ferguson was appointed chief justice of the County of San Patricio on May 5, 1841, which position he held until he resigned on September 1, of the same year, following his election to the House of Representatives. In the meantime, various charges were made against him, and Lindsay S. Hagler, his opponent in the congressional race, challenged his election to Congress. This matter will be discussed later in connection with the Dimitt case.

For a brief period following the President's instructions, there was considerable flurry to get the militia organized and brought up to full compliment; but as time passed and the Mexicans did not make their move, the Texans came to regard it as just another of those countless rumors that had circulated through the country since the summer of 1836. The former Secretary of the Treasury, Attorney General, and Secretary of State, James Webb, then in Houston preparing to go to Mexico to reopen negotiations, found "the people . . . rather doubtful as to the truth of Dr. Booker's report—they say the Mexicans are not coming," he informed Lamar, "but if they do come, they will give 'em h——l."[7] As the excitement over the "invasion" died down, it became increasingly difficult to perfect the organization of the militia and to get the men enrolled.

On the whole, the law providing for the organization of the "minute men" or ranging companies was believed to have met with general disapprobation, except in Milam, Robertson, and Béxar counties, where some good resulted from the exertions of brave and enterprising captains.[8] In most parts of the country it was thought that the law had rather aided in encouraging land speculators to venture out to make locations of land at public expense than in protecting the frontier. "It is said in some counties," reported the editor of the *Telegraph,* "parties of men have frequently met for the purpose of going to survey land

[6] "Petition of Citizens of the County of San Patricio, April 23, 1841," recommending A. Ferguson for the chief justiceship has not been found. See Joseph Waples to the Speaker of the House of Representatives, Nov. 6, 1841, Correspondence, State Department Letterbook, no. 1, ms., p. 249; Harriet Smither (ed.), *Journals of the Sixth Congress of the Republic of Texas,* II, 16.

[7] James Webb to M. B. Lamar, Houston, April 9, 1841, in *Lamar Papers,* III, 506.

[8] *Telegraph and Texas Register* (Houston), Dec. 15, 1841.

or to steal cattle, and then applied to the chief justice for certificates that they had been out on an expedition against the Indians!" [9] Reported Secretary of War Hockley on January 25, 1842,

It has been reported often to officers of the Department, and to others, that . . . in some instances false Muster Rolls have been made by reporting names of persons said to have perform'd service, and who really were not in existence; and by a Power of Attorney, Pay Drawn; and further, that in other cases certificates have been given for services never performed, because . . . the Chief Justice was aware that such person *did* reside in their Counties, and presumed that it had been done. . . . The Law, as it now stands, certainly admits of the perpetration of fraud to a great extent.[10]

The expense thus incurred in the several counties in which spy companies had been organized in the aggregate was believed to have exceeded by twice the allowance made by Congress for such bodies.

If there was to be no Mexican invasion, Lamar was determined to push his project for an expedition to Santa Fé, New Mexico. In company with Colonel William G. Cooke, he visited San Antonio, arriving there on May 15 and remaining several days.[11] Lamar was the first President of the Republic to visit Béxar and gain a first-hand knowledge of the problems confronting the frontier traders and settlers in that quarter. One of his principal objects in going to San Antonio, however, was to confer with José Antonio Navarro about the forthcoming Santa Fé Expedition.

In May a small group of Mexican soldiers descended upon Refugio, killed a few men, robbed the place, and carried off several citizens as prisoners. Captain John R. Baker immediately summoned a small party of volunteers and went in pursuit of the invaders. He followed them to the Río Grande, but failed to overtake the marauders. On the way back he encountered a *caballada* of horses that had been stolen in Texas. Baker's men attacked the small Mexican party and recovered the horses which they drove to Carlos' Rancho.[12] When Lamar, acting

9 *Ibid.*

10 George W. Hockley to Sam Houston, Department of War & Navy, Austin, Jan. 25, 1842, in Army Papers (Texas), ms.

11 R[euben] M[armaduke] P[otter] to the Editor of the *Morning Star*, San Antonio de Béxar, May 15, 1841, reproduced in *Telegraph and Texas Register*, June 9, 1841.

12 *Lamar Papers*, IV, pt. I, 214; 214; Hobart Huson, "Refugio: A Comprehensive History of Refugio County from Aboriginal Times to the End of World

After San Jacinto

through Colonel Kinney, notified General Arista that the men taken at Refugio were unoffending citizens, and not soldiers, they were released.[13] At this time Arista was rumored contemplating rising against Santa Anna and had no desire to offend the Texans. Reports from the Río Grande said he was fortifying San Fernando de Rosas and other towns.[14]

In consequence of the raid on Refugio, a company, known as the "San Patricio Rangers," was organized "for the mutual protection of our persons, property and civil and religious liberties" at Camp Independence, west of the Nueces River, May 18, 1841. The party included twenty-four men, headed by James P. Ownsby as Captain. Ewen Cameron and John H. Yerby, who formerly resided at Austin were among the privates.[15] It was stipulated that all spoils taken were to be held jointly until equally divided. A member was liable to the forfeiture of one-eighth to one-fourth of his share of the booty for breach of discipline or neglect of duty.[16] This company was apparently organized without authorization from the government.

The "San Patricio Rangers" made one successful sally not upon the Mexican raiders, but upon a party of traders, capturing goods, cash, and horses amounting to one thousand dollars, and murdering the eight Mexicans whom they had taken without resistance.[17] The thieves then fell out among themselves over a division of the booty. One man withdrew from the group and the remainder divided into two parties—one under Yerby and the majority under Ownsby. Ownsby's raiders descended to the Río Grande, and near Para encountered sixty to seventy Mexicans under Colonel Ramírez. A fight ensued in which

War II, vol. II, chap. 24, p. 4; John J. Linn, *Reminiscences of Fifty Years in Texas*, pp. 310–311.

[13] *Lamar Papers*, IV, pt. I, 214. A. S. Wright to William Bryan, Mexico City, Dec. 25, 1839, in Garrison (ed.), *Diplomatic Correspondence of Texas*, 1908, II, 518–520.

[14] "P. S. 23 May" to R[euben] M[armaduke] P[otter] to Editor of the *Morning Star* (Houston), Béxar, May 22, 1841, quoted in *Telegraph and Texas Register*, June 9, 1841.

[15] A list of the "rangers" may be found in Frederick C. Chabot, *Corpus Christi and Lipantitlán*. pp. 31–32.

[16] [Statement of Colonel H. L. Kinney], Lamar Papers, no. 2421, ms.; John T. Price to Branch T. Archer, Secretary of War and Navy, Victoria, July 2, 1841, Army Papers (Texas), ms.

[17] *Ibid.*

three Anglo-Texans were killed and the Mexicans suffered losses of five killed and sixteen wounded.[18] Meanwhile the search for Agatón continued. In a letter from a loyal Mexican of San Antonio de Béxar, dated July 1, General Rafael Vasquez was informed that the next day Antonio Parez would leave Béxar with a few less than two hundred men, including thirty Mexicans and the rest Americans, "with the sole object of surprising the force under Agatón Quinoñes." Béxar, he said, would be left unprotected against any Mexican division which might wish to advance against it. The informer also reported that one thousand men, including five hundred soldiers and the rest muleteers and merchants, had left for New Mexico twelve days before.[19]

General Arista, in the meantime, sought to break up the increasing illicit trade of Mexicans with the Texan enemy. From Sabinas on April 13 he issued a proclamation to his troops and to the people of the eastern frontier departments warning them to cease their trade with the Texans and reminding them that the penalty for such a crime was ten years' service in the regular army on the frontier, and confiscation of the goods, beasts, and all effects used in conducting the trade.[20] The Mexicans refused to sell any land west of the Nueces to any person who would not become a citizen of Mexico, and repeatedly asserted that no person would be permitted to live west of that river unless he acknowledged the authority of Mexico.

By way of enforcing the policy against illicit trading, and especially for the purpose of punishing "the Texan gangs who boldly advance to hostilize the frontier," General Ampudia, who commanded the First Division of the Second Brigade of the Army Corps of the North with headquarters at Matamoros, dispatched a Mexican force of two hundred rancheros under Captain Enrique Villareal in cooperation with a squadron of *defensores* from Matamoros under Don Macedonio Capistrán towards the Rancho del Oso. The Mexican troops descended upon Kinney's rancho. At the ranch, their leaders became convinced

18 *Ibid.*; *Telegraph and Texas Register*, July 14, 1841; *El Cosmopolita* (Mexico City), July 28, 1841.
19 *El Centinela de Nuevo León*, July 25, 1841, quoted in *El Cosmopolita*, Aug. 7, 1841.
20 Mariano Arista, *El C[iudadano] Mariano Arista, general de brigade del egército mégicano y en gefe del cuerpo de Egército del Norte*, dado en el cuartel general de Sabinas el dia 13 de abril de 1841, broadside; also, in *El Ancla*, May 3, 1841; *Texas Sentinel* (Austin), July 1, 1841.

that Colonel Kinney "had no agency in the affair," but had actually "endeavored to suppress & prevent such conduct." "Learning that a party of the enemy who he sought was passing the night in el paraje de los Leonistos," [21] Villareal traveled all night with a detachment of some forty rancheros with the hope of surprising the Texans the next day. The Mexicans came upon Captain Yerby and his nine men at daylight at Leonistos, not far from the Nueces and within thirty miles of the rancho. At daylight he ordered twenty-two men from the La Bahía squadron and *presidiales* to dismount. Near sunrise, June 13, the Mexicans commenced their assault under the command of Ensign (brevet Lieutenant) Ambrosio de la Garza. The attack continued until 9 o'clock, killing all of the Texan "cow-thieves," except Thomas Cabasos, who was "notorious for his guiding the Americans in such enterprises." [22] Cabasos succeeded in effecting his escape under protection of the forest. The Mexican losses consisted of two killed and two wounded, one gravely.[23] The bodies of Yerby's party were found by Captain John T. Price's company which reached the Nueces on June 23. Reported Price,

It appears that they (the robbers) had a short time before killed a party of traders and robbed them of several hundred dollars, a lot of blankets, etc. This party of Americans was led by a Mr. Yearby who formerly resided at Austin. We learned also from some Mexicans recently from Camargo that Owensby, with about fifteen men, had been surrounded by two or three hundred Mexicans, and that eight or nine of his men were killed and himself and five others taken prisoners.[24]

In the latter report Price seems to have been in error for other information indicates that upon learning of Yerby's fate Ownsby's party

[21] Pedro de Ampudia ál Sr. General gefe del cuerpo de Egército del Norte, cuerpo de egército del Norte, 1ª Division, 2ᵈ Brigada, Núm. 160 [161?], Matamoros, Junio 18 de 1841, in El Ancla, June 21, 1841.

[22] Ibid.; Telegraph and Texas Register, July 7, 14, and 21, 1841; Jesús Cárdenas, Prefecto del Norte de Tamaulipas, ál Gobernador del Departamento [de Tamaulipas], Matamoros, Junio 18 de 1841, in Gaceta del Gobierno de Tamaulipas, July 3, 1841. It was reported in the Telegraph and Texas Register that Yerby's men were captured and hung. Ampudia reported that all ten of the enemy were killed.

[23] Killed: Jesús Flores, Juan Cantú. Wounded: Eustaquio Cantú, father of Juan Cantú, gravely; Madrid (presidial soldier).

[24] John T. Price to Branch T. Archer, Secretary of War, July 2, 1841, Army Papers (Texas), ms.

became alarmed and disbanded, although some of the men attached themselves to the service of Kinney at Corpus Christi.[25] Upon withdrawing toward Matamoros, however, Captain Capistrán and his *defensores* had, on the morning of June 15 at 10 o'clock, suddenly come upon another party of Texans in *el paraje del Pastle*. In the distance the Mexican spies descried a *caballada* and a large herd of cattle, numbering some 230 head, being driven along a road leading toward the interior of Texas by fourteen men. The Mexicans immediately bore down upon the Texans at a gallop, hoping to attack them in the open plain that they were in the process of crossing, but the "Texan thieves," observing the approach of the enemy, fled to a nearby wooded area, where they surrendered at discretion without the firing of a shot and were taken to Matamoros.[26]

Villareal and his men had returned to the Río Grande before the arrival of Price on the frontier, leaving a force of twenty-five men under Lieutenant Norverto Galán to protect the passes of the Arroyo Colorado.[27] However, "it appears," said Price, "from the statement made by the traders who have visited our country of late, that it is the settled purpose of the Mexican authorities not only to assert, but *maintain* the control of the territory between the Nueces and Río Grande. I learn from a creditable source that the Mexican mail passes weekly between Kinney's Ranch and Matamoros."[28] Another party of cow thieves was captured on the Colorado and all were hung. A man named Hopkins, who had recently effected his escape from Matamoros, was overtaken by a pursuing Mexican party and shot. By mid-July 1841, it was reported at Houston that the Mexican troops had killed between the Río Grande and the Nueces River about 47 cow thieves within the space of a few weeks.[29] Although bandits still operated

25 [Statement of Colonel H. L. Kinney], Lamar Papers, no. 2421, ms.; John T. Price to [Branch T. Archer], Secretary of War, July 2, 1841, in Smither (ed.), *Journals of the Sixth Congress of the Republic of Texas*, III, 436–437.

26 *El Ancla*, June 21, 1841; Pedro de Ampudia ál Sr. General Gefe del cuerpo de Egército del Norte, cuerpo de egército del Norte, 1ª Division, 2d Brigada, Núm. 160 [161?], Matamoros, Junio 18 de 1841, in *El Ancla*, June 21, 1841.

27 *Ibid.*

28 John T. Price to Branch T. Archer, Secretary of War, July 2, 1841, Army Papers (Texas), ms.; Smither (ed.), *Journals of the Sixth Congress of the Republic of Texas*, III, 424–425; *Telegraph and Texas Register*, July 7, 1841; *Texas Sentinel*, July 1, 1841.

29 *Telegraph and Texas Register*, July 14, 1841.

427

between the Nueces and the Río Grande, the Mexican authorities began in the late spring and early summer of 1841 to show an increasing interest in reopening the frontier trade, indicated by the readiness of the military commanders to grant passports to all who wished to trade with the citizens of western Texas.[30]

Some time later, the sheriff of Refugio County, Jeremiah Findley, ordered the raising of a company of volunteers from Victoria, Refugio, and San Patricio for the purpose of tracking down and arresting the marauders infesting the frontier and of giving protection to the Mexican traders.[31] While the troops were being raised, the citizens of San Patricio commenced the erection of a fort at that place to give protection to the trade, for San Patricio, being closer to the settlements on the Río Grande than any other Texas community and being within fifteen miles of steam navigation at all seasons, could easily become a flourishing trade center.

While there seemed to be no peace on the frontier, the Texan government still had hopes of arriving at an amicable settlement with Mexico. Shortly after the adjournment of the Fifth Congress, while formulating his plans for the occupation of New Mexico, Lamar made a third attempt to effect a peaceful adjustment with Mexico with Great Britain acting in the role of mediator, according to the promises in the recent Anglo-Texan treaty. Why he should think that with one hand he could make peace with Mexico while with the other he extended the jurisdiction of Texas over an area that by the greatest stretch of the imagination had never been considered a part of historic Texas has never been explained by his most impassioned supporters.

Judge James Webb, former Attorney General and Secretary of State in Lamar's cabinet, was named minister plenipotentiary and envoy extraordinary to Mexico on March 20, 1841. His instructions concerning boundaries were the same as those given to Bee, but if Mexico objected to giving up the harbor of Brazos Santiago, lying just north of the mouth of the Río Grande, she was to be offered free use of the port, as well as the right of deposit. The general tone of his instructions indicated that this was the final effort of Texas to negotiate. They also contained a specific plan for aggressive action should his mission fail.

[30] *Telegraph and Texas Register*, June 23, 1841.
[31] John T. Price to Branch T. Archer, Secretary of War, July 2, 1841, Army Papers (Texas), ms.; Smither (ed.), *Journals of the Sixth Congress of the Republic of Texas*, III, 424–425; *Telegraph and Texas Register*, July 7, 1841.

If you are not permitted to open negotiations with the Government of Mexico, or having opened them, should find it necessary to discontinue them, without any beneficial results, you will after notifying this Government of the fact be at liberty, to return by the way of Yucatán and ascertain what part the government of that country would be willing to take in a war which Texas might be compelled to wage against Mexico. In doing this however it is only expected that you will sound the people of Yucatán on the subject as you are not furnished with authority to enter into any treaty stipulations, but you may suggest to the authorities the propriety of their sending an agent to this Government with full powers to treat and you may give them assurances of our friendship and willingness to receive such an agent.[32]

"How much better it would be," declared the *Brazos Courier* upon the eve of Webb's departure on the *San Bernard*, "if the Government had appointed Commodore Moore, to go down as minister, accompanied by the whole fleet. We could then have *treated* and *coerced* alternately, according to the circumstances."[33]

Upon his arrival at the harbor of Sacrificios, near Vera Cruz, at the end of May, Webb was denied permission to land. The Mexican government not only refused to receive the propositions which he was authorized to make for the adjustment of differences, but it "positively rejected the mediation of the British Government, in the settlement of those differences."[34] "They declare emphatically," Webb informed Lamar, "that they will never discuss, or even receive propositions, *from any source* whatever, which have for their object the separation of Texas from Mexico."[35]

On leaving Mexican waters, Judge Webb explained to Pakenham that the continuation of a pacific policy on the part of Texas would be extremely difficult in view of the overtures constantly being made by the Federalists of Yucatán, who were regarded by many in Texas as seeking to throw off the yoke of despotism.[36] In a communication

[32] J. S. Mayfield to James Webb, Department of State, Austin, March 22, 1841, in Garrison (ed.), *Diplomatic Correspondence of Texas*, 1908, II, 732–736.

[33] *Brazos Courier* (Brazoria), n.d., quoted in *New Orleans Picayune*, April 18, 1841.

[34] James Webb to James S. Mayfield, Galveston, June 29, 1841, in Garrison (ed.), *Diplomatic Correspondence of Texas*, 1908, II, 751–752.

[35] ———— to General [M. B. Lamar], Galveston, June 29, 1841, in *ibid.*, II, 760–766.

[36] James Webb to Richard Pakenham, Texan Schooner San Bernard, Sacrificios, June 16, 1841, in *ibid.*, II, 759–760.

to Lamar, however, Webb, believing that further negotiations with Mexico were useless, gave other reasons for resorting to war now.

I think if active steps are taken, the War may be renewed, and consequences most important to the Nation be atchieved by it, before your administration closes. At all events, the War can be renewed, and placed upon a footing by you as will preclude your successor from discontinuing it, and your administration will have the Credit for it. Should Genl. Houston succeed in the Presidential Canvass (and of this there is now the strongest probability) I understand that he will be opposed to a renewal of the war. Unless therefore it is done in your time, we may expect an additional three years of doubt, difficulty, and embarrassment.[37]

Webb recommended recognition of Yucatán and Tabasco and joining with them in joint declaration of war against Mexico.

General Huston was believed to be extremely anxious "to distinguish himself before the world in the adjustment of . . . [the Texan] differences with Mexico by the sword," wrote Miller, and it is believed "that he will seek every possible means of exciting our people. . . . "And what will be the accomplishment and consequences of opening the war and becoming the assailants"? he asked.

Why, Sir, nothing less than the disturbance, confusion, alarm and uprooting of our whole population, and, withal, the loss of many valuable lives. Distress will hover over the scene from its commencement to its close; and the issue, however favorable will certainly find us, as a nation, impoverished and bankrupt, the scoff and derision of our neighbors. We are doing well enough; and having nothing to apprehend from Mexico. When ever it shall become necessary to protect, in the field, the fair fame of our country, or preserve the integrity of her soil, I and all others are ready to stand by the staff of the tricolor whilst a Texian lives to uphold it.[38]

[37] James Webb to General [M. B. Lamar], Galveston, June 29, 1841, in *ibid.*, II, 760–766.

[38] W. D. Miller to Sam Houston, Gonzales, July 10, 1841, in W. D. Miller Papers, 1833–1860, ms.

CHAPTER EIGHTEEN

Mexican Military Commander
Requests Armistice

BEFORE WORD OF THE FAILURE of Webb's mission reached the Texan authorities, an unexpected overture for the cessation of hostilities came from the commander of the northern frontier of Mexico. A week after the issuance of his proclamation against engaging in illicit trade with the Texans, General Arista, reputedly a man of wealth and the owner of a great deal of land in northern Mexico,[1] addressed a letter to "Mr. Mirabeau Lamar," requesting an armistice to enable him to conduct a war against the Comanches which might entail crossing into Texan territory. "In that spirit of confidence, usual amongst men of honour," wrote Arista, "I address you this communication, which will be handed you by Dr. Rafael Uribe."

The Indians ferocious and sanguinary and perfectly faithless,[2] should be driven beyond the bounds of civilization, and to effect this, a force will soon move from the banks of the Río Bravo.

At the present time War should be carried on, with a frankness and gentlemanly generosity, compatible with the customs and civilizations, to which fortunately both men and Nations have arrived in this age.

Therefore, in accordance with these maxims, I make known to you, with the frankness of a soldier, and with that noble conduct, which should govern all hostilities that the expedition has not in view, as might be supposed, a surprise upon those Colonies, but simply to chastise the ferocious enemies of humanity. This expedition will not commit any acts, which injure any of the inhabitants or citizens of the country, through which it may pass.

This communication must only be interpreted as a manifestation of the anxiety I entertain, for the success of the campaign against the Indians; and not as a suspension of hostilities between us.

Our difficulties, originating, since those colonies declared their pretensions

---

[1] George L. Rives, *The United States and Mexico, 1821–1848*, II, 150.

[2] For ruthless and repeated Indian raids upon the northern frontier of Mexico, see *El Cosmopolita* (Mexico City), May 1, 29, July 23, 28, Aug. 28, Dec. 3, 22, 1841.

431

to Independence, will be settled at some better time, either by the force of reason and judgement, or if that fail, upon the field of battle.[3]

Arista's letter was carried to Texas by two commissioners who passed through San Antonio on their way to the seat of government at Austin. The principal commissioner, Don Rafael Uribe, requested Juan N. Seguin to accompany him to Austin. The Mexican emissaries, accompanied by Seguin, arrived in Austin on June 22 [4] and sought to discuss with Lamar the advisability of sending Mexican troops across the Río Grande for the purpose of subduing the Indians. Seguin attended several of the interviews between Uribe and Lamar. The letter that the commissioners bore to Texas was rejected because it had not been addressed to Lamar as "President of the Republic of Texas," [5] but the President at once availed himself of this opportunity to dispatch two secret commissioners, Cornelius Van Ness and John D. Morris, to Arista's headquarters for "the purpose of coming to some understanding . . . upon the subject of the irregular and brigand border warfare which has unhappily for so long a period desolated our western frontier," said Roberts, Acting Secretary of State, "stripping our citizens of their hard earned property, depriving them of their liberty, and even in many instances of their lives." [6] Another objective of the mission was to make an effort to "establish on a firm and . . . lasting footing a safe and friendly commerce with that portion of the Mexican territory bordering on and to the westward of the Río Grande," although the Texan authorities surely must have known of Arista's

[3] Mariano Arista to Mr. Mirabeau Lamar, Lampazos [Mexico], April 21, 1841 (Confidential), in *Quarterly of the Texas State Historical Association*, VII (1903–1904), 173–174.

[4] *Telegraph and Texas Register*, June 30, 1841, says the commissioners arrived at Austin on June 22. See also Juan N. Seguin, *Personal Memoirs of Juan N. Seguin, from the year 1834 to the Retreat of General Woll from the City of San Antonio in 1842*, p. 20.

[5] Samuel A. Roberts, Acting Secretary of State, to Don Rafael Uribe, Department of State, City of Austin, June 23, 1841, in Garrison (ed.), *Diplomatic Correspondence of Texas*, 1908, II, 747. The complete correspondence between Lamar, Van Ness, Morris, and Roberts, on the one hand, and the Mexican officials (Col. José María Carrasco, General Mariano Arista, and Dr. Rafael Uribe), on the other, may be found in Harriet Smither (ed.), *Journals of the Sixth Congress of the Republic of Texas*, III, 251–264.

[6] Samuel A. Roberts to C. Van Ness and John D. Morris, Department of State, Austin City, June 24, 1841, in Garrison (ed.), *Diplomatic Correspondence of Texas*, 1908, II, 748–749.

widely publicized order of April 13 to all the brigades of the Army Corps of the North that any person apprehended in trading with the Texan enemy was to be sentenced to ten years military service in one of the regular companies on the frontier, and that all goods and effects seized under these circumstances coming from Texas were to be declared "spoils of war." [7] The Texan commissioners were instructed not to commit Texas in the slightest degree to participation in any domestic war in Mexico, nor were they to intervene in any political movement in that country or to consent to any request for Mexican troops to invade Texas, "either under the pretext of chastizing the savages or any other."

At the same time, Lamar addressed a letter to General Arista, declaring

. . . the Government of Texas has witnessed with regret the sectional and border war now existing and which has existed several years past on the adjoining frontiers of Texas and Mexico, and which of late divested of almost every feature of a National contest between the two countries, has become little other than a system of predatory incursion and foray, attended with no other results than the pillage and ruin of exposed and unoffending citizens and settlements. This state of things is not only destructive of the interests of important sections of both countries, but is disreputable to the character of enlightened and honorable people, and should not be suffered to continue any longer. Degrading the profession of arms into robbery and murder, this species of warfare can only lead to crime and individual sufferings, without tending in the least degree towards the adjustment of the difficulties between the two nations.

He pointed to the negotiations then in progress in Mexico whereby it was hoped that permanent peace could be brought about—"a consideration sufficient of itself to induce a suspension of all hostilities for the present, and even more particularly for the abolishment of a petty and provoking mode of warfare, which is calculated to engender personal feuds and revengeful feelings which may linger upon the border even after peace has been established." [8]

Although he was not successful in his mission, during the few days that he was in Texas Uribe learned of the departure of the Santa Fé

[7] *El Cosmopolita*, May 19, 1841.

[8] Mirabeau B. Lamar to Genl. Arista, Executive Department, Austin, June 24, 1841, in Smither (ed.), *Journals of the Sixth Congress of the Republic of Texas*, III, 252–253.

Expedition and was able to inform his government regarding its objective. Finding that the expedition had departed from its camp on Brushy Creek the day before his arrival in Austin, Uribe immediately departed the Texan capital for San Antonio and Mexico, and shortly after his return to Mexico, Governor Francisco G. Conde of the Department of Chihuahua published the news of the Texan expedition toward Nuevo México and warned his people against being led astray by the flattering talk of the Texans.[9] Indeed, in Texas many believed that Arista's request for a cessation of hostilities to enable him to make a campaign against the Comanches was merely a ruse to get an agent to Austin for the purpose of gathering information about the troops being assembled in Texas for an expedition against some point on the Mexican frontier; and, possibly, to delay the march of those troops until the Mexican government could organize its forces to meet the threat to its far northern frontier.

While Uribe was in Texas, Seguin entered into an agreement with him to smuggle goods into Mexico. Seguin's object, in part, was to recoup his financial losses from having fitted out a. company in the Federalist War.[10] On the other hand, he and his associates, Messrs. Blow, Davis, Murphy, Ogden, and Chevallie, were interested in the promotion of illicit trade between San Antonio and the Río Grande settlements simply as a lucrative business proposition. For this object, Seguin obtained from Ogden and Howard a credit of three thousand dollars on part of his property.[11]

Thus, accompanied by Van Ness, Morris, Seguin, Blow, Davis, Murphy, Ogden, and Chevallie, the two Mexican commissioners returned to the Río Grande. On the tenth day, after leaving San Antonio, they reached Guerrero, where the Texan commissioners determined to remain a few days to recruit their horses before pushing on to Arista's headquarters at Monterey.[12] At Guerrero Uribe received a communication from Arista expressing surprise that Seguin was on the frontier in the character of a commissioner from Texas, an erroneous assumption on his part. Indeed, he seemed to be embarrassed by the arrival of emissaries from Texas, and "made a good deal of fuss to exculpate

[9] Francisco G. Conde, *El gobernador y comandante general del departamento, á sus habitantes,* Chihuahua, Julio 28 de 1841, broadside.
[10] Seguin, *Memoirs,* pp. 20–21.
[11] *Ibid.*
[12] John D. Morris to Samuel A. Roberts, San Antonio, Sept. 30, 1841, in Smither (ed.), *Journals of the Sixth Congress of the Republic of Texas,* III, 255.

himself in the eyes of his government." [13] Uribe was asked to report on the purpose of Seguin's mission. The Texan commissioners hastened to assure Uribe, and thereby Arista, that they did not "intend to broach the question of the recognition of the independence of Texas, or that of peace between the two governments," as these were "subjects alone for the consideration of the high powers of the Nation." [14] And then with considerable hypocrisy, they informed Uribe that "the rumours of the approach of a Texan force, to attack this frontier are entirely groundless. Nor will any party authorized by the Government of Texas make an exhibit or commit any act of hostility during our visit. Should any depredations be committed, we can assure you," they said, "that this will proceed from unauthorized banditti."

In a few days, Colonel José María Carrasco, who less than a year before had effected a reconciliation between Arista and Canales, arrived at Guerrero, bearing dispatches from Arista and instructions to open negotiations with the Texan commissioners in the name of his superior. He was instructed to treat the Texans with "marked attention and politeness," and to enter into formal discussions with them concerning the object of their mission. Carrasco informed Morris and Van Ness that "the whole country North of the Sierra Madre was then and had been in a state of violent commotion and agitation, that the federal cause far from being smothered and destroyed by the events of the past year had only been depressed for the moment, in order that it might break out in a form which would give a greater guarantee of success," and their conclusion from Carrasco's conversation, reported the two commissioners, was that the

. . . treaty with Canales was simply an agreement between him and Arista, that the federal cause which was then rather desperate, should be depressed for a while again to rise at a more favorable opportunity, under the guidance and with the assistance of Arista. . . . Col. Carrasco unhesitatingly declared, that he himself was a Federal, and Arista would head the party, in the revolution, which would break out at the very first moment when a favourable opportunity presented itself—that he was most anxious to conciliate the friendship and perhaps assistance of the Texans.[15]

[13] Seguin, *Memoirs*, pp. 20–21.

[14] C. Van Ness and J. D. Morris to Dr. Rafael Uribe [Guerrero, July 18, 1841], in Smither (ed.), *Journals of the Sixth Congress of the Republic of Texas*, III, 255–256.

[15] John D. Morris to Samuel A. Roberts, Acting Secretary of State, San Antonio, Sept. 30, 1841, in Garrison (ed.), *Diplomatic Correspondence of Texas*, 1908, II, 768–776.

Although the Texan commissioners appealed to Carrasco for an end to the "system of predatory incursions and forays, attended with no other results than the pillage and ruin of unoffending citizens and settlements," and hoped for an arrangement which would place intercourse between the two frontiers on a higher and more honorable footing they let it be known that they had not come to compromise "the character or dignity of either nation." Open and honorable war was neither shunned nor invited by Texas, and was far preferable to the species of hostility now being conducted upon the frontier. They went on to say that unless measures were taken to relieve the border settlements from the continued apprehensions they were under, Texas would be forced to take retaliatory measures.

You cannot but be aware that even at the present time, a considerable commerce is carried on between the inhabitants of the two frontiers, and notwithstanding the vigorous efforts which have been made by the authorities both military and civil to put an end to this trade, it continues to exist. That it is beneficial to both countries cannot be denied, nor do we believe it possible effectually to check it unless at an enormous expense and trouble— an expense entirely beyond any benefits to be expected. By authorizing that commerce and protecting, instead of persecuting it we entertain no doubt but that results of the most important character could be realized by you. And as it must exist why not place it upon that footing that will enable you to derive the great benefit which must necessarily arise from it.[16]

Carrasco declared officially that he was unable and unwilling to enter into any negotiations upon the propositions of the Texans, but, reported the Texan commissioners, he gave

. . . an absolute verbal pledge that so soon as the matter could be secretly arranged, the ranging parties who are now stationed on the frontier to intercept traders, and by whom our frontier has been continually harrassed, should be removed, every effort should be made to prevent any hostile movements by the citizens and that so far as they were concerned the trade should proceed free and uninterrupted.[17]

Carrasco pointed out that during the last two years Matamoros, once a flourishing port and growing city, had dwindled to almost nothing

[16] C. Van Ness and J. D. Morris to Col. [J. M.] Carrasco, Guerrero, July 25, 1841, in Garrison (ed.), *Diplomatic Correspondence of Texas,* 1908, II, 772–773.
[17] John D. Morris to Samuel A. Roberts, Acting Secretary of State, San Antonio, Sept. 30, 1841, in *ibid.,* II, 768–776.

and that only about one-fourth of the usual revenue was obtained at the customhouse for the area, and, hence, the principal support for the Centralist army in the north had greatly declined. He was in favor of encouraging and promoting the contraband trade as a means of weakening the Centralist party; and, therefore, was not inclined to facilitate legitimate trade. Finally, however, Carrasco gave way on this point and the other, for ending hostilities, and Morris and Van Ness, thinking that their mission had been accomplished, started for home.

No sooner were they across the river than they were overtaken by an express from Arista, bearing passports and a note urging them to proceed immediately to Monterey to confer with him. Morris and Van Ness, accompanied by the other Americans, proceeded to Monterey, but Seguin was ordered to remain at Guerrero. Chevallie, who was sick with the fever, had to remain with him, until the return of his associates.

Well might Arista embarrass Bustamante's government by dealing with the hated colonials in the face of rising revolution at home, and especially when it was being publicized in Mexico that a Texan military expedition had headed toward Santa Fé with the object of "closely uniting it with the rest of the Republic," so that "the supremacy" of the Texan constitution and laws might be asserted equally over the entire tract of country embraced within the claimed limits of Texas and all public property there taken possession of by force if necessary.[18] Already Arista had ordered troops marched from Matamoros to San Fernando to strengthen the northwestern defenses against the advance of the Texan expedition toward Santa Fé.

In Texas it was believed that Arista was on the verge of instituting a revolt against the Centralist government, headed by Bustamante, and that if he did issue a *pronunciamiento* it would be under the banner of "Federalism." [19] Colonel Juan N. Seguin had engaged, it was said, the services of about seventy volunteers to join the standard of Arista in the event he broke with the Mexican government. But, at this time, Arista and Ampudia seemed anxious to remove all suspicion of such an act, and, consequently, in the face of published reports of Seguin's activities, which were bound to make their way into Mexico,

---

[18] Samuel A. Roberts to William G. Cooke, Antonio Navarro, Richard F. Brenham, and William G. Dryden, Commissioners, Department of State, Austin, June 15, 1841, in Smither (ed.), *Journals of the Sixth Congress of the Republic of Texas*, III, 289–294.

[19] *Telegraph and Texas Register* (Houston), June 9 and 16, 1841.

437

Arista could not do otherwise than to order Seguin stopped at the frontier, for it was yet a month before General Mariano Paredes y Arrillaga raised the standard of liberalism at Jalisco. Eventually, Arista ordered Seguin to leave the country, and the goods that he had carried to Mexico to trade were left on consignment to be disposed of for him. Recorded Seguin in his *Memoirs*,[20]

When I heard that they had been sold I sent Chevallie with some men of San Antonio to the place appointed by my agent, to receive the proceeds of the sale, but the agent not having shown himself, Chevallie returned to San Antonio empty handed. Shortly afterwards, an American, who came from Mexico, informed me that a certain [Francisco] Cavillo, who was on the look out for smugglers, had seized upon my money.

Chevallie remained with Seguin, and after the latter's expulsion continued with him until the return of his associates.[21]

As the Texan commissioners proceeded inland they found the Mexicans east of the mountains and west of the Río Grande anxiously praying for peace and the reopening of a safe and direct trade with Texas. They found their present condition deplorable, not only because of the oppression of their government but also because of the destruction of their flocks and crops by the drought. From January to August there had been no rain in that section of the country, and as they passed through, the Texan commissioners found that "the atmosphere had become offensive from the number of cattle which had perished from the want of water." [22]

Five days after leaving Guerrero, the Texan commissioners reached Monterey, where they were received by Arista with marked attention and politeness. Arista was pictured at this time as "a thick set, corpulent Mexican of ordinary stature, about forty years old, with red hair, large bushy whiskers, and a beard ten inches long, also red." [23] He was

[20] P. 20; Mariano Arista to Pedro de Ampudia, Army Corps of the North, Dec. 26, 1841, no. 450, in *El Honor Nacional* (Matamoros), Dec. 27, 1841.

[21] Seguin, *Memoirs*, p. 20.

[22] *Austin City Gazette* quoted in *Telegraph and Texas Register*, Sept. 29, 1841.

[23] *Telegraph and Texas Register*, Jan. 6, 1841. Mariano Arista was born at San Luis Potosí on July 16, 1802, and died at Lisbon, Portugal, August 9, 1855, at the age of fifty-three years. He began his military career at the age of eleven as a cadet in the Spanish army, rising later to the rank of lieutenant. He served in the Spanish army until June 1821, when he joined the revolutionary cause. During General Victoria's administration in 1825 Arista became a captain and a

considered more of a politician than a soldier; yet, according to Doctor Francis Moore of the *Telegraph* of January 6, 1841, he seemed to be the "ablest and most enterprising of the generals now in the Mexican service; but like most other Mexicans, he is more distinguished for the attributes of the blustering braggadocio, than for true heroism." In the summer of 1841 Arista appeared to favor the Federalist cause and was

distinguished member of the "Yorkino" Party. After 1826 he was alternately a supporter and an opponent of Santa Anna, and for a time, while suffering under the latter's displeasure, lived at Cincinnati, Ohio, where he learned the saddler's trade. In 1832 he was made a lieutenant colonel and when Santa Anna came to office was promoted to the rank of general of division. In 1833 he was forced to leave Mexico for the United States, but returned to Mexico in June 1835, to accept the terms of the Amnesty Decree of May 2, 1835, and resumed his military position. In 1835 he was named judge of the Supreme Tribunal of War, which position he held until April 1837. In June 1837, he was named a member of the Junta de Código Militar, and a little later a member of the Consejo Consultivo de Guerra, and in October 1837, became inspector of the Active Militia. During Bustamante's second administration he was reinstated in the Mexican army and was in command of a force intended to relieve Vera Cruz when he was captured by the French on December 5, 1838, but was released after a short and easy captivity of two months. In 1839 he was given command of a brigade to suppress the revolution of General José Urrea in Tampico, afterwards becoming Commandant General of Tamaulipas. Towards the end of 1839, after the defeat of Col. Francisco G. Pavón by a combined Federal-Texas force, he was named commander in chief of the Army Corps of the North, and hurried north from Mexico City to organize the defenses of Monterey. In September 1841, Bustamante made him general of a division and he opposed Santa Anna's efforts to oust Bustamante from the control of the government in Mexico. Upon the fall of Bustamante's government, Arista renounced his command in November 1841, but was re-named (in 1842) shortly after being exonerated of the charge of fomenting a revolution. In March 1843, he was reported in a state of declining health at his hacienda of Mamoelique. For a brief period after the commencement of the war with the United States in 1846, he commanded the Mexican troops in the North. In June 1848, he was named Minister of War by President Herrera. He served as Commandant General of Durango in 1849 and of San Luis Potosí in 1853; soon, however, retiring to his hacienda (Lanos de Apam) because of the changed political situation, later going to Europe, where he lived for a while in Spain. Becoming ill, he started for France, but died at Lisbon, August 9, 1855, the same day that Santa Anna, who had usurped his position as president, fled from Mexico. George L. Rives, *The United States and Mexico, 1821–1848*, I, 442, 448; Hubert Howe Bancroft, *History of Mexico*, V, 133–135; *Telegraph and Texas Register*, Oct. 20 and 27, 1841; *El Cosmopolita*, March 25, 1843; *Diario official* (Mexico City), Oct. 19, 1881; Albert M. Carreño (ed.), *Jefes del ejército mexicano en 1847: biográfias de generals de division y de coronels del ejército mexicano por fines del año de 1847*, pp. 44–49.

only awaiting an opportunity to rise against the government, and, therefore, dared not enter into any formal arrangement in respect to trade relations and an armistice which might embarrass him with the Centralist authority.[24]

The Texan commissioners were requested by Carrasco and Arista to make their written communications "as mild and conciliating as the nature of things would permit," and were assured that their letters would be transmitted to Mexico City. Carrasco flatly told them that "it would be impossible openly and publicly to concede" to their propositions, "but that whilst a secret negotiation might take place in which all our propositions and plans might be carried out," they reported, "still . . . the answer which appeared to the world, and more especially that which would be sent to government authorities at Mexico, should contain a flat and positive refusal of all our propositions." The high authorities in Mexico wished to appear "most inverterately opposed to any thing like conciliation with Texas," and the reception of any Texan agent, no matter in what capacity he might go, would be considered a high crime in the eyes of the government, Reported Van Ness and Morris,

Gen. Arista, or rather his agent Col. Carrasco, was anxious to conciliate, and to accede to our propositions, but at the same time wishes to hoodwink his government. He therefore privately entered into an agreement with us, and publicly disclosed his utter refusal to comply with our propositions. The truth is, the whole Mexican country is in a perfect ferment, and on the eve of a great revolution.

Arista is still doubtful as to the probable result of this impending revolution, and with a fair prospect of the Presidential chair on one side, should he adhere to the Central cause, and the absolute certainty of his being elevated to the highest station in the nation should be espouse the Federal cause, and in case of their success. In this state of affairs Arista is halting, as to his decision, he is privately conciliating the Citizens, all of whom with but few exceptions belong to the Federal party, and inducing among them the belief that he inclines to their side, whilst all his public acts which he knows must reach to Government, would declare him the most uncompromising, and devoted Central. Hence arises the unmitigated abuse of Texas and the Texans, which daily emanates from all the newspapers.[25]

[24] *Cf.* John W. Bradley to J. G. Chalmers, San Antonio, Aug. 3, 1841, in Domestic Correspondence (Texas), 1836–1846, ms.

[25] C. Van Ness and John D. Morris to Samuel A. Roberts, San Antonio, Sept. 30, 1841, in Smither (ed.), *Journals of the Sixth Congress of the Republic of Texas*, III, 258.

Arista informed the Texan commissioners that the regular troops ranging on the frontier had always received specific orders from him not to cross the Nueces, which he implied was the boundary; and, he asserted that they had been instructed not to molest any unoffending citizens of Texas. These orders, he said, would still be enforced, but

. . . that for his own protection he should be compeled to use every means in his power to put a stop to the trade, on the grounds that such trade was illegal, since it was being carried on by belligerents.[26] He informed us, [continued Morris] that at present, and for a long time to come, no hope need be entertained by Texas of a recognition of her independence by Mexico, not only on account of the inveterate animosity entertained towards us, but because a Texas Campaign was always a sure means of raising money, when required by the Government. But that we might be well assured that no hostile operations would or could be made against Texas for the present,"

and Morris believed that Mexico had not "the most remote idea of ever invading Texas yet she has no stronger inclination," he said, "to recognize our independence than when Santa Anna first marched against us with his invading army." [27] Arista declared that he was un-

[26] This attitude on the part of Arista was in line with his proclamation of April 13, 1841, "To the troops under my command and to the Inhabitants of the Frontier of the Department of the East," prohibiting trade with the Texans. He announced that any citizen caught trading with the Texans would be arrested and made to serve ten years in a permanent frontier company of the army, and that all his effects and beasts engaged in the trade would be confiscated. He declared "booty of war all effects coming from Texas apprehended from the left bank of the Río Bravo toward the interior of the territory usurped by the Texians: those apprehended on the right side [of the river] would be considered as contraband." Those who assisted the Texans in conducting the contraband trade would likewise be punished. Mariano Arista, *El C[iudadano] Mariano Arista, general de brigada del egército mégicano y en gefe del cuerpo de Egército del Norte.* [Proclamation defining and imposing penalties for engaging in contraband trade with Texas and providing for the division of captured contraband.] "Á los tropos de mi mando y á los habitantes de la frontera de los Departamentos de Oriente . . ." [Dated and signed at the end:] Dado en el cuartel general de Sabinas de dia 13 de Abril de 1841. Broadside.

[27] John D. Morris to Samuel A. Roberts, San Antonio, Sept. 13, 1841; Mariano Arista to Cornelius Van Ness and John D. Morris, Aug. 8, 1841, in Garrison (ed.), *Diplomatic Correspondence of Texas,* 1908, II, 767-768, 776-777. Henry M. Morfit, President Andrew Jackson's secret agent to Texas, reported an interview he had near Orozimbo in September 1836, with Santa Anna, a prisoner in Texas, in which Santa Anna said, in substance, "he would avow frankly though with much mortification, that there were many men in Office in Mexico who did not

able, as an officer of the Mexican government, to entertain any conversation with the Texan commissioners on the subjects of an armistice and on the reopening of the frontier trade.

In breaking off the conferences with the Texan emissaries, Arista informed them on August 8 that

. . . there can be no doubt that Texas belongs to Mexico, and that the inhabitants of that territory have rebelled against the legitimate Govt. It is not to be presumed that in this case the rules and forms observed by different nations at issue with each other, at all exist, much less that international laws be recurred to.

Upon this principal then no relations or treaty whatever can be entered upon which does not have for its basis the *subjection of that country to the* Govt. of Mexico.

He then proceeded to inform Van Ness and Morris that the Mexican frontier commander was acquainted with and acted in conformity with the rules of war, with the instructions of his government, and the spirit of the age, and the laws of humanity. He reminded the Texan commissioners that the frontier commander "never attacks the innocent citizen, particularly as he is persuaded that in Texas there are many pacific persons who heartily desire to return to obedience to the Republic" of Mexico.[28]

Possibly, with the desire to show his good intentions towards peaceful Texans, Arista, upon learning of the arrest of Dimitt (discussed in chapter XIX), ordered him and the other Texan prisoners to be sent to Monterey with the object of liberating them, since it was felt that they could not be freed at Matamoros in view of the excitement against them in that city. At the time the Texan commissioners left Monterey, Dimitt and his companions had not arrived.[29] When they did reach Monterey, capital of Nuevo León, the turmoil of revolution had rolled northward making Arista's position quite uncertain, and the attitude

really know where Texas was, and that therefore it should not astonish anyone if their attention could easily be withdrawn from a war, about the cause of which they were ignorant and from a country which the most of them did not know they had ever claimed." Henry M. Morfit to John Forsyth, near Orazimba, Sept. 6, 1836, in Correspondence and Reports of American Agents and Others in Texas, 1836–1845, Justin H. Smith, "Transcripts," V, ms.

[28] Mariano Arista al Sres. Dn. C. Van Ness y Dn. T. [J.] Morris, Agosto 8 de 1841 (Particular), in Garrison (ed.), *Diplomatic Correspondence of Texas,* 1908, II, 776–777; *Telegraph and Texas Register,* Sept. 22, 1841.

[29] *Austin City Gazette* quoted in *Telegraph and Texas Register,* Sept. 29, 1841.

of the Mexican populace had been affected, too, by the late events on the Texas frontier. Thus, when the Texan prisoners reached Monterey, they were ordered on to Mexico City.

While the Texan commissioners were yet at Monterey, two Mexicans who had been captured by a party of Texans néar Goliad, succeeded in making their escape and arriving in town. Their report "produced a great excitement among the liberal party, the friends of Texas," reported Morris, "and two Americans, Drs. Tower and Cottle, were in a day or two placed under arrest." Hostile movements on the frontier on the part of Texans, he continued, could "result in no beneficial effect, but . . . render many who are now firm friends, in self-defence, our most inveterate foes. Could Matamoros be destroyed," he said, "good might result for these all are Centrals, and all most bitter enemies of Texas." [30]

After twelve days at Monterey, where they "received every attention from Arista, his officers, and all the people," Morris and Van Ness, feeling that nothing more could be accomplished, departed for home under an escort of an officer and eight soldiers, who accompanied them as far as the Río Grande. The two commissioners reached Béxar on the evening of September 7. [31] At San Antonio, they were reported as saying that General Arista had assured them that he contemplated no hostile movements against Texas, and that he had given orders that no Texan citizen should be molested east of the Río Grande and had remarked that if any of his officers had injured any citizens of Texas east of that stream, they should be punished. [32] At this time Arista probably had his hands full protecting the northern frontier against the barbarous Indians without wishing to antagonize the Texans by making raids across the Río Grande. Upon their return home the Texan commissioners reported that "the whole open country beyond the Río Grande" had been laid waste by the Comanches, who had extended their ravages close to the very streets of Monterey, driving off immense herds of cattle and droves of horses and mules. [33] "One thing is cer-

---

[30] John D. Morris to Samuel A. Roberts, Sept. 30, 1841, in Garrison (ed.), *Diplomatic Correspondence of Texas*, 1908, II, 776.

[31] *Telegraph and Texas Register*, Sept. 22, 1841. A week later (Sept. 29), this same paper reported that Van Ness and Morris reached San Antonio on the morning of September 6.

[32] *Ibid.*

[33] C. Van Ness and J. D. Morris to Samuel A. Roberts, San Antonio, Sept. 30, 1841 (and enclosures), in Garrison (ed.), *Diplomatic Correspondence of Texas*,

tain," reported the editor of the *Austin City Gazette*, "Texas need not anticipate an invasion from Mexico, no matter how much the Mexican Government and the papers under their control may talk about and threaten an invasion; it is merely done for effect, and *as a means of raising money,* but without even the most distant intention of making the attempt." [34]

1908, II, 768–777. A similar view was expressed by William E. Jones, from Gonzales County, in the House of Representatives on December 9, 1841, in Smither (ed.), *Journals of the Sixth Congress of the Republic of Texas,* II, 121–122.
[34] Quoted in *Telegraph and Texas Register,* Sept. 29, 1841.

CHAPTER NINETEEN

Capture and Death of Dimitt

IN THE MEANTIME, the Mexican raids on the southwestern frontier con-. tinued unabated throughout the summer and into the fall of 1841. Early in June Kinney & Aubrey were reported doing an excellent business with the Mexican traders.[1] Philip Dimitt, James Gourlay of Lamar and late a resident of Matamoros,[2] and John Sutherland, with the assistance of James C. Boyd and William Thompson, employees, began in May 1841, the establishment of a trading post on the Laguna Madre, near Flour Bluff, in the Corpus Christi area in competition with Aubrey and Kinney, whom they accused of having treasonable relations with the Mexican authorities on the Río Grande, particularly at Matamoros. Dimitt's establishment, located near the head of Padre Island [3] about fifteen miles below Aubrey & Kinney's rancho and about twenty-five miles southeast of the mouth of the Nueces was expected to cut into the latter's "excellent business with the Mexican traders." [4] Stephen W. Farrow and Henry Graham, traders, also resided nearby. In May, after the establishment of his competitor in a more favored position, Kinney paid a visit to Arista's headquarters, and was reported on June 9 as having received assurance from him that he would not be molested.[5]

On July 1, 1841, without a single vessel afloat in the Gulf, the Mexican government declared the ports of Texas and Yucatán to be in a state of blockade and prohibited the introduction of the products of

[1] *Telegraph and Texas Register* (Houston), June 9, 1841.
[2] Reuben M. Potter to Genl. M. B. Lamar, Velasco, Nov. 26, 1838, in *Lamar Papers*, V, 218.
[3] Vicente Sánchez described the location as on Padre Island, near its head. Vicente Sánchez á Sr. general commandante de la 2ª Brigada de la 1ª Division del Cuerpo de Ejército del Norte D. Pedro de Ampudia, Matamoros, Julio 9 de 1841, in *El Ancla* (Matamoros), July 12, 1841.
[4] *Telegraph and Texas Register*, June 9, 1841.
[5] *Ibid.*

either of these "republics" into the ports of Mexico.[6] "This silly attempt to assert the supremacy of the Supreme Government of Mexico, when they dare not set a single armed vessel afloat in the Gulf, will have no effect than to prove that the members of that Government, President and all, are supremely stupid," declared the editor of the *Telegraph*; "and their silly order should be styled the Blockhead's Blockade." [7]

In carrying out the terms of this proclamation and of Arista's of April 13, as well as to take alive or dead known enemies of Mexico operating below the Nueces, the historic Spanish-Mexican boundary of the former province of Texas, Lieutenant (Brevet Captain) Vicente Sánchez, aide-de-camp to General Ampudia at Matamoros, was assigned the task of eliminating the *contrabandistas*,[8] and especially of apprehending Dimitt (the "principal object" of the mission). Sánchez commenced his advance towards the Nueces with fourteen men, while the Texan commissioners were on their way to Arista's headquarters to treat on the subject of ending brigand warfare on the frontier. On July 4 Sánchez, accompanied by Blas Falcón, "well known as Aubrey and Kinney's spy, travelling agent or courier," [9] arrived at a distance of half a mile of the Isleta de la Posa (Dimitt's Island). From here he sent forward Lieutenant Chipita with five men to reconnoiter and see if any enemy force was near, for it had been reported in Matamoros that a Texan unit of some eighty men was operating in the vicinity of the Nueces. This rumor probably had reference to Captain Price's company that had reached the Nueces on June 23. If Dimitt was found at the island, he and his companions were to be arrested and brought to Matamoros. The Mexican detail arrived at the edge of the bay opposite the island, and while they were surveying the situation, saw a boat approaching about 2 P.M., which they hailed, indicating at the same time that they were rancheros come to buy goods to be smuggled into northern Mexico. The boat was manned by William Thompson, whom Dimitt had sent that morning to the pass to purchase lumber

[6] *Ibid.*, Sept. 22, 1841.

[7] *Ibid.*

[8] Pedro de Ampudia á Sr. general en gefe del cuerpo de ejército del Norte D. Mariano Arista, [dated:] Cuerpo de ejército del Norte, 1ª Division, 2ª Brigada, Matamoros, Julio 9 de 1841, *El Ancla*, July 12, 1841. Ampudia enclosed a copy of Vicente Sánchez á Sr. general comandante de la 2ª Brigada de la 1ª Division del cuerpo de Ejército del Norte D. Pedro de Ampudia, Matamoros, Julio 9 de 1841, in *ibid.*

[9] William Thompson's affidavit, Republic of Texas, Victoria County, July 10, 1841, in *Telegraph and Texas Register*, Aug. 11, 1841.

Capture and Death of Dimitt

from a vessel there. As Thompson hove to and landed, Chipita engaged him in a brief conversation and then suddenly told him that he was under arrest.[10] Thompson was taken inland to the main unit, where he was held under guard. In the meantime, a small Mexican detail crossed in the boat to the island; where Dimitt, James C. Boyd, Henry Graham, and Stephen W. Farrow, an old soldier who was said to have been in every battle of the Revolution except that of the Alamo, appeared and likewise, after a brief conversation were arrested and transferred to the mainland.[11] The Mexicans plundered Dimitt's establishment of all merchandise, money, and everything of value,[12] which along with the prisoners, were transferred to the mainland. Among the captured items were 100 barrels of tobacco and 229 silver pesos. The total value of the captured goods was estimated at $6,000. A part of

[10] Ibid.

[11] W. B. Goodman, who had returned from New Orleans with a stock of goods, landed at Corpus Christi on July 4, the day of Dimitt's capture near Flour Bluff. He later reported that Dimitt and his companions were taken near the head of Padre Island. W. B. Goodman, "A Statement of Facts, Washington, Feby 10, 1843," in W. D. Miller Papers, 1833–1860, ms. Goodman was nominated and appointed by Lamar on Oct. 6, 1841, chief justice of San Patricio County. State Department Letterbook, no. 1, ms., pp. 250–251.

William Thompson reported that after his capture he was moved inland a short distance, where he found Dimitt, Farrow, and Graham, also prisoners. This may well be the case since the Mexican force was divided, and he may not have been aware of the fact that his boat was used to go to the island and transfer his companions to the shore. "William Thompson's Affidavit, Republic of Texas, Victoria County, July 10, 1841," Telegraph and Texas Register, Aug. 11, 1841.

[12] James Gourlay, Jr., to Branch T. Archer, Lamar, July 8, 1841, copy in Army Papers (Texas), ms. Gourlay, age 35, was a partner of Dimitt's. He was arrested on August 10, 1837, in the streets of Matamoros and held prisoner at Tampico by General Filisola's orders until Sept. 16, when he was released upon protest by the U.S. consul that he was a citizen of the U.S. and native of Albany, N.Y. D. W. Smith to Gen. Vicenta Filisola, Consulate of the U.S.A., Matamoros, Aug. 24, 1837, in Consular Dispatches (U.S.), 1837–1839 (Matamoros), ms., microfilm. Previous to the raid, he had been obliged to go on business to Lamar, where his family was residing at the time. He did not get back to Corpus Christi until the day after the Mexican party had left. James W. Byrne to Branch T. Archer, Lamar, Refugio County, July 8, 1841; James Gourlay, Jr., to Branch T. Archer, Lamar, July 8, 1841; copies in Army Papers (Texas), ms. A native-born Irishman, James W. Byrne came to Texas from the United States in 1835 or early 1836 and served in the revolutionary army. He was one of the founders of Lamar. From 1839–1841 he served as clerk of Refugio County, and as Senator from the Refugio district in the Fifth, Sixth, and Seventh Congresses of the Republic. Handbook of Texas, I, 260.

the goods, but not the tobacco, was loaded on two vessels in the bay, and the remainder was packed away on mules. According to Arista's proclamation, the tobacco was not subject to division among the captors but became the property of the government. One of the vessels appropriated by the Mexicans was described as a "boat," found in the bay, managed by a decrepit old man named Manuel; the other was a lagoon skiff, which was seen approaching on the day following the capture of Dimitt and was taken without resistance. Its crew was tied up and held captive.

While these events were transpiring, the remainder of the Mexican party under Captain Sánchez reconnoitered carefully along the shore to learn if other enemies were in the vicinity, and, if so, in what force. Finding no signs of an enemy. Sánchez and his men passed to the island adjoining to take precautionary measures without delay and to keep news of their arrival from spreading, for fear that superior Texan forces, known to be a short distance away, would come to attack him.

During the afternoon of the 4th, Sánchez learned that at a place, three miles distant, called Sal de la Nación, several Texans were working.[13] The Texans working the salt deposits were said to be well armed. Fearing that should the smallness of his force become known to them he might be attacked, the Mexican captain decided to take the initiative and see if he could surprise and capture them. For this purpose he dispatched Lieutenant Chipita and five of his most trusted men, who succeeded in capturing the six men at the salt lagoon.

The Mexican troops spent the night in the vicinity of Kinney's rancho. During the evening Captain Sánchez and Lieutenant Chipita visited the ranch, but nothing at the ranch was disturbed, nor was any person connected with that establishment or in the employment of Kinney and Aubrey molested.[14] About daylight they returned from Colonel Kinney's with bottles of whiskey, pilot bread, and other supplies. Thompson later stated under oath that Don Juan, a trader who arrived about the same time as the Mexican force from the Río Grande, remarked to Sánchez that he had been up to Colonel Kinney's, to which "the Captain merely replied with a laugh."[15]

After spending a night of uneasiness and constant vigilance, the Mexican party prepared to return to Matamoros on the afternoon of

[13] *El Ancla*, July 12, 1841.
[14] *Telegraph and Texas Register*, July 14 and 21, 1841.
[15] "William Thompson's Affidavit, Republic of Texas, Victoria County, July 10, 1841," *ibid.*, Aug. 11, 1841.

the 5th. Dimitt protested his arrest, declaring that he was engaged in legitimate trade and did not deal in stolen cattle; but Sánchez informed him that he had been ordered arrested as a spy, presumably on the basis of a letter he had written on Mexican affairs which had appeared in the *Austin City Gazette*, October 14, 1840. His captors told him that he, along with the others, would be taken to Matamoros, some sixty leagues away, "but that he should not blame the Mexicans as he had been denounced by his own countrymen." [16] Later, William Thompson testified that a Mexican trader, who had joined the group, claimed that he had seen a letter from a certain Texan, whom the Mexican said he need not name, informing General Ampudia that Dimitt, who had been very active in the Texas revolutionary movement around Goliad, was stationed on the frontier by the Texan government to watch the movements of the Mexicans.[17]

Dimitt, Boyd, Farrow, Graham, Juan Gómez, a man stained by many horrible crimes, and another Texan were carried off as prisoners. The last two were among those taken from the salt lake. William Thompson, whom the Mexicans believed to be too sick to travel, and the other four taken at El Sal de la Nación were released at the time the Mexicans began their withdrawal, because, so the Mexicans said, they had an insufficient number of men to guard them, and because they were good men and laborers. Thompson, however, testified on the 10th, that when the salt workers were interrogated by Captain Sánchez, they declared that they worked for Colonel Kinney; whereupon, the Captain said, " 'Ah, very well, if they belong to Col. Kinney don't disturb them.' " [18]

Just as Sánchez was about to commence his march, José María Cabazos came up with a group of *vecinos*. Cabazos reported he had been commissioned by the sub-prefect of Reinosa to intercept illicit traders. The newcomers assisted Sánchez's men as much as they could and the tobacco was distributed among them, which seemed better than dumping it into the bay or burning it. All of the prisoners, except Dimitt and Boyd, were sent on the two vessels with the plunder and a guard of twelve men from Sánchez's *partida*. Dimitt and Boyd were

---

[16] Catherine George, "The Life of Philip Dimmitt," pp. 73–74.

[17] William Thompson's affidavit, Republic of Texas, *Victoria County*, July 10, 1841, in *Telegraph and Texas Register*, Aug. 11, 1841; see also James Gourlay, Jr., to Branch T. Archer, Lamar, July 8, 1841, copy in Army Papers (Texas), ms.

[18] Deposition of William Thompson of Corpus Christi Bay, July 10, 1841, *Telegraph and Texas Register*, Aug. 11, 1841.

considered too valuable to be entrusted to the vicissitudes of a voyage along the coast. They were securely tied, carefully guarded, and, under the immediate supervision of Sánchez marched to Matamoros. Among other things, Boyd was wanted in Mexico for having stolen one of the small guard boats from the port of Brazos de Santiago.[19]

Although Sánchez returned to Matamoros, other parties of Mexican troops guarded the crossings of the Arroyo Colorado to prevent the entry of hostile Indians and to keep robbers from Texas from depredating the Mexican settlements below.[20]

Up to this time, Philip Dimitt was probably the most important Texan to be captured by the Mexicans since the battle of San Jacinto. Dimitt came to Texas in 1822 from Kentucky, and for many years engaged in the frontier trade. At first he established himself at San Antonio and participated in the trade between northern Mexico and New Orleans. In 1828 he married María Luisa Lazo, daughter of Xavier Lazo and Josefa Calaona; became a naturalized Mexican citizen, a Roman Catholic, and a landholder, owning by 1838 more than thirty leagues of land in the southwest.[21] About 1832 he established a trading post on a site on Lavaca Bay, which became known as "Dimitt's Landing" or "Dimitt's Point." He traded in coffee, rice, dishes, hardware, corn, tobacco, and cotton seeding machines.[22] He took part in the capture of Goliad during the early days of the Texas revolution, and played an active part throughout the revolutionary period. Acting Governor James W. Robinson appointed him public storekeeper at Lavaca Bay, and his warehouse was designated the place for deposit of all government stores landed at that point. At the May 1841, term of the District Court for Refugio County Carlos de la Garza instituted suit against Dimitt for ejectment from a piece of land which he had

[19] Vicente Sánchez á Sr. general comandante de la 2ª Brigada de la 1ª Division del cuerpo de Ejército del Norte D. Pedro de Ampudia, Matamoros, Julio 9 de 1841, in *El Ancla*, July 12, 1841.

[20] Jesús Cárdenas á Antonio Salazar, Señor Secretaría del Gobierno del Departamento [de Tamaulipas], Matamoros, Julio 16 de 1841, in *Gaceta de Gobierno de Tamaulipas* (Ciudad Victoria), July 31, 1841.

[21] George, "The Life of Philip Dimmitt," pp. 1–61; Philip Dimitt to Henry Smith, Goliad, Dec. 29, 1835, in William C. Binkley (ed.), *Official Correspondence of the Texan Revolution, 1835–1836*, I, 251.

[22] Most of the trade through Texas with the inhabitants of the interior of northern Mexico before 1836 was carried on through Goliad. Eugene C. Barker, *The Life of Stephen F. Austin*, p. 336 n.

entered and held "forcibly without shadow of title." [23] At the same term of court the Republic of Texas accused both Dimitt and Edward Fitzgerald of violating the postal laws; each pleaded guilty and was fined.[24]

The news of Dimitt's capture spread quickly. It required five days for William Thompson, who had feigned sickness so well that the Mexicans had left him, to carry the news from Flour Bluff to Austin, via Lamar, Victoria, and Gonzales. En route Thompson collected and conveyed to Austin the resolutions of a public meeting at Victoria, letters from Captain Byrne and Gourlay at Lamar, and from "several highly intelligent gentlemen at Gonzales and other places." [25] At Victoria a public meeting was held on the 10th at the home of Charles Vincent, with Thomas Newcomb presiding, to protest the capture.[26] A preamble and resolutions offered by Major Richard Roman were adopted [27] declaring that

. . . it appears manifest to us, that the Mexican authorities are enforcing an open and avowed occupation of the Territory lying west of the Nueces River; and we would respectfully suggest, that the time has arrived when it is imperative upon this government to assert her claim to the said territory by a sufficient force, and occupation thereof; and that Government should adopt instant and energetic measures for the release of our patriotic and unfortunate fellow citizens.

[23] "Memo[randum] for Refugio District Court, May Term, A.D. 1841," Andrew Neill Papers, 1824–1874, ms. Andrew Neill was District Attorney at this time.

[24] *Ibid.*

[25] Samuel A. Roberts to M. B. Lamar, Austin, July 14, 1841 (at night), in *Lamar Papers*, III, 546–547.

[26] "Copy of Minutes of a Public Meeting of the Town of Victoria held July 10, 1841, in regard to the Capture of Captain Dimitt *et al.*, Army Papers (Texas), ms.

[27] "Copy of a Memorial of a Committee chosen and appointed by the Public Meeting of the Citizens of Victoria, July 10, 1841, addressed to the Hon. Branch T. Archer, Secretary of War and Navy," *ibid.* The memorial is signed by Richard Roman, John T. Price, A. S. McDonald, A. J. Cunningham, J. T. O'Reilly, and Thomas Newcomb. See also, *Texas Centinel* . . . . Extra. Austin, Thursday Morning, July 15, 1841. [At head of first column:] Important from the West— Recommencement of Mexican Hostilities upon Our Inhabitants. [Editorial comment on the abduction of Captain Philip Dimitt and others by the Mexicans under General Arista, followed by a report of the proceedings of a "Public Meeting at Victoria," protesting the abduction, signed and dated at end:] Thomas Newcomb, Chairman. J. T. O'Reilly, Secretary. Victoria, July 10, 1841. [Austin: Printed at the *Texas Centinel* Office, 1841], broadside.

They also recommended "an immediate retaliation be made on the exposed frontier of the enemy, and that they be reminded by proper action on our part, that such assumption and such outrage, will not be tolerated." In conclusion, the memorialists suggested that a sufficient militia or volunteer force should be "immediately authorized to effect that object" and to "remove from the western border of the Republic any individual or individuals, who, losing sight of their proper character as Texan citizens, admit the dominion of Mexico on any portion of the soil of this Republic or pay allegiance to the sovereignty of Mexico whilst residing in and claiming the benefits of our Government." By the latter suggestion, they probably had reference to Kinney, Aubrey, and Don Carlos de la Garza. The petitioners stated their readiness to retaliate if Dimitt and his companions were not immediately released and their property restored, and they requested permission of the government to go to their rescue, "and should it not be obtained," wrote James Wright, late member of Congress, "they will go on their own responsibility. . . . I have no doubt," he continued, "that Kinney is acting a double part." [28] Similar indignation meetings were held at Lamar, Gonzales, and other towns. Letters accompanying the resolutions declared the determination of the inhabitants in the various towns and surrounding areas to turn out en masse with, or without, official orders to make good the claims of Texas to the territory between the Nueces and the Río Grande and to retaliate for the injuries they had suffered.[29]

"The people in the more settled areas of the Republic, however, were less inclined to rush headlong to the Río Grande."

[28] J. Wright to B. T. Archer, Victoria, July 10, 1841, Army Papers (Texas), ms., copy.

[29] *Texas Centinel* (Austin), July 15, 1841 (extra). Being so ill that he was scarcely able to sit up, James W. Robinson appealed to the Secretary of War to rescue Dimitt.

I pray you, in God's name, secure him if you can, and the benedictions of millions of freemen will bless the act, and a weeping and desponding wife, and six helpless children, will breath the holiest prayer ever uttered for your happiness; but I need not say so—I know you will rescue him if you can. The sentiments of the people will be unanimously with you; and any expense will most assuredly be paid by Congress. This county would turn out, in my opinion nearly in masse, for this object.

J. W. Robinson to B. T. Archer, Gonzales, July 13, 1841, Army Papers (Texas), ms., copy.

Capture and Death of Dimitt

The people of Austin, [declared editor Dr. Francis Moore of Houston, making a dig at the new capital] are so cut off from the rest of the republic, that they imagine the little effervesance of public opinion in that little city is the will of the people of Texas. Thus the recent capture of Dimitt and his party on Corpus Christi has created so much excitement that the people of Austin are anxious to have war renewed at once; and the editor of the *Austin City Gazette* declares that it is his "firm conviction that it is the *will of the people of Texas to sustain Mr. Dimitt.*" Now if by this he means that it is the will of the people of Texas that Mr. Dimitt should be sustained in his settlement on Corpus Christi Bay, in order that he may sell goods to the Mexicans, at an expense of several thousand dollars to the government in keeping up a military post there, or that it is necessary to raise an army of volunteers to hold possession of the country west of the Nueces at this time, he is mistaken. The people of Texas wish to remain quiet and wait until the meeting of the next Congress.[30]

In the meantime, before the news of the seizure of Dimitt reached Austin, Webb's report of his efforts to reopen discussions with Mexico concerning the major issues between the two countries, had been received at the Texan capital and a different line of approach to Mexico was in the making. Lamar hastily left Austin on July 8 for Galveston to confer with Webb.[31] Disheartened at the failure of his several efforts at negotiation with Mexico, Lamar determined to become more aggressive, at least to the point of annoying the Mexican government. But how was this to be done? Already an expedition had departed for Santa Fé on what was considered to be a peaceful mission, and General Arista had recently sent an emissary to Austin proposing a cessation of hostilities, resulting in the dispatch of Van Ness and Morris to the Río Grande. If, however, some arrangement for peace on the southwestern frontier could be concluded with the Mexican commander in the north, it would be far better than attempting to take possession of northern Mexico by a military force and thereby incur an expense that Texas was in no condition to meet. Abner S. Lipscomb and James Love had both written Lamar earlier from Galveston upon the arrival of Webb proposing the use of the navy in sweeping Mexican commerce from the Gulf, the blockading of Mexican ports, and the fitting out of privateers "with letters of Marque and reprisal under such restrictions and limitations as may comport with the honor of

[30] *Telegraph and Texas Register*, Aug. 4, 1841.
[31] Samuel A. Roberts to James Webb, Department of State, Austin, July 7, 1841, in Garrison (ed.), *Diplomatic Correspondence of Texas*, 1908, II, 766.

453

the Country."[32] They both urged giving assistance and assurances to the liberals in the northern provinces of Mexico and to the revolutionists in Yucatán.[33] Wrote Love,

I am aware that in the exhau[sted] state of our finances, that no efficie[nt] force can be put on foot for land services, but the Federalists of the North, and [in] the South, may be strengthened by forming [so]me understanding with them of aid and [subs]istance, a few hundred soldiers would [do] this on [the] Rio del Norte, and a single vessel of War at Yucatán. . . . Is it not well to consider what means of aggressio[n] and annoyance we have in [our] power, and to make her *feel* th[at] peace with Texas is necessary [for] her own security?[34]

Very little additional expense would be incurred in the employment of the navy in an operation against Mexico since it was already equipped and manned.

John Henry Brown (later a well-known Texas historian) wrote at this time that while he was opposed to "another volunteer army from the U.S. entering Texas" and to "having anything to do with such a body," he believed that if it became necessary to prosecute the war against Mexico, it could be done best without expense to the government by having the navy blockade the Mexican ports and make reprisals.[35] "If Texas has the ships, and Yucatán has dollars to sail and fight these ships," declared the *Texas Sentinel* on September 23, "we say in God's name, let them go and do the work which cannot but be honorable and advantageous to both nations."

[32] James Love to M. B. Lamar, Galveston, June 30, 1841, in *Lamar Papers*, III, 541–542; Abner S. Lipscomb to M. B. Lamar, Galveston, June 29, 1841, in *ibid.*, III, 539–540.

[33] A Federalist uprising broke out in Yucatán in May 1839, and its leaders declared independence in June 1840. On the eve of the inauguration of the new Mexican constitution of 1843, the war with Mexico was brought to an amicable end, and a treaty was concluded at the City of Mexico on December 14, 1843, by which Yucatán agreed to recognize the government and constitution of Mexico with representation in the new congress, but was to enjoy complete autonomy. In January 1846, Yucatán again declared herself independent of Mexico. George L. Rives, *The United States and Mexico, 1821–1848*, I, 451–452, 462–463; II, 225; Hubert Howe Bancroft, *History of Mexico*, V, 244.

[34] James Love to M. B. Lamar, Galveston, June 30, 1841, in *Lamar Papers*, III, 541–542.

[35] Extract of a letter to Thomas M. Duke, dated Matagorda, July 12, 1841, in John Henry Brown Papers, 1835–1872; ms.; *Texas Sentinel*, Sept. 23, 1841.

Influenced by these ideas, and anxious to regain his popularity in the west, Lamar sent a letter to Governor Miguel Barbachano of Yucatán informing him of the desire of the Texan government to establish "relations of amity and friendship" and "to reciprocate, in the fullest manner, every evidence of good will manifested by the Federalists of Mexico" towards Texas.[36] Lamar informed him that the ports of Texas were open to the commerce of Yucatán on the same terms as the most favored nation, and invited him to send an agent to Texas "to enter into more permanent and specific relations." Upon the receipt of Lamar's friendly letter, Yucatán immediately availed itself of this opportunity to improve its foreign relations and dispatched an agent to Texas, in the person of Martin Peraza, to negotiate. Peraza reached Austin late in August 1841, and on September 17 signed a treaty with Texas, but not until the Texan State Department had made a careful check with Van Ness and Morris, who, having recently returned from Arista's headquarters, were delayed at San Antonio to attend the District Court then in session and had not yet made their official report. In response to Secretary Roberts' request for information on the outcome of their negotiations with Arista, Morris replied:

I only deem it necessary at this time to state that no treaty or stipulation has been entered into by General Arista, with us, which can in the slightest degree clash with any arrangement which may now be made with the commissioner from Yucatán—whether of a hostile or pacific character towards the government of Mexico, and that the Republic of Texas, so far as our Mission is concerned, is perfectly free and open to pursue any course which it may deem fit towards that Country. No stipulation has been entered into restraining the movements of Texas in any manner whatever, and so far we stand in the same position towards Mexico, which we have always occupied.[37]

The treaty pledged the cooperation of the Texas navy with the Yucatán naval force in preventing a Centralist invasion by sea[38] and

---

[36] Mirabeau B. Lamar, *Letter from the President of Texas to the Governor of Yucatán*; Mirabeau B. Lamar to the Governor of the State of Yucatán [Miguel Barbachano], Republic of Texas, Executive Department, Austin, July 20, 1841, in Harriet Smither (ed.), *Journals of the Sixth Congress of the Republic of Texas*, II, 91.

[37] John D. Morris to Samuel A. Roberts, San Antonio, Sep[t] 13, 1841, in Garrison (ed.), *Diplomatic Correspondence of Texas*, 1908, II, 767.

[38] Jim Dan Hill, *The Texas Navy: in Forgotten Battles and Shirtsleeve Diplomacy*, p. 145; Joseph William Schmitz, *Texan Statecraft, 1836–1845*, pp. 128–139;

in breaking up the blockade contemplated under the proclamation of July 1. A portion of the Texas fleet was virtually leased to Yucatán at the rate of $8,000 a month.

While Lamar was at Galveston, the resolutions and accompanying papers from Victoria, Gonzales, and other points pertaining to the Dimitt case arrived at Austin. The Victoria express reached the capital on July 14 and created quite a stir. In the absence of the President, the papers were handed to Samuel A. Roberts, the Acting Secretary of State. Since the Texan commissioners had already left on their mission to the Río Grande to negotiate with General Arista in regard to the frontier trade, Roberts was reluctant to do anything that might endanger their safety; yet, Thompson, the courier, assured him, and the spirit of the letters that he brought indicated that the country was ready to turn out en masse to rescue Dimitt and the other prisoners, or to retaliate with or without governmental authorization. A cabinet meeting was immediately summoned. Secretary of State Roberts opposed ordering out the militia, believing that no good could result from its being activated, for obviously Dimitt could not be rescued and the safety of Van Ness and Morris should not be jeopardized. After considerable argument, and having secured the approval of the other members of the cabinet to dispatch the next day a "trusty messenger" to the Río Grande to warn Van Ness and Morris of the threatened danger and to advise their immediate return, Roberts finally consented to the calling out of the militia. He reported to Lamar that he had consented for the sake of unanimity, "for I would not have it go abroad that we could not unite on *any* thing." "War," he concluded, "seems now inevitable." [39] "Under this critical state of affairs," in order to prevent any rash action on the part of the frontiersmen, the cabinet by unanimous vote decided "*to authorize* the turning out of the militia, tho' not to *order* them out." [40] The latter responsibility was taken by

Department of State (Texas), *Correspondence between the Secretary of State and Col. Peraza, Special Commissioner from the State of Yucatán*; the correspondence contained in the foregoing document is reprinted in Smither (ed.), *Journals of the Sixth Congress of the Republic of Texas*, III, 264–272.

[39] Samuel A. Roberts to M. B. Lamar, Austin, July 14, 1841 (at night), in *Lamar Papers*, III, 546–547.

[40] Branch T. Archer to Richard Roman, John T. Price, and Others, War Department, Austin, July 14, 1841, in *Telegraph and Texas Register*, Aug. 11, 1841; Samuel A. Roberts to M. B. Lamar, Austin, July 22, 1841, in *Lamar Papers*, III, 555–556; M. B. Lamar to Congress [Austin, Texas, Nov. 3, 1841], *ibid.*, V, 494–495.

the Secretary of War, Dr. Branch T. Archer (reputed to be the most accomplished swearer in the Brazos country)[41] who, without prior knowledge of the Secretary of State or the Secretary of the Treasury, authorized the petitioners at Victoria

. . . to assemble such force as you can command for the expulsion of the enemy. . . . Volunteers to any number necessary for the accomplishment of this object we authorize you to call out. You will of course use discretion in distinguishing between traders and soldiers of the enemy, taking care however to possess yourselves of traders and their effects as indemnity for the loss of our citizens and treat soldiers as the rules of war direct.[42]

At the suggestion of the Secretary of War, the Victoria committee had Colonel H. L. Kinney and William P. Aubrey arraigned on July 17 on a charge of having committed treason by conspiring with the Mexicans in Dimitt's abduction. The basis for the arraignment was affidavits of James Gourlay of Lamar and of William Thompson of Corpus Christi Bay, both of whom accused Kinney and Aubrey of treason and of having an agency in the late abduction. Gourlay declared that in the preceding November, Colonel Kinney came to him to translate two letters for him—one from Colonel Canales and the other from General Arista. The letter from Arista, it was said, informed Kinney that he was perfectly willing for the latter to operate his trading post at Corpus Christi peacefully, but that instead of paying customs duties to Canales he was henceforth to pay the duties to the Mexican government. This seems to have been a perfectly normal communication to one who operated in disputed territory. It was also reported that Arista requested Colonel Kinney to keep him informed, from time to time, of events in Texas.[43]

The letter from Canales merely informed Kinney, it was said, that the former had spoken favorably to Arista in behalf of his remaining at the Bay, and he (Canales) concluded by requesting Kinney to take good care of the cannon, ammunition and other articles he had left in his care.

Accordingly, orders were released for their arrest, and the sheriff of Victoria County, accompanied by the Victoria County Minute Men

---

[41] Herbert Pickens Gambrell, *Anson Jones: the Last President of Texas*, p. 51.
[42] B. T. Archer to Richard Roman and Others, War Department, Austin, July 14, 1841, in *Telegraph and Texas Register*, Aug. 11, 1841.
[43] "James Gourlay's Affidavit, Republic of Texas, Victoria County, July 17, 1841," *Telegraph and Texas Register*, Aug. 11, 1841.

under Captain Charles M. Creaner, proceeded to Corpus Christi to serve the warrants on Kinney and Aubrey. By way of reprisal, Captain Creaner was ordered to seize any enemy goods and traders he might find.[44] The posse, numbering twenty-three men,[45] reached Kinney's rancho on the 23rd and found ten Mexican traders there with a small *caballada* of horses recently from the Río Grande. The Texans made prisoners of the traders, and in two hours time they and their horses, mules, and money were on the road to Victoria. En route, Captain Creaner stopped at the Mission Refugio, and, after dividing the prisoners' property (their clothes, too, it was said) among his men, passed on to Victoria with his prisoners. At Victoria he learned that seven traders from Reinosa had recently passed the Mission Refugio going eastward with a drove of horses and mules. Creaner immediately detached a portion of his command to pursue and capture them,[46] which was accordingly effected on July 28, in spite of the fact that the Mexicans claimed the laws of Texas and the proclamations of two of its presidents invited, encouraged, and protected the trade between the western settlements of Texas and the citizens of Mexico on the Río Grande. Their protest was to no avail. They were held prisoners for eleven days, and stripped of their entire property, including horses, mules, saddles, bridles, guns, pistols, and other items.[47] They later claimed their losses amounted to $2,348. Both groups of prisoners and their property were reported late in July to be at Victoria, awaiting the disposition of the Texan government. Colonel A. S. McDonald, the mayor of Victoria, however, cautioned the Secretary of War, "that if

[44] A. S. McDonald, Col. 5th Regt., 1st Brig., T. M., to B. T. Archer, Victoria, July 28, 1841, Army Papers (Texas), ms.

[45] Goodman, "A Statement of Facts, Washington, Feby 10, 1843," in W. D. Miller Papers, 1833–1860, ms.

[46] Charles M. Creanor to Col. A. S. McDonald, Victoria, July 28, 1841, in Army Papers (Texas), ms. Among those captured on the 28th were José María Cantú, Francisco María Cantú, Francisco Guzmán, and Valentín Gutiérrez.

[47] Memorial of José María Cantue [Cantú] and Others to Congress, Dec. 20, 1841, Memorials and Petitions (Texas), ms.; Smither (ed.), *Journals of the Sixth Congress of the Republic of Texas*, II, 211, 269. November 11 the Committee on the State of the Republic in the House of Representatives, headed by John D. Morris, suggested that "the Pay-Master be required to retain all pay, if any due the company of Captain C. M. Creanor until further action of Congress." *Ibid.*, II, 23; I, 16 n. The committee's report has not been found. The traders' petition for compensation was favorably reported by a Select Committee of the House on January 3, 1842, but no law was ever enacted for their relief.

the government determined that the property should be restored to [the] Traders and they released, . . . some assurance from you would be necessary that the captors should be properly compensated." [48]

A few days after Creaner's return to Victoria, Captain Richard Roman led a group of Texans to Corpus Christi and effected the capture of some nine or ten Mexican traders, whom they carried a part of the way in the direction of Victoria; finally they stopped, divided their effects among the captors, and set the poor souls at liberty on foot.[49]

When Lamar returned to the capital and was fully apprised of what had happened to innocent traders, who apparently had no connection whatsoever with the capture of Dimitt and others, or were even suspected of having any, he countermanded as much of the order of the Secretary of War as related to peaceable traders and their property and ordered those in custody to be released forthwith and their property restored to them,

. . . because I believed [he later told Congress] it was essential to the end of private justice, and to the preservation of our national honor. These men wer[e] invited into our country for the purpose of lawful commerce, by an Executive Proclamation, based upon an act of Congress, authorizing the trade to be opened, by which faith the nation and the Government was solemnly pledged for their protection and security so long as they demeaned themselves as peaceful traders. I could not feel disposed to visit upon them any portion of that resentment which was due to the real offenders; neither could I perceive how I could, under the circumstances, hold them and their property in anywise responsible for the conduct of their Government, or its officers, without violating the plighted faith of the nation. Under these circumstances, I ordered that they should be set at liberty, and their property restored to them.[50]

[48] Col. A. S. McDonald to B. T. Archer, Victoria, July 28, 1841, in Army Papers (Texas), ms.; ——— to Secretary of State, Victoria, Sept. 21, 1841, in Domestic Correspondence (Texas), 1836–1846, ms. July 12, 1841, A. S. McDonald was appointed Chief Justice of Victoria County by President Lamar. State Department Letterbook, no. 1, ms., pp. 250–251.

[49] Goodman, "A Statement of Facts, Washington, Feby 10, 1843," in W. D. Miller Papers, 1833–1860, ms.

[50] Message of President Lamar to Congress, Austin, Nov. 3, 1841, in Smither (ed.), *Journals of the Sixth Congress of the Republic of Texas*, I, 7–25; Mirabeau B. Lamar, *The Annual Message of Mirabeau B. Lamar, President of the Republic of Texas, Communicated to Both Houses of Congress, Nov. 3d, 1841.*

The men were released, but their property, already distributed among their captors, was not returned to them. In the end, Lamar recommended to Congress that it "consider making some reparation for the forcible seizure of property which the Government had pledged itself to protect." [51]

The only part of the Secretary of War's order of July 14, 1841, rescinded by Lamar was that relating to the capture of peaceful and unoffending traders. Those portions designed to give protection to the west against marauding parties continued in effect, and the troops that had been collected under it were permitted to remain in the field, until they refused to obey orders of the government. For this disobedience they were dismissed from the service, but not until the necessary steps had been taken to supply their place by other troops, for which purpose Colonel Bell, adjutant general of the Republic, was sent to the frontier.

On July 30 Kinney, voluntarily, and Aubrey, under arrest in custody of James Wright, special deputy of the sheriff of Victoria County, appeared in Austin before Judge Anderson Hutchinson, of the Fourth Judicial District, to answer the charges preferred against them, according to S. L. Jones, "by unprincipled and interested individuals." [52] The case was heard on August 2, and in their defense were presented a number of letters and affidavits.

J. E. L. Solomon, who was at Kinney's ranch at the time of Dimitt's capture, reported under oath late in July that the first news of the capture was brought to the ranch by the salt workers from the rancho, who had been captured along with a man from Dimitt's station. The salt workers had been taken and held about twelve hours until the Mexicans were ready to withdraw. Solomon disclaimed seeing Sánchez or any of his men or hearing at the time of their coming to the rancho, and said he believed that Kinney's conduct was entirely exemplary, that Kinney and Aubrey were "the most enterprising and liberal Mexican traders" he had seen, and that by such means were concentrating a large amount of the frontier trade at their ranch. It was commonly said that they refused to purchase "stolen cattle." [53] William H. Chester of Matagorda, who had visited the rancho at least thirty times, and

[51] *Ibid.*

[52] S. L. Jones to Gen. M. B. Lamar, Corpus Christi, Aug. 18, 1841, in *Lamar Papers*, III, 563–565.

[53] J. E. L. Solomon to Editor of the *Colorado Gazette*, Matagorda, July 26, 1841, in *Telegraph and Texas Register*, Aug. 11, 1841.

Henry Redmond, who had been there many times, both declared that they saw no evidence of treasonable conduct on the part of the accused, or any of their alleged correspondence with Mexican officials. James Wright declared that he would not believe Thompson, even under oath; [54] and Albert C. Horton, a man of considerable wealth, stature, and influence in the Matagorda area (he had served in the First and Second Congresses, been a vice-presidential candidate in 1838, and served on the commission to locate the capital), wrote Lamar: "I believe the charges . . . [against Kinney] to be groundless—and the result of a system of persecution against him. I therefore take pleasure in recommending him to your favourable consideration—with confidence that you will do him that justice, which I believe he merits, by exculpating him from false charges." [55]

When no one appeared to give testimony against them, Aubrey and Kinney were adjudged not guilty by Judge Hutchinson, who ruled,

There being no evidence whatever to criminate the accused, and on the contrary satisfactory proof to place them on very high and unimpeachable ground as gentlemen of probity, and citizens not only of fidelity to the Republic but as having made great personal and pecuniary sacrifices in favor of the country, in the establishment and sustension of their fortress beyond the Nueces—Wherefore, they, and each of them, are fully, freely, and entirely discharged.

The undersigned take pleasure in stating, that the evidence given has been strongly corroborated by sundry communications recently addressed to the Hon. the Secretary of War, and which he has submitted for inspection of the undersigned. A Hutchinson, Judge 4th Jud. Dist.[56]

Just what the "sundry communications recently addressed to the Hon. the Secretary of War" may have been or from whom they may have come is difficult to say. One piece of evidence centers around Judge Alanson Ferguson, who was accused of receiving money from H. L. Kinney to pay his expenses to the seat of government at Austin to lay before the authorities the circumstances surrounding the abduction of Dimitt and other citizens by the Mexicans.[57] Thinking that

[54] *Telegraph and Texas Register*, Aug. 25, 1841.
[55] A. C. Horton to Gen. M. B. Lamar, Matagorda, July 25, 1841, in *Lamar Papers*, V, 483.
[56] *Telegraph and Texas Register*, Aug. 25, 1841.
[57] Simeon Newcomb to Judge [Alanson] Ferguson, San Patricio, [dated:] Victoria, Aug. 5, 1841, in Domestic Correspondence (Texas), 1836–1846, ms.

Ferguson had been bribed to present Kinney's side of the case, the friends of Dimitt held a "public meeting" at San Patricio and petitioned the President to remove him from the position of chief justice of San Patricio County, alleging that he had been bribed.[58]

[58] The petitioners for the removal of Ferguson, however, soon learned that the President was without authority to make such dismissals, as the removal of a chief justice could only be effected by impeachment and conviction. Simeon Newcomb and others believed that there were no ill-designs back of Kinney's "loan," as Ferguson attempted to explain the matter. Ferguson maintained that he had arrived upon the frontier at Corpus Christi shortly after Dimitt's abduction where he ascertained the facts concerning the case. He determined to repair to Austin to lay them before the Executive; but, being without money, and his horse unfit for the journey, he had borrowed, he said, twenty dollars from Kinney and purchased a horse for himself and another for one of the members of the San Patricio Company.

As Ferguson prepared to go to Austin, several of the men in the San Patricio ranging company gave him a power of attorney to draw for them the pay due for their services. At Austin he drew pay for twenty-five men for thirty-six days, and for one man for twenty-seven days; yet, only fourteen men had served as much as thirty-six days, one twenty-eight days, and three about twenty days each. (Those serving thirty-six days in the company of San Patricio Minute Men were: William Snodgrass, A. T. Miles, William J. Cairns, T. W. Murry, J. B. Parkes, H. D. Weeks, James McPherson, John Botham, J. M. Block, Patrick Quinn, John James, George Anderson, Lawson Mills, Charles Sherman; serving twenty-eight days: James Bennet; serving about twenty days each: Tipton Walker, ———— Sapp, and James Wilson. L. S. Hagler to Saml. A. Roberts, City of Houston, Oct. 5, 1841, in *ibid.*, ms.). Charges were also made that Ferguson had drawn pay for men who had not authorized him to do so and that pay had been drawn for others who had not been on active duty. "He has violated his oath of office for the purpose of swindling the Govt. and has retained the money which he received and defrauded the members of the company," declared L. S. Hagler.

As chief justice, it was charged, he had failed to order elections held at Corpus Christi for Congress. Thus, when he was elected to the House, his seat was challenged by Lindsay S. Hagler, his opponent to represent San Patricio County in the House of Representatives. Whereupon, the House appointed a Select Committee on November 2 to investigate the charges against Ferguson, especially the one concerning his election to Congress. He had, upon his election to the House, resigned the office of chief justice. In obtaining the chief justiceship Ferguson had the support of Aubrey and Kinney, who, not knowing him at the time, later claimed that they had supported him because he had pledged to support the Lamar administration. (As a replacement for him, they later recommended W. B. Goodman, "a Gentleman of good reputation and well versed in the duties of the office." Aubrey & Kinney to M. B. Lamar, Ranche Corpus Christi, Sept. 18, 1841, in *Lamar Papers*, III, 568–569.)

Ferguson characterized the petition against him as a *ruse de guerre* of a few individuals at Victoria who wished to see the mercantile establishment at Kinney's

It was revealed at the trial of Kinney and Aubrey, declared the *Telegraph* of August 11, 1841, that the arrest of Dimitt and his associates was not authorized by the Mexican government and was unknown to Arista. In consequence of this evidence, Lamar ordered the recently captured Mexican traders to be released and their property restored to them, and it was hoped that the Texan commissioners, Morris and Van Ness, already on their way to Mexico would upon arrival at Arista's headquarters be able to effect the release of the Texan prisoners.

It was Kinney's belief that he had become "obnoxious to some . . . Americans who disliked the successful trade" which he carried on with the Mexicans. Although he admitted having visited Mexico with the purpose of furthering his business as a trader, he declared that he was not a traitor. He had gone there, he said, to secure

. . . the title to the land we live on, having been advised that it would be absolutely necessary to make our title beyond a doubt. . . . No pains were

Ranch broken up. As for the failure to hold an election at Corpus Christi, Ferguson defended himself, saying, that as chief justice he had issued a writ of election for that precinct and had appointed a presiding officer for the election. He felt that his responsibility ended here, but "the true cause of the omission," he believed, "was due to the high excitement caused by the capture of Dimitt, which for the moment absorbed every other consideration."

The House Committee, however, seems to have been primarily concerned with the election issue. The Committee found that Ferguson had received thirty-nine votes to seventeen for Hagler, that there was no evidence submitted to expunge the legality of any of the votes cast, that Ferguson was "duly elected by the voters of San Patricio County, to represent them in the 6th Congress"; but that since "the member elect had not resided in the county of San Patricio six months, previous to the day of election, and was therefore Constitutionally ineligible to a seat in the House of Representatives," it was recommended that the seat then occupied by Ferguson be declared vacant and a new election for San Patricio be ordered by the President. The Committee's recommendations were adopted by the House on November 6. Affidavit of John D. James, Republic of Texas, County of Victoria, Sept. 22, 1841, in Domestic Correspondence (Texas), 1836–1846, ms.; Deposition of William Van Horne, Sept. 22, 1841, *ibid.*; L. S. Hagler to Saml. A. Roberts, City of Houston, Oct. 5, 1841, *ibid.*; Alanson Ferguson to S. A. Roberts, Secretary of State, Victoria, Aug. 5, 1841, *ibid.*; Smither (ed.), *Journals of the Sixth Congress of the Republic of Texas*, II, 6, 6 n. "House Committee Report on the Contested Election of San Patricio County," Friday, Nov. 5, 1841, *ibid.*, 6th Cong., 1 sess., II, 12–14; *Texas Sentinel* (Austin), Nov. 11, 1841. No answer has been found to the charge concerning the drawing of pay for members of the San Patricio Company of Minute Men.

spared to conciliate those in power on the Río Grande, as we were determined to sustain ourselves, if possible, by all honorable means. *We succeeded.* The result was, that the entire trade from the lower section of Mexico, came to our Ranche, it being so much nearer than any other trading point in Texas. This is the main cause of hostility to us, *the stopping of the trade,* as there are so many other points that are (in the opinion of the proprietors) truly eligible, but cannot be brought into market until such time as our Ranche is destroyed; every falsehood has been busily circulated, that would have a tendency to rouse the people to the most desirable object;—*they cannot succeed.*⁵⁹

"There was no alternative left us," declared Aubrey and Kinney "but either to sacrifice our *all* which is invested in the Rancho, or change our policy, and make our common enemy our friends." ⁶⁰ Later, in the state constitutional convention of 1845, Kinney revealed further his method of operation. He declared that the Nueces frontiersmen had occasionally been "placed in a situation where they were obliged to give assistance to the enemy for their own security and, safety, when they did not feel any disposition to do so." He readily admitted having been in such a situation himself, and "when Mr. Mexican came," Kinney said, "I treated him with a great deal of politeness, particularly if he had me in his power; when Mr. American came, I did the same with him; and when Mr. Indian came, I was also very frequently disposed to make a compromise with him." ⁶¹ Thus, for lack of adequate protection of life and property by the government, the frontiersmen often found it necessary to sacrifice political ideals and principles of well established moral conduct in order to ensure survival. He was confronted with realistic conditions, and found it necessary to solve each new problem concerning his security in the light of facts or actualities confronting him at the time.

Although Kinney and Aubrey were acquitted by the court, a public meeting later in Goliad petitioned the government to remove from

⁵⁹ *Telegraph and Texas Register,* Aug. 11, 1841; *Lamar Papers,* IV, pt. I, 213–214; *Austin City Gazette,* Aug. 11, 1841. Evidently Colonel Kinney was not always on the best of terms with the Mexican authorities, for in August 1842, we find him detained on parole at Matamoros. *Telegraph and Texas Register,* Aug. 3, 1842. For additional information bearing on Kinney and Aubrey, see pp. 405–408, 499–500 of this work.

⁶⁰ Affidavit of Aubrey and Kinney, *Telegraph and Texas Register,* Aug. 25, 1841.

⁶¹ William F. Weeks, *Debates of the Texas Convention,* p. 405.

office the judge who had presided at the trial because he had, it was said, accepted a bribe from Kinney.[62] John Sutherland, who was arrested in Mexico soon after the seizure of Dimitt, informed the British minister that he could prove that Kinney and Aubrey caused his arrest, for they had "wantonly abused and villified" him in many ways.[63]

Kinney returned to Corpus Christi on August 13, where he found, as he had expected, "a Gang of desperadoes on our frontier perfectly regardless of the rights of any one, robbing indiscriminately and not wishing to know or *hear* of any Orders to the contrary." Aubrey and Kinney informed Lamar that if this condition continued, their trading post would have to be abandoned, but that if the government "should determine to station men near the Nueces under a responsible Officer," they declared, "we shall be pleased to cooperate with them for the benefit and credit of our Country; otherwise a band of robber *Texians* will soon be in possession of the fairest portion of the Country." [64] Apprehensive for their own personal safety, they added in a postscript: "As we are at present more or less entirely at the mercy of the company of men spoken of we beg that this shall remain in your hands solely confidential."

Other traders in the Corpus Christi area, too, were not happy about the situation on the frontier. "I fully appreciate the motives of the Honble. B. T. Archer in sending out the Volunteer Companies from Victoria," wrote S. L. Jones, a newcomer in the Mexican trade, "but the Country will have much to regret if some immediate steps are not taken to restrain them in the proper discharge of their duty. At present," he continued, "I fear they are transgressing all authority vested in them, as a company came to this place a few days since and carried off several Horses amongst them some belonging to Aubrey & Kinney. This act was committed under the pretence that the Horses were Mexican property." [65] There seems to have been considerable delay, and possibly dragging of the feet, in getting through to the chief justice at San Patricio and to the frontier the government's order to the chief

[62] Thomas Newcomb to Alanson Ferguson, Aug. 8, 1841, in Domestic Correspondence (Texas), 1836–1846, ms.

[63] John Sutherland to Richard Pakenham, Feb. 25, 1842, in English-Mexican Diplomatic Correspondence, 1841–1842, Public Records Office, London, England.

[64] Aubrey and Kinney to M. B. Lamar, Corpus Christi, Aug. 15, 1841 (Confidential), in *Lamar Papers*, III, 562–563.

[65] S. L. Jones to Gen. M. B. Lamar, Corpus Christi, Aug. 18, 1841, in *ibid.*, III, 563–565.

justices, cancelling the Secretary of War's order in respect to the seizure of peaceful traders and their property.[66]

While Kinney was in Austin, Lamar suggested that upon his return to the frontier he visit Matamoros to intercede for the release of Dimitt and other Texan prisoners. A few weeks later, Kinney, still at his ranch, was informed by Colonel Peter H. Bell, then on an inspection tour of the frontier, that Lamar hoped he would proceed to Mexico. By September 18 Kinney was planning to leave immediately. However, a few weeks later he reported that he could not find out anything definite concerning Dimitt.[67]

In the meantime, Dimitt and his companions were taken to Matamoros, where they were joined by another party of Texans captured by Villareal in the neighborhood of the Nueces in December 1840. From Matamoros the Texan prisoners, numbering twenty-two according to the U.S. consul,[68] were ordered sent to Arista's headquarters at

[66] *Ibid.*

[67] William P. Aubrey and H. L. Kinney to M. B. Lamar, Sept. 18, 1841; Same to Same, Oct. 6, 1841, in *ibid.*, III, 568–569, 589.

[68] Those captured by Villareal included: James Ownsby (escaped), Barsilla Cottle, Thomas Gage, Thomas Pratt, David B. Fowler, Daniel Davis (died), James G. Fowler, George L. Frastrez [Fraster], E. McDowell, Stephen Duncastle, John Jameson, William Roysores, and two others. "Summary investigation held concerning the apprehension of fourteen foreigners, Texians, who were in the neighborhood of the Nueces River, Plaza de Matamoros, 1841." Archivo General, Secretaría de Guerra y de Marina, 1841–1842, Legájo, núm. 1.

According to the American consul's report from Matamoros at the end of September 1841, the following Americans (Texans) had been taken by the Mexican authorities on the frontier of Texas in recent months:

Captured by Prefecto Jorge S. de Lara on the Sauceda on the frontier of Texas with arms in hand (Jan. 6, 1841):

Captain	James P. Ormsby [Ownsby]
Lieut.	David B. Foulet [Fowler]
Sgt.	Daniel Davis
Soldiers	William Smith
	Berryman O. Stout
	R. W. Basil
	James G. Fowler
	James Gaites

Captured by Captain [Enrique] Villareal on the Range del Este:
George L. Fraster
Thomas Pratt
E. M. McGowen
Stephen Duncastle
John Jameson
William M. Romper

Monterey, where, it was said, Arista intended to free them, some of them having been held in close confinement at Matamoros for many months. The Texans were started for Monterey about the middle of August 1841, nearly a week after the outbreak of the Paredes y Arrillaga revolt at Jalisco. En route they suffered much from thirst and hunger. The officer in charge of the escort permitted them to buy water at ruinous prices from the rancheros. The Texans were charged with sundry crimes—robbery, murder, spying, cattle stealing, dealing in contraband and making attacks upon the villages near the Río Grande. Berryman O. Stout was seized "as a cattle stealer among those coming from Texas to make attacks upon the villages near the Río

---

Captured by Captain D. Vicente Sánchez in la Bahía:
Francisco McCafferty
John Seigmon
Philip Dimitt
James Boyd
Stephen M. Howison
Henry Graham
Benjamin Presswood
Ezekiel Ballard

D. W. Smith to Daniel Webster, Matamoros, Sept. 26, 1841, (no. 178) Consular Dispatches (Matamoros), ms., microfilm; Mariano Arista to D. W. Smith, Monterey, Oct. 25, 1841, enclosed in D. W. Smith to Daniel Webster, Matamoros, Nov. 5, 1841, in *ibid.*; Berryman O. Stout to Waddy Thompson, Mexico, April 29, 1842, in "Relaciones Exteriores Internacional Estados Unidos, 1842–1847," Barker Transcripts from Archivo de la Secretaría, ms.

George W. Grover, a Santa Fé prisoner, recorded in his "Minutes of Adventure from June 1841," ms., under date of Feb. 25, 1842, that at Santiago Prison, Mexico City, was the "San Patricio Party taken on the Nueces": J. P. Ownsby, J. C. Gage, D. B. Fowler, E. Ballard, [Francisco] McCafferty, William Roger, John Jamison, Louis Trastee, Stephen Dincans [Duncastle], W. McDowell, John Seigmon, Dan Davis, Tom Pratt; and taken from Corpus Christi: Philip Dimmit [error], Santiago [James] Boyd, S. W. Farrow, Ben Rondo, H. Graham, Dr. Cottle & Towers taken at Monterey.

George W. Kendall, editor of the *New Orleans Picayune* and Santa Fé prisoner, reported several men taken on the Río Grande in the early part of the winter of 1841–1842; namely, Tower, Cottell, Pratt, Sutherland, and several others, who, he said, were being held at the Acordada. *Telegraph and Texas Register*, June 1, 1842. As for Drs. Tower and Cottle being taken on the Texas frontier, he seems to be mistaken. They had been arrested at Monterey a day or two after "two Mexicans who had been taken by a party of Texans near Goliad . . . made their escape" and arrived at Monterey. John D. Morris to Samuel A. Roberts, Acting Secretary of State, San Antonio, Sept. 30, 1841, in Garrison (ed.), *Diplomatic Correspondence of Texas*, 1908, II, 768–776.

Bravo." [69] Sutherland was accused of having been an officer in the battle of San Jacinto, but Dimitt's crime was not stated in the report forwarded by the American consul from Matamoros; however, several of the prisoners were charged only with being in his company. Dimitt's crime was great, as he had been among the first to raise the flag of independence at Goliad, and the *New Orleans Commercial Bulletin,* reporting the news from Matamoros, says he was charged also with "selling goods to degraded Mexicans, who afterwards smuggled them into the Mexican provinces." [70]

The mistreatment of Mexican traders in Texas and the vicissitudes of recent political developments in Mexico [71] seem to have reacted against the Texas prisoners. The precarious position of Bustamante's government, whose cause had been flatteringly supported by Arista who was at this time negotiating with agents from Texas, may have caused the government to order the "odious Texians" on to the capital.

From Monterey the prisoners, plus three or four other Texans, were sent on toward Mexico City in irons and under a heavy guard commanded by Captain Chaffind. After a day's journey, the Captain ordered their irons removed. The Texans were inclined to go peacefully to Mexico, said Thomas Pratt, and "would have done so had it not been for the severe treatment they had received on the road and the representations that were made to them daily." There were all sorts of rumors afloat among their guard concerning the ultimate fate of the prisoners. They were told that they were to be sent to the mines, that at Mexico City they would be shot, that they would never reach San Luis Potosí, that they would be massacred on the road, and many other things. Thus, it was no wonder that by the time they reached Saltillo, they were determined to make an effort to escape.

Just beyond Saltillo, at the Hacienda de Agua Nuevo, on September 10 an unsuccessful attempt was made to drug the guards by adding morphine to a quantity of mescal which they had purchased for their

[69] Pedro de Ampudia to [D. W.] Smith, Army of the North, First Division, Second Brigade, Sept. 24, 1841, copy enclosed in D. W. Smith to Webster, Matamoros, Sept. 26, 1841, in Consular Dispatches (Matamoros), ms., microfilm. See also *Austin City Gazette* quoted in *Telegraph and Texas Register*, Sept. 29, 1841; Thomas Pratt to Richard Pakenham, Jan. 30, 1841 [1842]; Same to Same, Feb. 6, 1842, in English-Mexican Diplomatic Correspondence, 1841–1842, Public Records Office, London, England.

[70] Quoted in *Telegraph and Texas Register*, Aug. 25, 1841.

[71] Discussed on pp. 437–443, 473.

protectors. The quantity of morphine proved insufficient, but the guard was sufficiently impaired to enable eighteen of the men to escape. Eleven of them were overtaken by the guard and shot, and the others were pursued into the mountains.[72] Dimitt was not among the escapees, having been confined with three or four others, including Stout, apart from the main body of prisoners.[73] Captain Chaffind sent word that he would forgive those who had escaped, if they would return; otherwise, he would have Dimitt shot. This statement was made in the presence of Dimitt, who, no doubt, had been worrying much about what would happen to him at Mexico City. As soon as Dimitt saw that he was unobserved, he took a large dose of laudanum and committed suicide.[74]

[72] D. W. Smith to Daniel Webster, Matamoros, Sept. 26, 1841, (no. 178), in Consular Dispatches (Matamoros), ms., microfilm.

[73] Mariano Arista to Daniel W. Smith, Monterey, Oct. 25, 1841, copy in D. W. Smith to Daniel Webster, Matamoros, Nov. 5, 1841, (no. 179), in Consular Dispatches (Matamoros), ms., microfilm.

[74] James T. DeShields, *Border Wars of Texas: being an Authentic and Popular Account, in Chronological Order, of the Long and Bitter Conflict Waged between Savage Indian Tribes and the Pioneer Settlers of Texas*, p. 366; H. Yoakum, *History of Texas from Its First Settlement in 1685 to Its Annexation to the United States in 1846*, II, 319–320; Thomas Pratt to Pakenham, Jan. 30, 1841 [1842], in English-Mexican Diplomatic Correspondence, 1841–1842, Public Records Office, London, England. Grover reported in his "Minutes of Adventure from June 1841," p. 34 (Feb. 25, 1842): "Demit took poison and died at Ague Nueve." An editorial in the *Telegraph and Texas Register*, Dec. 8, 1841, discredits the rumors of suicide, stating that prisoners who had returned from Mexico generally concurred in the opinion that Dimitt was basely murdered.

 CHAPTER TWENTY

Marauders Prey on
Frontier Trade and Life

OTHER MEXICAN RAIDS occurred in 1841. Near the middle of July, three wagons loaded with tobacco and dry goods on the road from the coast to San Antonio were robbed near Victoria by a party of some twenty Mexicans. A "spy company" left Victoria on the 20th to ascertain the number and location of the enemy.[1] Public meetings were held at Victoria, Goliad, and San Patricio to devise measures to prevent further marauding attacks. The repeated acts of treachery on the part of the Mexicans had destroyed entirely the little confidence the Texans had placed in them. A committee of safety was created at Victoria to correspond with the Secretary of War, who, in the meantime, authorized the raising of volunteers to disperse the Mexican bands on this side of the Río Grande. The volunteers were scheduled to rendezvous at Goliad on August 1. "Another campaign," declared the editor of the *Morning Star*, "Would afford the most sincere delight to the hundreds of idle men who have gathered on the western frontier." [2]

In August 1841, about six weeks after the capture of Dimitt, a party of approximately fifty Texans consisting of the Minute Men of San Patricio and a few volunteers from Gonzales, reported L. S. Hagler,[3] made an excursion to the southern extremity of Padre Island, and in the afternoon of August 17 surprised and captured a Mexican captain by the name of Corsco and nine soldiers stationed at a rancho. The soldiers offered no resistance, and were taken with their horses to San Patricio and turned over to the chief justice of the county to be exchanged for the same number of Texan prisoners in Matamoros. The Mexican captain, it was reported, wrote to General Ampudia at Matamoros suggesting the exchange and requesting that Dimitt be included

[1] *Telegraph and Texas Register* (Houston), July 28, 1841.
[2] Quoted in *ibid.* For data on the status of the western trade, see *ibid.*, June 16, 23, July 28, and Dec. 8, 1841.
[3] *Ibid.*, Sept. 15, 1841.

among the Texan prisoners exchanged. The prisoners were held to September 14, during which time they were boarded by William Snodgrass at a cost of $10 per day for twenty-eight days.[4]

Based on information obtained from Captain Corsco and his men and several Irish settlers at the southern extremity of Padre Island, it was estimated that the whole Mexican force on the Río Grande did not exceed three hundred troops, distributed as follows: one hundred regular infantry in Matamoros; fifty men, part infantry and part cavalry, under Colonel Fernández at Camargo—the cavalry horses were said to be so poor they could scarcely walk; forty rancheros on the Arroyo Colorado under Colonel Villareal; and higher up and north of the Río Grande were an estimated fifty to a hundred men under Colonel Ramírez ranging the country as a robber band—"a terror to the traders of either party." No doubt the weakness of the Mexican military position along the line of the Río Grande was due to the outbreak of revolutionary disturbances in the interior of Mexico.

In spite of Arista's attitude and repeated orders from the Mexican authorities against the conduct of trade with Texas,[5] wagons loaded with beans, sugar, flour, leather, shoes, saddles, and silver bars molded in sand, each embracing $50 to $60 of pure silver, continued to cross the prairies to be exchanged for calico (bleached and unbleached), tobacco, and American hardware. The trade persisted, although the

---

[4] Petition of William Snodgrass [being a] Claim of Wm. Snodgrass to Com[mittee] on Military Affairs, Memorials and Petitions (Texas), ms. Snodgrass claimed that he boarded the prisoners from August 17–September 14, 1841 (28 days) at a cost of $10.00 a day, or $280. He presented his claim for reimbursement December 24, 1841, to the House of Representatives, where it was referred to the Committee on Military Affairs, and payment was ordered by a Joint Resolution of Congress, approved by President Houston on January 29, 1842. Harriet Smither (ed.), *Journals of the Sixth Congress of the Republic of Texas*, II, 211; III, 494.

[5] Jesús Cárdenas, Prefecto del distrito del Norte en el Departamento de Tamaulipas, á todos sus habitantes, Mier, Jan. 6, 1842, Matamoros Archives, 1840–1842, XL (photostat), broadside. Cárdenas, former president of the Republic of the Río Grande, announced that in accordance with the orders of the Minister of War and Marine of November 26, 1841, and of General Arista of December 26, 1841, the inhabitants of Laredo who traded with the Texans, as reported by D. Francisco Calvillo, would be sentenced to eight years in the regular army at Tampico and those not suitable for service in the army would be confined in the presidio de Matamoros. See also, Jesús Cárdenas en Cuidad Guerrero ál Alcalde de Matamoros, Feb. 12, 1842, concerning the apprehended "contrabandistas," in *ibid.*, and Mariano Arista to D. Pedro de Ampudia, Army of the North, Dec. 26, 1841, no. 450, in *El Honor Nacional* (Matamoros), Dec. 27, 1841.

471

area between the two frontiers of settlement remained infested with robbers, marauding bands, and small bodies of Mexican cavalrymen in search of the *contrabandistas*. At the suggestion of Launcelot Smithers, the City Council of San Antonio decreed on September 9, 1841, that foreigners entering the city make known their presence to the mayor.[6] At a meeting of citizens of Béxar County on November 24 a committee, with Samuel a Maverick as chairman and Edward W. Sanders as secretary, was appointed to draft a petition to Congress in behalf of frontier protection. The petition, as drafted and approved by the public meeting, requested the Congress then in session

. . . to take into consideration the very exposed, and truly suffering situation of this section of the Republic, and as the most probable means of stopping the incursions of murdering and robbing Indians and Mexicans, and preventing numerous other evils, that the Congress be pleased to consider the propriety of establishing, on an economical plan, two Military Posts, the one at, or near the ford of the Río Grande road, on the Medina River, the other post, at or near the ford of the Laredo road on the Atascoso; which two with the addition of one other post at San Patricio would, in the opinion of this Meeting under the management of active and trustworthy Captains, with a few soldiers, and a small complement of good corn fed Horses, and without much cost, do much to save the lives and property of the Citizens. For the present and under existing circumstances it is suggested that it would be better to limit the number, and narrow the circle of Posts to the points indicated, and to extend them further hereafter, if the proposed experiment should satisfy the expectations of the Country.

The proximity of the posts to the settlements would permit them to be manned by fewer troops and at less expense. By requiring each post to keep a portion of its force constantly scouring the country above and below, these outposts, declared the memorialists, would be sure to check, if not wholly arrest,

. . . that countless throng of pilfering Mexicans, and escaping Peons of Mexico, as well as put a check to the Indians, and secure the numerous runaway slaves of the Eastern Counties, all which operate very imperiously on us, and are of so much moment to the whole country, that if some immediate and effective means, are not adopted for their prevention the best interests of the Republic will be greatly endangered.[7]

[6] San Antonio, City of, "Journal A, Records of the City of San Antonio," Sept. 9, 1841, ms. For greater detail, see p. 419 of this work.

[7] Petition of Meeting of Citizens of Béxar County for Frontier Protection, Nov. 24, 1841, to the Congress of the Republic of Texas, presented in the Senate on

By December 1841, the trade at Béxar was greatly improved as a result of the internal political troubles in Mexico, beginning with the uprising in Jalisco on August 8 of General Mariano Paredes y Arrillaga, in secret understanding with Santa Anna, whose Bases of Tacubaya were accepted by those who sought to unseat Bustamante. The latter evacuated Mexico City on October 5, and the next day in an agreement at Estanzuela bowed out and soon left the country.[8] On October 7 Santa Anna made his triumphal entry into Mexico City and was declared provisional president. In the north, General Arista sought to stave off the collapse of Bustamante's government by raising the Texas question. "It increases my pain," he wrote the Minister of War, "to see disunited the interior of the Republic, at a time when the Texans everywhere cry to arms, and prepare to conduct the most cruel hostilities against us, dreaming that they can place their puny flag over that of Mexico."[9]

During the revolutionary disturbances and the preoccupation of Arista, commander of the Army of the North, in assisting Bustamante, the citizens of the eastern provinces were driven to the markets of Texas for their supplies of merchandise. In the north the Mexican troops were concentrated near Monterey, leaving the frontier virtually unprotected. Caravans of traders from the Río Grande arrived at Béxar and other places to purchase large quantities of goods.[10] One party of traders, it was reported,[11] brought in $10,000 in specie. Although an occasional party of traders was robbed while on the way to San Antonio (one party lost $5,000 in specie), such losses scarcely interrupted the trade. The ranger company under Captain Hays was most efficient and had "almost completely broken-up the old haunts of the Commanches in the vicinity of Béxar." In fact, declared the editor of the *Telegraph and Texas Register*,[12]

December 2, 1841, by William H. Daingerfield, where that portion of it dealing with frontier protection was referred to the Committee on Military Affairs and reported December 3 by bill. Smither (ed.), *Journals of the Sixth Congress of the Republic of Texas*, I, 84, 84 n; Memorials and Petitions (Texas), ms.

[8] Hubert Howe Bancroft, *History of Mexico*, V, 227–235.

[9] Mariano Arista ál Ministro de la Guerra, Cuartel general en Monterey, Septiembre 6 de 1841, in *Boletín Official* (Mexico City), Sept. 13, 1841.

[10] *Telegraph and Texas Register*, Dec. 8, 1841.

[11] *Ibid.*, Oct. 20, 1841.

[12] *Ibid.*, Dec. 8, 1841.

So great has been the protection and security resulting from the active enterprise of this excellent officer that the settlements are extending on every side around [San Antonio, and] the country is assuming the appearance of peace and prosperity that characterized it previous to the revolution. This must be cheering news to those families that have been so long waiting for "better times" to return to their homes in the fertile and healthy valley of the San Antonio and resume the occupations of husbandry.

It was rumored in the west that Arista had no intention of submitting to Santa Anna, but hoped to form an offensive and defensive alliance with Texas. "Should he carry these threats into execution," reported Francis Moore, "he would doubtless be able to maintain his position, and the trade with Chihuahua and other provinces, would probably be opened to our citizens. His movements are watched with eager eyes by the western traders, and many entertain sanguine hopes that within a few months they will reap a golden harvest from his favor." [13]

Conditions on the lower Nueces frontier in the summer and fall of 1841 were not as prosperous or as encouraging as those at San Antonio. The difference might be accounted for (1) by the character of many of the frontiersmen in this area as evidenced by their past activities; (2) by the greater volume of trade funneled through the adjacent ports which afforded more numerous opportunities to banditti groups; and (3) last, but by no means least, by the fact that there was no captain comparable to Hays to protect this segment of the frontier. Hays' daring, energy, and hard-fighting qualities were becoming known. He was a terror to all lawless groups, be they Texan, Mexican, or Indian; and his honesty and integrity were beyond reproach.

The several companies of volunteers which were gotten up around Victoria pursued a policy toward the Mexican traders which exasperated the frontier settlers of the Río Grande, who, reported S. L. Jones, after a visit to the frontier are "friends of this Country, but . . . [whose] traders are robbed of all their effects and turned adrift to make the best of their way home on foot. From men [so] treated . . . we have every reason," he declared, "to expect similar treatment if in their power." [14] In mid-August a company of Texan volunteers, operating from San Patricio, apprehended thirty-three traders, who subse-

[13] *Ibid.*
[14] S. L. Jones to Gen. M. B. Lamar, Corpus Christi, Aug. 18, 1841 [addressed: Victoria, Aug. 23, His Excellency Gen¹ M. B. Lamar, Austin], in *Lamar Papers*, III, 563–565.

quently escaped or were set free; but were no sooner free of their captors than they were followed by another company under Captain January.[15]

In view of this situation on the lower southern frontier, Lamar sought to restore law and order in the area. Hence, on August 14, through the Secretary of War, he ordered the disbandment of the recently formed frontier companies, but not before others were available under more dependable leadership to replace them. The adjutant general was sent to the theater of disturbance with full authority to raise whatever number of men he might consider necessary "for the expulsion of the enemy and to ensure the complete protection of the inhabitants in that quarter."[16] Captain A. T. Miles, whose real character was apparently not known by the authorities, was commissioned to head a ranger company to be stationed at San Patricio for the maintenance of order and the discouragement of freebooters. His command of the San Patricio "Minute Men" was of brief duration, for he soon became so "odious" that Adjutant General Bell,[17] while on an inspection tour of the frontier in September 1841, found it necessary to replace him by Captain W. J. Cairns, a Scotsman, who, according to some persons, was suspected of being engaged in robbing. One thing for sure, Cairns was not inclined to be lenient toward Mexican marauders, having been captured several years previously on the Nueces, and having spent a year inside a Matamoros jail before effecting his escape about October 1838.[18] By October 4 the adjutant general of the militia, having returned to Austin, was able to report that all of the companies along the lower southwestern frontier, except that of Captain Cairns had been discharged in conformance to the order of the War Department, dated

---

[15] *Ibid.*

[16] "Message of President Lamar to Congress, Austin, Nov. 3, 1841," in Smither (ed.), *Journals of the Sixth Congress of the Republic of Texas*, I, 7–25.

[17] For a brief summary of Bell's brilliant career as a civil and military officer in Texas, see Harold Schoen (comp.), *Monuments Erected by the State of Texas to Commemorate the Centenary of Texas Independence*, p. 71, and C. Luther Coyner, "Peter Hansbrough Bell," *Quarterly of the Texas State Historical Association*, III (1898–1899), 49–53. The Muster Rolls for Captain A. T. Miles' Company for the period from May 14 to August 28, 1841, are in Muster Rolls, 1838–1860 (Rangers), ms., and are reproduced in the Appendix of this work. Among Miles' command were such well known men of the Mier Expedition of 1842 as Thomas W. Murray, W. H. Van Horn, Patrick Maher, H. D. Weeks, L. F. Mills, Ewen Cameron, William Ripley, J. M. Simon, Henry Whalen, and George Anderson.

[18] *Telegraph and Texas Register*, Oct. 20, 1838.

August 14.[19] By this time, also, all Mexican traders had been released and furnished with passports to the Río Grande, but their property had not been restored. The government's order for the restitution of the property taken from them or its equivalent could not be carried out, because, consisting largely of mules and horses, it had been divided amongst the captors and was within a few hours scattered throughout the western country and could no longer be identified. The only recourse that seemed to be open to the traders was to bring suit in court against the individuals who had made off with it, or for the government to compensate the rightful owners for their losses.

[19] P. Hansbrough Bell, Adjt. Genl. Militia, to Branch T. Archer, Secretary of War & Navy, City of Austin, Oct. 4, 1841, in Army Papers (Texas), ms., copy.

CHAPTER TWENTY-ONE

Frontier Issues in the
Presidential Election of 1841

THE EXCITEMENT IN THE SPRING and summer of 1841 was neither all caused by nor all limited to the frontier. Toward the end of the year Lamar's term as President would expire, and since he would be ineligible to succeed himself, his supporters turned their eyes toward David G. Burnet, the Vice President, and Lamar endeavored to promote his election. His opponent was Houston, who sought a second term and represented the anti-Lamar-Burnet faction. There was no such thing as political parties, and the presidential campaign of 1841 turned as much upon personalities as upon issues, if not more so. Houston had represented San Augustine County in the House of Representatives in the Fourth and Fifth Congresses and had been anything but cooperative with the Lamar administration. Recorded Anson Jones in 1840 in his diary,[1]

I had hoped something from Gen. Houston but he appears only intent upon making Lamar's administration as odious as possible in order that the contrast with his own may be favorable to him. He is willing the government should be a failure in order that he may have it to say there is no one but *"Old Sam"* that the people can depend upon, and that he is the only man that can successfully administer the Govt. of Texas. Lamar is certainly no statesman and he and his friends are ruining the country and going to the Devil as fast as Gen. Houston can possibly wish. This he sees and chuckles at—hence nothing can be expected from him, more than to save appearances. He is skillful to destroy his enemy; but will do nothing to stay the impending ruin.

The campaign was bitter and full of vituperation. Among the issues were the claims to the eleven-league land grants, both Burnet and Houston being accused of securing such grants; the removal of the

[1] Anson Jones, Memorandum Book No. 2, Jan. 1, 1840, ms.

477

seat of government; the Franco-Texienne Bill [2] sponsored by Houston; the Cherokee land question; retrenchment; and the redemption of the nation's honor, desecrated by Mexico. As to the latter, it was charged that if Houston were elected, he would not vindicate the national honor in respect to Mexico and would let matters drift rather than settle the issues by the sword or make another attempt at negotiation. Houston was pictured as representing the east (except in Nacogdoches County where his attitude on the Cherokee land question made Burnet the favorite), and as being "generally inimical to the welfare of the West." Burnet was represented as the supporter of the true interests of the west.[3]

You are represented by many of your opponents [Miller wrote Houston from Gonzales] as rejoicing in the anticipation of power to dissever from us, in the day of our depression, the strong arm of our defence, protection and prosperity, by a removal of the present seat of government—as viewing us beyond the pale of common justice and equal privileges with the rest of our countrymen—as deeming us unworthy of governmental consideration, or even mercy—as partial to the East because of its strength and hostile to the West because of its weakness.[4]

Houston lost no time in attempting to dispel the belief in the west that he considered their problems unimportant. In a letter to W. D. Wallach, editor of the *Colorado Gazette and Advertiser*, a former Lamar supporter, who by 1841 had become one of Houston's staunchest friends and advocates, in response to some delicate inquiries from Wallach, Houston wrote, "I deem the efficient protection of the frontier against the Indians, as a desideratum in the policy of Texas, and should I be elected, it shall be protected!!" [5] It is only fit, he con-

2 "A Bill to be entitled an Act to Incorporate a Company, to be called the Franco-Texienne Company, and granting certain privileges to the same," Texas Congress, *Journals of the House of Representatives of the Republic of Texas, Seventh Congress, Appendix*, pp. 395–399.

3 W. D. Miller to Sam Houston, Gonzales, Feb. 27, 1841, in W. D. Miller Papers, 1833–1860, ms., copy; Thomas W. Bell to Brother, Rutersville, Texas, July 25, 1841, in Llerena Friend (ed.), "Thomas W. Bell Letters," *Southwestern Historical Quarterly*, LXIII (1959–1960), 457–460.

4 W. D. Miller to Sam Houston, Gonzales, Feb. 27, 1841, in W. D. Miller Papers, 1833–1860, ms., copy.

5 Sam Houston to W. D. Wallach, Cedar Point, May 31, 1841, in *Writings of Sam Houston*, II, 367–369; *Colorado Gazette and Advertiser* (Matagorda), July 10, 1841.

tinued, to state "that whilst I was President, the whole amount placed at my disposition for that purpose was only $50,000. I was denounced because I did not render the protection required. I had no newspapers to tell the cause. Millions have been expended by the present Executive, and nothing done; yet I hear no complaints made." On the question of the removal of the seat of government, a matter on which the people of the west also felt very strongly, Houston in the true style of a politician, "rode the fence."

I never have entered upon the discharge of any public office or national trust, embarrassed by any pledge, which, to maintain it, might in any event prejudice the welfare of my country. I did not think well of the removal of the seat of government, at the time it was made, because I thought it unnecessary and unwise, for we were poor, and I doubt not but it cost the nation at least $300,000, and violated a pledge given, by a former act of Congress, (which could not be cancelled before 1841)[6] for it to remain at Houston. I never was in favor of it being located at Houston, in the first instance, but once being located, I thought it well for it to remain there for some time to come. . . .
The course which I pursued in relation to the subject of removal, while a member of congress (session before last) was in strict obedience to the instructions of my immediate constituents, and if I had not done so, it would have been my duty to resign my seat, as their representative. I was opposed to molesting the subject at the last session, because I was unwilling to see any matter mooted, that might by possibility create any feelings which in the end might add to the present embarrassments and calamities of the country.
The seat of government being *now* at Austin, would present many considerations connected with any change in future. I have no prejudice against Austin; I have no interest in its removal to any other place; and therefore, if the subject shall be agitated, so as to be presented to me as a chief magistrate, in the event of my election to that station, I would give it my calm and unbiased consideration, as a matter of national interest, and without advertency to either local or sectional feeling or interest.

A short while later, Houston's views on frontier protection were reported to be acceptable to the people in the Gonzales section of the Republic; however, wrote Miller, the enactment of the last session of

[6] By an act passed on December 15, 1836, Congress, while in session at Columbia, provided that the capital should be located at Houston until the close of the legislative session of 1840. Stanley Siegel, *A Political History of the Texas Republic, 1836–1845*, p. 58.

Congress "to encourage frontier protection" is "too much disjointed to be effectual. I think," he continued, "a better one would be to authorize some three or four well mounted ranging companies to traverse the frontiers across their whole extent, without cessation. Let them be organized upon the plan, pretty much, of similar companies upon the western frontier of the United States." [7]

Houston's position in the west, too, was undoubtedly improved by his according his blessing in the vice-presidential race to Edward Burleson of Bastrop over General Memucan Hunt and thus giving a sectional balance to the ticket as well as offsetting to some extent Houston's acknowledged preference for the east. Houston also had the support of many of the leading newspapers. The *Austin City Gazette,* the *Houstonian,* the *Morning Star* (Houston), the *Red-Lander* (San Augustine), and *Colorado Gazette and Advertiser* (Matagorda) gave their support to him; whereas, the *Telegraph and Texas Register* (Houston) and *Texas Sentinel* (Austin) favored Burnet and Hunt.

When election day rolled around on September 6, the results showed Houston the winner by a vote of more than two to one over Burnet; in the vice-presidential race the vote was much closer, yet Burleson, the Houston-sanctioned candidate, won over Hunt by a vote of 6,161 to 4,336.[8] Thus, as James Morgan phrased it, "Old Sam H. with all his faults appears to be the only man for Texas—He is still unsteady, *intemperate,* but drunk in a ditch is worth a thousand of Lamar and Burnet." [9] "In short," as one writer puts it, "Burnet's identification with the disastrous mistakes and extravagances of the Lamar administration and Houston's powerful, compelling personality had returned the Old Hero to the Executive Chair." [10]

[7] W. D. Miller to Sam Houston, Gonzales, July 10, 1841, in W. D. Miller Papers, 1833–1860, ms.

[8] Dudley G. Wooten (ed.), *A Comprehensive History of Texas, 1685 to 1897,* I, 377–378; Hubert Howe Bancroft, *History of Texas and the North Mexican States,* II, 341.

[9] Quoted in Siegel, *A Political History of the Texas Republic,* p. 182.

[10] *Ibid.*

CHAPTER TWENTY-TWO

Frontier Raids, Threats,
and Counter-Threats of Invasion

DURING THE TWO MONTHS INTERVAL between election day and inauguration the raids on the frontier continued and there was talk of invasion and counterinvasion. To the fire-eaters who favored direct military action against Mexico, protection was not enough. Upon Judge Webb's failure to open negotiations with Mexico, a "wild scheme" for invading Mexico was discussed in certain circles in Texas. Meetings were soon reported being held "in all the considerable places in Eastern Texas for the purpose of recommending offensive measures" against Mexico.[1] The grand meeting was to be held in Jackson, Mississippi, on July 4, 1842, "for the purpose of devising means and of organizing and embodying troops to act under the jurisdiction of Texas in a campaign against Mexico." The proponents of such a campaign proposed to furnish all the funds and troops necessary for the enterprise, and would only require the sanction of the Texan government. "What is the meaning of this?" asked W. D. Miller. "Are we to be pushed into a war, whether we will or not, and Gen. Felix [Huston] to be sent upon a military mission to the grand *plaza* of Mexico, upon his 'own hook'? You may rest assured, that there will be a strong effort made to precipitate the Government into active war before the present administration ceases its functions."[2] And one would gather that those who favored a campaign against Mexico were working relentlessly. Thomas Jefferson Green on September 22 urged Lamar to transfer Colonel Barnard E. Bee, Texan chargé d'affaires at Washington, to the Court of France, and send Secretary of War, Doctor Archer, to the United States as the Texan diplomatic representative.[3] Apparently, Green still

[1] W. D. Miller to Sam Houston, Gonzales, July 10, 1841, in W. D. Miller Papers, 1833–1860, ms.

[2] *Ibid.*

[3] Lamar to Thomas Jefferson Green, Austin, Sept. 22, 1841, in Records of Executive Documents from the 10th Dec. 1838 to the 14th Dec. 1841, ms., pp. 253–266.

hoped to obtain the War Office for General Felix Huston. Lamar, however, informed Green in a lengthy reply to his request, that he could not agree with him in his reasons for removing Bee, "notwithstanding every disposition in me to gratify your wishes in the matter, I feel that I cannot do it, without offering violence to my convictions of what is just and right." [4]

Not long after the return of the Texan commissioners from the Río Grande with assurance from Arista that his troops would not molest the Texas frontier, Captain Agatón Quinoñes with a force numbering sixty men was again on the frontier. For a while he had his headquarters near the mouth of the Medina. On September 18 he sacked the Mission of Refugio,[5] probably supposing it to be the home of Captains Creaner and Roman,[6] since they had gone there to divide the property seized from the Mexican traders. In the west there was also the report that "the sack of Refugio was made by a party of Mexicans who have been regarded as citizens of Texas, and resided near Carlos' Rancho." Their object was not so directly for the purpose of plunder, as to destroy the records of the District Court, which contained bills of indictment against several of them as accessories and principals in the robbery of Colonel Karnes, and other merchants on the San Antonio, a few years since while returning from Aransas, with several teams loaded with merchandise.[7]

[4] *Ibid.*

[5] *Telegraph and Texas Register* (Houston), Sept. 29, 1841.

[6] Goodman, "A Statement of Facts, Washington, Feb⁷ 10, 1843," in W. D. Miller Papers, 1833–1860, ms.; B. T. Archer to Col. P. Hansbrough Bell, War Department, Austin, Sept. 25, 1842, in Harriet Smither (ed.), *Journals of the Sixth Congress of the Republic of Texas*, III, 431.

[7] *Telegraph and Texas Register*, Dec. 1, 1841. The citizens of Refugio County, forced to give constant vigilance to the protection of their homes, petitioned Judge Anderson Hutchinson of the Fourth Judicial District to suspend the regular term of the District Court to be held in the fall of 1841. They believed that "the documents and papers appertaining to the district court of Refugio County had been destroyed and all cases must be commenced *de novo*, wherefore they were unanimous in requesting the court not to proceed to that county at this time." The matter was referred to Congress and the request of the people of Refugio County was granted. Petition of Citizens of Refugio County to His Honor Anderson Hutchinson, Judge from the Judicial District, Republic of Texas, Victoria, October 23, 1841, in Memorials and Petitions (Texas), ms.; Smither (ed.), *Journals of the Sixth Congress of the Republic of Texas*, II, 166 n; *ibid.*, II, 77, 166, 184; I, 128, 142, 154, 164.

Appearing before the Mission of Refugio just before daybreak, the marauders launched their attack, and after a short skirmish the inhabitants of the place surrendered, with the exception of Henry Ryals, justice of the peace of Refugio County,[8] who was at his store at the eastern end of the settlement. He fought desperately and kept the whole Mexican party at bay until some of the local citizens came to him and persuaded him to surrender, which he did on condition he be treated as a prisoner of war. One Mexican was reported killed and three wounded by Ryals in the attack.[9]

Captain Benjamin F. Neal, John W. B. McFarlane, and John R. Talley made their escape in safety to Victoria, while the rest of the citizens of Refugio, except the women, were made prisoners, and the town plundered of its valuables. Most of the residents of Refugio were absent at the time of the attack, having gone down to the bay a day or two previous. Those who could speak Spanish, it was reported, were released, while the others were stripped of their clothing and carried away by Agatón, who commenced his retreat at 8 A.M. of the same day as the attack. Ryals was treated with great rudeness, and the Mexicans declared "they should kill him at a short distance from the town." Among those carried off were Henry Ryals, John Fox, James Fox, Michael Fox,[10] Israel Canfield, Bartlett Annibal, James St. John, William St. John, one Mexican [Rafael Gonzales?], and one Negro boy.[11] The outlaws bound the prisoners' hands before them and tied them to the tail of their horses and started off at a brisk trot.

Shortly after the Mexican withdrawal, five persons were found murdered on the Aransas.[12] Whether or not these were of the party carried off from Refugio, or some other deed perpetrated by Agatón's men, it has been impossible to determine.[13] But as for Ryals, there is no doubt. For his resistance, this brave frontiersman was left "sus-

---

[8] Hobart Huson, "Refugio: A Comprehensive History of Refugio County from Aboriginal Times to the End of World War II," Vol. II, chap. 20, p. 11.

[9] *Telegraph and Texas Register*, Sept. 29, Oct. 6, and Dec. 8, 1841; Heirs of Henry Ryals, Refugio County, to the Legislature of the State of Texas, Nov. 21, 1849, Memorials and Petitions (Texas), ms.; Huson, "Refugio," vol. II, chap. 24, p. 13, reports that Ryals killed one soldier and wounded another. I have not found proof of this.

[10] Huson, "Refugio," vol. II, chap. 23, p. 14.

[11] *Telegraph and Texas Register*, Sept. 29, 1841.

[12] *Ibid.*, Oct. 6, 1841.

[13] It is highly probable that Agatón's men had nothing to do with these murders.

pended by his heels and quite dead" at Burke's Hollow,[14] six miles south of the Mission, where the Mexicans paused briefly. While the unit rested here, "Sabina Brown, who was then the wife of Michael Fox, one of the prisoners, came up with the party," having followed her husband on foot all the way from town. Crazed with grief, the poor woman pleaded for his release. One of Agatón's men struck her on the head with his pistol, which proved too much for the bandit chief, cruel as he was; so, he graciously freed Michael Fox and permitted them both to return to Refugio.[15]

News of the raid spread quickly and Texans were soon in pursuit of the marauders. A party of about twenty-five Texan volunteers from the region from the San Antonio River to beyond Aransas quickly assembled under the leadership of Captain Cairns and took up the trail the day after the sacking of Refugio, but failed to overtake them. Agatón's party left Texas by way of Laredo and carried its prisoners to Lampazos, where they were subsequently released by order of General Rafael Vasquez. Several of the released men requested passports to visit Arista's headquarters at Monterey to ask for redress, but their request was rejected and the unhappy men returned home to report that the country west of the Río Grande was in a wretched condition. The garrisons were small and the soldiers were reported to be "ill armed, ill clothed, and so cowardly" that they could afford little protection to the unfortunate rancheros who were constantly subjected to the inroads of the warlike Comanches and other Indians.[16] Arista was reported at Monterey with seven to eight hundred men under his command; Vasquez was at Lampazos with three hundred men; and forty soldiers were said to be at Laredo.

Upon Agatón's return to Mexico, he was summoned to Arista's headquarters at Monterey to "answer for the outrage he had committed, as he had express orders not to injure any Texian citizens east of the Nueces."[17] Unable to justify his conduct, it was said, he was placed under guard until his punishment could be determined. In the meantime, he attempted to escape and was shot by one of the guards and

---

[14] Huson, "Refugio," vol. II, chap. 23, p. 14. Ryals was apparently hung by his heels and then shot. See Goodman, "A Statement of Facts, Washington, Feb? 10, 1843," in W. D. Miller Papers, 1833–1860, ms. Huson says that Ryals was tied to a horse's tail and dragged to death, as well as riddled with bullets.
[15] Huson, "Refugio," vol. II, chap. 23, p. 14.
[16] *Telegraph and Texas Register*, Dec. 8, 1841.
[17] *Ibid.*, Jan. 5, 1842.

wounded so severely that his recovery at the end of the year (1841) was considered doubtful.

The citizens of Victoria assembled in a public meeting at the Pavilion on September 20 with S. O. Tarpley as chairman and G. Everrette as secretary, for the purpose of providing for their own defense and of soliciting the authorities at Austin for assistance from a blood-thirsty Mexican foe who have carried into captivity "some six or eight valuable citizens" and plundered the town of Refugio of much property. The citizens of Victoria proceeded to create a committee of vigilance of six persons, whose duties were: (1) "to visit every house [in the town], ascertain as near as possible the state of the arms, and the quantity or number on hand, and if in order for actual and immediate use and service"; (2) to establish and provide support for a night guard; (3) to provide for continuation of the recently embodied spy company, but if this company were not in readiness, then for the immediate creation of another; and (4) to petition the Secretary of War for fifty stands of guns, one six-pound field piece, and a supply of ammunition.[18]

A verbal report of the sacking of Refugio reached Austin on Saturday, September 25, and immediately, in consequence of this new attack upon the frontier, Colonel Peter Hansbrough Bell, adjutant general of the Texas militia, was instructed by the War Department to inquire into the affair at Refugio and report to the government at Austin. He was ordered to take whatever steps he deemed "necessary for the future protection of Refugio and other exposed towns and settlements on the western frontier."

You are hereby further ordered to report to the Government, as early as practicable, your opinion, as to the influence which the Trade no[w] carried on with the Mexicans upon the Río Grande, has in producing the difficulties arising in the west—and whether said trade should be closed, or still continued.

It is the object of the Executive to clear the Country of its enemies, and to repel them when, and wherever they make their appearance; and for this purpose you are invested with ful[l] powers to raise whatever force is necessary to this end—to appoint your own Quarter Masters, and other officers, and to give receipts for such supplies as you may procure for the support & subsistence of your force. But whilst the Executive is thus anxious

---

[18] Report of a Public Meeting at Victoria, September 20, 1841, in *Texas Sentinel* (Austin), Oct. 14, 1841; G. Everrette, Secretary of the Committee of Vigilance, to Branch T. Archer, Secretary of War, Victoria, Sept. 21, 1841, in *ibid.*

to give protection to the west, he does not wish you to prosecute any war beyond the limits of our own Territory. To invade Mexico at this time, and push a war on the west of the Río Grande, is a measure frought with too many important consequences, in his opinion, to this country, to justify his ordering it without consulting the Congress of the Nation upon its propriety and policy.[19]

The President, however, a week later still "finding great difficulty in ascertaining the true state of affairs" on the southern frontier ordered Captain John C. Hays to repair as speedily as practical to the seat of government.[20] Hays was authorized to raise one hundred men under the terms and conditions specified in his orders of May 27, 1841, and to report to Colonel Bell after first reporting himself at Austin to get more specific explanation as to his duties, and should he fail to make contact with Bell, he was to carry out the orders issued to the latter, a copy of which was enclosed to him.

You will perceive by these orders, [wrote Lamar] that it is the desire of the Government to have the entire Western country cleared of the enemy, and protected from further pollution until the meeting of Congress; when it will be the duty [of] that body to devise some more efficient mode of giving security to that portion of the frontier, than can possibly be afforded by the operation of temporary volunteers or extended by the Minute Men system.[21]

The President had neither the means of supporting, nor the authority to raise a regular army for the defense of the country, but he was determined to do all that was within his power to give relief to the frontier. Unless it were Mathew Caldwell, John H. Moore, or Edward Burleson, the assignment now made could have been entrusted to no one in whom the frontier people had greater confidence than in Hays, whose fidelity, obedience to orders, and soldierly conduct was unquestioned.

At Victoria when the attack on Refugio took place, Bell hastened to San Patricio, where he found a company of men assembled upon the Nueces under Captain Cairns. He instructed Cairns to take the

[19] B. T. Archer, Secretary of War & Navy, to Col. P. Hansbrough Bell, War Department, Austin, Sept. 25, 1841, in Army Papers (Texas), ms., copy.
[20] Mirabeau B. Lamar to Captain [John C.] Hays, Executive Department, Oct. 2, 1841, in Record of Executive Documents from the 10th Dec. 1836 to the 14th Dec. 1841, ms., p. 250.
[21] *Ibid.*

trail and ascertain the movements of the marauders. Cairns' Company was composed of men originally belonging to the Minute Men of San Patricio County. These men had completed the term of service for which they had been enrolled under the law of February 4, 1841, and had been discharged, but with the attack on Refugio many of them had readily re-enlisted for the defense of their lives and property. Upon Cairns' return from his unsuccessful pursuit of Agatón, Bell reorganized his company for scouting purposes and arranged with Kinney and Aubrey to furnish them ammunition and subsistence.[22] Cairns' Company, it was believed would be effective in breaking up small marauding parties, and, as long as the trade was permitted to continue, would afford some confidence to those engaged in it.

Cairns was instructed to select a convenient point on the east side of the Nueces, at or near the river, as a base for military operation on either side of that stream. He was cautioned to engage only in defensive operations and to "be careful to do no act or make any movement calculated to induce attack from the Mexican enemy," as "it was considered unnecessary and useless to invite attack without the capacity to repel it." [23] He was to be constantly on the alert to intercept and break up all marauding parties, give protection to the traders going to and from the Río Grande, and to detail from his command scouts to gather "information of any suspicious bodies of men lurking on the Nueces, Agua Dulce, San Fernández or any watering places adjacent." Peace to the western frontier was desired, Bell informed Cairns,

. . . and it will be your duty, as far as practicable to promote it. You should at all times be ready to afford when called on, prompt assistance to the citizens; and to the civil authorities any aid necessary for their enforcing a due execution of the Laws. The Gov[ernmen]t expects that the irregularities and disorders heretofore common amongst volunteer commanders, on this frontier, will be avoided by you, by maintaining over your company a proper discipline.[24]

Cairns was to make a monthly report of his operations and of frontier conditions to the Secretary of War.

[22] P. Hansbrough Bell, Adjt. Genl. Militia, to Branch T. Archer, City of Austin, Oct. 4, 1841, in Army Papers (Texas), ms., copy.
[23] *Ibid.*; P. Hansbrough Bell, Adjt. Genl. Militia to Capt. [W. J.] Cairns, Comdg. Minute Men, San Patricio County, San Patricio, Sept. 20, 1841, copy in *ibid.*
[24] *Ibid.*

Having instructed Cairns and made a visit to all the settled portions of the southwestern frontier—Victoria, Lamar, Live Oak Point, La Bahía, San Patricio, Refugio, Lipantitlán, Corpus Christi, and other points, Colonel Bell returned to Austin to make his report to the War Department. He found that "the sum of the evils on the frontier, complained of from time to time to the . . . [War] Department, is far less, and of a character less aggravated than has been represented to you," he informed the Secretary of War; "it is nevertheless true that the condition of the western frontier is at this time such as to ask from your Department a serious consideration." Bell reported that there were no armed bands of Indians or Mexicans on the frontier, except an estimated 150 to 200 armed rancheros under Colonel Villareal stationed at the three principal crossings of the Arroyo Colorado, a small tidal creek, 125 miles from Corpus Christi, for the purpose of protecting the ranches in the neighborhood, and of intercepting the trade between the two countries.[25]

Villareal's position and activities were deemed purely of a defensive nature and were expected to remain so. Several parties of "mustangers," of from fifty to one hundred men, were declared to be ranging chiefly the Palo Blanco, Santa Rosa, and Los Olmos streams, some sixty to one hundred miles south of San Patricio. "These parties," reported Bell, "though hostile to and injurious to the trade, do not excite any serious apprehensions, or threaten any danger to the citizens of the west. But there are," he said, other bodies of armed men, commanded by Agatón, Ramírez, and others

. . . of a different character . . . whose frequent attacks upon our citizens have and do yet excite the most serious alarm. There is little doubt but that they are Commissioned by the Commander[s], of the Mexican frontier, for the expressed and ostensible purpose of intercepting and breaking up the existing Trade, [if not at times turning it to their own personal advantage[26]] and indeed to stop all intercourse with the Río Grande; but they are held to no responsibility for plundering or butchering Texan citizens in their lawless excursions. They are equally the terror of all Mexican Traders, and our citizens upon the Nueces, of the Peninsular, Lamar, Copano, the Mission and San Antonio Rivers—indeed the Guadalupe does not claim any exemption. Their object is plunder; no matter when, or where found; and there is no

[25] P. Hansbrough Bell, Adjt. Genl. Militia, to Branch T. Archer, Secretary of War & Navy, City of Austin, Oct. 4, 1841, in *ibid.*, ms., copy.
[26] Hubert Howe Bancroft, *History of Mexico*, V, 262 n; *Telegraph and Texas Register*, June 9, 1841.

sacrifice that they will not make, but that of their own cowardly blood. Our citizens have too often witnessed their success.[27]

"The merciless Indian savage is, if possible," declared the Secretary of War in his annual report in September 1841, "eclipsed in cruelty by our semi-barbarian Mexican foe; who are at this time engaged in the work of murder, plunder and rapine, desolating in their bloody career, the fairest portion of our Western frontier." [28] Some of the Mexican freebooters, wrote Kinney and Aubrey from their post on Corpus Christi Bay, are "believed to be leagued with merchants of Matamoros who have a hatred to this place, as we have positive information that it is not with the sanction of those in power." [29]

Bell made it plain that the Indians often got the blame for acts committed by others. Mexicans disguised as Indians, he declared, are "formidable in depredating on the property of Citizens on the Border," but "in speaking of disguised Mexicans," he continued, "I would by no means omit to mention that there are strong reasons to believe they have the co-operation of disguised Americans. Of the latter I am glad to believe there are but few." [30]

Bell found the citizens of the west "united in opinion that some strong and decided movement should be made towards visiting upon these daring hordes, a just punishment, and of driving them beyond the Río Grande." As to just what procedure should be followed in exacting retribution, the citizens of the west seemed to be divided into two classes. A portion of the westerners desired unrestricted orders from the government to intercept and break up the trade with the Río Grande, expel the Mexicans residing on and east of that river, and appropriate their property as an indemnity. "To use their own language," reported Bell, "they would 'rake down every thing west of the Nueces and pay themselves'—for this purpose some would cross the Río Grande." Among those who advocated such strong and sweeping action against the Mexicans, were "the most experienced and

[27] P. Hansbrough Bell, Adjt. Genl. Militia, to Branch T. Archer, Secretary of War & Navy, City of Austin, Oct. 4, 1841, in Army Papers (Texas), ms., copy.
[28] B. T. Archer, Secretary of War and Navy, to the President of the Republic of Texas, War and Navy Department, City of Austin, September 30, 1841, in Smither (ed.), *Journals of the Sixth Congress of the Republic of Texas*, III, 358.
[29] Letter of W. P. Aubrey and H. L. Kinney, Corpus Christi, Dec. 15, 1841, in *Daily Bulletin* (Austin), Dec. 31, 1841.
[30] P. H. Bell to B. T. Archer, Secretary of War and Navy, Victoria, Nov. 21, 1841, in *Lamar Papers*, III, 592–594.

respectable citizens." The other, and larger group, desired much the same privileges of retaliation, but wished to make a distinction between Mexicans east of the Río Grande, who were friendly, and those who were not. The friendly rancheros and others of unsuspicious character engaged in trade should be permitted to continue that trade, while all others should be annihilated or expelled beyond the Río Bravo. It was Bell's belief that a majority of the people of the western country favored a policy of closing the trade, "basing their objections to it mainly on the idea that it increased the channels of observation and intelligence from Mexico, and exposed the frontier more openly to the depredations of marauders." [31] There seemed to be no question but that some of the traders were later recognized in the ranks of the marauders, but the dangers from spy activity on the part of incoming traders would appear to have little weight so long as Mexican citizens, whose government was at war with Texas, continued to reside in Texas. "I frankly confess I have not been able to see the full force of the opposition to the existence of the Trade," declared Bell.

It certainly has its evils; but many of the inhabitants of the West are its beneficiaries, from a supply through it of various articles which they need, and which at this time they cannot procure elsewhere. Most of them ride Spanish horses and mules, with Spanish Saddles—wear Mexican Blankets, and it is not unusual to see and handle Mexican Plata; all procured in the way of Trade. With such a force as has been suggested, the Trade might go on, for the present, with some advantage to the west; and with a proper scrutiny into the manner of conducting it, I believe that many of the citizens now arrayed against it, would waive their opposition.

Any force ordered out by the War Department, he thought, should be well organized and with very definite and restrictive orders concerning the trade and distinction to make between friendly rancheros and suspicious and irresponsible Mexicans. He felt that if the government announced its policy in positive and unqualified terms, the people of the west would give their full cooperation in carrying out that policy. He, therefore, recommended raising and stationing on the frontier from 150 to 200 volunteers, or drafted men, enrolled for three months' service, unless sooner discharged. These men, or "rangers" as they were called, were to be well armed, mounted, and equipped to

[31] P. Hansbrough Bell, Adjt. Genl. Militia, to Branch T. Archer, Secretary of War & Navy, City of Austin, Oct. 4, 1841, in Army Papers (Texas), ms., copy.

operate between the Nueces and the Río Grande, and "from the Agua Dulce, or even from the Coast, and as high up as the movement of an enemy may require." The subsistence for the troops should be supplied from two points—San Antonio and Kinney's & Aubrey's ranch. Declared Bell,

These gentlemen have shown much liberality in expressing a willingness to afford every aid they can in maintaining a sufficient force west of the Nueces. The utility of such a force is increased from the consideration that there has already been formed an interesting nucleus of a settlement below the mouth of the Nueces, consisting of from seventy to one hundred souls; and by this measure, protection would be afforded at once to the San Antonio and Mission settlements, to the Peninsular, and to the settlements on the different Bays. Such a measure would also go far towards establishing in fact, that which now exists, only in empty declaration—*jurisdiction to the Río Grande.*[32]

Almost two months later, after another tour of all the western counties, where he sought to explain the nature of the War Department's plan of defense through the use of volunteer companies, properly organized, led, and disciplined, Bell made another report, this time detailing, in part, why his efforts to organize such companies had generally failed. The lack of sufficient response on the part of the citizens to the Department's efforts to organize such companies was, he believed, "found in the fact that many [of t]he Citizens have so long borne the brunt of frontier troubles that they are truly War worn, and in means worn out. The west has constituted a chain of sentinels to the Republic until the relief-hour has arrived."[33] Because this condition was recognized by the War Department as peculiar to the western frontier, its new policy for that area was for the government itself to furnish supplies of beef, sugar, coffee, and ammunition for 100 to 150 men who would operate beyond the line of settlements as a cordon to intercept, and, if interception failed, to retaliate upon the principal marauders. The initial period of enlistment was to be for three years, with the expectation that when Congress met some permanent plan of defense would be devised. Bell's efforts to assemble a sufficient force to carry out the objectives and orders of the War Department met with failure, and he turned his attention to organizing an efficient

[32] *Ibid.*
[33] P. H. Bell to B. T. Archer, Victoria, Nov. 21, 1841, in *Lamar Papers*, III, 592–594.

corps of spies.[34] The men were enlisted for three months, unless discharged sooner. The spy group was headed, as previously noted, by W. J. Cairns, a tried soldier, and was to do the service of Minute Men. These men were to be supplied by the government and not by themselves as the law provided for Minute Men. Bell pointed out that on the southwestern frontier it would be impossible for the men to furnish their own supplies; and, in view of his promises to the men, he hoped no deductions would be made from their pay for failure to equip themselves. He strongly urged the drafting of an efficient plan of defense for the western frontier and the establishment of a permanent force there. He thought the plan embraced in the law of December 21, 1838, establishing the First Regiment of Regular Infantry, was a sound one, and that "three or four or even two military posts properly manned and provided would be sufficient for present protection." [35]

In his annual report, Secretary of War Branch T. Archer declared that the militia plan, now in use, had proven "totally abortive." The duty of organizing the militia, he said, "has heretofore been confided to the Chief Justices of the respective counties, without the slightest obligation on their part to perform the duty." Many of them have aided in this important work and given their attention to perfecting the organization of the militia in their counties; yet, "little has been done towards its accomplishment," he declared.[36] For placing the militia on a sound footing, Archer recommended

. . . the appointment of some competent and responsible individual, (and were I authorized to nominate such an individual, I should fix on the present Adjutant General of Militia, Col. P. H. Bell,) with others to visit the several counties of the Republic; ascertain their military strength, classify and arrange them into battalions, regiments, and brigades; reporting to each Brigadier General, the strength of his brigade, and to the War Department, the whole strength of the nation, with the classification for order of service. The cost attending this plan for organizing the militia, would be comparatively small, when contrasted with the importance of the work.[37]

[34] *Ibid.*
[35] *Ibid.*
[36] B. T. Archer, Secretary of War and Navy, to the President of the Republic of Texas, War and Navy Department, City of Austin, Sept. 30, 1841, in Army Papers (Texas), ms.; Smither (ed.), *Journals of the Sixth Congress of the Republic of Texas*, III, 359.
[37] Smither (ed.), *Journals of the Sixth Congress of the Republic of Texas*, III, 359.

Archer was more than critical of the President's policy in regard to the southwestern frontier, and spoke out firmly for bold action.

It is not without regret that I have to acknowledge the difference of opinion existing between your Excellency and the head of this Department on the subject of our Western military operations. The territory claimed by us extends to the Río Grande. Our citizens have been authorized to locate and settle within this territory. Many have availed themselves of this authority, without the aid or protection of Government. Invasions of this section of country have been of daily occurrence. Our Mexican enemy have no restraints upon their action. Under pretence of a licensed trade, they enter and depart, unmolested, with the profits of their traffic; thus presenting to the world an anomaly in the prosecution of border war—free trade between belligerents—free interchange of commodities, between men in arms against each other; a facility, I think, never before given or practised, but by the most adroit and skilful spies. This state of things is not the most material disadvantage, under which our Western fellow-citizens have been laboring. The authorized Central Troops of Mexico, invade at will, for the purpose of murder and plunder; whilst our Troops are not permitted to enter their territory, either for purposes of revenge or reprisal. A border war prosecuted on this plan, cannot fail to be disastrous to the restrained party. We know this fact, from the repeated complaints of our Western fellow-citizens, and their continued and loud demands on the Government for permittance to prosecute this border war on equal terms with the enemy. My order of date the 14th of July was countermanded by your order, of date the 14th of August following. This recession of the orders of the 14th of July, has been attended with consequences fairly to have been anticipated. The murder of our citizens, the violation of our women, and the sacking of our towns. If this state of things is to continue, I would most earnestly advise my brethren of the West, to abandon that frontier, as in a contest so unequal it cannot be sustained.[38]

Lamar's term of office was too near its close for him to lay down a policy in the light of these suggestions, and the problem of frontier defense was left to the incoming Houston administration to work out. But it was not too late to put into effect the new policy developed with Yucatán—a policy designed as much to embarrass his successor as to aid Yucatán and retaliate upon Mexico. The Texas naval expedition, consisting of the *Austin, San Bernard,* and *San Antonio,* sailed from Galveston on December 13, 1841, the last day of Lamar's administration and the day that Houston began his second term as President,

[38] *Ibid.,* III, 361–362.

with instructions to capture Mexican towns and levy contributions, destroying public works and seizing public property. It was suggested that these acts would "strike terror among the inhabitants, which may be very useful to us." [39] But, as for a military operation by land against Mexico, even Lamar could see the impracticality of such an enterprise. His whole administration had been one of general frustration on both the international and domestic fronts, and as Congress assembled amid a "scene of *tumult* and *vexation*" for the last time in Austin, Lamar was constrained to ask in his last annual message to Congress on November 3:

Whilst we are . . . annoying our enemy by water, the question naturally arises, what shall be our course toward them upon land? I have already expressed my aversion to military invasion of their territory. If there were no other reasons which would indicate the impropriety of such a step, the condition of the country, in a pecuniary point of view, utterly forbids it at present. We have not the means to raise, equip, and continue in the field an army of sufficient force to chastise that nation into an acknowledgment of our independence, without involving ourselves in pecuniary difficulties and embarrassments, infinitely greater than those which now surround us, and which it is admitted by all, are as great as the country at this time can bear, without materially retarding its prosperity and the development of its resources. I am aware that an opinion prevails among many of my fellow-citizens that an army once organized and put in motion, can support itself off the enemy. But how is this to be done? Shall it be permitted by sacrilege and robbery—by plundering the churches, and strip[p]ing peaceful citizens of their private property without giving them any thing in compensation for it? This would hardly be consistent with civilized and honorable warfare. Besides the violence would be offered to a people who are neither hostile to us, nor adverse to their Government's acknowledging our rights; for it is known that the Mexicans on the Río Grande, have always evinced a disposition for peace and a desire to cultivate with us, amicable and commercial relations. It is emphatically their interest to do so; for if a violent war be awakened upon that border, they will be the sufferers, no matter which of the contending parties may prevail; as both will equally prey upon them. They also desire peace upon other grounds. Their proximity to, and intercourse with us, have inspired them with more enlarged and liberal views than are entertained by the interior State of Mexico; and instead of being at war with our institutions, they would prefer to see them introduced

[39] Branch T. Archer, Secretary of War & Navy, to E. W. Moore, Sept. 18, 1841, in E. W. Moore, *To the People of Texas: An Appeal in Vindication of His Conduct of the Navy*, pp. 12–13.

into their own country, to the extirpation of that bigotry and despotism that enslave the land.[40]

Apparently by the end of his administration Lamar had given up any ideas that he may have had relative to an extension of the Republic's boundaries beyond the line set by Congress in December 1836, and had become more concerned with maintaining full sovereignty over the area lying between the Nueces and the Río Grande, within the claimed boundary of the nation.

Although . . . opposed to any active operations beyond the Río Grande, I am equally clear in the opinion that we should no longer delay enforcing our claims to the territory lying east of that river; for unless this be effectually done, the western country, where population is mostly needed, will be more slowly settled than any other section. As the best means of directing emigration to that quarter, and giving strength to the border, which it so much needs, I would recommend to congress the propriety of establishing such military posts, west of the Nueces, as may be deemed sufficient to the maintenance of our rights to the country, and to give security to its citizens. It is believed that this can be done without involving the Government in any serious expenditure; for the force necessary to this object, need not be large, inasmuch as we shall in all probability not very shortly, if ever, have to contend with any other enemy than the savages, and the marauding parties that may occasionally infest that region, until they shall be finally expelled. Should Mexico, however, seriously contemplate another invasion of our territory, this measure becomes the more important from the fact that the success of the enemy in penetrating our country, will depend entirely upon the condition of the west; which if permitted to remain unsettled and defenceless, can offer no barrier to the advances of the invaders; but if strengthened and sustained by means of military posts, it will soon be able of itself, to hold the enemy in check, until the forces of the nation can be rendered available, and be brought to bear upon our foes, before they can overrun the country as was done in the campaign of 1836.[41]

The heavy debt of the Republic, much of which had been incurred during his administration, made any active campaign by land against Mexico most impractical, and Lamar saw little prospect of any speedy

[40] M. B. Lamar to the Senate and House of Representatives, Executive Department, Austin, November 3, 1841, in Smither (ed.), *Journals of the Sixth Congress of the Republic of Texas*, I, 11–13; also in Record of Executive Documents from the 10th Dec. 1838 to the 14th Dec. 1841, ms., pp. 267–291.
[41] *Ibid.*

alleviation of the current situation in the nation's finances, for emigration into the country, "from which much had been expected, [had] proved generally not to be of that industrious and laboring class," which adds to the vigor and wealth of the nation through the cultivation of the soil. "The influx into our country," he informed Congress, "was of that adventureous character, which rather destroyed than strengthened the hopes that our fertile plains would be shortly subjected to the plow-share." [42]

Even Burnet, in defense of his conduct while acting as President the year before, was constrained to say in his valedictory to the Senate that the charges made during the past year against him by "partisan editors" and "respectable friends" that he was "in favor of getting up a military invasion of Mexico," were totally unfounded. They "have entirely misunderstood my acts and the motives which induced them," he declared.

I have never desired to be instrumental in calling my fellow-citizens from their peaceful occupations at home, to endure the toils, and dangers, and vicissitudes of "the tented field," in a foreign land: I have seen enough of war, its "pride and circumstances," in my youth; and enough in Texas, too, to repress every ambitious aspiration that could prompt me to wish a repetition of its calamities here—and I have been too long conversant with the affairs of Texas, not to know, that her best policy consists in cultivating the nobler and more profitable arts of peace.

But, two certain messages, which I had the honor to transmit to Congress, have been denounced with all the vehemence of party strife, as "*war messages.*" The plain import and the true intention of those communications, have been grossly misrepresented by others. At the time they were made, the minds of men here, were strongly impressed with the expectation of an immediate and formidable invasion by Mexico. Intelligence from highly respectable authorities was crowded upon us with a startling rapidity, that the enemy was actively embodying his forces, for the purpose of invading our territory, and again committing his vaunted claim to dominion over us, to the arbitrament of the sword . . . and I am still of the opinion it was founded in truth; but that circumstances entirely extraneous to us, and independent of any intervention on our part, diverted the attention of the enemy and dissolved the militant powers arrayed against us. . . .

A fair interpretation of the two messages will admit of but one understanding:—that the whole matter was founded on the presumption that Mexico would certainly invade us, and that "very soon." And is there a

[42] Smither (ed.), *Journals of the Sixth Congress of the Republic of Texas*, I, 20.

Texian patriot who would not advocate a similar policy, in the event of a serious invasion? Who would be content with simply *repelling* the invaders; and then to relapse into the inert, and, so far as *peace* is concerned, unproductive quietude of the last five years? If there be such, he and I differ essentially, as to the most efficient and expeditious means of securing what we all desire, the peace, independence and happiness of Texas. I could not be satisfied with a mere *repulsion* of the invading host; and then to give our faithless enemy another five years of undisturbed tranquility to reanimate his drooping spirits; replenish his exhausted coffers; and again, at a convenient season, to marshal his recruited forces for another desolating inroad. No! I would not. If our citizens must again be impelled to the battlefield, I would not remit our labors, until the great work of the revolution should be accomplished; and the hardened pride of Mexico be humbled in the dust, before the banner of Texian freedom.[43]

For a brief spell after Bell's visit all was quiet on the frontier, until some time in November when the Texan spies on the Nueces discovered a party of Mexicans collecting some thirty miles away.[44] Their movements were carefully observed for several weeks by the Texan scouts. Finally, it was announced that the Mexican force was advancing toward Corpus Christi. The cannon was drawn up in front of the gate of Kinney's post, "well charged and man[n]ed."[45] Late in the evening of December 23, Cairns' men, numbering some twenty-eight, re-enforced by twenty-five citizens, ordered the Mexicans into the post, disarmed them, and placed their horses under a strong guard for two days; when becoming convinced of their peaceful intentions, they were permitted to trade and leave. After the Mexicans had been gone several days, reported Goodman, "Capt. Carnes with some volunteer citizens, proceed[ed] west in order to rout the Enemy."[46] Discovering a camp, Cairns' party of twenty men charged it, thinking it was the enemy, but found that the camp was that of a small party of traders. After running some distance, the traders halted and indicated they desired not to fight, but Cairns again charged them, killing one.

[43] David G. Burnet to the Senate, Saturday Morning, Dec. 4, 1841, in *ibid.*, I, 92–97.
[44] Goodman, "A Statement of Facts, Washington, Feby 10, 1843," in W. D. Miller Papers, 1833–1860, ms.
[45] *Ibid.*
[46] *Ibid.*; ———— to William L. Hunter of Goliad [in Austin], Victoria, Dec. 24, 1841, in *Daily Bulletin*, Dec. 31, 1841.

The Texans now returned to the Mexican camp, took possession of the mules and other belongings and returned to the post.[47]

A few months later, in March 1842, Cairns' small party, now reduced to eight men, was attacked near San Patricio on the Nueces by a part of Valero's troops.[48] The Mexicans succeeded in killing Cairns, Miles, Snodgrass, White, and one other and capturing Marvin and Wells. Ewen Cameron, however, effected his escape by swimming the river.[49] Cairns was said to have killed a Mexican after he, himself, had been mortally wounded. Colonel Kinney was able to have Marvin released the day after he was taken. Wells was carried to Matamoros, where Kinney met him later, and obtained his release.

[47] Goodman, "A Statement of Facts, Washington, Feby 10, 1843," in W. D. Miller Papers, 1833–1860, ms.; *Telegraph and Texas Register*, Jan 12, 1842. The editor of the *Telegraph* reported that Cairns' men had captured the Mexicans below the Nueces, believing them to be the advance guard of a large Mexican invading force. The *Morning Star* (Houston) reported on January 11, 1842, that word had been received in Houston the evening before from Austin that Captain Cairns and the twenty men under him had been captured by an advance guard of 400 Mexicans under Gonzales. The news, it was said, had been conveyed to Austin in a letter from Major Roman to William E. Jones, a member of the House of Representatives from Gonzales. *Morning Star* of Jan. 11, 1842, quoted in *Telegraph and Texas Register*, Jan. 12, 1842.

[48] The *Morning Star*, quoted in *Telegraph and Texas Register*, March 30, 1842, reported the attack occurring around March 14.

[49] "Information derived from Col. [H. L.] Kinney, Corpus Christi" concerning difficulties between Mexicans and Texans, 1840–1842, in the vicinity of Corpus Christi, *Lamar Papers*, IV, 211–214; *Telegraph and Texas Register*, Jan. 12, 1842.

CHAPTER TWENTY-THREE

The Republic's Colonization Program

BESIDES INCREASED TEXAN ACTIVITY on the frontier, another development which no doubt drew Mexico's attention to Texas was the Texas colonization program. The Indian disturbances of 1838 and 1839 had caused a renewal of the discussion of colonizing the area beyond the frontier of settlement. When the Indian campaign of 1839 removed the most immediate danger to the settlements, the government turned its attention to the problem of establishing frontier posts and promoting a colonization plan. Early in 1841 a bill was introduced in the House of Representatives providing for the incorporation and establishment of a French colonization company to introduce eight thousand Frenchmen, over seventeen years of age, into Texas as colonists. This company, previously mentioned, to be known as the Franco-Texienne Company, was to station its colonists at twenty forts to be erected and maintained by it for twenty years along the western frontier, and to enjoy exclusive trading privileges with the New Mexican settlements; its settlers were to be exempt of all taxes and tariffs for a period of twenty years. When the required number of settlers had been introduced and located at these forts, the company was to receive three million acres of land, to be divided into sixteen tracts scattered along the frontier. The eastern boundary of the proposed grant was substantially the line of frontier posts which had been suggested by Johnston, in 1839, "while the tract as a whole covered a strip of territory varying from twenty to one hundred miles in width from east to west." [1] The bill contained a number of objectionable features,[2] and failed to pass the Senate,

[1] William C. Binkley, *The Expansionist Movement in Texas, 1836–1850*, p. 55.
[2] For details concerning this bill and the opposition thereto, see Binkley, *The Expansionist Movement in Texas*, pp. 54–56; Rupert N. Richardson, *Texas: The Lone Star State*, pp. 157–158; Bernice Barnett Denton, "Count Alphonso de Saligny and the Franco-Texienne Bill," *Southwestern Historical Quarterly*, XLV, (1941–1942), 136–146; *Texas Sentinel* (Austin), May 27, July 1, Aug. 5, 12, Oct. 7, 1841; *Telegraph and Texas Register* (Houston), Aug. 4 and 11, 1841; *Austin City Gazette*, Dec. 8, 1841; and *Red-Lander*, Oct. 23, 1841.

499

probably because of Lamar's opposition, although it was strongly supported in the House by ex-President Houston. Lamar offered a counterproposition known as the Santa Fé Bill for developing the trade of West Texas, but Houston actively fought Lamar's proposal and helped defeat it in Congress in January 1841. The two bills were among the leading issues in the presidential election campaign of 1841; and, in spite of the opposition, Houston, who had been one of the principal supporters of the Franco-Texienne Bill in the House, was elected. When the bill was presented again in the Sixth Congress, however, there was still very little enthusiasm for it. It had proven decidedly unpopular among Texans, and was allowed to die.

Even before the Santa Fé Expedition was organized, plans for colonizing the area between Austin and Santa Fé were being formulated by Lamar's administration and were no doubt a part of the general program to secure a monopoly of the Santa Fé trade for the Republic. By an act approved January 4, 1841, every head of family or single man who immigrated to Texas after January 1, 1840, but before January 1, 1842, was to be given 640 acres and 320 acres, respectively, provided he became a citizen, settled on the land for three years, and cultivated not less than ten acres. The law also authorized the President to form a contract for settling vacant and unappropriated lands "beyond the limits of the present settlements." [3] This law allowed a single company—that of W. S. Peters and Associates—to colonize along the northern frontier. Later, President Houston and his Secretary of State, Anson Jones, proposed the establishment of alternate colonies of French, English, and Belgians along the lower reaches of the Río Grande to serve as a buffer against Mexican attacks. The passage by the Texas Congress of a law in January 1841 (amended on February 5, 1842), permitting the President, under certain conditions, to conclude contracts with individuals for colonizing the country, soon resulted in the signing of a number of agreements with foreign companies or other agents.

Hoping to take advantage of the amended colonization law, Henri Castro, a former citizen of France who had taken out naturalization papers in the United States, arrived in Austin on January 29, 1842, and applied for permission to establish a colony in Texas. On February 15 the Texas government awarded Castro and his partner, Jean Jassaud, a contract to introduce six hundred families or single men over seven-

[3] H. P. N. Gammel (ed.), *Laws of Texas*, II, 554–557.

teen years of age within the next three years. They were given two tracts of land, one of which was "situated upon the Río Grande, commencing at a point nearly opposite Camargo and running to *El Sal del Rey*, thence in a parallel line to a point opposite Dolores, below Laredo." [4] This tract, however, was never settled by the contractors as it was too near areas occupied by Mexican troops and subject to Mexican marauding parties. The other grant was located west of San Antonio and included that section "now comprising parts of Medina, Uvalde, Frio, Atascosa, Béxar, McMullen, LaSalle and Zavalla counties." [5] At the same time Houston appointed Castro, a trustworthy and educated Frenchman, to be consul general for the Republic in France.

Without visiting the land which had been granted to him, Castro returned to France in the spring of 1842 and began recruiting colonists to settle a colony in southwest Texas on the Medina River. In the meantime, those French immigrants who had arrived at Galveston and other points on the Texas coast [6] were authorized to proceed at once at their own expense to San Antonio and select and occupy the vacant houses in that place, and to cultivate such farms as might be unoccupied, taking due care, however, not to interfere with the rights of any citizen who might wish to do the same.[7] These immigrants were assured that at San Antonio they would find a French consul who

[4] *Ibid.*, 785–786; Proclamation of a Colonial Contract between the Republic of Texas and Henri Castro and John Jassaud, February 5, 1842, in *Writings of Sam Houston*, II, 483–484; Florence Johnson Scott, *Historical Heritage of the Lower Río Grande: A Historical Record of Spanish Exploration, Subjugation and Colonization of the Lower Río Grande Valley and the Activities of José Escandón, Count of Sierra Gorda, together with the Development of Towns and Ranches under Spanish, Mexican and Texas Sovereignties, 1747–1848*, p. 105; "Report of Joseph Waples, Acting Secretary of State, to the Senate, July 6, 1842," in Harriet Smither (ed.), *Journals of the Sixth Congress of the Republic of Texas*, III (Called Session), 10–12; *Telegraph and Texas Register*, Feb. 16, 1842. El Sal del Rey (the Royal Salines or the King's Salt) was a salt lake in the lower Río Grande Valley.

[5] Julia Nott Waugh, *Castro-Ville and Henry Castro: Empresario*, p. 4.

[6] The *Atlante*, a barque of five hundred tons from Le Havre, arrived off Galveston on February 9 with sixty immigrants (chiefly farmers) and a considerable cargo of merchandise, and the *Amanda*, a French vessel, reached Matagorda on June 25, 1842, with "a fine company of emigrants to lay the foundation of a large settlement, which," declared the *Telegraph*, "we understand is to be composed mostly of Swiss, from the neighborhood of Lucerne." *Telegraph and Texas Register*, Feb. 16 and July 6, 1842.

[7] Houston to Major George T. Howard, Washington, Jan. 24, 1842, in *Writings of Sam Houston*, II, 440–441.

would afford them protection and assistance. At the time this contract was made with Castro, another was made with William Kennedy and the latter's confidential agent, William Pringle of London, for settling an English colony between the Nueces and the Río Grande.[8] Similar colonization contracts were made during 1842 with interested Germans and others for settling along the southern and western borders. Alexander Bourgeois d'Orvanne and Armand Ducos received two contracts. One, dated June 3, called for the establishment of a colony of twelve to sixteen hundred German families or single men on the headwaters of the Frio and Medina rivers;[9] and the other, granted also in the summer of 1842, provided for the location of five hundred families along the Río Grande from its mouth up to Reinosa. A third contract, granted to Henry Francis Fisher and Burchard Miller, on June 7, 1842, called for the settlement of six hundred families from Germany within eighteen months on three million acres of land located between the Colorado and Río Grande, and west of the Llano River.[10] Interest in settling one thousand Europeans (Belgians, Hollanders, and Swiss) in Texas along the Río Grande was shown by Captain Victor Pirson, a Belgian agent who arrived in Texas in February–March 1842, and concluded a contract to that effect in November, which he proposed to transfer to a company to be chartered by the Belgian government. The Belgian government, however, having recently organized a company to colonize in Guatemala, vetoed this proposal for a second company.[11]

---

[8] Binkley, *The Expansionist Movement in Texas,* p. 99; "Report of Joseph Waples, Acting Secretary of State, to the Senate, July 6, 1842," in Smither (ed.), *Journals of the Sixth Congress of the Republic of Texas,* III, 10–12; "Colonization Contract of William Kennedy signed by Sam Houston, William Kennedy, and William Pringle (by William Kennedy), City of Austin, February 15, 1842, in Sam Houston, Unpublished Houston Correspondence, 1842, III; William Kennedy to the Earl of Aberdeen, Haymarket, Nov. 12, 1841 (Private), in Ephraim D. Adams (ed.), "Correspondence from the British Archives Concerning Texas, 1837–1848," in *Quarterly of the Texas State Historical Association,* XV (1911–1912), 249–251.

[9] *Telegraph and Texas Register,* June 8, 1842; Anson Jones to Ashbel Smith, City of Houston, June 7, 1842, in Garrison (ed.), *Diplomatic Correspondence of Texas,* III, 963–965; colonization contract given to A. Bourgeois and A. Ducos, City of Houston, June 3, 1842, signed by: Sam Houston, in Texas Colony Contracts, Feb. 1842–Jan. 1844, ms., pp. 158–163.

[10] R. L. Biesele, *The History of the German Settlements in Texas, 1831–1861,* pp. 71, 72 n, 80, and map on p. 152.

[11] Joseph William Schmitz, *Texan Statecraft, 1836–1845,* pp. 163, 167, 215.

The Republic's Colonization Program

Such colonizing activities indicated to the Mexican authorities that the Texas government definitely intended to settle and develop the area west of the San Antonio River, and thus the so-called "no-man's land" would soon become distinctly a part of the rebel country to the north. That Congress had such an object in mind in granting liberal land bounties for the introduction of settlers was openly admitted in Texas. The object of Congress, wrote "Civilian," is "to augment our population as fast as possible under our present relations with Mexico and thus strengthen the defensive powers of the country. After our independence has been formally acknowledged by that nation we shall have no necessity for granting rewards to those who come to dwell among us."[12] Furthermore, if German, French, Belgian, Dutch, and British colonists were established in Texas, a Mexican invasion would tend to ally the mother countries of the imperilled immigrants to the Texas cause. While the efforts of the Republic to occupy the territory within its asserted boundaries and outside the limits of old Mexican Texas excited some attention in Mexico, the efforts themselves proved largely unsuccessful. There was some dubious infiltration into the County of San Patricio. "Land boards of the Republic issued certificates to lands which were surveyed and located in the [county, but] . . . there was in fact little, if any, settlement on these grants" until after General Zachary Taylor reached the Nueces at the end of July 1845.[13] On January 29, 1842, an act to organize the County of Guadalupe was passed over the President's veto.[14]

[12] *Telegraph and Texas Register*, Oct. 26, 1842.
[13] Walace Hawkins, *El Sal del Rey, Fixing Title to*, pp. 19–20. General Zachary Taylor landed at St. Joseph's Island, July 26, 1845, and at Corpus Christi, July 31. W. A. Croffut (ed.), *Fifty Years in Camp and Field: Diary of Major General Ethan Allen Hitchcock*, pp. 193–194.
[14] Gammel (ed.), *Laws of Texas*, II, 750–755.

CHAPTER TWENTY-FOUR

Growth of a War Spirit in the West

As THE MEXICAN INVASION failed to materialize in the spring of 1841, the business of organizing an expedition in Texas was directed toward another point—Santa Fé. Many eyes in Texas, however, still turned south toward the Río Grande. Lamar's administration saw the only attempt made by the Republic to realize the boundary fixed by the law of December 19, 1836. An ill-advised, preposterous, and inadequately equipped expedition of approximately 321 men left Kenney's Fort on Brushy Creek, twenty miles north of Austin, on June 19, 1841, for Santa Fé. This so-called Santa Fé Expedition, sponsored by President Lamar, the successful candidate of the west in the presidential election of 1838, lacked congressional support [1] and in East Texas was looked upon as "a National outrage," [2] and "as a chimerical project, without force to maintain itself." [3] The expedition, which had been

[1] Although Congress had discussed the question of dispatching an expedition to Santa Fé and sending the navy to Yucatán, it had authorized neither action. In outfitting and sending the expedition to Santa Fé, Lamar probably exceeded the authority given the President in the Constitution. To allege that he was merely extending the authority of the government over the area claimed by Texas is not enough, for only Congress had the power "to call out the militia to execute the law, to suppress insurrection, and repel invasion." Certainly no law was being violated by the New Mexicans in 1841 any more than in 1836, when Texas began its claim of jurisdiction over the inhabitants of Sante Fé. Furthermore, the Constitution imposed upon Congress the authority "to provide and maintain an army and navy," and declared that "no money shall be drawn from the public treasury but in strict accordance with appropriations made by law." (Art. I, sec. 25.) It seems, therefore, a bad policy for the President to have committed the nation to the expenditure of large sums of money in fitting out the expedition to Santa Fé, especially after the matter had been so recently discussed in Congress and not authorized.

[2] David S. Kaufman to W. D. Miller, Sabine Town, Aug. 15, 1841, in W. D. Miller Papers, 1833–1860, ms.

[3] *Telegraph and Texas Register* (Houston), Sept. 29, 1841. A subsequent investigating committee of the House found that *"the enormous sum of eighty-nine thousand, five hundred and forty-nine dollars and sixty-nine cents"* had been drawn

assembled quietly, possibly so as not to attract the attention either of Mexico or that of other powers whose interests might be affected by it, was expected to accomplish a two-fold purpose—to open direct trade between the Texas settlements and Santa Fé by a route known to be much nearer than the great Missouri trail connecting Santa Fé with the United States, and to establish peaceably the Republic's jurisdiction over her western territory, which included Santa Fé as claimed under her own laws. It was the last major effort of the administration to add luster to its political star; and, yet, more than any of its other efforts to court popularity, it was to culminate in abject failure.

The sending of this expedition beyond the historic boundaries of Texas was an act of war-provoking character, and was regarded by the Mexican government as an effort of her "rebelled province" to take further territory from her. By September this most ambitious and ill-advised "caravan" was a complete failure. Its members, "broken, dispirited, desperately hungry, and almost dying with thirst," were easily captured by Governor Manuel Armijo of New Mexico and sent in bondage to Mexico City.[4]

In the meantime, as the administration of Lamar ground to a halt, "everything and every body" appeared, "to be waiting the 'moving of the waters' by old Sam." [5] The conditions under which the Sixth Congress [6] assembled in Austin on November 1, in regular session, to hear

---

from the treasury to fit out this expedition. Texas Congress, *Report of Select Committee on Resolutions relative to the Santa Fé Expedition; Austin City Gazette*, Dec. 15, 1841.

[4] For excellent accounts of the Santa Fé Expedition see George W. Kendall, *Narrative of the Texas Santa Fé Expedition Comprising a Description of a Tour through Texas and across the Great Southwestern Prairies, the Comanche and Caygua Hunting-Grounds with an Account of the Sufferings from Want of Food, Losses from Hostile Indians, and Their March, as Prisoners, to the City of Mexico*; A. K. Christian, "Mirabeau Buonaparte Lamar," *Southwestern Historical Quarterly*, XXIV (1920–1921), 87–139; William C. Binkley, *The Expansionist Movement in Texas, 1836–1850*, pp. 68–95; H. Bailey Carroll, *The Texan Santa Fé Trail*; and Thomas Falconer, *Letters and Notes on the Santa Fé Expedition, 1841–1842*. The Santa Fé men were imprisoned at Mexico City, Puebla, and Perote. Many of them were placed in chains and forced to work on the streets and undergo other hardships and indignities.

[5] Anson Jones to Mary Jones, Austin, Nov. 19, 1841, in Anson Jones Papers, ms.

[6] Duncan W. Robinson, in *Judge Robert McAlpin Williamson: Texas' Three-Legged Willie*, p. 184, says,

The personnel of the House of Representatives at the time was international, cosmopolitan, and colorful: three representatives were from North Carolina;

the "swan song" of the Lamar administration were anything but favorable to Texas. Its southwestern frontier was the scene of constant attacks by Texan renegades and parties of Mexicans from the Río Grande; the nation was heavily in debt, almost on the verge of bankruptcy; and, although the fact was not yet known in Texas, the Santa Fé Expedition had been a complete and dismal failure. The people, in general, were in low spirits. Prices were greatly depressed. There was no money in the country, and people were moving "back to the States faster than they came in." [7] The effects of the Panic of 1837 in the United States had begun to have adverse effects upon the Texas economy. The city of Austin was pictured as "more dull than you could imagine," and the Congress was described as doing little, "except prying into the different offices to find the leaks by which the money has all run out, and contriving the means to stop some of them." [8]

Partisanship was at its height. The recent presidential election had terminated in favor of the "Houston crowd," and all the ills that beset the country, it was felt by the supporters of "Old Sam," must be pictured as the fruits of the Lamar administration. On motion of Tod Robinson of Brazoria County on November 8 the Naval Affairs Committee of the House of Representatives was instructed to inquire into the expediency of recalling the navy from the service of Yucatán. [9] The committee reported on November 13 that it was inexpedient for the House to act upon the subject of the recall of the Texan navy until action had been taken by the Senate on the Convention entered into

four from South Carolina; three from Kentucky; four from Virginia; one from Pennsylvania; eight from Tennessee; one from Wales (Simeon L. 'hello-roaring' Jones); one from Arkansas; one from Ohio; one from Austria; one from Ireland; one from Vermont; and ten from Georgia. In the group were eighteen farmers, eighteen lawyers, and four merchants. The oldest was fifty-four, and the youngest, twenty-five.

[7] J. M. Odin to Monsieur J. Timon, July 16, 1841, in [James M. Kirwin and others], *Diamond Jubilee, 1847–1922, of Galveston and St. Mary's Cathedral*, p. 66. Ralph Bayard, *Lone-Star Vanguard: The Catholic Re-occupation of Texas, 1838–1848*, pp. 144–145, 257–258.

[8] Anson Jones to Mary Jones, Austin, Nov. 19, 1841, in Anson Jones Papers, ms.

[9] Harriet Smither (ed.), *Journals of the Sixth Congress of the Republic of Texas*, II, 17. The Naval Affairs Committee was composed of Louis P. Cooke (Travis County), Gustavus A. Parker (Fort Bend County), Thomas F. Smith (Fannin County), Thomas M. Dennis (Matagorda County), and Jesse Grimes (Montgomery County). On November 11 Robert M. Williamson (Washington County) and on the 12th John B. Jones (Galveston County) were added to the committee.

by the Executive with the state of Yucatán.[10] The report was read the
first time and, not being what the opponents of Lamar had in mind,
was ordered laid on the table for further consideration.

Immediately following this action, Nicholas H. Darnell of San
Augustine County introduced a joint resolution calling for the appointment of a Select Naval Committee to inquire into "the expediency of
recalling the Navy from the service in which they are at present engaged under contract or agreement made by the Executive of this
country with the State of Yucatán." This proposal passed its first reading on November 13, its second on November 15, and at that time
was referred with the report of the Naval Affairs Committee to a Select
Committee composed of Darnell (chairman), Cooke (Travis County),
Tod Robinson (Brazoria County), Van Zandt (Harrison and Panola
counties), Wynns (Harris County), Mayfield (Nacogdoches County),
John B. Jones (Galveston County), Hewett [11] (Shelby County), and
Williamson [12] (Washington County). The majority of the Select Naval
Committee made its report on November 19, recommending that Con-
gress require the President to recall the navy, and the minority pre-
sented its report three days later.

In the meantime, the Lamar administration was attacked along
another line. On November 23, the day following the presentation of
the report of the minority of the Select Committee on the Recall of
the Navy, Archibald Wynns of Harris County, one of the signers of
the majority report of said committee, introduced a resolution in the
House censuring the President for fitting out the Santa Fé Expedition,
and on the 26th upon motion of William N. Porter from the newly
created county of Bowie the resolution was referred to a Select Committee, consisting of Van Zandt (chairman), Porter, Brown, George T.
Wood [13] of Liberty County, and William E. Jones of Gonzales County.
On Monday, December 6, the committee presented a lengthy report [14]
recommending rejection of the resolution of censure because (1) it

---

[10] *Ibid.*, II, 28, 128 n.   [11] *Ibid.*, II, 31.

[12] *The Weekly Texian* (Austin), Nov. 25, 1841.

[13] George T. Wood organized a company and fought under General Andrew
Jackson in 1814 in the Battle of Horseshoe Bend against the Creeks. Wood served
as governor of Texas, 1847–1849. *Biographical Directory of the Texan Conventions
and Congresses*, p. 194; *Handbook of Texas*, II, 929–930.

[14] Texas Congress, *Report of Select Committee on Resolutions relative to the
Santa Fé Expedition*; Smither (ed.), *Journals of the Sixth Congress of the Republic
of Texas*, II, 99–109; *Austin City Gazette*, Dec. 15, 1841.

doubted that the House had the power to censure another department of government; (2) the resolution arraigned the Executive upon a high charge, without affording him an opportunity of defense; and (3) such a resolution, if adopted, would show to the country that the House "had witnessed a violation of the Constitution and laws," and had failed to discharge its duty. Instead, it raised the question of impeachment of President Lamar,[15] Vice President Burnet,[16] and Secretary of the Treasury John G. Chalmers, for their conduct in the fitting out of the Santa Fé Expedition, but refrained from recommending to the House any definite action in regard to impeachment.[17] The Select Committee, unanimously, except for Jones of Gonzales, found "the President, in fitting up and sending out the Santa Fé Expedition," had

[15] A scathing denunciation of Lamar for fitting out the Santa Fé Expedition and for other actions, signed by "A"—subsequently identified as General Memucan Hunt—appeared in the January 26, 1842, issue of the weekly *Texian*. Its author proposed that Lamar should be delivered up to the vengeance of Mexico for the redemption of the unfortunate Santa Fé prisoners, and that he should be prevented from leaving Texas until the proposition could be made to Mexico and responded to by her. At first, Lamar thought that the article had originated with Anson Jones, the Secretary of State, and if so, he thought, it wore "the aspect of a Government measure," and "I cannot allow him to escape from his responsibility to me." In conclusion, Lamar remarked: "Had the production eminated from the Editor of the *Texian* or from any irresponsible scoundrel like him, it might be suffered to pass unnoticed without any detrim[en]t to my own character or that of the country." Mirabeau B. Lamar to James Webb, Galveston, Feb. 23, 1842, in *Lamar Papers*, IV, pt. I, pp. 1–2. See Anson Jones to Mirabeau B. Lamar, Galveston, Feb. 27, 1842; P. Edmunds to M. B. Lamar, Galveston, Nov. 15, 1843; both in *ibid.*, IV, pt. 1, pp. 2, 28.

[16] Burnet's reply to the charges made against him was written on January 17, 1842, but an earlier publication was delayed by factors beyond his control. Congress adjourned in the meanwhile and publication did not take place until the eve of the convening of the Sixth Congress in special session in June, in order "that a 'report' of a select committee of the Hon. House of Representatives, charging me," he said, "with a violation of '*every obligation* which is held sacred by man,' should not remain on file among the archives of the Republic, without an effort to expose the error of its positions, and the fallacy of its arguments." David G. Burnet to the Hon. I. Van Zandt, G. T. Wood, John Brown, and W. N. Porter, Select Committee on Resolutions relative to the Santa Fé Expedition, Oakland, 17th January 1842, in Smither (ed.), *Journals of the Sixth Congress of the Republic of Texas*, II, 176–182; David G. Burnet to the Editor of the Telegraph, Oakland, June 25, 1842, in *ibid.*, II, 176 n; [David G. Burnet], *Reply to the Report of Committee on the Santa Fé Expedition*.

[17] "Report of Select Committee on Resolutions relative to the Santa Fé Expedition," in Smither (ed.), *Journals of the Sixth Congress of the Republic of Texas*, II, 99–109.

"acted without the authority of law or the sanction of reason"; that the reasons assigned by the President were

. . . strange, unnatural and unsatisfactory, and that the course pursued by his Excellency meets the disapprobation of Congress . . . that whatever amount of public funds may have been appropriated to the fitting out of the expedition cannot be regarded in any other light than in direct violation of the 25th section of the first article of the Constitution, which declares that no money shall be drawn from the Treasury but in strict accordance with appropriations made by law;

therefore, if the House agreed with the committee, the report declared, "it will be the duty of the House to vindicate the outraged laws and Constitution by applying the only proper remedy—impeachment," even though it might be contended with some degree of plausibility that the term of office of the several officers had nearly expired. The near expiration of the term of office, it was declared, should not check the House in the discharge of its duties. "The trial of the articles of impeachment, if once prepared," declared the committee, "can be conducted as well after the expiration of their terms of office as before," for the penalty was not only removal from office but also disqualification from holding any office of honor, trust, or profit under the government in the future.

In the discussion that followed Porter explained that "the committee had not made a positive recommendation to impeach, because the report would have gone abroad over the country, that a *packed* committee had reported in favor of the impeachment of the President and all who had acted under him"; and that the committee had to bring the matter fairly before the House; have it fully investigated; and give the accused, "through their friends upon the floor, an opportunity to make their defence."[18] The discussion then being brought to a close, the resolutions for impeachment were made the special order of Thursday next,[19] after which the House commenced consideration of the Joint Resolution for the recall of the navy.

In making its report on the naval alliance with Yucatán, the committee severely arraigned Lamar for not carrying out the provisions

[18] Smither (ed.), *Journals of the Sixth Congress of the Republic of Texas,* II, 110.
[19] December 9; however, the reconstructed Journal of the House makes no further reference to this particular matter until Friday, December 17, four days after the inauguration of Houston, when the articles of impeachment were voted down without discussion.

of the law of January 18, 1841, directing the Texas navy "to be laid up in ordinary," and declared:

That the enterprise has been undertaken contrary to law; that it is in violation of the agreement entered into with Great Britain; that it is calculated to involve us in difficulties and perplexities with neutral powers, and promises to subject us to greater responsibilities and losses than we are able to sustain; that the manner in which the undertaking has been commenced and carried out, is calculated to add nothing to national honor; that it promises no efficient results; and in a word that it is contrary to good policy.[20]

Then, too, there was the danger of becoming involved with neutral powers for the illegal acts that might be committed by the vessels of Yucatán. In the arrangements made with Yucatán, the committee saw other objections,

. . . such as the injury . . . to national credit; the undignified attitude in which we are placed in subsidizing for hire one of the arms of national power, and becoming as it were the mercenary alley of Yucatán; the great danger of the entire loss of the vessels, they having been represented by the commandant as unsuited to the purposes of war; the utter insufficiency of the enterprize of effecting any object of importance commensurate with the risk which is run, and the probabilities of incurring further expense and greater than we can bear.[21]

The committee concluded by recommending the immediate recall of the navy.

During the ensuing days, the resolution to recall the navy, with its preamble censuring the President,[22] was discussed. Lamar, however, had his defenders on the committee. A minority report,[23] signed by

[20] Report [of Majority] of Select Naval Committee to the Hon. the Speaker of the House of Representatives, Committee Room, Nov. 19, 1841, in Smither (ed.), *Journals of the Sixth Congress of the Republic of Texas*, II, 46–49; *The Weekly Texian* (Austin), Dec. 1, 1841; Texas Congress, *Report [of the Majority] of Select Naval Committee, November 19, 1841.* The committee members signing the report were: N. H. Darnell, chairman; Isaac Van Zandt; R. M. Williamson; W. M. Hewett; Tod Robinson; and Archibald Wynns.

[21] *Ibid.*

[22] Smither (ed.), *Journals of the Sixth Congress of the Republic of Texas*, II, 128.

[23] Louis P. Cooke and J. S. Mayfield to the Hon. the Speaker of the House of Representatives, Committee Room, November 22, 1841, in *ibid.*, II, 55–59; *Report of the Minority of the Select Naval Committee, November 22, 1841.*

Louis P. Cooke and James S. Mayfield and presented in the House on November 22, pointed to the *de facto* government of Yucatán and emphasized that, according to their belief, "a formal declaration of independence" was not a necessary attribute of sovereignty. The "treaty," they declared, had been made with "an accredited agent" of the *de facto* government of the State of Yucatán. They could not see how the British efforts at mediation between Texas and Mexico might be jeopardized, "when that mediation [through Richard Pakenham, her Britannic Majesty's Minister at Mexico] has been attempted, in accordance with the spirit of the understanding between this government and Great Britain, and the State Department contains the official information of its having utterly failed." This, however, was denied by Van Zandt, who asserted that the mediation "had not yet been attempted," and he read letters from Pakenham to sustain his position.[24] The Lamar supporters disagreed with the majority report, contending that the contingencies contemplated under the law of the preceding January, fixing the naval establishment, had arisen. Declared the minority report,

Our territory has been invaded by armed Central Mexican forces; our western border has been the scene of continued strife, apprehension and hostility; our western villages have been attacked and destroyed; our civil officers have been driven from their jurisdiction, and with their suffering fellow citizens, either murdered or carried away into the vilest captivity; . . . the Executive is assured that [the] Central Mexican Government is preparing, in the most serious manner, for a maritime war with Texas; [and] that they are building vessels for that purpose, and in anticipation of these designs, have already declared our coast in a state of blockade. . . . Under these circumstances, the only guide of the President was his best discretion; and whether that discretion has been wisely used or not, the undersigned are not called on by the preamble and joint resolution to consider.[25]

The minority report concluded by recommending that the Preamble and Joint Resolution for the recall of the navy, together with the report of the Naval Affairs Committee on the same subject, be returned to the House, "with the opinion that the popular branch of Congress ought not to legislate upon the subject in its present condition."

[24] Smither (ed.), *Journals of the Sixth Congress of the Republic of Texas*, II, 128–131.
[25] *Ibid.*, II, 55–59.

In defense of the President's conduct in agreeing to use the navy to aid Yucatán, Jones of Gonzales declared: "The course that Mexico was pursuing was one detrimental to Texas, but not at all so to herself. It injured her in no wise. The nominal existence of the war [with Texas] served her rulers as a pretext for extorting money from the people, and for maintaining a standing army." [26] Jones believed that the Mexicans would not attack Texas again, for "they knew too well the result of such a struggle." Under existing conditions, he declared, some benefit might be obtained from the navy on which large sums had been spent for outfitting and getting officers and men. The navy could raid Mexican commerce, wreak destruction upon her ports, cut off the principal source of Mexico's revenue by blockading her ports and engaging in an extensive contraband trade from the islands scattered along her coast, and thus "by extortion procure the recognition" of Texan independence; or, if Yucatán were successful, and "the party she belonged to should regain power in Mexico, she would recognize our independence," he declared. "She would be bound by every principle of honor to do so; but if we should refuse to cooperate, we could expect nothing from them." Those supporting the resolution to recall the navy, however, seemed horrified that the Lamar men should consider Yucatán the friend and ally of Texas. "God save me from such friends or allies!" exclaimed Darnell. "Others may consider them as such, but with such, I beg leave to differ in opinion; and Mr. Speaker, when I recur back to the fields of San Jacinto, I am informed that about two-thirds of the Mexicans whose bones lie bleaching on that field, were from the State of Yucatán. Is it not reasonable then, sir, to conclude, without any good cause for a change, that they are now our enemies?" he asked.[27]

Mayfield of Nacogdoches, vehement in his defense of Lamar, leaned so far toward a liberal construction of the Constitution and laws, that Darnell rose to show how quickly the gentleman could change his views to fit partisan spirit, saying,

It will be recollected sir that at the beginning of this session of Congress, and while the vote for President and Vice President was being counted, that gentlemen objected to the counting of the vote of San Augustine, Montgomery and other counties, upon the ground, not that there was any thing illegal, or even irregular in the mode of conducting the election, that

[26] *Ibid.*, II, 121–122.
[27] *Ibid.*, II, 152–153.

there were illegal votes polled, or any other substantial objection, but solely because the votes had been returned to the State Department instead of to the Speaker of the House of Representatives, as directed by the Constitution.

It was not pretended that any thing was radically wrong in the votes thus returned. Yet no latitude of construction would then be allowed. The Constitution must be pursued to the very letter. This construction prevailing, reduced the majority of Gen. Houston about one fourth. I will not impeach his motives, because I have no right to do so. But how stands the case now sir? The tables are turned; the conduct of Gen. Lamar is under consideration, therefore a different rule of construction must prevail—the utmost latitude of construction must be allowed, for it is only by implication and remote influence [inference?], that the power now claimed for the Executive, can be derived from the Constitution and laws. Consistency, thou art a jewel.[28]

Robert M. Williamson of Washington County forcefully presented the constitutional issue.

Violence has been done to the only king in the country—the law. [he declared] Gentlemen have contended that it was policy to send out the navy—yes, it was policy that the Executive should put the laws and constitution under foot. I have been taught when I was a boy that honesty is policy. Sir, this is a policy that will break the social compact; policy, sir; yes, sir, policy. . . . Have not laws been made, and yet gentlemen contended that *policy* should govern. Sir, policy is the course of the ex-Executive. [Williamson spoke two days after the inauguration of Houston.] Give the privilege of the same course to the Executive just appointed. Sir, we had better adjourn *sine die* at once, than sustain such a course. I would sooner adjourn to the infernal regions than to do it. The country has been trampled under foot by the Executive.[29]

On the other hand, Wood of Liberty County doubted the power of Congress to lay up the navy while the country was still at war. The west, he declared, was "subject to constant depredations, and yet Gentlemen said there was peace. . . . If is [it] was a peace, it was a kind that brought much pain and difficulty upon the people. . . .

[28] *Ibid.*, II, 148–149. As to the Montgomery County votes, Darnell seems to be in error. "From the counties of Montgomery, Galveston, Brazoria, and Jackson there were no returns at all. From the counties of San Augustine, Washington, Bowie, Burnet, Lamar, Bastrop and Gonzales, the returns were informal, having been made to the Secretary of State instead of the Speaker of the House, as required by the constitution." *Ibid.*, I, 69 n.
[29] *Ibid.*, II, 155.

Gentlemen contend," he said, "that we had no right to notice a paper blockade—no right to oppose it." When then, he asked, should one prepare to prevent an actual blockade? [30] Louis P. Cooke of Travis County, Chairman of the Naval Affairs Committee, wanted "to know how much longer the wretched people of the West were to endure the sacking of their towns, the plunder of their property and the carrying off of their citizens; how much longer was it to be subject to devastation and gentlemen to contend that we were not invaded?" [31] Cooke then went on to paint a vivid picture of the suffering and misery of the people of the west, and was highly critical of the policy which permitted this state of things. He thought the effort to censure the President and recall the navy an eastern measure, and in subsequent debate was severely taken to task by Chairman Darnell for this bold assertion. Cooke declared that the country had already been invaded, that Mexico had declared and published a blockade of the Texas coast; and that "other nations would suppose the actual existence and enforcement of the blockade," unless the administration had otherwise demonstrated. He contended that under these circumstances "the ordering out of the Navy was necessary and proper."

Witnessing the belligerent attitude of the western leaders, Van Zandt rose to ask, "What was the true state of things?" "There was," he declared, "news upon news, brought here last winter to induce Congress to invade Mexico; . . . some of it was created not far from here. But this House," he said, "had stamped its disapprobation upon it. But the President had attempted to carry out the principle which the House had refused to sanction, and involve the nation in a war." [32] He ridiculed the suggestion that had been made by Lamar's defenders that the navy had been sent out to defend Texas against the vessels which were yet upon the stocks in New York, building for the Mexican government. He declared that the argument was "a petty sub[t]erfuge [and] . . . that the excuses for sending off the navy were false and palpable." Van Zandt concluded by drawing "a picture of a wretched female, ragged and almost naked, with her children around her, wringing her hand in bitterness, on account of the money which had been drawn from her for taxes, and paid out to send the navy to Yucatán." He represented the "female as calling upon the Government, in varied and pathetic terms, to know what had become of their money; whether

30 *Ibid.*, II, 126–127.
31 *Ibid.*, II, 123–125.
32 *Ibid.*, II, 129.

they had paid off the national debt, or what they had done with it." [33]
Van Zandt was followed in debate by John W. Dancy of Fayette
County, who probably made one of the ablest defenses of the Lamar
policy.

I stand on this floor, not as an apologist to the President, nor as his
accuser, but to advocate that course which is best calculated to advance the
prosperity of our infant Republic.

I would ask those who are loudest in their denunciations, if our territory
has not been invaded by armed enemies? Have they not kidnapped and
carried into captivity a citizen of our Republic? Have they not sacked
Refugio, and robbed and murdered the inhabitants of that unprotected
country? Still we hear from the opposite side of this House the cry of peace!
peace! when there is no peace. Heaven defend us from such peace! Do they
wish us to fold our arms and remain in a state of inactivity until the enemy
shall plant their daggers in our hearts, and die ingloriously, without lifting
an arm in our own defence?

I regard the policy of keeping our navy in ordinary as the worst which
we could pursue with respect to it. . . .

Let us take a view of the relative positions of Texas and Mexico, when
the President issued the order for our navy to cooperate with that of Yucatán
against our common enemy. We had made every proposition which a just,
honorable and magnanimous nation should do, and had been treated with
contempt. When our Commissioner applied, during the last summer, to the
Mexican Government, through her Britannic Majesty's Minister, to make
a treaty of peace, and offered to assume the payment of one million of
pounds of sterling of the foreign debt of Mexico, what answer did he
receive? He was told that they would not consent to a dismemberment of
the territory of the Mexican Republic, and that they would never "bind
themselves to an act equivalent to the sanction and recognition of slavery."
All hope of succeeding by a pacific policy had vanished; news had reached
this country that Mexico was endeavoring to procure a navy which could
drive that of Texas from the Gulf, and that they designed blockading our
ports. Yucatán had thrown off the Government of central Mexico, and
driven every hostile foot from her soil. Mexico was preparing an expedition
against Yucatán to reduce her to subjection. Peraza, as Commissioner from
Yucatán, applied to Texas for assistance in order to prevent the contemplated
invasion. He offered the means necessary to prepare the navy for active
operations against Mexico as a common enemy. The proposition was
accepted, not merely to assist Yucatán, but to protect our commerce and
maintain that ascendancy upon the Gulf of Mexico which is essential to

[33] *Ibid.*, II, 131.

our prosperity. . . . But we are told that we have no right to act in concert with Yucatán, because she is an integral part of Federal Mexico, and must be our enemy. And we are asked in triumph what is Mexico? and what is Yucatán? A set of faithless murderers the northern Mexicans have proved themselves to be, say gentlemen on the opposite side of the question, those of Yucatán are no better. Those gentlemen have as much confidence in Mexicans in general as I have. I will tell them, however, that there is a difference between the northern Mexicans and those of Yucatán. . . . [The latter] have more intelligence and are more worthy of confidence than the northern Mexicans on the Río Grande. Admit that they are the faithless wretches that they are described to be, their interest still makes them our friends. Admit that they are our enemies, and according to the laws of nations, we have a right to use them as a means to weaken a more powerful enemy; to keep up the Kilkenny catfight until they shall destroy each other. Like an young Hercules, we have a right to clip off the heads of the Hydra one by [one], and sear them with a hot iron, until it shall have no power to do us harm. . . .

It has been said that there are war men in this House. I am as much opposed to war when it can be honorably avoided as any member of this House; but, Sir, when negotiation has become useless, when our overtures for peace have been spurned, and insult has been added to injury; when I see the loveliest portion of my country languishing and desolate on account of the hostile attitude of our vain, proud and imbecile enemy, my voice is then for War! Not for an invasion by land, because we would only accommodate Mexico by destroying a population which will ever be troublesome to that distracted country whenever an artful demagogue shall excite them to rebellion. Let us attack her at her most vulnerable point;—attack by sea, destroy her commerce and we destroy her revenue. . . . Deprive her of her revenue and she dies for want of sustenance. With a coast depending upon foreign nations for support, war will then be presented to her in its most horrid form, and she will be forced into a recognition of our independence. . . .

Let us use the means which we have under our control to annoy our perfidious and vindictive adversary. Let us make her feel some of the evils which have heretofore afflicted us; let us keep our navy on the Mexican coast, and lay every town, village and hamlet under contribution, until our independence is recognized by the Mexican Government. The more violent the storm, the shorter will be its duration.[34]

While the debate on the Preamble and Joint Resolution for the recall of the navy extended over a period of several days, it boiled down to a fight between the Lamar and Houston supporters, with the east and

[34] *Ibid.*, II, 131–135.

"Old Sam's men" being accused of sponsoring the censure of Lamar, the idol of the west. For all practical purposes the main objective in the Joint Resolution for the recall of the navy and in the efforts to impeach Lamar and others was accomplished on December 13 by the inauguration of Houston as President. Lamar, by the completion of his term of office, was no longer President; and the new President was in a position to recall the navy by executive order. Consequently, on December 15 the Preamble and Joint Resolution were rejected by the House by a vote of 18 to 20. Two days later (December 17) the House voted down the impeachment charges against Lamar, Burnet, and Chalmers, by a vote of 13 to 25. In only one instance (George T. Wood of Liberty County) did a negative vote for the recall of the navy become a vote in favor of impeachment; whereas, six individuals who favored recall of the navy cast their ballot against impeachment.[35] All

[35] The vote was as follows on these two important issues:

County	Recall of Navy		Impeachment	
	Yea	Nay	Yea	Nay
Austin	1			1
Bastrop		1		1
Béxar		2		2
Bowie	1			1
Brazoria	1	1		2
Colorado	1		1	
Fannin		1		1
Fayette		1		1
Fort Bend	1		1	
Galveston		1		1
Goliad		1		1
Gonzales		1		1
Harris	1			
Harrison & Panola	1		1	
Houston	1		1	
Jackson		1		1
Jasper	1		1	
Jefferson		1		1
Lamar		1		1
Liberty		1	1	
Matagorda	1		1	
Montgomery		1		1
Nacogdoches	1	1	1	1
Navasota	1		1	
Red River		1		1
Refugio		1		1
Robertson		1		1
Sabine		1		1
San Augustine	2		2	
Shelby	2		2	

517

of the northern frontier counties, western frontier counties, southwestern frontier counties with the exception of Victoria, and coastal counties with the exception of Matagorda and Brazoria (divided) voted against impeachment and the recall of the navy. Taking into consideration Liberty County, already mentioned, the only interior counties supporting Lamar were Montgomery and Nacogdoches (divided). Montgomery County supported a firm policy against Mexico, and its militiamen comprised later an important segment of the Somervell Expedition to the Río Grande in 1842.

While the debate on the recall of the navy was in progress, news of the capture of the Santa Fé Expedition was published at Houston on December 8 by the *Telegraph and Texas Register,* quoting from the *New Orleans Bulletin* under date line of Villa de Passo, September 28; and on the eve of the second inauguration of "Old Sam" the information reached Austin from San Antonio.[36] Three days later, at Austin, the *Weekly Texian* was able to declare that the sad fate of the expedition was "almost indisputably confirmed." Further confirmation of the failure of Lamar's ambitious project was received at Houston on January 19 from the *Missouri Republican.*[37] News of the failure of the expedition, wrote the new Secretary of State from Austin,

. . . has thrown a perceptible gloom over our city for several days past. . . . I now occupy the room a short time since used by H. McLeod, the Commander of that ill-starred and *foolish* enterprise. It is now the office of Secretary of State. In this room the expedition was principally planned. Here was the headquarters of the late administration. Now ask for all that crowd, of fools and knaves and flatterers of power who basked in the smiles of

County	Recall of Navy		Impeachment	
	Yea	Nay	Yea	Nay
Travis		1		1
Victoria	1		1	
Washington	1			1
	—	—	—	—
	18	20	13	25

Ibid., II, 160, 175–176.

[36] Anson Jones to Mrs. Mary Jones (wife), Austin, Dec. 13, 1841, in Anson Jones Papers, ms.

[37] As quoted in the *Telegraph and Texas Register,* Dec. 8, 1841; Jan. 5 and 19, 1842; *Weekly Texian,* Dec. 15, 1841; José María Elias González, Comandancia principal del distrito del Paso á Escmo. Sr. Comandante general del departamento de Chihuahua, Villa del Paso, Septiembre 28, 1841 (conveys news of Salazar's defeat of Texan Santa Fé Expedition), *El Cosmopolita* (Mexico City), Oct. 16, 1841.

518

executive influence, and where are they. Gone and scattered for ever. Some are dead, others doomed to hopeless misery and to spend the remainder perhaps of a cheerless existence, in the mines of Mexico, the rest powerless, weak—accursed and despised and wishing themselves with the others,
"and like the baseless fabric of a vision,"
have "Left not a wreck behind!" or rather
nothing but a wreck.[38]

Had the expedition been successful it might have encouraged Mexico to seek negotiations with Texas, but the ignominy of surrender on the soil of the enemy not only showed the Lamar policy at its worst but was to set in motion a series of developments that were to have far-reaching consequences for Texas, and "from the point of view of territorial activities in Texas," wrote Professor Binkley, "the four years from the failure of the Santa Fé expedition to annexation to the United States may be characterized as a prolonged effort to overcome the effects of that failure."[39] As it was, the failure of the expedition not only affected adversely immigration and financial aid to Texas from Europe and elsewhere[40] and impeded the carrying out of the colonization contracts, but it also lessened the prowess of the Texans in the minds of the Mexicans and stimulated a demand among the former for an invasion of Mexico to force a release of the prisoners. The British diplomatic agent in Texas informed his government that the principal result of the expedition was "something little short of the breaking up of the whole Western Country of Texas."[41] The Santa Fé Expedition, therefore, served to keep alive the bitter animosities between the two countries—Texas and Mexico—which had been growing for more than a decade.

From Kenyon College in Ohio, Guy M. Bryan, nephew of Stephen F. Austin, advocated force to release the Texans held in Mexican dungeons. "Texas to the rescue!" he exclaimed.

Your brave countrymen fought for you, now *you*, if necessary, die [for them] . . . Are there no Deaf Smith's or Karnes's left to lead the daring and the brave into the enemies country to seize the wealthy and influential . . .

[38] Anson Jones to Mrs. Mary Jones, Austin, Jan. 3, 1842, in Anson Jones Papers, ms.
[39] Binkley, *The Expansionist Movement in Texas*, p. 96.
[40] Ashbel Smith to Anson Jones, Legation of Texas, France, March 31, 1843, in Garrison (ed.), *Diplomatic Correspondence of Texas*, 1908, III, 1429.
[41] Charles Elliot to Lord Aberdeen, Nov. 2, 1842, in Adams (ed.), *British Diplomatic Correspondence Concerning the Republic of Texas*, 1836–1846, p. 122.

and hold them as hostages for the safety and well treatment of our captured countrymen. . . . Let the press send forth its thunders, and Lamar and Burnet ply their pens and unfurl to the breeze the broad folds of the tricolored [flag] whose star shall cast its rays of hope into the inmost recesses of the mind and the darkest corner of the dungeon.[42]

Over at Natchez, an individual (presumably General Felix Huston) addressed a letter to the editor of the *New Orleans Bulletin* on December 20 calling upon "Gen. [Leslie] Combs of Kentucky, whose son was in the expedition, and the friends of [George W.] Kendall, of the *Picayune*, to rally around the standard of freedom and come to the rescue." [43] And in Texas, "A Citizen," describing himself as "A Voice from the West," appealed to his "Fellow Citizens" for vengeance against the Mexicans for the capture of the Santa Fé Expedition. "The Piteous cries, and dying groans of our imprisoned and slaughtered countrymen, come to our ears in every breeze that sweeps over the Western prairies," he declared.[44] A memorial from a public meeting at Nacogdoches urged that the navy and privateers "scour the Gulf and attack, burn, and destroy every town upon the coast of Mexico," and "that a land force be organized to carry on the same species of warfare along the Río Grande. Vengeance should be meted out with a liberal hand." [45] As the weeks passed, the chorus for revenge mounted. But, according to President Houston and a number of his able supporters, any attempt to invade Mexico would likely prove not only inexpedient and "ineffectual but destructive to the prisoners"; and, hence, he sought to discourage the idea,[46] and in his second administration reversed Lamar's policy by seeking to promote peace along the Indo-Mexican frontier. In his inaugural message Houston recommended

---

[42] Guy M. Bryan to James F. Perry, Gambier, Ohio, Jan. 8, 1842, in James F. Perry Papers, 1842–1843, transcripts. James F. Perry was Bryan's stepfather.

[43] Quoted in "A Voice from the West!!!" [Jan. 1842], broadside (incomplete).

[44] *Ibid.*

[45] Memorial of the Citizens of Nacogdoches County, Memorials and Petitions (Texas), ms.; see "Santa Fé Expedition" in *Austin City Gazette*, Feb. 2, 1842; Smither (ed.), *Journals of the Sixth Congress of the Republic of Texas,* I, 259 n.

[46] Houston to George William Brown and Others, Galveston, March 3, 1842, in *Writings of Sam Houston,* IV, 73–74; *Telegraph and Texas Register,* March 16, 1842; *ibid.*, Oct. 6, Dec. 1 and 8, 1841; *Weekly Texian* (Austin), Dec. 15, 1841, quoted in *ibid.*, Jan. 5, 1842; W. D. Miller to Sam Houston, Austin, Feb. 23, 1842 (Private), no. 3, and Same to Same, Austin, Wednesday night, Feb. 23, 1842 (Private), no. 4, in W. D. Miller Papers, 1833–1860, ms., copy.

that the frontier be protected by a string of military stations of twenty-five men each, and that trading houses for the double purpose of conciliating the Indians and protecting the frontier from depredations of the heathen barbarians should be established.[47]

For two years, various persons had talked of invading Mexico for conquest, but more thoughtful persons considered the idea impractical, since Texas lacked the necessary resources. It was estimated that at least five thousand troops would be required to insure the success of an invasion.[48] Such persons as Judge Anderson Hutchinson of the Fourth Judicial District, wondered if James Hamilton should succeed in getting a five million dollar loan from France if the country would "squander it in redemption of the promissory notes, or what would be more mad apply it in creating up invading battalions for Felix Huston." [49]

Many thought, however, "We should not wait for a demonstration from the enemy; we must carry the war into Carthage. Let the tocsin be sounded. . . . Five thousand volunteers raised on this plan would be . . . sufficient with the cooperation of the Navy, to conquer the country to Monterey." [50]

Quite a number of men in the west believed that the Santa Fé prisoners were in a hopeless, merciless captivity and that their inevitable fate was death. Throughout her history, Mexico, it was argued, had in no single instance shown respect to the laws of civilization and humanity that was not dictated by unworthy considerations, or produced by circumstances which they could not control. Texans, then, had no choice. Vengeance was all that was left to them, it was argued. Texas was fast reaching the point where she could no longer afford to refrain from hostilities, for the peace that existed was, in fact, no peace. It handicapped the growth of the nation's population, and the development of its resources. It was, therefore, of paramount importance that a war to force recognition and peace from Mexico be brought about at the earliest practicable time. But when the advocates of a war against Mexico were asked how would Texas finance such an

[47] No copy of Houston's inaugural message has been found. The substance of his address is found in the *Telegraph and Texas Register*, Dec. 22, 1841.
[48] Edmund J. Felder to W. D. Miller, March 1, 1842, in W. D. Miller Papers, 1833–1860, ms., copy.
[49] A. Hutchinson to W. D. Miller, Austin, July 28, 1841, in *ibid*.
[50] Quoted in *Houston: A History and Guide*, p. 55.

undertaking, they often answered, "If *we* have not the means, *Mexico* has," and as for an army,

. . . what we cannot furnish will *furnish themselves* from the United States. It is known to all that there is at this time a state of things in that country that would enable us at any time upon very short notice to enlist in such a cause any number of men that we ask, or that the occasion might require—men, too, who would neither ask nor receive from our hands expenses—men who merely ask the permission of our government to march through its territory.[51]

Infrequently it was said, "Never before in this lower world has there been offered to mortal man an opportunity to acquire a fame so enduring, so brilliant, so dazzling, as that which is now within the grasp of General Sam Houston."

In 1841–1842 the citizens of Gonzales held several meetings in regard to Mexican relations. "We have had a great many patriotic meetings here [Gonzales] and played the d——l," quoted Washington D. Miller from one of his Gonzales correspondents.

The people all pretend to believe the Mexicans are coming and every one is trying to see who can make the most noise. At a meeting held here last Saturday [February 19], for the purpose of organizing the county, the people did everything but start to Mexico. I wish you had been here to hear the speakers. Each slew his Richmond and withdrew his blade for what is called the "big meeting" which is to take place on the first Saturday in March. The people by that time are to be organized by companies, and all meet here to elect their officers;—then Wo be to the Mexicans!![52]

The "big meeting" at Gonzales was set for March 5, and William E. Jones, known as "fiery Jones of Gonzales," a member of the House of Representatives, gave notice that at that meeting he would present a preamble and resolutions "*censuring the President and the presses at Austin for refusing their cooperation with the people in an offensive war with Mexico.*"[53] The tide of public opinion in the west was rolling with tremendous force against Mexico.

[51] As quoted in W. D. Miller to Sam Houston, Austin, Feb. 23, 1842 (Private), no. 3, in W. D. Miller Papers, 1833–1860, ms., copy.
[52] W. D. Miller to Sam Houston, Wednesday night, Austin, Feb. 23, 1842 (Private), no. 4, in *ibid.*
[53] *Ibid.*

It is for war they make demands;
Their shouting cry will never cease,
Till armies and invading bands
Shall wring from Mexico, a peace.[54]

By the end of 1841, France, England, Holland, and Belgium had recognized the independence of Texas. Treaties of commerce and navigation had been signed with several European countries, and the western trade with northern Mexico had taken a change for the better. At the turn of the year, large numbers of traders from the Río Grande were arriving almost daily at the western towns, where it was soon reported they purchased nearly all the dry goods in that section of the country, causing more than one merchant at Béxar, Victoria, and the region of Corpus Christi Bay to go to New Orleans to procure new supplies.[55] With the arrival of the news concerning the fate of the Santa Fé Expedition, the Mexican traders became more wary about coming in for fear of retaliation. The unwholesome fate of a party of Mexican traders who had recently been to Béxar served as a warning to others. The traders, it seems, had purchased approximately $10,000 worth of goods and upon their return toward Laredo had been robbed, and a few of their number murdered, by an unknown party about forty miles from San Antonio.[56] It was supposed that the robbery had been committed by citizens from Béxar and the ranches below.

During the next several months, the Mexican marauders on the frontier became more troublesome, killing one or two Texans at Aransas Bay. Sometime early in February a Texan spy company on the frontier intercepted and routed a large number of Mexican marauders, killing several and taking a large quantity of plunder.[57] General Vasquez's expedition to Texas, then being planned in Mexico, no doubt also had much to do in February and March 1842 with interrupting the friendly relations being developed with the Río Grande peoples.

Shortly after resuming the office of President, Houston sent James Reily, a former Texas Congressman whose wife was Henry Clay's niece, as chargé d'affaires to the United States to reopen, if possible, negotiations for annexation. In the meantime, the President's policy toward

54 *Daily Texian* (Austin), Feb. 2, 1842, contains a twenty verse poem on the cry for war with Mexico.
55 *Telegraph and Texas Register*, Jan. 12, 1842.
56 *Ibid.*, March 2, 1842.
57 *Ibid.*, Feb. 23, 1842.

Mexico became one of watchful waiting. On December 16, three days after entering office, he repudiated the Yucatán alliance and ordered Commodore E. W. Moore,[58] who had sailed from Galveston the very day that Lamar turned over the reins of government to Houston, to bring the navy home; and in May 1842, the vessels were ordered to New Orleans and Mobile to undergo repairs, preparatory to enforcing the blockade which had been proclaimed in March against Mexico and for the purpose of transporting troops in the forthcoming Texan invasion of Mexico. A week after his inauguration at Austin, "that scene of tumult and vexation," [59] Houston submitted on December 20 his first message to the Texas Congress. In it he outlined what he thought should be the attitude of Texas toward Mexico. Since his predecessor's overtures for an amicable adjustment of existing difficulties between Texas and Mexico had, as often as made, been rejected under circumstances which had not exempted the Texas government from humiliation,

the present Executive of Texas [he said] will neither incur the expense nor risk the degradation of further advances [until a disposition is evinced on the part of Mexico herself to solicit friendly relations.]

Aware of the Mexican character, and believing as I always have that Mexico is and will remain unable to invade us with any hope of success, I would recommend the kindest treatment of her citizens;—so far, at least, as they might be disposed to engage in commerce with ours. But in every instance where they shall enter our territory with inimical or hostile intentions they should be treated as common enemies. I believe that any interference with the revolutions and distractions of Mexico, is not only incompatible with the dignity and interests of Texas, but directly calculated to exasperate our national enemy, while it weakens our resources, by sacrificing those of our citizens who may engage in their partizan quarrels, to their proverbial perfidy and to certain destruction. This is demonstrated by the issue of every enterprise of the kind, in which our countrymen have been participants. The feuds and contests, which have arisen and may continue to arise, have for their object personal aggrandizement, the leaders

[58] Yucatán made peace and returned her allegiance to Mexico on December 28, 1841. George W. Hockley to Sam Houston, Dec. 22, 1841, in Army Papers (Texas), ms.; E. W. Moore, *To the People of Texas: An Appeal in Vindication of His Conduct of the Navy*, pp. 12–14, 21–31; *Lamar Papers*, IV, pt. 2, p. 32; Christian, "Mirabeau Buonaparte Lamar," *Southwestern Historical Quarterly*, XXIII (1919–1920), 156–162.

[59] W. G. Hide to Isaac Van Zandt, Franklin [Texas], Oct. 27, 1841, in Isaac Van Zandt Papers, 1839–1843, ms.

in which are better entitled to the appellation of bandits than of either patriots or statesmen. These individuals have no exalted principles of action, and should receive no encouragement from us. The Executive, therefore, should be fully empowered to arrest and prevent the predatory warfare occasionally carried on within our territories to the injury of our Western settlers.

It is my desire that this government should assume a station in relation to this subject, not inconsistent with national respectability and conducive to our best interests. Mexico has more to lose in a contest with Texas than Texas has with Mexico. Her civil commotions will exhaust her resources and diminish her means of aggression; while emigration to Texas will give us population and resources—and they will give us power to resist aggression.[60]

Houston's policy was in line with the recommendation made by England's minister to Mexico, Richard Pakenham, to James Webb, the Texan secret agent to Mexico in June 1841. Pakenham had written:

I have, on various occasions, taken the liberty to express to the gentlemen acting for the Government of Texas with whom I have had the honor to communicate, my conviction that it is entirely for the interest of Texas to forbear from any acts of hostility or aggression towards Mexico, so long as Mexico refrains from active hostilities against that country.

The Government of Texas, I have no doubt, possess sufficient information as to what passes in this country, to enable them to judge how far it is possible that Mexico will be able, and how soon, to undertake an expedition upon a scale to endanger the safety and independence of Texas. The longer such an expedition is postponed, the less likely it becomes that it should ultimately take place, unless Texas should, in the meantime by some act of aggression, offend the pride of the Mexicans, and lead them to put in action the means which they undoubtedly possess, if properly directed, of causing serious annoyance to Texas.[61]

In cabinet council, December 22, two days after the President's message to Congress, Dr. Anson Jones, the new Secretary of State, in substance, made similar recommendations.

Our policy as it regards Mexico should be to act strictly on the *defensive*. So soon as she finds we are willing to let her alone, *she will let us alone*.

[60] Houston to the Senate and House of Representatives, City of Austin, Dec. 20, 1841, in *Writings of Sam Houston*, II, 399–408.
[61] R. Packenham to James Webb, Her Britannic Majesty's Mission, Mexico, June 10, 1841, in "Report of the Secretary of State to Mirabeau B. Lamar, Department of State, Austin, October 12, 1841, reproduced in Smither (ed.), *Journals of the Sixth Congress of the Republic of Texas*, III, 246–247.

The navy should be put in ordinary; and no troops kept in commission, except a few Rangers on the frontiers. The Indians should be conciliated by every means in our power. It is much cheaper and more humane to purchase their friendship than to *fight* them. A small sum will be sufficient for the former; the latter would require millions. By a steady, uniform, firm, undeviating adherence to this policy for two or three years, Texas may and will recover from her present utter prostration. It is the stern law of necessity which requires it, and she must yield to it or perish! She cannot afford to raise another crop of "Heroes." [62]

Eight days later the President warned Congress that the War Department had received information, which, if true, left "no doubt that some movements against Texas" were in preparation by Mexico.[63] Word had just been received at the War and Navy Department by letters from the United States that two "brig schooners" of about 170 tons each were being built at New York for the Mexican government and that in England other war vessels were under construction for that same government. Considering "a demonstration as most probable," Houston suggested that Congress authorize the President to procure as many Paixhan cannon as necessary for "the protection of at least Galveston and Matagorda Bays," as no invasion by land would likely be attempted unless supported by a naval force.

A week later, the President called Congress' attention to the fact that the law regulating frontier protection failed to achieve its real objective. "It seems," he said, "to have been inefficient and is certainly enormously expensive." No reports were made to the War Department concerning the operations of the several companies acting under provisions of the law; consequently, little information could be obtained about the state of the frontier or the services the companies rendered the country. "In this way, too," said the President, "frauds are liable

---

[62] Quoted in "Biographical Sketch of Anson Jones Written in the Summer and Fall of 1880. Prepared with a view to publication in the 'Biographical Encyclopedia of the West,'" in Anson Jones Papers, ms.

[63] Message of the President [Executive Department, City of Austin, Dec. 30th, 1841] and Accompanying Document. [Austin: Printed at the *Austin City Gazette* Office, 1842], 4 p.; [Houston] to the House of Representatives, Executive Department, City of Austin, December 30th, 1841, accompanied by a report of the Secretary of War and Navy, George W. Hockley to Sam Houston, Department of War & Marine, Decr 22, 1841, in Smither (ed.), *Journals of the Sixth Congress of the Republic of Texas*, I, 173–175; II, 237–239. Houston's message without the document will be found in *Writings of Sam Houston*, II, 415–416.

to be practiced upon the Treasury." [64] He carefully pointed out that the arsenal at the seat of government in Austin was almost destitute of lead, possessing only seven hundred pounds on February 1, 1842. Six weeks later, on March 10, at the time of the Mexican invasion, there were at Houston only 2,128 pounds of lead and 1,550 of powder.[65] Congress responded by providing for a company of mounted men to "act as Rangers" on the southern frontier on such terms as the President might deem beneficial to the public interest.[66] As for the fortifying of Galveston and Matagorda Bays, the Senate Committee on Naval Affairs, headed by James W. Byrne from the Goliad, Refugio, and San Patricio District, reported on January 8 adversely on the proposal to fortify those two points along the coast. Mexico's efforts to create a naval force on the Gulf was viewed as "the vain boasting of the vainest and most imbecile nation on earth," and the committee did not believe that "the enemy would venture within our Bays or Harbours with any force—he could bring on the Coast." The committee admitted that Galveston and Matagorda Bays could be made defensible, but pointed out that a long line of coast, several harbors, and inlets would remain in a defenseless condition, open at all times to an invading force. In view of this situation, coupled with the entire prostration of the nation's credit and the need to economize in public expenditures, the committee recommended "that no action be taken on the subject of harbour defence for the present." [67]

Just as Congress was about to adjourn on February 5, Houston reminded it of "the exposed condition of the National Archives." Since the establishment of the government at Austin, he said,

. . . a constant military force has been at the disposition of the President. The large amount of money placed at the disposition of the former Executive gave him the means of rendering every necessary protection to this

[64] Houston to the House of Representatives, Executive Department, City of Austin, Jan. 6, 1842, in *Writings of Sam Houston,* II, 423.
[65] Same to George W. Hockley, Galveston, March 10, 1842, *ibid.,* IV, 76–77. See also Same to House of Representatives, Executive Department, City of Austin, Feb. 2, 1842; Same to Same, City of Austin, Feb. 2, 1842 (Veto Message), *ibid.,* II, 466–471.
[66] H. P. N. Gammel (ed.), *Laws of Texas,* II, 746. The law was approved by the President on January 29, 1842.
[67] Texas Congress, Committee Reports, Sixth Congress, No. 2582. Endorsed: Report of Naval Committee, January 8, 1842, ms.; printed in Smither (ed.), *Journals of the Sixth Congress of the Republic of Texas,* I, 215–217.

section of the country. No such means have been placed at my disposal and when Congress adjourns, I have every reason to believe that the available force remaining at Austin will not be such as to guarantee the undoubted safety of the archives, and other public property. The loss of the archives would be an irreparable injury to the Country. Therefore, to the representatives of the people, I submit the question as to measures proper to be adopted for the protection and security of an object so important to the whole nation. The enemy must be apprised of the true situation of affairs at Austin; and can it be reasonably supposed that they will not endeavor to take advantage of our condition? [68]

A bill to locate the seat of government at some other place from and after March 1, 1842, had been presented in the House of Representatives on January 17 by Robert M. Williamson and ten days later passed its first reading,[69] but received no further attention during that session of the Congress.

While the administration in Texas sought to promote peace and the economic development of the Republic, her declared enemy south of the border was planning a renewal of hostilities. Having for the first time in several years re-established a semblance of· order at home, Mexico late in 1841 began to turn her attention to the problem of Texas. Having persuaded the French to leave, subdued the Federalist uprising, and captured the Texan Santa Fé Expedition, the "war-dogs of Santa Anna," began to howl "furiously in Mexico, reporting themselves in full outfit, and determined to quell the rebellion in Texas and plant the Mexican flag on the Sabine." [70] "What stupid illusions [of invasion] occupy the brains of our Texans!" declared a correspondent of *El Sol* from Santa Ana de Tamaulipas under the date of March 13, 1842. "Wretched ones! The hour approaches for your extermination, and the immortal leader [Santa Anna] whose name fills you with terror, will not delay in clutching tightly his victorious sword to give the order of subjecting you to obedience. The fatherland will revenge itself! Ungrateful ones! Do not doubt it!" [71]

Motivated by the desire to retaliate for the Santa Fé Expedition and

[68] Sam Houston to the Senate and House of Representatives, Executive Department, City of Austin, Feb. 5, 1842, in *ibid.*, I, 357.

[69] *Ibid.*, II, 396, 424.

[70] Z[enos] N. Morrell, *Flowers and Fruits in the Wilderness: or Forty-Six Years in Texas and Two Winters in Honduras*, p. 157; *Diario del Gobierno* (Mexico City), Nov. 20, 1841, quoted in *Telegraph and Texas Register*, Dec. 22, 1841.

[71] Quoted in *El Cosmopolita* (Mexico City), March 26, 1842.

previous Texan attacks upon Laredo, to disrupt the economic development of the western frontier of Texas, and to strengthen the argument
of the anti-annexationists in the United States that to annex Texas
would be tantamount to annexing a war with a foreign power, Mexico
in 1842 resumed the offensive by launching three invasions of Texas.
In the fall of 1841, General Arista, the Centralist leader in the North,
issued a manifesto, calling upon the Federalists and Centralists to forget their differences in the interest of greater harmony at home, and
to give their attention to the real enemy. "In Texas," he declared,
"there is a field open to gather fresh and glorious laurels that . . . false
aspirations . . . calumny and envy cannot wither. In Texas you can
find a field in which to display your warlike ardor without the pain
and mortification of knowing that the blood you shed and the tears
you occasion are from your brethren." [72] From Monterey, Arista issued
an address on January 9, 1842, to the inhabitants of the "Department
of Texas," carefully pointing out the hopelessness of their struggle for
independence and promising amnesty and protection to all who refrained from taking up arms during his contemplated invasion. At the
same time he warned them that while his country held out "the olive
branch and concord" with one hand, she would direct with the other
"the sword of justice against the obstinate." [73] Thereupon, Mexico
began to strengthen her northern garrisons and to make preparations
for invading Texas,[74] but thoughtful persons in Texas believed Mexico

[72] *Telegraph and Texas Register,* Oct. 17, 1841.

[73] Mariano Arista, general de division y en gefe del cuerpo de ejército de Norte
de la republica mexicana, á los que habitan el departamento de Tejas, Cuartel
general en Monterey, Enero 9 de 1842, in *El Cosmopolita,* March 30, 1842
(English translation in *Telegraph and Texas Register,* March 9, 1842); Eugene C.
Barker (ed.), *Texas History for High Schools and Colleges,* p. 363.

[74] José A. Quintero, *José A. Quintero en Cuidad Victoria; un decreto del presidente sobre una contribución establecida durante la guerra con Téjas, Abril 7 de
1841,* in Matamoros Archives, XXXVIII, 192–195. On January 17, 1842, Santa
Anna ordered the establishment of companies of *auxiliares* and *rurales* for the
protection of the inhabitants from robbers and marauding bands. The governors
of the Departments and the public officials of the towns were directed to establish
companies of *caballeria* to be known as *auxiliares,* subject to the orders and
inspection of the governor of the respective departments. On the principal
haciendas armed guards, known as *rurales,* were to be organized under the
leadership of the proprietors of the haciendas. The governors were to supply both
groups with arms and munitions, and they were to designate at three months
intervals the size of the force and arms to be maintained by the towns and

would not be so foolish as to launch a campaign in the spring or summer by troops brought from the interior of Mexico, for such troops would be so susceptible to disease when brought down from the tablelands that they would be wholly unfit to endure a campaign during those seasons of the year.[75]

While preparations were in progress in Mexico for a campaign against Texas, news reached Galveston that the two vessels of war, reported building at New York for the Mexican navy, had been completed and were lying at the wharf in New York ready for sea. Each was described as having been fitted out with a forty-two–pound Paixhan gun amidship, six eighteen-pound carronades, and an American crew under Mexican officers.[76] At the same time it was reported that a steam frigate had been purchased for $40,000 in England for the "new" Mexican navy. Formerly the *City of Dublin* (under Captain Cobb), the steamer was a first rate one of 388 tons with two superior engines of sixty horsepower each. The vessel was schooner-rigged and mounted six eighteen-pound cannons and one long eighteen-inch pivot gun.[77]

A few days later it was reported that the two vessels fitted out in the United States had cleared the New York customhouse as merchantmen under bond of $170,000 to guarantee their nonemployment for belligerent purposes against Texas before being delivered to the authorities of Mexico in the ports of that country.[78] The two schooners set sail for Mexican waters late in January or early February. One was wrecked and lost in the Gulf and the other succeeded in reaching Vera Cruz, where Commodore Moore saw it the first week in February tied up under the guns of the fortress of San Juan de Úlloa. The new addition to the Mexican navy had been in the harbor since about the first of the month. About the same time, P. Edmunds, Texan consul at New

---

haciendas. M. Galindo en Matamoros, Un decreto del Presidente Sobre la formación de compañías para protección contra los malhecheros, Feb. 20, 1842, in *ibid.*, XL.
   [75] *Telegraph and Texas Register*, Feb. 23, 1842.
   [76] Samuel Swartwout to Sam Houston, New York, Dec. 26, 1841, in Domestic Correspondence (Texas), 1836–1846, ms.
   [77] *Telegraph and Texas Register*, March 2, 1842.
   [78] *Ibid.*, Jan. 26, 1842, quoting the *Morning Star*, Jan. 26, 1842; Jim Dan Hill, *The Texas Navy: in Forgotten Battles and Shirtsleeve Diplomacy*, pp. 152–153; *Telegraph and Texas Register*, Feb. 23, 1842. The February 23, 1842, issue of the *Telegraph* reported from New Orleans newspapers of as late as February 14, 1842.

Orleans, wrote that the Mexican government had purchased the steamship *Natchez* to blockade Galveston harbor.[79] A short time later, it was discovered that, besides a steamship being acquired in England, two heavily armed warships, the *Montezuma* and the *Guadaloupe*, were being built there for the Mexican navy.[80]

News of the fitting out of vessels in the United States for the Mexican navy first appeared in the press at Houston on January 25, 1842, and produced considerable excitement. It gave some of the fire-eaters an opportunity again to kick up the wind against Mexico. In response to a public notice, the citizens of Houston assembled in the courthouse at 4 P.M., January 28, where, upon motion of Charles J. Hedenberg, Dr. Francis Moore, Jr., editor of the *Telegraph and Texas Register*, was called to the chair and Peter W. Gray was named secretary.[81] In a brief, but eloquent speech, interrupted from time to time by rapturous applause, Moore explained the purposes for which the local citizens had been called together. Following Moore's address, Major James D. Cocke, a printer who had come to Texas in 1837,[82] moved the appointment of a committee of five to draft a preamble expressing the objects of the meeting together with such resolutions as they might deem expedient to carry out those objectives. Upon the adoption of Cocke's motion, Chairman Moore named to the committee of five James D. Cocke, chairman; B. P. Buckner, R. C. Campbell, John N. O. Smith, and Charles J. Hedenberg, after which the meeting adjourned until 7:30 P.M.

Following a brief intermission, the public meeting was resumed at the appointed time, and the preamble and resolutions which had been drafted by the committee were presented, discussed, and after some alteration in the resolutions were adopted unanimously. "The position toward Mexico, now occupied by the government and people of Texas, is peculiar and critical" declared the preamble.

---

[79] Sam Houston to Alexander Somervell, City of Houston, March 25, 1842, in *Writings of Sam Houston*, IV, 85–86.

[80] Details concerning the fitting out of these two vessels may be found in E. D. Adams, *British Interests and Activities in Texas, 1838–1846*, pp. 79–96; Garrison (ed.), *Diplomatic Correspondence of Texas*, 1908, III, 955–962, 1004–1008; H. Yoakum, *History of Texas from Its First Settlement in 1685 to Its Annexation to the United States in 1846*, I, 389.

[81] "Meeting of the Citizens of Houston," *Telegraph and Texas Register*, Feb. 2, 1842.

[82] *Handbook of Texas*, I, 368.

We now learn that . . . Santa Anna, after a singular series of military and political reverses, is again raised by the popular voice to the Presidency of Mexico, and that he is endeavoring to call forth all the energies of that country, for the purpose of prosecuting his hitherto unsuccessful war upon Texas. Authenticated as is this intelligence, by information of a character which almost challenges contradiction, it is strengthened by the conviction, that the vanquished of San Jacinto, a great and successful hero, however, in previous and succeeding battles, must from his known temperament, entertain the fertile ambition to blot out the memory of his degradation in Texas, by directing another campaign against this country. Internal dissensions in Mexico, we are told, are for the present quieted; Yucatan, even, having sent in its notice of submission to the government of Santa Anna. Since the capture of the Santa Fé Expedition, unadvisedly sent out from this country, the arch leaders of the enemy have been artfully busy in getting up a rallying point, at which all parties, it was supposed, would unite, lay down their domestic bickerings and feuds, *namely: the subjugation of Texas.*

In the approved resolutions, the citizens of Houston indicated their willingness to cooperate promptly "in any measures adopted by the Government in reference to our Mexican enemies, whether they shall be *offensive* or *defensive* in their character." It was recommended that the regimental and company officers of the Harris County militia "forthwith . . . appoint and hold early drills and parades, for the purposes of military instruction, and that the citizen-soldiers be requested to turn out with alacrity, to carry that purpose into effect." [83]

Under authorization of other resolutions, Chairman Moore appointed E. S. Perkins and J. F. Randel, as a committee of two, to take up voluntary subscriptions of money from citizens in the community to purchase a supply of ammunition; he also appointed a committee of vigilance of five persons whose duty it was to give "such early intelligence to the community as they may from time to time receive," relating to the present status of affairs with Mexico. To the latter committee Moore appointed S. S. Tomkins, R. C. Campbell, John Scott, Colonel A. S. Thurston, and Dr. William McCraven, and on motion from the floor Dr. Moore's own name was added to the list.[84]

A week later, in an open letter to the editor of the *Telegraph and Texas Register*,[85] James D. Cocke, captain of the Border Guards in 1840 who was referred to by the anti-Lamar press as the "fighting cock" because of his extreme partisanship,[86] set forth in clear, unmis-

[83] *Ibid.*   [84] *Ibid.*   [85] Feb. 9, 1842.
[86] *Handbook of Texas*, I, 368; *Texas Sentinel* (Austin), Aug. 15, 1840.

takable language "the views and temper," he said with considerable exaggeration, "of the most considerate of my fellow citizens at this juncture."

The position of Texas toward Mexico has been said to be "peculiar and critical." It is true, that it is "peculiar and critical," but not so much from the fact that Texas is in any immediate imminent danger of being overrun by Mexico, as that the latter power is on the eve of a great disaster and humiliation—which *must* ensue, if the councils and energies of the former are directed in wisdom.

As to the justification in the eyes of the world, of any expedition which Texas may set on foot against Mexico, *under the banner of Texas,* the several Powers which have recognized her Independence are, by virtue of their acts of recognition, precluded from raising an objection. And if I believed that the rest of the civilized world would need an excuse for acts of *hostility* on the part of the Texians, I would necessarily have to write anew, and in blood, the history of the perfidy and barbarity of the Mexicans; and, with a pen of diamond, of the clemency, magnanimity, and too patient endurance of my countrymen.

We are universally considered to have fairly won our Independence— nearly six years having elapsed since the glorious battle of San Jacinto which sealed it, and since the inglorious retreat of the enemy, *by gracious permission,* from our territory. But we hear that the haughty enemy—having, as he vainly supposes, outlived the shamefulness of defeat, and shaken off the trammels of domestic discord and revolution—is arming to the teeth, by land and water, for the purpose of again invading and desolating the country. What, then, must Texas do?—Does not every patriot answer: "To your tents, O Israel!" "To arms!" "War to the knife, and the knife to the hilt!"

But it becomes a serious question, among those who reflect, what is the best course to be adopted in the emergency which besets us: whether to undertake offensive operations ourselves, or to await the desperate onset of the enemy, and leave our country exposed to the ravages of his savage hordes? For my humble self, I would not be slow to choose. One needs no prophetic vision to see that Texas now has it in her power to [make] a complete conquest of Mexico, if she will offer the proper inducements to the daring and enterprising spirits of the Southern and Western States of America to join her standard as *citizen soldiers.* Let but the banner of the Lone Star be flung to the breeze, preparatory to an invasion of Mexico, and the noble hearted sons of Kentucky, Tennessee, Mississippi, Louisiana, Missouri, and other States of the Union, self-equipped and munitioned, will rush to join the standard in such numbers as to ensure its being planted upon the strongest battlements of Mexico. And all this can be done, *if the government wills,* without cost to the nation—and without taking so many of our own citizens from their families and business as to retard the regular growth of the country. There are ambitious young men, born in the United States, and Texas (and that sort of ambition has been wisely said to be a virtue) who will swell the ranks of an army for invasion—assured of subsistence and reward from the honorable spoils of war, without plundering the country of the enemy.

The only way in which we can ever expect to force upon Mexico our own terms—which must now be as rigorous as she has been contemptuous and insolent—is to invade her territory. By making *that country* the theatre of the contest, we secure *our own* from the ravages of war. . . .

But practically speaking—Texas can furnish a force of 8,000 men, who can concentrate at a given point, to march to the Río Grande, and capture and fortify the frontier towns of the enemy upon and near that river. She has a Navy consisting of one Steamer, one Corvette or Sloop, two Brigs, and two Schooners, making, in all, six vessels of war. This naval force, besides being employed afterward in blockading the Ports of Mexico, can transport the emigrant soldiers of Texas, from the United States, so as to invest, capture, and fortify Matamoros, Tampico, and Vera Cruz. And we may be assured that Missouri alone, with, perhaps, a little aid from the adjacent States, will send out a number of men sufficient to march upon and conquer that rebellious portion of Texas comprehending Santa Fé, and likewise the adjoining Northern Provinces of Mexico.

To accomplish these objects will require not more than $2,000,000, and 12,000 of our former countrymen and brothers. We are assured, upon high authority—from the action of the Legislature of Kentucky itself [condemning the capture and treatment of some of its citizens who were members of the ill-fated Texan Santa Fé Expedition]—that the spirit of that State is sensibly aroused in our behalf. We hear reiterated the glad tidings that 20,000 men from the Valley of the Mississippi alone, may be expected to emigrate to Texas, whenever the war cry shall be raised for the conquest of Mexico. And of course, when such a spirit prevails, the aid of money will not be wanting. . . .

Have we not shown, by our forbearance and endeavors to conciliate the enemy, that we love the arts and the repose of peace? But since the necessity is imposed upon us by the hardihood of our foes, let us teach them *again*, as at Conception, San Antonio and San Jacinto, that we can make a direful business of the havoc of war. . . .

I will not speculate upon the advantages to Texas of an offensive war against Mexico. My genius is not equal to the calculation. First, the peace and independence of Texas—in the next place, the multiplied population, the increased growth and resources of the country, together with the extension of Free Principles over a land enchanted, but lovely beyond description, and over a People now firmly bound in the chains of Superstition and Despotism—these form the high incentives to *action—action—action, on our part.*

It must be enforced upon Texians and upon those who would co-operate with them in a war with Mexico, that, when the enterprise is undertaken, *we must strike at her vitality—we must supplant all the vestiges of her changeful but always licentious and despotic government, with Anglo-Saxon Institutions.*

Cocke's ideas were typical of those found among Galvestonians and other Texans anxious to take direct, forceful action against Mexico; but, as is evident from subsequent action during 1842, these views did not represent the general opinion of the people of Texas. Even among those in favor of strong measures against Mexico, there were very different opinions as to procedures and objectives. Dr. Edmund J. Felder, who had acted as surgeon on Ross' Federalist campaign, was asked by the President's private secretary to comment on the public attitude at Houston toward the Republic's relations with Mexico and to express himself. His remarks, contained in his letter of March 1 to Washington D. Miller,[87] are extremely interesting in the light of subsequent events, and may have had some part in molding the thinking of both Miller and the President after the Vasquez raid.

The voice of this people [he wrote from the City of Houston] is for war, as you may find from the proceedings of a town meeting held not long since and published in the papers of the city—at which they unanimously passed upon Resolutions requesting President Houston to permit our Navy to remain at sea, for the purpose of hampering the enemy, and if need be punish them for injuries done to the prisoners of the Santa Fé expedition; and should they be injured this people in my opinion, will be for invasion almos[t] unanimously. This is my desire. I have been in favor of such measures all of two years, but for different objects than excites most persons who are favouring the project both here and in the United States.

With me conquest is out of the question, for already we have more territory than can be disposed of for less than a pep[p]er corn p[e]r acre. We have not money and means to defend effectually our present limited borders from the Indian & Robber. I am aware many calculate on much assistance from the people of the United States; but this is a very fallacy; there cannot be greater excitement gotten up in that country in favour of an invasion for the conquest of Mexico than was in favour of Texas during

[87] Edmund J. Felder to W. D. Miller, City of Houston, March 1, 1842, in W. D. Miller Papers, 1833–1860, ms.

the Revolution; and if you will examine the muster rolls of that period the fighting men were but few from the large proportion of them being on useless recruiting service in the U. S. But even supposing 20 or 30,000 men could be raised to join the expedition, with means to overrun the country, it could not be held any length of time. It would take that number to garrison sufficient military posts to keep the Mexicans in subjection—a task that will be found more difficult than many may imagine. . . . We can not keep the Comanches from forcing our frontier . . . and they fight mostly with bows and arrows. Mexicans are more advanced in the arts of warfare and when a foreign army shall have entered the heart of the nation, they will fight with a desperation not surpassed by Texians themselves. I know the Mexican reputed cowardice. I know they are cowards; but even a coward will fight desperately when driven to the wall. They will hover about your fortifications and camp with an eagle eye, and hang on the flanks, and rear of an army with the tenacity of a Seminole Indian, killing the soldiers by detail, and cutting of[f] subsistence untill the whole 20 or 30,000 shall have perished either by the sword or starvation.

In fact, taking into consideration what it has cost Texas to obtain and retain her independence, with the present value of the country, the whistle would be dearly paid for. . . . They can no more than the Indian conmingle with us, and will recede as we approach, untill time shall find the whole Mexican Republic peopled with an Anglo-American race. To render this more easy and hasten its consumation, as well as for Texian prosperity, we must compell them to acknowledge our independence, and be on peacible terms with us. This *can* be accomplished with our little navy to harrass their co[a]st and commerce; at the same time sending a military force of 4 or 5,000 men into the interior of the country, who shall take and destroy property as they go, and at the same time let them know our object is the peace and independence of our country, and that as soon as we have attained that object we would return to our homes. But even this should not be attempted untill the destiny of our Santa Fé friends shall be known. The Mexicans are an excitable people governed by demagogues, and should they be made to believe we will invade their country, especially with the object of conquest, they more than probably would be urged to acts of cruelty by some aspiring demagogue. Whereas, by remaining passive yet for a time our people may be released.

Should we ever come to the conclusion to invade the country, I think 5,000 men well equipped would be amply sufficient. With [the] exception of one or two instances Texians have conquered them ten to one, and by a little harder fighting it can be done twenty to one, which is probably a larger force than they could possibly bring into the field at once, and an army of that size divided into five divisions could be more easily subsisted while passing through the country, and could be brought together when there was some important point to attack.

The best point to redizvous would be at La Casa Blanca on the Nueces; where there is an abundance of the very best pasturage for horses and cattle, good water and a healthy region.

I am so little acquainted with the military tallent of that country, that it would be difficult for me to select a leader. The man is not in my knowing who possessess sufficient qualification to command such an expedition as is in contemplation—he must be a good tactician, a good disciplinarian, affable and courtious, possessed of much firmness, great energy, quick of apprehension, and much reflection. Find such an one and he will lead 5,000 men through the Mexican Republic.

Again, in February 1842, it was reported at Corpus Christi and San Patricio that the Mexicans to the number of three hundred were collecting at a point some thirty miles below the Nueces. An express was sent to Victoria for aid, but none was forthcoming.[88] In the meantime, a hunter came in to Kinney's rancho to report seeing thirty Mexicans cross the Nueces, going east. Cairns and a few of his men were still around, although he had discharged his company some time previous to this. Cairns and six companions headed up the Nueces River about March 1 on a reconnaissance and ran into trouble.

"It is believed here," wrote the President on February 15, shortly after his arrival in Houston, "and I do not doubt the truth of the assertion, that Santa Anna intends, and will if he can, send a large force, and station it upon the Río Grande," from which cavalry parties will be sent out to "annoy" and "assail all frontier points." The predatory incursions may be expected to "bear off such goods and citizens, as they may think will do us greatest injury. If this should not be done within one year," he informed his private secretary, "I'll answer, that we shall have peace upon our Río Grande border!"[89]

Let the battalions of the redoubtable Santa Anna come, declared the President's private secretary, "they will be the heralds of their own destruction. Their presence on our soil will but *precipitate* their in-

---

[88] Goodman, "A Statement of Facts, Washington, Feby 10, 1843," in W. D. Miller Papers, 1833–1860, ms.

[89] Houston to Washington D. Miller, Houston, Feb. 15, 1842, in *Writings of Sam Houston*, II, 484–485.

evitable fate. Let them come then, and quickly. God and the friends of freedom will smile upon their funeral march."[90]

While Cairns was out, two Mexicans, represented as soldiers from the Mexican army, arrived at Kinney's rancho on March 6 before daylight and informed the men there as they had previously promised "if ever an expedition was got up against us," reported Goodman, "that San Antonio was or would be in possession of a command of 700 Mexicans," and that some three hundred Mexicans had gone to Goliad and the Mission Refugio and "would be at our place in one or two days for friendly purposes."[91]

The failure of the Fifth Congress in 1841 to make appropriations for maintaining the regular army, caused President Lamar on March 24, 1841, to issue orders for disbanding the Republic's army,[92] which had been raised for the protection of the northern and western frontiers in accordance with an act of Congress approved on December 21, 1838. The possible danger of this policy of leaving the nation unprotected by a regular standing army soon began to taunt the public mind, and there was considerable discussion in and out of official circles as to the best policy to pursue in respect to frontier defense.

William H. Daingerfield presented in the Senate on December 2 a petition from citizens of Béxar County requesting the establishment of two military posts near enough to the settlements to protect them from the incursion of Mexicans and Indians. They recommended that one of these be located at or near the ford of the Río Grande road on the Medina, and that the other be at or adjacent to the ford of the Laredo road on the Atascosa. These two posts, with an additional one at San Patricio, would do much to protect the lives and property of the frontiersmen at small cost.[93] That the frontiersmen lived in a state of jitters is quite evident from the fact that several months before, when a report was circulated from Gonzales that a large party of Comanches had gone down towards Victoria, "about three hundred

[90] W. D. Miller to Sam Houston, Austin, Feb. 16, 1842 (Private), no. 2, in W. D. Miller Papers, 1833–1860, ms., copy.

[91] Goodman, "A Statement of Facts, Washington, Feby 10, 1843," in W. D. Miller Papers, 1833–1860, ms.

[92] Christian, "Mirabeau Buonaparte Lamar," *Southwestern Historical Quarterly,* XXIII (1919–1920), 256; B. T. Archer, Secretary of War and Navy, to Col. William G. Cooke, War Department, Austin, March 2, 1841, Special Order No. [blank], Army Papers (Texas), ms., copy.

[93] Smither (ed.), *Journals of the Sixth Congress of the Republic of Texas,* I, 84, 84 n.

men from the Colorado, on reception of the news, drove over post haste to Gonzales in pursuit of the enemy, but were met with the unwelcome intelligence that the reported Indians were merely mustangs . . . quietly feeding in the prairie." [94]

In the Cross Timbers near the source of the west branch of the Trinity, in Fannin, Red River, and several other eastern counties there had been adopted with considerable degree of success a system of defense with settlements based on stations similar to "Coffee's Station" and the old station of Kentucky pushed directly into the Indian country fifty or sixty miles from the main settlements.[95] The system worked somewhat like this. Each station consisted of several families protected by a strong stockade and blockhouses, which formed an impregnable fortress against the Indians. At the station would be placed a garrison of fifty to sixty men, who cultivated a large cornfield in common. The settlers from the adjoining districts clubbed together and furnished, by private subscription, corn, beef, pork, and other provisions which were conveyed regularly every two or three months to the families at the station.

Arista's proclamation and preparations, plus the fact that the first authentic information of the capture of the Santa Fé Expedition reached Austin on January 18, spurred the Texas Congress to pass a bill providing for the establishment of a chain of seventeen military colonies along the western and northern frontier, some forty to one hundred miles from the established settlements to serve as bulwarks against Mexican and Indian raids. The posts were to be located as follows: *one* post at some convenient point in the Upper Cross Timbers near Red River, to be called the Military Colony of Red River; *one* post at or near the Hackbury Fork on Elm Creek of the Trinity to be called the Military Colony of East Trinity; *one* post on the main prong of the Trinity in the Cross Timbers to be called the Military Colony of Trinity; *one* post at or near the head of Burnett's prong of the Trinity in the Cross Timbers to be called the Military Colony of West Trinity; *one* post at or near the head of Chambers Creek, sometimes known as Pecan Creek, to be called the Military Colony of Cross Timbers; *one post* at or near the Toweash Village on the Brazos to be called the Military Colony of the Brazos; *one* post on the Little River at or near where a line from the Toweash Village to the mouth

[94] *Telegraph and Texas Register,* June 2, 1841.
[95] *Ibid.,* Dec. 15, 1841.

of the Pedernals on the Colorado River crosses the same which shall be called the Military Colony of Little River; *one* post on the Pedernales or Colorado near the junction of the Colorado and Pedernales to be called the Military Colony of Colorado; *one* post on the Río Blanco on and north of the Post Road from Austin to San Antonio to be called the Military Colony of Blanco; *one* post on the Guadalupe at or near the crossing of the old San Antonio and Nacogdoches road to be called the Military Colony of Guadalupe; *one* post at or near the head of the Cíbolo to be called the Military Colony of the Cíbolo; *one* post at or near the head of the Canon ford of the Medina to be called the Military Colony of the Medina; *one* post at or near the mouth of the Río Frio to be called the Military Colony of Río Frio; *one* post at or near San Patricio to be called the Military Colony of San Patricio; *one* post forty miles above Fort Houston on the west side of Trinity River; *one* on the Sabine; and *one* post on the Atascoso [Atascosito] at or near the Béxar County line to be called the Military Colony of Atascoso [Atascosito].[96]

Senator Clark L. Owen, representing Matagorda, Jackson, and Victoria counties believed that the most sensible plan for defense of the southwestern frontier was one company of fifty-six men, rank and file, who he thought could "at all times make a successful resistance against any depredatory band of Mexicans who might be disposed to extend their robberies to that section of the country. . . . Ten armed men," he declared, "could have prevented the sacking of Refugio, and twenty would have annihilated the robbers who committed the deed." Thus, "for the want of protection," he said, "the citizens of that place were carried into captivity and the brave and unfortunate Ryals, was hung up like a dog, a spectacle to our treacherous enemies, of the imbecility of a government which affords no protection to its citizens." [97]

The bill for frontier defense was vetoed by President Houston on February 2 as a very unsatisfactory plan, although Houston, himself, had recommended the establishment of trading-posts on the frontier, each protected by a garrison of twenty-five men. According to the President, the government neither possessed the power nor the means to furnish arms, ammunition, ordnance, nor provisions to sustain such

[96] Texas Congress, Bills, Sixth Congress, Nos. 2450, 2455, ms.; *The Weekly Texian*, Jan. 19, 26, 1842; Smither (ed.), *Journals of the Sixth Congress of the Republic of Texas*, I, 232 n, 254 n, 298; II, 358 n.
[97] *Ibid.*, I, 226–227.

colonies, even for a year until the settlers could begin to grow their own food. Furthermore, as most of the land in the area in which the posts were to be located had already been deeded to individuals, the government lacked the money with which to purchase it.[98]

Under the apprehension of a Mexican invasion, the Senate quickly passed on January 27 a bill authorizing the President to call into service as many militiamen as necessary to repel the expected enemy force and to take command, in person, of the land forces whenever he should "deem proper"; "to send out the Navy, and to raise the men and use the means sufficient to man and equip it properly." [99] Action on this measure in the House, however, was indefinitely postponed on January 31.[100] The opposition to the President's taking command of the militia in person was led by Owen of the District of Matagorda, Jackson, and Victoria, and Robert Potter from the district of Red River and Fannin counties.

At about the same time, the "Reform Congress," revived an old idea dating back to the beginning of the Republic. It passed on January 27 a bill to extend the boundaries of the Republic to the Pacific Ocean, beyond the coast islands, from the Tropic of Cancer to the forty-second degree north latitude. "A Bill to be entitled an act establishing the Texas Californian Territory" had been presented in the Senate during the dying days of the Lamar administration on November 4 by Clark L. Owen. It was read the first time on November 4 and upon its second reading on November 5 had been referred to the Committee on Public Lands, where it apparently lay when the act redefining the boundaries of the Republic arrived in the Senate from the House on January 25, 1842. On the 27th the Committee on Public Lands reported favorably, through its chairman, Robert Potter, on the creation of the Texas-Californian Territory and the bill was passed the same day.[101]

[98] Houston to the House of Representatives, City of Austin, Feb. 2, 1842 (Veto Message), in *Writings of Sam Houston*, II, 466–471; Executive Records of the Second Term of General Sam Houston's Administration of the Government of Texas, December 1841–December 1844, ms., pp. 35–39; Bancroft, *History of Texas and the North Mexican States*, II, 344.

[99] *Weekly Texian*, Feb. 2, 1842; Smither (ed.), *Journals of the Sixth Congress of the Republic of Texas*, I, 312–315.

[100] *Ibid.*, I, 332.

[101] Smither (ed.), *Journals of the Sixth Congress of the Republic of Texas*, I, 26, 26 n, 298, 308.

The Select Committee on Boundaries, headed by John W. Dancy, declared that "Texas is merely the nucleus of a mighty republic."[102] In his inaugural address of December 10, 1838, Lamar had referred to the boundaries of Texas as "stretching from the Sabine to the Pacific and away to the South West as far as the obstinacy of the enemy may render it necessary for the sword to make the boundary."[103] By the joint resolution now enacted, Congress proposed to add nearly five hundred million acres of land to the national domain by including in Texas portions of the states of Tamaulipas, Coahuila, Durango, Sinaloa, and all of Chihuahua, New Mexico, Sonora, and Upper and Lower California. As a plan for occupying the territory, the committee recommended the chartering of one or more commercial companies, "with authority to take possession of the most important points on the coast of California and to give them privileges which would justify them in keeping in their employ a sufficient number of soldiers to protect them against any hostile movement which might be made against them by the Mexicans."[104]

The extension of the boundary by Congressional resolution, declared the editor of the *Telegraph*,[105] is mere "legislative humbug." "This is about as sensible as the act of the Mexican Congress, declaring the ports of Texas under blockade, when the Mexican government had not even a cockboat afloat on the Gulf. We think the two governments may now turn to each other with the self-complacency of two boys that have been playing tag, and say—'*now we are even*.'"

This bill, too, was vetoed by the President on the grounds that it was "visionary" and that the government was powerless to exercise jurisdiction over the area. It was ridiculous to think that one hundred thousand Texans who were unable to sustain a regular military force could govern successfully two million Mexicans. "A legislative jest" of this type could only affect adversely the safety of the Santa Fé prisoners

[102] Texas Congress, *Report of Select Committee on Boundaries of Texas*; the report is reprinted in Smither (ed.), *Journals of the Sixth Congress of the Republic of Texas*, II, 363–366; "A Bill to amend an act entitled an act to define the boundaries of the Republic of Texas," in Texas Congress, Bills, Sixth Congress, no. 2491, ms.

[103] Smither (ed.), *Journals of the Sixth Congress of the Republic of Texas*, I, 26–27, 27 n, 312; Records of Executive Documents from the 10th Dec. 1838 to the 14th Dec. 1841, p. 8; *Lamar Papers*, II, 320.

[104] Smither (ed.), *Journals of the Sixth Congress of the Republic of Texas*, II, 363–366.

[105] Feb. 23, 1842.

and Britain's proposed mediation in the dispute between Texas and Mexico.[106] Houston renewed his plea for peace with all nations, if possible, including Mexico, for only through peace could Texas grow in population, wealth, and prosperity. Houston succeeded, for the time being in curbing the enthusiasm for war, and Texans were forced to await further developments.

Before adjourning on February 5 Congress passed a joint resolution authorizing the President to employ one company of mounted men to act as rangers on the frontier on such terms as he believed would be "most beneficial to the public interest." [107] especially since "the Indians had been driven to the highest degree of exasperation" by Lamar's "savagism." It appropriated $20,000 to be used at the President's discretion for purposes of protecting the frontier.[108] Such an appropriation, however, was regarded as insufficient to sustain a single company upon the border for one year.[109] An effort in the Senate to get the members of Congress, in view of the prostrated financial condition of the Republic, to donate five of their eight dollars per diem for the protection of the frontier got hopelessly sidetracked, but in the end Congress, due to the insistence of the House,[110] agreed to set the pay of its members at five dollars per diem instead of eight dollars as formerly.[111]

The Senate adopted a resolution to give "the President . . . power, in case of actual invasion by Mexico, to employ the Army, and fit out and employ the Navy on the Gulf," but this resolution was rejected by the House of Representatives.[112] In the interest of economy, the Congress abolished the offices of paymaster general and of quartermaster and commissary general of subsistence, and Houston found it

[106] Houston to the House of Representatives, City of Austin, Feb. 1, 1842, in *Writings of Sam Houston*, II, 462–465; Smither (ed.), *Journals of the Sixth Congress of the Republic of Texas*, II, 434–436. There is no record of any attempt of the House to repass the boundary bill over the President's veto.

[107] "Joint Resolution for the Protection of the Southern Frontier, Approved January 29, 1842," in Gammel (ed.), *Laws of Texas*, II, 746.

[108] *Ibid.*, II, 770–771; Bancroft, *History of Texas and the North Mexican States*, II, 342.

[109] Houston to Richard Roman, H. Ledbetter, and Others, City of Houston, Aug. 10, 1842, in *Writings of Sam Houston*, III, 142–145.

[110] Smither (ed.), *Journals of the Sixth Congress of the Republic of Texas*, I, 272, 272 n, 325–326, 345–346; *Weekly Texian*, Jan. 26, Feb. 6, 1842.

[111] Gammel (ed.), *Laws of Texas*.

[112] Houston to George William Brown, Galveston, March 3, 1842, in *Writings of Sam Houston*, IV, 73–74.

necessary to combine the functions of these offices under that of adjutant and inspector general, to which post he appointed Colonel Jacob Snively.[113]

Thus, the "Reform Congress" adjourned on February 5 without making adequate provision for protecting the frontier, although thoughtful, intelligent citizens within and without the government expected that an invasion would soon be attempted by Mexico.

A few days after the adjournment of Congress, the Secretary of War expressed his anxiety to the President about the movement of Indians on the frontier. "The Indians generally," he wrote, "are at their respective points to commence their crops, but why should parties remain so long at places mentioned in my last, except as a corps of observation until a junction with the Mexicans (if such be intended) can be made, and that intended to be at *an earlier day than we have been used to expect them.* Their movements are entirely different from former custom." Eight Lipans, who "have kept remarkably sober," he said, "will leave today [February 16] on an excursion towards the Río Grande under Captain Castro of that tribe" to gather information for the Texans. The Secretary estimated that six companies, comprising 310 men could be called into service "at the shortest time" on the frontier; but, he declared, "we have no horses or accoutrements—no arms for rangers—no commissioner of subsistance, no supplies to issue. . . . We," however, "have an appropriation of 20,000 Dollars for the protection of the frontier in general—but this is a special service—and requires a distinct Law for its payment" if it is to be used for the maintenance of a regular ranger company.[114]

As news began to come in late in February of the hardships, sufferings, and mistreatment of the Santa Fé prisoners, sentiment in the Republic in relation to Mexico, especially in the west, became stronger in favor of direct military action against Mexico. Even many thoughtful men who had counseled peace and negotiation began to demand and support a more vigorous treatment of Mexico. "Let the avenging

---

[113] Houston to Col. J. Snively, Executive Department, City of Austin, Feb. 5, 1842, in Army Papers (Texas), ms.; Texas Congress, *Report of the Retrenchment Committee to the Hon. Speaker of the House of Representatives*; also in *The Weekly Texian*, Dec. 1, 1841, and Smither (ed.), *Journals of the Sixth Congress of the Republic of Texas*, II, 59–62.

[114] George W. Hockley to Sam Houston, Austin, February 16, 1842 (Private), in Sam Houston, Unpublished Houston Correspondence, 1842, III, ms.

sword be drawn!" wrote Houston's private secretary on the day scheduled for the "big meeting" at Gonzales.

Let the battle cry be raised, and the indignant countrymen of Cooke and his men will levy condign and fearful punishment. . . . It strikes me that we are upon the eve of a great and important crisis in the history of America. Think, General, and think betimes, of the complexity and grandeur of the movements about to be exhibited to the gaze of astonished millions. A great drama is in progress. Two acts have already raised. The first was the settlement and establishment of the independence of the United States—the second, the settlement and liberation of Texas—the third *will be the conquest of Mexico.*

He continued in the spirit of "manifest destiny."

"Westward the *Star* of empire makes its way"; and, like the wise men of old, the Anglo-American race will be true to its course. They will follow its light as a bad son of glory. General, I am not raving. I am in earnest. Fully do I believe, that as the morrow's sun will rise, the irrevocable destiny of that people points to an absolute dominion as extended as the continent itself. Heaven has decreed it; and will employ agents equal, by benign favor, to the splendid accomplishment. "Delen[d]a est Carthago." [115]

"Need I say . . . that ought in this life would give me more profound satisfaction, than to behold you once more directing the tide of conquest—the champion of civilization, religion and Liberty," Miller had written the President earlier, "To me it would, indeed, be a 'consummation devoutly to be wished.' The world expects it from you. I trust in God it may not be destined to disappointment; but that the period may shortly arrive when your victorious sword shall cut the meshes of priestly bigotry and slavish ignorance, and your name be heard in every valley and enregistered upon every mount of Mexico, as the liberator of all her people." [116] "Never again," in his opinion, "will circumstances so admirably concur for the achievement of unfailing renown and extended empire. The harvest of glory is ripe, and invites the reaper." [117]

[115] W. D. Miller to Sam Houston, Austin, March 5, 1842 (Private), no. 5, in W. D. Miller Papers, 1833–1860, ms., copy. *"Delenda est Carthago"* in the words of Cato the elder, "Carthage must be destroyed."
[116] W. D. Miller to Sam Houston, Austin, Feb. 16, 1842 (Private), no. 2, in W. D. Miller Papers, 1833–1860, ms., copy.
[117] Same to Same, Austin, March 2, 1842 (Private), no. 5, in *ibid.*

Epilogue

THE INTERNAL POLITICAL and economic difficulties in Mexico, coupled with the memories and rumors of the savage fighting qualities of *los Tejanos diablos* operated strongly after San Jacinto to help Texas maintain its independence. Although those who occupied responsible leadership in the Mexican government always felt compelled publicly, for political effect at home, to agitate periodically for a war against Texas, privately they often expressed the view that Texas was forever lost to Mexico. Texas, however, while existing in relative security during the early years of her independence, was prevented by her own economic problems from bringing her differences with Mexico to a satisfactory conclusion.

As long as Mexico talked of renewing the war to reconquer Texas and encouraged the Indians and disgruntled Mexicans in Texas to attack the Texas frontiersmen, it was no easy task for Texas leaders to maintain the defensive policy that even Lamar knew was correct in regard to Mexico. The adventurers from the United States, who were eager for a chance to fight the enemy, and the Texan frontiersmen, who had suffered much during the revolution, could see little advantage to a policy which did not provide adequate security to life and property from Mexican brigands, lawless Texan freebooters, and hostile Indians who roamed the frontier. In answer to the repeated threats of an invasion from Mexico, each successive Texas President at one time or other, for political effect at home and abroad, talked of administering a severe retribution to any hostile Mexican force that might be so bold as to cross to the Texan side of the Río Grande, and at times was even provoked into boasting of conducting vigorous offensive operations against the enemy's country.

In May 1837, however, President Sam Houston, who understood well the necessity of leaving Mexico alone, ordered most of the men

546

in the army to be furloughed to relieve the financial strain upon the treasury and to forestall any unauthorized attack upon Mexico, which might cause that country to renew its efforts to subjugate Texas. After the disbandment of the army the defense of the Republic came to rest upon a poorly organized militia, upon a series of ranger companies of short term enlistment, upon small "minute men" companies formed in the frontier counties, and upon a limited infantry and cavalry force enrolled for three years.

Upon the basis of a law enacted by the Texan Congress in December 1836, Texas claimed the Río Grande as her boundary, and Mexico, refusing to recognize the loss of Texas, was successful in keeping Texas from exercising its jurisdiction beyond the Nueces, even though her own authority could not be made effective over the area north of the Río Grande. As time passed, Mexico doubtless realized she could never reconquer Texas, and directed her energies toward preventing the new republic from annexing significant portions of the states of Tamaulipas and Coahuila. Thus, the area between the Nueces (the historic boundary of Texas) and the Río Grande became a sort of no-man's land which was traversed at great risk to life and property.

Nevertheless, by the spring of 1838 enterprising Texans and Mexicans had commenced a profitable smuggling trade across this area, a trade which was to expand during the French blockade of the Mexican coast late in 1838 and early 1839, and which persisted thereafter in spite of many handicaps. The frontier trade was complicated by the activities of the so-called Texan "cowboys" who robbed the Mexican ranches in the vicinity of the Sal Colorado, the Nueces, and the San Antonio rivers of their cattle and other livestock, and penetrated even to the Río Grande to get more. Their only excuse was that those whom they robbed were Mexicans, that the war had not ended, that the Mexican army in its retreat from Texas had carried off cattle and horses without remuneration as provided for in the treaty of Velasco (which, of course, had not been ratified by the Mexican government), and that their actions were only retaliatory. The "cowboys," however, were not always too careful about whose cattle they drove off, often stealing stock belonging to their fellow citizens for sale in the east.

While the Texan raiders forced the abandonment of many of the Mexican ranches between the Nueces and the Río Grande, Mexican gangs also penetrated the area and sometimes even crossed the Nueces to drive away cattle and horses. Mexican brigands and Texan cutthroats infested the frontier, robbed the traders, despoiled them of their money and goods, and sometimes killed them in cold blood. Both governments sought unsuccessfully to exterminate the "gangs"; yet, each accused the other of abetting them.

Meanwhile, the Federalist wars in Mexico, which helped to secure Texas from Mexican attack, also helped to increase the ill-will between the two nations.

It was difficult for Mexico to realize that the Texans who participated in the Federalist wars from 1838 to 1840 did so as private parties and not as representatives of the Texan government. The motives of the Texans in aiding the Federalists were varied and not always altruistic, and, in the long run, the Texans probably did more harm than good to that cause. The most significant result, however, was to intensify the bitterness on both sides of the border, to destroy confidence, and to adversely affect Texas-Mexican border relations for many years to come.

The acrimony of the presidential election in 1841 between the Houston and Lamar factions carried over into the Sixth Congress where an effort was made by each side to blame the other for the country's woes, largely emanating from a nearly bankrupt treasury, a defenseless frontier, a frustrated foreign policy, and a feeling of utter hopelessness and despair resulting from the depression. Many resented the wasteful expenditures of the Lamar administration, and, in particular, the sending of the army to Santa Fé and the renting of the navy to Yucatán, which could only further antagonize Mexico. The persistence of marauders on the frontier, and the failure of the Sixth Congress, before its adjournment early in February 1842, to make adequate provision for frontier defense were very disheartening.

The prospects for rapid growth and prosperity of the country seemed at low ebb. Then as news of the failure of the Santa Fé Expedition was confirmed and reports trickled in of the mistreatment of its members, and as new rumors circulated of a Mexican invasion, men began to talk boldly of taking matters into their own hands and of marching across the Río Grande to force a release of the Texan prisoners and to punish Mexico severely. The situation on the frontier was daily becoming more ominous. Lamar's poor judgment in sending out the Santa Fé Expedition in the summer of 1841 unleashed a chain of events that brought the first significant body of Mexican troops into Texas since the battle of San Jacinto and made the year 1842 the most exciting one in the frontier history of Texas since the decisive events of the spring of 1836.

APPENDIX

Muster Rolls of Certain Select Frontier Forces, 1839 to 1841

Colonel Edward Burleson's command in pursuit of Córdova, as listed in the *Telegraph and Texas Register,* April 17, 1839.

Adkisson, A. J.
Alderson, Henry
Alexander, P. D.
Allen, George
Anderson, J. D.
Andrews, M.
Barnhart, Joseph
Barton, Wayne
Bennett, S. C.
Billingsley, Jesse
Brown, A. C.
Brown, John W.
Burleson, Edward
Burleson, John
Burleson, Jonathan
Byers, Ross
Caldwell, John
Campbell, B. A.
Carter, William
Caruthers, William
Childress, Hugh M.
Clopton, William A.
Colver, Samuel
Conley, Preston
Conn, Napoleon
Crockeron, Henry
Cunningham, J. R.
Dancer, John
Durst, John G.
Eaken, John J.
Engelhart, Lewis
Fentress, James
Flesher, Nelson
Foster, John L.
Gillet, S. S.
Gilmore, D. C.
Glas[s]cock, G. J.
Gorman, James P.
Hardeman, Owen B.

Hardeman, William P.
Haynie, Dr. S. G.
Hemphill, C. M.
Hemphill, W. A.
Hicks, M.
Highsmith, Samuel
Holmes, William
Hornsby, M. M.
Hornsby, William M.
Johnson, Enoch S.
Lester, J. S.
Lloy[d], Richard J.
Lynch, John L.
McGary, Isaac
McKennon, Thomas
Mabry, James L.
Miller, James
Miller, R. W.
Mills, R. M.
Moore, John
Moore, Thomas A.
Morgan, H. S.
Newcomb, W.
Norris, J.
Pendleton, J. W.
Rice, J. O.
Robinson, John B.
Robison, W. M.
Robison, J. N.
Sanders, Thomas
Scott, G. W.
Sharp, G. W.
Shelp, D. C.
Smith, J. L.
Turner, Winslow
Vandever, Logan
Walker, Martin
Whiting, F. P.
Wilson, ———
Woods, Henry G.

549

Muster Roll, Captain Mathew Caldwell's Gonzales Rangers
March 16, 1839–June 16, 1839 [1]

1. Caldwell, Mathew	Capt.	
2. Campbell, James	1st Lt.	
3. Colley, Canah C.	2nd Lt.	
1. Miller, George D.	1st Sergt.	
2. King, John R.	2nd Sergt.	
3. Henry, William N.	3rd Sergt.	
4. Archer, John	4th Sergt.	

1. Baber, M. L.	Private	23. Minter, T. N.	Private
2. Baldridge, Seth	Private	24. Nichols, G. H.	Private
3. Burgett, Nathan	Private	25. Nichols, G[eorge] W.	Private
4. Caldwell, Curtis	Private	26. Nichols, James W.	Private
5. Clinton, William	Private	27. Nichols, John W.	Private
6. Day, J[ames] M.	Private	28. Nichols, Sol. G.	Private
7. Dikes, Miles G.	Private	29. Nichols, Thomas R.	Private
8. Emmitt, A. S.	Private	30. Osbourne, William S.	Private
9. Forrester, James	Private	31. Pinchback, James	Private
10. Gray, Daniel	Private	32. Poore, D. M.	Private
11. Gray, John B.	Private	33. Putman, William	Private
12. Grubbs, Thomas	Private	34. Reynolds, David	Private
13. Happle, F[rederick] W.	Private	35. Roberts, Abram	Private
14. Harris, Everett H.	Private	36. Roberts, Alexander	Private
15. Henderson, Vaughter	Private	37. Roberts, James B.	Private
16. Henson, David	Private	38. Roberts, Jeremiah	Private
17. Hodges, John S.	Private	39. Russell, D. W.	Private
18. Irvin, Maury	Private	40. Russell, John H.	Private
19. Jones, E. R.	Private	41. Smith, Ezekiel	Private
20. Killin, William H.	Private	42. Smith, French	Private
21. King, Henry B.	Private	43. Smith, William	Private
22. McCulloch, Henry	Private	44. Sowell, A. J.	Private
		45. Sowell, Asa J. L.	Private
		46. Sowell, J. N.	Private
		47. Stump, John S.	Private
		48. Swift, James A.	Private
		49. Symonds, T. W.	Private
		50. Wadkins, Nathan	Private
		51. Wallace, Isaac	Private
		52. Wolfin, John D.	Private

[1] Muster Rolls (Rangers), ms. I have rearranged the names of "privates" in alphabetical order.

Muster Roll, Captain Micah Andrews' Rangers
March 10–June 10, 1839 [2]

1. Andrews, Micah	1st Lt.	11. Duncan, Francis	Private
2. Rice, J. O.	2nd Lt.	12. Fowler, Samuel	Private
		13. Harness, Abel	Private
1. Eakin, J. J.	O[rderly] S[ergeant]	14. Hudson, David	Private
		15. Leffingwell, Ira	Private
1. Adkisson, A. J.	Private	16. Lowe, Winfield	Private
2. Alderson, Henry	Private	17. McCluskey, Phillip	Private
3. Anderson, Mathew	Private	18. McKaman, Thomas	Private
4. Bassford, B. B.	Private	19. Merrill, Nelson	Private
5. Brown, A. E.	Private	20. Mills, Richard	Private
6. Brown, J. W.	Private	21. Newcomb, William	Private
7. Burleson, John	Private	22. Norris, Isaac	Private
8. Castleberry, B. B.	Private	23. Parker, Milton	Private
9. Chandler, R. T.	Private	24. Parrish, C. S.	Private
10. Davis, A. J.	Private	25. Smith, R. T.	Private

Muster Roll, Captain J. P. Ownsby's Company of the ———— Regiment ———— commanded by Lieutenant Colonel D. J. Woodlief of the ———— Brigade of the Militia of the Republic of Texas, March 2–Sept. 9, 1839 [3]

1. Ownsby, James P.	Capt.		
2. Woodhouse, M. P.	1st Lt.		
3. Murphy, Daniel	2nd Lt.		
1. Low, Hannibal A.	1st Sgt.		
2. Homan, Harvey	2nd Sgt.		
3. Kirkman, Green	3rd Sgt.		
4. Waddell, R. H.	4th Sgt.		
1. Saunders, John	1st Cpl.		
2. Hilbert, John	2nd Cpl.		
3. Lindsay, James	3rd Cpl.	[enrolled:]	May 20th
4. Robinson, John	4th Cpl.		
1. Atroff, Joseph	Private	[enrolled:]	May 15th
2. Barrett, J. G.	Private		

[2] Muster Roll (Rangers), ms. I have rearranged the names of the "privates" in alphabetical order and numbered the men.

[3] Militia Rolls (Texas), ms. I have rearranged the names of the "privates" in alphabetical order. See also Receipt Roll, in *ibid.*

3. Boyle, James	Private	[enrolled:]	May 20th
4. Cochran, E. S.	Private		
5. Cooke, George	Private		
6. Craddock, W. B.	Private		
7. Croggan, Samuel	Private	[enrolled:]	May 7th
8. Cunningham, Horatio	Private		
9. Daley, Edward	Private	[enrolled:]	May 20th
10. Daniels, John	Private		
11. Dibble, Henry	Private		
12. Dikeman, W. P.	Private	[enrolled:]	April 17th
13. Edgy, James	Private	[enrolled:]	May 20th
14. Everett, Joseph M.	Private		
15. Faholger, Fidel	Private		
16. Findley, William	Private	[enrolled:]	June 15th
17. Follett, Robert	Private		
18. Frazer, Alexander	Private		
19. Gillmer, W. Rhea	Private	[enrolled:]	April 2nd
20. Hand, Moses	Private		
21. Harrell, B. C. F.	Private		
22. Hayes, James	Private		
23. Haynes, Samuel	Private		
24. Horsler, William	Private	[enrolled:]	May 17th
25. Hughes, Frances	Private		
26. Johnson, William	Private		
27. Kelker, A. D.	Private		
28. Kennedy, W. H.	Private		
29. King, James	Private		
30. Labrick, Francis	Private	[enrolled:]	April 17th
31. Lafayette, John	Private		
32. Lockhart, J. C.	Private	[enrolled:]	April 2nd
33. Lockridge, E. B.	Private		
34. Lysaught, John	Private		
35. McCartney, M.	Private		
36. McCreary, Neil	Private		
37. McDermott, J. P.	Private		
38. McKay, Daniel	Private		
39. Mail, W.	Private		
40. Moore, James W.	Private		
41. Moore, John	Private		
42. Morrison, Lewis	Private	[enrolled:]	May 20th
43. Ogsbury, C. A.	Private		
44. Padget, J. F.	Private		
45. Rayhouse, William	Private	[enrolled:]	May 20th
46. Rinehart, Henry	Private		
47. Saunders, R. G.	Private	[enrolled:]	June 1st
48. Seeley, Alexander	Private		

49. Talbot, John D.	Private	[enrolled:]	May 20th
50. Vitch, T. S.	Private		
51. Wamock, B. F.	Private		
52. Welman, George	Private		
53. Wheeler, T. R.	Private		
54. Woodriff, E.	Private		

Deserted
1. Bell, William W.
2. Butler, J. O.
3. Jackson, John F.
4. McCoy, C. B.
5. Mahar [Maher], P.
6. Murray, J.
7. Noland, J.
8. Robinett, James
9. Welch, James

Discharged

1. Atkinson, George	March 2, 1839	
2. Butler, J. S.	July 2, 1839	
3. Byrne, Isaac	July 2, 1839	
4. Copeland, Richard	July 2, 1839	
5. Crooks, Samuel	March 2, 1839	discharged dishonorably
6. Gillom, Richard	April 2, 1839	
7. Jones, Francis	May 6, 1839	
8. Mathewson, Hugh	May 17, 1839	
9. Russell, Thomas	April 2, 1839	
10. Thomas, E. B.	March 2, 1839	
11. Walker, William D.	March 2, 1839	
12. Watkins, J. D.	March 2, 1839	

After San Jacinto

Muster Roll of Captain John T. Price's Company of Spies
January 3–May 2, 1841 [4]

1. Price, John T.	Capt.	11. Jenkins, S.		Private
		12. Layne, Thomas [7]		Private
2. Ballard, E.	Private	13. Lees, George		Private
3. Blackwell, O. M.	Private	14. Mozier, A[dam]		Private
4. Cameron, E[wen]	Private	15. Perat, A.[8]		Private
5. Carnes [Cairns], W. J.	Private	16. Rouch, Pierre [9]		Private
6. Elliott, Jacob	Private	17. Rupley, William		Private
7. Estrevon, N.	Private	18. Snodgrass, W.		Private
8. García, A.	Private	19. Stemm, W.		Private
9. Guthrie, George [5]	Private	20. Tresten, J. S.		Private
10. Guthrie, Joseph [6]	Private			

Muster Roll of Captain A. T. Miles' San Patricio Minute Men
May 14–28, 1841 [10]

Miles, A. T.	Capt.	McPhearson, James	Private
		Mills, L. F.	Private
Anderson, George	Private	Murry, T. W.	Private
Bennett, James	Private	Parks, J. B.	Private
Black, John M.	Private	Quinn, P.	Private
Bosharn, John	Private	Roach, Peter	Private
Cairns, W. J.	Private	Sapp, A.	Private
Dolan, Joseph	Private	Sherman, Charles	Private
Ferguson, A.	Private	Snodgrass, William	Private
Geary, George M.	Private	Van Horn, W. H.	Private
Gonzales, Christopher	Private	Walker, T.	Private
Hackett, James	Private	Weeks, H. D.	Private
James, John	Private	Wilson, James	Private
Lenard, James W.	Private		

[4] Militia Rolls (Texas), ms. The Receipt Roll of Capⁿ J. T. Price's Compy of Spies, Janʸ 3–May 2, 1841, in *ibid.*, has a penciled notation on the back that under the law of Congress only 15 men could be raised in each county. A penciled notation at the bottom of the roll states that it is overpaid by $42.00. The correct audit is given as 15 men for the whole time, or $5778.00. I have rearranged the names of the privates in alphabetical order by surname."

[5] *Ibid.*, shows that this person signed his name "George W. Guthrie."
[6] *Ibid.*, shows this name as "Joseph Rogers."
[7] *Ibid.*, shows that this person signed his name "Thomas Lane."
[8] *Ibid.*, shows that this person signed his name "A. Pieratt."
[9] *Ibid.*, shows that this person signed his name "Peter Rouche."
[10] Muster Rolls (Rangers), ms.

Appendix

Muster Roll of Captain A. T. Miles' San Patricio Minute Men
June 1–15, 1841
[Same as Muster Roll for May 14–28, 1841][11]

Muster Roll of Captain A. T. Miles' San Patricio Minute Men
June 16–30, 1841
[Same as Muster Roll for May 14–28 and June 1–15, 1841,
except for the omission of "T. Walker"][12]

Muster Roll of Captain A. T. Miles' San Patricio Minute Men
July 12–26, 1841 [13]

Miles, A. T.	Capt.	Hackett, James	Private
		McPhearson, James	Private
Anderson, George	Private	Mills, L. F.	Private
Black, J[ohn] M.	Private	Parks, J. B.	Private
Bosharn, John	Private	Quinn, P.	Private
Cairns, W. J.	Private	Snodgrass, William	Private
Dolan, Joseph	Private	Weeks, H. D.	Private

Muster Roll of Captain A. T. Miles' San Patricio Minute Men
July 27–Aug. 10, 1841 [14]

Miles, A. T.	Capt.	Mills, L. F.	Private
		Neil[l], J[ohn] C.	Private
Anderson, George	Private	Parks, J. B.	Private
Black, J. M.	Private	Quinn, P[atrick]	Private
Bosharn, John	Private	Ripley [Rupley], W[illiam]	Private
Brown, J. W.	Private	Senan, J[ames] W.	Private
Cairns, W. J.	Private	Senan, Thomas	Private
Cameron, E[wen]	Private	Smith, F.	Private
Duggan, Michael	Private	Snodgrass, William	Private
Gerard, F.	Private	Taylor, F. R.	Private
Hagler, L[indsay] S.	Private	Weeks, H. D.	Private
Heffron, John [15]	Private	Wells, W[illiam]	Private
McEvoy, P.	Private	Whalen, Henry	Private
McPhearson, James	Private	Wheeler, Thomas	Private
Maher, P[atrick]	Private	White, J[ohn] B.	Private
Marvin, S. B.	Private	Wilson, John	Private

[11] Muster Rolls (Rangers), ms.
[12] *Ibid.*
[13] *Ibid.*
[14] Muster Rolls (Rangers), ms.
[15] Signature on Receipt Roll, *ibid.*, shows the name as "Hefferon."

555

After San Jacinto

Muster Roll of Captain A. T. Miles' San Patricio Minute Men
Aug. 11–25, 1841

Miles, A. T.	Capt.	Mills, L. F.	Private
		Neil[l], John C.	Private
Anderson, George	Private	Parks, J. B.	Private
Black, J. M.	Private	Quinn, Patrick	Private
Bosharn, John	Private	Ripley [Rupley], William	Private
Brown, J. W.	Private	Senan, James W.	Private
Cairns, W. J.	Private	Senan, Thomas	Private
Cameron, E[wen]	Private	Smith, F.	Private
Dolan, Joseph	Private	Snodgrass, William	Private
Dug[g]an, Michael	Private	Taylor, F. R.	Private
Gerard, F.	Private	Weeks, H. D.	Private
Hagler, L[indsay] S.	Private	Wells, William	Private
Heffron, John	Private	Whalen, Henry	Private
McEvoy, P.	Private	Wheeler, Thomas	Private
McPhearson, James	Private	White, John B.	Private
Maher, Patrick	Private	Wilson, John	Private
Marvin, S. B.	Private		

BIBLIOGRAPHY

A. Primary Sources

1. PUBLIC DOCUMENTS

a. MANUSCRIPTS

Adjutant General's Records. *See* Webb, W. P., Collection.

Arista, Mariano. "Proceso institutido contra los extranjeros Victor Lupín y Benito Watman acusados de haber tomado armas contra el gobierno de la Republica. Marzo 26 de 1840." Archivo de la Secretaría de Gobierno, Saltillo, Coahuila, Vol. XLI, Exp. Núm. 1360, Legájo Núm. 34 (1839–1842). Transcript in Archives Collection, University of Texas.

Arizpe, Ignacio de. Nota del Gobernador de Coahuila Ignacio de Arizpe al Ministro de la Guerra, Saltillo, 5 de Noviembre de 1840, in Archivo de la Secretaría de la Defensa Nacional, Operaciones Militares, 1840.

Army Papers (Texas). Texas State Archives.

Barker, [Eugene C.]. Transcripts from Archivo de la Secretaría de Relaciones Exteriores International. *See* "Relaciones Exteriores International . . ."

———, [Eugene C.]. Transcripts from Archivo de la Secretaría de Relaciones Asuntos Varios Comercio. *See* "Relaciones Exteriores Asuntos Varios Comercio . . ."

Bills. *See* Texas Congress.

City Records (Matamoros), Vols. 1–57 (1811–1859). Photostats in Archives Collection, University of Texas Library.

Colony Contracts. *See* Texas Colony Contracts.

Committee Reports. *See* Texas Congress.

Comptroller's Military Service Records (Texas). Texas State Archives.

Consular Correspondence (Texas), 1838–1875. Texas State Archives.

Consular Dispatches (United States), 1837–1848 (Matamoros). Microfilm in Archives Collection, University of Texas Library.

Consular Dispatches (United States), 1838 (Tampico). Microfilm in Archives Collection, University of Texas Library.

Consular Letters (Texas), 1835–1844. Microfilm in Archives Coltion, University of Texas Library.

Defunciones, Vol. II, p. 24, entries nos. 108–110. Archives of San Augustine Church, Laredo, Texas.

"Diligencias practicadas sobre la mala conversación de Don Manuel Rosas, jefe político del Partido de Río Grande, de los intereses que tuvo en su cargo pertenecientes al ejército del Norte." Archivo de la Secretaría de Gobierno, Saltillo, Coahuila, Vol. XLI, Legájo Núm. 33 (1838). Photostat in Archives Collection, University of Texas Library.

Documents under the Great Seal (Texas), Record Book. Texas State Archives.

Domestic Correspondence (Texas), 1836–1846. Texas State Archives.

Domestic Correspondence (Texas), Undated. Texas State Archives.

English-Mexican Diplomatic Correspondence, 1841–1842. Public Records Office, London, England.

Executive Department Journals (Texas), March 1836–September 1836. Texas State Archives.

Executive Department Journals (Texas), April 1836–October 1836. Texas State Archives.

Executive Documents (Texas). *See* Record of Executive Documents; Executive Department Journals; Executive Records.

Executive Records (Texas), 10th December 1838 to the 14th December 1841 (Mirabeau B. Lamar). Texas State Archives.

Executive Records, of the Second Term of General Sam Houston's Administration of the Government of Texas, December 1841–December 1844. Texas State Archives.

Filisola, Vicente. "Commander in Chief [of the] Army of the North to the Justice of the Peace, Laredo," [dated:] Matamoros, July 30, 1838. English translation in Laredo Archives.

Freeman, W. G. "Report of an Inspection of Eighth Military District, April 23, 1853," Appendix V, Old Records Section, A. G. O. Washington, D.C.: War Department, 1853.

Galindo, M., en Matamoros. "Un decreto del Presidente sobre la formación de compañias para protección contra los malhecheros, Feb. 20, 1842." Matamoros Archives, XL. Photostat in Archives Collection, University of Texas Library.

"Journal A, Records of the City of San Antonio." *See* San Antonio, City of.

Laredo. *See* Defunciones.

Laredo Archives. Records of the City of Laredo. Laredo, Texas.

Matamoros City Records. *See* City Records (Matamoros).

Memorials and Petitions (Texas). Texas State Archives.

Military Service Records. *See* Comptroller's Military Service Records.

Militia Rolls (Texas). Texas State Archives.

Muster Rolls, 1830–1860 (Rangers). Texas State Archives.

Petitions. *See* Memorials and Petitions (Texas).

President (Texas). *See* Executive Department Journals; Executive

Records; Proclamations of the Presidents; Record of Executive Documents.
Proclamations of the Presidents (Texas). Texas State Archives.
Rangers (Texas). *See* Muster Rolls; Webb, W. P., Collection.
Record of Executive Documents from the 10th December 1838 to the 14th December 1841. Texas State Archives.
"Relaciones Exteriores Asuntos Varios Comercio Estados Unidos, 1825–1849," Barker Transcripts from the Archivo de la Secretaría. Archives Collection, University of Texas Library.
"Relaciones Exteriores Internacional Estados Unidos, 1842–1847," Barker Transcripts from Archivo de la Secretaría. Archives Collection, University of Texas Library.
Republic of Texas Papers. *See* Texas Republic Papers.
Reyes, Isidro. "Informe de Isidro Reyes g[ene]ral de brigada de ejército mejicano 2d en jefe de la Division Auxiliar del Norte y com[andan]te general inspector del Departamento de Coahuila y Tejas, Abril 10 de 1840." Archivo de la Secretaría de Gobierno, Saltillo, Coahuila, Vol. XLI, Exp. Núm. 1360, Legájo Núm. 34 (1839–1842). Transcript in Archives Collection, University of Texas Library.
San Antonio, City of. "Journal A, Records of the City of San Antonio." Typed ms. in Archives Collection, University of Texas Library.
San Augustine Church. *See* Defunciones.
Seguin, Town Book of. *See* Town Book of Seguin.
Smith, Justin H. "Transcripts," Vols. V–VI. Latin American Collection, University of Texas Library.
State Department (Texas). Department of State Correspondence, December 1835–February 1836. Texas State Archives.
State Department (Texas). Department of State Letterbook, November 1836–December 1841. Texas State Archives.
State Department (Texas). Department of State Letterbook, no. 1 (November 1836–January 1842). Texas State Archives.
State Department (Texas). Department of State Letterbook, no. 2 (November 1836–March 1841). Texas State Archives.
Stephens, W. B. "Collection." Latin American Collection, University of Texas Library.
"Summary investigation held concerning the apprehension of fourteen foreigners, Texians, who were in the neighborhood of the Nueces River, Plaza de Matamoros, 1841." Archivo General, Secretaría de Guerra y de Marina, 1841–1842; Legájo Núm. 1. Transcript in Archives Collection, University of Texas Library.
Texas Adjutant General's Records. *See* Webb, W. P., Collection.
Texas Colony Contracts, February 1842–January 1844. Texas State Archives.
Texas Congress. Bills, Texas State Archives.
———. Committee Reports. Texas State Archives.

Texas Consular Correspondence. *See* Consular Correspondence.
Texas Consular Letters. *See* Consular Letters.
Texas Documents under the Great Seal. *See* Documents under the Great Seal.
Texas Domestic Correspondence. *See* Domestic Correspondence.
Texas Executive Records. *See* Executive Department Journals; Executive Records; Record of Executive Documents.
Texas Memorials and Petitions. *See* Memorials and Petitions.
Texas Military Service Records. *See* Comptroller's Military Service Records.
Texas Militia Rolls. *See* Militia Rolls.
Texas Rangers. *See* Muster Rolls; Webb, W. P., Collection.
Texas Republic Papers, 1835–1846. Archives Collection, University of Texas Library.
Texas State Department. *See* State Department.
Town Book of Seguin, in Guadalupe County Deed Record, Vol. A (entry no. 86).
United States Consular Dispatches. *See* Consular Dispatches (U.S.).
United States War Department. *See* Freeman, W. G.
Webb, W. P., Collection, Texas Rangers (typed transcripts of Adjutant General's Records, 1838–1865). Archives Collection, University of Texas Library.

b. PRINTED

Adams, Ephraim D. (ed.), *British Diplomatic Correspondence Concerning the Republic of Texas, 1836–1846.* Austin, Texas: Texas State Historical Association, 1917.

———. (ed.), "Correspondence from the British Archives Concerning Texas, 1837–1848," *Quarterly of the Texas State Historical Association,* XV (1911–1912), 201–265, 294–355; XVI (1912–1913), 75–98, 184–213, 291–327, 423–429; XVII (1913–1914), 67–92, 188–206, 306–314, 415–427; XVIII (1914–1915), 83–108, 208–214, 305–326, 410–417; XIX (1915–1916), 91–99, 195–206, 283–312, 405–439; XX (1916–1917), 59–95, 154–193, 277–307, 381–403; XXI (1917–1918), 69–98, 185–213.

Address of Congress to All the People of Texas, November 12, 1838. *See* Texas Congress, Joint Committee of.

[*Address to the Army on the Subject of Desertion, March 14, 1840*]. *See* Lamar, Mirabeau B.

Adjutant-General, Report of. See Texas Adjutant General.

Amador, Juan V. and others. *Manifiesto del ejército que ha operado contra los tejanos á la nación mejicana.* [Dated and signed at end:] Cuartel General en Matamoros, Octubre 16 de 1836. El General en Gefe, Juan V. Amador. El Mayor General, Adrián Woll [and twenty-three others] [Matamoros:] Imprenta del Mercurio de Matamoros, [1836]. Broadside. Copy in Thomas W. Streeter Collection, Yale University Library.

Bibliography

Ampudia, Pedro de. *See* Filisola, Vicente.

Annual Message of Mirabeau B. Lamar. See Lamar, Mirabeau B.

Annual Report of the Secretary of War. See Texas War Department.

Archer, Branch T. *Report of the Secretary of War, September, 1841. See* Texas War Department.

Arista, Mariano. *El C[iudadano] Mariano Arista, general de brigada del egército mégicano y en gefe del cuerpo de Egército del Norte.* [Proclamation defining and imposing penalties for engaging in contraband trade with Texas and providing for the division of captured contraband.] [Text begins:] "Á las tropas de mi mando y á los habitantes de la frontera de los Departamentos de Oriente . . ." [Dated and signed at the end:] Dado en el cuartel general de Sabinas el dia 13 de abril de 1841. Mariano Arista. [1841]. [Sabinas: 1841]. Broadside. Matamoros Archives, XXXVIII, 196. Photostat in Archives Collection, University of Texas Library.

————. "Cuerpo del Ejército de Norte. General en gefe [Mariano Arista], Monterey, Enero 23 de 1841," in *Gaceta del Gobierno de Tamaulipas,* March 13, 1841. Circular. Matamoros Archives. Photostat in Archives Collection, University of Texas Library.

————. *General en gefe del cuerpo de Ejército del Norte, á Exmo. Sr. Gobernador del Departamento de* ————. Cuartel general en el Saltillo, Diciembre 15 de 1840. [Saltillo: 1840]. Broadside. Copy in Archives Collection, University of Texas Library.

————. *El general en gefe del cuerpo de ejército del Norte, á la 1ª Division.* Cuartel general en Arroyo Colorado, Agosto 30 de 1840. [Matamoros? 1840] Broadside. Copy in Thomas W. Streeter Collection, Yale University Library.

————. *El general en gefe del cuerpo de Egército del Norte á los habitantes de los departamentos de Tamaulipas, Nuevo León y Coahuila.* Cuartel General en Victoria de Tamaulipas a 13 de Octubre de 1840. [Ciudad Victoria? 1840]. Broadside. Matamoros Archives, XXXIX, 150. Photostat in Archives Collection, University of Texas Library.

————. *El general en gefe del cuerpo de Ejército del Norte á los habitantes de los departamentos de Tamaulipas, Coahuila y Nuevo León.* Cuartel General en Monterey, Enero 3 de 1841. [Monterey: 1841]. Broadside. Matamoros Archives, XXXIX, 151. Photostat in Archives Collection, University of Texas Library.

————. *General en gefe de la Division Auxiliar del Norte, á los habitantes de los departamentos de Tamaulipas, Coahuila y Nuevo León.* Cuartel General en el Saltillo, Diciembre 12 de 1839. [Saltillo? 1839]. Broadside. Copy in Thomas W. Streeter Collection, Yale University Library.

————. "To Mr. Mirabeau Lamar, Lampazos [Mexico], April 21, 1841 (confidential)," in *Quarterly of the Texas State Historical Association,* VII (1903–1904), 173–174.

561

Army of the North (Mexico). *See* Arista, Mariano; Canalizo, Valentín; Filisola, Vicente; Reyes, Isidro; Bravo, Nicolás.

Binkley, William C. (ed.), *Official Correspondence of the Texas Revolution, 1835–1836.* 2 vols. New York: D. Appleton and Company, Inc., 1936.

Blanchard, P. and A. Dauzats. *San Juan de Ulùa: ou Relation de l'expédition Francaise au Mexique, sous les ordres de M. le Contre-Amiral Baudin . . . Suivi de notes et documents, et d'un apercu général sur l'état actuel du Texas, par. M. E. Maissin . . .* Paris: Gide, 1839.

Brabo [Bravo], Nicolás. *El general en gefe del Ejército del Norte, á las tropas de su mando.* Cuartel general en San Luis Potosí, Noviembre 9 de 1826 [i.e. 1836]. [San Luis Potosí: 1836]. Broadside. Copy in Yale University Library.

Burnet, David G. *Message of the President, on the Subject of Our Mexican Relations.* [Austin: Austin City Gazette Office, 1840].

———. *Reply to the Report of Committee on the Santa Fé Expedition.* Houston: Telegraph Press, [1842]. 7 + [1] pp.

———, President, and A. Somerville, Secretary of War. [Proclamation to the People of Texas]. Done at Velasco, the 20th day of June, 1836. [Brazoria: F. C. Gray, 1836]. Broadside. Copy in Archives Collection, University of Texas Library.

Canalizo, Valentín. *El general en gefe de la Division del Norte á sus subordinados,* Cuartel General de Matamoros y Noviembre —— de 1839. [Matamoros: 1839]. Broadside. Copy in Yale University Library.

———. *El gral. . . . segundo en gefe del Ejército del Norte á los indiviudos [sic] que componen la segunda division.* Cuartel General en Matamoros, Abril 3 de 1838. Matamoros: Imprenta del Ancla, 1838. Broadside. Copy in Yale University Library.

———. *See also,* Filisola, Vicente.

Cárdenas, Jesús. *Prefecto del distrito de Norte en el Departamento de Tamaulipas, á todos sus habitantes,* Mier, Enero 6 de 1842. Broadside. Matamoros Archives, 1840–1842, XL (photostat), Archives Collection, University of Texas Library.

Castañeda, Carlos E. (trans.). *The Mexican Side of the Texan Revolution [1836]: By the Chief Mexican Participants . . .* Translated with Notes by Carlos E. Castañeda. Dallas, Texas: P. L. Turner Co., c1928.

Colección de leyes y decretos, publicados en el año de 1839, [and 1840]. Mexico City: Imprenta en Palacio, 1852.

Conde, Francisco G. *El gobernador y comandante general del departamento á sus habitantes.* Chihuahua, Julio 28 de 1841. Francisco G. Conde. [Chihuahua:] Imprenta del Gobierno, [1841]. Broadside. Copy in Huntington Library, San Marino, California.

Congress (Texas). *See* Texas Congress.

Bibliography

Corro, José Justo. [Decree of the *Congreso general,* approved by José Justo Corro, President *ad interim,* July 16, 1836, opening the port of Matamoros to the importation of provisions during the war with Texas, assigning those provisions to the expeditionary force, and exempting from seizure mules and wagons carrying supplies to that army from within the country]. Mexico, Julio 16 de 1836. [Mexico City: 1836]. 4 p. printed folder headed: "Secretaría de Hacienda. Seccion 1ª." Copy in Thomas W. Streeter Collection, Yale University Library.

————. [Decree of José Justo Corro, Presidente *ad interim,* dated July 16, 1836, is extended to all the ports at the north occupied by the expeditionary force against Texas]. Mexico, Octubre 15 de 1836. [Mexico City: 1836]. 4 p. folder printed on p. [1] and headed: "Secretaría de Hacienda. Seccion 1ª." Copy in Yale University Library.

————. [Decree of José Justo Corro, President *ad interim,* promulgated October 15, 1836, by Alas, Secretary of the Treasury, establishing a commissary department for the army now proceeding to Texas], Mexico City: 15 de Octubre de 1836. Broadside, headed: "Secretaría de Hacienda. Seccion 1ª." Copy in Bancroft Library, University of California.

Crimmins, M. L. (ed.). "W. G. Freeman's Report of the Eighth Military Department," *Southwestern Historical Quarterly,* LI (1947–1948), 54–58, 167–174, 252–258, 350–357; LII (1948–1949), 100–108, 227–233, 349–353, 444–447; LIII (1949–1950), 71–77, 202–208, 308–319, 443–473; LIV (1950–1951), 204–218. Crimmin's editing is based on a copy in the Office of Quartermaster General, File Box No. 1, Item 51, San Antonio, National Archives.

Department of State (Texas). *Correspondence between the Secretary of State and Col. Peraza, Special Commissioner from the State of Yucatán.* [Austin:] printed by order of the House of Representatives [by] G. H. Harrison, Printer, [1841]. 12 pp.

Documentos para la historia de la guerra de Tejas. Mexico City: Editora Nacional, 1952.

Documents from the Heads of Department. See Houston, Sam. *Documents.*

Documents on Indian Affairs. See Houston, Sam. *Documents.*

Emory, William H. *Report on the United States and Mexican Boundary Survey, Made under the Direction of the Secretary of the Interior.* 3 vols. Washington, D.C.; Cornelius Wendell, printer, 1857.

Filisola, Vicente and others. *Los generales y gefes del Ejército del Norte á sus subordinados y á todos sus conciudadanos.* Cuartel General en Matamoros. Marzo 6 de 1838. Vicente Filisola, Valentín Canalizo, Adrián Woll, Pedro de Ampudia [and twenty-one others]. Matamoros: Imprenta del Ancla . . ., 1838. Broadside. Copy in Yale University Library.

Gammel, H. P. N. (ed.). *Laws of Texas.* 10 vols. Austin: The Gammel Book Co., 1898.

Garrison, George P. (ed.). *Diplomatic Correspondence of Texas,* in *Annual Report of the American Historical Association,* 1907, vol. II; 1908, vol. II, pts. 1–2. Washington: Government Printing Office, 1908–1911. This work will be cited in the present study as "1907, I," "1908, II," and "1908, III."

General Order, No. 24, dated June 5, 1840. See Texas War Department.

Herrera, José J. de. [Letter of the Secretary of War, dated October 5, 1836, to Nicolás Bravo, General in Chief of the Army of the North, relating to the decree of the same date on the organization of the staff for the war in Texas. Dated and signed at end:] Mexico, Octubre 11 de 1836. José J. de Herrera. [Mexico City: 1836]. 4 p. printed folder. Copies in Yale University Library and California State Library.

Hockley, George W. *See* Texas War Department, [Proclamation].

Houston, Sam. *Documents from the Heads of Departments, Submitted to Congress by the President. By order of Congress.* Houston: Telegraph Power Press, 1838.

———. *Documents on Indian Affairs, Submitted to Congress by the President, November 15, 1838. By order of Congress.* Houston: Telegraph Power Press, 1838.

———. *General Order.* Nacogdoches, Texas, August 11th, 1838 [signed by:] Sam Houston [and] H. McCleod [McLeod], Adjutant General. [Nacogdoches?: Texan Chronicle Office? 1838]. Broadside. Copy at Dallas Historical Society, Dallas, Texas.

———. *A Message from the President, Relative to Indian Affairs, with Accompanying Documents.* Houston: Telegraph Power Press, 1838. 13 pp.

———. *Message of the President,* [Executive Department, City of Austin, Dec. 30th, 1841] and Accompanying Document. [Austin: Austin City Gazette Office, 1842].

———. *Rules and Regulations Promulgated by the President, for the Direction of the Army and Navy of Texas.* Houston: Office of the Telegraph, 1838. 7 pp.

[Houston, Sam]. *To the Chief Justice of the County of San Patricio, Houston, June 13, 1836.* [Houston: National Banner Office? 1838]. Broadside. English text at left of sheet, Spanish at right. Copy in Bancroft Library, University of California.

Impugnación, Matamoros, Febrero 23 de 1837 [by] Varios Gefes del Egército, amigos de la verdad. Matamoros: Imprenta del Mercurio, 1ª calle de Terán, á cargo de Juan Southwell, [1837]. Broadside. Copy in Yale University Library.

Johnston, Albert Sidney. *Annual Report of the Secretary of War. See* Texas War Department.

Bibliography

———. *Reply of the Secretary of War to a Resolution of the Senate* ... [of] *Dec. 10, 1839*. See Texas War Department.

———. *Government of the Army* . . . *1839*. See Texas War Department.

Lamar, Mirabeau B. [Address to the army on the subject of desertion, dated:] Executive Department, Austin, March 14, 1840. [Text begins:] Soldiers: I am constrained by feelings of deep regret and mortification, to address you in the language of admonition. . . . [Published with General Order, no. 6. Austin: Adjutant and Inspector General's Office, March 14, 1840]. Broadside. Archives Collection, University of Texas. Printed in Gulick, C. A., and Others (eds.). *Papers of Mirabeau Buonaparte Lamar*, III, 352–353.

———. *The Annual Message of Mirabeau B. Lamar, President of the Republic of Texas, Communicated to Both Houses of Congress, Nov. 3d, 1841*. Austin: S. Whiting, 1841. 20 pp.

———. *Letter from the President of Texas to the Governor of Yucatán*. Austin: S. Whiting, printer [1841]. 3 pp.

———. *Message of the President, Submitted to Both Houses, December 21, 1838. Published by Order of Congress*. Houston: Telegraph Power Press, 1838.

Laws of the Republic of Texas. Printed by order of the Secretary of State. 2 vols. Houston: Office of the Telegraph, 1838.

López de Lara, Jorgé. *El Ciudadano Jorgé López de Lara, alcalde 1° constitucional de esta ciudad á sus habitantes*. Matamoros, Noviembre 8 de 1839. [Matamoros]: Imprenta del Ancla [1839]. Broadside. Matamoros Archives. Photostat in Archives Collection, University of Texas Library.

Laws of the Republic of Texas, Passed at the Session of the Fifth Congress. Printed by Order of the Secretary of State, Houston: Telegraph Power Press, 1841.

McLeod, Hugh. See Houston, Sam, *General Order;* Texas Adjutant General.

Manifestación que hace ... *Francisco G. Pavón*. See Pavón, Francisco G.

Manifiesto del ejército . . . *Octubre 16 de 1836*. See Amador, Juan V.

Manning, William R. (ed.). *Diplomatic Correspondence of the United States: Inter-American Affairs*, vols. 8 and 12. Washington, D.C.: Government Printing Office, 1937 and 1939.

Menchaca, Manuel. Noticia extraordinaria [Report from Lieutenant Don Manuel Menchaca, "comandante militar de la Villa de Guerrero," dated August 24, 1839, to Valentín Canalizo. Published by the Secretario de Gobierno de Nuevo León and dated and signed at the end:] Monterey, Agosto 28 de 1839 [by] Francisco Margain, oficial 2°. Monterey: Imprenta del Gobierno, á cargo del C. Froylan de Mier, 1839. Broadside. Copy in Yale University Library.

Messages of the Presidents. See name of President.

After San Jacinto

Mexican Diplomatic Correspondence with England. *See* English-Mexican Diplomatic Correspondence.

Miracle, Pedro Julian. "Memorandum Book [of Pedro Julian Miracle]," in "Report of the Secretary of State . . . Relative to the Encroachments of the Indians of the United States upon the Territories of Mexico, Washington, Jan. 11, 1853," *Senate Executive Documents*, 32nd Cong., 2nd Sess., no. 14.

Montoya, José Cayetano de. *Comandancia militar del Saltillo. A Señor Goneral [sic] en Gefe D. Mariano Arista.* Saltillo, Octubre 30 de 1840, Saltillo. Imprenta del Gobierno de Coahuila, 1840. 4 p. folder printed on first 3 pages. Copy in Thomas W. Streeter Collection, Yale University Library.

Pavón, Francisco G. [Account of the Revolutionary Activities of the Texans], San Luis Potosí, Noviembre 30 de 1839, published as a 5 p. double column Suplemento á *la Gaceta*, numero 101, San Luis Potosí, Diciembre 3 de 1839. Copy in The Archivo General de Estado, San Luis Potosí, México.

———. *Manifestación que hace de su conducta militar, a la nación, el Coronel del 1er Regimento de Caballeria, Francisco G. Pavón.* Mexico City: 1841. 24 pp.

Peraza, Col. *See* Department of State (Texas).

Quintero, José A. *José A. Quintero en Ciudad Victoria; un decreto del presidente sobre una contribución establecida durante la guerra con Téjas, Abril 7 de 1841.* [Ciudad Victoria: 1841]. Matamoros Archives, XXXVIII, 192–195. Photostat in Archives Collection, University of Texas Library.

Roberts, Samuel A., Secretary of State. *See* Department of State (Texas). *Correspondence . . . [with] Yucatán. Rules and Regulations . . . for the Army and Navy* [1838]. *See* Houston, Sam.

Rusk, Thomas J. [Proclamation to the People of Texas], Guadalupe-Victoria, June 27, 1836. [Brazoria: F. C. Gray, 1836]. Broadside. Copy in Texas Memorial Museum, Austin, Texas.

Smither, Harriet (ed.). *Journals of the Fourth Congress of the Republic of Texas.* 3 vols. in 1. Austin, Texas: Von Boeckmann-Jones Co., [1931?].

———. *Journals of the Sixth Congress of the Republic of Texas.* 3 vols. Austin, Texas: Von Boeckmann-Jones Co., 1940–1945.

Somervell, A. *See* Burnet, David G., President.

Texas Adjutant General. *Report of the Adjutant-General, November, 1839. Printed by order of Congress.* [Signed at the end: H. McLeod, Adjutant-Gen.]. [Austin]: Whiting Press, [1839]. 3 + [1] pp. Copy in Texas Masonic Grand Lodge Library, Waco, Texas.

Texas Centinel . . . Extra, Austin, Thursday Morning, July 15, 1841. [At head of first column:] "Important from the West—Recommencement of Mexican Hostilities upon Our Inhabitants." [Editorial comment on the abduction of Captain Philip Dimitt and others by

Bibliography

the Mexicans under General Arista, followed by a report of the proceedings of a "Public Meeting at Victoria," protesting the abduction, signed and dated at end:] Thomas Newcomb. Chairman J. T. O'Reilly, Secretary. Victoria, July 10, 1841. [Austin: *Texas Centinel* Office, 1841]. Broadside. Copy in Thomas W. Streeter Collection, Yale University Library.

Texas Congress. *An Accurate and Authentic Report of the Proceedings of the House of Representatives from the 3d of October to the 23d of December.* Columbia: G. & T. H. Borden, Public Printers, 1836.

———. *Appendix to the Journals of the House of Representatives.* See appropriate Congress below.

———. *Journals of the House of Representatives of the Republic of Texas: First Congress, First Session.* Houston: Office of the Telegraph, 1838.

———. *Journal of the House of Representatives of the Republic of Texas, at the Second Session of the First Congress, held by Adjournment at the City of Houston, and commencing Monday, May 1st, 1837.* Houston: Telegraph Office, 1838.

———. *Journal of the House of Representatives of the Republic of Texas: Called Session of September 25, 1837, and Regular Session, commencing November 6, 1837.* Houston: National Banner Office, Niles & Co., Printers, 1838.

———. *Journal of the House of Representatives of the Republic of Texas: Second Congress, Adjourned Session.* Houston: Telegraph Office, 1838.

———. *Journal of the House of Representatives of the Republic of Texas: Regular Session of Third Congress, Nov. 5, 1838.* Houston: Intelligencer Office, S. Whiting, Printer, 1839.

———. *Journals of the House of Representatives of the Republic of Texas: Fifth Congress, First Session, 1840–1841.* Austin: Cruger and Wing, Public Printers, 1841.

———. *Journals of the House of Representatives: Fifth Congress, Appendix.* [Austin]: Gazette Office, [1841].

———. *Journals of the House of Representatives of the Seventh Congress of the Republic of Texas, convened at Washington, on the 14th November 1842.* Washington, Texas: Thomas Johnson, Public Printer, 1843.

———. *Journals of the House of Representatives: Seventh Congress, Appendix.* [Washington, Texas]: Vindicator Office, [1843].

———. *Journals of the House of Representatives of the Eighth Congress of the Republic of Texas.* Houston: Cruger & Moore, Public Printers, 1844.

———. *Journals of the House of Representatives of the Ninth Congress of the Republic of Texas.* Washington, Texas: Miller and Cushney, Public Printers, 1845.

————. *Journals of the Ninth Congress of the Republic of Texas, Appendix*, Washington, Texas: Miller & Cushney, Public Printers, 1845.

————. *Journals of the Senate of the Republic of Texas: First Congress, First Session*. Columbia: G. & T. H. Borden, Public Printers, 1836.

————. *Journals of the Senate of the Republic of Texas: First Congress, Second Session*. Houston: Telegraph Office, 1838.

————. *Journals of the Senate, of the Called Session of Congress Convened at the City of Houston, on the 25th day of September, 1837; and of the Regular Session, on the Sixth Day of November, 1837*. Houston: National Banner Office, Niles & Co., Printers, 1838.

————. *Journals of the Senate of the Republic of Texas: Adjourned Session, Second Congress*. Houston: Telegraph Power Press, 1838.

————. *Journals of the Senate, of the Republic of Texas: First Session of the Third Congress—1838*. Houston: National Intelligencer Office, 1839.

————. *Journals of the Senate of the Republic of Texas: Fifth Congress, First Session*. Houston: Telegraph Office, 1841.

————. *Journals of the Senate of the Republic of Texas: Sixth Congress—1841–1842*. Austin: S. Whiting, Public Printer, 1842.

————. *Journals of the Senate of the Seventh Congress of the Republic of Texas, Convened at Washington on the 14th Nov., 1842*. Washington, Texas: Thomas Johnson, Public Printer, 1843.

————. *Journals of the Senate: Eighth Congress of the Republic of Texas*. Houston: Cruger & Moore, Public Printers, 1844.

————. *Journals of the Senate of the Ninth Congress of the Republic of Texas*. Washington, Texas: Miller & Cushney, Public Printers, 1845.

————. *Report [of the Majority] of Select Naval Committee, November 19, 1841*. Austin: Texian Office [1841]. 7 pp. Copy in Thomas W. Streeter Collection, Yale University Library.

————. *Report of the Minority of the Select Naval Committee, November 22, 1841*. Austin: Texian Office, [1841]. 7 pp.

————. *Report of the Retrenchment Committee to the Hon. Speaker of the House of Representatives*. [Austin]: G. H. Harrison, Printer, [1841]. 4 pp.

————. *Report of the Select Committee of the House, and the Joint Committee of Both Houses, to whom were Referred the Several Messages of His Excellency the President, on the Anticipated Invasion by Mexico; with Accompanying Documents*. Austin: Gazette Office, 1841.

————. *Report of Select Committee on Boundaries of Texas*. [Austin: Austin City Gazette Office, 1842]. 4 pp.

————. *Report of Select Committee on Resolutions relative to the*

Bibliography

Santa Fé Expedition. By order of the House of Representatives.
Austin: S. Whiting, Public Printer, 1841. 14 pp.
————. *Rules and Articles for the Government of Armies of the*
Republic of Texas. Houston: Telegraph Power Press, 1839. 20 pp.
[Texas Congress, Joint Committee of]. *Address of Congress to All the*
People of Texas. [Text begins:] Your Committee, who were ap-
pointed to act in conjunction with a Committee from the House of
Representatives, for the purpose of preparing an address to all the
citizens of Texas, urging them to rush to the rescue of the inhabit-
ants of our frontiers . . . respectfully submit the following address
for the adoption of the honorable the Congress. . . . [Signed at end
by Richard Ellis and Isaac Campbell, chairmen, respectively, of the
Senate and House committees; also by the Speaker of the House,
the President pro tem of the Senate, and others. Dated: at end:]
Senate Chamber, 12th Nov. 1838. [Houston: Telegraph Office,
1838]. Broadside. Copy in Library of the Texas Masonic Grand
Lodge, Waco, Texas.
Texas Department of State. *See* Department of State (Texas).
Texas War Department. *Annual Report of the Secretary of War,*
November, 1839. Printed by order of Congress. Austin: Whiting's
Press, [1839]. 52 pp.
————. *Government of the Army of the Republic of Texas, printed*
in accordance with a Joint Resolution of Congress, approved January
23rd, 1839. By order of the Secretary of War. Houston: Intelligencer
Office, S. Whiting, Printer, 1839.
————. *Reply of the Secretary of War to a Resolution of the Senate,*
Passed Dec. 10, 1839, Instructing Him to Report a Plan for the
Defence of Our Northern and South-Western Frontiers. [Signed at
the end: A. Sidney Johnston, Secretary of War]. Austin: Whiting's
Press [1839].
————. *Report of the Secretary of War, November 1840. Printed by*
order of the House of Representatives. [Signed at the end: B. T.
Archer, Secretary of War]. Austin: Whiting's Print, [1840]. Copy
in Texas Masonic Grand Lodge Library, Waco, Texas.
————. *Report of the Secretary of War, September 1841.* [Signed
at the end: B. T. Archer, Secretary of War and Navy]. Austin:
Texian Office, [1841]. Copy in Texas Masonic Grand Lodge
Library, Waco, Texas.
————. [Proclamation beginning:] War Department, City of Austin,
June 6, 1840: Fellow Citizens: Information has been received by
the Department, of such a nature as to render necessary an appeal
to arms. [Proclamation signed by B. T. Archer, Secretary of War,
and publishing:] General Order, No. 24. Adjutant and Insp'r Gen's
office, Austin, June 5th, 1840. The Brigadier Generals of the First
and Second Brigades are required to immediately bring into the
field, the full militia of the counties named below . . . By Order of

the Sec'y of War. Geo. W. Hockley, Acting Adj't and Insp'r Gen'l. [Austin: *Texas Sentinel* Office, 1840]. Broadside. Copy in Yale University Library.

Tornel y Mendivil, José [Circular giving the organizational setup of the staff of the army which is to undertake the campaign against Texas. Dated and signed at the end:] Mexico 5 de Octubre de 1836. Tornel. [Mexico City: 1836]. 4 p. printed folder. Copy in Yale University Library.

United States Congress. "Difficulties on the Southwestern Frontier," *House Executive Documents,* 36th Cong., 1st Sess., no. 52.

———. *House Executive Documents,* 36th Cong., 1st Sess., no. 52.

———. *House Executive Documents,* 30th Cong., 1st Sess., no. 60.

———. *Senate Executive Documents,* 24th Cong., 2d Sess., vol. I, no. 1. [Washington, D.C.]: Gales & Seaton [1836].

———. *Senate Executive Documents,* 32d Cong., 2d Sess., vol. III, no. 14. [No imprint].

Urrea, José. *Proclama. José Urrea, general de brigada y comandante de la division de reserva en el ejército de operaciones sobre Tejas, á las tropas de su mando.* Matamoros, Junio 5, de 1836. [Matamoros:] Imprenta de Mercurio, [1836]. Broadside. Copy in Texas State Archives. Reprinted in *Documentos para la historia de la guerra de Tejas.* No. 3. Mexico City: Editora Nacional, 1952.

———. *Proclama. El general en gefe del egército de operaciones sobre Tejas á sus subordinados.* Matamoros, Agosto 10 de 1836. [Matamoros:] Imprenta del Mercurio, [1836]. Broadside. Copy in Yale University Library.

———. *Proclama. José Urrea, general en gefe del egército de operaciones sobre Téjas á los valientes que lo forman.* Matamoros, Junio 8 de 1836. [Matamoros:] Imprenta del Mercurio, [1836]. Broadside. *Reprinted in Documentos para la Historia de la Tejas.* no. 4. Mexico City: Editora Nacional, 1952.

Voice from the West!!!, A [Jan. 1842]. [Austin: Austin City Gazette Office, 1842]. Broadside (incomplete). Copy in Texas Masonic Grand Lodge Library, Waco, Texas.

War Department (Texas). *See* Texas War Department.

Weeks, William F. *Debates of the Texas Convention.* Houston: [Telegraph and Texas Register Press], 1846.

Winkler, E. W. (ed.). *Secret Journals of the Senate: Republic of Texas, 1836–1845.* [Austin]: Austin Printing Co., 1911.

Woll, Adrián. *See* Amador, Juan V.; Filisola, Vicente.

2. PRIVATE PAPERS, LETTERS, AND MEMOIRS

a. MANUSCRIPTS AND TYPESCRIPTS

Anaya, Juan Pablo de. Papers, 1792–1867. Latin American Collection, University of Texas Library.

Bibliography

Austin, Henry. Papers. Archives Collection, University of Texas Library.

Barrett, Don Carlos. Papers, 1800–1897 Typescript in Archives Collection, University of Texas Library.

Billingsley, Jesse. Papers. Archives Collection, University of Texas Library.

Brown, John Henry. Papers, 1835–1872. Typescript and original in Archives Collection, University of Texas Library.

Ford, John S. "Memoirs." Archives Collection, University of Texas Library.

Grover, George W. "Minutes of Adventure from June 1841." Typed copy in Texas State Archives from original in Rosenberg Library, Galveston, Texas.

Houston, Sam. Unpublished Houston Correspondence, 1837–1842, Vols. II and III. Archives Collection, University of Texas Library.

Jenkins, John H., Sr. "Personal Reminiscences of Texas History Relating to Bastrop County, 1828–1847." Typescript in Archives Collection, University of Texas Library.

Jones, Anson. Memorandum Books, nos. 1–3. Archives Collection, University of Texas Library.

————. Papers. Archives Collection, University of Texas Library.

Karnes, Henry W. Papers. Archives Collection, University of Texas Library.

Lamar, Mirabeau Buonaparte. Papers. Texas State Archives.

Maverick, Samuel A. Papers, 1825–1888. Archives Collection, University of Texas Library.

Menefee, John S. Papers. Archives Collection, University of Texas Library.

Miller, W. D. Papers, 1833–1860. Texas State Archives.

Morgan, James. Papers. Rosenberg Library, Galveston, Texas.

Neill, Andrew. Papers, 1824–1874. Texas State Archives.

Perry, James F. Papers. Transcripts in Archives Collection, University of Texas Library.

Ross, Reuben. Papers, 1825–1861. Archives Collection, University of Texas Library.

Rusk, Thomas J. Papers. Archives Collection, University of Texas Library.

Seguin, Juan N. Papers. Texas State Archives.

Smith, Ashbel. Papers. Archives Collection, University of Texas Library.

Starr, James H. Papers. Archives Collection, University of Texas Library.

Van Zandt, Isaac. Papers, 1839–1843. Transcripts in Archives Collection, University of Texas Library.

After San Jacinto

b. PRINTED

Barker, Eugene C. (ed.). *The Austin Papers*, in *Annual Report of the American Historical Association for the year 1919*, Vol. II, pts. 1–2, and 1922, Vol. II. 2 vols. Washington, D.C.: Government Printing Office, 1924–1928.

———— (ed.). *The Austin Papers*. Vol. III. Austin: University of Texas Press, 1927.

———— (ed.). "James K. Holland's Diary of a Texan Volunteer in the Mexican War," *Southwestern Historical Quarterly*, XXX (1926–1927), 1–33.

Bassett, John S. (ed.). *Correspondence of Andrew Jackson*. 7 vols. Washington, D.C.: Carnegie Institution of Washington, 1926–1935.

Bell, Thomas W. *A Narrative of the Capture and Subsequent Sufferings of the Mier Prisoners in Mexico, Captured in the Cause of Texas, Dec. 26th, 1842 and Liberated Sept. 16th, 1844*. DeSoto County, Mississippi: R. Morris & Co., 1845.

Bustamante, Carlos María. *El gabinete mexicano durante el segundo periodo de la administración del Exmo. Señor Presidente D. Anastacio Bustamante, hasta le entrega del mando al Exmo. Señor Presidente Interino D. Antonio Lopez de Santa-Anna*. 2 vols. Mexico City: 1842.

Croffut, W. A. (ed.). *Fifty Years in Camp and Field: Diary of Major General Ethan Allen Hitchcock*. New York: G. P. Putnam's Sons, 1909.

Duval, John C. *Early Times in Texas*. Austin, Texas: The Steck Company, 1935. (facsimile reproduction of the original, including title-page, of Austin, Texas, edition of 1892). Bound with Duval, *The Young Explorers*.

————. *The Young Explorers*. Austin, Texas: The Steck Company, 1935. (facsimile reproduction of the original, including title-page, of Austin, Texas, edition of 1892). Bound with Duval, *Early Times in Texas*.

Falconer, Thomas. *Letters and Notes on the Santa Fé Expedition, 1841–1842*. New York: Dauber & Pine Bookshop, Inc., 1930.

Filisola, Vicente. *Memorias para la historia de la guerra de Téjas*. 2 vols. Mexico City: Impr. de I. Cumplido, 1849.

Freund, Max (trans. and ed.). *Gustav Dresel's Houston Journal: Adventures in North America and Texas, 1837–1841*. Austin: University of Texas Press, 1954.

Friend, Llerena (ed.). "Thomas W. Bell Letters," *Southwestern Historical Quarterly*, LXIII (1959–1960), 98–109, 299–310, 457–468, 589–599.

Green, Rena Maverick (ed.). *Memoirs of Mary A. Maverick: Arranged by Mary A. Maverick and Her Son George Madison Maverick*. San Antonio, Texas: Alamo Printing Company, 1921.

572

Bibliography

——— (ed.). *Samuel Maverick, Texan, 1803–1870; A Collection of Letters, Journals and Memoirs.* San Antonio: [privately printed (H. Wolff, printer, N. Y.)], 1952.

Gulick, C. A., and Others (eds.). *The Papers of Mirabeau Buonaparte Lamar.* 6 vols. Austin, Texas: A. C. Baldwin & Sons, 1921–1927.

Jenkins, John Holmes, III (ed.). *Recollections of Early Texas: The Memoirs of John Holland Jenkins.* Austin: University of Texas Press, [1958].

Jones, Anson. *Memoranda and Official Correspondence Relating to the Republic of Texas, Its History and Annexation: Including a Brief Autobiography of the Author.* New York: D. Appleton & Company, Inc., 1859.

Kendall, George Wilkins. *Narrative of the Texas Santa Fé Expedition Comprising a Description of a Tour through Texas and across the Great Southwestern Prairies, the Comanche and Caygua Hunting-grounds with an Account of the Sufferings from want of Food, Losses from Hostile Indians, and Their March, as Prisoners, to the City of Mexico. With illustrations and a map.* 2 vols. Austin, Texas: The Steck Company, 1935. (facsimile reproduction of the original including title page of London edition of 1844).

Kennedy, William. *Texas: The Rise, Progress, and Prospects of the Republic of Texas.* 2nd ed. 2 vols. London: R. Hastings, 1841.

Linn, John J. *Reminiscences of Fifty Years in Texas.* New York: D. & J. Sadlier & Co., 1883. Austin, Texas: The Steck Company, 1935 (facsimile reproduction of the original, including title-page of New York edition of 1883).

Lubbock, Francis R. *Six Decades in Texas: or Memoirs of Francis Richard Lubbock.* Austin, Texas: Ben C. Jones & Co., 1900.

McCalla, W. L. *Adventures in Texas, Chiefly in the Spring and Summer of 1840: with a Discussion of Comparative Character, Political, Religious and Moral.* Philadelphia: 1841.

Maissin, Eugene. *The French in Mexico and Texas (1838–1839).* Translated from the French with introduction and notes by James L. Shepherd, III. Salado, Texas: The Anson Jones Press, 1961.

———. *Notes et Documents et d'un apercu général sur l'état du Texas, avec un grand nombre de belles gravures.* Paris: Blanchard & Dauzats, 1839. Published also in Blanchard, P., *San Juan de Ulua. . . .* Paris: Gide, 1839, pp. [522]–572.

Menchaca, Antonio. *Memoirs,* Compiled by Charles M. Barnes. Yanaguana Society *Publications,* II, (Yanaguana Society, San Antonio, 1937, Artes Gráficas, San Antonio, Texas).

Moore, E. W. *To the People of Texas: An Appeal in Vindication of His Conduct of the Navy.* Galveston, Texas: [*Civilian and Galveston Gazette* Office], 1843.

Morrell, Z[enos] N. *Flowers and Fruits in the Wilderness: or Forty-*

Six Years in Texas and Two Winters in Honduras. 4th ed. rev. Dallas, Texas: W. G. Scarff & Co., Publishers, 1886.

Nance, Joseph Milton (ed.). "A Letter Book of Joseph Eve, United States Chargé d'Affaires to Texas," *Southwestern Historical Quarterly,* XLIII (1939–1940), 196–221, 265–377, 486–510: XLIV (1940–1941), 96–116.

[Page, Frederic Benjamin]. *Prairiedom: Rambles and Scrambles in Texas or New Estremadura by a Suthron.* New York: Paine & Durgess, 1845.

Ramos Arizpe, Miguel. *Memoria sobre el estado de las provincias internas de oriente presentada a las cortes del Cádiz.* Mexico City: Bibliofilos Mexicanos, 1932.

———. *Memorial of the Natural, Political, and Civil State of the Province of Coahuila, One of the Four Internal Provinces of the East, in the Kingdom of Mexico, and Those of the New Kingdom of León, New Santander, and Texas . . .* [Translated from original Spanish printed at Cadiz, 1812]. Philadelphia: Printed for John Melish, G. Palmer, Printer, 1814.

Reid, John C. *Reid's Tramp: or a Journal of . . . Travel Through Texas, New Mexico, Arizona, Sonora, and California.* Selma, Alabama: J. Hardy & Co., 1858.

Rivera Cambas, Manuel. *Historia antigua y moderna de Jalapa y de las revoluciones del estado de Vera Cruz.* 5 vols. Mexico City: Impr. de I. Cumplido, 1869–1871.

Seguin, Juan N. *Personal Memoirs of Juan N. Seguin: from the Year 1834 to the Retreat of General Woll from the City of San Antonio in 1842.* San Antonio, Texas: Ledger Book and Job Office, 1858.

Smither, Harriet (ed.). "Diary of Adolphus Sterne," *Southwestern Historical Quarterly,* XXX (1926–1927), 139–155, 219–236, 305–324; XXXI (1927–1928), 63–83, 181–187, 285–291, 374–383; XXXII (1928–1929), 87–94, 165–179, 252–257, 344–351; XXXIII (1929–1930), 75–79, 160–168, 231–242, 315–325; XXXIV (1930–1931), 69–76, 159–166, 257–265, 340–347; XXXV (1931–1932), 77–82, 151–168, 238–242, 317–324; XXXVI (1932–1933), 67–72, 163–166, 215–229, 312–316; XXXVII (1933–1934), 45–61, 136–148, 215–222, 320–323; XXXVIII (1934–1935), 53–70, 149–152, 213–228.

Thwaites, R. G. (ed.). *Early Western Travels, 1748–1846.* 32 vols. Cleveland, Ohio: A. H. Clark Co., 1904–1907.

Webb, Walter Prescott. Collection. Copies of newspaper clippings, 1841–1846, dealing with Texas Rangers. Archives Collection, University of Texas Library.

Williams, Amelia, and Eugene C. Barker (eds.). *The Writings of Sam Houston.* 8 vols. Austin: University of Texas Press, 1938–1943.

Bibliography

3. MAPS

Austin, Stephen F. *Map of Texas with parts of the adjoining states.* Philadelphia: H. S. Tanner, 1837.

Bache, Alexander D. *Maps Galveston Entrance, Galveston Bay and Aransas Pass, Texas.* Washington: U. S. Coast Survey, 1853.

————. Notes on the Coast of the United States. Section IX. Coast of Texas, with 10 maps. June, 1861. [This memoir was prepared by Captain C. P. Patterson, Hydrographic Inspector, and revised by Supt. A. D. Bache. M.S. in Texas State Archives. A complete survey of the Texas Coast made in 1859–1860.]

Brue, A. *Carte du Texas. Extraite de la Grande Carte du Mexique par A. Brue, Géographe du Roi.* Paris: 1840.

Castañeda, Carlos E. (ed.). *Three Manuscript Maps of Texas by Stephen F. Austin; With Biographical and Bibliographical Notes by Carlos E. Castañeda . . . and Early Martin, Jr.* Austin, Texas: Privately printed, 1930.

DeCórdova, J. *A New and Correct Map of the State of Texas.* Philadelphia, 1857. Copy in Texas State Archives, Austin, Texas.

García y Cubas, Antonio, *Atlas geográfico estadistico é histórico de la republica mexicana.* Mexico City: J. M. Fernandez de Lara, 1858.

Hunt, Richard S. and Jesse Randel. *Map of Texas: Compiled from surveys on record in the General Land Office of the Republic.* New York: Sherman & Smith, 1845.

Mapa de los Estados unidos méjicanos arreghida a la distribución que en diversos de . . . ha hecho del territorio al Congreso general Méjicano. Paris: Publicado por Rosa, 1837.

Map of the Republic of Texas, from the most recent authorities. Philadelphia: C. S. Williams, 1845.

Young, J. H. *A New Map of Texas, with contiguous American and Mexican States.* Philadelphia: H. Augustus Mitchell, 1837. Copy in Texas State Archives.

4. NEWSPAPERS

El Ancla (Matamoros), 1839–1840.

Austin City Gazette, 1839–1842.

Boletín del Gobierno (Mexico City), July 1840.

Boletín Official (Mexico City), September–October, 1841.

Brazos Courier (Brazoria), 1839–1840.

La Brisa (Matamoros), August 30–November 15, 1839.

El Centinela de Tamaulipas (Ciudad Victoria), January 10–March 22, 1839.

Civilian and Galveston Gazette (Galveston), 1838–1843.

Colorado Gazette and Advertiser (Matagorda), 1839–1842.

La Concordia (Ciudad Victoria), 1837–1840.

El Cosmopolita (Mexico City), December 19, 1835–July 1843.

Le Courrier (New Orleans), January–March 1840
Daily Bulletin (Austin), 1841–1842.
Daily Texian (Austin), 1841–1842.
El Desengano Periodico del Puerto de Santa-Ana del Tamaulipas,
    December 1840.
Diario del Gobierno (Mexico City), 1835–1846.
Diario Official (Mexico City), October 19, 1881.
Gaceta Constitucional (Monterey), September 13, 1832.
Gaceta de Gobierno de Tamaulipas (Ciudad Victoria), 1840–1844.
Gaceta de Tampico, July–December 1839
Galvestonian (Galveston), May 16, 1839.
Guadalupe Gazette-Bulletin (Seguin), Historical Centennial Edition,
    April 30, 1936.
El Honor Nacional (Matamoros), December 27, 1841.
Matagorda Bulletin, 1837–1839.
Morning Star (Houston), 1839–1845.
El Mosquito Mexicano (Mexico City), February–May 1839.
New Orleans Picayune, April 18, 1841.
Niles' Weekly Register (Baltimore), 1811–1849.
The Red-Lander (San Augustine), 1841–1845.
Richmond Telescope, 1839–1840.
San Antonio Daily Express, March 10, 1910.
Seminario del Gobierno de Nuevo León (Monterey), August 1839–
    November 1840. Variant title: *Seminario Politico del Gobierno de
    Nuevo León.*
Telégrafo de Tampico, December 1838.
Telegraph and Texas Register (Houston), 1835–1846.
Texas Sentinel (Centinel), (Austin), 1840–1841.
The Weekly Texian (Austin), November 25, 1841–March 9, 1842.
Williamson County Sun (Georgetown), September 28, 1950.

B. Secondary Sources

1. MANUSCRIPTS AND TYPESCRIPTS

Affleck, J. D. "History of John C. Hays," Pts. I–II. Typed MS. Archives
    Collection, University of Texas Library.
Brown, Frank. "Annals of Travis County and the City of Austin." Typed
    MS. Archives Collection, University of Texas Library.
Brown, Maury Bright. "The Military Defenses of Texas and the Río
    Grande Region about 1766." Masters' thesis, University of Texas, 1924.
Christian, Asa K. "The Tariff History of the Republic of Texas." Masters'
    thesis, University of Texas, 1917.
Crane, Robert Edmund Lee, Jr. "The Administration of the Customs
    Service of the Republic of Texas." Masters' thesis, University of Texas,
    1939.

Crawford, Polly Pearl. "The Beginnings of Spanish Settlements in the Lower Río Grande Valley," Masters' thesis, University of Texas, 1925.

Davie, Flora Agatha. "The Early History of Houston, Texas, 1836–1845." Masters' thesis, University of Texas, 1940.

Gambrell, Thomas DeWitt. "The Army of the Republic of Texas." Masters' thesis, University of Texas, 1937.

George, Catherine. "The Life of Philip Dimmitt," Masters' thesis, University of Texas, 1937.

Goodman, H. H. "Presidential Elections of the Republic of Texas." Masters' thesis, University of Texas, 1918.

Gore, Walter Reece. "The Life of Henry Lawrence Kinney," Masters' thesis, University of Texas, 1948.

Harrison, Horace V. "Juan Pablo Anaya: Champion of Mexican Federalism." Ph.D. dissertation, University of Texas, 1951.

Highsmith, Kige, "Biographical Sketch of Jesse Billingsley," in Jesse Billingsley Papers, Archives Collection, University of Texas Library.

Huson, Hobart. "Iron Men: A History of the Republic of the Río Grande and the Federalist War in Northern Mexico." [1940]. One of the Sextuplicate typed copies of the original MS., Archives Collection, University of Texas Library.

————. "Refugio: A Comprehensive History of Refugio County from Aboriginal Times to the End of World War II." 3 vols. Typescript in Archives Collection, University of Texas Library.

Hutchinson, Cecil Alan. "Valentín Gómez Farías," Ph.D. dissertation, University of Texas, 1948.

Moore, Robert Lee. "History of Refugio County." Masters' thesis, University of Texas, 1937.

Reinhardt, Mrs. Ina Kate (Hamon). "The Public Career of Thomas Jefferson Green in Texas." Masters' thesis, University of Texas, 1939.

Scott, Mrs. Florence Johnson. "Spanish Land Grants in the Lower Río Grande Valley." Masters' thesis, University of Texas, 1935.

Vigness, David Martell, "The Republic of the Río Grande: An Example of Separatism in Northern Mexico." Ph.D. dissertation, University of Texas, 1951.

————. "A Survey of the Lower Río Grande Valley, 1836–1846." Masters' thesis, University of Texas, 1948.

2. PRINTED

a. BOOKS

Adams, E. D. *British Interests and Activities in Texas, 1838–1846.* Baltimore, Maryland: Johns Hopkins Press, 1910.

Alessio Robles, Vito. *Coahuila y Texas desde la consumación de la independencia hasta el tratado de paz de Guadalupe Hidalgo.* 2 vols. Mexico City: 1945–1946.

————. *Saltillo en la historia y en la leyenda.* Mexico City: [A del Bosque, impresor], 1934.

577

After San Jacinto

Bancroft, Hubert Howe. *History of Mexico.* 6 vols. San Francisco: The History Co., 1886–1887.

———. *History of Texas and the North Mexican States.* 2 vols. San Francisco: A. L. Bancroft and Company, 1889.

Barker, Eugene C. *Life of Stephen F. Austin,* Austin, Texas: The Texas State Historical Association, 1949.

——— (ed.). *Texas History for High Schools and Colleges.* Dallas, Texas: Turner Company, 1929.

Bayard, Ralph F. *Lone-Star Vanguard: The Catholic Re-occupation of Texas, 1838–1848.* St. Louis, Missouri: The Vicentian Press, 1945.

Biesele, R. L. *The History of the German Settlements in Texas, 1831–1861.* Austin, Texas: Von Boeckmann-Jones Co., [1930].

Binkley, William C. *The Expansionist Movement in Texas, 1836–1850.* Berkeley, California: University of California Press, 1925.

Biographical Directory of the American Congress, 1774–1927. [Washington, D.C.]: Government Printing Office, 1928.

Biographical Directory of the Texan Conventions and Congresses: Austin, Texas: Book Exchange, Inc., [1941].

Bishop, Curtis, and Bascom Giles. *Lots of Land.* Austin, Texas: The Steck Company, 1949.

Bolton, Herbert E. *Texas in the Middle Eighteenth Century.* Berkeley: University of California Press, 1915.

Brown, John Henry. *History of Texas, from 1685 to 1892.* 2 vols. St. Louis, Missouri: L. E. Daniell, [1892–1893].

———. *Indian Wars and Pioneers of Texas.* Austin, Texas: L. E. Daniell, [190?].

Carreño, Alberto M. (ed.). *Jefes del ejército mexicano en 1847: biografías de generals de division y de coronels del ejército mexicano por fines del año de 1847* [Fly leaf says to the end of "1840"] Mexico City: Imprenta y Folotipia de la Secretaría de Fomento, 1914.

Carroll, H. Bailey. *The Texan Santa Fé Trail.* Canyon, Texas: Panhandle Plains Historical Society, 1951.

Castañeda, Carlos E. and Jack Autry Dabbs (eds.). *Guide to the Latin American Manuscripts in the University of Texas Library. Edited for the University of Texas and the Committee of Latin American Studies of the American Council of Learned Societies.* Cambridge, Massachusetts: Harvard University Press, 1939.

Chabot, Frederick C. *Corpus Christi and Lipantitlán.* San Antonio, Texas: Artes Gráficas, 1942.

———. *With the Makers of San Antonio.* San Antonio, Texas: Artes Gráficas, 1937.

Conrad, Howard Louis. *Nathaniel J. Brown: Biographical Sketch and Reminiscences of a Noted Pioneer.* Chicago: Byron S. Palmer Printing Company, 1892.

Corpus Christi: A History and Guide. [Corpus Christi, Texas]: Corpus Christi Caller-Times, 1942.

Bibliography

Crane, William Carey. *Life and Select Literary Remains of Sam Houston of Texas.* Philadelphia: J. B. Lippincott Company, 1884.

Cravens, John Nathan. *James Harper Starr: Financier of the Republic of Texas.* Austin, Texas: The Daughters of the Republic of Texas, 1950.

Crocket, George Louis. *Two Centuries in East Texas: A History of San Augustine County and Surrounding Territory from 1685 to the Present Time.* Dallas, Texas: Southwest Press, [1932].

DeShields, James T. *Border Wars of Texas: being an Authentic and Popular Account, in Chronological Order, of the Long and Bitter Conflict Waged between Savage Indian Tribes and the Pioneer Settlers of Texas.* Tioga, Texas: The Herald Co., 1912.

Dixon, Sam Houston. *Romance and Tragedy of Texas History: being a Record of many thrilling Events in Texas History under Spanish, Mexican and Anglo-Saxon Rule.* Houston, Texas: Texas Historical Publishing Co., [1924].

——— and Louis Wiltz Kemp. *The Heroes of San Jacinto.* Houston, Texas: Anson Jones Press, 1932.

Dobie, J. Frank. *Coronado's Children: Tales of Lost Mines and Buried Treasures of the Southwest.* New York: Grosset & Dunlap, Inc., [1930].

———. *The Longhorns.* Boston: Little, Brown and Company, 1941.

Gambrell, Herbert Pickens. *Anson Jones: the Last President of Texas.* Garden City, New York: Doubleday & Company, Inc., 1948.

———. *Mirabeau Buonaparte Lamar: Troubadour and Crusader.* Dallas, Texas: Southwest Press, [1934].

Garrett, Kathryn. *Green Flag Over Texas: a Story of the Last Years of Spain in Texas.* New York and Dallas: The Cordova Press, Inc., 1939.

Hawkins, Walace. *El Sal del Rey, Fixing title to.* Austin, Texas: Texas State Historical Association, 1947.

Hill, Jim Dan. *The Texas Navy: in Forgotten Battles and Shirtsleeve Diplomacy.* Chicago, Illinois: University of Chicago Press, 1937.

Hodge, Frederick Webb (ed.). *Handbook of American Indians North of Mexico.* 2 vols. Washington, D.C.: Government Printing Office, 1907–1910.

Horgan, Paul. *Great River: The Río Grande in North American History.* 2 vols. New York: Rinehart & Company, Inc., 1954.

Houston: A History and Guide. Compiled by Workers of the Writer's Program of the Work Projects Administration in Texas. *American Guide Series.* Houston, Texas: The Anson Jones Press, 1942.

Huson, Hobart. *District Judges of Refugio County.* Refugio, Texas: Refugio Timely Remarks, 1941.

Jack Hays: The Intrepid Texas Ranger. [Bandera, Texas: Frontier Times, n.d.]

579

Jarrett, Rie. *Gutiérrez de Lara, Mexican Texan: The Story of A Creole Hero.* Austin, Texas: Creole Texana, 1949.

Johnson, Frank W. *A History of Texas and Texans.* 5 vols. Chicago and New York: The American Historical Society, 1914.

Johnston, William Preston. *The Life of Gen. Albert Sidney Johnston: Embracing His Services in the Armies of the United States, the Republic of Texas, and the Confederate States.* New York: D. Appleton & Company, Inc., 1879.

Kilman, Ed., and Lou W. Kemp. *Texas Musketeers: Stories of Early Texas Battles and Their Heroes.* Richmond, Atlanta [etc.]: Johnson Publishing Co., [1935].

[Kirwin, James Martin, and Others]. *Diamond Jubilee, 1847–1922, of the Diocese of Galveston and St. Mary's Cathedral.* [Galveston, Texas: Knapp Bros., printers, 1922].

Lott, Virgil N., and Mercurio Martinez. *Kingdom of Zapata.* San Antonio, Texas: The Naylor Company, [1953].

McCampbell, Coleman. *Saga of a Frontier Seaport.* Dallas, Texas: Southwest Press, [1934].

Madray, Mrs. I. C. *A History of Bee County with Some Brief Sketches about Men and Events in Adjoining Counties.* Beeville, Texas: Beeville Publishing Co., 1939.

Marshall, Thomas Maitland. *A History of the Western Boundary of the Louisiana Purchase, 1819–1841,* University of California Publications in History, Vol. II. Berkeley: University of California Press, 1914.

Parmenter, Mary Fisher. *The Life of George Fisher, 1795–1873, and the History of the Fisher Family in Mississippi.* Jacksonville, Florida: H. & W. B. Drew Co., 1959.

Pierce, Frank C. *A Brief History of the Lower Río Grande Valley.* Menasha, Wisconsin: George Banta Publishing Co., 1917.

Quarterly of the Texas State Historical Association. See *Southwestern Historical Quarterly.*

Rader, Jesse L. *South of Forty: From the Mississippi to the Río Grande.* Norman: University of Oklahoma Press, 1947.

Raines, C. W. *A Bibliography of Texas: Being a Descriptive List of Books, Pamphlets, and Documents Relating to Texas in Print and Manuscript since 1536, including a Complete Collation of the Laws; with an Introductory Essay on the Materials of Early Texas History.* Austin, Texas: The Gammel Book Co., 1896.

Richardson, Rupert N. *Texas: The Lone Star State.* Englewood Cliffs, New Jersey: Prentice-Hall, Inc., 1958.

Riva Palacio, Vicente. *Mexico á través de los siglos.* 5 vols. [Mexico City: Publicaciónes Herrerias, 1939?]

Rivera Cambas, Manuel. *Los gobernantes de México.* 2 vols. Mexico City: Imprenta de J. M. Aguilar Ortiz. 1872–1873.

Rives, George L. *The United States and Mexico, 1821–1848.* 2 vols. New York: Charles Scribner's Sons, 1913.

Robinson, Duncan W. *Judge Robert McAlpin Williamson: Texas' Three-Legged Willie.* Austin, Texas: Texas State Historical Association, 1948.

Robinson, Fay[ette]. *Mexico and Her Military Chieftains: from the Revolution of Hidalgo to the Present Time.* Hartford, Connecticut: S. Andrus & Son, 1851.

Rose, Victor M. *The Life and Services of Gen. Ben McCulloch.* Philadelphia: Pictorial Bureau of the Press, 1888.

————. *Some Historical Facts in Regard to the Settlement of Victoria, Texas: Its Progress and Present Status.* Laredo, Texas: Daily Times Print, [1883].

Saldivar, Gabriel. *Historia compendiada de Tamaulipas.* Mexico City: [Editorial Beatriz de Silva], 1945.

Schmitz, Joseph William. *Texan Statecraft, 1836–1845.* San Antonio, Texas: The Naylor Company, 1941.

Schoen, Harold (comp.). *Monuments Erected by the State of Texas to Commemorate the Centenary of Texas Independence.* Austin, Texas: Commission of Control for Texas Centennial Celebration, 1938.

Scott, Florence Johnson. *Historical Heritage of the Lower Río Grande: A Historical Record of Spanish Exploration, Subjugation and Colonization of the Lower Río Grande Valley and the Activities of José Escandón, Count of Sierra Gorda together with the Development of Towns and Ranches under Spanish, Mexican and Texas Sovereignties, 1747–1848.* San Antonio, Texas: The Naylor Company, [1937].

Siegel, Stanley. *A Political History of the Texas Republic, 1836–1845.* Austin, Texas: University of Texas Press, 1956.

Silver, James W. *Edmund Pendleton Gaines: Frontier General.* [Baton Rouge]: Louisiana State University Press, 1949.

Smith, Justin H. *The Annexation of Texas.* Corrected ed. New York: Barnes & Noble, Inc., 1941.

Southwestern Historical Quarterly. Vols. I–LXV (July 1897–April 1962). Austin: Texas State Historical Association, 1897–1962.

[Sowell, A. J.]. *Benjamin F. Highsmith: One of Hays' Rangers.* [Extract from Sowell's *Early Settlers and Indian Fighters*]. Houston, Texas: The Union National Bank, 1937.

Sowell, A. J. *Early Settlers and Indian Fighters of Southwest Texas.* Austin, Texas: Ben C. Jones & Co., Printers, 1900.

————. *Incidents Connected with the Early History of Guadalupe County.* Seguin, Texas: n.d.

Streeter, Thomas W. *Bibliography of Texas.* 3 parts. Cambridge, Massachusetts: Harvard University Press, 1955–1960.

Taylor, Paul S. *An American-Mexican Frontier: Nueces County, Texas.* Chapel Hill: University of North Carolina Press, 1934.

After San Jacinto

Taylor, Virginia H. *The Spanish Archives of the General Land Office of Texas.* Austin, Texas: The Lone Star Press, 1955.
Tinkle, Lon. *13 Days to Glory: The Siege of the Alamo.* New York: McGraw-Hill Book Company, Inc., 1958.
Warren, Harris G. *The Sword Was their Passport: A History of American Filibustering in the Mexican Revolution.* Baton Rouge: Louisiana State University Press, 1943.
Waugh, Julia Nott. *Castro-Ville and Henry Castro: Empresario.* San Antonio, Texas: Standard Publishing Company, 1934.
Webb, Walter Prescott. *The Texas Rangers.* Boston: Houghton-Mifflin Company, 1935.
—— and H. Bailey Carroll (eds.). *The Handbook of Texas.* 2 vols. Austin, Texas: The Texas State Historical Association, 1952.
Wilbarger, J. W. *Indian Depredations in Texas,* 2nd ed. Austin, Texas: Hutchings Printing House, 1890.
Wooten, Dudley G. *A Comprehensive History of Texas, 1685 to 1897.* 2 vols. Dallas, Texas: W. G. Scarff, 1898.
Yoakum, H. *History of Texas from Its First Settlement in 1685 to Its Annexation to the United States in 1846.* 2 vols. New York: J. S. Redfield, 1855.
Young, Philip. *History of Mexico: Her Civil Wars, and Colonial and Revolutionary Annals, from the Period of the Spanish Conquest, 1520, to the Present Time, 1847; including an Account of the War with the United States.* Cincinnati, Ohio: J. A. & U. P. James; New York: J. S. Redfield, 1847.

b. ARTICLES

Barker, Eugene C. "The Tampico Expedition," *Quarterly of the Texas State Historical Association,* VI (1902–1903), 169–186.
——. "The Texan Revolutionary Army," *Quarterly of the Texas State Historical Association,* IX (1905–1906), 227–261.
Barton, Henry W. "The Problem of Command in the Army of the Republic of Texas," *Southwestern Historical Quarterly,* LXII (1958–1959), 299–311.
Binkley, William C. "The Activities of the Texan Revolutionary Army after San Jacinto," *Journal of Southern History,* VI (1904), 331–346.
Christian, A. K. "Mirabeau Buonaparte Lamar," *Southwestern Historical Quarterly,* XXIII (1919–1920), 153–170, 231–270; XXIV (1920–1921), 39–139, 194–234.
Cox, I. J. "The Southwest Boundary of Texas," *Quarterly of the Texas State Historical Association,* VI (1902–1903), 81–102.
Coyner, C. Luther. "Peter Hansbrough Bell," *Quarterly of the Texas State Historical Association,* III (1899–1900), 49–53.

582

Bibliography

Davenport, Harbert. "General José María Jesús Carabajal," *Southwestern Historical Quarterly*, LV (1951–1952), 475–483.

Denton, Bernice Barnett. "Count Alphonso de Saligny and the Franco-Texienne Bill," *Southwestern Historical Quarterly*, XLV (1941–1942), 136–146.

Dienst, Alex. "The Navy of the Republic of Texas," *Texas State Historical Association Quarterly*, XII (1908–1909), 165–203, 249–275; XIII (1909–1910), 1–43, 85–127.

Dobie, J. Frank. "The First Cattle in Texas and the Southwest Progenitors of the Longhorns," *Southwestern Historical Quarterly*, XLII (1938–1939), 171–197.

Graf, Leroy P. "Colonizing Projects in Texas South of the Nueces, 1820–1845," *Southwestern Historical Quarterly*, L (1946–1947), 431–448.

McCaleb, Walter F. "The First Period in the Gutiérrez-Magee Expedition," *Quarterly of the Texas State Historical Association*, IV (1900–1901), 218–229.

Muckleroy, Anna. "The Indian Policy of the Republic of Texas," *Southwestern Historical Quarterly*, XXV (1921–1922), 229–260; XXVI (1922–1923), 1–29, 128–148, 184–206.

Potter, R. M. "Escape of Karnes and Teal from Matamoros," *Quarterly of the Texas State Historical Association*, IV (1900–1901), 71–85, 232–233.

Reagan, John H. "The Expulsion of the Cherokees from East Texas," *Quarterly of the Texas State Historical Association*, I (1897–1898), 38–46.

Shields, James T. "Jack Hays: Famous Texas Ranger," *The American Home Journal*, June 1906. Clipping in John Henry Brown Papers, University of Texas Archives.

Smith, W. Roy. "The Quarrel between Governor Smith and the Council of the Provisional Government of the Republic," *Quarterly of the Texas State Historical Association*, V (1901–1902), 269–346.

Terrell, Alexander W. "The City of Austin from 1839 to 1865," *Quarterly of the Texas State Historical Association*, XIV (1910–1911), 113–128.

Tilloson, Cyrus. "Espantosa Lake," *Frontier Times*, XXVI (1948–1949), 132–135.

———. "Lipantitlán," *Frontier Times*, XXV (1947–1948), 27–29.

Traylor, Maude Wallis. "Those Men of the Mier Expedition," *Frontier Times*, XVI (1938–1939), 299–309.

Vigness, David M. "Relations of the Republic of Texas and the Republic of the Río Grande," *Southwestern Historical Quarterly*, LVII (1953–1954), 312–321.

Warren, Harry. "Col. William G. Cooke," *Quarterly of the Texas State Historical Association*, IX (1905–1906), 210–219.

Webb, Walter Prescott. "The Texas Rangers," in E. C. Barker (ed.), *Texas History for High Schools and Colleges.* Dallas, Texas: Turner Company, 1929, pp. 592–598.

Wilcox, Seb. S. "Laredo During the Texas Republic," *Southwestern Historical Quarterly,* XLII (1938–1939), 83–107.

INDEX

"A": on Lamar (M. B.), 508
Abasolo, Mexico: Federalists in, 161
Abispa (*Wasp*): in Federalist service, 306, 372
acequias: 254
Acordada prison, Mexico: 467
Acosta, Juan José: to Houston (S.), 120
adjutant and inspector general, Texas: report of, 384; functions of, 544
adjutant-general, Texas: mention of, 215; annual report of, 242; ordered to the frontier, 475
Adkisson, A. J.: and pursuit of Flores (M.), 134; in frontier companies, 549, 551
agents, Mexican: work of, among Texas Indians, 118, 140; correspondence of, 139
Agua Dulce: wild horse on, 48; Cairns (W. J.) at, 188; cowboys at, 188; Federalists at, 188; Ross (R.) at, 211; mention of, 487, 491
Agua Leguas, Mexico: garrison at, 171
Agua Nueva, Mexico: 351
Agua Nuevo, *hacienda de*: escape of prisoners at, 468–469
Aguayo, Mexico: Federalist army halts at, 340–341
Aikins, John: death of, 229
Alabama: volunteers from, 15; mention of, 84, 104
Alabama Indians: mention of, 115; assignment of land to, 138–140
Alamo: mention of, 174; Howard's (G. T.) headquarters at, 383. SEE ALSO San Antonio, Texas
Alamo, Battle of the: 447
"Alamo and their Rifles": tune of, 178
Alamo River, battle of the: mention of, 219, 257; account of, 225–230
Albany, New York: 447
Alcantro, battle of: SEE Alamo River, battle of the
Alderson, Henry: in frontier companies, 549, 551

Aldrete, José Miguel: cattle stolen from, 107
Alessio Robles, Vito: on battle of Saltillo, 357
Alexander: at Aransas, 50; brings volunteers to Galveston, 211
Alexander, ———: murder of, 59; as member of Cox's company, 65
Alexander, P. D.: 549
Alexander's ranch: visit of Savariego to, 59
Allen, A. C.: on invading Mexico, 20; mention of, 22
Allen, George: 549
Allen, James C.: suspected of cattle stealing, 107; as chief justice, 107; commands "Buckeye Rangers," 107
Allen, John: capture of, 380
Allen, John M.: as mayor of Galveston, 160
Allen, Thomas: in Federalist army, 215, 264, 357; on Canales (A.), 258; suspects treachery, 354
Almonte, Juan N.: as Mexican secretary of war, 237
Alsbroke, ———: 357
Alsbury, Horace (Horatio) Alexander: on Federalist sympathies, 155; biographical sketch of, 249–250; commands "Life Guards" for Canales (A.), 249–250
Alsbury, Juana Navarro: petition of, 249–250
Altamira, Mexico: 164
Alto Limpia, Mexico: 226
Altos, Los (ranch): Miracle (P. J.) at, 117
Amador, Juan V.: 28
Amanda: arrival of, at Matagorda, 501
Americans: SEE Anglo-Americans; Texans
Ames, N. P.: ordnance purchases from, 95
amnesty decree, Mexican: 439
Ampudia, Pedro de: as commander at

585

Index

593

Index

ploitation of nationalism by, 224; in battle of Alamo River, 230; defend Matamoros, 233; at Concepción, 334; trick Zapata (A.) at Santa Rita de Morelos, 260; in battle of Santa Rita de Morelos, 266; at Peyotes, 268; alleged intentions of, 271; smuggling by, 306; influence of Texan troops on, 318; forces of, at Saltillo, 353, 357. SEE ALSO army, Mexican (Army of the North)

Chacón, Arroyo: location of, 34

Chaffind, Captain: 468–469

Chalmers, John G.: proposed impeachment of, 508, 517

Chamber of Deputies, Mexico: on conquest of Texas, 182

Chambers Creek: Cooke (W. G.) at, 96; mention of, 539

Chandler, Eli: raises frontier companies, 399, 402

Chandler, R. T.: 551

Chapa, José Antonio: 186

Charleston: purchased by Texas, 277

Chaucart, ———: 166

Chenoweth, John: and Federalists, 202

Cherokee Indians: killed by Comanches, 45; negotiations of, with Mexico, 54, 113–114, 117, 118, 120–122, 139, 140; visit of, to Matamoros, 54, 113–114, 140, 240; in Mexican service, 113, 275; mention of, 115, 137, 141, 332; Mexican agents among, 117, 118, 120–122; driven from Texas, 138, 139, 179, 184, 208, 212–214; Hawkins (L.) killed by, 240; Federalist pursuit of, 290; concentration of, for attack on Texas, 313

Cherokee land question: 382, 478

Cherokee Nation: SEE Cherokee Indians

Cherokee War: mention of, 138; financial burden of, 179; end of, 208; Jordan (S. W.) in, 212–214

Chester, William H.: on Kinney (H. L.), 460–461

Chevallie, Michael: as member of Hays' (J. C.) ranger company, 410–411; in battle near Laredo, 413; goes to Río Grande, 434; illness of, 437; mention of, 438

Chiapas, Mexico: revolt in, 143; mention of, 191, 205

"Chicharron": SEE Rodríquez, Captain

Chickasaw Indians: Mexican agents among, 118

Chihuahua, Mexico: relations of Texas with, 21, 140, 216; border trade with, 78, 415; mention of, 142, 174–175, 186, 254, 282, 434, 542; silver from, 155; Federalists in, 318

Chihuahua trail: Cooke (W. G.) follows, 96–97

Childress, Hugh M.: 549

China, Mexico: Federalist armies at, 246, 334–335

Chipita, Lieutenant: 446–448

Choctaw Indians: mention of, 7, 115; en route to Río Grande, 65; Mexican agents among, 118

Cíbolo River: proposed military post on, 86, 244, 540

Cincinnati, Ohio: 439

City of Dublin: purchased by Mexico, 530

Ciudad Canales: SEE Guerrero, Mexico

Ciudad Victoria de Tamaulipas: Quijano (B.) enters, 162; mention of, 227; Arista (M.) at, 330, 335; Federalist regime at, 338–339, 340; Canales (A.) contemplates march against, 362

"Civilian": on colonization plans, 503

Civilian and Galveston Gazette: on trans-Nueces country, 6

Clareño, Rancho: Canales (A.) at, 363

Clark County, Mississippi: 91

Clay, Henry: 523

Clements, William: desertion of, 240; death of, 261; as member of Snell's (M. K.) company, 262

Clendennin, Adam: in recruiting service, 90; on the Trinity River, 96, 97; escorts Baudin (C.), 160

Clifton, Caswell R.: recruiting for Texas by, 279

Clinton, William: in frontier companies, 129, 550

Clopton, William A.: 549

cloth: duties on, in Texas, 80; trade in, 102, 417; capture of, 470

clothing: for recruits, 91; for Federal army, 304

Index

(A. S.) visits, 29, 31; arms for Texas at, 92, 93; Mejía (J. A.) fits out expedition from, 145; *Pontchartrain* from, 165; Santángelo (O. de A.) at, 173–174; Anaya (J. P.) at, 191; battle of, 191; Bryan (W.) at, 199; Bee (B. E.) at, 283; Hamilton (J.) at, 283; Karnes (H. W.) at, 317; Kelsey (J. P.) at, 375; Woll (A.) seeks supplies at, 381; Mexican consul at, 382; Lamar (M. B.) visits, 384; Plummer (S. A.) at, 395; Goodman (W. B.) at, 417; trade with, 417, 523; Texas ships repaired at, 524

New Orleans Bulletin: mention of, 518; on Santa Fé prisoners, 520

New Orleans Commercial Bulletin: on Indo-Mexican alliance, 14

New Orleans Picayune: on Mexican invasion preparations, 11

New Spain: 218

New York: mention of, 92, 305, 387, 530; Austin (H.) at, 111

Nichols, G. H.: 550

Nichols, George W., Sr.: 129, 550

Nichols, James W.: 550

Nichols, John W.: 128, 550

Nichols, Sol G.: 550

Nichols, Thomas R.: 128, 129, 550

Nina, Manuel: and Republic of the Río Grande, 252, 289; at Victoria, 289

Noble, James: 262

Noland, J.: 553

Norias (ranch): mention of, 47; Federalist army at, 246

Norris, Isaac: 551

Norris, J.: 549

Norris, Nathaniel: in Córdova (V.) rebellion, 115, 120; to Houston (S.), 120

North Carolina: volunteers from, 16; mention of, 215, 503

north Mexican federation: proposal for, 174; proposal of alliance with Texas, 175–176

north Mexican republic: talk of, 142

north Mexican states: independence of, rumored, 189; independence of, desired by Texas, 224

"Novedad": SEE Guajardo, Eusebio

Nueces River: as boundary of Texas, 3–

4; mention of, 8–9, 11, 23–24, 47, 49–50, 54–55, 59, 80, 84, 86, 91, 100–102, 107, 185, 188, 211, 213, 215, 217, 254, 257, 268–269, 272, 275–276, 282, 292, 296, 305, 307–309, 311–312, 318, 323, 333, 360, 367, 372, 383, 399, 409, 414–415, 418, 424–426, 445–446, 452, 486–488, 491, 503, 537; cattle on, 21, 46; Parker (J. M.) killed on, 46; Santa Margarita Crossing of, 49; Mexican troops on, 54, 67, 441; Texan troops on, 55, 82, 368, 375, 406, 410; need for defenses along, 60, 86, 87, 105–107, 244, 301, 465, 474; valley of, 60; marauding near, 66, 291; country beyond, 100, 102; Federalist camp on, 188, 198, 203, 205, 268, 290, 312; Canales (A.) on, 322, 325; Jordan (S. W.) on, 328; Price (J. T.) on, 405; Hays (J. C.) on, 410; Texans captured near, 466

Nuevo León, Mexico: mention of, 142, 161, 171, 174–175, 186, 232, 246, 252–255, 288, 330, 373, 442; growth of discontent in, 144; Centralist troops in, 147; Cós (M. P. de) in, 147; Federalist cause in, 189; independence for, 224

Nuevo Mexico: trade with, 80; mention of, 142, 174–175, 186, 254, 428, 434, 505, 542; independence for, 224; Texas expedition to, 425

Nuevo Santander, Mexico: 3–4

Oaxaca, Mexico: mention of, 115; revolt in, 143

O'Dorharty, William: 296

O'Driscoll's Tavern: at Refugio, 206

Ogden, Duncan C.: mention of, 90; and Seguin (J. N.), 434; to Río Grande, 434

Ogsbury, C. A.: 552

Ohio: 235, 439, 506, 519

Oja del Agua, El: 355

"Old Leather-Breeches": SEE Huston, Felix

"Old Longshanks": SEE Huston, Felix

"Old Pike": 129–130

Olivera, Geronimo: removal of, from office, 339

Index

Small, W. B.: 411
Small, William G.: deserts Johnson's (B. H.) command, 240
Smith, Ashbel: mention of, 71, 189; entertains Baudin (C.), 160; on economic conditions in Texas, 208, 211, 303; criticizes Archer (B. T.), 313
Smith, D. W.: as United States consul at Matamoros, 148; on size of Federalist army, 217; mention of, 466–467
Smith, Erastus ("Deaf"): at Columbia, 29; at San Antonio, 29, 34; as Texan scout, 29, 70; attacks Laredo, 34–35; criticized by Houston (S.), 35–36; mention of, 519
Smith, Ezekiel, Sr.: 129, 550
Smith, French: in frontier companies, 129, 550, 555–556
Smith, Henry: as governor, 38
Smith, J. L.: 549
Smith, James: as brigadier general, 89
Smith, John: arrest of, 64; as cowboy, 64
Smith, John N. O.: at public meeting, 531
Smith, John W.: and Federalists, 206; as mayor of San Antonio, 271; on Centralists, 271
Smith, R. T.: 551
Smith, Thomas F.: on Naval Affairs Committee, 506
Smith, William: capture of, 466; as member of Gonzales ranger company, 550
Smith, William H.: as major of militia, 42
Smithers, Launcelot: on San Antonio city council, 472
smuggling: at Corpus Christi, 81; at Purgatory Hill, 117; Mexicans engaged in, 156, 158, 306, 415. See also trade, frontier
Snell, Martin K.: biographical sketch of, 261–262; at Santa Rita de Morelos, 261; kills Sprowl (J. T.), 262; death of, 262; at Saltillo, 357
Snively, Jacob: mention of, 90, 140; as appointed adjutant and inspector general, 544
Snodgrass, William: boards Mexican

prisoners, 471; death of, 498; as member of San Patricio Minute Men, 462, 554–556
Sol, El: on campaign against Texas, 528
soldiers, Mexican: See army, Mexican (Army of the North)
soldiers, Texas: See army, Texas
Solomon, J. E. L.: on Kinney (H. L.), 460
"Sombrero de Manteca": See Zapata, Antonio
Somervell, Alexander: as secretary of war, 11; as brigadier general, 89; mention of, 518
Sonora, Mexico: trade through, 80; Urrea (J.) in, 143, 161; mention of, 542
Soto, Juan Bautista: with Flores (M.), 131
Soto la Marina, Mexico: pronunciamiento at, 149; Federalists avoid French blockade of, 152
South America: Treat (J.) in, 182
South Carolina: 282, 506
Sowell, Asa J. L.: at Seguin, 125; as member of Gonzales ranger company, 550
Sowell, J. N.: 550
Sowell, John: at Seguin, 125
Spain: George Fisher seeks diplomatic mission to, 196; Wright (A. S.) in, 197; king of, 407; mention of, 439
Spaulding, Turner: 65
specie: 79, 81, 102, 149, 154–155, 416
spies, Centralist: trial and execution of, 335
spies, Federalist: 206
spies, Mexican: in Texas, 24, 69, 111; from Savariego's (M.) command, 111; in Refugio, 118; on Copano, 118; arrest of, 408; suspicion of, 408–409
spies, Texan: authorization of, 42; capture of, 50; on Matamoros, 76; sent by Burleson (E.), 124, 126; mention of, 383; detailing of, 402; on Mexican troops in Texas, 407. See also spy companies, Texas
Spooner, William: death of, 261
Springfield, Massachusetts: 95
Sprowl, J. T.: death of, 262
spy companies, Texas: authorization for,

634